AMERICAN FURNITURE in The Metropolitan Museum of Art

This publication has been made possible
by a generous grant from
MR. AND MRS. GEORGE M. KAUFMAN

AMERICAN FURNITURE

in The Metropolitan Museum of Art

II

Late Colonial Period:
The Queen Anne and Chippendale Styles

MORRISON H. HECKSCHER

Edited by Mary-Alice Rogers
Photographs by Richard Cheek

THE METROPOLITAN MUSEUM OF ART
RANDOM HOUSE
New York

PUBLISHED BY
The Metropolitan Museum of Art and Random House, New York

Bradford D. Kelleher, *Publisher, The Metropolitan Museum of Art*
John P. O'Neill, *Editor in Chief*
Polly Cone, *Project Coordinator*
Peter Oldenburg, *Designer*

PHOTO CREDITS: All photographs are by Richard Cheek, with the exception of those at catalogue numbers 74, 77, 78, 79 (easy-chair frames), 212, 213, and details at the back of the book of inscriptions on cat. nos. 72, 81, 100, 139, 178, 181, 192, which are by the Photograph Studio, The Metropolitan Museum of Art.

Type set by National Photocomposition Services, Inc., Syosset, New York

Printed and bound in Italy by Amilcare Pizzi, s. p. a., Milan

LIBRARY OF CONGRESS CATALOGING IN PUBLICATION DATA

Metropolitan Museum of Art (New York, N.Y.)
   American furniture in the Metropolitan Museum of Art.

   Includes bibliography and index.
   Contents: -- v. 2. The late colonial period,
Queen Anne and Chippendale styles.
   1. Furniture--United States--Catalogs. 2. Furniture--
New York (N.Y.)--Catalogs. 3. Metropolitan Museum of
Art (New York, N.Y.)--Catalogs. I. Heckscher,
Morrison H. II. Rogers, Mary-Alice. III. Title.

NK2405.M47 1985   749.214'074'01471   85-7298
ISBN 0-87099-427-1 (v. 2)
ISBN 0-394-55101-X (Random House)

CONTENTS

IV. Frames

FOR FENELLA

FOREWORD

With the inauguration of the new American Wing in May of 1980, space was at last provided for the proper display of the Metropolitan's comprehensive collections of American art. To accommodate the Museum's extensive and superior collections in the decorative arts, former period settings have been refurbished, new rooms opened, and several galleries installed. These follow the evolution of and focus on the finest moments and loci of American cabinet work from the seventeenth century to the end of the nineteenth.

Soon, with the completion of the Henry R. Luce Center for the Study of American Art on the mezzanine of the American Wing, all the Museum's permanent holdings will be on view in both primary and study galleries, and, through direct contact with the originals themselves, the lay visitor and student alike will be able to enjoy the quality of workmanship and design in all the American decorative arts, the furniture in particular. This appreciation will be considerably enhanced, and critical assessments facilitated, by the rare opportunity to view the Museum's holdings not only piece by piece but in the aggregate as well. As such, as a carefully ordered and articulated physical entity, the holdings reflect in their installation and labeling the most up-to-date scholarship and discriminating judgment on the part of the curators who care for them.

Now, clearly, the Museum's highest priority is to communicate fully and exhaustively what is known about its collections in catalogues such as the present one. The first of three volumes covering the entire field of American furniture, it is devoted to the achievements of American cabinet- and chairmakers in the mid-eighteenth century, and in it curator Morrison Heckscher is able to furnish not only both a synoptic and detailed account of the period but also invaluable information on methods of manufacture and on stylistic considerations, since his points of departure are the objects themselves, ultimately the most direct and secure evidence from which accurate conclusions can be drawn.

For the realization of Morrison Heckscher's catalogue, specifically for his extensive research and for the photography, we are deeply indebted to Mr. and Mrs. George M. Kaufman, themselves distinguished collectors of American furniture, for without their generous support this volume could not have been produced.

PHILIPPE DE MONTEBELLO
Director
The Metropolitan Museum of Art

PREFACE

The American Wing, the result of the pioneering vision of such men as Robert W. de Forest, Henry Watson Kent, H. Eugene Bolles, and George S. Palmer, has from its conception and first days of existence focused attention on the finest American furniture of the colonial and early republican periods. The Museum's holdings in these treasures, probably the earliest of the many remarkable public collections of American furniture, are surely one of the greatest glories not just of the American Wing but of the entire Metropolitan Museum. Beginning with the acquisition of the Bolles collection, made possible in 1910 by the generosity of Mrs. Russell Sage, and augmented by many subsequent gifts and purchases, the core of the Museum's collection was in place by the time the original American Wing opened in 1924. Since then, the Museum has been able to expand its holdings through continuing gifts and acquisitions, fulfilling the purpose for which the Wing was intended. As expressed in an address by its founder, Robert de Forest: "The reason for opening our American Wing with this degree of formality . . . is because for the first time an American museum is giving a prominent place to American domestic art and exhibiting it in such a way as to show its historical development." The Wing's immediate success and its long enjoyment of public recognition and attendance prove the wisdom of that farsighted decision.

Because of the inevitable constraints of space even within the enlarged Wing, reopened in 1980, the growing collection, constantly being added to, developed, and refined, has never before been presented in its entirety. Though most of it—certainly the cream of it—has been on continuous display, some of the major pieces, placed among many other objects in period rooms, cannot be examined as easily as they can be described; some pieces are on loan at other institutions; still others are in storage. Our strong desire is therefore to present through this and subsequent publications all acknowledged and illustrious objects in the Museum's collection.

That several catalogues are forthcoming is not to say that American furniture has been overlooked in past Metropolitan publications. Innumerable articles have appeared in the Museum *Bulletin*; a survey of American furniture was contained in the 1924 *Handbook of the American Wing* and its six revised editions published from 1925 to 1948; and other books on the subject have included *The American High Chest* (1930) and *American Chippendale Furniture* (1942). In addition to books on colonial furniture drawing heavily on the Museum's holdings for illustrations—Marshall B. Davidson's *American History of Colonial Antiques* (1967) and Marvin Schwartz's *American Furniture of the Colonial Period* (1976), to name but two—exhibitions of special facets of American furniture mounted at the

Museum have been accompanied by detailed, illustrated catalogues such as *In Quest of Comfort* (1971), *The Art of Joinery* (1972), and *Baltimore Federal Furniture* (1972).

The need for the planned series of catalogues is nevertheless obvious. The books in the series will be arranged more or less chronologically, according to style: Volume I, with the furniture of the seventeenth century and in the William and Mary style (1630–1725); Volume II (the present book), the Queen Anne and Chippendale styles (1730–1790); Volume III, the Federal or neoclassical styles (1790–1825). A subsequent volume or volumes on the later nineteenth-century collection still in the process of formation is contemplated. We are pleased to present this, the first; we look forward to the publication of those to follow.

JOHN K. HOWAT
The Lawrence A. Fleischman Chairman
of the Departments of American Art
The Metropolitan Museum of Art

ACKNOWLEDGMENTS

I am indebted first to The Metropolitan Museum of Art—its Board of Trustees and its director, Philippe de Montebello—for the unique privilege of studying and publishing the Museum's collection of late colonial American furniture.

I am further indebted to Mr. and Mrs. George M. Kaufman, whose generous grant in 1977 in support of the publication of this catalogue gave me the impetus to begin it and whose unfailing encouragement and great patience have sustained me in my efforts to complete it.

The catalogue could not have been realized without the help of many people. I have drawn heavily upon the diverse talents of my colleagues in different departments at the Museum: in Administration, James Pilgrim, champion of the cause of American art; in Archives, Patricia F. Pellegrini and Jeanie M. James, for information on the history of the collection and of its individual objects; in European Sculpture and Decorative Arts, James Parker and William Rieder, for their knowledge of English and European furniture, and Clare Vincent, for her knowledge of clocks; in Musical Instruments, Laurence Libin and Stewart S. Pollens, for their knowledge of spinets. I willingly acknowledge the debt I owe the staff of the Objects Conservation department, John Canonico in particular, both for what I learned while examining pieces under their guidance and for their skilled and sensitive treatment of the collection in preparation for the photography for this book. Mr. Canonico, Rudolph Colban, and Susan Klim did necessary restoration and refinishing work; Victor von Reventlow carved missing ornament; Shinichi Doi patinated restored elements; Charles Anello added his upholstery skill to my research into eighteenth-century techniques to rebuild easy chairs to their original shape; Henry F. Wolcott, Jr., restored clocks; and Richard E. Stone provided radiography and technical analysis.

Wood analysis was courteously performed by the staff of the Center for Wood Anatomy Research at the U.S. Department of Agriculture. Under a contract made possible by a gift from Mr. and Mrs. Herbert J. Coyne, Peter Lawrence Fodera worked at the Museum to conserve the painted surfaces of the japanned furniture. I am grateful to Nora Beeson and Beverley Placzek for their preliminary editorial work on the book, and to Marvin D. Schwartz, a fellow author at the Museum, who offered helpful suggestions on our mutual subject.

Scholars in the realm of American furniture have been most helpful. My colleagues in other museums have been generous not only with their wisdom and expert opinions but also with their time, which permitted my lengthy and innumerable examinations of objects in their collections. My special thanks go to staff members at many institutions: William Voss Elder III, at The Baltimore Museum of Art; David B. Warren and Michael K. Brown, of the Bayou Bend Collection, The Museum of Fine Arts, Houston; Diane Pilgrim, at The Brooklyn Museum; Graham Hood and Wallace B. Gusler, at Colonial Williamsburg; Robert F. Trent, at the Connecticut Historical Society; Clement E. Conger and Gail Daley Serfati, at the Diplomatic Reception Rooms, Department of State; Christina H. Nelson, at the Henry Ford Museum; Charles F. Hummel, Nancy E. Richards, Karol A. Schmiegel, and the late Benno Forman, at the Henry Francis du Pont Winterthur Museum; J. Peter Spang and Philip Zea, at Historic Deerfield, Inc.; Christopher P. Monkhouse, at the Museum of Art, Rhode Island School of Design; Margaret Stearns, at the Museum of the City of New York; Bradford L. Rauschenberg and Luke Beckerdite, at the Museum of Early Southern Decorative Arts; Jonathan L. Fairbanks and Wendy A. Cooper, at the Museum of Fine Arts, Boston; Mary Alice Mackay, at The New-York Historical Society; Beatrice B. Garvan, at the Philadelphia Museum of Art; Robert P. Emlen, at the Rhode Island Historical Society; Joseph T. Butler, at Sleepy Hollow Restorations, Inc.; Brock Jobe, at the Society for the Preservation of New England Antiquities; Phillip M. Johnston, at the Wadsworth Atheneum; and Patricia E. Kane and Gerald W. R. Ward, of the Mabel Brady Garvan collection at Yale University Art Gallery.

Other experts in the field who have graciously shared their long experience with me include Ralph E. Carpenter, Jr., Dean A. Fales, Jr., Benjamin Ginsburg, Joe Kindig III, John T. Kirk, Edward F. LaFond, Jr., Bernard Levy, S. Dean Levy, Michael Moses, Joseph K. Ott, Charles S. Parsons, Richard H. Randall, Jr., Albert Sack, Donald Sack, Harold Sack, Robert Sack, David Stockwell, and John S. Walton.

For their invaluable and often time-consuming genealogical research I am obliged to a number of persons, some of whom volunteered their services: for Newport families, Richard L. Champlin of the Redwood Library, Newport, Rhode Island; for New York families, Joyce Geary Volk; for Philadelphia families, Carl M. Williams; for their labors at the New York Genealogical and Biographical Society, May Hill and Clinton Savage. Additional information was culled for me at the Henry Francis du Pont Winterthur Museum by Wendy Kaplan.

All my colleagues in the American Wing have been of support to me over the course of this endeavor. In particular, John K. Howat, the Wing's Chairman, and Lewis I. Sharp, its Administrator, have provided constant encouragement. Prior to his retirement as Curator of American Decorative Arts, the late Berry B. Tracy advised me in my efforts and gave unstintingly of his brilliant knowledge. Frances Gruber Safford, in addition to sharing with me her vast store of information on early colonial furniture, assumed administrative tasks to free me to write. Don E. Templeton, Gary Burnett, and the late Don Devine, departmental technicians, treated the collection as their own as they patiently and with professional care moved every piece of furniture many times for its examination, conservation, and photography. Frances Bretter efficiently scheduled the original restoration and photographic work for the book; Sue Hazlett, Terese Bienfait Blake, and, especially, Ellin Rosenzweig typed correspondence and provided drafts of entries far above and beyond the call of duty; and volunteer interns Judith Coyne and William Straus also provided cheerful help.

For the catalogue's production at the Museum I am greatly obligated to Bradford Kelleher, Vice President and Publisher; John P. O'Neill, Editor in Chief and General Manager of Publications; and Polly Cone, Executive Editor. Peter Oldenburg, Design Consultant, was responsible for the timeless, classic quality of the design. Richard Cheek labored painstakingly to achieve the perfection of the photographs.

Most of all, however, Mary-Alice Rogers, my editor and wordsmith par excellence, must be credited with any clarity of writing and elegance of style the book possesses and for nurturing an ever-changing manuscript to its eventual completion.

I cannot end these acknowledgments without honoring the memory of the late Charles F. Montgomery, who introduced me to the subject of American furniture. Finally, Fenella G. Heckscher and her Tory tendencies must be publicly recognized for keeping the subject in proportion, the author in subjection.

MORRISON H. HECKSCHER
New York City
October 1985

NOTES ON THE CATALOGUE

Explanation of the abbreviations, acronyms, and short titles used throughout the entries will be found in the section beginning on p. 367. Where a book or article is quoted only once in the text, full details of publication are given at that reference.

Each chapter begins with a brief paragraph outlining the general characteristics, original function and nomenclature, and strengths and weaknesses in the Museum's holdings in the group of furniture to follow. Each entry follows the same format. The comment with which the entry begins contains whatever there is to tell about the object or the maker, if he is known. Also included are a listing of what related objects have come to light, with particular attention given to those having some kind of documentation that could suggest the attribution of the Museum's example, and a brief discussion of the general type to which the object belongs.

Each entry is illustrated with a photograph of the object. A cross reference under some of the photographs refers to the page(s) at which an illustration of a detail, or details, will be found.

The Provenance lists what original or former owners, including dealers, are known. If the object was part of a collection, that too is included.

The section on Construction describes variations on traditional methods of joinery for the most part. A detail clearly visible in the entry photograph is not explained in the text. The directions are those seen by the viewer: "the right side," for example, is actually the object's left side, but to the right in the illustration. The workings of movable parts are explained, as are elements no longer present—the ropes that originally controlled the hangings on a bedstead, for instance. Where possible, eighteenth-century terminology is used, especially in the names of the various furniture types.

The Condition segment is concerned with the object's present state; that is, what restorations, losses, replace-

ments, or alterations that have been made to it. Those elements not mentioned are still as originally made. The current finish and color of the woods are described, as is any fabric covering on seating furniture.

In Inscriptions, the marks, labels, signatures, instructions, records, or accounts that appear on the object are faithfully transcribed, and illegible inscriptions are noted. Cross references at some entry inscriptions are to the page at the back of the book where a photograph will be found. Unless otherwise stated, all inscriptions are cursive and apparently from the eighteenth century.

The Dimensions are in inches, taken to the nearest eighth of an inch, followed by centimeters, in italics and parentheses. Only the dimensions of original elements are given, not those of replacements. With chairs, the measurements have been taken at the wood, not at the upholstery. The seat height is to be understood as the top of the seat rail; the seat depth is that from center front to center back. With tables, the width and depth of both top and skirts, or frame, are given; with round tables, the dimensions of the top are those of its diameter. With case furniture, the width and depth are of the case's individual units, exclusive of moldings. If not otherwise stated, where an entry includes more than one object the dimensions of each are the same.

The Woods are divided into primary, those exterior and visible, and secondary, those used in the interior construction. All elements made of a secondary wood are listed. Only the woods of original elements are included. Where no listing is present, the interior elements are all of the same kind of wood.

The References pertain only to published information on the actual catalogue entry, not to any related object. Short titles are used where possible in order to conserve space.

Each entry ends with the Museum's credit line and accession number.

MARY-ALICE ROGERS
Editor

15

INTRODUCTION

American Furniture in the Late Colonial Period

For the English-speaking world the mid-eighteenth century—the early and middle Georgian periods—was a time of relative peace and unparalleled prosperity. Coincident with the accession to the British throne of George I, in 1714, the Treaty of Utrecht brought an end to decades of war with France. When after more than a generation of peace the two countries again fought, in the Seven Years War (1755–62), England was able to consolidate and vastly enlarge her naval power and her colonial holdings. During the eighteenth-century expansionary period her trade grew manyfold, leading to new wealth, which, while primarily in the hands of the greatest landowners and merchants, was also shared to an unprecedented extent with a growing middle class. In London, that newly affluent consumer society, hungry for the fashionable trappings of the good life, sought in its own modest way to emulate the fashions of the nobility. To gain its patronage, a growing number of skilled craftsmen issued engraved trade cards and advertised in the popular press wares of wood, textile, and precious metal. Defoe's description of "the middle sort, who live well," could as well be applied to the American merchants who availed themselves of the lucrative opportunities of the so-called Triangle Trade, exporting raw materials to the West Indies, Africa, and southern Europe in order to buy manufactured goods from England.

THE FURNITURE TRADE.   In the eighteenth century, household goods and clothing formed a much greater proportion of personal net worth than they do today, with furniture particularly highly prized among them. Some English furniture was shipped to America to be sold through cabinet and upholstery shops. Trade was greatest with the South; in the North, except for looking glasses and upholstered furniture, the imports for resale to the public were generally insignificant in amount or value. By far the largest amount of English-made furniture was brought over by government officials, immigrants, and colonial merchants for their own use, leaving the large market of the local population to be served by a home industry. The American colonists continued to buy both English- and American-made furniture for most of the century.

Workable native woods—walnut and cherry, white pine and tulip poplar—could be had in abundance; West Indian mahogany was easily come by. These, as craftsmen in America soon learned, were not subject to worm infestation, nor did they split in the dry climate, as woods brought from England did. The local preference for solid wood rather than veneers clearly stemmed not just from its ready availability but also from its ability to withstand the rigors of an intemperate climate. The capital cost of setting up shops where mostly hand tools were used was low; the cost of shipping bulky pieces across the Atlantic Ocean was high. Thus, American woodwork generally cost less than comparable English pieces and was at the same time more practical in use. In rural towns, where cabinetmaking was a seasonal occupation, done only when agricultural chores permitted, furniture was made just for the local market. In some of the large port cities, where woodworking was a year-round activity and more goods were produced than the citizens needed, an export trade developed. Boston, long the center of the chairmaking industry, exported her so-called Boston Chairs to Philadelphia and points south. Desks and tables were shipped from Newport to New York and the West Indies. Not surprisingly, then, furnituremaking was one of the largest and most widespread of manufacturing industries in eighteenth-century America, and the thousands of examples that survive form the most extensive category of physical evidence from colonial America.

THE CRAFTSMEN.   Very little is known about the individuals who crafted that furniture. Biographical information, scanty at best, consists mainly of account books and occasional newspaper notices; church records for births and deaths; tax lists, wills, and inventories for an indication of worldly success. That is about all. Cabinetmakers generally lived below the level of historical scrutiny. Because as a rule they did not commission portraits, we don't know what they looked like. One exception is Ralph Earl's painting of Marinus Willett of New York (acc. no. 17.87.1), but it is not Willett the cabinetmaker but Willett the soldier who is portrayed.

Extant account books and bills of sale give an idea of the organization and scope of American cabinet shops. Christopher Townsend's tiny one survives, attached to his Newport house; in all New England, the largest had only seven work benches. Most of them had no more than a handful of men at any one time—the master, one apprentice or more, and perhaps one or two journeymen. While the apprentices were theoretically bound for a fixed term—usually seven years—there was no tightly structured guild system like England's, and urban journeymen came and went largely at will. As a consequence, a number of different hands can have participated in the manufacture of furniture from a single shop. In addition, there was considerable specialization in the furniture trades, with turners, carvers, japanners, and upholsterers plying their individual skills. One cabinetmaker might sell round tea tables for which he had ordered the pillar from a turner and the legs from a carver; a chairmaker might employ a carver to ornament the chair frame and an upholsterer to provide the seat. The cabinet shops made two kinds of furniture. For the first kind, the ready-made, craftsmen had designs or templates of standard patterns from which they could mass-produce component parts to assemble as needed—in effect, off the rack, or "ready to wear." For the second kind—the bespoke, or custom-made—craftsmen executed more or less original designs to a customer's specifications. Schedules of prices listed the base costs of the furniture as well as additional charges for a choice of extras that ranged from the substitution of a more expensive wood to variations in elements or a proliferating series of embellishments.

Such an industrial organization renders identification of the work of any master or shop extremely difficult. Few makers signed or labeled their handiwork, but notable among those who did are William Savery of Philadelphia, Benjamin Frothingham of Charlestown, Massachusetts, and John Townsend of Newport. Savery's chair production, which demonstrates a fair range not only of types but also of construction practices, suggests that he employed journeymen to help with pieces he subsequently labeled. Frothingham's work exhibits a moderate degree of uniformity, possibly the result of his being one of a family of joiners working together. The large numbers of pieces carefully dated and signed or labeled by Townsend over a forty-year period are of such remarkable consistency in design and execution that similar pieces can be attributed to him with confidence (cat. no. 139). His documented oeuvre indicates that Townsend, who was the most prosperous and, in many respects, the most accomplished of the Newport dynasty of Townsend and Goddard furnituremakers, personally attended to all aspects of the work in his shop throughout that period; that he took great pride in his work; and that, unlike many another successful American craftsman, he had no interest in abandoning his craft as soon as he could afford to in favor of the more lucrative and prominent life of a merchant or land speculator.

The great majority of pieces of American furniture remain unattributable. Who made them and for whom or by whom they were commissioned is not known. The number of pre-Revolutionary houses that retain their original furnishings can be counted on one hand. The norm in American families has been for household possessions to be distributed among multitudinous heirs and ultimately sold. More often than not, they have lost their histories in the vicissitudes of the marketplace. Their American origin is nevertheless readily apparent, proclaimed not just by the distinctive regional style that identifies the handicraft of one colony or city from that of another but also by the native woods of which they have been fashioned.

THE STYLES. The furniture made on these shores during the late colonial period was predominantly in what have come to be called, for want of anything more accurate, the Queen Anne and Chippendale styles. The names immediately conjure up certain images. For Queen Anne, walnut furniture with gracefully curved cabriole legs and pad feet; chairs with baluster splats and rounded backs and seats; case pieces with architecturally inspired round-arched pediments, molded cornices, and fluted pilasters come to mind. For Chippendale, the images are of mahogany furniture with elaborate naturalistic carving; cabriole legs with claw-and-ball feet; chairs with pierced splats, eared crest rails, and square seats; architecturally conceived case pieces having carved scrolled pediments and an overlay of rococo carving.

These English style terms, which serve as appropriate reminders that colonial American cabinet- and chairmakers and their clients were still English provincials, have obvious shortcomings. For one, they fail to account for the colonial experience: Queen Anne was an English monarch who died in 1714, more than a decade before the manufacture of furniture in the style named for her began on this side of the Atlantic; Thomas Chippendale's *Gentleman and Cabinet-Maker's Director* of 1754, the most famous of all furniture pattern books, had little or no influence in much of America. For another, two totally different styles are implied by the terms, though the styles themselves are inextricably interconnected.

A few new furniture types, such as Pembroke tables, were introduced only with the Chippendale style, but many other forms—easy chairs, round tea tables, high chests and dressing tables, for instance—remained in fashion and changed little throughout the late colonial period. Often, the only difference between Queen Anne and Chippendale pieces is in their decorative detail. Then again, other types, such as the ubiquitous side chair, underwent a significant change in basic design, from the self-contained curves of the Queen Anne to the rectangular and flared shapes of the Chippendale. Even so, to assign a stylistic label is not always easy. A magnificent Philadelphia armchair of pure Queen Anne form can be embellished with naturalistic carving in the fully developed Chippendale manner (see cat. no. 45). What to call it? These hybrids—pieces that do not fit into stylistic straitjackets—are commonly labeled "transitional." The implication, often undeserved, is that they are of inferior quality because they do not represent a classic design.

In the *Prices of Cabinet & Chair Work* published by James Humphreys in Philadelphia in 1772, nearly every piece described was available in walnut or mahogany and in plain or carved versions. Only if the basic form had changed during the late colonial period, therefore, can the date range of undocumented examples be more precisely defined. For instance, despite its claw feet, an easy chair with narrow, high proportions (cat. no. 76) can be dated earlier than another (cat. no. 77) having pure Queen Anne pad feet but the broad overall proportions of classic Chippendale examples (see cat. no. 78).

A final weakness in the Queen Anne and Chippendale labels is that they presuppose one consistent American style, whereas the single most compelling fact about eighteenth-century American furniture is that there is no one "colonial" style; rather, each individual cabinet-making center evolved its own distinctively regional one. The reason is clear. The colonies were basically separate entities, settled at different times by groups of immigrants from different places. Except when forced together for common defense, as in the face of French and Indian threats, and except to the extent that coastal trade developed between them, their natural relationship was not with each other but directly with the mother country. To establish the qualities unique to each regional center, they must be looked at individually.

BOSTON.   Though sometime around 1740 her economy faltered and her population began a gradual decline, Boston was New England's dominant city in the seventeenth and eighteenth centuries. She was home to an immense number of craftsmen: between 1725 and 1760, some 225 employed in fields related to the manufacture of furniture—cabinetmakers, joiners, turners, japanners, carvers, chairmakers, and upholsterers. The great majority were native-born, many into families in which the craft had been handed down for generations. The furniture styles that evolved in Boston, the first American cabinetmaking center, set the design standards for the craftsmen of northeastern New England, including such important centers as Salem, Newburyport, and Portsmouth.

The introduction of the Queen Anne style to Boston is well documented in the account books of cabinetmakers and upholsterers. Chairs with round seats were being made in 1729; with cabriole legs in 1730; with splat backs and pad feet in 1732. High chests with bonnet tops and with carved and gilded shells set into their flat fronts were made as early as 1733, either veneered with figured walnut and inlaid with stringing and compass stars or japanned in imitation of oriental lacquerwork. On desks and chests, in contrast, the facades were usually shaped in block, serpentine, or bombé form. Of these, the earliest known is a block-front desk and bookcase dated 1738. Those furniture types, of patrician simplicity, remained the standard New England design models through the seventeen-sixties and, in some cases, much longer. Their continued popularity, long after the introduction into Boston of the Chippendale style, reflects the conservatism that paralleled the city's loss of her commercial primacy; it was also the natural outcome of an indigenous craftsman-population unwilling to admit outsiders— even London-trained ones—into its ranks.

The effect of the Chippendale style on Boston and on its area of influence was consequently comparatively modest; the time of its initial appearance has not even been pinpointed. The bombé case form, which was known by 1753, distinguishes a number of monumental desks and secretaries (cat. no. 183), but only later, with the much more common serpentine-front desk (cat. no. 179) or chest, does the playful elegance of the rococo become evident. In the seventeen-sixties and seventies the best high chests, while still Queen Anne in design, now have a sprightly and vivacious quality not previously seen. In seating furniture, a distinctive group of carved pieces was produced in the decade after 1765 on which the knees have sharp edges and flat, static leaf-carving; the claw feet have raked-back talons. One of the splat patterns favored for these chairs is a direct copy from an engraved plate in Robert Manwaring's *Cabinet and Chair-maker's Real Friend and Companion* (London, 1765), the only obvious influence of a printed English pattern book on Boston furniture design (cat. no. 13). Manwaring excepted, English pattern books—even Chippendale's *Director*—did not affect the designs of cabinetmakers in the Boston orbit. The *Director* was advertised only once by a Boston book shop, and though Salem's leading cabinetmaker is known to have owned a copy, his furniture shows no evidence of it (cat. no. 181). Instead, the inspiration for the most elaborate Boston furniture derives from the fashionable English furniture imported by Boston's mercantile leaders for their own use, such as Charles Apthorp's clothes press and the Hancock family double-chairback settee.

NEWPORT. The Boston style had but a limited influence in Rhode Island. That colony, founded by Roger Williams as a haven of religious liberty, retained its cultural identity throughout the eighteenth century. Newport, in the colonial period its major city, was taking its place among the most active and important American seaports during the seventeen-forties just as the commercial decline of Boston was beginning. And it was in Newport that a local school of cabinetmaking renowned for the originality of its design and for quality unsurpassed elsewhere in America was soon to emerge.

During the twenty-year period before the Revolution, Newport had nearly as many furniture craftsmen as Boston. Many were engaged in making plain desks and tables for export to New York and to the West Indies. What is today thought of as Newport furniture, however, is the costly bespoke kind commissioned by the mercantile elite of Newport and nearby Providence. Much of it is the work of the members of two intermarried families of Quaker cabinetmakers, the Townsends and the Goddards. Numerous signed and dated pieces by members of that clan document a progression of styles. The Queen Anne style was established in the mid-seventeen-forties with high chests, dressing tables, and tea tables, all delicate, angular, and with pointed slipper feet (cat. no. 115), a variation on Boston design, maturing in the 1750s to massive baroque tables having serpentine fronts and circular pad feet. The Chippendale style had virtually no influence on Newport furniture. John Goddard owned a copy of Chippendale's *Director*, but, as in Boston, to no discernible effect. Beginning in the late 1750s, in place of the progression toward a regional version of the Chippendale style found elsewhere, the Boston block-front treatment was reinterpreted, emerging as the remarkable Newport version: a lobed shell crowning the blocking. For nearly thirty years, between 1765 and 1792, John Townsend, possibly the originator of the style and its best-known practitioner, made block-and-shell case pieces of almost unchanged design (cat. no. 139). In addition, the Townsends and Goddards executed cabriole-leg furniture with knees embellished by elegant, stylized leafage (cat. no. 99); tables with stop-fluted legs (cat. no. 100); and stands and screens with tiny cat's-paw feet (cat. no. 133). All are illustrious for their precision of execution and for the rare quality of their wood, a dense purplish Honduras mahogany; all are fashioned in a uniquely American design. Newport's prosperity came to an abrupt end with the British occupation of 1776–79, and her mercantile economy never recovered after the war.

Nevertheless, the peace in 1783 marked the beginning of a decade during which the Townsends and Goddards produced some of their finest work, much of it for the merchants of Providence, a city then in ascendancy.

CONNECTICUT.   Furniture made in Connecticut often has a characteristically crisp, sharp-edged quality that is at least in part the result of the regional preference for working with the hard, native cherry wood. Aside from that, there is no single Connecticut style, for the simple reason that there was no dominant urban center to establish one. Instead, a number of local styles developed, produced by the craftsmen of coastal and river towns for their local markets. Pattern books appear to have played no part in their designs, and, unlike what is found elsewhere, the styles show more the influence of their neighboring regions than of England.

One of the most prolific centers was in New London County, in the southeast, adjacent to Rhode Island, where magnificent case furniture was made in the towns of Norwich and Colchester. The Newport influence is greatest there, as might be expected, extending even to a version of the block-and-shell motif. Some pieces share Massachusetts and New York features (cat. no. 178). Up the Connecticut River, in the colony's central region and in the city of Hartford, there were a number of regional styles: at Windsor, a group of exceptionally designed chests painted in a disarmingly unorthodox manner (cat. no. 152); at East Windsor, a Connecticut interpretation of the Philadelphia Chippendale, the inspiration of the Chapin family of craftsmen (cat. no. 10); and at Hartford itself, serpentine-fronted case pieces owing a debt to Massachusetts design. Distinctive Queen Anne and Chippendale furniture from the western coastal towns of New Haven County—centers of a lively furniture business in the seventeenth century—has not been identified, though manufacture of turned chairs continued there throughout the century. Other groups of Connecticut pieces have yet to be assigned to a region (cat. no. 141).

NEW YORK CITY.   New York City, which was not to experience rapid growth until the Federal period, had approximately the same number of furnituremakers as had Newport during the late colonial period. Some Queen Anne chair models made in both cities are so similar that where any given one originated is still open to question (cat. nos. 7, 8, 21), a direct result of the close trade connections between the two colonies. In all other respects, however, the furniture made in Newport and in New York City could hardly be less alike. Where Newport's craftsmen created distinctive, uniquely American designs, New York makers followed English practice with but little change. Since New Yorkers, from the royal governor on down, wanted familiar English furniture regardless of what side of the Atlantic it was made on, New York work tends to be as broad and heavy as the English furniture it copies. Its Englishness, a clear reflection of the dominance of Loyalists in the city's population, was made possible by the large numbers of English craftsmen who emigrated to New York in mid-century, turning their London training to good advantage. The upholsterer Joseph Cox, to name one, advertised himself as "from London" for some sixteen years, from 1757 until 1773 (cat. no. 81).

A certain number of pieces must have been imported. Among the few still identifiable today are a japanned Queen Anne desk and bookcase and a gilt rococo looking glass (acc. nos. 39.184.1, 13), which descended in the Verplanck family with furniture of New York manufacture (see cat. no. 24), and an easy chair that descended from Peter Townsend of Albany (acc. no. 33.26). Though the first two pieces bear no resemblance to New York work, the third one does. With its leaf-carved knees and claw-and-ball feet, it was thought to be locally made when it was acquired by the Museum, but it is unquestionably English, albeit a chair that may have served as a model for local makers. Understandably, such quintessentially American models as high chests and dressing tables were rarely produced in New York. The market was for familiar English forms—the chest-on-chest (cat. no. 146) or the clothes press. The influence of New York City cabinetmakers extended to Long Island, to western New Jersey, and especially up the Hudson River to Albany. How much of the furniture used by the Schuylers, the Van Rensselaers, and the Livingstons was from the city and how much was made upriver has never been determined (cat. no. 127).

Relatively little New York furniture of the late colonial period is now known. In 1776, in the first of a series of catastrophic fires, a third of the city was destroyed; at the British evacuation in 1783 many Loyalists fled to Canada or back to England, taking their household furnishings with them. Of the surviving pieces, a sizable number retain histories that link them to distinguished New York families, including the Beekmans, the Verplancks, and the Van Rensselaers, but since labeling was uncommon, very few can be dated or documented to a specific maker.

Evidence to fix precisely the introduction of the Queen Anne style has not been established. The fragmentary accounts of Joshua Delaplaine suggest that he was working in the style by about 1740: a "mahogany dressing table" in 1737; a "large claw table" in 1740; a pair of mahogany chests-on-chests in 1741. Leaf-carved knees and claw feet in the Chippendale style were in fashion by the late seventeen-fifties (cat. no. 81), but almost no dated New York Chippendale furniture exists. When and by whom even that most famous of New York table-types, the serpentine-sided card table, was introduced remains to be determined.

PHILADELPHIA. The meteoric growth of Philadelphia began in the seventeen-thirties. Her prosperity was based on direct trade with the British Isles—England (London and Bristol) and Ireland. By the seventeen-forties only Boston was larger in population and shipping; by 1765 Philadelphia's population had more than doubled to about 25,000, while Boston's had stabilized at about 15,000. Philadelphia was now the fourth largest city in the English-speaking world—coming after London, Edinburgh, and Dublin—and the influence of its furniture designs rapidly spread to eastern Pennsylvania, western New Jersey, Delaware, and Maryland. Woodworking was a big local industry. The names of 172 woodworkers are recorded between 1730 and 1760; in 1783, just after the Revolution, 111 are listed on the tax rolls; three years later, the number had risen by another 50.

Concurrent with Philadelphia's expansion in the seventeen-thirties was the introduction of the Queen Anne style and the attendant growth or revitalization of a local chairmaking industry. The new style presumably made its first local appearance not long after its arrival in Boston, in about 1730, but the earliest documented reference to it is the half dozen "Crookt foot Chairs" (that is, with cabriole legs) sold by the chairmaker Solomon Fussell in 1738. At about that time, at the end of that decade, the golden age of Philadelphia chairmaking dawned. Its prime mover or catalyst, judging from his numerous newspaper advertisements, was Plunket Fleeson, a native-born chairmaker. To stem the flood of inexpensive Boston Chairs, he employed local chairmakers to produce similar leather-covered maple examples.

Of greater importance, he "ingaged, and for many Months, employed several of the best Chair-makers in the Province to the End he might have a Sortment of Choice Walnut Chair Frames . . . of the newest and best Fashions." Chairs like those, whose curved stiles, elaborately outlined splats, balloon seats, and slipper feet form a symphony of curves, are the perfect manifestation of the American Queen Anne style (cat. nos. 36–43). They were made in considerable numbers, normally in sets of six or more, until at least the seventeen-sixties.

At the same time, though with less dramatic results, the city's cabinetmakers also turned to the Queen Anne style, creating round, or pillar-and-claw, tea tables and straight-fronted case pieces of solid walnut that depended for ornamentation on the grain of the wood. Those forms were interpreted in an unmistakable Philadelphia manner; only rare examples (e.g., cat. no. 162) show any direct influence from New England.

The Chippendale style, or, rather, some of its best-known features—claw-and-ball feet, leaf-carved knees, pierced splats, shell-carved drawers, all executed in mahogany—came into fashion in the early seventeen-fifties. The earliest of several documented examples is a high chest dated 1753, the year before the first edition of Chippendale's *Director* was published. During the next decade, those same features were grafted many a time onto Queen Anne forms (cat. no. 45). It was the seventeen-sixties and seventies, however, the years of Philadelphia's undisputed colonial supremacy, that witnessed the full flowering of the Philadelphia school of cabinetwork. Craftsmen trained in London's finest shops had located there: the cabinetmaker Thomas Affleck, a Scot who had apprenticed in Edinburgh before moving to London in 1760, arrived in 1763; the carver Hercules Courtenay, an apprentice of the famous London designer and carver Thomas Johnson, had arrived by 1765. If they had remained in London they would have been in the employ of one of the great shops, perhaps Chippendale's very own; in Philadelphia they worked for themselves. London styles, those of Chippendale in particular, were the acknowledged ideal. The *Director* was widely available: one of the four copies known to have been in Philadelphia could be had from the Library Company prior to 1770, and a local publication modeled on it was proposed in 1775.

In case furniture, playful rococo carved ornament was applied to severely architectural forms, the classic English mixture of Palladian and rococo (perhaps Philadelphians thought their city to be to the American colonies what London was to England). Though to identify English furniture that was in Philadelphia during the eighteenth century is now difficult, many a Pennsylvania merchant traveled to London and ordered his furniture there. As political relations worsened, the importation of English goods was curtailed, but by then there were craftsmen in place who were well able to work in the London manner. That the London-style trade card (about 1771) of Benjamin Randolph was decorated with designs copied from Chippendale, Johnson, and other London pattern books was symptomatic. The costliest bespoke pieces proudly display whole decorative motifs borrowed from the most popular books (cat. no. 168). If members of Philadelphia's merchant class could not buy London furniture, they would have it made in their own city.

WILLIAMSBURG AND CHARLESTON.   Southern furniture of the late colonial period is characteristically English in design and proportion, but each of the leading cabinetmaking centers—chiefly Williamsburg and Charleston—nonetheless has its own distinct regional style.

Williamsburg, the capital of Virginia, was also the colony's cabinetmaking center. Objects attributed to its leading shops, those of Peter Scott and Anthony Hay, are generally in a somewhat heavy, Early Georgian style. In Charleston, the capital of South Carolina and a city notable for its opulence and grace, some sixty cabinetmakers were active between 1735 and 1780. What furniture has been associated with Charleston is of standard English form and shows the influence of Chippendale's *Director*.

These southern styles were only recently recognized. Settlement patterns in the South differed from those in the North in that they were established around a plantation economy; the great houses were widely scattered and far from town or city; and the wealthy land-owners imported their furniture, largely from England. Until fairly recently, therefore, the misconception existed that there were not enough settlements and markets necessary to man-ufacturing enterprises and that as a result little or no southern furniture was made in the fash-ionable eighteenth-century styles. Since there was held to be no native southern furniture, none was sought-after during the early twentieth-century heyday of buying and studying American antique furniture. For these reasons, there is little furniture from the South in the great public collections. The only southern pieces in the Museum's holdings are two corner cupboards from Virginia's Eastern Shore and a magnificent Charleston easy chair (cat. no. 79), which because of its basic design was thought to be from New York City until chairs with comparable refinement of handling were proved to have a Charleston origin.

THE STYLES OUTMODED. The late colonial era came to a close with the Declaration of Independence in 1776, but in terms of furnituremaking it continued until about 1790. The war disrupted normal commerce, and the business of cabinetmaking came to a near-stand-still in the years between 1775 and 1783. Many craftsmen—Benjamin Frothingham of Charlestown, Massachusetts, and Thomas Affleck of Philadelphia among them—took up arms, Frothingham on the side of the Patriots, Affleck as a Loyalist. After the peace treaty was signed in Paris, some cabinetmakers never went back to the business; others picked up where they had left off, at the height of the Chippendale style. John Cogswell of Boston made his masterpiece, a bombé chest-on-chest with rococo scroll pediment, in 1782, the same year that Thomas Tufft of Philadelphia fashioned a claw-and-ball-footed serpentine-back sofa. In Newport, John Townsend kept to his practice of making classic block-and-shell chests until as late as 1792.

The ratification of the Constitution in 1788 coincided with the appearance in London of two illustrated furniture books: *The Cabinet-Maker's London Book of Prices, and Designs of Cabinet Work* and George Hepplewhite's *Cabinet-Maker and Upholsterer's Guide*. These volumes were the first to make widely known a version of the classical style that had been de-veloped a quarter of a century earlier by Robert and James Adam for their noble clientele. The books, interpreting the Adam neoclassicism and making it available for middle-class use, had a revolutionary effect on American furniture design. The style, characterized by straight lines, simple geometric shapes, and veneered and inlaid surfaces, was enthusiastically adopted by a new generation of craftsmen. In the urban centers of America, the Queen Anne and Chippen-dale styles of the late colonial period were suddenly outmoded.

A History of the Collection

The Metropolitan Museum of Art's collection of eighteenth-century American furniture is the result of the generosity and foresight of numerous persons—collectors and curators, for the most part—over a span of seventy-five years. Though the Museum was founded in 1870, at least four decades passed before it would make a serious commitment to the decorative arts of the American Colonial and Federal periods. To be sure, an interest in American art was implicit from the Museum's beginnings, for the founding members of the Board of Trustees included such distinguished representatives from the artistic community as Richard Morris Hunt, architect; John Quincy Adams Ward, sculptor; and John F. Kensett, painter. The first piece of American sculpture, an 1858 version of Hiram Powers's *California*, was acquired in 1872; the first painting, in 1874, was Henry Gray Peters's 1849 *Wages of War*. The year 1874 also saw a gift from Kensett's brother of thirty-eight of the artist's unfinished landscapes. Five years later, the Museum's first director, General Louis Palma di Cesnola, then newly appointed, encouraged the addition of pictures by early American artists—Trumbull and Stuart among them—to the permanent collection.

The collecting of American decorative arts was another matter. The acquisition of examples from the shops of New York's finest practicing designers and craftsmen was begun as early as 1877, a symbol of the Museum's determination to foster artistic progress in the nation. In that year, William Cullen Bryant gave to the Museum the silver vase, made by Tiffany in 1875, that a group of friends had commissioned in honor of his eightieth birthday. The gift of H. O. Havemeyer in 1896 of his collection of art glass made by Louis Comfort Tiffany rounded out two decades that the Metropolitan had dedicated to the acquisition and display of American design at its best. Among the furniture being collected at the same time were grandiose exposition pieces: chairs in the Henri II style made by Pottier and Stymus for the Philadelphia Centennial Exposition and presented to the Museum in 1885, and a standing cabinet made by Charles Tisch in 1884 for the New Orleans Exposition and given in 1889, all objects manifesting "the application of arts to manufacture and practical life," one of the Museum's stated purposes as outlined in its charter.

Concurrently, Americans were developing an interest in their colonial past, a nostalgic looking back to what was perceived as a simpler, more noble time. Men such as Cummings Davis (1810–1890) of Concord and author Benjamin Perley Poore (1820–1887) of Washington, who continued to maintain his family residence in West Newbury, amassed in their Massachusetts houses American objects of historical and sentimental association. Not surprisingly, the first piece of American antique furniture the Museum acquired, in January 1891, was described by the donor as "a relic of Washington, in the shape of one of [the] Mount Vernon chairs," and in 1900, an armchair used by Henry Clay in the United States Senate Chamber was presented by one of his descendants. Because both chairs were valued solely for their association with famous Americans—an approach laudable for a historical society but hardly suited to an art museum—they were never exhibited. (In 1902, at the donor's request, the Museum relinquished the Washington chair to the Society of Colonial Dames at Van Cortlandt Manor; in 1973, it sold the Clay chair to the Smithsonian Institution.)

In 1907, on receipt of the Georges Hoentschel collection of French medieval and eighteenth-century decorative arts, the Museum publicly recognized that category of artistic endeavor as worthy of display by creating, for the first time, a Department of Decorative Arts, with W. R. Valentiner as curator. (Previously, the Museum's only individual curatorial departments were for paintings, sculpture, and casts.) To house the immense collection—a gift of J. P. Morgan—a new decorative arts wing was begun in 1908, completed in 1910, and renamed the Morgan Wing in 1918.

In the same spirit, the Museum purchased in 1908 twenty-seven pieces of English Chippendale furniture from Tiffany Studios, part of a collection that Louis Comfort Tiffany, acting on the advice of furniture authority Luke Vincent Lockwood, had acquired in 1906 from Thomas B. Clarke of New York. Lockwood published the collection under the title *A Collection of English Furniture of the XVII & XVIII Centuries* in 1907, though it was subsequently found to be a mixture of original and reproduction English furniture, even including a few American pieces. One of the chairs, an exceptionally elaborate example (cat. no. 58) originally thought to be English but actually of Philadelphia manufacture, constituted the first piece of American antique furniture to be acquired by the Museum as a work of art. In the *Bulletin* of June 1908, Lockwood wrote glowingly about the recent acquisitions of "English" furniture, concluding with the plea that the Museum begin to add early American furniture to its galleries:

> The ideal collection . . . for the Museum would be a combination of English and American pieces, the former to show the models from which the colonial workmen acquired their inspiration and the latter to show the independent development of the style far away from the influences of fashion.

A carved and gilded Boston picture frame (cat. no. 213, the first object in the book to be acquired) came to the Museum that same year as an adjunct to the principal acquisition, a Copley pastel, but the February 1908 issue of the *Bulletin* did make passing reference to it as "contemporaneous with the picture and . . . itself attractive in its quaintness." The few sporadic purchases of American furniture made around the same time included two seventeenth-century oak case pieces from the collection of Irving P. Lyon of Buffalo, a William and Mary-style high chest, and a Chippendale dressing table.

When Henry Watson Kent (1866–1948) joined the Museum staff in 1905, he provided the mainspring of interest in things American. Kent, a New Englander whose enthusiasm for early American decorative arts was first kindled during his tenure as curator of the Slater Memorial Museum in Norwich, Connecticut, came to the Metropolitan to assist Robert W. de Forest, Secretary of the Board of Trustees. In 1909, in a series of new exhibition galleries, the Museum mounted an exhibition in honor of the Hudson–Fulton Celebration, a city-wide event "commemorative of the tercentenary of the discovery of the Hudson River by Henry Hudson in the year 1609, and the centenary of the first use of steam in the navigation of said river by Robert Fulton in the year 1807." De Forest agreed to chair the subcommittee on Art Exhibits, choosing to display for the Hudson section seventeenth-century Dutch paintings in American collections.

For the Fulton section, Kent suggested a display of the arts of Colonial America, his particular passion. De Forest agreed with Kent's proposal, thus presenting him with the opportunity to begin to amass a collection for this museum that would become one of its glories. Of the 176 pieces of furniture displayed at the exhibition, only seven were actually owned by the

Museum. For the rest Kent called upon the collectors Francis Hill Bigelow, R. T. Haines Halsey, Luke Vincent Lockwood, and, especially, H. Eugene Bolles and George S. Palmer. As de Forest was later to say, in an address at the opening of the American Wing, he himself viewed the exhibition as an opportunity "to test out the question whether American decorative art was worthy [of] a place in an art museum."

The Hudson–Fulton Celebration's tremendous popular success gave a resoundingly positive answer to de Forest's question. The Museum lost no time in altering its acquisitions policy, abandoning its pursuit of late-nineteenth-century objects in favor of a permanent collection of American decorative arts of the Colonial and early Federal periods. Even before the Celebration had ended, a major part of the furniture in it had been given to the Museum.

Eugene Bolles (1838–1910), a Boston lawyer, had acquired parts of the celebrated collections of the early Hartford collectors Irving W. Lyon and Albert Hosmer to supplement his own extensive holdings. In addition to great numbers of seventeenth-century case pieces and seventeenth- and eighteenth-century turned tables and chairs, his 434 objects, largely of New England origin, included representative pieces in the Queen Anne and Chippendale styles that account for twenty-five entries in this catalogue. Among them are three absolute masterpieces of their kind: a Newport block-and-shell bureau table (cat. no. 135), a Massachusetts walnut high chest with carved and gilded shells (cat. no. 157), and a Salem block-front desk and bookcase (cat. no. 181). De Forest and Kent, on learning that Bolles was considering the sale of his collection, arranged for Mrs. Russell Sage, widow of the well-known financier, to purchase it and give it to the Museum. Bolles wrote to Kent in October 1909 of his sale to the Museum:

> I sincerely hope that it will be the basis of a much larger and complete collection, and inspire a genuine and abiding interest in that range of things from the simple and quaint to the really beautiful, which are commonly called colonial. It is a line of collecting which has hitherto been wholly neglected, to my great surprise, by our large museums, although among the people of New England and their descendants throughout the United States, I think there is hardly any kind of collection which appeals so directly to their hearts or gives them so much simple reminiscent pleasure.

The next year, in the June issue of the *Bulletin*, Kent wrote of the purchase:

> With [a few] exceptions, no activity has as yet been displayed by our public museums in the conservation and exhibition in a dignified and discriminating manner—such as would be displayed in the treatment of the art of any other country—of the art of our own land. It is to Mrs. Sage's wise liberality that we, in New York, are enabled to save the evidence of our forefathers' appreciation of art before they shall have been scattered beyond recall and to show with becoming respect the work of their hands.

The Bolles collection—the nucleus of what was to become the American Wing—was temporarily exhibited in galleries in the decorative arts wing, but a decision was rapidly made that these examples of the American arts would be shown to best advantage in appropriate domestic settings. What was needed was a separate wing consisting of rooms taken from colonial houses. In 1914 Durr Friedley was named Acting Curator of Decorative Arts and R. T. Haines Halsey, a Trustee and an avid collector of Duncan Phyfe furniture, was appointed chairman of the newly formed Committee on American Decorative Arts. With de Forest and Kent to encourage them, the two men began systematically to expand the collection and to acquire suitable architectural elements.

The Museum's permanent holdings of American furniture were magnificently augmented in 1918 with the purchase of the Palmer collection. George S. Palmer (1855–1934) was a New London, Connecticut, textiles manufacturer and a cousin of Eugene Bolles. The two men formed complementary collections: Bolles focused on early New England pieces; Palmer preferred richly carved mahogany furniture, especially that from Philadelphia. Of the sixty-six pieces the Museum purchased from Palmer, forty-one were American, twenty-eight of them in the Queen Anne or Chippendale style. Preeminent among the latter, seventeen of which appear in this catalogue, are the Cadwalader slab table (cat. no. 97)—perhaps the finest known piece of American carved furniture—and the Philadelphia high chests and dressing tables (cat. nos. 165–168) enthusiastically attributed to the newly discovered cabinetmaker William Savery by Halsey in a December 1918 *Bulletin* article. While negotiating the sale with Halsey, Palmer, in a July 1918 letter to him, displayed a remarkable understanding of an art museum's requirements:

> . . . In bringing the matter before the Trustees, will you kindly state that in making an offering of our things to the Museum I have constantly kept in mind the value of space in the Museum and that the Museum should have only things of the highest quality and in general types representing progression of styles, etc. . . . I worked in unison with my cousin Mr. Bolles, whose collection the Museum now owns, for twenty years or more, more or less with the hope that our things might be placed in permanent relation with each other in some museum. Since his death, many of the finest things I offer have come to me, so that his things and mine together form such a complete representation of American artistic craftsmanship in wood as can never be matched.
>
> I asked Mr. Erving of Hartford, a well-known connoisseur, and Mr. Lockwood of New York, also a connoisseur and author of high repute, separately, to value the things which I am offering, stating to them the sentiment I felt that these things should be joined to my cousin's in the Metropolitan Museum. Their estimates are surprisingly similar but I have fixed a sum total somewhat less than that of either of these gentlemen. This way of arriving at the value seems to me fair.

In November 1922, the Museum announced that Robert W. de Forest, who had been its president since 1913, and Mrs. de Forest, a dedicated collector of antiques, were giving a new wing to be devoted entirely to American art of the Colonial, Revolutionary, and Early Republican periods. When the American Wing was formally opened, on November 10, 1924, the dreams of de Forest, Kent, and Halsey were finally realized. Each of the three floors of the new wing, at the northwest corner of the Museum and entered through the Morgan Wing, corresponded with one of the three periods into which Halsey had divided America's decorative arts, a division based on homogeneity of form and decoration: the late gothic of the first period (1630–1725); the baroque or cabriole, with rococo influence, of the second period (1725–1790); and the classical revival of the third period (1790–1825). The catalogues of the American furniture collection (this book, the first to be published, represents the second period) will follow the same stylistic divisions, if under different names.

The years following the opening of the American Wing saw a steady growth in the Museum's acquisition of American furniture, primarily through the gift or purchase of private collections. In 1925, Louis Guerineau Myers (1874–1932) of New York sold to the Museum forty-one pieces of Queen Anne-style furniture, twenty-three of which are included in this catalogue. Myers, an enthusiastic student and collector of American furniture, had two primary concerns: to acquire the most aesthetically pleasing pieces and to identify regional cabinetmaking styles. For instance, he was the first person to distinguish the characteristic features of Philadelphia Queen Anne chairs. Outstanding among the eleven from his collection appearing in the catalogue are a corner chair (cat. no. 43), two armchairs (cat. nos. 36, 45), and the famous Logan family settee (cat. no. 80).

From a descendant of the original owner the Museum purchased in 1927 three supreme examples of Newport cabinetwork, each bearing the label of John Townsend (cat. nos. 100, 139, 192). Their mellow, undisturbed surfaces attest to continuous tenure in one New England family. Forty years later, again directly from a New England family, the Museum purchased another magnificent and wonderfully preserved piece of Newport furniture: a card table attributable to John Goddard (cat. no. 99).

In 1930, George Coe Graves presented to the Museum his large and varied collection of American and English decorative art. Ten of its approximately eighty pieces of American furniture are included in this catalogue, notable among them a perfect rococo settee (cat. no. 83) and four clocks (cat. nos. 190, 196, 200, 201). Additional gifts made by Graves in 1932 include four fine Philadelphia Chippendale chairs he purchased at the 1931 auction of the Myers collection (cat. nos. 50, 54, 56, 57). The gifts, identified as "The Sylmaris Collection," are named for the country house in Osterville, Massachusetts, where Graves kept them. Graves made the generous stipulation that all the objects he had given could be sold or exchanged for better examples at the Museum's discretion.

In 1933, on the death of Joseph Breck, who had been appointed curator in 1917 to succeed Valentiner, the Department of Decorative Arts was divided into three separate departments: Medieval Art, Renaissance and Modern Art, and the American Wing. Where possible, the furniture in the American Wing was matched according to place of origin and style to the period rooms in which it was displayed, but until 1939 no room was devoted to furniture made exclusively for one family. In that year James De Lancey Verplanck and John Bayard Rodgers Verplanck gave a large and important group of family heirlooms—paintings, porcelains, and furniture—on the condition that they be permanently installed in a suitable eighteenth-century room to be named the Verplanck Room. The family's furniture, save for two English pieces, is all of New York manufacture, and accounts for eight catalogue entries that include a card table (cat. no. 105) en suite with six side chairs (cat. no. 24) and a settee (cat. no. 82)—a rare survival of a pre-Revolutionary American matched set. Subsequent gifts by Verplanck family members include eight chairs from the family's great Gothic-splat set (cat. no. 34). An equally auspicious acquisition of en suite furniture was realized in 1940 with the purchase of five pieces of japanned furniture that had come down in the Pickman and Loring families of Salem, Massachusetts. In addition to the splendid Boston bonnet-top high chest with matching dressing table and looking glass (cat. nos. 155, 156, 210), the group included a William and Mary high chest and an English dressing glass. No other such group is known. Combined at the Museum with the japanned high chest and dressing table from the Bolles collection (cat. nos. 153, 154), it constitutes the largest existing representation of the type.

Of the mere handful of women collectors of note in the first half of the twentieth century, one from New York made a lasting mark on the American Wing. For many years Natalie K. Blair (Mrs. J. Insley Blair) of Tuxedo Park unerringly bought the very best of seventeenth- and eighteenth-century American furniture. In 1939, her most active collecting days behind her, she put about fifty pieces of furniture on long-term loan to the Museum, making gifts of most of them over the course of the ensuing decade: in 1943, the so-called Dunlap chairs from New

Hampshire, with their original crewelwork seat covers (cat. no. 19); in 1945, a group of early painted chests and a unique, painted tilt-top tea table (cat. no. 128); in 1946, other pieces of painted furniture, including a Connecticut high chest from Windsor (cat. no. 152) and four Queen Anne side chairs with crewelwork seats (cat. no. 5); in 1947, a rare New York tall clock by Henry Hill (cat. no. 197); and, in 1950, a Newport easy chair (cat. no. 72), signed, dated, and with its remarkable upholstery intact, the crown jewel of American upholstered furniture. In 1952 and 1953, after Mrs. Blair's death, her benefactions were continued by her daughter, Mrs. Screven Lorillard (cat. nos. 63, 88, 142, 179).

The American Wing was further enriched by the 1962 bequest of Cecile L. Mayer of Tarrytown, New York. Twenty years earlier, Mrs. Mayer (then Mrs. Harold M. Lehman) had asked the Museum to choose from her fine collection of eighteenth-century furniture those pieces it would be interested in having one day. The selection of twenty-one objects she subsequently bequeathed, subject to life estates, includes nine in this volume. Particularly felicitous additions to the American Wing are a unique New England high chest (cat. no. 149) now reunited with its matching dressing table (cat. no. 150); a rare bombé dressing glass (cat. no. 204); and some especially pleasing Philadelphia chairs (cat. nos. 42, 48). More recently, the Museum has been able to select material from two other important New York collections: in 1971, that of Flora E. Whiting—six catalogue entries, a Boston block-front desk of exceptional quality (no. 177) among them; in 1974, that of Lesley and Emma Sheafer—three catalogue entries, of which one (cat. no. 117) is the only known Massachusetts square tea table to have knees with rococo carving.

Over the years, and never more so than recently, the collection has been fleshed out by gifts of single objects of great distinction: in 1980, the only Newport high chest with four carved knees and open-talon claw feet (cat. no. 161); in 1981, a graceful square tea table from Newport (cat. no. 115); in 1984, one of the set of New York chairs from the Apthorp family (cat. no. 22). Others are promised gifts: a fine Connecticut armchair (cat. no. 10) and, currently on loan, the only known Massachusetts Masonic armchair (cat. no. 12).

Gifts of funds for the acquisition of these treasures have been just as important as the gifts of the objects themselves. For the major early purchases the Museum remains indebted to Mrs. Russell Sage's munificence for the Bolles collection; to the John Stewart Kennedy Fund for the Palmer collection; to the Rogers Fund for the Myers collection and the John Townsend Newport pieces; and to the Joseph Pulitzer Bequest for the Pickman family japanned furniture. The tradition continues: in recent years important acquisitions have been made possible by increasing numbers of generous friends and benefactors.

American Furniture of the Late Colonial Period is a record of the Museum's holdings in the Queen Anne and Chippendale styles as of October 1984. The book contains a number of objects not now on view which are either bequests subject to life estates or promised gifts. Excluded from these pages are pieces that have been deemed unsuitable for reasons of authenticity, condition, or quality. Furniture made in America during the late colonial period but neither in the Queen Anne or Chippendale styles nor in the English tradition—the Windsor style of turned-leg seating forms and characteristic furniture from the Pennsylvania German communities, essentially—has also been omitted.

The Metropolitan's collection, even though it is one of the largest and finest and in many ways the most comprehensive in the country, is not an entirely accurate reflection of the full range of American cabinetwork. Its emphasis is overwhelmingly on high-style objects, with an unabashed prejudice in favor of those of great aesthetic merit. And it is still uneven—exceptional riches in Boston japanned case pieces and in the Philadelphia Chippendale style generally, but a regrettable paucity of examples from rural areas and an almost total lack of representation from the South.

The catalogue's primary purpose, therefore, must be to serve as a work of reference: to provide comprehensive descriptions and histories of each of the Museum's pieces. The book is divided into four categories according to the basic functions for which furniture is made: accommodation (seating and sleeping), service (tables and stands), storage (case furniture), and protection (frames). Each of these categories is subdivided into chapters, usually according to recognizable types. Among the tables, for example, these are slab, card, dining, and tea. The order of the chapters and the order of entries within each chapter follow an essentially visual progression. Like objects are grouped together, and, where possible, are listed according to chronological or geographical arrangement.

I SEATING AND SLEEPING FURNITURE

1 New England Chairs

Chairs are the most numerous of American late colonial furniture. Household inventories record large numbers of them in both parlors and bedchambers, where they were apparently lined up against the walls when not in use. That they were almost always made in matching sets—side chairs in groups of at least six; armchairs in pairs or en suite with the side chairs—is proved by the code their makers employed to keep the separate parts from being mixed up when the chairs were sent to be upholstered. The code consisted of numerals incised on the seat rails and seat frames of those with slip seats and on the shoe and splat or rear seat rail of those to be upholstered over the rail. The chairs are divided among three chapters in the catalogue, according to place of origin. Chapter 1 includes diverse types from New England's leading furniture centers. The classic New England Queen Anne chair with baluster splat, cabriole front legs, and pad feet was introduced into Boston in about 1730; the seats, or bottoms, as they were called, were usually leather-covered. Regional renditions from Massachusetts, Rhode Island, and Connecticut are present in the Museum's collection, though armchairs are not. The individual features of those regions became more pronounced with the coming of the Chippendale style. The collection, while particularly rich in the finest carved versions from Boston, also contains important examples from New Hampshire and Connecticut.

1. Side Chair

New England, 1730–60

ON THIS CHAIR, number V in a set of at least six, the molded rear stiles and the upholstered rectangular splat are carryovers from the William and Mary style, and suggest an early date. A chair now at the NHS (acc. no. 1885.2), with a similar back but with turned legs and Spanish feet and hence an even earlier date, has a history of having come from the William Ellery house, Thomas Street, Newport. On that basis, the only known mate to cat. no. 1 has been attributed to Rhode Island (*Antiques* 77 [April 1960], p. 331; Ott 1965, no. 1). Though on the chairs the treatment of the seat rails and legs is typical of large numbers of New England counterparts (e.g., cat. no. 2), the ample circular pads of the feet are characteristic of Newport work.

PROVENANCE: Ex coll.: Walter Hosmer, Hartford; H. Eugene Bolles, Boston. On loan by the MMA to the Kenmore Association, Fredericksburg, Virginia, from 1931 to 1978.

CONSTRUCTION: The back is serpentine in profile. On the posts, the stiles are molded in front and flat behind; the rear legs are beveled on all four corners between the seat and the stretchers. Rectangular vertical supports tenoned to the crest and the bottom rail frame the splat. The bottom edges of the front and side seat rails are shaped: on the front, with symmetrical scallops; on the sides, with flat arches ending at the rear in serpentine curves. A flat, bevel-edged shoe is nailed to the rear rail. The crest rail, the front and side seat rails, and the side stretchers are pegged.

CONDITION: The wood is a mellow walnut brown in color. Except at the right front, the knee brackets are replaced. The vertical framing members of the splat have been refitted—one may be a replacement—and the crest rail repegged. The slip seat has its original muslin and stuffing. An old photograph of the chair (MMA files) shows similar splat upholstery but nails more closely spaced. That covering was apparently added when the splat frame was restored. The chair is here illustrated with the old reddish brown leather in which it was covered in 1978, the nailing pattern conforming to that on the original leather of the chair's mate (Ott 1965, no. 1).

INSCRIPTIONS: Incised, on front seat-rail rabbet: *V*; on slip-seat frame: *II*. A paper label (20th-century) pasted inside rear skirt rail printed: *Included in the collection of Antique Furniture transferred to Mr. H. E. Bolles, and Mr. Geo. S. Palmer.* In brown ink, on the label: *A chair, Leather back embroidered* [signed] *Walter Hosmer.* In ink, within a printed red lozenge on a paper label inside right skirt rail: *368.* Stamped, under side stretcher blocks: *3* (left); *4* (right). In pencil, on slip-seat frame: *Bolles/23 + 17.*

DIMENSIONS: H.: overall, 41½ (*105.4*), seat, 17 (*43.2*); W.: seat front, 19¼ (*48.9*), seat back, 14¾ (*37.5*), feet, 20¾ (*52.7*); D.: seat, 16⅛ (*41.*), feet, 20 (*50.8*).

1

WOODS: Primary: walnut. Secondary: maple (splat side and bottom rails, slip-seat frame).

Gift of Mrs. Russell Sage, 1909   (10.125.212)

2. Side Chairs (Two)

New England, 1730–90

CHAIRS OF THIS TYPE, with yoke crest, straight stiles, inverted baluster splat, and scalloped front skirt, were made in large sets and survive in great numbers. They have descended in colonial families of Massachusetts, Rhode Island, and Connecticut (Randall 1965, no. 135). Connecticut examples often exhibit distinctive regional features (see cat. no. 5), but to separate those made in Rhode Island from those made around Boston is difficult. On the MMA pair, numbers V and XII in their set, the boldly shaped circular pads of the front feet are suggestive of documented Newport examples (e.g., cat. no. 72), which may indicate their place of origin.

The shape of the scalloped skirts and the use of turned or chamfered rear legs, as well as the more subtle differences in shape and proportion of the splat, crest rail, and pad feet, distinguish the members of different sets. A chair at Dearborn (Hagler 1976, p. 16, top) is identical in every detail to the MMA pair, but not in every proportion. Other examples—at Boston (Randall 1965, no. 135), Sturbridge (Kirk 1972, no. 99), and Williamsburg

2

(Greenlaw, no. 50)—are identical save for the shaping of the side skirts. Boston was the chairmaking and exporting center of New England, and the greatest number of chairs of this type were undoubtedly made there. In 1732, Mrs. Andrew Oliver was portrayed by John Smibert in just such a chair (Bishop, fig. 81).

PROVENANCE: Ex coll.: Charlotte E. Hoadley, Darien, Connecticut.

CONSTRUCTION: On each chair: The back is markedly serpentine in profile. On the posts, the rectangular stiles are beveled at the back edges and become rounded at the crest rail; the rear legs are turned between the seat rails and the stretchers. The seat rails are similar in shape to those of cat. no. 1. The side stretchers and the rails are pegged.

CONDITION: The chairs, which have been refinished, are dark brown in color. The glue blocks are old replacements. Chair no. V, the one illustrated, has been disassembled and reglued, with new pegs inserted. On chair no. XII, the right front knee bracket has been replaced and a piece of the left side bracket is missing. When the pair were acquired, the slip seats were finished in leather, not their first covering. Their present cover, shown here, is an eighteenth-century blue silk damask, probably French.

INSCRIPTIONS: Incised, on front seat-rail rabbet: *IIIII* (no. V); *VIIIIII* (no. XII).

DIMENSIONS: H.: overall, 42 (*106.7*), seat, 17¾ (*45.1*); W.: seat front, 20¼ (*51.4*), seat back, 14⅞ (*37.8*), feet, 22 (*55.9*); D.: seat, 16½ (*41.9*), feet, 21½ (*54.6*).

WOODS: Primary: walnut. Secondary: cherry (slip-seat frame).

REFERENCES: Myers, fig. 4. Downs 1948, p. 81.

Bequest of Charlotte E. Hoadley, 1946 (46.192.2, 3)

3. Side Chair

New England, 1730–90

NUMBER VII IN ITS SET, this is one of a large number of New England Queen Anne side chairs of similar design. Its splat is narrower than those at cat. no. 2, examples of the same genre. The marquetry device inlaid on the splat, while not an uncommon feature on English prototypes (e.g., Kirk 1982, fig. 786), is not known on any other piece of American furniture. It may have been salvaged from an English chair and inserted here during the eighteenth century.

PROVENANCE: Ex coll.: Louis Guerineau Myers, New York City.

CONSTRUCTION: The chair's construction is similar to that at cat. no. 2. Within the floral surround of the marquetry device is a bird (an eagle?), its face turned to the left. On the slip-seat frame, the side rails are half-lapped over the front and rear rails.

CONDITION: The chair is a dark walnut brown in color. The marquetry inlay has a number of inexpert repairs. The left seat rail, the knee brackets, and the glue blocks are restorations. The slip-seat frame (old, but possibly not the original) has been reupholstered. The chair is illustrated here with a reproduction red wool moreen seat cover.

INSCRIPTIONS: Incised, on front seat-rail rabbet: *VII.*

DIMENSIONS: H.: overall, 42 (*106.7*), seat, 18 (*45.7*); W.: seat front, 20¼ (*51.4*), seat back, 14⅞ (*37.8*), feet, 21⅞ (*55.6*); D.: seat, 16½ (*41.9*), feet, 21 (*53.3*).

WOODS: Primary: walnut. Secondary: white pine (slip-seat frame).

Rogers Fund, 1925 (25.115.20)

4. Roundabout Chair

New England, 1730–60

THIS IS ONE OF A SMALL number of corner chairs with crossed stretchers and identically shaped splats and turnings (*Antiques* 79 [April 1961], p. 350; ibid. 108 [November 1975], p. 855; SPB sale no. 4048, 11/19/77, lot 1218). Another chair, similar to those of the group except for variations in the designs of splat and stretcher, has an identical rush seat (*Antiques* 76 [October 1959], p. 298).

On the MMA chair, the almost circular top of the splat's inverted baluster and the crisply cut trumpet turnings are characteristics of Newport work (see cat. no. 65). A set of chairs with similar splats was once the property of Joseph Wanton, governor of Rhode Island (*Antiques* 105 [April 1975], p. 550). Nevertheless, where in New England the group originated is still in question. An identical roundabout chair now at the CHS (acc. 1969-55-6) descended in the Royce family of Wallingford, Connecticut, home of two members of the Lothrop family of woodworkers from Norwich. On the basis of intermarriages between the Royces and the Lothrops, an attribution of the chair to Samuel Lothrop has been advanced (information from Robert Trent, CHS).

3

4

PROVENANCE: Ex coll.: George Coe Graves, Osterville, Massachusetts.

CONSTRUCTION: The crest rail, rounded in front, flat in back, and with cut-out ends, is affixed to the armrest rail with eight roseheads. The armrest rail is in two pieces butted together at the left of the rear stile. The three stiles are pegged to the armrest rail. The seat rails are pegged to the turned back and side posts and to the cabriole front leg. The rush-covered slip-seat frame rests on corner braces nailed with roseheads to the rails at the back and sides and on a bracket centered in the right rail. The turned stretchers, half-lapped and screwed together at their crossing, are pegged to the legs.

CONDITION: The chair, now reddish tan in color, was originally painted or stained red, and remnants of that color can be seen on the front corner block of the slip seat under the applied strips. The top of the right-hand splat has been patched. Small pieces are missing from the bottom of two legs. The flat strips that hold the seat in place are replacements. The rush seat, probably early nineteenth-century, has sagged, and is broken on the left side.

DIMENSIONS: H.: overall, 31½ (80.), seat, 16⅞ (42.9); W.: seat, 25⅝ (65.1), arms, 29⅜ (74.6), feet, 23½ (59.7); D.: seat, 25 (63.5), feet, 25 (63.5).

WOODS: Primary: maple. Secondary: walnut, ash (corner braces).

The Sylmaris Collection, Gift of George Coe Graves, 1930 (30.120.43)

5. Side Chairs (Four)

Connecticut, 1740–60

THE FOUR CHAIRS were owned by the prominent Hartford collector William B. Goodwin in 1927. In September and October of that year, Goodwin illustrated one of the four in an advertisement in *Antiques* magazine. Identifying himself only as "Box W.B.G.," he requested, as "essential to tracing [the chair's] history," the identity of the owner of another chair from the set which had been sold by a Boston dealer to a western collector in 1925. Goodwin was apparently successful in his quest, for in Nutting's *Furniture Treasury*, published the next year, he was recorded as owning a set of six, "Made by the South-meads of Middletown," and dated 1712 (Nutting 2, no. 2131). The caption for the illustration of the slip seat was: "A Mrs. Southmead of Middletown, Connecticut, Embroidered the Work. About 1720" (ibid., no. 2156). No cabinetmaker of that name has been identified. In 1965, Houghton Bulkeley questioned the Southmead attribution, noting that the name, also given as "Southmayd," had been a very common one in Middletown until the

1850s, and adding that he was "quite sure that Mr Goodwin bought [the four MMA chairs] from a Mrs Derby in Middletown and her sister who lived in Guilford" (1965 correspondence, MMA files). Meanwhile, in 1953, Mrs. Lorillard, daughter of Mrs. Blair, the last private owner of the chairs, gave the Museum a needlework purse (acc. no. 53.179.15) that had a paper label inscribed "1720 / no. 66 / Mrs. Elmer G. Derby, Middletown /Mrs. L.G. South-mayd." If that was the Mrs. Derby whom Bulkeley

5

5

referred to, her sister can then be identified as having married a Southmayd. And if the chairs and the purse acquired by Mrs. Blair came from the same source, presumably the chairs descended in the Southmayd family and the seats were worked by one of the Southmayd wives. A chair advertised in *Antiques* (111 [May 1977], p. 940) appears to be one of the two unlocated chairs from the set.

Chairs at Winterthur (Downs 1952, no. 102) and at Dearborn (Bishop, fig. 80) are from another set, similar, but subtly different in the proportion and shape of their individual parts. Evidently by the same maker as these four, they have been traced back to Colonel Simon Lothrop (1689–1774) of Norwich, Connecticut (Bulkeley correspondence). On the seat frame of one (Hagler, p. 31) is inscribed: "No ³ June 17th 1756 Elizabeth Lothrop," possibly referring to Simon's daughter (1733–1763). The MMA chairs were likely made about the same time. Since a number of Lothrop family members were carpenters and joiners (information from Robert Trent, CHS), the chairs may have been made by one of them. A pair of chairs with turned front legs and rush seats (*Antiques* 111 [June 1977], p. 1113), but otherwise matching the Lothrop set, are apparently by the same hand. The rectilinear rear legs and the stretchers appear to have been inspired by the "Boston chairs" (Randall 1963, pp. 12–20) that were widely exported from that city throughout the mid-eighteenth century.

PROVENANCE: Ex coll.: William B. Goodwin, Hartford; Mrs. J. Insley Blair, Tuxedo Park, New York.

CONSTRUCTION: On each chair: The back is gently serpentine in profile. The cabriole legs and the posts are both square in section. The front edge of the shoe is a molded quarter round. The double-pegged seat rails are unusually deep; those at front and sides have sharply scalloped skirts. The knee brackets are glued to the downward extensions of the rails, the side rails continued in ovolo curves to join the stiles in back. The crest is pegged, as are the side and rear stretchers.

CONDITION: The original finish—reddish brown paint streaked with black to suggest figured mahogany—is remarkably intact, with a dull mat surface. The slip seats have been reupholstered, but they retain their original crewelwork covers, each embroidered in the foreground with trees and flowers or fruit emerging from hills over which assorted shepherds, sheep, dogs, lions, and stags are disposed. The red, blue, green, and brown colors of the crewelwork wool are somewhat faded; the linen backgrounds, darkened with the years, have been much mended. The chairs here illustrated are numbers III and IV in the set.

INSCRIPTIONS: Cut into front seat-rail rabbet of each chair and its matching slip-seat frame, identifying notches: two, three, four, and six, respectively.

DIMENSIONS: H.: overall, 43¼ (*109.9*), seat, 18⅛ (*46.*); W.: seat front, 19½ (*49.5*), seat back, 16½ (*41.9*), feet, 21¼ (*54.*); D.: seat, 17 (*43.2*), feet, 20 (*50.8*).

WOODS: Primary and secondary: maple.

REFERENCES: *Antiques* 12 (September 1927), p. 174; ibid. (October 1927), p. 279 (Goodwin queries). Nutting 2, nos. 2131, 2156 (slip seat). Downs 1948, p. 79 (slip seats); p. 82. W. Johnston, p. 120; figs. 1, 3 (seat-rail detail). Davidson 1967, fig. 170. Kirk 1967, no. 227. Bishop, figs. 60, 60a. Kirk 1972, fig. 184.

Gift of Mrs. J. Insley Blair, 1946   (46.194.1–4)

6. Side Chair

New England, 1740–90

OTHER CHAIRS from the set in which this one is number V are at the Wadsworth Atheneum (numbers II and VI; slip seats numbered IIII and V [Kirk 1972, no. 171, ill.]) and at Deerfield (number IIII; seat numbered VI [Fales 1976, fig. 79]). The latter chair was owned in the Williams family of Deerfield, presumably first by Dr. Thomas (1718–1775) and thereafter by his son Ephraim (1760–1835) and his grandson John (1817–1899), who was a president of Trinity College, Hartford. In the late nineteenth century the Atheneum chairs were owned in Hartford, as was cat. no. 6. Consequently, it has been suggested that the set may have been made in central Connecticut (Fales 1976, fig. 79; P. Johnston, p. 1018, right). The hypothesis seems unlikely, since the chairs bear no stylistic relationship to any recognizable examples of Connecticut manufacture. On cat. no. 6, the tall narrow back and simple inverted baluster splat are reminiscent of a popular, uncarved New England Queen Anne-style chair (see cat. no. 2). The overall design is otherwise similar to that of cat. no. 7, whose knee shells these closely resemble, and cat. no. 8, whose claw feet are very like these. The chairs in this group have been traditionally associated with Newport (see cat. no. 7).

PROVENANCE: Ex coll.: Walter Hosmer, Hartford; H. Eugene Bolles, Boston. In his notes (MMA files), Bolles recorded: "This chair is the original of figure 72 in Dr. Lyon's book. It was formerly in the Hosmer collection and was purchased from him by me in 1894." Lyon states (pp. 161–162): "A chair in the Hosmer collection . . . is made of black walnut and was bought a few years since in Hartford, Conn."

CONSTRUCTION: The back is serpentine in profile. On the posts, the stiles are flat in front, rounded behind, and pieced at the inside curves; the rear legs are chamfered on all four corners between the seat rails and the side stretchers; below the stretchers, only in front. The thick, flat-arched seat rails have straight inner edges. Triangular glue blocks reinforce the front corners. The crest and seat rails are pegged; the side stretchers are pegged at the back.

CONDITION: The chair has a lustrous reddish brown patina. The crest rail is split where it meets the stiles. The right stile is spliced and patched midway up the back. According to MMA records, the chair was originally upholstered in leather. It is illustrated here with a reproduction red wool moreen seat cover.

INSCRIPTIONS: Incised, on front seat-rail rabbet: *V*; on slip-seat frame: *I*.

DIMENSIONS: H.: overall, 41⅛ (*104.5*), seat, 16¾ (*42.5*); W.: seat front, 20½ (*52.1*), seat back, 14¾ (*37.5*), feet, 21⅝ (*54.9*); D.: seat, 17 (*43.2*), feet, 20½ (*52.1*).

WOODS: Primary: walnut. Secondary: maple (slip-seat frame); white pine (glue blocks).

REFERENCES: Lyon, pp. 161–162; fig. 72. Esther Singleton, "The Chippendale Chair," *The Antiquarian* I (September 1923), pp. 3–8; ill., p. 7. Myers, fig. 6. *The Home Craftsman* (November–December 1934), pp. 43–46 (measured drawings). Cescinsky and Hunter, p. 110 (as English). Price, fig. 2.

Gift of Mrs. Russell Sage, 1909   (10.125.252)

6 See also p. 336

7. Side Chair

New England, 1740–90

OF THE QUEEN ANNE chairs of this type that survive in considerable numbers, examples at Bayou Bend (Warren, no. 40) and in the Stone collection (Rodriguez Roque, no. 49) are nearly identical to cat. no. 7, number II in its set; one at Dearborn (Hagler, p. 28) looks to have been carved by the same hand.

These chairs have little to identify them with any particular chairmaking center, and may have been made in more than one place. The flat-arched skirts of the seat rails, the square rear legs with chamfered corners, and the turned stretchers proclaim New England work. A number of the chairs (Jobe and Kaye, no. 99; Hagler, p. 28), including cat. no. 7, have histories of ownership in Massachusetts. The carved shells, particularly the reeded ones with pendent bellflowers on the knees, are of a pattern found both on New York chairs (Fairbanks and Bates, pp. 100–101) and on Newport ones (Ott 1965, no. 8). The chair pattern (cf. cat. nos. 6, 8) has in fact long been associated with Newport (Downs 1952, no. 103; Carpenter, no. 5), an attribution that appears to have been based upon a certain resemblance between the lobate shell emerging from a C-scroll in the crest rail and the shells on Newport case furniture. The only chairs having Newport histories, however, are a variant model with pad feet and uncarved knees (Carpenter, no. 11, said to be by John Goddard for Moses Brown) and square seats (ibid., no. 7), one owned in Newport in 1948 (correspondence, MMA files).

PROVENANCE: Ex coll.: H. Eugene Bolles, Boston.

CONSTRUCTION: The back is straight in profile. On the posts, the stiles are pieced at the inner projections; their chamfered back edges become rounded at the juncture with the crest rail; the rear legs are chamfered on all four edges between the seat and the stretchers; below the stretchers, only in front. The seat rails, straight on the inner edges, are pegged to the stiles and legs. The knee brackets are nailed with double roseheads.

CONDITION: The wood is nut brown in color. The crest rail is broken at its juncture with the right stile, and the shoe is split. The chair is illustrated here with a modern blue wool moreen seat cover.

INSCRIPTIONS: Incised, on front seat-rail rabbet: *II*; on slip-seat frame: *II*. In pencil, on slip-seat frame, front: *H—C—y/ Biffield Mass*; *Oliver D. Rohgers/—Mass*; side: *Oliver D. Rohgers/—s Mass*.

DIMENSIONS: H.: overall, 38¾ (*98.4*), seat, 16½ (*41.9*); W.: seat front, 20⅞ (*53.*), seat back, 15⅛ (*38.4*), feet, 21⅞ (*55.6*); D.: seat, 17½ (*44.5*), feet, 20 (*50.8*).

WOODS: Primary: walnut. Secondary: maple (slip-seat frame).

7 See also p. 336   8 See also p. 336

REFERENCES: MMA 1909, 2, no. 123; ill. facing p. 56. Myers, fig. 3a.

Gift of Mrs. Russell Sage, 1909   (10.125.696)

8. Side Chair

New England, 1740–90

AS WITH CAT. NO. 7, a chair of the same general type, the exact place of origin of this side chair, number I in its set, has not been determined. At the MMA it was thought to be New England until 1939; thereafter, New York. While it is a New England chair in overall design and construction—especially the turned stretchers and the rear-leg treatment—in its carved ornament it reveals motifs employed both in Newport and in New York. The small claw feet, the webbing between the claws covering much of the ball, are a type known on chairs from both regions (see cat. no. 6; Kirk 1972, no. 131), but the knee shells with alternating raised and recessed lobes and no defining bottom scroll are found more often in New York (see cat. no. 22). The shell on the crest rail is like no other known. Rising from a base of symmetrical acanthus leafage, it has a scalloped border and blind-pierced lobes in the rococo manner, but its execution gives no hint of where it was made. Though certain of the chair's features bear comparison with New York work (e.g., cat. no. 21), the overall impression conveyed is New England, specifically Newport.

PROVENANCE: Ex coll.: Louis Guerineau Myers, New York City.

CONSTRUCTION: In front, the crest rail is cut away deeply around the carved shell; in back, it is rounded on either side of a flat middle. On the posts, the stiles are straight in profile; their exaggerated inner curves are pieced; their chamfered back edges become round at the crest rail; the rear legs are turned below the rear rail; below the stretchers, they are beveled at the front edges. The splat is slightly curved in profile. The front of the shoe is cut out in a deep cavetto. The front and side seat rails are straight on the inner edges and flat-arched at the bottom.

The front legs are reinforced with triangular glue blocks. The side rails and side stretchers are pegged. The back surface of the chair is roughly worked.

CONDITION: The rear legs and stretchers have a fine reddish patina and the original thin finish, somewhat decayed. On the chair front, another finish, now dark and crazed, has been applied over the original one. The crest rail has been patched at its juncture with the stiles. The projecting tips of the shell are missing. The pieced part of the left stile has been screwed on; that of the right stile has been patched at the bottom. The left leg brackets are old replacements. The chair is here illustrated in a modern red wool moreen seat cover.

INSCRIPTIONS: Incised, on front seat-rail rabbet: *I*; on slip-seat frame: *IIII*.

DIMENSIONS: H.: overall, 40 (*101.6*), seat, 17 (*43.2*); W.: seat front, 20½ (*52.1*), seat back, 15⅛ (*38.4*), feet, 21¼ (*54.*); D.: seat, 18½ (*47.*), feet, 21¾ (*55.2*).

WOODS: Primary: walnut. Secondary: maple (slip-seat frame); white pine (glue blocks).

REFERENCES: Halsey and Cornelius, fig. 55. Price, fig. 30.

Rogers Fund, 1925   (25.115.11)

9. Side Chair

Newport, 1760–85

ITS INCISED NUMBERS record this as chair number I from a set of at least fourteen. Another chair from the same set was on loan to the MMA from 1954 to 1957 (Ralph E. Carpenter, Jr., "Discoveries in Newport furniture and silver," *Antiques* 68 [July 1955], p. 45, fig. 3); what looks to be a third has been published (*Antiques* 31 [June 1937], p. 310, fig. 7, left); and a fourth appears in nineteenth-century photographs (MMA files) of the interior of the Samuel Powel house, 23 Bowery Street, Newport. Two others, numbered XII and XIII on their front seat rails, are also known (SPB sale no. 5142, 1/28/84, lot 865). The set is unusual among Rhode Island cabriole-leg chairs in having square seat frames and anthemionlike relief carving on sharp-edged knees. Another example with those features is a corner chair (*Antiques* 91 [March 1967], p. 260). Chairs of a second set, certainly by the same hand as cat. no. 9, differ only in their more angular crest rails, in the lack of the bottom C in their crest shells, and in their rounded seat rails and uncarved knees (Hipkiss, no. 80, or Nutting 2, no. 2155; Rodriguez Roque, no. 52; and one at Dearborn). Another chair would be identical to the second set but for its solid splat (Ott 1965, no. 7). Other related examples have variant crest-rail and pierced-splat patterns; some have pad feet (Carpenter, no. 14).

All are of the densest mahogany with areas of light-colored heartwood, and all have straight, square rear legs, flat-arched seat rails, and thin, undistinguished turned stretchers. The combination proclaims common authorship, and the design of the claw-and-ball feet of cat. no. 9 suggests the hand of John Goddard (1723–1785). The feet, in particular the fleshy bulges separating the rear talons from the legs, are like those now attributed to Goddard (Moses 1982, pp. 1132–33). Similar feet appear on the corner chairs that once belonged to John Brown, for whom Goddard is known to have made chairs in 1760 and 1766 (Cooper 1973, pp. 333–334), as well as on a serpentine chest long attributed to Goddard (cat. no. 140).

PROVENANCE: Purchased from Elmer D. Keith, Clintonville, Connecticut. Keith had inherited the chair from Mary Wilbour, younger sister of his great-aunt by marriage Sarah Elizabeth Wilbour Marcy (1829–1916), of Washington Street, Newport. Mary had moved into the house after her sister's death. The chair is described in a "notebook of her best furniture . . . made by Mary not too long before she passed away in 1934" as "One chair with claw feet owned once by my grandmother Dyer, who had, I think, eight or more, perhaps twelve—do not know" (Keith letter, 1/6/56, MMA files). Mary and Sarah's grandmother was Sara Lyon Dyer. Chairs numbered XII and XIII descended through three generations of Charles Morris Smiths of Providence.

CONSTRUCTION: The back is straight in profile. On the posts, the stiles have flat backs and rounded sides and are pieced at the inside curves; the rear legs are rectangular. The splat, its edges unbeveled, is double tenoned into the shoe. The rear seat rail is the thickness of the shoe nailed to it. The flat-arched front and side seat rails are pegged to the front legs and double pegged to the rear ones. The crest rail, rear rail, and side stretchers are also pegged.

CONDITION: The mahogany has a rich reddish brown color. The bottoms of the rear legs are restored. The slip seat, here illustrated with a modern red wool moreen cover, retains the original webbing, stuffing, and muslin.

INSCRIPTIONS: Incised, on front seat-rail rabbet: *I*; on slip-seat frame: *XIIII*; on back of crest, splat, shoe, and rear seat rail, to identify for assembly: *XII*.

DIMENSIONS: H.: overall, 39⅝ (*100.7*), seat, 17⅜ (*44.1*); W.: seat front, 19⅞ (*50.5*), seat back, 15¾ (*40.*), feet, 21¾ (*55.2*); D.: seat, 16¼ (*41.3*), feet, 20½ (*52.1*).

WOODS: Primary: mahogany. Secondary: maple (slip-seat frame).

REFERENCES: W. Johnston, p. 121; fig. 5. Kirk 1972, p. 50; figs. 38, 172.

Rogers Fund, 1955   (55.134)

9 See also p. 336

10.   Armchair

East Windsor, Connecticut, 1770–90

ONE OF THE MOST distinctive groups of Connecticut seating furniture is represented by this chair. Its basic design and several of its decorative and structural details are in the Philadelphia manner: the strapwork splat is the most popular of Philadelphia patterns (see cat. nos. 44–51), the seat rails have notched flat arches and exposed rear tenons, the glue blocks reinforcing them are two-part vertical quarter rounds, the rear legs are stump-shaped, and the armrests are knuckled. Nevertheless, owing in part to the hard, unyielding nature of the cherry wood with which the chairs of the group are made, they

10

are utterly unlike their Philadelphia counterparts in overall effect. The framing members are thin, cut with sharp, hard edges, and, apart from the claw feet, the carving is limited to the lobed shell, molded ears, and knuckles.

All the chairs of the group have been associated with Eliphalet Chapin (1741–1807), cabinetmaker of East Windsor, Connecticut. In 1877, Irving W. Lyon purchased a pair of chairs, now at Yale, for which he was shown a bill of sale, dated 1781, purportedly from Chapin to Alexander King of South Windsor, Connecticut (Kane, no. 117). References to the bill, which has been lost, are the basis for the Chapin attribution. Chapin was born in Somers, Connecticut. Little is known about his early years, although he is said to have trained as a cabinetmaker in Philadelphia—an appealing explanation for the marked Philadelphia style of his furniture (ibid.). Chapin was in East Windsor by 1769, and two years later he acquired land for the house and shop that were to be his until his death. Aaron Chapin (1751–1838), a cousin, moved to East Windsor in 1774, built a house next to Eliphalet's, and probably shared his shop. In 1783 Aaron moved to Hartford, where he advertised that he now carried on "the Cabinet and Chair Making business, in as great variety perhaps as is done in any one shop in the State, in both Mahogany and Cherry Tree" (Kihn, pp. 113–114). The account books of William and Russell Stoughton, Eliphalet's East Windsor blacksmith neighbors, record his frequent purchases of nails and furniture hardware between 1778 and 1786, transactions continued in the accounts of the clockmaker Daniel Burnap between 1788 and 1796. Eliphalet was still offering buyers an array of case furniture and chairs in 1797. It can therefore be concluded that after 1771, when he acquired his own shop, he was active for another twenty-six years and that Aaron, at least in the nine years he worked with Eliphalet, probably made chairs similar to his. Cat. no. 10 matches the Eliphalet Chapin side chairs documented by Lyon in all but a few respects: the crest shell, which begins in the splat, has eight lobes rather than nine, and in the articulation of the strapwork—three layers rather than two—certain elements are of slightly different proportions and sizes. That could imply either a different set of chairs or two different hands.

Except for the crest shell's flatter arch, armchairs at Yale (Kane, no. 119), at the Wadsworth Atheneum (P. Johnston, p. 1020), and in a private collection (Kirk 1967, no. 238, converted from a side chair) appear identical to cat. no. 10. A set of chairs of the same general type but not the work of the same man was originally owned by Joseph Barnard (died 1785), who between 1768 and 1772 built the Old Manse in Deerfield, Massachusetts (Fales 1976, no. 98). Another set, with an interlaced-diamond motif in the splat, belonged to the Reverend John Marsh of Wethersfield, Connecticut (Kirk 1967, no. 239). And Anna Barnard, who married Joseph Clarke of Northampton, Massachusetts, in 1772, owned a set of chairs with a wider and more complexly pierced splat (*Antiques* 10 [November 1926], p. 236, where chairs are attributed to her father, Abner). How many of these distinctive Connecticut chairs were made by Eliphalet and how many by Aaron (or even by other local artisans) is still unknown.

PROVENANCE: Ex coll.: Mr. and Mrs. Mitchel Taradash, Ardsley-on-Hudson, New York. The chair, now in the collection of Mr. and Mrs. Erving Wolf, New York City, has been promised to the MMA.

CONSTRUCTION: On the crest rail, the scrolled ears and lobed shell are carved from the solid; the bottom part of the shell is carved from the splat. In back, the crest rail is flat, with beveled edges; an additional strip reinforces its juncture with the splat. The splat has unbeveled edges; the stiles are rounded in back. The rear legs, of rectangular stock, are rounded. The rear rail is made up of two vertical boards glued together, tenoned to the rear legs, and double pegged. The side rails are tenoned through the rear legs. The bottom edges of front and side rails are cut out in flat arches. The glue blocks, huge vertical quarter rounds attached with double roseheads, are made in two pieces at the front; at the back, in one piece, they are cut out below to conform to the arches of the side rails. Each rounded serpentine armrest support is secured to the side rail with two screws through the inside rabbet and with one screw through the outside bottom beveled edge. The tops of the knuckle arms and the tops of the ears are similarly molded. The knee brackets, sawed out, are attached with cut nails.

CONDITION: The chair has a fine reddish brown color. The strapwork at the upper left of the splat and the top front of the right arm support are patched. The slip seat now has the modern blue silk cover illustrated here.

INSCRIPTIONS: Incised, inside front seat rail: a small triangle and an illegible inscription.

DIMENSIONS: H.: overall, 41 (*104.1*), seat, 16½ (*41.9*); W.: seat front, 23⅛ (*58.7*), seat back, 16¾ (*42.5*), feet, 24¾ (*62.9*); D.: seat, 18⅜ (*46.7*), feet, 22¼ (*56.5*).

WOODS: Primary: cherry. Secondary: white pine (glue blocks). Slip-seat frame not examined.

REFERENCES: Alice Winchester, "Living with Antiques" (the house of Mr. and Mrs. Mitchel Taradash), *Antiques* 63 (January 1953), pp. 45–47; ill. p. 47, in bedroom, in front of secretary. For information on Eliphalet Chapin, see Emily M. Davis, "Eliphelet [*sic*] Chapin," *Antiques* 35 (April 1939), pp. 172–175; Kihn, pp. 113–114 (see also Aaron Chapin entry, pp. 112–113).

Promised Gift of Mr. and Mrs. Erving Wolf

11 See also p. 335

11. Side Chair

Massachusetts, 1760–90

JUDGED BY ITS sharp-edged knees, straight seat rails, and triangular glue blocks, the chair, number VII in its set, is clearly of Massachusetts origin. A side chair from the same set was advertised by a Boston firm in 1931 (*The Antiquarian* 16 [February 1931], p. 10). A set of six chairs once owned by Joseph Willard (1738–1804), president of Harvard College from 1781 until his death, would be identical except for the shape of the curve joining the crest rail and splat (Harvard Tercentenary, no. 252, pl. 45; P-B sale no. 2080, 1/20/62, lot 134). Another chair with flatter ears, rounded knees, and plain brackets is otherwise similar (P-B sale no. 2080, lot 135; Sack 5, p. 1149). All these examples, executed in a distinctive angular style and with the lower part of their splats drawn from the same template, look to be the work of one hand.

A chair at Winterthur (Yehia, fig. 146), its knees and feet elaborately carved, the knees with an asymmetrical C-scroll in classic Boston style, has an identical splat. Numerous other chairs with the same splat pattern, but lacking the knoblike projections at top and bottom, have leaf-carved knees (like those of cat. no. 14) and crest rails carved in C-scrolls and rocaille designs, both in the Boston manner (e.g., Kirk 1972, nos. 117, 118).

Cat. no. 11 was adapted from a popular English chair pattern. On English examples, the splat design consists of pairs of C- and S-scrolls with carved volute ends surrounding interwined diamond and figure-eight strapwork under a drapery swag with pendent tassel (e.g., Lockwood 2, fig. 550; Kirk 1982, figs. 1000–1004). Those carved details created a pattern that was abstracted by the maker of this chair, who retained from the original concept only a suggestion of the strapwork's overlapping elements.

PROVENANCE: Purchased from John S. Walton, Inc., New York City.

CONSTRUCTION: The round-edged crest rail is flat in back. On the posts, the stiles are stop-fluted in front and rounded in back; the square rear legs are slightly tapered and rounded before splaying out at the foot. The seat rails are double pegged to the rear stiles and pegged to the front legs. The rear rail is the thickness of the shoe nailed to it. The upper front edges of the front and side rails are molded in quarter rounds. Shaped horizontal brackets are attached with roseheads at the rear of the side rails. The triangular glue blocks are nailed with roseheads.

CONDITION: The dense mahogany has a dark and velvety old finish. The top of the left front leg is split. The chair is illustrated here with an antique red silk damask seat cover.

INSCRIPTIONS: Incised, on front seat-rail rabbet: VII; on slip-seat frame: III.

DIMENSIONS: H.: overall, 37¼ (94.6), seat, 16⅜ (41.6); W.: seat front, 21½ (54.6), seat back, 16¼ (41.3), feet, 23½ (59.7); D.: seat, 17¼ (43.8), feet, 21¾ (55.2).

WOODS: Primary: mahogany. Secondary: maple (rear seat rail, slip-seat frame); white pine (glue blocks).

Rogers Fund, 1973   (1973.207)

12. Masonic Armchair

Boston, 1765–90

THE ARRANGEMENT OF certain of the Masonic devices appearing on the splat of this superb chair has caused it to be regarded as that of a Senior Warden (Randall 1966), but in the eighteenth century a ceremonial object of such size and rich ornamentation can surely have been used only by the Master of the lodge (Gusler, p. 113, n. 79). The back of the chair is made up of Masonic symbols. The stiles form columns (the pillars of King Solomon's temple), and the crest rail is arched (the arch of heaven). On the splat, the compass and square (faith and reason), mason's level (equality), serpent swallowing its tail (rebirth), trowel (the cement of brotherly love), and mallet (untimely death) are sawed out. In the splat's central tablet are a carved and gilded sun and crescent moon (vigilance), two globes (the universality of Freemasonry) on turned and gilded columns, and, in a pattern of white and black (good and evil), a mosaic pavement (the floor of King Solomon's temple). Below the tablet are a carved and gilded pick and spade (required in the search for Divine Truth) and sprig of acacia (immortality). The grid pattern and the compass directions on the central tablet are not typical Masonic symbols, nor is the serpent swallowing its tail (which dates from ancient times), though the serpent appears with Masonic symbols on a Chinese Export bowl dated 1781, as well as on a somewhat later Masonic apron, both objects found in Boston (Randall 1966, p. 286). It has consequently been suggested that the motif had significance to a Massachusetts Masonic lodge (ibid.), but which lodge it was is not known.

The history accompanying the chair is tantalizingly vague. The catalogue of the 1928 auction at which it was sold reported only that it was "known to have been made to the order of a New Hampshire lodge of Free Masons." The arms, with their horizontally scrolled ends, are of a type found on Queen Anne chairs made throughout New England (Downs 1952, nos. 19–22) and even into New York (see cat. no. 67). The framing of the seat, the shape of the legs and the stretchers, and the style of the knee carving, however, are characteristic of a distinctive group of carved furniture from Boston (see also cat. nos. 13, 14, 74, 117). This armchair stands out from the group because of the brilliance and individuality of its carving: on the knees, the leaves flanked by tiny scrolls are deeply incised; on the feet, the talons are beautifully articulated. The carver left the heavy mahogany rough-cut on the splat and just below the leaves, causing each facet of the plain surface to catch and reflect the light. This magnificent Massachusetts example is the only one known to have been made in New England; other American Masonic armchairs made in the carved, cabriole-leg Chippendale style are of Virginia origin (Bradford L. Rauschenberg, "Two Outstanding Virginia Chairs," *Journal of Early Southern Decorative Arts* 2 [November 1976], pp. 1–20; Gusler, pp. 110–112).

PROVENANCE: Ex coll.: Joe Kindig, Jr.; Joe Kindig III, York, Pennsylvania. The chair was previously owned by Israel Sack,

12 See also p. 335

Boston and New York City, who added it to the 1928 auction of the George S. Palmer collection, where the senior Kindig acquired it. Now on loan to the MMA by Mr. and Mrs. George M. Kaufman, Norfolk, Virginia.

CONSTRUCTION: The thick arched crest rail is flat in back with rounded edges; in front it is incised with masonry joints pointed with white composition material. On the back posts—single pieces of wood whose tenons break through on the outer edge of the arched top—the stiles, turned and fluted columns with square caps and bases above the arms, are rounded in back below them; the square rear legs have chamfered corners except below the stretchers in back. The splat, a single board sawed out in C-scrolls and Masonic emblems, is tenoned into the crest rail and the rear rail, the latter pegged to the rear legs. On the splat's scallop-edged central tablet, the cutout serrated border, points of the compass, central grid, and patterned pavement are filled with composition material. The arms are tenoned into the fronts of the stiles and the arm supports are tenoned into the tops of the side rails; in each case, arms and supports overlap the sides. Shaped vertical brackets flank each rear leg.

CONDITION: The fine dense wood has the original finish, with deep red luminous highlights in the worn areas. Most of the gilding has been somewhat sloppily applied: on the keystone it covers the continuous masonry joints of the arch; on the points of the compass it covers the composition inlay; on the compass and square it has a rough surface, suggesting that it was applied over the old finish. The date 1790 (see Inscriptions) may indicate when that gilding was done. On the columns and globes of the splat and on the balls of the feet the gilding, more carefully applied, may date from the chair's manufacture. The right arm has been broken at its juncture with the stile. The inner talon of the right foot is missing. Under a cover of plain horsehair the seat retains the original striped black horsehair as well as the original webbing, stuffing, and canvas. X-rays show that the brass nails on the front rail originally formed a more graceful pattern: four swaglike curves instead of the present two.

INSCRIPTIONS: In gilt paint, large numbers on the back of the splat's central square: *1790*.

DIMENSIONS: H.: overall, 50½ (*128.3*), seat, 17¾ (*45.1*); W.: seat front, 25⅝ (*65.1*), seat back, 20½ (*52.1*), feet, 28 (*71.1*); D.: seat, 19⅝ (*49.9*), feet, 24¾ (*62.9*).

WOODS: Primary: mahogany. Secondary: maple (seat rails).

REFERENCES: Nutting 2, no. 2212. *Antiques* 13 (April 1928), inside front cover. Anderson Galleries sale no. 2280, October 18–20, 1928, lot 209. Randall 1966, pp. 286–287. Fales 1972, fig. 132. MFA 1975, no. 335. For meaning of Masonic symbols, see Barbara Franco, *Masonic Symbols in American Decorative Arts*, Lexington, Massachusetts, Scottish Rite Masonic Museum of Our National Heritage, 1976, pp. 47–62.

Promised Gift of Mr. and Mrs. George M. Kaufman (L.1978.24)

13. Side Chairs (Two)

Boston, 1765–90

ROBERT MANWARING'S modest pattern book *The Cabinet and Chair-maker's Real Friend and Companion*, which was published in London in 1765, was advertised in the *Boston Newsletter* of January 1, 1767, by Cox and Berry, Booksellers (Dow, pp. 222–223). Many popular Massachusetts "Chippendale" chair patterns appear to have been inspired by Manwaring's plates. The back illustrated in plate 9, left, was copied exactly for these two chairs, numbers I and II in a set. Five other chairs from the set are known: a single one with original seat stuffing and canvas intact, at the MHS (Yehia, fig. 152), and two pairs in private collections (*Antiques* 49 [January 1946], pp. 48–49; ibid. 66 [October 1954], inside front cover). A number of other chairs are known with crests and splats of the same pattern but not carved, though varying degrees of modeling in small areas of the strapwork on some suggest that the splats may be not uncarved but unfinished. On examples from one set, at Williamsburg (Greenlaw, no. 55), at the Lynn (Massachusetts) Historical Society, and at Deerfield (Fales 1976, no. 87), the splats are from the same template as that of cat. no. 13 and the knee carving is by the same hand. The central stem of the acanthus leafage covering the surface of the knee divides sharply along the corner into two flat sides outlined with punched circular dots, with the areas between the fronds of the leafage and immediately below them stippled. On the chairs of another uncarved-back set, examples of which are at Deerfield (ibid.), at the Boston MFA (Randall 1965, no. 144), at the Essex Institute (Fales 1965, no. 55), and at Winterthur (Kirk 1972, no. 113), the flatter knee carving and the lack of stippling suggest a different hand. An inscription on the Winterthur chair reads, "Bottumd June 1773 by WVE Salem."

PROVENANCE: Purchased for the MMA from Frances Nichols, The Antique Galleries, Boston. The vendor acquired the chairs from a Mrs. Loring of North Andover, Massachusetts. According to her (notes, MMA files, based upon a now missing letter), the chairs were originally made for Clark Gayton Pickman (1746–1781), who married Sarah Orne in 1770. (Pickman was a son of the original owner of cat. no. 155.) The chairs descended to the Pickmans' daughter Sarah Orne Osgood (1771–1791); to her sister Rebecca Taylor Osgood (1772–1801); to Rebecca's daughter Sally (1796–1835), who in 1816 married the Reverend Bailey Loring (1786–1860). The chairs remained in the house the Lorings built in Andover in 1818 through the ownership of Isaac Osgood Loring (1819–1867); John O. Loring (born 1860); John Alden Loring (1895–1947); and Jane Gertrude Loring (born 1927).

CONSTRUCTION: On each chair: In back, the crest rail is flat and has rounded ends. The straight stiles have molded fronts

13 See also p. 335

and rounded backs. The rounded rear legs end in square feet. The shoe fits around the splat, which is tenoned into the thick rear rail. Shaped brackets are applied under the side rails at the rear. There are four triangular glue blocks, each with four rose-heads. The knee brackets are attached with single roseheads.

CONDITION: The wood, dark brown in color, has a thin old finish. There are holes for casters on the front feet. On chair no. I, the splat is split; on chair no. II, the knob centered at the top of the crest rail is replaced. The upholstery on each chair has been replaced and does not correspond in shape with the original stuffing on another chair from the set (Yehia, no. 152). On the MMA chairs it is flatter and has sharper corners and brass nails. The finish fabric, illustrated here on chair no. I, is an eighteenth-century silk brocade with salmon-colored flowers and green leaves on a light green ground.

INSCRIPTIONS: Incised, on underside of one chair's shoe: *I*; of the other's: *II*. Punched, under shoe on splat of chair no. II: two dots.

DIMENSIONS: H.: overall, 38¾ (*98.4*), seat, 16½ (*41.9*); W.: seat front, 21⅝ (*54.9*), seat back, 16¼ (*41.3*), feet, 23⅝ (*60.*); D.: seat, 17½ (*44.5*), feet, 21 (*53.3*).

WOODS: Primary: mahogany. Secondary: maple (front and side seat rails); white pine (glue blocks).

REFERENCES: Joseph Downs, "A Pair of Chairs," *MMAB* 34 (October 1939), pp. 227–229, fig. 2. Powel, p. 206. W. Johnston, pp. 123–124, fig. 7. Davidson 1967, fig. 256. Kirk 1972, no. 114. For the Loring family, see Charles Henry Pope, *Loring Genealogy*, Cambridge, Massachusetts, 1917; Edward P. Loring, *Loring Genealogy, A Continuation and Revision*, Farmington, Maine: Knowlton & McLeary, 1971.

Gift of Mrs. Paul Moore, 1939   (39.88.1, 2)

14. Side Chair

Boston, 1760–90

THIS CHAIR, NUMBERED I, belongs to a set of which one other is privately owned and two, numbered VII and VIII, are at Winterthur. One of the latter has a modern paper label inscribed *Property of | Estate of Mr. Grafton* [Grayson?] (Hummel 1970a, pp. 901–902, fig. 3). The Winterthur chairs and the privately owned one came from the De Wolf family of Bristol, Rhode Island, a family said to have descended from the De Wolfs of Boston (9/21/60 letter, MMA files, from Ginsburg & Levy, Inc., vendor of the Winterthur chairs). The chairs of the set have straight, shallow seat rails, square-cornered knees with acanthus-leaf carving, and claw feet with raked-back talons, all characteristic of rococo chairs from Bos-

ton (Yehia; see also cat. nos. 12 and 13). The carving is of the highest quality: on the splat it is crisper and in higher relief than that of the related cat. no. 15; on the knees, it looks to be by the same hand as that of an easy chair (cat. no. 74)—the turnings of the stretchers of the two chairs are virtually identical. That same hand has been credited with the carving on a chair at Winterthur of a different pattern (Yehia, p. 210; fig. 150).

Except for an uncarved version of similar design still with its original green worsted seat cover in the SPNEA collection (Jobe and Kaye, no. 118), the unusual splat pattern is found elsewhere in America only on a few straight-legged chairs. One set of these (see cat. no. 15) also has a Boston history. The splat pattern is inspired by Manwaring's 1765 *Cabinet and Chair-maker's Friend*, the splat's scrolled outlines following those of plate 9, left. The strapwork interior is a graceful Gothic adaptation; another Boston chair has a splat copied line for line from the same plate (cat. no. 13).

PROVENANCE: Ex coll.: Mrs. J. Amory Haskell, Red Bank, New Jersey. Purchased at the May 20, 1944, sale of her collection. According to the sale catalogue, the chair originated in Salem, Massachusetts; was sold to Mrs. Haskell by Henry V. Weil, New York City; and had been exhibited at the Monmouth County Historical Association.

CONSTRUCTION: The crest rail, flat in back, has beveled edges. The stiles, rounded in back, have a rope-carved outer front edge and, with the splat, are gently curved in profile. The rear legs are square, with beveled edges between the rails and stretchers and with front edges beveled below the stretchers. The front and side seat rails have front edges molded in quarter rounds. The knee brackets are double nailed. The backs of the side stretchers are pegged.

CONDITION: The dense mahogany has a rich dark brown patina. The seat rails are reinforced inside with modern wooden strips. The slip seat has been reupholstered. The chair is here illustrated with an antique red silk damask seat cover.

INSCRIPTIONS: Incised, on front seat-rail rabbet: *I*; on slip-seat frame: *I*. Branded (20th century), on bottom of rear seat rail: *PROPERTY | MRS J.A. HASKELL*.

DIMENSIONS: H.: overall, 38 (*96.5*), seat, 16⅞ (*42.9*); W.: seat front, 21⅞ (*55.6*), seat back, 17 (*43.2*), feet, 23¾ (*60.3*); D.: seat, 17¾ (*45.1*), feet, 22 (*55.9*).

WOODS: Primary: mahogany. Secondary: maple (slip-seat frame).

REFERENCES: Haskell sale 2, lot 753 (ill.). Downs 1944, p. 81 (ill.); idem 1949, fig. 14. Comstock, no. 272.

Rogers Fund, 1944   (44.55)

14 See also p. 335

15. Side Chair

Massachusetts, 1760–90

OTHER CHAIRS from the set in which this is number VII are at SPNEA (Jobe and Kaye, no. 117), at Winterthur (Hummel 1970a, pp. 902–903, fig. 5), and a pair at the Tryon Palace Restoration, New Bern, North Carolina. Another chair (Lockwood 2, fig. 568) has pierced knee brackets but seems otherwise identical. An armchair at the Brooklyn Museum (ibid., fig. LXXXIII), while of the same design, looks to be by another carver. The splat pattern on these chairs was favored in the Boston area. Both the set from which cat. no. 15 comes and another set with a splat of similar pattern (see cat. no. 14) have Boston histories; the cabriole legs of the latter are carved with stylized acanthus leafage in the archetypal Boston manner. Cat. no. 15 and its mates have straight legs and are by a less skilled hand. The carving is flatter and softer, the backs of crest and stile are shaped differently, and the chairs are somewhat larger.

PROVENANCE: Purchased for the MMA, together with the two chairs now at New Bern, at auction on May 22, 1971. The chair is said to be part of a set of eight acquired by Abigail

15

Phillips and Josiah Quincy, Jr., in 1769, at the time of their marriage (Jobe and Kaye, no. 117). When Quincy died, in 1775, his inventory included "8 Chairs" valued at £18, probably a reference to this set. The chairs descended in the family along with a desk-and-bookcase, also listed in the inventory, on which an 1846 inscription by Eliza Quincy records that it had belonged to Josiah and Abigail, probably from the time of their marriage, and that it was moved from Pearl Street, Boston, to the Quincy house in Braintree, Massachusetts, in 1806 (ibid., n. 2). Photographs taken in the house in about 1880 illustrate one of the chairs in the east parlor (ibid., n. 3) and three others in the west parlor (ibid, fig. 117a). The presumed descent was from Abigail and Josiah to their granddaughter Abigail Phillips Quincy (1803–1893); to her nephew Josiah Phillips Quincy (1829–1910); to his son Josiah Quincy (1859–1919); to Edmund Quincy, the last family owner.

CONSTRUCTION: The crest rail and stiles are rounded in back. The inner edge of each square rear leg is chamfered along the full length; the outer front edge, below the side stretchers. The shoe fits around the splat, which is tenoned to the rear rail. Corner braces are dovetailed to the front and side rails. On the front legs, the inner edges are chamfered. The front stretcher is attached with horizontal tenons to the side stretchers, which are pegged.

CONDITION: The dense mahogany is brown in color, faded at the crest rail. The front legs and the adjacent rails and stretchers have been apart, and the back glue blocks are new. The seat, which has been restuffed, is illustrated here with an eighteenth-century red damask cover. Patches and repairs to the seat rails have obscured any evidence of the existence or positioning of original brass nails. The present ones are placed according to the pattern of those on cat. no. 16.

INSCRIPTIONS: Punched, on top of rear seat rail and on underside of shoe: seven dots.

DIMENSIONS: H.: overall, 39 (99.1), seat, 17 (43.2); W.: seat front, 21⅝ (54.9), seat back, 17⅛ (43.5); D.: seat, 18½ (47.), feet, 22 (55.9).

WOODS: Primary: mahogany. Secondary: maple (seat rails); white pine (corner brackets).

REFERENCES: P-B sale no. 3215, May 22, 1971, lot 128.

Purchase, Mrs. Russell Sage Gift, 1971   (1971.132)

16. Side Chair

Massachusetts, 1760–90

THE UNBROKEN FLOW of strapwork from the crest into the splat of this chair produces a well-integrated back. The splat pattern—the so-called owl's-eye, because of the two large open circles—while a variant of the Manwaring design that can be seen at cat. no. 13, was probably adopted directly from an English chair (e.g., Kirk 1982, no. 849). The most common pierced-splat design found in

16

Massachusetts work (idem 1972, nos. 25, 103–109), it appears on chairs carved or plain, with straight or cabriole legs, upholstered over the rail or with slip seats.

The Massachusetts attribution of these owl's-eye chairs is supported by the large numbers of them that have histories of ownership in Boston and its environs (Sack 3, p. 623; Randall 1965, no. 143; Greenlaw, no. 54; Warren, nos. 74, 94; Kane, no. 125; Jobe and Kaye, no. 110), including one said to have been saved from the residence of Massachusetts Lieutenant Governor Thomas Hutchinson when it was sacked by the Sons of Liberty in 1765 (Warren, no. 73). Another is recorded as having been lent to George Washington in 1775 by William Greenleaf of Boston (Sack 1, p. 243). The most thoroughly documented examples, however, are two chairs from a set of twelve made in 1770 by George Bright of Boston for Jonathan Bowman of Pownalborough, Maine (Jobe and Kaye, no. 113). As with cat. no. 16, the chairs have straight legs and are upholstered over the rails with the original leather, but differences in the carving of the crest rail from that of the MMA example indicate that the chairs of the set were made in a different shop. Bright's bill (ibid., fig. 15a) lists them as "12 Mahogany Chairs with Leather Seats" at thirty shillings each. They lack certain ornamental features found on cat. no. 16, including the gently bowed front rail, molded front legs, and two rows of brass upholstery nails—niceties that would certainly have increased this chair's price.

PROVENANCE: Purchased from Israel Sack, Inc., New York City.

CONSTRUCTION: The crest rail is flat in back with beveled edges. The stiles are rounded in back; the rear legs are square, with chamfering all along the inner edge and below the stretchers on the outer front edge. The splat is tenoned into the rear rail, which is the thickness of the stiles; the shoe fits around the splat. On the front legs, the outer sides are molded; the inner edge is beveled. The outer top edge of each stretcher is a molded quarter round. The front stretcher is dovetailed. The leather seat covering is attached to the sides of the front and side rails with double rows of brass nails.

CONDITION: The well-preserved original finish is dark, with red highlights in the areas of wear. The original seat upholstery—webbing, canvas, stuffing, leather, and brass nails—is intact. The leather is much decayed, and a piece at the back of the right side is missing.

DIMENSIONS: H.: overall, 38⅛ (96.8), seat, 16⅛ (41.); W.: seat front, 21⅞ (55.6), seat back, 16⅝ (42.2); D.: seat, 18⅛ (46.), feet, 20½ (52.1).

WOODS: Primary: mahogany. Secondary: maple (front and side seat rails).

REFERENCES: Sack 4, p. 939 (ill.).

Purchase, The Wunsch Foundation, Inc., Gift, and Friends of the American Wing Fund, 1975   (1975.269)

17. Side Chairs (Six)

Massachusetts, 1760–90

THESE, NUMBERS III–V, X–XII, are the only known survivors from a set of at least twelve chairs, but identical patterns of crest rail and splat are found on a number of others: some with slip seats and cabriole legs (Downs 1952, no. 156; Randall 1965, no. 150); some with slip seats and straight legs (Yehia, fig. 150); some with seats upholstered over the rail and with cabriole legs (*Antiques* 91 [June 1967], p. 696); some with seats upholstered over the rails but with straight legs, as here. On all the chairs, molded stiles and raised beading around crest and splat are to be found; the crest rails are carved with a central acanthus sprig and with flanking C-scrolls having rocaille mantels; and the splat strapwork is subtly modeled. An uncarved example (P-B sale no. 551, 3/31/44, lot 604) is an exception.

The chairs can all be attributed to the Boston area. Those with cabriole legs have sharp-edged knees with straight acanthus leafage and claw feet with raked-back talons, characteristics of Boston carving (Yehia). On one such chair, which descended in the Lane family of Boston until acquired by the Boston MFA (Randall 1965, no. 150), the splat is cut from the same template as are those of cat. no. 17. Two chairs at Deerfield (Fales 1976, nos. 104, 105)—one with a local history—having straight legs and the same splat in an uncarved version look to be rural adaptations of the Boston pattern.

On the MMA chairs, the combination of strapwork, or ribbon-back, splat and straight legs is suggestive of the least pretentious of the designs in Manwaring's *Cabinet and Chair-maker's Friend*, which was well known in Boston. The quatrefoil in the bottom of the splat is in fact similar to that on chairs copied directly from Manwaring (see cat. no. 13). The entire splat design, however, is identical to that on a number of English chairs (Kirk 1982, figs. 901–905), and must have been copied from an imported example.

PROVENANCE: Ex coll.: H. Eugene Bolles, Boston.

CONSTRUCTION: On each chair: The crest rail is flat in back and has beveled edges. The stiles, straight in profile, are rounded in back. On the square rear legs the inner edge is chamfered; below the side stretchers the outer front edge is chamfered. The splat is tenoned to the thick mahogany rear rail; the shoe fits around it. The rails are pegged, as are the side stretchers. The front stretcher is dovetailed. On all the stretchers the outside upper edge has a quarter-round molding. Shaped brackets are nailed at the insides of the front legs. Double roseheads secure the triangular glue blocks.

CONDITION: The original thin finish has a mellow nut brown patina. A photograph (MMA files) of one chair with its original stuffing and muslin more or less intact shows a higher crown than the present, reupholstered one. The chairs' present cover is illustrated on no. X: a reproduction raspberry red wool moreen with an impressed vermicelli pattern. The brass nails follow the pattern of the original nail holes.

INSCRIPTIONS: Punched, on each chair, on top of rear seat rail and on underside of shoe, identifying dots: 3, 4, 5, 10, 11, and 12, respectively. In pencil (19th-century), outside rear seat rail: *Boston Massachusetts* (no. X); an illegible inscription (no. III).

DIMENSIONS: H.: overall, 37⅛ (*94.3*), seat, 16¼ (*41.3*); W.: seat front, 21 (*53.3*), seat back, 15⅞ (*40.3*); D.: seat, 17¾ (*45.1*), feet, 20¾ (*52.7*).

WOODS: Primary: mahogany. Secondary: maple (front and side rails); white pine (glue blocks).

REFERENCES: Salomonsky, pl. 23 (measured drawings). Yehia, p. 208, no. 4.

Gift of Mrs. Russell Sage, 1909   (10.125.289–294)

18. Armchair

New England, 1770–90

WHEN THE MMA ACQUIRED this chair, it was thought to be of Rhode Island origin. Indeed, the modeled crest shell and the flat intaglio carving at the juncture of crest rail and splat and on top of the armrests do bear comparison with some Newport carving (cf. cat. no. 9). Nevertheless, the splat design is a variation on two Massachusetts types (for the quatrefoil and ogival arch of the lower half, see cat. no. 17; for the interaction of crest rail with splat, see cat. no. 16), and similarly molded crest rail, stiles, and front legs are found on a side chair thought to be from Salem, Massachusetts (Sack 6, p. 1514). In most other respects, however, the decorative details on the chair are atypical of American furniture from any known regional

17

18

center. The stiles are molded only above the armrests. The molded fronts of the serpentine sides of the crest rail end in scallops where they meet the flat strapwork. Below the crest shell, an opening of inverted-tulip shape is surmounted by an acanthus sprig. Above the seat rails, sharp-edged flanges break the curves of the rounded arm supports. The tops of the seat rails are cavetto-molded. Although of unusual design and an as yet unidentified origin, the chair has been executed with uncommon assurance and skill.

PROVENANCE: Ex coll.: Harold Huber, New York City. Huber purchased the chair and its mate from Ginsburg & Levy, Inc., New York City.

CONSTRUCTION: The back of the crest rail is rounded except where it conforms to the undulation of the front central shell. The stiles, gently curved in profile, have rounded backs. The wide, rectangular rear legs are chamfered on the inner edges. The splat's edges are unbeveled. On the front legs, the inner edge is chamfered and the molded outer sides project beyond the rails. The arm supports are triple screwed to the side rails, which are cut out to receive them. The front stretcher is dovetailed. The pierced knee brackets are nailed in place. The slip-seat frame is half-lapped together.

CONDITION: The chair, which has been refinished, is a rich reddish brown in color. Nail holes indicate that there were once pierced brackets at the sides of the front legs. The left side of the chair bears evidence of past breaks: at the juncture of side rail and stile; at the arm, which has been off; on the rail, now patched and veneered on both sides with figured mahogany; at the beaded bottom edge of the crest rail, where there is a patch. The glue blocks are replaced. The slip seat has been reupholstered. The chair is illustrated here with an eighteenth-century red silk damask seat cover.

DIMENSIONS: H.: overall, 38½ (97.8), seat, 17¼ (43.8); W.: seat front, 21⅝ (54.9), seat back, 16¾ (42.5); D.: seat, 16⅝ (42.2), feet, 19½ (49.5).

WOODS: Primary: mahogany. Secondary: spruce (slip-seat frame).

Rogers Fund, 1953   (53.88)

19. Side Chairs (Two)

New Hampshire, 1770–90

THESE CHAIRS, TWO of four virtually identical examples, are made in an engaging rural interpretation of the Chippendale style. Each of the remaining two retains its old painted surface and original seat cover: one, at Winterthur (Downs 1952, no. 157), appears to have been a robin's-egg blue, now much darkened; the other, in the Stone collection (Rodriguez Roque, no. 65), is now a dark

green. The original appearance of the MMA pair must be seen with the mind's eye: chairs of brilliant green or blue, their brown seats strewn with multicolored flowers. When the chairs were acquired, they were attributed to Samuel Dunlap of Salisbury, New Hampshire, on the basis of similarities—the carved fans of the crest and skirt rails and the pierced S-scrolls of the splat—to motifs on a number of case pieces found in the Salisbury area and attributed to him (Downs 1944, p. 80). The pair were later reattributed, this time to Samuel's brother John (Parsons, p. 9; fig. 78).

Major John Dunlap (1746–1792) was born in Chester, New Hampshire, but by the late seventeen-sixties had settled, and was working, in Goffstown. In 1777 he disassembled his house and moved it to nearby Bedford, where he resided until his death. In his account book spanning the years 1768 to 1787 he recorded the sale of five hundred chairs. In 1773, John's brother Samuel (1752–1830) began to work for him in Goffstown before moving out on his own, first to Henniker in 1779, then in 1797 to Salisbury (Parsons, p. 35). Mrs. De Witt Clinton Howe, who pioneered in the collecting of New Hampshire furniture, found the chairs of cat. no. 19 in Goffstown (ibid., p. 9), a provenance that would support an attribution either to John or to Samuel, both of whom worked there.

On these chairs, the molded profile of the stiles, the legs, and the stretchers is unique. The S-scrolls, cut out from the splat, are paired vertically (counterparts carved in the skirts of Dunlap pieces are horizontal). Only the fanlike shells in the crest and seat rails suggest a direct connection with Dunlap work. Their round lobes have thumbnail-molded ends characterized by a flat surface followed by a narrow raised ridge, the whole contained within a semicircle and typical of Dunlap work. The marks of the compass that plotted them (see Construction), also visible around the shells of a chest-on-chest found in Bedford and attributed to Major John (Parsons, figs. 3, C, G), might be considered a further, if tenuous, link. Otherwise, except for the provincial exuberance of their design, the chairs exhibit little specific evidence to tie them to the case furniture of the Dunlap school.

PROVENANCE: Ex coll.: Mrs. J. Insley Blair, Tuxedo Park, New York.

CONSTRUCTION: On each chair: The wide crest-rail board is sawed out with flat edges to form an arched central section and exaggerated ears. The board is flat in back, except behind the central arch, where it is tapered; in front it tapers at the ears, which are fashioned as continuations of the molding of the stiles; on the board are visible the marks of the compass with which the concave central rayed shell was plotted. The fronts of the rectangular stiles are molded. The bevel-edged pierced splat is seated in a pegged rail that extends upward as a cavetto-molded shoe. The seat rails, double pegged to the rear legs and pegged to the front ones, are rabbeted at the top edges to accommodate the solid seat board. The seat board is slightly hollowed in the center to receive the stuffing. Molded strips nailed on top of the rails secure the upholstered seat. The side rails are scalloped; the front rail is scalloped on either side of the recessed central shell. The front and side stretchers are pegged. Their fronts are molded, as are the fronts and sides of the front legs.

CONDITION: The chairs are stripped of their original painted finish and the cherry wood is now shellacked. The insides of the seat rails are painted an off-white, presumably a remnant of the undercoat for the original green or blue finish. The original seat covers are entirely worked in crewel in an allover pattern of flowers in red, green, and blue on a brown ground. The slip seats have been restuffed, the low crown (cf. Downs 1952, no. 157) now somewhat reduced. The horsehair filling, possibly a later replacement, is secured by a goatskin cover, which has been turned over and renailed.

INSCRIPTIONS: In pencil (20th-century?), on bottom of one seat board: *Moore*.

DIMENSIONS: H.: overall, 44⅞ (*114.*), seat, 16⅜ (*41.6*); W.: seat front, 22 (*55.9*), seat back, 16 (*40.6*); D.: seat, 15¼ (*38.7*), feet, 17 (*43.2*).

WOODS: Primary: cherry. Secondary: ash (rear stretcher).

REFERENCES: Downs 1944, p. 80. *Antiques* 47 (March 1945), p. 168; ibid. 81 (May 1962), p. 542 (ill.). W. Johnston, p. 122, fig. 6, left; p. 126. The Currier Gallery of Art, *The Decorative Arts of New Hampshire 1725–1825*, Manchester, 1964, nos. 38, 39. Parsons, p. 9; no. 78a/b. *The Currier Gallery of Art Bulletin*, April–June 1970, cover. Fales 1972, fig. 11. MMA 1976, no. 21.

Gift of Mrs. J. Insley Blair, 1943   (43.149.1, 2)

19

2 New York Chairs

Except for the earliest Queen Anne examples, some of which can be confused with Newport work, New York chairs have a distinctive character. In overall design and proportions they adhere closely to the precedent of Early Georgian chairs. Their characteristic and oft-noted heaviness results from their being shorter and proportionally squatter than other American chairs and from a regional preference for unrelieved individual elements: the surfaces of the stiles left flat; the seat rails not cut out in arches. The Museum's collection encompasses fine examples of most of the late colonial splat types made in New York. The chapter begins with a Hudson River valley rush-seated chair—the only chair in the catalogue to have turned supports in the William and Mary manner—whose Queen Anne-style baluster splat and pad feet justify its precedence even though the type was made only from the latter half of the century on. Some of the best-known Chippendale patterns, including tassel-back and gothic versions, represented in multiple examples, complete the chapter.

20. Side Chairs (Two)

New York, 1780–1800

TURNED CHAIRS OF THIS type, with only the shape of the baluster splats and pad feet to relate them to prevailing eighteenth-century styles, were made in great numbers in New York City and in the Hudson River valley beginning in about 1750. The chairs carry on a rural tradition from the north of England. In Lancashire and Cheshire, for example, rush-bottomed chairs whose turned front legs, some bearing on top the maker's stamp, terminate in pad feet were widely produced in the later years of the century. Unlike their New York counterparts, those chairs have ladder or spindle-type backs (William Cotton, "Vernacular Design: The Spindle Back Chair and Its North Country Origins," *Working Wood* [U.K.], 1980, pp. 41–50). On some domestic examples, the turned legs continue above the seat and the chairs have roughly rounded seat rails; a woodcut of such a chair appeared in James Chestney's advertisement in the *Albany Gazette* of July 11, 1798 (Rice, p. 38, ill.). On others, including those of cat. no. 20, seat rails are rectangular boards mortised and tenoned to exposed corner blocks that rest on the front legs.

Several American makers of such chairs also stamped their work on top of the front legs. The largest number of marked examples were made by Jacob Smith, who was listed in the New York City Directories from 1787 to 1795 as a "rush bottomed chair maker" and afterward, at least until 1812, as a turner (Blackburn 1981, p. 1136). His chairs can be seen at the Albany Institute, at the NYS Museum, and at Williamsburg. The MMA pair are similar to those of his making, particularly in the turnings of the front stretchers and the tops of the front legs, but they were marked by a Michael Smith. They are the only known examples of Michael's work, and whether he was related to Jacob is not recorded. Other rush-bottomed chairs are marked by David Coutant (Butler, no. 56) and by Vincent Tillou of New York City (Blackburn 1981, p. 1137).

A number of these chairs are branded, in the Hudson River valley tradition, with the initials of their first owners: an armchair with PVR for Philip Van Rensselaer (ibid., no. 41); a side chair with GGR at the Schuyler Mansion; a pair with JJL at Williamsburg; and the Museum's two, with TVV. Two other chairs branded TVV and from the same set are known, one in a midwestern collection (*Americana: Midwest Collectors' Choice*, Henry Ford Museum, 1960, p. 9, no. 19), the other in a New York City private collection in 1961. (A green-painted tavern table at the Albany Institute has the same TVV brand.) No history of descent accompanies any of the chairs of this set, but of the eighteenth-century New York Dutch family surnames beginning with double Vs, only in the Van Vechtens can given names beginning with the letter *T* be found. Tobias (born 1777), of New York City, or three members of the Kingston-area branch of the Van Vechten family—Teunis (1707–1785), Teunis-Teunissen (1749–1817), or Teunis (born 1784)—are likely candidates to be the original owner of these chairs. Of the four, Teunis-Teunissen is chronologically the most apt. Rushed-bottom chairs of this type are also known on Long Island (see Huyler Held, "Long Island Dutch Splat Backs," *Antiques* 30 [October 1936], pp. 168–170; Hummel 1968, pp. 260–263).

PROVENANCE: Purchased from Winick and Sherman, New York City.

20

CONSTRUCTION: On each chair: The turned stiles extend into the yoke crest and are nailed, and nails secure molded blocks above the front legs into which the rectangular seat rails are tenoned. The rail under the splat is tenoned and nailed. The rear and side stretchers were fashioned with a spoke shave.

CONDITION: The chairs have what looks to be their original paint, applied after they were branded and rushed. The frames are a dark red, now somewhat worn and decayed; the white rush seats are now darkened. On both chairs, part of the central ring turning of the front stretcher is broken off. On one chair, the rush is broken behind the front rail.

INSCRIPTIONS: Branded, on the back of the rail supporting the splat of each chair: *TVV*. Stamped, on top of each left front leg: *MICHAEL*; on top of each right front leg: *SMITH*.

DIMENSIONS: H.: overall, 40⅞ (*103.8*), seat, 17½ (*44.5*); W.: seat front, 20⅜ (*51.8*), seat back, 15¾ (*40.*), feet, 21¾ (*55.2*); D.: seat, 15¾ (*40.*), feet, 17¾ (*45.*).

WOODS: Primary: maple; ash (side and rear stretchers). Seat frame not examined.

REFERENCES: Downs and Ralston, p. 2, no. 7. Blackburn 1981, p. 1136, caption, fig. 12a; pp. 1143, 1145.

Rogers Fund, 1933   (33.121.1, 2)

21. Side Chair

New York, 1750–90

CHAIR NUMBER V from the same set in which this chair is number VI is now in a New York City private collection (Kirk 1972, no. 170); other examples, apparently identical, have been advertised (*Antiques* 76 [September 1959], p. 173; SPB sale no. 4938, 10/22/82, lot 392). These chairs have usually been published as of Newport origin. Their backs, particularly the crest shells and splat patterns, resemble a New England, probably Rhode Island, design (e.g., cat. nos. 7, 8), though backs with the same configuration are also found in New York work (e.g., Kirk 1972, no. 126).

From the seat down, however, the chairs exhibit details of design and construction that are characteristic only of New York. The bottom edges of the front and side seat rails are flat, and there are shaped brackets at their junctures with the rear legs; the rear rail is made of local hardwood and is the thickness of the shoe; the rear legs are tapered and end in square pad feet; and there are no stretchers (see also cat. no. 24). Further, the knee shells are carved with alternately projecting and receding lobes and lack bottom C-scrolls, and the knee brackets have circular ends. All these are precisely the features of a number of chairs with histories of ownership in New York families, including the Van Cortlandts (Downs and

Ralston, no. 54; Downs 1952, no. 26); the Van Rensselaers (*Antiques* 66 [August 1954], p. 80); the Yateses (Sack 1, no. 73); and the Apthorps, theirs with the addition of flat stretchers (cat. no. 22).

PROVENANCE: Ex coll.: Mrs. Evelyn T. Mackenzie, New York City.

CONSTRUCTION: The crest rail is cut out deeply around the high-relief central shell. The stiles are straight, with pieced inside curves; the rounded rear legs taper to pad feet that are square and have rounded inner corners. Glued beneath the rear seat rail and to the rear legs are two-piece brackets. The upper part is pegged to the leg; the lower part, identical to the rear side brackets in shape, is laid vertically. The seat rails have straight inner edges and are pegged; in each corner is a triangular glue block.

CONDITION: The heavy, dense wood is dark brown in color. The glue blocks have been renailed. There is a patch on the top of the right front leg. The chair is here illustrated with a reproduction blue wool moreen seat cover.

21 See also p. 336

INSCRIPTIONS: Incised, on front seat-rail rabbet: *VI*; on slip-seat frame: *VI*.

DIMENSIONS: H.: overall, 40½ (*102.9*), seat, 16½ (*41.9*); W.: seat front, 21⅛ (*53.7*), seat back, 15⅛ (*38.4*), feet, 22 (*55.9*); D.: seat, 18¼ (*46.4*), feet, 21¾ (*55.2*).

WOODS: Primary: mahogany. Secondary: maple (slip-seat frame); cherry (rear seat rail); white pine (glue blocks).

REFERENCES: Price, pp. 91–93; fig. 24.

Purchase, Mrs. Russell Sage Gift, 1958   (58.154)

22. Side Chair

New York, 1750–70

NUMBER I IN THE APTHORP family set, the chair represents the most elaborate version of a well-known New York Queen Anne chair-type, which is distinguished by a veneered splat—of a bulbous ginger-jar shape on the upper part and a sagging baluster on the lower—seated in a cupid's-bow shoe and by stiles whose compound curves conform to the design of the splat. These features are borrowed directly from a popular English chair pattern (e.g., Kirk 1982, fig. 805). In the shaping of the feet and the construction of the seat frame the chairs of the type are markedly consistent, but cat. no. 22 is unique of its kind in having the flat stretchers that are also found on some Newport examples (e.g., Carpenter, no. 13). The set of eight to which the chair belongs includes four at Bernard & S. Dean Levy, Inc., New York City (Levy, p. 10); one owned by Benjamin and Cora Ginsburg; and two sold at auction (Christie's, 10/15/83 sale, lots 737, 738).

What separates one chair of this type from another is the ornamentation of the crest rail: in some, a simple carved central shell (Kirk 1972, no. 131); in others, notably the one that belonged to Henry Bromfield of Boston (Fairbanks and Bates, p. 100), a shell embellished on either side by emerging flowering vines. On the most ornate examples a deeply undercut shell is supported only by projections of the surrounding mantel of leafage or, in the case of this chair and one other (Sack 7, p. 2007), by strapwork decorated with fish-scales. The shell, which is almost freestanding, is noticeably similar to those on some carved and gilded picture frames of American origin—for example, one at Yale, on Copley's 1769 portrait of Mr. Isaac Smith. The fish-scale decoration, a motif popular in English furniture of the seventeen-twenties and thirties, is a further indication of the chairs' English antecedents. Sets of this prized Queen Anne type were owned by the Van Cortlandts (Downs 1952, no. 26), the

Van Rensselaers (*Antiques* 66 [August 1954], p. 80), the Beekmans, possibly (Downs 1952, no. 106, with legs identical to those of a Beekman sofa), and the Apthorps.

PROVENANCE: Ex coll.: Benjamin and Cora Ginsburg, Tarrytown, New York. According to Apthorp family tradition, the chairs of this set originally belonged to Grizzell Eastwick (1709–1796), who in 1726 married Charles Apthorp (1698–1758) of Boston, a wealthy merchant and paymaster of the British forces. The chairs descended in the female line: to Susan Apthorp Bulfinch (1734–1815); to Elizabeth Bulfinch Coolidge (1777–1837); to Elizabeth Coolidge Swett (1797–1880); to Elizabeth Swett Sargent (1822–1866); to Elizabeth Sargent McCalla (1850–1920), author of the label on the chair (see Inscriptions); to Elizabeth McCalla Miller (born 1875); to Mary Elizabeth Miller Symington, from whom they were acquired in 1960 by Ginsburg & Levy, Inc. The early part of this history is unlikely on two counts: it would have been most unusual for an eighteenth-century Boston merchant to buy New York furniture, and the chairs look to date stylistically from the 1750s or 1760s, long after Grizzell's marriage and about the time of her husband's death. It seems more plausible that the chairs were made for Charles Ward Apthorp (1729–1797), son of Charles and Grizzell, who married Mary McEvers of New York in 1755. The first two of their thirteen children were born in Boston, the others in New York (Stokes 6, p. 70). In 1763, Apthorp purchased a three-hundred-acre farm in the "Out Ward of the city of New York," and the following year constructed on it his mansion, Elmwood, at what is now Columbus Avenue and Ninety-first Street (ibid., pl. 108). The house was described in 1780 as "An exceeding good house, elegantly finished. . .(ibid. p. 70). Its furnishings presumably included this set of chairs, but how they were returned to the Boston branch of the family is not known.

CONSTRUCTION: On the crest rail, the shell and its strapwork mantel, both freestanding, are carved from the solid; the flanking leaf fronds, in low relief. The stiles, rounded in back, are pieced at the inner curves. The rear legs, which end in pad feet, are rounded except where they join the side stretchers. The bevel-edged splat board is veneered with walnut of a rich, flamelike figure. The top edge of the shoe is molded in a double serpentine, or cupid's-bow. The shoe and the rear rail are of one piece. The inner sides of the seat rails are straight. The side rails are pegged to the rear legs. The front knee brackets, affixed with small nails, have chiseled lobate sides. The rear side brackets are in two parts: a horizontal upper and a thick, vertical lower. There are triangular front glue blocks. The front stretcher is pegged in place.

CONDITION: The chair has its original finish, with a fine reddish brown patina. There is a break at the middle of the left stile. A shim has been inserted in back between the base of the splat and the shoe. The front glue blocks have been screwed in place. On the original slip seat, the webbing and linen are replaced, but the swamp-grass stuffing and dark and white curled horsehair layers remain. Fragments of the first upholstery materials, including a pale yellow silk damask cover, are still nailed to the edge. The chair is illustrated here with an alternate slip-seat frame covered with an antique damask matched to the original fragments.

22 See also p. 336

INSCRIPTIONS: Incised, on front seat-rail rabbet and on slip-seat frame: *I*. In brown ink, on paper label (19th-century) pasted to the inside edge of front rail:

This "Apthorp Chair" which —
to the Eldest daughter of each generation,
Elizabeth–belonged to my Great-Great-G[reat]
-Grandmother—Madam Apthorp —
& is at my death to be given to my eldes[t]
daughter Elizabeth, to be left to her descen[dants]
[in] the same manner

[signed] *Elizabeth H. McCalla.*

DIMENSIONS: H.: overall, 38⅝ (*98.1*), seat, 16⅛ (*41.*); W.: seat front, 20¾ (*52.7*), seat back, 15¼ (*38.7*), feet, 22 (*55.9*); D.: seat, 18½ (*47.*), feet, 21½ (*54.6*).

WOODS: Primary: walnut; walnut veneer. Secondary: maple (splat, slip-seat frame); white pine (glue blocks).

REFERENCES: Comstock, fig. 161. Davidson 1967, fig. 160. Kirk 1972, nos. 130, 33 (detail). Bishop, fig. 91. Montgomery and Kane, fig. 147. Price, pp. 86–89; fig. 11. Fairbanks and Bates, p. 94.

Gift of Mr. and Mrs. Benjamin Ginsburg, 1984   (1984.21)

23. Side Chairs (Two)

New York, 1760–90

THESE CHAIRS ARE numbers VII and XII in a set; numbers I and II (with slip seats numbered II and VIII) are at Winterthur (Hummel 1970, 2, p. 905; fig. 10); a virtually identical chair, also numbered II, is at Van Cortlandt Manor (*Antiques* 78 [November 1960], pp. 472, ill.; 473). The set is a rococo-carved version of a Queen Anne chair pattern popular in New York in the middle years of the eighteenth century (Price, pp. 89–91; figs. 17–22). A related chair at Winterthur (Downs 1952, no. 105), which was found on Long Island, is constructed in the same manner and appears to be from the same shop. The simplest form of the pattern, visible in the family set at Schuyler Mansion, Albany, consists of a plain-yoked crest rail, an eared, thin-waisted baluster splat whose contour is repeated in the compound curves of the stiles, a balloon seat, and claw-and-ball feet. A number of similar sets are known with shell carving in the yoke and on the knees (e.g., *Antiques* 88 [September 1965], p. 256); on other sets, the knee shells are replaced by leaf carving (e.g., Downs 1952, no. 105). On the MMA pair, the splat is enriched by rosettes with pendent leaf streamers; the carving, now more extensive and an integral part of the outline on crest rail, splat, and knees, is of a pronounced rococo flavor.

PROVENANCE: According to tradition (letter, MMA files, from the agent for the vendor, a Mrs. Dodge), these chairs came down in the family to Mrs. Dodge from Cornelius Willett. Cornelius (about 1708–1781) lived in Westchester County, New York. In his will, he left to his wife, Elizabeth, his "worked chairs," which may have been these. The chairs are said to have descended through their daughter Mary, who married Augustine Graham in 1770 (William S. Pelletreau, *Wills of Early Residents of Westchester Co., N.Y., 1664–1784*, New York, 1898, p. 343). In 1940, Mrs. Dodge owned three chairs from the set, and two others were in a cousin's possession (correspondence, MMA files). The chair now at Van Cortlandt Manor is apparently Mrs. Dodge's third one; the two at Winterthur, the cousin's. The history of descent from Cornelius contradicts the provenance given by the vendor of the Winterthur chairs (see Hummel 1970, 2, p. 907): that they had been acquired from descendants of Marinus Willett (1740–1830), the illustrious New York City soldier, merchant, mayor, and sometime cabinetmaker.

CONSTRUCTION: On each chair: The stiles, straight in profile, have rounded backs and are pieced at their inner projections. The rounded rear legs taper to ovoid pad feet pointed at the outer back edge. The splat board is thin. The double-pegged

23 See also p. 337

rear seat rail is built up inside with a thin board to the thickness of the stiles. The front and side seat rails have straight inner edges. The knee brackets and the serpentine-shaped brackets applied at the juncture of side rails and rear stiles are reinforced with vertical quarter-round glue blocks. A medial brace is dovetailed into the slip-seat frame of chair no. XII.

CONDITION: The chairs, of a light, porous wood, have been refinished and are dark red in color. On chair no. VII, the top of the central lobe of the crest-rail shell is gone; the front legs have been reinforced with screws; the side brackets and the glue blocks are replaced. On no. XII, the chair illustrated, the front right bracket and part of the left side bracket are replaced. The slip seats are covered in the modern yellow silk damask shown here.

INSCRIPTIONS: Incised, on front seat-rail rabbet of one chair: *VII*; *III* (19th-century); on slip-seat frame: *IX* [or *XI*]; *III* (19th-century); in brown ink, on slip-seat frame: *55 / 38 Recd B— / Tea Table 55 / 61*. Incised, on front seat-rail rabbet of the other: *XII*; *IIII* (19th-century); on slip-seat frame: *IIII* (19th-century).

24 See also p. 337

DIMENSIONS: H.: overall, 38⅞ (*98.7*), seat, 16¾ (*42.5*); W.: seat front, 21 (*53.3*), seat back, 16⅛ (*41.*), feet, 22½ (*57.2*); D.: seat, 18½ (*47.*), feet, 21½ (*54.6*).

WOODS: Primary: mahogany. Secondary: mahogany (glue blocks, inner rear seat rail); cherry (rear seat rail, part of slip-seat frame); white oak (part of slip-seat frame).

REFERENCES: W. Johnston, p. 120 (ill.). Kirk 1972, fig. 133.

Harris Brisbane Dick Fund, 1940   (40.100.1, 2)

24. Side Chairs (Six)

New York, 1760–90

A SET OF AT LEAST twelve chairs that descended en suite with a settee (cat. no. 82) and a card table (cat. no. 105) in the Verplanck family includes these six. Two others, numbered VIIII and XII, remain in the family, and number V was exhibited at the MCNY in 1957 (V. I. Miller, no. 50). One of the chairs appears in a 1931 photograph of Mrs. Bayard Verplanck's parlor (Reynolds, pl. 156). Queen Anne features—the heavy walnut frame, balloon-shaped seat, and absence of rococo carving—suggest that the set was made for Samuel Verplanck shortly after his return from Holland in 1763 with his bride, Judith Crommelin.

A few other New York chairs with strapwork splats of similar pattern are known. Those from the General Philip Schuyler set (Kirk 1972, no. 148) also have balloon-shaped seats, a feature relatively rare on New York pierced-splat chairs. The splats of another set with balloon-shaped seats are cut out in the cipher of Robert Livingston and Margaret Beekman, who were married in 1744 (ibid., no. 127). The Verplanck and Livingston sets have virtually identical feet: large circular balls with wiry, webless talons. The same carver may have executed the legs of each set, but variations in the rail construction and in the handling of the rear legs and stiles denote another hand.

PROVENANCE: Part of a group of furniture (cat. nos. 24, 68, 75, 82, 92, 93, 105, 125) inherited by the brothers James De Lancey Verplanck and John Bayard Rodgers Verplanck, whose family had "owned these particular pieces since their first acquisition" (5 / 3 / 39 letter, J.B.R. Verplanck to MMA). Since some of the pieces (cat. nos. 75, 92, 93) may be dated stylistically prior to 1750, they could have been made for Gulian Verplanck (1698–1751), a successful merchant who built a house in New York City on what he referred to in his will as his "Lott of ground with the houses and buildings thereon in Wall Street near the City Hall" (William Edward Verplanck, *The History of Abraham Isaacse Ver Planck*, Fishkill, New York, 1892, p. 106). He also built Mount Gulian, a country house at Fishkill Landing, in Dutchess County, New York. Most of the furniture, however, having Chippendale features and looking to date from the 1760s, was probably made for Gulian's son Samuel (1739–1820). Samuel, in 1758 a member of Columbia College's first graduating class, went to Holland to study banking, and there, in 1761, married his cousin Judith Crommelin. Back in New York City in 1763, Samuel and Judith took up residence in Wall Street (No. 3), in the house for which the furniture was presumably made. In 1776, with the British occupation of New York City, Samuel moved to Mount Gulian, but Judith, a Loyalist, stayed behind. In 1804, the year after her death, the house was rented and the furnishings removed to Fishkill Landing. (The house was demolished in 1822 to make way for the Branch Bank of the United States, through whose facade, now at the MMA, one enters the American Wing.) Samuel's will, dated 1793 and probated May 1, 1820 (now at the N-YHS), named as his sole heir his only son, Daniel Crommelin Verplanck (1762–1834). After his mother's death, Daniel moved from the house in Wall Street to Mount Gulian. The furniture descended from him to his son James De Lancey Verplanck (1805–1881); to his grandson Samuel Verplanck (1840–1911); to his great-grandsons James De Lancey Verplanck (1870–1958) and John Bayard Rodgers Verplanck (1881–1955), the donors.

CONSTRUCTION: On each chair: The crest rail is concave in front; in back, the middle is flat and the rounded sides end in boldly scrolled ears. The stiles, straight in profile, are rounded in back. The square rear legs taper with rounded edges to square spade feet. The splat, seated in the rear rail, has overlapping strapwork, also with scrolled ears. Only the splat's back edges are beveled. The molded shoe is fitted around the splat. The inner edges of the double-pegged seat rails are straight. The flat, shieldlike carved knees terminate in scroll-carved brackets. At the juncture of the side rails and rear legs are similar brackets, rough-hewn in back. There are two vertical triangular glue blocks for each front leg; a vertical quarter round for each rear leg. The front and back boards of the slip-seat frame are tenoned into the side boards. The frame's inner edges are gently shaped.

CONDITION: The wood has a fine mellow reddish walnut color. The seat frames have been reupholstered, and are now covered with a modern yellow worsted, a 1965 reproduction of an antique fabric that was acquired from Mrs. Bayard Verplanck.

INSCRIPTIONS: Incised, inside rear seat rail of each chair, a Roman numeral: *I, II, VII, VIII, X, XI*, respectively; on corresponding slip-seat frames: *II, V, VII, VIII, X, XI.*

DIMENSIONS: H.: overall, 38½ (*97.8*), seat, 17 (*43.2*); W.: seat front, 23 (*58.4*), seat back, 16⅞ (*42.9*), feet, 24½ (*62.2*); D.: seat, 18¼ (*46.4*), feet, 21¾ (*55.2*).

WOODS: Primary: walnut. Secondary: white oak (slip-seat frame); white pine (glue blocks).

REFERENCES: Downs 1941, pp. 8–9; idem 1941a, pp. 218, 224; 222–223 (ill.). [Downs], p. 155 (ill.). Kirk 1972, no. 146. Levy, p. 10.

Gift of James De Lancey Verplanck and John Bayard Rodgers Verplanck, 1939   (39.184.3–8)

25

25. Roundabout Chair

New York, 1760–90

THERE ARE TWO TYPES of New York roundabout chairs. One has serpentine front rails and cabriole arm supports and legs (Warren, nos. 86, 87); the other, represented by cat. no. 25, is more common. Examples of the second type—earlier, and probably dating from mid-century—have quadrant-shaped seats, three front cabriole legs, and one turned leg at the rear. Most have heavy, high crest rails; arms with flat round ends; squat, solid baluster splats; and the heavy, pointed pad feet that are a well-known New York characteristic.

The traditional attribution of these corner chairs to Albany (Kane, no. 60) has yet to be documented. Chairs at Yale (ibid.), at the N-YHS (*Antiques* 64 [December 1953], p. 474, fig. 2), and at Winterthur (Downs 1952, no. 62) are typical, as is another that descended in the Bogart and Onderdonk families of Roslyn, Long Island (photographs, MMA files). Others have leaf-carved knees (*Antiques* 70 [November 1956], p. 400) or pierced splats (Failey 1976, no. 140). Cat. no. 25, with claw feet, a low, elongated crest rail, finely wrought knuckle arms, and pierced splats, is the most thoroughly rococo of its type and probably the latest in date. A similar version of the chair was sold in New York at auction (Christie's, 10/13/83, lot 282).

PROVENANCE: Ex coll.: Howard Reifsnyder, Philadelphia; Harold M. and Cecile Lehman (later Cecile L. Mayer), Tarrytown, New York.

CONSTRUCTION: The arc-shaped crest rail—two pieces butt-joined at left of center—overlaps the armrests and is pegged to the central stile. Each serpentine-shaped armrest, pieced at its molded knuckles, is supported by a splat and by a front stile, to which it is pegged. Each splat is seated in an applied shoe. The turned columnar stiles continue as cabriole legs at the sides and a turned spade foot in back. The deep seat rails are double pegged to the stiles. An inner strip that once supported a commode unit is nailed with roseheads to each rear rail. There are four serpentine-shaped knee brackets.

CONDITION: The chair, of fine dense wood, has a dark red patina. The lower left corner of the right splat is split. Nail holes in the bottom of each front rail suggest that strips of gadrooning were once present. In place of the commode unit, now gone, modern strips have been nailed to the seat rails to support the slip seat. The chair is here illustrated with a modern black horsehair seat cover.

INSCRIPTIONS: Typewritten, on a shipping label (20th-century) pasted inside right rear seat rail: *Howard Reifsnyder, /3914 Walnut Street, / Phila.Pa / One (1) Roundabout Chair*.

DIMENSIONS: H.: overall, 31⅝ (*80.3*), seat, 16½ (*41.9*); W.: arms, 29 (*73.7*), seat, 25 (*63.5*), feet, 28 (*71.1*); D.: seat, 17¾ (*45.1*), feet, 20½ (*52.1*).

WOODS: Primary: mahogany. Secondary: northern white cedar (rear-rail strips). Slip-seat frame not examined.

REFERENCES: *Antiques* 11 (June 1927), front cover; p. 453 (as Philadelphia). Reifsnyder sale, lot 626 (ill.).

Bequest of Cecile L. Mayer, subject to a life estate, 1962 (62.171.13)

26. Side Chair

New York, 1755–90

ON THIS CHAIR, number VIII in a set, the splat—a pierced diamond centered within scrolled strapwork—has long been recognized as a New York state type (Homer Eaton Keyes, "A Clue to New York Furniture," *Antiques* 21 [March 1932], pp. 122–123). Of the many such chairs known (e.g., Kirk 1972, nos. 139–144) the most elegant are those believed to have been made for Sir William Johnson of

Johnson Hall, Johnstown, New York (see Downs 1952, no. 149). Those chairs have balloon seats, shaped rear legs, and fine rococo carving, but most examples are somewhat heavy and boxlike, having thick stiles and crest rails and square seats and rear legs. Some, like the sets made for Philip Van Rensselaer (Blackburn 1976, nos. 43, 44) and Abraham Yates (DAPC 74.847), both of Albany, have carved crests and knees; others, like cat. no. 26, are uncarved. The splats of all the chairs are perfectly flat, with no differentiation in surface planes to suggest the lapping of one strap over another. The splat pattern is based on a popular English design (Kirk 1982, figs. 870–877). Three chairs with diamond-and-strapwork splats from a set originally at Vlie House, a Van Rensselaer family residence at Rensselaer, New York, are signed: "Made by Gilbert Ash in Wall Street New York" (Roderic H. Blackburn, "Gilbert Ash inscriptions reconsidered," *Antiques* 123 [February 1983], pp. 428–431). Since their splats, though closely resembling that of cat. no. 26, were cut from a different template and their legs are entirely unlike these, Ash could not have been the maker of the set to which the MMA chair belonged.

PROVENANCE: Ex coll.: W. Gedney Beatty, Rye, New York.

26

CONSTRUCTION: The crest rail is slightly concave in front; in back it is flat, with rounded edges. The backs of the stiles and rear legs are rounded. The splat, its edges slightly beveled, is seated in the shoe. The side rails are unusually thin. There are double quarter-round vertical glue blocks in front and single quarter-round blocks with fillets in back.

CONDITION: The dense reddish brown wood has a glossy finish. The slip seat has a replaced frame. The chair is illustrated here with a modern red silk damask seat cover.

INSCRIPTIONS: Incised, inside rear seat rail: *VIII*. Chalk inscriptions on the front and rear seat rails are mostly illegible, but one may read: *J B — M*.

DIMENSIONS: H.: overall, 38½ (*97.8*), seat, 16⅝ (*42.2*); W.: seat front, 20½ (*52.1*), seat back, 15½ (*39.4*), feet, 22⅜ (*56.8*); D.: seat, 16½ (*41.9*), feet, 20½ (*52.1*).

WOODS: Primary: mahogany. Secondary: white pine (glue blocks).

Bequest of W. Gedney Beatty, 1941   (41.160.637)

27. Side Chair

New York, 1755–90

TASSEL-BACK, or tassel-and-ruffle, chairs were made in America only in New York, where they were one of the most popular of patterns. This one, number IV in a set, is a classic example of those chairs, which are remarkably consistent in overall design. On the crest rail, a central C-scroll with rocaille mantel is flanked by carved acanthus leafage. In the center of the pierced splat, a tassel and a ruffled band appear between fronds of pendent acanthus leafage. At the bottom are three vertical slots, as here, or a spade-shaped opening (e.g., cat. nos. 28, 29). The front legs have acanthus-carved knees and blocklike claw feet. Gadrooning is applied to the front rail. The known triple-slotted tassel-back chairs differ one from another only in minor details of their carving. On the crest rails of some (SPB sale no. 4663, 7/10/81, lot 650; sale no. 4692Y, 9/26/81, lot 442), the rocaille mantel is modeled in rough parallel gouges like those found on cat. no. 29. On others, at the Brooklyn Museum (*Antiques* 66 [October 1954], p. 249, ill.; Schwartz, pl. VI), in the Stone collection (Rodriguez Roque, no. 54), and at the Carnegie Institute, the crest-rail motifs differ in size and shape. These chairs must all have originated in the same shop, since their splats are cut from the same template and their carving is of a common technique.

Tassel-back chairs have descended in a number of New York families, including those of Whitehead Hicks, mayor of New York City from 1766 to 1776 (Kirk 1972, no. 138), and Stephen Van Rensselaer (ibid., no. 137). The design follows closely an English or Irish chair-type

(Kirk 1982, fig. 934; Hinckley, fig. 713), although no example imported into eighteenth-century New York is recorded.

PROVENANCE: Ex coll.: Mr. and Mrs. George Sands Bryan, Pelham, New York.

CONSTRUCTION: The crest rail, attached to the stiles with round pegs, is concave in front; in back it is rounded except in the middle, where it is flat with beveled edges. The stiles are rounded in back. The square rear legs, tapered and with rounded edges, end in spade feet. The bevel-edged pierced splat is seated in the shoe, which is nailed to the rear rail. All the rails are double pegged. The side rails form serpentine-shaped brackets where they join the rear legs. The gadrooned strip is nailed to the front rail. Triangular glue blocks reinforce the front legs.

CONDITION: The chair, fashioned from extremely heavy wood, is a light brown in color. The upper tips of the ears are broken off. The front bracket on the left cabriole leg was carved in 1979, replacing an inaccurate restoration. The glue blocks have been reattached with modern screws. The side rails have been built up inside with poplar strips (19th-century). The slip seat has been reupholstered. The chair is here illustrated in an antique yellow and white damask seat cover.

27

INSCRIPTIONS: Incised, inside rear seat rail: *IIII*.

DIMENSIONS: H.: overall, 38¼ (*97.2*), seat, 17 (*43.2*); W.: seat front, 22 (*55.9*), seat back, 15¾ (*40.*), feet, 24⅛ (*61.3*); D.: seat, 18½ (*47.*), feet, 22½ (*57.2*).

WOODS: Primary: mahogany. Secondary: maple (slip-seat frame); white pine (glue blocks).

REFERENCES: Downs 1948, p. 83. W. Johnston, pp. 125–126; fig. 13.

Gift of Mrs. George Sands Bryan, in memory of her husband, 1946   (46.152.1)

28. Side Chairs (Two)

New York, 1755–90

NEW YORK TASSEL-BACK chairs are often called Van Rensselaer chairs, and not without reason; at least four different sets have associations with the Van Rensselaer

family. They include the well-known set, or sets, believed to have belonged to Stephen Van Rensselaer II, builder of the Manor House at Albany, 1765–68 (Kirk 1972, no. 137); the set at Winterthur (Downs 1952, no. 52; see Provenance, cat. no. 146); the chairs said to have descended from Jeremias Van Rensselaer (cat. no. 29); and, finally, these chairs, numbers VI and VII in a set made for a Nicoll descendant of Kiliaen Van Rensselaer. Chair number V from the same set (Sack 5, p. 1341) is now at the High Museum, Atlanta.

These Van Rensselaer chairs appear to have a common source. The splats, all with a spade-shaped lower opening, are cut either from the same template or from identical ones. Differences are limited to the carving—particularly that on the crest rail—and to the treatment of the rear legs, some shaped, some square. On the crest rails of these two, for example, large acanthus leaves flank a simple C-scroll and softly modeled rocaille; at cat. no. 29, smaller leaves flank two C-scrolls and a gouge-cut rocaille. On all three chairs, the rear rails are similarly incised with Roman numerals and the slip seats are made of sweet gum.

PROVENANCE: According to the last private owners, the chairs descended in the Nicoll family of New York. The presumed line of descent was from Benjamin Nicoll (1718–1760), grandson of Kiliaen Van Rensselaer, the first patroon of Rensselaerwyck, or from Benjamin's son Matthias (1758–1827); to Ann Nicoll Clinch; to Sarah Clinch Smith; to Bessie Springs Smith (Mrs. Stanford White); to Lawrence Grant White; to F.L. Peter White and Alida White Lessard, from whom the MMA acquired them.

CONSTRUCTION: On each chair: The rails are not pegged and there are no glue blocks. Otherwise, the construction is like that of cat. no. 27.

CONDITION: The chairs, made of light-weight wood, have a reddish brown color. On no. VII, the chair illustrated, the juncture of the left stile with the crest rail has been reinforced with a spline. The slip seats have been reupholstered, and now have the antique green and white damask cover shown here.

INSCRIPTIONS: Incised, inside rear seat rail of each chair: *VI*; *VII*, respectively; on corresponding slip-seat frame: *III*; *VIII*.

DIMENSIONS: H.: overall, 38⅞ (*98.7*); seat, 17 (*43.2*); W.: seat front, 22 (*55.9*), seat back, 16 (*40.6*), feet, 24¼ (*61.6*); D.: seat, 18⅛ (*46.*), feet, 22¼ (*56.5*).

WOODS: Primary: mahogany. Secondary: sweet gum (slip-seat frame).

Purchase, The Sylmaris Collection, Gift of George Coe Graves, by exchange, 1957   (57.158.1, 2)

28 See also p. 337

29

29. Armchair

New York, 1755–75

THIS CHAIR, NUMBER VII in a set from the Van Rensselaer family, is one of a small group of New York tassel-backs readily distinguishable by their somewhat tall and narrow backs and by the double C-scroll with gouge-cut rocaille mantel in the middle of the crest rail. Two armchairs, numbers V and VIII from the same set, are at the White House (*Antiques* 116 [July 1979], p. 117, ill.), with the chalked initials D S on the rear rail of one of them. The White House chairs are the same as cat. no. 29 in size and construction and in bearing the ink inscription "Cathalina E. Groot," but their arms and armrest supports are altogether different in detail. Those of cat. no. 29, which began life as a side chair, are later additions—realistically carved versions of the eagle's-head terminals present on every New York tassel-back armchair. A pair of armchairs apparently identical in every detail to the ones at the White House belonged to the New York collector Thomas B. Clarke (Lockwood 1907,

pl. CXX). Though carved by a different hand, a side chair at Dearborn inscribed "1757 Philena Barnes" (Campbell, p. 25) is also identical—the splat even appears to be cut from the same template; another chair (P-B sale no. 1202, 12/1/50, lot 497) looks to be from the same set. Six side chairs and one armchair at Winterthur (Downs 1952, no. 52), also with a Van Rensselaer history (see Provenance, cat. no. 146), are of similar construction and carving, but their rear legs are rounded and tapered. The Winterthur set was on loan in the American Wing's Van Rensselaer Hall at the MMA from 1934 to 1946.

PROVENANCE: Purchased from the firm of Harry Flayderman, King Hooper Mansion, Marblehead, Massachusetts. According to Benjamin Flayderman (December 1932 telegram, MMA files), the chair was "... originally the property of Jeremiah Van Rensselaer and purchased at the present time from a direct descendant whose name is also Jeremiah Van Rensselaer. From what I can find out about him he is an architect and formerly lived in Scotia, but now lives in Schenectady." The first "Jeremiah" was perhaps Jeremias (1738–1764) or his son John Jeremias (1762–1828). The latter had a son named Cornelius Glen Van Rensselaer, whose grandson and namesake was an architect in Schenectady, New York, in 1932. That descent would seem to relate to the provenance of the chair given by the vendor. Alternatively, the "Randolph" inscription on the MMA chair conforms to the history of the matching White House pair, which are thought to have belonged to a granddaughter of Thomas Jefferson named Eleanora Wayles Randolph (1796–1876), who married Joseph Coolidge of Boston in 1825 (provenance, White House files). From Eleanora, the chairs would have descended to Thomas Jefferson Coolidge; to Sarah Lawrence Coolidge, who married Thomas Newbold; to Mary Edith Newbold Morgan; to Gerald Morgan, Jr., the last private owner. But whom they belonged to prior to Eleanora Randolph remains uncertain, as does the identity of Cathalina E. Groot.

CONSTRUCTION: The front legs are reinforced with thin triangular glue blocks. The square rear legs are slightly beveled on the front edges. Otherwise, the construction is like that at cat. no. 27.

CONDITION: The chair's finish looks to have been scraped down at one time, but the wood is a rich dark red in color. The curved arm supports and the finely carved arms were added sometime after the chair was made: their patina is brown; the arm supports are cut out to conform to the profile of the side rails; the screws that secure them are modern; behind the supports, the seat rails retain an old, undisturbed finish. The slip seat has been reupholstered. The chair is here illustrated with an antique green and white damask seat cover.

INSCRIPTIONS: Incised, inside rear seat rail: *VII*; in brown ink (18th-century?), on bottom of left front glue block: *Cathalina E. Groot*. In brown pencil (19th-century?), inside rear seat rail: *Randolph*(?).

DIMENSIONS: H.: overall, 39⅛ (*99.4*), seat, 17¼ (*43.8*); W.: seat front, 20⅞ (*53.*), seat back, 15½ (*39.4*), feet, 23 (*58.4*); D.: seat, 18 (*45.7*), feet, 22 (*55.9*).

WOODS: Primary: mahogany. Secondary: tulip poplar (rear seat rail): sweet gum (slip-seat frame); white pine (glue blocks).

REFERENCES: *MMAB* 28 (February 1933), p. 35 (ill.). Kirk 1972, no. 136.

Rogers Fund, 1932   (32.107)

30. Side Chair

New York, 1765–90

THE SPLAT DESIGN of this chair derives ultimately from plate XII, center, of the third edition of Chippendale's *Director* (1762). Whether the chair was actually inspired by that plate or, as is more likely, by an imported English chair based on it is as yet undocumented. Numerous straight- or cabriole-leg side chairs with this splat pattern are known, several having histories of descent in New York families. They were apparently made only by New York chairmakers, who followed Chippendale's advice (plate IX) for the height of their chairs but who made the seats both wider and deeper.

With cabriole legs and claw feet, the side chair is slightly larger than other New York chairs of the pattern.

30

Numbered VIII, it is apparently from the same set as a pair from the Cox family of Piping Rock, Long Island (Downs and Ralston, no. 88), and now at the MCNY (*Antiques* 64 [October 1953], p. 289, fig. 3; Comstock, no. 277, where an erroneous Thompson family provenance is given). A similar set, a dozen in number, descended from the famous New York revolutionary war general Matthew Clarkson (Fairbanks and Bates, p. 152). A chair from a third set, also at the MCNY and said to have descended in the Thompson family of Brooklyn, New York, has acanthus-leaf-carved knees (Kirk 1972, no. 149).

PROVENANCE: Purchased by the donor from Bernard & S. Dean Levy, Inc., New York City.

CONSTRUCTION: The crest rail is concave in front; in back, it is flat at the middle and has rounded ends. The stiles are molded in front and rounded in back. The square rear legs, slightly rounded at the edges, taper to spade feet. The splat, its sides slightly beveled, is tenoned into the shoe, which is glued to the double-pegged rear rail. Serpentine-shaped horizontal brackets are nailed at the junctures of side rails and rear legs. On the front rail the gadrooning is applied. There are triangular front glue blocks.

CONDITION: The chair, which has been refinished, is reddish brown in color. The upper right part of the splat and the left rear foot have been patched. The rear glue blocks are replaced. The slip seat has been reupholstered. The chair is illustrated here with a seat cover of modern yellow wool damask.

INSCRIPTIONS: Incised, inside rear seat rail: *VIII*.

DIMENSIONS: H.: overall, 38½ (*97.8*), seat, 17⅛ (*43.5*); W.: seat front, 23 (*58.4*), seat back, 18⅞ (*47.9*), feet, 25 (*63.5*); D.: seat, 18⅝ (*47.3*), feet, 23½ (*59.7*).

WOODS: Primary: mahogany. Secondary: tulip poplar (slip-seat frame); white pine (glue blocks).

Gift of Wunsch Foundation, Inc., 1984   (1984.334)

31. Side Chair

New York, 1765–90

A FEW SETS OF CHAIRS with this Chippendale-inspired splat pattern have cabriole legs and claw feet (see cat. no. 30), but the majority have straight legs with pierced corner brackets. Alternative ways of ornamenting the latter are illustrated at cat. nos. 31 and 32: the legs either plain with a quarter-round-molded outer edge or molded; the brackets either double C-scrolls or arcs and right angles. This chair, numbered I, is part of a set of at least twelve. Eight others, numbered III, IIII, V, VI, VII, VIIII, X, and XI, and almost certainly from the same set, were advertised (*Antiques* 67 [June 1955], p. 453), later exhibited at Philipse Manor (Comstock, fig. 279), and subsequently acquired at auction (SPB sale no. 3371, 5/19/72, lot 113) by a New York collector. Joseph Downs claimed (notes, MMA files) that cat. no. 31 was identical to a set of chairs originally owned by Stephen Van Rensselaer and was possibly part of the set. A set of six chairs like this one but for having arc-and-right-angle brackets descended in the Floyd family of Setauket, Long Island (Failey 1976, no. 104). Except that they have no brackets, six others now at Williamsburg (acc. 1930-161, 1-6) are identical, even to the splat template.

PROVENANCE: Purchased at auction (P-B, 2/16/46), to which the chair had been consigned by a "Newport Private Collector."

CONSTRUCTION: The crest rail, flat in back and with rounded edges, is affixed to the stiles with round pegs. The stiles are molded in front and rounded in back. The square rear legs are slightly beveled on their inner edges, as are the back edges of the splat. The seat rails are pegged. The upper edges of the front and side rails are molded quarter rounds. The front legs, beveled on the inner edges and with quarter-round molding on the outer edges, are reinforced with triangular glue blocks. The front stretcher is dovetailed and nailed to the side stretchers; the pierced brackets are also nailed.

CONDITION: The heavy dark wood has a reddish color. There is a buildup of old finishes, but the effect is pleasing. The side bracket on the left front leg is replaced. The slip seat has been reupholstered. The chair is illustrated here with an eighteenth-century English gold and white silk brocade seat cover.

INSCRIPTIONS: Incised, inside rear seat rail: *I*; on slip-seat frame: *VI* and (probably later) *X*.

DIMENSIONS: H.: overall, 37⅞ (*96.2*), seat, 16½ (*41.9*); W.: seat front, 22 (*55.9*), seat back, 19 (*48.3*), feet, 22 (*55.9*); D.: seat, 18 (*46.7*), feet, 20¼ (*51.4*).

WOODS: Primary: mahogany. Secondary: cherry (slip-seat frame); white pine (glue blocks).

REFERENCES: P-B sale no. 739, 2/16/46, lot 311 (chair said to be English). Downs 1948, p. 83.

Rogers Fund, 1946   (46.45)

32. Side Chair

New York, 1765–90

THOUGH IDENTICAL in overall design to cat. no. 31, the set in which this chair is number VI is the product of another shop, as is demonstrated by such different construction details as the treatment of the edges of the splat and the beveled back edges of the front legs. The deeper and crisper stile moldings and ear carvings and the

31

32

molded front legs contribute to a lighter and more delicate general effect than displayed at cat. no. 31. The chairs of another set, with seats upholstered over the rails (private collection; for a similar chair see Bishop 1972, no. 179), look to be by the same hand as cat. no. 32. Brass plaques on the rear rail identify them as having belonged to William and Mary Nicoll of Middle Hope, Orange County, New York, who were married in 1823. Chairs at Williamsburg (Blackburn 1976, no. 45) from a set thought to have belonged to Philip Van Rensselaer (1747–1798) have front legs molded on two sides, but are otherwise identical to cat. no. 32.

PROVENANCE: Ex coll.: The Reverend George Drew Egbert and Mrs. Egbert, Flushing, New York. On loan to the MMA from the Egbert children from 1940 until given in 1966.

CONSTRUCTION: The crest rail is rounded in back except for the middle, which is flat with beveled edges. The stiles are molded in front, rounded in back. The square rear legs are slightly beveled on the inner edge. The splat is flat in back and has unbeveled edges. The upper edges of the front and side rails are molded quarter rounds; their inner rabbets, which receive the slip seat, are unusually thin. In front, triangular glue blocks are attached with double roseheads; in back are small vertical quarter rounds. On the front legs, the front surface is molded with a central bead-and-reel pattern; the inner edges are chamfered below the seat rails. The front stretcher is dovetailed and nailed to the side ones; the pierced brackets are also nailed.

CONDITION: The front surface of the chair has an opaque, decayed finish; the rear surfaces have the original thin finish, a reddish brown in color. The side bracket on the left front leg is replaced. The slip seat has been reupholstered. The chair is here illustrated with an eighteenth-century English gold and white silk brocade seat cover.

INSCRIPTIONS: Incised, inside rear seat rail: *VI*. In white chalk, on the right triangular glue block: *23*; on the left one: *24*.

DIMENSIONS: H.: overall, 37⅝ (*95.6*), seat, 16 (*40.6*); W.: seat front, 22¼ (*56.5*), seat back, 18¾ (*47.6*); D.: seat, 18⅝ (*47.3*), feet, 21 (*53.3*).

WOODS: Primary: mahogany. Secondary: tulip poplar (slip-seat frame); white pine (glue blocks).

Given in memory of George Drew Egbert and Estelle Powers Egbert by their children, 1966   (66.108.6)

33. Side Chairs (Two)

New York, 1760–90

AMERICAN CHAIRS with this ornate back design—stop-fluted stiles and a splat intricately pierced with owl's-eyes and pointed arches and carved with ruffles and rosettes—were made almost exclusively in New York,

33

though a side chair at the Boston MFA has cabriole legs and claw feet executed in a characteristically Massachusetts manner (Randall 1965, no. 149). The design of these chairs, two from a set, must have been based on imported examples. An English chair at the MMA (acc. no. 10.125.297) has a back that is similar to those of its American counterparts, if of different proportions. Acquired by H. Eugene Bolles, an early collector (1880s–1910), it may well have been in this country in the eighteenth century. On these two New York straight-legged chairs of excellent quality the embellishment has been executed with assurance, but not by either of the hands that carved the Verplanck family set with the same back design (cat. no. 34).

PROVENANCE: Ex coll.: Adeline R. Brown, St. Alban's, Long Island, New York.

CONSTRUCTION: On each chair: The crest rail, deeply concave and splayed in front, is outlined at the top and bottom edges by scratch beading. In back, the crest rail and stiles have beveled edges that meet at a rounded point. The splat's back edges are also beveled. The shoe is the same thickness as the rear rail. The side rails are pegged to the legs. The top edges of the front and side rails and the front edges of the front legs are molded in narrow quarter rounds. The square front and rear legs have beveled inner edges. A narrow wooden strip is nailed to the rear rail between the small triangular glue blocks, these affixed with double roseheads.

CONDITION: The chairs are of dense wood and have a deep reddish brown patina. Chair no. VIII has a rectangular patch set into the right rail. The other chair, the one illustrated, has a repair in the splat below the owl's-eyes. The front glue blocks of both chairs are replaced. The slip seats have been reupholstered, and are now covered with the modern red silk damask shown here.

INSCRIPTIONS: Incised, inside rear seat rail of one chair: VIII; of the other: —I [2 or 6?]; on one of the slip-seat frames: IIV.

DIMENSIONS: H.: overall, 37½ (95.3), seat, 16¾ (42.5); W.: seat front, 21¾ (55.2), seat back, 16¾ (42.5); D.: seat, 18 (45.7), feet, 21½ (54.6).

WOODS: Primary: mahogany. Secondary: mahogany (rear glue blocks); white oak (rear-rail strips); beech (slip-seat frames).

Bequest of Adeline R. Brown, 1947   (48.135.94, 95)

34. Armchair and Seven Side Chairs

New York, 1770–90

THE CHAIRS OF CAT. NO. 34, here divided into two subgroups,* are part of a set, or sets, consisting of twelve chairs that descended in the Verplanck family (see Provenance). The MMA owns these eight chairs of the twelve; two others appeared at auction in 1977 (SPB sale no. 4004, 6/10/77, lot 311); and of the remaining two unaccounted for, one may have been in the Wanamaker Collection (*The Antiquarian* 14 [November 1930], ill., p. 17). The shaped rear legs, the thick red-oak seat rails, and, on the armchair, the carved eagle's-head armrests are characteristics of New York workmanship. The two side chairs given to the MMA in 1940 for installation in the Verplanck Room of the American Wing retain their old finishes, as does the armchair, which was given in 1984. These three chairs are now covered in the pumpkin-colored fabric used throughout that room; the five chairs given in 1962–63 have been refinished and are now covered in green silk.

These visual differences, resulting from the chairs' separate recent histories, are misleading. All the chairs exhibit close similarities in design and construction and may have been made in one shop. A more thorough ex-

*The chairs are referred to throughout the entry as nos. 1–8. The corresponding accession numbers of the six chairs of the the first subgroup are: 40.137.1 (1); 62.250.1 (2); 62.250.2 (3); 62.250.3 (4); 63. 22.1 (5); 1984.287 (6); of the two chairs of the second subgroup: 40.137.2 (7); 63.22.2 (8).

amination, however, reveals splats from two different templates, carving by two different hands, and the incised marks of two separate sets. For example, on the armchair, on one of the chairs sold at auction, and on the five chairs of the first subgroup: the beaded upper edge of the crest rail forms a rounded projection at the center but gradually turns into an incised line at the sides; on the splat, the ruffle carving on the central owl's-eyes projects into the plain C-scrolls above, and carved rosettes with clearly defined quatrefoil profiles are squeezed into the pointed-arch openings below. In contrast, on the second of the chairs sold at auction and on the two chairs of the second subgroup: the projecting beaded upper edge of the crest rail is continuous, the ruffle carving on the owl's-eyes does not project up into the C-scrolls, the carved rosettes have circular profiles and are comfortably spaced within the pointed-arch openings, and the carving has been executed with greater assurance.

PROVENANCE: The eight chairs all have Verplanck family histories, the line of descent being from Samuel (1739–1820) or Daniel Crommelin Verplanck (1762–1834); to Gulian Crommelin Verplanck (1786–1870); to William Samuel Verplanck (1812–1885), at whose death the set was split up. Nos. 1 and 7 descended to Robert Newlin Verplanck, thence to Mrs. Robert Newlin Verplanck, the donor. Nos. 2–5 and 8 descended to Gelyna Verplanck Fitzgerald (born 1852); to Geraldine Fitzgerald Adee (1873–1956), from whose estate the chairs were acquired by Dr. Charles A. Poindexter, the donor. No. 6, which was owned in 1900 by William E. Verplanck, Fishkill, New York (Singleton 1, p. 290), descended from Mrs. Adee; to Geraldine F. Kurtz; to Barbara Bradley Manice, the donor. The chairs must have come from the house of Samuel and Judith (Crommelin) Verplanck at No. 3 Wall Street, New York City. When the house was closed, in 1804, the furnishings were taken to Samuel Verplanck's country house, Mount Gulian, Fishkill Landing, New York; one of the chairs appears in a photograph of the dining room there (Reynolds, pl. 63). In May 1940, Mrs. Adee knew of ten of the twelve chairs (letter, MMA files). The six chairs she owned included the eagle-armed chair described in 1900 as "one of a set of twelve" that had belonged to Judith and Samuel Verplanck (Singleton 1, p. 290).

CONSTRUCTION: On each chair: The concave crest rail is rounded in back. The stiles are stop-fluted in front and rounded in back. On the splat, which is seated in the rear rail, the back edges are beveled. The shoe fits around the splat and is nailed over the upholstery. The rear legs, square at the top, are tapered and rounded and end in oval spade feet. The seat rails are thick, the rear one a full two inches deep. Corner braces are dovetailed into the tops of the front and side rails. The carved knee brackets are glued to horizontal blocks attached to the front legs and the bottom of the seat rails. On chairs nos. 1–6, the side and rear rails are pegged to the rear legs. On no. 6, the inner surfaces of the thick side rails are cut out for the double screws that secure the rounded arm supports.

CONDITION: Chairs 1, 6, and 7 have a fine, thin old finish with a dark reddish brown mahogany color; the other five, which have been refinished, now have a bright red mahogany

color. No. 1 is intact. On no. 2, the crest is patched at its juncture with the splat; the right front bracket is a 1980 replacement; the rear legs are split where they join the rails; the frame has been reinforced with four blocks. On no. 3, the crest is patched where it joins the splat. On no. 4, the back of the splat is patched at the bottom; the right front bracket is replaced and the tips of the others are patched; the junctures of rear legs and side rails are reinforced with modern wooden blocks and old but not original angle irons. On no. 5, the crest rail is patched where it broke free of the stiles and splat; the splat is an old replacement; the rear seat rail is patched at the left side. On no. 6, the top of the right arm support is patched; the left side knee bracket is replaced; and the front braces and rear glue blocks are gone. On no. 7, the crest rail, stiles, and splat have been repaired at their juncture. On no. 8, the crest rail is patched where it broke free of the stiles and splat; the splat is patched at the top front and center bottom; the rails have been reinforced with corner brackets. On all the chairs, the oak seat rails show the effects of numerous reupholsterings. X-rays of no. 2 indicate that a round-arched pattern of brass-headed nails may once have ornamented the rails. The pumpkin-colored wool damask that covers the seats of side chair no. 1 and the armchair, both illustrated, and no. 7 is a reproduction of fabric from the Verplanck family (see cat. no. 82). The seats of the other five side chairs are now covered in an antique green silk damask.

INSCRIPTIONS: Incised, on top of rear seat rail and on underside of shoe on the chairs of the first subgroup: *I* (no. 3); *II* (no. 2); *III* (no. 5); *V* (no. 4); *VII* (no. 1); *VIII* (no. 6); of the second subgroup: *I* (no. 8). No. 7 is unmarked. Engraved, on an oval silver plaque (20th-century) screwed to back of nos. 2, 3, 4, 5, 6, and 8: *Judith Crommelin 1761*. In pencil, inside rear seat rail of no. 7: *Herman Wille* (?) *June 7 1901*.

DIMENSIONS: armchair: H.: overall, 39½ (*100.3*), seat, 17¼ (*43.8*); W.: arms, 30 (*76.2*), seat front, 25⅜ (*64.5*), seat back, 18½ (*47.*), feet, 27 (*68.6*); D.: seat, 18⅜ (*46.7*), feet, 23½ (*59.7*); side chairs: H.: overall, 38½ (*97.8*), seat, 16½ (*41.9*); W.: seat front, 22¼ (*56.5*), seat back, 16 (*40.6*), feet, 24 (*61.*); D.: seat, 17½ (*44.5*), feet, 22 (*55.9*).

WOODS: Primary: mahogany. Secondary: red oak (seat rails); ash (corner braces of no. 8); sweet gum (corner braces and glue blocks of nos. 1–7).

REFERENCES: Singleton 1, p. 290; opp. p. 286 (armchair ill.). [Downs], p. 156. MMAB n.s. 22 (October 1963), pp. 58–59; p. 59 (ill.). *Antiques* 91 (April 1967), p. 481 (ill.). Bishop, fig. 176 (no. 7 ill. with previous upholstery).

Gift of Mrs. Robert Newlin Verplanck, 1940 (40.137.1, 2); Gift of Charles A. Poindexter, 1962, 1963 (62.250.1–3; 63.22.1, 2); Bequest of Barbara Bradley Manice, 1984 (1984.287)

34 See also p. 337

3 Pennsylvania Chairs

The flowering of the chairmaking industry in Philadelphia in the seventeen-forties led to the production of great numbers of chairs, in the purest American expression of the Queen Anne style, distinguished by their high narrow backs, balloon seats, and absence of stretchers. The pronounced curves of the balloon seat were made possible by a unique method of construction: broad and flat seat rails forming a frame into which the front legs are doweled. The Museum's holdings, which include armchairs and a roundabout chair, demonstrate the nearly infinite variety that was achieved within a standard form; the only notable variant missing is an example of the recessed-blocked and applied-shell front-skirt type. The earliest pierced-splat pattern—the so-called strapwork splat introduced in the mid-seventeen-fifties—appears on both Queen Anne and Chippendale chair forms at the same time. Succeeding designs, mostly with gothic trefoils and pointed arches, demonstrate the unmistakable influence of Chippendale's *Director*. Oddly, most of the great sets of chairs in the fully developed rococo style did not include armchairs, and only one is in the collection.

35

35. Side Chair

Philadelphia, 1740–60

THE SEAT FRAME and legs of this simple chair, number III in a set, follow those of well-known Pennsylvania Queen Anne patterns, but the outline of the back is wider and rounder than the norm, and the splat is a variation of the standard baluster type.

PROVENANCE: Ex coll.: Louis Guerineau Myers, New York City.

CONSTRUCTION: The back of the yoke-shaped crest rail is flat in the middle and rounded at the ends. The rail is pegged to the stiles. The stiles, gently serpentine in profile, are pieced at their lower curves. The rear legs are octagonal. The thick boards of the curved front and side seat rails are straight on the inside. The side rails are tenoned into the front rail and double pegged;

the rails are cut away at the top to create a rim that contains the slip seat. The slip seat is also supported by a strip nailed to the rear rail. The tops of the front legs continue as large dowels through the seat rails; the side rails and their cavetto-shaped rear brackets are tenoned through the rear legs. The knee brackets are attached with double roseheads.

CONDITION: The wood has a mellow brown color. The knee brackets of the left front leg have been replaced. The slip seat has been reupholstered. The chair is here illustrated with an eighteenth-century blue silk damask seat cover.

INSCRIPTIONS: Incised crescent-shaped marks, on front seat rail: *III*; on slip-seat frame: *IIII*.

DIMENSIONS: H.: overall, 40¼ (*102.2*), seat, 16¼ (*41.3*); W.: seat front, 20¼ (*51.4*), seat back, 15¼ (*38.7*), feet, 18⅜ (*46.7*); D.: seat, 16¾ (*42.5*), feet, 17¼ (*43.8*).

WOODS: Primary: walnut. Secondary: walnut (rear-rail strip); yellow pine (slip-seat frame).

Rogers Fund, 1925　　　　　　　　　　　　　(25.115.3)

36. Armchair and Side Chair

Philadelphia, 1740–60

THESE CHAIRS from the same set are particularly fine examples of the fiddleback-splat Philadelphia Queen Anne chair, so named because the lower splat silhouette resembles that of a violin. Numerous variants of the fiddleback pattern are known, including a set from the Shoemaker (Schumacker) family of Philadelphia (Downs 1952, no. 112; PMA 1976, no. 27). The MMA chairs, the side chair numbered III, are notable not only for their clean, graceful lines but also for the unusual care with which they were made—witness the use of the same board for the seat rails and their applied rims. Louis Guerineau Myers, the chairs' previous owner, knew of two other side chairs from the same set (1925 notes, MMA files), possibly those numbered I and II now in a Philadelphia private collection. An apparently identical side chair has been advertised (*Antiques* 65 [March 1954], p. 197); another is said to have descended in a Chester County, Pennsylvania, family (ibid. 89 [February 1966], p. 165). The set's maker is probably also responsible for an armchair, identical but for a crest-rail shell (ibid. 32 [December 1937], p. 273).

On the knees of all the chairs is a carved, tonguelike intaglio, a motif found on several pieces of furniture labeled by or otherwise documented to William Savery (1722–1787), the famous Philadelphia cabinet- and chairmaker (e.g., Comstock, fig. 176; *Antiques* 88 [December 1965], p. 743). Because the chairs of cat. no. 36 have tongues—bulbous on top and with a long narrow bottom, and also

36 See also p. 338

found on a generally similar armchair branded IF (DAPC folio 68.3226)—and oval pad feet, both differing in shape from those of any piece of Savery's documented work, an attribution to that craftsman is not warranted.

PROVENANCE: Ex coll.: Louis Guerineau Myers, New York City.

CONSTRUCTION: On each chair: The back is gently serpentine in profile. In back, the yoke-shaped crest rail is flat and has rounded edges; the stiles, pieced at their curves, are rounded. The rear legs are octagonal. The splat is seated in the molded shoe nailed to the rear rail. The front and side seat rails, thick horizontal boards, form the boldly curved balloon seat. Their straight inner edges frame a square opening; an applied rim, cut from the same stock, holds the slip seat in place. The side rails are pegged to the front rail. The straight inner edge of each front leg continues as a large dowel through the front rail and the side-rail tenon. The knee brackets, their serpentine sides chiseled, are secured with four roseheads each. The side rails and their cavetto-shaped rear brackets are tenoned through the rear legs and pegged; the brackets are pegged to the seat rails; the rear rail, roughly sawed on the inside, is double pegged. On the armchair: The side rails are double pegged to the front rail. The armrest supports overlap the seat rims and are double screwed into the side rails and pegged to the armrests. The armrests are secured by screws through the stiles.

CONDITION: The chairs have a warm walnut brown color. On the side chair: The stiles have been patched at their juncture with the crest rail. The pieced lower curve of the right stile and a section of the applied rim on the right seat rail have been replaced. Modern steel bolts reinforce the junctures of side rails and rear legs. On the armchair: The applied rim on the front rail is slightly pushed back from the seat-rail front. An arc-shaped piece has been roughly cut from the back surface of the front rail. On both chairs, the slip seat has been reupholstered. The chairs are illustrated with an antique yellow silk bourette seat cover.

INSCRIPTIONS (on side chair only): Incised, on front seat rail: *III*; on slip-seat frame: *V*. Under front seat rail: fragmentary remains of a large gummed paper label. In brown ink, on a large paper label (20th-century) pasted inside rear seat rail: *These chairs were the property of Robert Montgomery (2nd) of "Eglinton," Upper Freehold, Monmouth Co.—belonged originally to the 2nd Elisha Lawrence of Chesnut Grove Monmouth Co. N.J.—from whence they were brought.* [Signed] *Hetty N. Watson.*

DIMENSIONS: armchair: H.: overall, 41 (*104.1*), seat, 16¼ (*41.3*); W.: arms, 31½ (*80.*), seat front, 23¼ (*59.1*), seat back, 17 (*43.2*), feet, 23¼ (*59.1*); D.: seat, 18½ (*47.*), feet, 21¼ (*54.*); side chair: H.: overall, 40 (*101.6*), seat, 17 (*43.2*); W.: seat front, 19⅝ (*49.9*), seat back, 14⅛ (*35.9*), feet, 19½ (*49.5*); D.: seat, 16¼ (*41.3*), feet, 19¾ (*50.2*).

WOODS: Primary: walnut. Secondary: walnut (most elements of slip-seat frames); yellow pine (back of side chair's slip-seat frame).

Rogers Fund, 1925   (25.115.36, 37)

36

37. Side Chairs (Two)

Philadelphia, 1740–60

THE HIGH, NARROW BACK and the simple pad feet of these two chairs, numbers II and III from a set of at least six, typify Philadelphia Queen Anne chairs of an early date. The splat pattern is a variant on the fiddleback at cat. no. 36, with four carved scrolls, or volutes, now defining the upper section. The pattern, while well represented in the MMA collection (cat. nos. 38, 39), is relatively uncommon in Queen Anne chairs made in

37 See also p. 338

Philadelphia. A chair apparently from the same set as cat. no. 37 was identified as being from the "collection of Amelia Foulke Custard, 1789" (Haskell sale 3, lot 597). Chairs from two other sets (Girl Scouts, no. 575; SPB sale no. 3638, 5/11/74, lot 443) look to be the work of the same hand, differing from cat. no. 37 and from each other only in details of the shell carving.

PROVENANCE: Ex coll.: Louis Guerineau Myers, New York City.

CONSTRUCTION: On each chair: The back is gently serpentine in profile. The scrolled crest rail is flat in back with rounded edges. Its shell is carved from the solid. The stiles, pieced at their curves, are rounded in back. The rear legs are octagonal. The splat is seated in the molded shoe nailed to the rear rail. Thick horizontal front and side rails whose straight inner edges frame a square opening form the boldly curved balloon seat. The side rails, their applied rounded rim cut from the same stock, are tenoned into the front rail. The rim's sections are tenoned together horizontally. The straight inner edges of the front legs continue as large dowels through the front rail and the tenons of the side rails. The serpentine sides of the knee brackets are chiseled; the brackets, secured with four roseheads each, overlap in back. The side rails and the rear brackets, the latter's front edges cavetto-shaped, are tenoned through the rear legs. The front legs end in oval pad feet, each with a central raised tongue.

CONDITION: The chairs have a fine mellow brown color. On no. II, a section of the rim above the right front leg has been replaced and the knee brackets renailed. On no. III, the dowellike extension of the left front leg has been replaced. The slip-seat frames have been reupholstered, and now have a reproduction red worsted cover illustrated here on chair no. II.

INSCRIPTIONS: Incised, on one chair, on front seat rail: *II*; on slip-seat frame: *V*; on the other, on front and side seat rails: *III*; on front and sides of slip-seat frame: *VI*.

DIMENSIONS: H.: overall, 42¾ (*108.6*), seat, 16¾ (*42.5*); W.: seat front, 20 (*50.8*), seat back, 15 (*38.1*), feet, 19 (*48.3*); D.: seat, 16⅛ (*41.*), feet, 19¾ (*50.2*).

WOODS: Primary: walnut. Secondary: walnut (front and sides of slip-seat frame); yellow pine (back of slip-seat frame).

Rogers Fund, 1925   (25.115.6, 7)

38. Side Chair

Philadelphia, 1740–60

THE CHAIR, WITH ITS boldly splayed trifid feet, is number I in a set. The chairs of another set (SPB sale no. 5094, 10/22/83, lot 254; *Antiques* 70 [September 1956], p. 173), two of which are now at Williamsburg, are similar to this one except for the treatment of the bottom of the shells. The two sets of chairs, their unusually wide splats cut from the same template, are the work of the same maker.

38

The Williamsburg chairs, which retain their original needlework seat covers, have a history of descent from William Penrose, son of the Samuel Penrose who acquired Graeme Park with its contents in 1801 (Eberlein and Hubbard, pp. 133–141). The house, originally known as Fountain Low, had been built in about 1722 in Horsham, north of Philadelphia, by Sir William Keith (1680–1749), governor of Pennsylvania from 1717 to 1726. On that basis it has been said (*Antiques* 70, p. 173) that the Williamsburg chairs were made for Sir William—the same history as that given for the MMA chair (see Provenance). While it is therefore reasonable to assume that both sets of chairs were once at Graeme Park, they cannot have belonged to the governor, for they are executed in a style introduced in about 1740. Sir William returned alone to England in 1728, deeding the property to his wife, who sold it in 1737. Her son-in-law Dr. Thomas Graeme bought it back two years later, just about the time the sets would probably have been made.

PROVENANCE: Ex coll.: Louis Guerineau Myers, New York City. As recorded in Myers's notes (MMA files), "The original owner of this particular chair was Governor Keith of Pennsylvania, according to family tradition."

CONSTRUCTION: The figured wood of the splat is unusually thick. The rear legs are rounded in front and back and flat at the sides. The side rails are pegged to the rear legs and to the front rail. The front legs have trifid feet. Otherwise, the construction is like that at cat. no. 37.

CONDITION: The wood has a rich dark brown color. There are splits in the crest rail at its junctures with the splat and the stiles. The rim applied to the front and side seat rails has been replaced. Nail holes in the rails' tops and sides indicate that the chair was upholstered over them at one time. The front legs have been reglued and their knee brackets renailed; the right front knee bracket has been reshaped. The slip-seat frame has been reupholstered. The chair is here illustrated with a reproduction green silk damask seat cover.

INSCRIPTIONS: Incised, on front seat rail: *I*; branded: *PS*.

DIMENSIONS: H.: overall, 42 (*106.7*), seat, 16½ (*41.9*); W.: seat front, 21¼ (*54.*), seat back, 16⅛ (*41.*), feet, 20½ (*52.1*); D.: seat, 17½ (*44.5*), feet, 20½ (*52.1*).

WOODS: Primary: walnut. Secondary: white pine (slip-seat frame).

Rogers Fund, 1925   (25.115.9)

39. Side Chairs (Two)

Philadelphia, 1750–75

OTHER CHAIRS APPARENTLY from the same set in which this pair are numbers III and VI have been recorded: two from the Thomas B. Clarke collection (Lockwood 1907, pl.

39 See also p. 338

XXIX) and another, numbered VII, in a private Philadelphia collection. Possibly of a later date than the chairs at cat. nos. 37 and 38, the pair are made of mahogany rather than walnut and their front seat rails are blocked-in, as though in anticipation of the chair type's final stylistic evolution: with an applied shell centered in the front rail, leaf carving on the knees, and claw feet (e.g., Downs 1952, nos. 115, 116).

PROVENANCE: Ex coll.: Louis Guerineau Myers, New York City.

CONSTRUCTION: On each chair: The rear legs are rounded in front and back and flat at the sides. The side rails are pegged to the rear legs and the front rail. The balloon seat is cut out in a flat arch at the front and in half arches at the sides. A rounded rim is applied to the front and side rails. The serpentine sides of the knee brackets are chiseled; the rear brackets are serpentine-shaped. The front legs have trifid feet. Otherwise, the construction is like that at cat. no. 37.

CONDITION: The chairs, of dense wood, now have a deep red color. Old breaks at the junctures of stiles and crest rail are repaired and reinforced with iron straps (18th-century). The feet have holes for casters. On chair no. III, the chair illustrated: The left front leg has been reset; the shoe has split and been patched in back; the upper right volute on the splat has been repaired. On no. VI: The seat-rail rim has been patched above the left front leg and at the right rear; the tenon at the juncture of the left side rail and the rear leg has been reinforced with a modern dowel. The slip seats have been reupholstered on both chairs, and are now covered with mid-eighteenth-century needlework in an allover pattern, much faded, of red, blue, green, and yellow leaves and flowers on a brown ground.

INSCRIPTIONS: Incised, on one chair, on front seat rail: *III*; on slip-seat frame: *IIII*; on the other, on front seat rail: *VI*; on slip-seat frame: *V*.

DIMENSIONS: H.: overall, 41½ (*105.4*), seat, 16⅞ (*42.9*); W.: seat front, 20¾ (*52.7*), seat back, 16⅛ (*41.*), feet, 20½ (*52.1*); D.: seat, 15⅞ (*40.3*), feet, 20 (*50.8*).

WOODS: Primary: mahogany. Secondary: yellow pine (slip-seat frames).

REFERENCES: Nutting 2, nos. 2121–22 (the pair). Myers, fig. 8. W. Johnston, figs. 1, 2 (detail of seat-rail construction). Bishop, figs. 61, 61a.

Rogers Fund, 1925   (25.115.5, 8)

40. Side Chair

Philadelphia, 1740–60

NUMBER II OF A SET, this example is generally similar to the preceding fiddleback-splat chairs, but its splat is the classic baluster, or vase-shape, one of the most frequently encountered Philadelphia patterns. The outline of its upper part conforms closely to the curves of the stiles; the lower part is scalloped and sharply pointed. A pair of side chairs (SPB sale no. 3947, 1/29/77, lot 1169), though not from the same set as this one, look to be by the same hand.

PROVENANCE: Ex coll.: Louis Guerineau Myers, New York City.

CONSTRUCTION: In profile, the back forms an exaggerated serpentine curve. The stiles are pieced at the lower curves. The rear legs are rounded in front and back and flat at the sides. The rear and side rails are double pegged to the stiles; the side rails are pegged to the front rail. The inner surface of the front rail is cut out in a flat arch. The knee brackets, their serpentine sides sawed out, are attached with triple roseheads. The front legs end in trifid feet. Otherwise, the construction is like that at cat. no. 37.

CONDITION: The chair has a fine mellow brown color. The slip-seat frame has been reupholstered. The chair is here illus-

trated with an antique Italian yellow silk damask seat cover.

INSCRIPTIONS: Incised, on front seat rail: *II*; on slip-seat frame: *III*.

DIMENSIONS: H.: overall, 42¾ (*108.6*), seat, 17¼ (*43.8*); W.: seat front, 20⅛ (*51.1*), seat back, 15 (*38.1*), feet, 20 (*50.8*); D.: seat, 16⅛ (*41.*), feet, 20½ (*52.1*).

WOODS: Primary: walnut. Secondary: tulip poplar (slip-seat frame).

Rogers Fund, 1925   (25.115.14)

40 See also p. 338

41 See also p. 338

41. Side Chair

Philadelphia, 1740–60

THOUGH AT FIRST GLANCE the chair, number VI in a set, appears identical to cat. no. 40, differences in their construction show that they are not the work of the same hand. Here, unusual features in a chair of this pattern are the carved volutes on the knee brackets and the six lobes on the crest shell instead of the normal five. An armchair

at Winterthur (acc. 60.1172) and cat. no. 41 look to be from the same set; the splat of the MMA chair and that of another at Winterthur (acc. 60.1034.1) were cut from the same template. Wallace Nutting sold reproductions of cat. no. 41 with and without arms (Nutting, *Checklist of Early American Reproductions*, 1930; rev. ed., Watkins Glen, New York, American Life Foundation & Study Institute, 1969, nos. 399, 499).

PROVENANCE: Ex coll.: Wallace Nutting, Framingham, Massachusetts; Louis Guerineau Myers, New York City.

CONSTRUCTION: The stiles, which are not pieced, are beveled to a rounded point in back. The rear legs, rounded at the edges, end in oval feet. The rear and side rails are double pegged. The top of the applied rim on the front and side rails is molded in a quarter round. The knee brackets, sawed out and ending in carved volutes, are attached with three roseheads each. There are thick horizontal triangular glue blocks for the rear legs. Otherwise, the construction is like that at cat. no. 37.

CONDITION: The wood has a crazed finish and a dark brown color. The knee brackets are attached with modern nails. The rear glue blocks, probably added in the eighteenth century, have been rescrewed. The slip seat has been reupholstered. The chair is here illustrated with an eighteenth-century Italian green and red silk-and-linen brocade seat cover.

INSCRIPTIONS: Incised, on front seat rail and on slip-seat frame: *VI*.

DIMENSIONS: H.: overall, 42¼ (*107.3*), seat, 17⅝ (*44.8*); W.: seat front, 21 (*53.3*), seat back, 15⅛ (*38.4*), feet, 20 (*50.8*); D.: seat, 17½ (*44.5*), feet, 19½ (*49.5*).

WOODS: Primary: walnut. Secondary: walnut (rear glue blocks); tulip poplar (slip-seat frame).

REFERENCES: Nutting 2, no. 2120.

Rogers Fund, 1925   (25.115.10)

42. Side Chair

Philadelphia, 1740–60

THE SPLAT ON THIS CHAIR is an unusual variant on the classic baluster model (e.g., cat. no. 41). The set in which this is number II and a number of others look to be by the same maker. All have crest-rail S-curves with unusually deep and sharply carved scrolled ends, rounded stiles, fanlike shells, and blunt trifid feet. Nutting (3, pp. 217–219) illustrates one with a pierced splat; another (*Antiques* 60 [October 1951], p. 279) has scroll-carved knee brackets. The chairs of other sets with the same knee brackets display variations in the lower part of the baluster splat (Downs 1952, no. 27; *Antiques* 114 [October 1978], p. 603; ibid. 79 [March 1961], p. 229, this last originally owned by a Colonel Ash of Germantown, Pennsylvania). A dressing table at Winterthur (Downs 1952, no. 324), with legs all but identical to those of cat. no. 42, must be by the same maker.

Affixed to the slip seat of chair number IV from the same set as cat. no. 42 (Warren, no. 46) is a paper label that reads: "This chair belonged to 'Aunt Shoemaker'/a great Aunt of Grand Mother H. Williams/it is probably 150 years old April 8 1892." The unusual splat also appears on a set of yoke-back chairs, by a different maker, once owned by Caspar Wistar (1696–1752), founder of the famous New Jersey glassworks (Hornor 1935, pl. 303).

PROVENANCE: Ex coll.: Harold M. and Cecile Lehman (later Cecile L. Mayer), Tarrytown, New York.

CONSTRUCTION: The crest rail, with four carved volutes flanking its central shell, is rounded at either end. The stiles, pieced at their upper curves, are circular. The rear legs are rounded at front and back and flat at the sides. The rim on top of the front and side rails is cut from the solid. The side rails and the serpentine-shaped rear brackets nailed to them are pegged to the stiles. The front knee brackets, with scrolled relief carving along their serpentine edges, are triple nailed. The sides of each truncated trifid foot are cut away to create the central tongue. Otherwise, the construction is like that at cat. no. 37.

CONDITION: The chair has a fine mellow reddish brown color. The back has been repaired and shims added at the juncture of crest rail, splat, and right stile. The ends of the front seat rail and the dowels of both front legs have been repaired. Modern glue blocks have been added at the back. The slip-seat frame is a replacement. The chair is here illustrated with a reproduction red worsted seat cover.

INSCRIPTIONS: Incised, inside rear seat rail: *II.*

DIMENSIONS: H.: overall, 42 (*106.7*), seat, 17¼ (*43.8*); W.: seat front, 20⅛ (*51.1*), seat back, 14¾ (*37.5*), feet, 19 (*48.3*); D.: seat, 16⅜ (*41.6*), feet, 18 (*45.7*).

WOODS: Primary and secondary: walnut.

Bequest of Cecile L. Mayer, subject to a life estate, 1962 (62.171.21)

42 See also p. 338

43. Roundabout Chair

Philadelphia, 1740–50

THE MOST FULLY developed Philadelphia roundabout, or corner, chairs combine cabriole legs, inverted cabriole stiles, and serpentine front seat rails. Only a handful are known: an unusually large one at Bayou Bend (Warren, no. 50); two others, apparently by one maker (Downs 1952, no. 60; *Antiques* 57 [March 1950], inside front cover); and cat. no. 43 and a chair from the Richard Waln Meirs family (Hornor 1935, pl. 71), both clearly by another maker. The last two chairs exhibit a number of

minor differences, but their legs, stiles, splats, and knuckle arms look to be identical. The angular, "wrought" quality of the twisted stiles, which is particularly distinctive, justifies the attribution of both chairs to the same man. It has been claimed that the Meirs family chair was "Made by Joseph Armitt" (Hornor 1935, pl. 71, caption) and, again, "believed to have been made by Joseph Armitt before 1747" (ibid., p. 200). That chair, two different side chairs (ibid., pls. 23, 24), a chest-on-chest (ibid.,

pl. 37), and a dressing table (ibid., pl. 39) whose legs and feet look to match those of the corner chair apparently all descended in the Meirs family from Joseph Armitt. Armitt, who was married in 1738 and died in 1747, is thought to have been a cabinet- and chairmaker. According to tradition, he made all these pieces for his family's own use (Hornor 1935a, nos. 27–33). If the tradition is correct, Armitt can be identified as the maker of cat. no. 43.

PROVENANCE: Ex coll.: Francis Hill Bigelow, Cambridge, Massachusetts; Louis Guerineau Myers, New York City. When the chair was first published, by Frances Clary Morse in 1902, it was part of the Bigelow collection. In an early twentieth-century photograph album of the collection (MMA library), it is illustrated (pp. 17, 25) and said to be a "Roundabout chair—1710—*English*—all curves" (p. 32, no. 86). At the Bigelow sale in 1924, the chair, described as English but with a Philadelphia history, was purchased by Myers. The MMA acquired it from him the following year.

CONSTRUCTION: The crest rail and arms are in the shape of a horseshoe. The crest rail, rounded in front and concave in back, is half-lapped over the armrests and nailed to them where they meet the splats. The armrests terminate in large molded knuckles built up with two applied layers and having scrolled ends. The inverted-cabriole stiles, extensions of the cabriole legs, are square in section. The rear stile is tenoned into the crest rail; the sides ones, into the armrests. The sharply beveled baluster splats are seated in molded shoes above the double-pegged rear rails. The serpentine front rails have straight inner edges and are pegged to the side legs, as are the concave brackets above their knees which are glued under the rails. The right front rail is half-lapped over the left one. The applied rim that secures the slip seat is in two pieces butted together above the front leg. The dowellike extension of the front leg is fitted through both front rails. Wooden strips, which once supported a commode, are nailed inside each rail. The knees and ankles of all four legs are rounded; the chiseled knee brackets are nailed on. On the octagonal pad feet, the inner side is rounded and three of the outer sides form projecting tongues.

CONDITION: The chair has a fine dark walnut color. A modern glue block reinforces the front leg at its juncture with the seat rails. The front of the left foot and the tip of the left front-leg bracket are restored, as, possibly, are parts of the pieced arm knuckles. The commode framework is missing. The feet have holes for casters. When Bigelow owned the chair (see Provenance), the seat had what may have been the original leather. The slip seat has been reupholstered, and is now covered in the replacement leather illustrated on the chair.

INSCRIPTIONS (all 20th-century): In brown ink, on a paper label pasted under the left front seat rail: *Property of / —Bigelow / —Mass*. In gray ink, on a Copley Society Exhibition printed paper label pasted over it: *F H Bigelow / Cambridge*. Printed, on a paper label glued to the left front seat-rail strip: *527*. In red pencil, on right rear-rail strip: *H. F. 83.1*, in reference to the Hudson–Fulton Celebration held at the MMA in 1909.

DIMENSIONS: H.: overall, 30½ (*77.5*), seat, 16¾ (*42.5*); W.: arms, 28½ (*72.4*), seat, 25¾ (*65.4*), feet, 26¼ (*66.7*); D.: seat, 26 (*66.*), feet, 27 (*68.6*).

WOODS: Primary: walnut. Secondary: yellow pine (slip seat, commode-frame support strips).

REFERENCES: Morse, p. 166 (ill.). MMA 1909, 2, no. 124. *Retrospective Exhibition of the Decorative Arts*, Boston, The Copley Society, 1911, p. 27, no. 595. Lockwood 2, fig. 520. Bigelow sale, lot 139. Nutting 2, fig. 2075. Lee 4, p. 66 (ill.); p. 67 (measured drawings). Myers, fig. 9. Halsey and Cornelius, fig. 54.

Rogers Fund, 1925   (25.115.15)

44. Armchair
Philadelphia, 1750–90

THE ARMCHAIR, NUMBER I of a pair, and the two following chairs (cat. nos. 45, 46) incorporate pierced and scrolled strapwork splats and claw feet—elements associated with the Chippendale style—into frames having the rounded shoulders and balloon seats of the earlier Queen

44 See also p. 339

Anne. With a relatively low back and small central shell area on the crest rail, the chair lacks the overall grandeur of cat. no. 45, but some of its features are among the most pleasing to be found on any Philadelphia example. These include, most notably, its beautifully shaped knuckled arms. The matching armchair, numbered II (Sack 6, p. 1545), is in a Philadelphia private collection.

PROVENANCE: Ex coll.: Louis Guerineau Myers, New York City.

CONSTRUCTION: The back is boldly serpentine in profile. The stiles are pieced at their lower curve. The rear legs are octagonal. The rear rail is double pegged. The balloon seat, rounded in front, is cut out in a shallow arc behind each arm support. The inside edge of the front rail is also cut out in an arc. The side rails, double pegged in front and pegged in back, and the cavetto-shaped rear brackets are tenoned through the rear legs. The rim on the front and side rails is cut from the solid. The side rails are cut out to receive the curved arm supports triple screwed to them and pegged to the arms. The molded ends of the arms are scroll-carved only at the front. The knee brackets are chiseled.

CONDITION: The chair is dark brown in color. The crest rail is patched at its juncture with the left stile. The splat, made in 1978 to duplicate that on the matching armchair, supersedes an old replacement. Nail holes in the seat rails remain from the upholstery that once covered them. On the left side of the front rail, the rim has been replaced. Thin tulip-poplar strips nailed to the inner edges of the side and rear rails to support a commode frame appear to be from the nineteenth century. The slip seat has been reupholstered. The chair is here illustrated with a reproduction yellow worsted seat cover.

INSCRIPTIONS: Incised, on rear seat rail: *I*; crescent-shaped marks on slip-seat frame: *II*.

DIMENSIONS: H.: overall, 42½ (*108.*), seat, 17½ (*44.5*); W.: arms, 32½ (*82.6*), seat front, 23¼ (*59.1*), seat back, 17⅛ (*43.5*), feet, 25 (*63.5*); D.: seat, 18½ (*47.*), feet, 21 (*53.3*).

WOODS: Primary: walnut. Secondary: yellow pine (slip-seat frame).

Rogers Fund, 1925   (25.115.19)

45. Armchair

Philadelphia, 1750–90

DISPLAYED HERE, on a chair whose massive size and stately grandeur are matched by only a few other Philadelphia examples (e.g., Downs 1952, no. 27), is that city's ultimate stylistic achievement in the continuously curvilinear Queen Anne form. With more fully developed rococo ornament than almost any of its local counterparts, its knees and splat are enriched by naturalistic leaf carving; its crest rail, by a blind-pierced rocaille shell. The

carving has now come to define the chair's outline rather than being contained within the individual members, as on earlier examples.

An armchair at Bayou Bend (Warren, no. 49) is identical to cat. no. 45 not only in design and decoration but also in the upper part of the splat, which is cut from the same template. Differences in the carving technique and in the shape of the punched motif around the leaves on the knee surfaces, however, indicate another hand. There are also dramatic variations in the chairs' proportions: on the Bayou Bend one, the back is lower, the curves of the stiles begin higher up, and on each arm support the curved part (which resembles a shoehorn in outline) begins lower. A side chair with a solid splat at Winterthur (Downs 1952, no. 115), though by yet another hand, shares with these armchairs crest-shell and knee carving of the same rococo patterns.

PROVENANCE: Ex coll.: Louis Guerineau Myers, New York City.

CONSTRUCTION: The back is serpentine in profile. The stiles are pieced at their curves. The pierced splat is cut from thin stock. The rear legs are octagonal. The double-pegged rear rail has thin, cavetto-shaped brackets at either end. The balloon seat, formed of thick horizontal rails, is cut out in an arc behind each arm support. The side rails are double pegged to the front rail and tenoned through the stiles. Cavetto-shaped rear brackets are screwed to the side rails and tenoned through the stiles. On the front rail, the upper half of the inner edge has been chiseled out, forming a narrow shelf. The carved knee brackets, their sides chiseled, are secured with four roseheads each. The arm supports, pegged to the arms, are rounded behind their shaped fronts; their bottom blocks, rounded in front and with serpentine back edges, are triple screwed to the side rails, which are cut out to receive them. The arms are screwed to the stiles. The sides of the molded knuckles are scroll-carved.

CONDITION: The dense wood has a dark red color. The chair has been refinished except in back, where the old decayed varnishes remain. The chair back has been broken: the crest rail is reinforced at its junctures with the stiles with iron straps (18th-century) let in behind and screwed in place. On the splat, the pierced part is split in a number of places, wooden reinforcements have been added in back, and there are some small patches in front. Both arms have been repaired where they join the back. The dowel of the left front leg has been replaced. Rims apparently originally cut from the solid have been replaced on the front and side seat rails. Nail holes in the rails and the shoe remain from the upholstery that once covered them, and holes in the arms and stiles show that iron brackets (probably 18th-century) once reinforced their joints from behind. The inner half of the right rear bracket is missing. The slip-seat frame, a modern replacement, now has the reproduction red silk damask cover illustrated here.

DIMENSIONS: H.: overall, 44 (*111.8*), seat, 15¾ (*40.*); W.: arms, 33¼ (*84.5*), seat front, 23¾ (*60.3*), seat back, 17½ (*44.5*), feet, 24 (*61.*); D.: seat, 18⅝ (*47.3*), feet, 21½ (*54.6*).

WOODS: Primary: mahogany. No secondary woods.

45 See also p. 339

REFERENCES: Nutting 2, no. 2152. Myers, fig. 12. Miller 1, no. 67. Halsey and Cornelius, fig. 56. *MMAB* n.s. 12 (March 1954), p. 206 (ill.). Davidson 1967, fig. 272.

Rogers Fund, 1925　　　　　　　　　　　　　　(25.115.18)

46. Side Chair

Philadelphia, 1750–90

ON THE PHILADELPHIA chairs that combine rococo ornament with the rounded back and seat of the earlier Queen Anne form, the backs are usually serpentine in section (e.g., cat. nos. 44, 45). This one, number VI in a set, is straight and slightly canted in the Chippendale manner. The acanthus-leaf carving on the knees—enclosing a plain, triangular-shaped central field—is an atypical design.

PROVENANCE: Ex coll.: Louis Guerineau Myers, New York City.

CONSTRUCTION: The back of the crest rail is flat in the middle and tapers to a thin top edge. The stiles and splat arch gracefully backward. The stiles are pieced: the left one at both curves, the right, only at the lower. The rear legs are oval. The rear rail is double pegged. Thick horizontal rails form the balloon seat.

46　See also p. 339

The through-tenoned side rails are pegged at the front, double pegged at the back, and have rear brackets with serpentine front edges. The rims of the front and side seat rails are cut from the solid. Each of the carved knee brackets is affixed with four small nails.

CONDITION: The wood has a mellow brown color. The junctures of crest rail and stiles have been restored with iron straps covered by wooden patches. The slip seat has been reupholstered. The chair is illustrated here with an eighteenth-century yellow silk serge seat cover.

INSCRIPTIONS: Incised, inside rear seat rail: *VI*; on slip-seat frame: *IIII*.

DIMENSIONS: H.: overall, 40 (*101.6*), seat, 16¾ (*42.5*); W.: seat front, 20⅞ (*53.*), seat back, 15¾ (*40.*), feet, 19¾ (*50.2*); D.: seat, 17¼ (*43.8*), feet, 20½ (*52.1*).

WOODS: Primary: walnut. Secondary: yellow pine (slip-seat frame).

REFERENCES: Nutting 2, no. 2154. Myers, fig. 11 (profile).

Rogers Fund, 1925　　　　　　　　　　　　　　(25.115.17)

47. Side Chair

Philadelphia, 1760–90

A RECESSED, STYLIZED rocaille ornament centered in the crest rail and delineated at the bottom by a continuation of the beading of the crest rail's edge distinguishes a common type of scrolled-strapwork-splat Philadelphia chair. On this—a good example of one of the plainer versions—the splat's straight-sided high base compensates for a template pattern that was too short for the stiles (see cat. no. 50). Large numbers of the type are known, including one identical except for having plain knees (*Antiques* 91 [April 1967], p. 455) and another with voluted ears and knee brackets but the same shell and knee carving (ibid. 118 [October 1980], p. 553), both apparently by the hand that fashioned cat. no. 47. The stencil of Trenton upholsterer Charles B. Cogill on the chair, number VII in a set, shows that it was at one time in New Jersey. Cogill, of 86 Warren Street, is listed in Mains and Fitzgerald's 1877 Trenton Directory as "furniture, undertaker and upholsterer."

PROVENANCE: Ex coll.: Louis Guerineau Myers, New York City.

CONSTRUCTION: In back, the crest rail has rounded edges; the stiles are beveled to a rounded point. The rear legs are oval. The front and through-tenoned side rails are cut out in flat arches; the shell centered in the front arch is applied. The seat rails are double pegged; the knee brackets are triple nailed. The triangular glue blocks are set vertically, the rear ones slightly rounded.

CONDITION: The wood, whose modern finish has begun to craze, has a good dark brown color. The slip-seat frame has been reupholstered. The chair is here illustrated in a 1766 needlework seat cover with an allover pattern of leaves and flowers. The colors—once bright reds, greens, and yellows on a dark brown ground—are much faded. Originally made for a larger chair (the edges, on which initials and a date are embroidered, are folded under), it was put on cat. no. 47 at the MMA in 1938. When it was taken off for cleaning in 1961, the slip seat's original canvas, curled hair, burlap, and webbing were discovered.

INSCRIPTIONS: Incised, on front seat-rail rabbet: *VII.* Worked into the back edge of the needlework slip-seat cover: *RB 1766.* Stenciled (19th century) onto the eighteenth-century burlap formerly nailed to the slip-seat frame and now mounted separately: *FROM/CHA^S B. COGILL/UPHOLSTERER/TRENTON/N.J.*

DIMENSIONS: H.: overall, 41¼ (*104.8*), seat, 17¼ (*43.8*); W.: seat front, 21¾ (*55.2*), seat back, 16¾ (*42.5*), feet, 23⅝ (*60.*); D.: seat, 16¾ (*42.5*), feet, 21¼ (*54.*).

WOODS: Primary: mahogany. Secondary: Atlantic white cedar (corner blocks); cherry (slip-seat frame).

REFERENCES: Myers sale 1921, lot 612. *MMAB* 16 (April 1921), p. 86. Lee 4, p. 68 (ill.); p. 69 (measured drawings).

Rogers Fund, 1921   (21.44.4)

48. Side Chair

Philadelphia, 1750–90

THE SET OF SCROLLED strapwork splat chairs in which this is number X is one of a number of related sets distinguished by certain features: on the crest rail, shell ears and acanthus fronds flanking a central shell; on the splat, a five-lobed rosette at the junctures of the uncarved central straps and, below acanthus fronds, a bellflower centered between two raised knobs; on the stiles, four flutes; on either side of the junctures of crest rail and stiles, a peglike knob.

Though this boldly carved walnut chair had arms at one time, it must originally have been a side chair: its dimensions match those of a chair at RISD numbered VIII (XI on its slip-seat frame) from the same set (Kirk 1972, no. 70). Still others of the set are illustrated in the Reifsnyder sale catalogue (lot 646) and in *Antiques* magazine (90 [December 1966], p. 749).

A set of chairs now at the Department of State, identical to cat. no. 48 except for a modification in the carved motif under the central crest shell, descended in the fam-

47 See also p. 339

48 See also p. 339

ily of Vincent Loockerman of Dover, Delaware. Loocker-man's inventory, taken in 1785, lists "6 Leather Bottomed Walnut Chairs (old)" and "1 Ditto arm Chair," presumably a reference to that set (Sack 3, pp. 616, 617). Loocker-man brought furniture from the cabinetmaker Benjamin Randolph (1721–1791), including some in 1774 for which he paid £38-8-0 (PMA 1976, no. 101). It does not necessarily follow, however, that Randolph made the chairs of the Loockerman set, which, stylistically datable to the mid-1760s, are unlike any known labeled Randolph example. A variant of the same general type, by a different hand, has been attributed to Thomas Affleck (Hornor 1935, pp. 217–218; fig. 220).

PROVENANCE: Ex coll.: Louis Guerineau Myers, New York City. Purchased by the MMA at the auction of the Myers collection.

CONSTRUCTION: Both crest and stiles are unusually wide. In back, the crest rail and stiles are rounded. The rear legs are oval. The seat rails are double pegged. The front and through-tenoned side rails are cut out in flat arches; the shell centered in the front rail is applied. The left side rail is unusually thick. The double-nailed knee brackets are roughly sawed out in scrolls. The glue blocks are two-part vertical quarter rounds.

49 See also p. 340

CONDITION: The chair, walnut brown in color, has a pleasing old finish. Patches in the stiles and side seat rails where arms and their supports were attached show that it was an armchair at one time. The decorative peg at the top of the right stile is missing. The slip seat, which has been reupholstered, now has the antique green and white silk brocade cover with which the chair is illustrated.

INSCRIPTIONS: Incised, on front seat-rail rabbet and on slip-seat frame: X. In chalk, inside left rail: 4; inside right rail: 3.

DIMENSIONS: H.: overall, 41 (104.1), seat, 17½ (44.5); W.: seat front, 22 (55.9), seat back, 17⅜ (44.1), feet, 23 (58.4); D.: seat, 17 (43.2), feet, 21 (53.3).

WOODS: Primary: walnut. Secondary: walnut (glue blocks); tulip poplar (slip-seat frame).

REFERENCES: Myers sale 1921, lot 663 (ill.). *MMAB* 16 (April 1921), p. 86. Nutting 2, fig. 2183.

Rogers Fund, 1921   (21. 44. 5)

49. Side Chairs (Two)

Philadelphia, 1755–90

THESE CHAIRS, NUMBERS IV and VIII in a set, are classic specimens of the Philadelphia scrolled-strapwork-splat type. Of particularly pleasing proportions, they have a dramatic visual impact resulting from the use on them of striped "tiger" maple, a blond wood with pronounced parallel stripes running at right angles to the grain. The figure of the wood imparts to the chairs the illusion of shimmering, as though seen through gently flowing sunlit water.

PROVENANCE: Ex coll.: Harold M. and Cecile Lehman (later Cecile L. Mayer), Tarrytown, New York.

CONSTRUCTION: On each chair: The splat and stiles arch backward. On the splat, the strapwork overlaps; the straps that end in carved volutes are slightly hollowed. The stiles are rounded in back. The rear legs are rounded at front and back and flat at the sides. The front and side rails are cut out in flat arches and pegged; the rear rail is double pegged. The front-rail shell is applied. The tenons of the side rails are exposed. The serpentine sides of the knee brackets are sawed.

CONDITION: The wood has a glowing honey brown color. The finish, not the original, has begun to craze. On chair no. IV, there are splits in the splat. On no. VIII, the chair illustrated, the tips of the left scroll terminal of the crest rail have been broken off, there is a large patch in the right seat rail, and all the glue blocks have been replaced except for the shims of the rear ones. The modern slip-seat frame is covered with eighteenth-century needlework, probably English, showing an urn and flowers against a red background.

INSCRIPTIONS: Incised, on one chair, on front seat-rail rabbet: *IIII*; on the other, on front seat-rail rabbet and on rear seat rail: *VIII*.

DIMENSIONS: H.: overall, 39¼ (*99.7*), seat, 16¾ (*42.5*); W.: seat front, 21⅜ (*54.3*), seat back, 16¾ (*42.5*), feet, 22⅞ (*58.1*); D.: seat, 17⅛ (*43.5*), feet, 21¼ (*54.*).

WOODS: Primary: maple. Secondary: Atlantic white cedar (rear glue-block shims).

REFERENCES: Sack 1950, p. 35, lower left (ill.). Biddle, nos. 16, 17.

Bequest of Cecile L. Mayer, subject to a life estate, 1962 (62.171.1, 2)

50. Side Chairs (Two)

Philadelphia, 1755–90

THESE CHAIRS REPRESENT the Philadelphia scrolled-strapwork-splat type at its refined best. On the crest rail, acanthus fronds grow out of the central shell and loop back to form the serpentine top edge. The stiles are stop-fluted, the top of the shoe is gadrooned, and a tassel fills the splat's central void; the ornament, carved in high relief, is judiciously placed. Other chairs from the set in which this pair are numbers I and II are known: one acquired in Charleston, South Carolina, by the collector W.A. Hitchcock (Nutting 2, fig. 2216), and others that have been advertised (*Antiques* 78 [September 1960], p. 217; ibid. 106 [July 1974], inside back cover; see also Kindig, no. 44). No. V of the set was auctioned in New York (Christie's, 12/12/80, lot 638).

Except for variations in height, two other sets of chairs are virtually identical to this one. On the first, the back is an inch shorter and the shell on the front rail has five lobes rather than seven (Hipkiss, no. 85, or Downs 1952, no. 125); on the second, the back is an inch taller (Hipkiss, no. 86, or Comstock, no. 263). The splats of these two sets were cut from one template (Zimmerman 1981, p. 297), the same as that employed for cat. no. 50's: the differences in height were achieved simply by modifying the proportions of the splats' straight-sided bases. The chairs of all three sets exhibit the bold, high-relief carving

50 See also p. 340

of the finest Philadelphia work, and look to be the product of a single shop. An armchair, now at the PMA (1976, no. 66), of the same pattern but carved by another hand descended in the Shoemaker family and has been attributed to Jonathan Shoemaker, a cabinetmaker active between 1767 and 1793 (Hornor 1935, pl. 159).

PROVENANCE: Ex coll.: Howard Mansfield, New York City; George Coe Graves, Osterville, Massachusetts.

CONSTRUCTION: On each chair: The crest rail is flat in back with rounded edges. The stiles are beveled in back to a rounded point. The rear legs are oval. The edges of the splat are slightly beveled; the shoe, in which the splat is seated, is gadrooned at the top. All four seat rails are cut out in flat arches and double pegged; the arch of each through-tenoned side rail ends at the rear in a serpentine curve. The shell on the front rail is applied. The knee brackets are double nailed. The glue blocks are vertical quarter rounds.

CONDITION: The wood is dark brown in color. On chair no. I, the lobes at the top of the crest shell are worn away; the splat and the tops of the stiles are split and patched where the back was broken. On no. II, the bottom lobes of the ears are missing. The slip seats have been reupholstered and now have the antique red silk damask seat covers illustrated here on chair no. II.

INSCRIPTIONS: Incised, on one chair, on front seat-rail rabbet and inside rear rail: *I*; on the other, on front seat-rail rabbet, inside rear rail, and slip-seat frame: *II*.

DIMENSIONS: H.: overall, 40½ (102.9), seat, 17 (43.2); W.: seat front, 21¾ (55.2), seat back, 16½ (41.9), feet, 23½ (59.7); D.: seat, 17½ (44.5), feet, 21¼ (54.).

WOODS: Primary: mahogany. Secondary: white pine (slip-seat frame); Atlantic white cedar (glue blocks).

REFERENCES: Girl Scouts, no. 635. Davidson 1967, fig. 282.

The Sylmaris Collection, Gift of George Coe Graves, 1932 (32.57.1, 2)

51. Side Chair

Philadelphia, 1765–90

THIS CHAIR IS from the well-known set said to have been made for the Lambert family of Lambertville, New Jersey. The first of the set to be published, a chair now at Winterthur, was described in the 1929 Reifsnyder catalogue as "From the Lambert Family." Cat. no. 51 came without provenance to the MMA the following year. Another chair, one of a pair now at the PMA, was cited in 1935 (Hornor, p. 216) as from the "Lambert family chairs . . . believed to have consisted of a set of eight (some of which are now in England)." In 1954, two of three more chairs from the set which had been acquired by a dealer in Lambertville were advertised. The vendor, a woman who

was descended from Emanuel Coryell and who lived in the Coryell house, believed that the chairs, which she said had just previously been brought back from England, had belonged originally to Emanuel (notes, MMA files). Since the chairs are of too late a design to have been owned by the first Emanuel Coryell, who died in 1749, and since Emanuel II, born in 1754, never had sufficient wealth to have ordered them, a more likely first owner is John Lambert (1746–1823). Lambert was an important public figure, an acting governor of New Jersey and, later, a United States senator. In 1812, the town of Coryell's Ferry was renamed Lambertville at his request. Chair numbered VIIII from the set was advertised as "President James Monroe's side chair attributed to Benjamin Randolph" (*Antiques* 78 [October 1960], p. 287). In subsequent advertisements of the same chair the Monroe provenance was abandoned in favor of a Lambert one, although the conjectural Randolph attribution was retained (ibid. 80 [September 1961], p. 189). Of the twelve or more chairs that formed the original set nine are now known: an unnumbered one (private collection); II (cat. no. 51); IV and VIII (PMA); V (Stone collection); VII (private collection); IX (Dietrich collection); X (Williamsburg); XII (Winterthur).

The chairs, lavishly endowed with ornate carving, appear bigger and heavier than most Philadelphia Chippendale patterns. Other chairs comparable in scale and ornament to cat. no. 51 include one at Dearborn (Bishop, fig. 152), whose back has a similar program of carving, and those of other sets from the same shop which have been identified on the basis of identical splat templates or similar construction details (Zimmerman 1981, pp. 292–299, figs. 4, 9, 10); in addition, a chair at RISD (Lockwood 1904, pl. IV) looks to have been carved by the same hand. Though different patterns for crest, stiles, and front skirt are employed on these chairs, they are all notable for having the same massive quality.

PROVENANCE: Ex coll.: George Coe Graves, Osterville, Massachusetts.

CONSTRUCTION: The splat and stiles arch gracefully backward. In back, the crest rail is flat, with beveled edges and an applied strip at its juncture with the splat. The backs of the stiles are beveled to a rounded point. Scratch-beading outlines the continuous low-relief carving on crest and stiles. The rear legs are rounded at front and back and flat at the sides. The rear rail is double pegged. The front and through-tenoned side rails, of unusually thick stock, are carved at the top in an egg-and-dart pattern, as is the shoe. The front rail is sawed out in a scallop; the side rails, in flat arches. The glue blocks are vertical two-part quarter rounds.

CONDITION: The chair has a mellow brown color. A shim has been inserted in back between the splat and the shoe. The slip seat has been reupholstered. The chair is illustrated here with an antique green and white silk brocade seat cover.

INSCRIPTIONS: Incised, on front seat-rail rabbet: *II*.

DIMENSIONS: H.: overall, 41¾ (*106.*), seat, 17½ (*44.5*); W.: seat front, 22⅝ (*57.5*), seat back, 17¼ (*43.8*), feet, 24¼ (*61.6*); D.: seat, 17¾ (*45.1*), feet, 22½ (*57.2*).

WOODS: Primary: mahogany. Secondary: mahogany (glue blocks); white pine (fillets of rear glue blocks, slip-seat frame).

REFERENCES: Edward Warwick, "The Source of an American Chippendale Chair," *Antiques* 15 (March 1929), pp. 213–215. Reifsnyder sale, lot 688. Hornor 1935, p. 216; pl. 336. *PMA Bulletin* 38 (January 1943), p. 4. Downs 1952, no. 128. *Antiques* 65 (May 1954), p. 340; ibid. 66 (November 1954), p. 383; ibid. 78 (October 1960), p. 287; ibid. 80 (September 1961), p. 189; ibid. 82 (July 1962), p. 9. Kirk 1972, no. 71. Sack 6, pp. 1676–77. Bishop, fig. 153. Rodriguez Roque, no. 68. For the Coryell family, see Ingham Coryell, *Emanuel Coryell of Lambertville, New Jersey, and His Descendants*, Philadelphia, 1943. For the Lambert family, see James P. Snell, comp., *History of Hunterdon and Somerset Counties, New Jersey*, Philadelphia, Everts & Park, 1881, p. 270.

The Sylmaris Collection, Gift of George Coe Graves, 1930 (30.120.58)

52. Side Chair

Philadelphia, 1760–90

WITH ITS PERFECT proportions, elegantly integrated crest and splat design, and unsurpassed carving, this is perhaps the best of all Philadelphia Chippendale chairs. The splat pattern, its dominant figure-eight motif flowing from the crest rail, is a free adaptation from plate XVI, lower right, in the 1762 edition of Chippendale's *Director*. Four other side chairs from the set in which this is number XI, their slip-seat frames numbered VII–X, are at Winterthur (Downs 1952, no. 137); possibly by the same hand is a set of Gothic-splat chairs with identically scalloped front skirts and similar cabochon-carved knees (Hornor 1935, pl. 364; *Antiques* 105 [January 1974], p. 1, as from the Gouverneur Morris family; Rodriguez Roque, no. 60).

A few other sets like that of cat. no. 52 in design and with Philadelphia family histories are known, but, with unscalloped front skirts and scrolled acanthus knee leafage, they are clearly the work of other hands. According to Hornor (1935, pl. 119), one of the sets belonged to John Dickinson (1772–1808), and an identical set belonged to Isaac Cooper (ibid., pl. 341). Two chairs from the Dickinson set are now at the PMA; the Cooper armchair is now at Winterthur. A variant set (ibid., pl. 225), upholstered over the seat rails and with plain molded stiles, belonged to Charles Thompson (1729–1824), secretary of the Continental Congress. Dickinson married in 1770 and Thompson, for the second time, in 1774, both men during the period in which furniture inspired by the *Director* was being made in Philadelphia.

51 See also p. 340

On cat. no. 52, the projecting bead near the top of the shoe is an unusual feature that can compare with work by Benjamin Randolph. It appears on a Gothic-splat chair bearing Randolph's label (Kane, no. 108), and on a number of chairs (ibid., nos. 90, 93; Kindig, no. 53) with splats similar to those on a labeled Randolph pair (Hipkiss, no. 89). Of itself, however, that one feature is not proof of Randolph authorship.

PROVENANCE: The chair descended from Mr. and Mrs. Delancey Kane of New York and Newport; to Miss Sybil Kent Kane; to Mrs. Peter A. Jay, in 1928. It was acquired by the dealer R.G. Hall in 1950; by Winterthur, in 1950; and by the MMA, by exchange, in 1951. According to Kane family tradition, the chair came down in the Langdon branch of the family.

CONSTRUCTION: The configuration of the bottom edge of the crest rail matches the double curve at the top. The crest rail and the stiles are rounded in back. The rear legs are oval. The back edges of the splat are slightly beveled. The figure-eight motif is so realistically wrought as to resemble actual strapwork. The shoe is notched into the stiles and nailed. The rear rail is the thickness of the rear legs. The side rails, tenoned through the rear stiles, are cut out in flat arches that end at the rear in a serpentine curve. The knee brackets, their shaped edges chiseled, are triple nailed. The glue blocks are vertical quarter rounds; the rear ones in one piece, the front ones in two.

CONDITION: The chair, which retains its original finish, has a lustrous dark reddish brown patina. Both the rear legs and rear glue blocks are split at their junctures with the side rails. The slip seat has been reupholstered. The chair is here illustrated with an antique red silk damask seat cover.

INSCRIPTIONS: Incised, on slip-seat frame: *XI*.

DIMENSIONS: H.: overall, 38 (*96.5*), seat, 17 (*43.2*); W.: seat front, 21⅞ (*55.6*), seat back, 17⅜ (*44.1*), feet, 23¾ (*60.3*); D.: seat, 17¼ (*43.8*), feet, 21½ (*54.6*).

WOODS: Primary: mahogany. Secondary: Atlantic white cedar (glue blocks); yellow pine (slip-seat frame).

REFERENCES: Downs 1952, no. 137. W. Johnston, p. 122. Margon 1971, p. 169.

Bequest of W. Gedney Beatty and Rogers Fund, by exchange, 1951 (51.140)

52 See also p. 341

53. Side Chair

Philadelphia, 1770–75

OTHERS OF THE SIX-CHAIR set in which this is number II include one that remains with descendants of the original owners. The rest are in a private Philadelphia collection (no. III), at Winterthur (no. VI), and at the PMA (no. I). The set has been attributed to the cabinetmaker Thomas Affleck (Hornor 1935, pp. 91, 204, 212); moreover, it has the same eighteenth-century provenance as a chest-on-chest that may be the one referred to in payments made by William Logan in 1772 to Affleck and to the carver James Reynolds (see cat. no. 147). It is, however, by a different hand from the one that fashioned the elaborate set for General John Cadwalader (cat. no. 59), also often associated with Affleck (Beckerdite, pp. 1129–31). The carver of the brilliant ornament on cat. no. 53, while as yet unidentified, must have been one of Philadelphia's leading craftsmen. The chair's splat design follows closely that of a pattern in plate IX of the 1762 edition of Chippendale's *Director*. As such, it exemplifies the predilection of wealthy Philadelphia patrons (see cat. nos. 168, 205) for ordering elaborate furniture that incorporated major design motifs literally translated from

53 See also p. 340

the illustrated pattern books of Chippendale and his contemporaries.

PROVENANCE: The chair, believed to be part of a set originally made for Sarah Logan Fisher, descended to Elizabeth Rodman Fisher in the same line as did cat. no. 147. The set was thereafter divided, the MMA chair passing to Sarah Logan Fisher Wister (died 1891); to John Wister, of Belfield Farm, Philadelphia; to Mrs. Charles Stuart Wurts; to Mrs. George Cavendish; to S. Grey Dayton, Jr., and Mary Dayton McNeely.

CONSTRUCTION: The crest rail, flat in back and with beveled edges, is pierced above its juncture with the splat. The stiles are rounded in back and notched to receive the shoe, in which the splat is seated. The splat is flat in back and has slightly beveled edges. The seat rails are double pegged. The front and side rails are cut out in flat arches. On the side rails, which are tenoned through the stiles, the arch is serpentined at the rear. The inner side of the rear rail is faced with poplar. The knee brackets have smoothly shaped sides. The glue blocks are two-part vertical quarter rounds.

CONDITION: The chair has an attractive aspect. An old (19th-century) finish, somewhat crackled and decayed, covers the original surface. There are old, repaired splits at the junctures of the left stile with the crest and seat rails. Two of the knee brackets have been reglued; one of the glue blocks is a replacement. The slip seat has been restuffed. The chair is illustrated here with a modern needlework seat cover.

INSCRIPTIONS: Incised, on front seat-rail rabbet: II. Engraved, on a nineteenth-century calling card nailed inside rear rail: *Mrs. John Wister/Belfield/Germantown.* In red paint, on the rear rail: *28-1924-1* and *53-1928-1*, documenting loans to the PMA.

DIMENSIONS: H.: overall, 39¼ (99.7), seat, 17¼ (43.8); W.: seat front, 22⅜ (56.8), seat back, 16⅞ (42.9), feet, 24¼ (61.6); D.: seat, 17 (43.2), feet, 22¼ (56.5).

WOODS: Primary: mahogany. Secondary: tulip poplar (inner rear rail, glue blocks); yellow pine (slip-seat frame).

REFERENCES: *PMA Bulletin* 19 (May 1924), p. 164, pl. IV. Hornor 1935, pls. 113, 115; pp. 91, 204, 212; idem 1935a, nos. 16, 17 (attributed to Affleck). Kirk 1972, pl. 94. Hummel 1976, figs. 69, 69a.

Purchase, Anonymous Gift, in memory of Elizabeth Snow Bryce, 1983   (1983.395)

54. Side Chair

Philadelphia, 1760–90

THIS CHAIR AND THE TWO that follow are examples of the trefoil-pierced-splat chair, the so-called Gillingham type that enjoyed great popularity in Philadelphia in the second half of the eighteenth century. The chairs might better be called after Thomas Chippendale, for the

splat—indeed, the design of the entire back save for the scroll-like central part of the crest rail—was taken line for line from a plate in his *Director* (1754 edition, pl. XIII; 1762 edition, pl. X). The treatment of the front skirt derives from that on one of Chippendale's settees (1762 edition, pl. XXIV); the shape and carving of the knee brackets, from one of his chairs (1762, pl. XIIII). Cat. no. 54, number VI in its set, is a well-executed chair of fine proportions. The carving on its knees—acanthus leafage and a bellflower suspended from a knob—is a pattern not elsewhere known. A second chair from the set was owned by Eliza Davids in 1935 (Hornor, pp. 210–211; pl. 347). (For other chairs of the same set, see *Antiques* 60 [September 1951], p. 177; Kindig, pl. 55.)

The Gillingham appellation stems from a much-published set of four sparsely carved trefoil-pierced-splat chairs, three bearing the engraved label of James Gillingham (*Antiques* 76 [November 1959], p. 394). One is illustrated in Lockwood (2, figs. 558, 559); a second, from the Cushing and Taradash collections, is now at the White House (*Antiques* 49 [June 1946], p. 359; ibid. 116 [July 1979], p. 116). The second chair was on loan to the MMA between 1936 and 1952, and has been mistakenly identified as part of the Museum's collection (see caption, Comstock, fig. 268). James Gillingham (1736–1781) set up his own shop in Philadelphia on Second Street, the address given on his label, in 1768. He remained active there until 1773, suggesting the five-year period during which those chairs must have been made. Other identical chairs (Comstock, fig. 268; *Antiques* 65 [April 1954], p. 261) may also be attributable to Gillingham, but cat. nos. 54–56 are demonstrably the work of three separate hands, none of them his.

PROVENANCE: Ex coll.: Louis Guerineau Myers, New York City; George Coe Graves, Osterville, Massachusetts. Eliza Davids inherited a chair from this set. Its presumed line of descent is from Isaac Greenleafe (1715–1771), who married Catherine Wistar (1730–1771) in 1753; to Sarah Greenleafe Davids; to Benjamin Davids; to Richard Wistar Davids; to Richard Wistar Davids, Jr.; to Eliza Davids (born 1895).

CONSTRUCTION: The chair back is canted at an unusually sharp angle. In back, the crest rail is flat in the middle and has beveled edges; the edges of the stiles are beveled to a rounded point. The rear legs are oval. The splat's edges are slightly chamfered. The rails are double pegged. The side rails, which are not tenoned through the stiles, are cut out in flat arches having a serpentine rear curve and, at the front, a circular scroll. The carving on the front rail is cut from the solid. The inner sides of the double-nailed, leaf-carved knee brackets are chiseled. The front glue blocks are two-part vertical quarter rounds.

CONDITION: The chair, of dense wood with some figure in the front rail, has a fine dark brown color. The bottom tip of the central leaf carving on the front rail has broken off. The rear glue blocks have been replaced except for the shims glued to the rear rail. The slip-seat cover shown on the chair in the Myers sale catalogue—a piece of allover floral needlework—was possibly the original one. The slip seat has been reupholstered. The chair is illlustrated here with an eighteenth-century red silk damask seat cover.

INSCRIPTIONS: Incised, on front seat-rail rabbet and on slip-seat frame: *VI*.

DIMENSIONS: overall, 39 (*99.1*), seat, 17⅛ (*43.5*); W.: seat front, 21½ (*54.6*), seat back, 16⅝ (*42.2*), feet, 23½ (*59.7*); D.: seat, 17¾ (*45.1*), feet, 21½ (*54.6*).

WOODS: Primary: mahogany. Secondary: Atlantic white cedar (glue blocks); tulip poplar (slip-seat frame).

REFERENCES: Myers sale 1932, lot 521 (attributed to James Gillingham). *MMAB* 27 (June 1932), p. 165. Rogers, fig. 30. Comstock, fig. 268. For the Wistar family, see Richard Wistar Davids, comp., *The Wistar Family*, Philadelphia, 1896.

The Sylmaris Collection, Gift of George Coe Graves, 1932 (32.55.5)

55. Side Chair

Philadelphia, 1760–90

THE CHAIR, NUMBER II in a set, differs from most others of the trefoil-pierced-splat type in having a taller back, lower seat, narrower splat, carved C-scrolls on the side rails, and the egg-and-dart-carved shoe found in Chippendale's *Director* (pl. XIII, left, 1754 edition; pl. X, left, 1762 edition). Another chair from the same set was the property of Mrs. Charles Pemberton Fox in 1935 (Hornor, pl. 346). Hornor claims that chairs with trefoil-pierced splats were known in the eighteenth century as fan-back chairs; he implies that the Fox chair was part of the "1 doz Mahogany Carved Fan back'd Chairs, In the S.E. Room up one pair Stairs" listed in the 1754 inventory of the Charles Willing mansion (ibid., pp. 203, 220). It is nevertheless unlikely that chairs with backs duplicating a design in the *Director* could have been made in America prior to the arrival of that book's first edition. Other chairs with carved front skirts and knees identical to cat. no. 55's, but with Gothic splats, are known (Nutting 2,

54 See also p. 341

55 See also p. 341

56 See also p. 339

no. 2194; Hornor 1935, pl. 163). These chairs and the MMA example look to be the work of the same anonymous maker.

PROVENANCE: Ex coll.: Harold M. and Cecile Lehman (later Cecile L. Mayer), Tarrytown, New York.

CONSTRUCTION: In back, the crest rail is flat in the middle and has rounded edges; the stiles are rounded. The rear legs are oval. The splat's edges are slightly chamfered. A thin strip of wood glued to the rear rail below the shoe prevents the slip seat from shifting. The side rails, tenoned through the stiles, are cut out in shallow C-scrolls. The carving on the front rail is cut from the solid. The knee brackets, smoothly chiseled on their inner sides and rounded in back, are secured with single rose-heads. The front glue blocks are two-part vertical quarter rounds.

CONDITION: The chair has a warm dark brown patina, with a buildup of old varnish around the carving. The knee carving is scuffed. The crest rail has splits at the left and central junctures with the splat; the pointed rolled ends of the concave center have been sawed off. The tips of the front knee brackets are old restorations. The rear glue blocks are old replacements. The slip seat retains its original webbing, horsehair, and canvas. The chair is illustrated here with an eighteenth-century red silk damask seat cover.

INSCRIPTIONS: Incised, on rear seat-rail strip: *II*; on slip-seat frame: *I*.

DIMENSIONS: H.: overall, 40 (*101.6*), seat, 16¾ (*42.5*); W.: seat front, 21¾ (*55.2*), seat back, 17⅜ (*44.1*), feet, 23½ (*59.7*); D.: seat 17¼ (*43.8*), feet, 21½ (*54.6*).

WOODS: Primary: mahogany. Secondary: white oak (front glue blocks); yellow pine (slip-seat frame).

Bequest of Cecile L. Mayer, 1962   (62.171.19)

56. Side Chair

Philadelphia, 1760–90

WITH STILES AND CREST rail finely carved in alternating long and short lozenges, this chair, number IV in its set, represents the most richly embellished version of the trefoil-pierced-splat type. The lozenge motif was adapted from Chippendale's *Director* (pl. XII, 1754 edition; pl. XIIII, 1762 edition). Chair number V of the set is at the Boston MFA (Hipkiss, no. 88). That chair, or an identical one, was advertised in *Antiques* magazine (29 [May 1936], inside front cover). Chairs VI and IX are at the White House (acc. 970.670.1, 2; for another from the set, see Kindig, pl. 56). A pair of chairs from a second set match those of the first except for minor variations in the handling of the knee brackets and the upper splat openings (*Antiques* 61 [January 1952], p.37; ibid 119 [March 1981], p. 471). Both sets are evidently the work of the same man. Straight-legged chairs with this lozenge motif

and with splats either trefoil-pierced (Downs 1952, fig. 140) or Gothic (ibid., fig. 141) have also been identified as being from the same shop (Zimmerman 1981, p. 297).

PROVENANCE: Ex coll.: Howard Mansfield, New York City; George Coe Graves, Osterville, Massachusetts.

CONSTRUCTION: The crest rail and stiles are rounded in back. The rear legs are oval. The splat's back edges are slightly beveled. All four rails are double pegged. The side rails, cut out in flat arches serpentine-curved at the rear, are tenoned through the stiles. The carving on the front rail is cut from the solid. The inner sides of the knee brackets are chiseled. Each of the front glue blocks consists of two vertical rectangular blocks.

CONDITION: The chair, of fine heavy wood with some figure in the front rail, has a deep reddish brown color. Part of the carving on the side bracket of the left front leg has been replaced. The rear glue blocks are missing. The feet have holes for casters. The slip seat has been reupholstered. The chair is illustrated here with an eighteenth-century red silk damask seat cover.

INSCRIPTIONS: Incised crescent-shaped marks, on front seat-rail rabbet: *IIII*; on slip-seat frame: *VII*. Scratched, on rear rail and on slip-seat frame: two vertical marks and the letter *M*.

DIMENSIONS: H.: overall, 38¾ (*98.4*), seat, 17¼ (*43.8*); W.: seat front, 22⅜ (*56.8*), seat back, 17 (*43.2*), feet, 24 (*61*.); D.: seat, 17½ (*44.5*), feet, 21½ (*54.6*).

WOODS: Primary: mahogany. Secondary: northern white cedar (glue blocks); yellow pine (slip-seat frame).

REFERENCES: Girl Scouts, no. 641. Bjerkoe, pl. 26, no. 1.

The Sylmaris Collection, Gift of George Coe Graves, 1932 (32.57.3)

57. Side Chair

Philadelphia, 1760–90

ON THE CLASSIC Philadelphia pierced Gothic splat-type chair, a central ogival arch and a large vee surmount a pierced quatrefoil and are flanked by half quatrefoils. On this modestly carved version, number VII in a set, the vee overlapping the arch rather than the arch the vee is an unusual treatment. The splat design, which is a synthesis of a number of motifs found in plates X, XI, XIII, and XVI of Chippendale's *Director* (1762 edition), appears to have originated in Philadelphia. Though on the chair the front seat rail and knee carving appear similar to those at cat. no. 55 and on a chair labeled by Thomas Tufft (Downs 1952, no. 134), and though its seat rails and distinctive claw feet with raked-back talons resemble those at cat. no. 56, the same hand is not evident anywhere.

PROVENANCE: Ex coll.: Howard Mansfield, New York City; George Coe Graves, Osterville, Massachusetts.

57 See also p. 341

CONSTRUCTION: In back, the crest rail, flat at the middle and with beveled edges, is pieced at each of its three junctures with the splat, and the molded stiles are rounded. The rear legs are oval. The back edges of the splat are slightly beveled. The shoe is notched into the stiles. The rails are all double pegged. The rear rail is nearly the width of the stiles. The side rails are sawed out in flat arches with a serpentine curve at the rear and a circular scroll at the front. The carving of the front skirt is cut from the solid. The inner sides of the knee brackets are smoothly chiseled. The two-part vertical glue blocks are slightly rounded.

CONDITION: The chair is a dark reddish brown in color. The wood has a buildup of old finishes. The lower part of the shoe and the molded top edge of the front and side seat rails are mutilated by nail holes that remain from the upholstery that once covered them. On the left front leg, the scroll tip of the front bracket and the outside talon of the foot are replaced. The slip-seat frame is modern. The chair is illustrated here with an antique red silk damask seat cover.

INSCRIPTIONS: Incised, on rear seat rail: *VII*.

DIMENSIONS: H.: overall, 38⅛ (*96.8*), seat, 17 (*43.2*); W.: seat front, 22¼ (*56.5*), seat back, 17 (*43.2*), feet, 24 (*61.*); D.: seat, 17½ (*44.5*), feet, 22¼ (*56.5*).

WOODS: Primary: mahogany. Secondary: yellow pine (glue blocks).

REFERENCES: Girl Scouts, no. 637. Kirk 1972, no. 90.

The Sylmaris Collection, Gift of George Coe Graves, 1932 (32.57.4)

58. Side Chair

Philadelphia, 1760–90

THE SQUAT PROPORTIONS of the back and the carved skirts applied to the rails on this chair are English design features seldom encountered in American work. (The richly carved skirt boards do, however, appear on two elaborate Philadelphia easy chairs: see Downs 1952, no. 94; PMA 1976, no. 89.) The massiveness of the white oak seat rails nevertheless suggests a native origin, and the oval, or stump, rear legs, the side rails with through tenons, and the design and carving of the back are in the classic Philadelphia manner. The chair, number VII in its set, was one of a pair in the Clarke Collection (Lockwood 1907, pl. CXLIX); a chair from the same set belonged to C.W. Lyon; to Norvin Green (P-B sale no. 1202, 11/12/50, lot 659); and to Mr. and Mrs. Donald S. Morrison (*Antiques* 73 [May 1959], p. 455) before being given to Princeton University. Since the feet of that chair and those of cat. no. 58 were restored in the same manner, the Princeton chair is presumably the other of the Clarke Collection pair. Assuming the restoration to have been correctly done, the chairs may be related to chairs, tables, and screens made for John Cadwalader (see cat. nos. 59, 133), all having similar paw feet.

The refined carving that accentuates the integrated design of crest and splat on cat. no. 58's back represents the fullest development of the Gothic-splat pattern in Philadelphia. Identical backs are found on a number of other sets of chairs from that city. Examples from a set at Winterthur (Downs 1952, no. 129) that was made en suite with a pair of Cadwalader family card tables (ibid., no. 345) have straight mahogany rails with applied gadrooning, but clearly come from the same shop as cat. no. 58. On the chairs of both sets, the seats are upholstered halfway over the rails, the front legs end in hairy paw feet, and the splats were cut from the same template (Zimmerman 1981, pp. 297–298), though that on this chair is somewhat reduced in height. The chairs of other sets, all having straight rails, slip seats, and claw-and-ball feet, differ from each other in the carved motifs on their knees and the ornamentation of their seat rails (see Hornor 1935, pl. 364; Sack 5, p. 1168); chairs from the Wharton (Hornor 1935, pl. 352; Sack 4, pp. 2086–87) and Edwards (Downs

1952, no. 130) family sets have additional splat openings. A chair at Yale labeled by Benjamin Randolph (Kane, fig. 108) shares with cat. no. 58 the same splat design but differs in all details of construction. Any attribution of the MMA chair to Randolph is therefore implausible.

PROVENANCE: Ex coll.: Thomas B. Clarke, New York City; Tiffany Studios, New York City.

CONSTRUCTION: The crest rail and stiles are rounded in back. The rear legs are oval. On the splat, which is seated in the rear rail, the back edges are slightly beveled. The shoe, its upper edge gadrooned, is fitted around the splat and secured to it with two screws. The rear rail is thicker than the rear legs. The front and side rails, visible in an old photograph (Lockwood 1907, pl. CXLIX), are finely worked rectangular pieces of oak tenoned into the front legs and through the rear ones. The front rail is slightly serpentine in shape; its inner surface is sawed out in a conforming curve. Smoothly chiseled horizontal oak blocks are tenoned into the legs and glued to the bottom of the rails behind the thin, richly carved knee brackets. The carved skirt boards, also smoothly chiseled on their inner surfaces, are glued to the bottom of the rails.

CONDITION: The chair has an old finish with a dark, reddish brown patina. The carved hairy paws on the front legs and the bottom of the rear legs are restorations. The applied carved skirt board on the right side rail has been replaced. There are splits in the shoe. The seat has been reupholstered. The chair is illustrated here with an antique red silk damask seat cover.

INSCRIPTIONS: Incised, on shoe back and on splat behind it: *VII*.

DIMENSIONS: H.: overall, 36¾ (*93.3*), seat, 16½ (*41.9*); W.: seat front, 23 (*58.4*), seat back, 17½ (*44.5*), feet, 24¾ (*62.9*); D.: seat, 19⅛ (*48.6*), feet, 21 (*53.3*).

WOODS: Primary: mahogany. Secondary: white oak, American or European (front and side seat rails, corner blocks).

REFERENCES: Lockwood 1907, pl. CXLIX. *MMAB* 3 (June 1908), p. 111 (as English). Halsey and Cornelius, fig. 65. Downs 1949, fig. 16. P-B sale no. 1202, 11/12/50, lot 659 (attributed to Randolph). *Antiques* 62 [August 1952], p. 135; ibid. 75 [May 1959], p. 455 (also as Randolph). Comstock, fig. 274. Margon 1971, pp. 170–171 (measured drawings). Zimmerman 1981, pp. 297–298; fig. 16.

Rogers Fund, 1908   (08.51.10)

59. Side Chair

Philadelphia, about 1770

THE FULLEST AND MOST elaborate interpretation of the Chippendale style in Philadelphia seating furniture is demonstrated in this chair. Its stump rear legs, side rails tenoned through the rear stiles, and northern white cedar glue blocks, all characteristic regional construction fea-

58 See also p. 341

tures, proclaim its Philadelphia origin. In common with cat. no. 58, it has several English features: a somewhat low back; front and side seat rails upholstered on the upper half, richly carved on the lower; and hairy paw feet. It has other English features apparently unique in Philadelphia side chairs: the hollowed, or saddle, seat; the scalloped curves of the seat rail followed on the upholstery's bottom edge; and the splat splayed out to join the stiles. The splat pattern looks to have been inspired by engravings for "Ribband Back Chairs" in Chippendale's *Director* (1754 edition, pl. XVI; 1762 edition, pl. XV): from the design on the left, the C-scrolls joining the stiles; from the design on the right, the double figure-eight at the bottom.

The chair is number VII in a set of at least twelve chairs, seven of which are now located. Listed in order of the set numbers incised on the top of the rear rail and on the underside of the shoe, these are: I, private collection; II, Winterthur; VII, MMA; VIII, private collection; IX

59 See also p. 341

(with an inscription identical to that on cat. no. 59) and X, private collection; XI, Williamsburg. Number I was found in Italy in 1982 (Solis-Cohen, pp. 14A–15A); number II, in Philadelphia prior to 1942 (Zimmerman 1979, p. 203). Numbers VII–XI appeared in Ireland (see Provenance) and were included in a London sale (Sotheby's, 1/25/74, lot 68), but were withdrawn and later sold in New York (SPB sale no. 3691, 11/16/74, lots 1477–79). A pair of card tables (PMA 1976, no. 91) unique among Philadelphia cabinetwork were made en suite with the set of chairs; the identical decorative scheme is found on the legs and skirts of both forms. One of the card tables appears in Charles Willson Peale's portrait of General John Cadwalader with his wife and child, painted in the summer of 1772 (one of the tables remained in the Cadwalader family until acquired by the PMA). In a companion portrait of the general's bachelor brother Lambert, which Peale painted in the summer of 1770, one of the chairs is recognizable, its back depicted in every detail save for the carving on the stiles.

John Cadwalader (1742–1786), who emerged from the revolutionary war a general, married Elizabeth Lloyd, an heiress from Maryland, in 1768. The following year he purchased a large but relatively plain house on Second Street in Philadelphia and immediately undertook to rebuild it to the richest possible taste. In addition to spending more than £3,600 on architectural improvements, he employed Philadelphia's leading artisans, including cabinetmakers Benjamin Randolph and Thomas Affleck and carvers James Reynolds and the partners Bernard and Jugiez, to provide the furnishings. He also hired William Savery to make modest furniture for the lesser rooms, and commissioned Peale to paint five family portraits to enliven the walls of the large front parlor. Affleck's statement for furniture supplied to Cadwalader between October 13, 1770, and January 14, 1771 (Wainwright, p. 44), included "2 Commode Card Tables @ £5." The curved front of the table portrayed by Peale fits that description; the table was obviously one of the pair. The charges for the carving by James Reynolds and Bernard and Jugiez were added at the bottom of the Affleck bill; the two tables, though en suite, exhibit differences in carving techniques that suggest that Reynolds worked on one and Bernard and Jugiez on the other. Six elaborate but dissimilar chairs, including the one now at Winterthur that matches cat. no. 59, were published (Woodhouse 1927) as Randolph's work, but the firmly documented Cadwalader–Affleck connection with the set of tables and chairs controverts the claim that the Winterthur chair was a sample belonging to Randolph, though he is known to have worked for Cadwalader. The chairs that match the tables do not appear in Affleck's October 1770 bill, but

that does not diminish the likelihood that he made them; they may have been recorded in one of his bills (now missing) for work he supplied prior to that date. On October 18, 1770, the upholsterer Plunket Fleeson charged Cadwalader "To covering over Rail finish'd in Canvis 32 Chairs" (Wainwright, p. 40). If the chairs of the set were among them, Fleeson would have finished them just in time for Peale to include one in his portrait of Lambert.

PROVENANCE: Ex coll.: Anthony Francis Nugent, eleventh earl of Westmeath, Pallas, County Galway, Ireland; Nancy Hone Connell; Major R.G. Fanshawe, Stowe-on-the-Wold, Gloucestershire, England. Purchased for the MMA at auction in November 1974. The chair was made for General John Cadwalader, but its history between the general's death in 1786 and Westmeath's possession in the twentieth century is uncertain. Cadwalader's property was divided among a son and four daughters, with most of the known furnishings apparently descending through son Thomas (1779–1841); to Thomas's grandsons Dr. Charles E. (1839–1907) and John (1843–1925) Cadwalader. The chair was still in Philadelphia at the beginning of the twentieth century, as is proved by inscriptions (q.v.) on its shoe (Charles Hanlon was an upholsterer listed in the Philadelphia directories between 1901 and 1905 [Loughlin, p. 78]). Beyond that, one may speculate that the chair was taken to England by Dr. Charles in 1904, when he and his Irish wife moved permanently to London; it was not among the Cadwalader heirlooms that he auctioned off prior to his departure. He died in London, without issue, three years later.

CONSTRUCTION: The crest rail curves gracefully in at the middle in front; in back, it is rounded except at the flat middle. The stiles are rounded in back. The rear legs are oval. The splat, seated in the rear rail, is in three pieces: a vertical board, its back edges beveled, forms the bottom three-quarters; it is tenoned into a thick, horizontal board tenoned into the stiles, its rounded edges overlapping the first board in back; tenoned to it and to the crest rail is the vertical top board, built up in back to the thickness of the middle board. Two screws through the back of the splat secure the shoe, its upper edge gadrooned and its bottom edge conforming to the saddle shape of the thick rear seat rail. Thick pieces of mahogany form the front and side rails and the skirts that are carved from them. The side rails are tenoned through the rear stiles and pegged at front and back. The front rail is hollowed out at the middle to form a saddle seat. The knee brackets are attached with double roseheads.

CONDITION: The chair, with a considerable buildup of old finishes, has a dark reddish brown color. The left rear glue block is missing. The seat was reupholstered at the MMA in 1975 and covered with the modern yellow silk damask illustrated here on the chair. The choice of color was dictated by manuscript references to yellow silk upholstery on some of John Cadwalader's furniture (Wainwright, p. 69), which appears to have included this chair. The use of brass nails conforms to the original treatment evident in the nail holes on the seat rails.

INSCRIPTIONS: Incised, on bottom of shoe and top of rear seat rail: *VII*. In pencil (20th-century), on bottom of shoe: *C. Hanlon*; in chalk: *J Wannamakers Phila.*

DIMENSIONS: H.: overall, 37 (*94.*), seat at center front, 16¼ (*41.3*); W.: seat front, 22¼ (*56.5*), seat back, 16⅞ (*42.9*), feet, 24½ (*62.2*); D.: seat, 19¾ (*50.2*), feet, 23 (*58.4*).

WOODS: Primary: mahogany. Secondary: northern white cedar (glue blocks).

REFERENCES: Woodhouse 1927; idem 1930, fig. 3. Downs 1952, no. 138. Wainwright, pp. 116–117 (ill.). SPB sale no. 3691, 11/16/74, lot 1479. MMA 1975, p. 24. MMA 1976, no. 15. PMA 1976, no. 90 (attributed to Benjamin Randolph and John Pollard). Zimmerman 1979 (attributed to Affleck).

Purchase, Sansbury-Mills and Rogers Funds; Emily C. Chadbourne Gift; Virginia Groomes Gift, in memory of Mary W. Groomes; Mr. and Mrs. Marshall P. Blankarn; John Bierwirth and Robert G. Goelet Gifts; The Sylmaris Collection, Gift of George Coe Graves, by exchange; Mrs. Russell Sage, by exchange; and funds from various donors, 1974   (1974.325)

60.   Side Chair

Philadelphia, 1760–90

AN UNUSUAL RENDITION of the Gothic taste in Philadelphia is seen on this chair. The posts splay outward, forming an uncommonly broad crest rail. The carved or-

60 See also p. 340

nament, particularly the paired C-scrolls on the knees, is of remarkably small scale. The distinctive splat consists of two tiers of pointed arches. The chair is number IV in a set of side chairs en suite with an armchair and a dressing table, all with identical legs, that descended in the Carpenter, Howell, Lloyd, and Wister families of Philadelphia (Hornor 1935, p. 112; pls. 165, 167). Two other side chairs of the set are known (see Kindig, pl. 47, for one of them). Five straight-legged chairs from another set have splats identical to these, and must be the work of the same hand (Haskell sale 2, lot 367). Two chairs with seats upholstered over the rails, from still another set, belonged to William White, the first bishop of Pennsylvania, and are now in his restored Philadelphia house. A variation on the type, with three tiers of arches, is also known (Downs 1952, pl. 450).

PROVENANCE: Ex coll.: Joseph Hergesheimer, West Chester, Pennsylvania.

CONSTRUCTION: The crest rail and stiles are rounded in back. The rear legs are oval. The double-pegged rear rail is the thickness of the rear stiles. The side rails, cut out in flat arches serpentine-curved at the rear, are tenoned through the rear stiles and pegged. The front rail is also pegged. The carved knee brackets are double screwed, the lower screws countersunk. The glue blocks, probably the originals, are vertical quarter rounds.

CONDITION: The wood, a dark reddish brown in color, has a buildup of old finishes. There are splits at the top in the splat's outer straps. The seat rails have been reglued and the glue blocks stained. The left front and right side knee brackets are replacements. The slip seat has been reupholstered. The chair is illustrated here with an antique red silk damask seat cover.

INSCRIPTIONS: Incised, on rear seat rail: *IIII*; on slip-seat frame: *V*.

DIMENSIONS: H.: overall, 38¼ (*97.2*), seat, 17 (*43.2*); W.: seat front, 20½ (*52.1*), seat back, 16⅛ (*41.*), feet, 22¼ (*56.5*); D.: seat, 16⅛ (*41.*), feet, 20¾ (*52.7*).

WOODS: Primary: mahogany. Secondary: yellow pine (glue blocks, slip-seat frame).

REFERENCES: Hornor 1935, pl. 167. Joseph Hergesheimer auction, Samuel T. Freeman & Co., Philadelphia, 12/15/43, lot 601. Downs 1944, p. 81. Kindig, no. 47.

Rogers Fund, 1943   (43.160)

61.   Armchair

Pennsylvania or Maryland, 1760–90

ITS BALUSTER SPLAT of identical design to that on some mid-eighteenth-century English examples (e.g., Nutting 2, no. 2218), the chair is one of a small group, all of

61 See also p. 340

unusually large scale, having tassel-carved crest rails terminating in exaggerated scrolled ears, pierced baluster splats, triple-fluted stiles, stepped and molded shoes, and concentric incised vees amid the leaf carving on the knees. An armchair at the Department of State (Acc. 73.7), except for once having had a commode, is a virtual match to this one. Among other sets (e.g., *Antiques* 68 [October 1955], p. 313) is a cherry-wood one, said to have belonged to George Washington, that descended in the Morton family of Philadelphia (Sack 1, p. 6); a matching armchair is at the Art Institute of Chicago (Rogers, fig. 31). The crest-rail carving on cat. no. 61 and that on a chair at Winterthur (Downs 1952, no. 123) look to be by the same hand. Two armchairs at Winterthur (ibid., nos. 37, 38), though with different splat patterns, are also massive in scale and have the same tassels and scrolled ear crests.

The chairs of the group have the fluted stiles and stump rear legs, seat rails cut out in flat arches, and scrolled armrests and tonguelike arm supports characteristic of Philadelphia work. Their unusual size and exaggerated ears, however, indicate a provincial origin; Maryland or Chester County, Pennsylvania, have been suggested (ibid., no. 37).

PROVENANCE: Ex coll.: George S. Palmer, New London, Connecticut.

CONSTRUCTION: In back, the edges of the crest rail are beveled, the knuckled ears are fully carved, and the stiles are rounded. The rear legs are rounded at front and back and flat on the sides. The splat's outer edges are beveled. The base of the shoe is stepped and molded at front and sides. The front and side rails, cut out in shallow flat arches, are pegged; the rear rail, cut out in a deeper flat arch, is double pegged. Small rounded brackets are tenoned into the stiles below the side rails. The molded top edges of the side rails are cut away to receive the arm supports, which are secured by screws that extend through the rails into thin blocks nailed to them. The arms are screwed to the stiles. The inner sides of the double-nailed knee brackets are sawed. The square glue blocks, the front ones in two parts, are laid vertically.

CONDITION: The chair is dark brown in color. The top of the left stile has split in back. There are small patches behind the right ear and on the flanges of the right arm and its support. The top of the crest rail, the bottom of the splat, and the right rail have splits. The arms and supports have been rescrewed and the holes plugged. The left front and right side knee brackets are replacements. The small rear bracket is missing from the left rail. The slip-seat frame has been reupholstered. The chair is illustrated here in an antique red silk damask seat cover.

INSCRIPTIONS: Incised, on front seat-rail rabbet: *I*.

DIMENSIONS: H.: overall, 39¼ (*99.7*), seat, 16⅜ (*41.6*); W.: seat front, 23½ (*59.7*), seat back, 17¾ (*45.1*), feet, 24¾ (*62.9*); D.: seat, 18¼ (*46.4*), feet, 23 (*58.4*).

WOODS: Primary: walnut. Secondary: walnut (arm-support blocks), white cedar (glue blocks); yellow pine (slip-seat frame).

REFERENCES: Nutting 2, no. 2219 (ownership incorrectly given as C.P. Cooley). Downs 1949, no. 12. Marion Day Iverson, *The American Chair*, New York, Hastings House, 1957, fig. 104.

John Stewart Kennedy Fund, 1918   (18.110.54)

62. Side Chairs (Two)

Philadelphia, 1785–95

IN THE LATE EIGHTEENTH century, a stylish mahogany version of what was then called a slat-back, or splat-back, chair (Hornor 1935, p. 222) emerged as an alternative to the traditional vertical-splat Chippendale chair. This pair, numbers II and VI in a set of at least six chairs, now called ladderbacks, represent a version being made in Philadelphia in the mid-seventeen-eighties. The straight Marlborough legs described in the price book of 1772 as without bases or brackets (Weil, p. 183) are like those of the simplest chair designs in Chippendale's *Director*. The back, with rectangular rosettes in the ears and central ovals with carved anthemions in the swaglike slats, is a portent of the emerging Federal period's neo-classicism. Other chairs with backs of similar design are known (e.g., Montgomery, no. 82; Comstock, no. 282);

the anthemion in each slat not infrequently lacks an oval frame (Hornor 1935, pls. 267, 268). A set of chairs, similar to those of cat. no. 62 except that they have serpentine front rails and tapered and stop-fluted front legs, was made for Stephen Girard in 1786 by the Philadelphia cabinetmaker Daniel Trotter (Naeve, p. 442). As a result, all chairs of this type have routinely been assigned to Trotter. On the MMA pair, however, differences in the execution of certain of their details suggest that they did not come from Trotter's hand.

PROVENANCE: Ex coll.: George Horace Lorimer, Wyncote, Pennsylvania. Purchased by the MMA at the 1944 auction of Lorimer's collection.

CONSTRUCTION: On each chair: The crest rail and the three thick, horizontal, runglike splats below it are pierced. In back, the crest rail is flat, with rounded top and bottom edges. The triple straps flanking the carved central anthemion are convex in front and have beaded edges; the stiles are similarly molded in front and are rounded in back. The rectangular rear legs are beveled on their inner edges. The outer edges of the square front legs are molded in quarter rounds; the inner edges are beveled. The rear seat rail, scratch-beaded along its top edges, is the thickness of the stiles. The glue blocks are vertical quarter rounds.

CONDITION: The chairs have a good reddish brown color. The molded quarter-round top edges of the front and side rails are restored. Nail holes in the rails remain from the upholstery that once covered them. On chair no. II, marks indicate where wooden strips were once nailed to the seat rails to support a commode. The slip-seat frames (old, but possibly not original) have been reupholstered. The chair seats are now covered with the green and white antique silk damask illustrated here on no. VI.

INSCRIPTIONS: Incised, on front seat-rail rabbet of one chair: *II*; of the other: *VI*.

DIMENSIONS: H.: overall, 38½ (*97.8*), seat, 17 (*43.2*); W.: seat front, 22 (*55.9*), seat back, 17⅛ (*43.5*); D.: seat, 17¼ (*43.8*), feet, 20½ (*52.1*).

WOODS: Primary: mahogany. Secondary: yellow pine (glue blocks); white pine (slip-seat frame).

REFERENCES: Lorimer sale 2, lot 956. Downs 1945, p. 71. Bjerkoe, pl. XII, no. 2. Naeve, fig. 4.

Rogers Fund, 1944   (44.109.2, 3)

62

4 Stools, Couches, and Upholstered-back Chairs

Grouped together in this chapter are seating-furniture forms that do not fit readily elsewhere. Stools, the most commonplace of medieval furniture, had by the late seventeenth century acquired ceremonial significance in England, for court etiquette prescribed that only they could be used in the presence of the seated monarch. By the eighteenth century stools had attained a certain popularity with England's middle classes, but in the colonies they were almost nonexistent, perhaps a conscious rejection of symbols of a royal hierarchy. The two included here are among but a handful of American cabriole-leg examples. What was known in colonial America as a couch (in form, a side chair with immensely extended seat) is today called a daybed. It knew its greatest popularity in the William and Mary style. A number in the Queen Anne manner are known from New England—Rhode Island, especially—and from Philadelphia, though none of the latter are in the collection. A few in the Chippendale style survive from Connecticut. All interpretations employ a local splat pattern for the back. Couches, placed in the parlor during the daytime, were for reclining. Their seats have sacking bottoms like those of bedsteads; some examples have adjustable backs. While none with intact cushions are known, English survivals suggest that there was originally a thick seat cushion plus, at the back, three fat pillows in graduated sizes. In the Chippendale period, couches were superseded by sofas. The upholstered-back chair was a common English furniture form that for reasons unknown was seldom made in America. A number of such armchairs appear in the collection, but the upholstered-back side chair, sometimes called a back stool, does not. The armchairs from Newport and New York are plain versions of standard English types; one from Philadelphia shows the direct inspiration of designs for French Chairs in Chippendale's *Director*.

63

64

63. Stool

New England, 1730–60

NOTCHES ON THE SLIP SEAT and on a seat rail of this, one of the few known New England cabriole-leg stools, signify that it was one of a pair. Its place of origin is uncertain. The rounded front edge and the boldly shaped knee and pad of the leg are evocative of Massachusetts or Rhode Island work; the use of cherry and the design of the knee brackets, of Connecticut. The curve of the knee is continued by brackets that instead of being nailed to the bottom edge—the standard New England practice— are glued to the front of the seat rails. Among the few chairs with that same feature are some in a distinctive rural interpretation of the Queen Anne style, including those of a set said to be from Middletown, Connecticut (cat. no. 5). Middletown is downriver from Hartford, which bolsters the claim that the stool was made in the Hartford area (see Provenance), but the rounded, sculptural form of the stool's legs is the work of a different hand from the one that fashioned the staid and angular chairs at cat. no. 5.

PROVENANCE: Ex coll.: Mrs. J. Insley Blair, Tuxedo Park, New York; Mrs. Screven Lorillard, Far Hills, New Jersey. Purchased in 1930 by Mrs. Blair from Willoughby Farr, an Edgewater, New Jersey, dealer. According to Farr, the stool was made in the vicinity of Hartford, Connecticut, and was formerly in the collection of Herbert Newton, Holyoke, Massachusetts.

CONSTRUCTION: The rails, their bottom edges cut out in flat arches, are pegged to the legs. The knee brackets are glued to the front of the rails. On one leg, the knee and pad foot are pieced on one side; on a second, on two sides.

CONDITION: The wood has a mellow brown patina. Four of the knee brackets and the pieced part of one pad foot are replacements. Glue blocks, which were not original, were removed in 1978, when the stool was disassembled and reglued. The eighteenth-century needlework covering, purchased by Mrs. Blair from Hare & Coolidge, New York City, was added in 1933.

INSCRIPTIONS: On one of the seat-rail rabbets: a single notch; on the slip-seat frame: two notches.

DIMENSIONS: H.: overall, 16 (40.6); W.: seat, 17⅝ (44.8), feet, 19¼ (48.9); D.: seat, 15¾ (40.), feet, 17⅜ (44.1).

WOODS: Primary: cherry. Secondary: yellow pine (slip-seat frame).

Gift of Mrs. Screven Lorillard, 1952   (52.195.14)

64. Stool

Probably New York, 1760–90

AMERICAN STOOLS ARE remarkably rare, particularly those with cabriole legs and rococo carving. Although on the claw feet of this one the undefined handling of the front and side talons and the finlike projection of the back talon are in the English manner, the stool appears to be of New York manufacture. The glue blocks have been microscopically examined, and are identified (7/30/79, Gordon Saltar, Winterthur Museum) as *Fagus grandifolia*—American beech. The bow shape of the scalloped edges of the long rails was a popular motif in eighteenth-century New York, and the flat carving with its somewhat crude, gougelike finishing strokes, notably on the knees, is typical of local practice. Another carved stool of similar oval shape but of unmistakable Philadelphia design is at Winterthur (Downs 1952, no. 296).

PROVENANCE: Ex coll.: Joe Kindig, Jr., York, Pennsylvania.

CONSTRUCTION: The four thick rails that form the oval top are pegged to the legs. The recessed blocking on each inner surface is chiseled out. On the long sides, rocaille shells flanked by acanthus fronds are carved in relief above the scalloped bottom edges; on the shorter sides, the bottom edges are sawed out in flat arches. The inner edges of the stiles are notched to receive quadruple-nailed triangular glue blocks. On the knee brackets, the flat area above the leaf carving is stippled; the back surface is roughly chiseled.

CONDITION: The heavy dense wood has a fine old dark reddish finish. There is a large patch at the top on one of the long sides; a small patch inside the top edge on the other long side. The feet have holes for casters.

DIMENSIONS: H.: 16¾ (*42.5*); W.: seat, 19⅝ (*49.9*), feet, 17¾ (*45.1*); D.: seat, 18⅝ (*47.3*), feet, 15 (*38.1*).

WOODS: Primary: mahogany. Secondary: American beech (glue blocks).

Gift of Joe Kindig, Jr., 1969   (69.208)

65. Couch

Newport, 1740–90

WITH TWO SQUARE, chamfered rear legs, six pad-footed cabriole legs, turned cross-stretchers, and an adjustable back, this is a classic example of the New England cabriole-leg couch. The form is relatively uncommon. A number of different hands are discernible in the execution of the known pieces, and the form's origin cannot be narrowly localized. The couch, however, looks to be from Newport. The shape of the knees and the size of the pad feet match features on a documented Newport easy chair of 1758 (cat. no. 72); the stretchers are also similar. The distinctive outline of the baluster splat is related to that on a set of chairs said to have been made by Job Townsend in 1743 for the Eddy family of Warren, Rhode Island (Flayderman sale, lot 492); indeed, cat. no. 65 has long been identified with Eddy family furniture and attributed to Townsend, though without confirmed documentation (see Provenance). This couch has straight skirt rails and stiles that end in turned finials (see also Lockwood 2, fig. 644; Ott 1965, no. 87, now at RIHS); a number of Newport couches, otherwise similar, have scalloped rails and stiles that end in outward-scrolled ears. These include ones at Winterthur (Downs 1952, no. 212), at the Boston MFA (Randall 1965, no. 190), and in the Stone collection (Rodriguez Roque, no. 90), all of which have been published as the work of Job Townsend on the basis of the similarities of their legs and stretchers to those of cat. no. 65. Whoever the maker of this couch, he produced a unique interplay in the curves of its back and stiles and endowed its legs and stretchers with an assurance unmatched on any other New England example.

PROVENANCE: Purchased by the donors in 1945 for the MMA from Israel Sack, Inc., New York City. That firm had acquired it in 1930 at the Flayderman sale, where it was described simply as "New England, circa 1720–30." In the same sale were a set of six Queen Anne walnut side chairs and a matching walnut easy chair of characteristic Newport style (lots 492–493), which Flayderman had acquired as the work of Job Townsend in Warren, Rhode Island, from a descendant of the original owner. In 1932, at the sale of the Israel Sack Collection, the couch was associated with the Newport chairs, all said to have been made by Townsend in 1743 for the Eddy family of Warren, in whose possession "one of these pieces, which bears Townsend's label, still remains" (Sack sale, lot 80). On the basis of that description and of a letter (1/26/45) from Israel Sack to the MMA, the couch has been attributed to Job Townsend (Downs 1945, p. 67); later, Downs even refers to a 1743 Townsend bill for it (idem 1952, no. 212). That documentation still awaits confirmation. The bill of sale has not been found; the only Eddy in Warren in 1743 was Joseph (1729–1800), then aged fourteen and later a shipwright; and the couch differs from the chairs said to be by Townsend in the woods employed, as well as in the handling of seat rails, knees, and stretchers.

CONSTRUCTION: The square posts of this eight-leg couch are chamfered on all four edges above the stretchers on the leg part and on the back edges on the stile part. In profile, the stiles are serpentine; the adjustable back unit, convex. On the back unit, the narrow sides are pegged to the crest and bottom rails; the bottom rail, cavetto molded, is attached to the stiles with dowellike extensions. The yoke crest rail, flat in back, is dovetailed into the backs of the stiles. The top surfaces of the square seat rails are scratch-beaded in front; in back, they are cut out in a shallow rabbet so as to contain the canvas bottom. The seat rails are pegged to the corner legs; the intermediate legs are pegged to the rails, with concave transverse braces tenoned just in front of each pair. The knee brackets are double nailed.

CONDITION: The wood, dark brown in color, has a thin old finish. The turned finials were made in about 1930 to replace the missing originals. The back unit was originally secured to the stiles with iron chains through holes in the dovetail-shaped extensions, thus permitting the back to be raised or lowered. Then, presumably in the eighteenth century, it was nailed with pairs of roseheads into an upright position. The front transverse brace has been restored. The right front knee bracket is a replacement. In 1962, the canvas bottom and the leather cushion illustrated here replaced the old canvas (Flayderman sale, lot 345, ill.) and a cushion made in 1945.

DIMENSIONS: H.: overall, 39⅝ (100.7), seat, 14¾ (37.5); W.: seat, 22 (55.9), front feet, 24 (61.); D.: seat, 67½ (171.5), feet, 70¼ (178.4).

WOODS: Primary and secondary: maple.

REFERENCES: Flayderman sale, lot 345. Sack sale, lot 85. Downs 1945, p. 67. *Antiques* 50 (October 1946), p. 251, fig. 19. Bishop, fig. 83.

Gift of Mr. and Mrs. Paul Moore, 1945   (45.32)

66. Couch

Connecticut, 1760–90

A COUCH STRIKINGLY similar in appearance to this one is at the Wadsworth Atheneum (Kirk 1967, no. 258). The crest rails and the upper part of the pierced splats of both pieces are identically fashioned, suggesting a common source. The two nevertheless have disparate overall proportions and exhibit numerous differences in construction. The Atheneum couch, which is en suite with a side

chair (ibid., no. 244), is lower and wider; its rails are maple, its stretchers poplar; its splat passes behind the shoe to seat in the rail; and the knobs on its rails, of a variant shape, are fewer in number. Features of Philadelphia and Connecticut craftsmanship are combined on both couches. The seat rails tenoned through the back stiles, the applied gadrooning (cf. cat. no. 113), and the interlaced, Gothic-arched splats (cf. cat. no. 57) are characteristics of Philadelphia work, while typically Connecticut are the use of cherry wood and the hard angularity of the shaped parts of the back, particularly the sharp top edge of the crest rail's central arch.

A similar combination of regional features distinguishes a large group of Connecticut pieces, all now commonly attributed to Eliphalet Chapin (1741–1807), a Connecticut cabinetmaker thought to have been apprenticed in Philadelphia prior to his establishing a shop in East Windsor, Connecticut, in about 1771. The attribution is based solely on Chapin's bill of sale, now lost, for a set of chairs (see cat. no. 10). Since the two couches appear not to be by the hand, or hands, that fashioned the

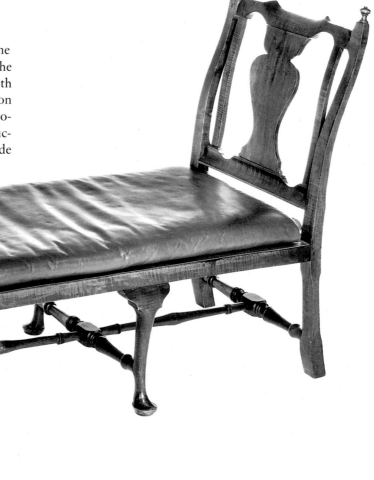

65

documented chairs, an attribution of cat. no. 66 to Chapin cannot be sustained. The couch is nonetheless an outstanding Connecticut piece in the Philadelphia manner, and, with its sacking bottom intact, an important document of eighteenth-century upholstery.

PROVENANCE: Ex coll.: H. Eugene Bolles, Boston.

CONSTRUCTION: The back surface of the crest rail is flat: at the top, the edge is beveled; at the bottom, behind the central C-scrolls, it is ɩollowed out as if to provide finger grips. The splat is seated ɪɪɪ the shoe. The stiles are rounded in back. On the front and side seat rails, the upper edge is molded into a quarter round. On all four rails, the upper inside edge is rabbeted to accommodate the turned knobs—eight at each end, twenty-four at each side—to which the sacking bottom is laced; on the bottom, strips of gadrooning are secured with roseheads. The end rails are cut out to receive the side rails. The side rails are tenoned through the rear legs. The rails are pegged to the corner legs; the middle legs, to the side rails. On the front and middle legs, the outer edges are molded into a quarter round. The two sets of crossed stretchers, half-lapped and nailed at the crossings, are tenoned into the chamfered inner edges of the legs and pegged diagonally. The transverse stretchers that join both rear and middle legs are also pegged.

CONDITION: The wood, light reddish brown in color, has a mellow old finish. The gadroon strips have been reset, their roseheads countersunk. Holes just behind the middle legs, now filled with diamond-shaped plugs, may have accommodated an iron reinforcing rod. In the right rear leg, below the stretchers, is a patched slot. Except for a tear at the foot end, the original canvas sacking is intact with its laces. The original cushions and pillow are gone.

INSCRIPTIONS: In white chalk, on underside of sacking bottom: *W H—ss* [Harris?]. In blue pencil (19th-century), on both sides of the sacking bottom: *15/4P*. In pencil (20th-century), on back of splat: *609.26*.

DIMENSIONS: H.: overall, 43½ (*110.5*), seat, 17⅝ (*44.8*); W.: seat, 24⅝ (*62.6*); D.: seat, 72¼ (*183.5*), feet, 74½ (*189.2*).

WOODS: Primary: cherry. No secondary woods.

REFERENCES: Lockwood 2, fig. 647. Miller 1, no. 506.

Gift of Mrs. Russell Sage, 1909   (10.125.178)

67. Upholstered Armchairs (Pair)

New York, 1740–60

A SMALL GROUP of Queen Anne armchairs with upholstered backs, open arms, and balloon seats can be assigned a New York origin on the basis of their family histories. Among the group are a pair at Winterthur (Downs 1952, no. 17) from the Tibbetts, or Tibbits, family of New York; a closely related chair from a family of the same name but from Hoosick Falls, New York (Sack 5, pp. 1322–23); and one other (ibid., p. 1190). The arms and legs of the MMA pair, which are from the Ludlow family, are similar to those of a chair at Winterthur (Downs 1952, no. 16) that differs from the group only in its upholstered upper section, which is wider and flatter at the top.

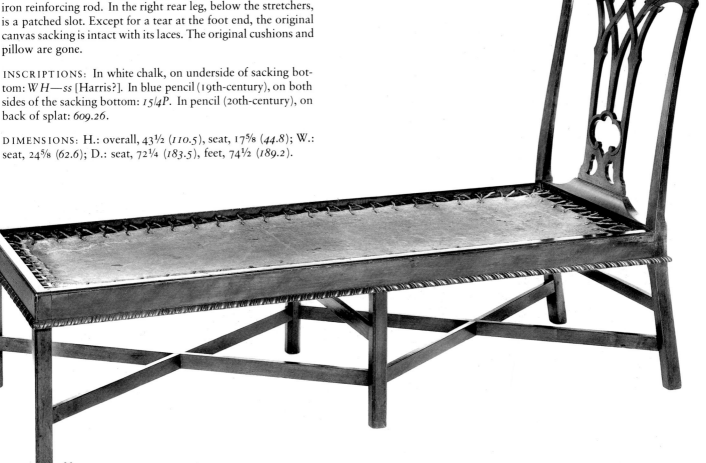

66

A Newport version of the type (Sack 7, pp. 1724–25) is distinguishable from New York examples in having turned stretchers, continuous arms, and a shaped crest. Its mate (Downs 1952, no. 18) retains its original leather covering and decorative brass nails along the edges of the seat and back, suggesting how the chairs of cat. no. 67 may have originally been finished.

PROVENANCE: The chairs, which descended in the Ludlow family of New York City, were probably made originally for William Ludlow (born 1707), who married Mary Duncan in 1731. They would have then descended to the Ludlow son Gabriel William (1734–1805); to grandson Charles; and to great-granddaughters Elizabeth Ludlow and Cornelia Ann Ludlow Willink. The donor, née Maria Selleck, lived with the two sisters as one of the family, and inherited from them a large collection of their family possessions, including important New York Federal furniture, all of which she left to the MMA. These armchairs appear to have been part of that collection rather than having descended in the family of her husband, W.K. James of Flushing, New York, as has been suggested (Downs 1952, no. 17).

CONSTRUCTION: On each chair: The arched crest rail is pegged to the rectangular posts. The posts, pieced at the shaped outer side, continue as rounded rear legs that curve sharply backward and are splayed at the foot. The front and side seat rails, thick boards laid flat, are shaped at the inner edges to conform to the balloon outline of the seat. The side rails are tenoned into the front rail and double pegged. The front legs continue through the seat rails in immense dovetail-shaped tenons double wedged and pegged diagonally from either side. Serpentine-shaped rear brackets are applied on the side rails and are cut out on the rear rail. The front glue blocks, double screwed, are triangular; the rear glue blocks are vertical quarter rounds. The armrest supports, let into the seat rails and triple screwed, are pegged to the armrests. The armrests are screwed to the stiles.

CONDITION: On one chair, illustrated here in the frame, the finish is old and much decayed; the bottom of the right rear leg, which is restored, has lost some of the flare at the foot. The rear glue blocks are missing. Evidence remains of original ornamental brass-headed nails. On the other chair, a mellow brown in color, the left arm support and the bottom of both rear legs are split. The stuffing and upholstery fabric are replacements. Once covered in a plain dark velvet (Nutting 2, no. 2132), the chair was re-covered by 1924 with the antique crewelwork, probably originally made for bed hangings, in which it is shown here.

DIMENSIONS: H.: overall, 36 (91.4), seat, 14¾ (37.5); W.: seat front, 22¾ (57.8), seat back, 14⅛ (35.9), feet, 21¾ (55.2); D.: seat, 18¾ (47.6), feet, 20¾ (52.7).

67

WOODS: Primary: walnut. Secondary: ash (front and side seat rails); white pine (glue blocks of upholstered chair); mahogany (glue blocks of chair shown in the frame).

REFERENCES: "Bequest of Mrs. Maria P. James," *MMAB* 6 (April 1911), p. 89. For the Ludlow family, see William Seton Gordon, "Gabriel Ludlow (1663–1736) and His Descendants," in the *NYGBS Record* 50 (1919), pp. 34–55, 134–156.

Bequest of Maria P. James, 1910   (11.60.148, 149)

68. Upholstered Armchair

Probably New England, 1755–90

THE OVERALL DESIGN of this chair, fully upholstered on the back and seat and having padded armrests, is based upon the so-called French Chairs that first became popular in England in the 1730s (*DEF* 1, p. 234, fig. 82). It is a type not commonly found in American furniture. Of the few extant examples, some of mahogany with maple and white pine have the stop-fluted legs characteristic of Newport (Ott 1969, pp. 11–15; *Antiques* 71 [April 1957], p. 292); another, of cherry wood, may be from Connecticut (*Antiques* 108 [October 1975], p. 574).

Despite its history of descent in the Verplanck family of New York (see Provenance), cat. no. 68 too appears to be of New England origin. It has maple and white pine secondary woods, and it conforms to the regional type except that on each arm support the base, which forms the top of the front legs, is not straight but rounded. While the back is higher than that specified for a "French Chair" in Chippendale's *Director* (1762 edition, pl. XIX), the seat dimensions follow his precepts exactly. Richly carved versions of the chair type, based upon Chippendale's designs, were made in Philadelphia (see cat. no. 69).

PROVENANCE: See cat. no. 24.

CONSTRUCTION: The serpentine-crested back is fully upholstered. The stiles rest on the side rails and against the wedge-shaped tops of the rear legs. The legs are square and chamfered on the inner edge. The rear legs, slightly rounded at the outer rear corner, splay back sharply below the side stretchers. At the level of the top of the seat rails the front legs are butted into the armrest supports, which are curved and have rounded fronts.

CONDITION: The wood is a light reddish brown in color. The right front leg is an old replacement; the front and side stretchers are later replacements. The originals were dovetailed into the legs approximately an inch higher up. The tops of the front legs, until 1965 covered with upholstery fabric, are patched where they were defaced by upholstery nails. All four legs formerly had casters. The seat rails are reinforced with modern corner braces. The chair has been reupholstered and is illustrated here with a modern pumpkin-colored worsted cover, a 1965 reproduction of the eighteenth-century fabric with which the chair was covered in 1940.

68

DIMENSIONS: H.: overall, 42⅛ (*107.*), seat, 12 (*30.5*); W.: seat front, 27 (*68.6*), seat back, 23 (*58.4*); D.: seat, 23¾ (*60.3*), feet, 28 (*71.1*).

WOODS: Primary: mahogany. Secondary: red maple (seat rails); white pine (armrests, back frame).

Gift of James De Lancey Verplanck and John Bayard Rodgers Verplanck, 1939   (39.184.15)

69. Upholstered Armchair

Philadelphia, 1765–90

THIS IS ONE OF A SMALL number of large and elegant Philadelphia chairs that can be divided into two general groups. The overall design of the chairs—upholstered backs and seats, open arms, and Marlborough legs—is based upon the two French Chairs of plate XIX in Chippendale's *Director* (1762 edition). On cat. no. 69, one of a pair (its mate is at Williamsburg; see Reifsnyder sale, lot 682; Nutting 2, no. 2311A; Girl Scouts, no. 613; Comstock, fig. 253), the hollow-cornered panels cut into the front legs and the leaf-carved handholds of the arms are motifs adopted with little change from the left-hand illustration of plate XIX, although the chair's dimensions, especially its height, are somewhat greater than those recommended by Chippendale. The crest rail's serpentine curve with projecting points is a shape found on many Philadelphia camel-back sofas. In the same group is another pair, one at Winterthur (Palmer sale, lot 173; Hornor 1935, pl. 259; Downs 1952, no. 57) and one whose location is unknown (Nutting 2, no. 2279), which are identical to these except for slight differences in the carving of the bellflowers and beads on the front legs. On the second group of the *Director*-type chairs, the fronts of the arm supports are leaf-carved and the legs are carved in pointed arches, Chinese trellises, and rosettes. Examples of these are at Winterthur, Bayou Bend, the Department of State, and on deposit at the PMA (1976, no. 79).

Both groups of chairs are unusually large and of a pattern more common in London than in Philadelphia. They are the work of a gifted craftsman and must have been made for a particularly prominent client. Hornor (1935, pl. 259, caption) claimed that the first group was made by Thomas Affleck for John Penn between 1763 and 1766; elsewhere (ibid., p. 176) he noted that between 1766 and 1792/93 Penn and his wife purchased Marlborough-leg furniture from Affleck that included the chairs of the second group. Thomas Affleck (1740–1795), a Scot trained in London, came in 1763 to Philadelphia, where he achieved preeminence as a cabinetmaker. That same year, Penn (1729–1795), grandson of William, arrived from England to serve as lieutenant governor of the Province of Pennsylvania. He married in 1766 and moved into a grand house on Third Street. Hornor's attribution (ibid., p. 73) rests upon evidence in Affleck's manuscript accounts and receipt book, whose whereabouts remain a mystery. Other evidence, however, does support the Penn–Affleck history. The carved legs of the second group of French Chairs are similar to those on the Chew family's massive sofa now at Cliveden, their country estate. A long-standing Chew family tradition has it that Benjamin Chew, the distinguished Philadelphia jurist, bought the sofa, among other furnishings, from the Penns (Raymond V. Shepherd, Jr., "Cliveden and Its Philadelphia-Chippendale Furniture: A Documented History," *The American Art Journal* 8 [November 1976], p. 6). There is also a traditional link between the Penns and the MMA chair: the chair's last private owner recalled in 1933 that the family had always called it the "William Penn" chair, obviously a mistaken reference to John. Further, the design for both groups of French Chairs owes an unquestioned debt to an illustra-

tion in the *Director*'s third edition, and while the Library Company of Philadelphia had a copy of the book in 1770, the only local cabinetmaker known to have owned one independently was Affleck.

PROVENANCE: Ex coll.: The Misses Alice and Ida Cushman, Philadelphia; Mrs. J. Insley Blair, Tuxedo Park, New York; Mrs. Screven Lorillard, Far Hills, New Jersey; Screven Lorillard. On loan to the MMA from 1953 to 1959. According to a letter from Alice Cushman to Mrs. Blair (7/15/33, MMA files), the armchair "was part of the furniture of our father's studio in Philadelphia when a young man, before he married our mother in 1849." The father was George Hewitt Cushman (1814–1876), a Connecticut portrait- and miniature-painter who moved to Philadelphia in about 1842 and married Susan Wetherill in 1849. Mrs. Blair's 1933 notes mistakenly identify him as James Wetherill Cushman, and it was on that basis that Hornor (1935, pl. 259) described the chair as the "Newly Discovered James–Wetherill–Cushman Example."

CONSTRUCTION: The junctures of stiles and crest rail are reinforced with corner braces. The stiles end at the seat rails, into which they are slotted, and are held in place by the tapered top edges of the square rear legs. On the rear legs, the front surface is canted back at a slight angle above the stretcher and at a sharp angle below it; the back surface is gently curved. Mahogany strips, their fronts carved in a bead-and-reel pattern, are nailed to the bottom of the front and side seat rails. There are no glue blocks. The serpentine arm supports, rounded in front and back and flat at the sides, are screwed to the side rails. The pierced C-scroll knee brackets are nailed on. On the applied molded cuffs that form the feet, the fronts and backs overlap the sides. The cuffs extend well below the bottoms of the legs, concealing brass casters.

CONDITION: The chair has an old finish, probably the original, and a fine reddish brown patina. Splits where the carved armrests meet the arm supports have been screwed together. The supports are reinforced with modern screws through the bottom of the side rails. On the front legs, the outer edges are badly scuffed; the beaded molding set into a deep groove between the recessed panels on front and sides is a replacement. The original bead, which survives on the matching chair at Williamsburg, was shouldered. The two carved front knee brackets and the front stretcher are restorations, as is the back of the right cuff. The seat, back, and armrests have been reupholstered. The armchair is illustrated here covered in an antique silk damask with a gold background on which a broad central red panel is flanked by narrow, ribbonlike stripes of light and dark green.

DIMENSIONS: H.: overall, 43 (*109.2*), seat, 16¾ (*42.5*); W.: seat front, 28 (*71.1*), seat back, 22¼ (*56.5*), feet, 28¼ (*71.8*); D.: seat, 24¾ (*62.9*), feet, 30 (*76.2*).

WOODS: Primary: mahogany. Secondary: white oak (rear stiles and rails, seat rails).

REFERENCES: Hornor 1935, p. 182; pl. 259, caption. Davidson 1967, fig. 270. *Antiques* 109 (January 1976), p. 34.

Purchase, Mrs. Russell Sage and Robert G. Goelet Gifts; The Sylmaris Collection, Gift of George Coe Graves; and funds from various donors, 1959   (59.154)

69

5 Easy Chairs

Easy chairs—what have now come to be called wing chairs—are large, fully upholstered chairs with wings projecting from the back, above the arms. The form originated
in Restoration England, in the sixteen-sixties, and was popularly made in the William
and Mary and Queen Anne styles before fading from fashion. The chairs, introduced
into America by about 1720, were made continually for a century. The word "easy," derived from the old French *aisié* ("conducive to ease or comfort"), described their function. The seat was roomy and the inner surfaces generously padded; the wings provided
headrests and protection from drafts. Made to be used in bedchambers by the aged and
the sick, easy chairs often had casters on the feet and a frame for a close stool, or chamber pot, in the seat. Copley employed the easy chair as an obvious symbol of great age in
his portraits. Exceptionally elaborate examples, sometimes made en suite with other
furniture, were intended for the parlors of the well-to-do. The chairs were the product of
two different craftsmen: the chairmaker, whose wooden armature determined the
chair's outline, and the upholsterer, whose stuffing determined its ultimate shape. The
upholstery materials and the finish fabric—wool harrateen, or moreen, silk damask,
embroidered needlework—were the most costly parts of the chair, and few examples
survive intact. An almost perfectly preserved specimen from Newport is the highlight
of the Museum's rich and extensive representation of the cabriole-leg type from New
England and Philadelphia, the two areas where the form was most popular. Marlborough-leg examples were made in Newport and Philadelphia, but are not represented
in the collection. The entries are arranged within geographic areas, beginning with New
England and ending splendidly with Charleston.

70. Easy Chair

New England, 1730–90

THE LOW, ARCHED crest rail, conical arm supports, rounded front seat rail, turned stretchers, and pad-footed cabriole legs of this frame typify large numbers of Queen Anne easy chairs made in Massachusetts, Rhode Island, and Connecticut in the mid-eighteenth century, but the block-and-spindle front stretcher is a type more commonly found on chairs with rococo features (e.g., cat. no. 74). The frame matches almost exactly one of a chair in the Brooklyn Museum (Jobe, fig. 25), which retains its original upholstery stuffing and cover of red wool worsted. Cat. no. 70 was doubtless first finished in a similar moreen or harrateen.

PROVENANCE: Ex coll.: Mrs. Giles Whiting, New York City.

CONSTRUCTION: The rear legs, chamfered above the stretcher, are continuous with rear stiles that are rounded along the outer edge. Dovetail-shaped tenons continue the front legs into the front seat rail. The knee brackets are secured with roseheads. The side rails are tenoned into the front seat rail. On the seat rails, both inner and outer sides are contoured. The armrests are nailed to the two-piece conical arm supports and double screwed to the wing stiles. All mortice and tenon joints are pegged except for those of the front and rear seat rails, the crest and lower rear rails, and the front stretcher.

CONDITION: The front legs and the front and side stretchers have a walnut brown color; the rear legs and stretcher are stained reddish brown. The bottom two inches on the rear legs is restored; on the front legs, about a quarter inch. There is an old split in the knee on the left front leg, and the foot is patched. The chair was stripped of its modern upholstery in 1977 for exhibition in the frame. Notches in the framing members remain from upholsterer's strips that were once added (cf. cat. no. 73, frame).

DIMENSIONS: H.: overall, 47 (*119.4*), seat, 12⅞ (*32.7*); W.: seat front, 30⅝ (*77.8*), seat back, 23¾ (*60.3*), arms, 37 (*94.*), feet, 30⅞ (*78.4*); D.: seat, 23⅜ (*59.4*), feet, 25¾ (*65.4*).

WOODS: Primary: walnut (front legs, front and side stretchers); maple (rear legs, rear stretcher). Secondary: white pine (outer half of arm supports); maple (all other framing members).

REFERENCES: *Antiques* 77 (January 1960), p. 91 (ill.).

Bequest of Flora E. Whiting, 1971 (1971.180.31)

71. Easy Chair

New England, 1730–90

THIS EASY CHAIR is a variant of cat. no. 70. Its crest and front seat rails are flatter, and its front stretcher, doweled directly into the side ones, is of the most common New

70

71

England type. The pads of the front feet stand on deep disks, a feature believed to be contemporaneous with the claw-and-ball foot (Randall 1965, no. 154). A similar chair frame, now with restored front legs, was made by Clement Vincent or George Bright and upholstered in 1759 by Samuel Grant of Boston (Jobe and Kaye, no. 101). A Newport version (cat. no. 72) is dated 1758.

PROVENANCE: Ex coll.: H. Eugene Bolles, Boston.

CONSTRUCTION: The frame construction has not been examined, but, on the basis of a photograph (about 1910, MMA files) made when the chair was stripped, it appears to resemble that of cat. no. 70, except that on the rear stiles the outer edges are square.

CONDITION: The front legs and front and side stretchers have an old finish and a mellow walnut color; the rear legs and stretcher are stained a matching brown. The seat frame has been reinforced with corner blocks. The rear feet have holes for casters. None of the original upholstery materials survive. The chair was reupholstered at the MMA in 1966 and covered with the eighteenth-century striped bourette in which it is illustrated here. Originally, there were no brass-headed nails lining the skirts.

DIMENSIONS: H.: overall, 45¾ (116.2), seat, 12⅝ (32.1); W.: seat front, 31½ (80.), seat back, 24⅝ (62.6), arms, 35¾ (90.8), feet, 33⅛ (84.1); D.: seat, 22¾ (57.8), feet, 24¾ (62.9).

WOODS: Primary: walnut (front legs, front and side stretchers); maple (rear legs, rear stretcher). Secondary: white pine (arm supports); maple (all other framing members).

REFERENCES: Little, fig. 55.

Gift of Mrs. Russell Sage, 1909   (10.125.268)

72. Easy Chair

Newport, 1758

THE CONICAL ARM supports, turned stretchers, and uncarved front legs with pad feet on this example are general features of New England Queen Anne easy chairs, but the high arch of the crest rail, the generous scale of the feet, and the heavy, unchamfered, square rear legs are distinctive features that because of their presence on a documented Newport piece (see Inscriptions) can be considered characteristics of work from that city.

In terms of quality, condition, and documentation, this chair must count as one of the most remarkable pieces of all eighteenth-century American furniture. With a frame of stately proportions and cabriole legs and pad feet formed with an effortless, bold assurance, the chair's woodwork ranks it among the best of New England seating furniture. One of only two such easy chairs now

known to have their original stuffing and finish fabric in place and intact (the other is at the Brooklyn Museum), cat. no. 72 stands as a Rosetta stone to illustrate the form and technique of eighteenth-century upholstery. While other examples (their stuffing restored) are finished in front in similar Irish-stitch needlework (Downs 1952, no. 73; Warren, no. 90), on this chair the back covering—an embroidered bucolic landscape—is unique.

The inscription on the crest rail locates the chair in Newport, in 1758, in association with someone named Gardner. He may be a Caleb Gardner who died in 1761, since his son and namesake, said to have been born in 1750 and to have had a long and active career as an upholsterer, was possibly carrying on a family business. In Newport, on September 14, 1774, he billed Abraham Redwood for making crimson silk bed and window curtains (mss., NHS collection); on December 31, he charged Mrs. Rachel Wright £40 "To making a Easy Chair" (Haight mss., NHS). By 1780 he had moved to Providence, where in January 1790 he charged Enos Hitchcock "To making a Easy Chair and Case £1-16" (Ott 1969b, p. 117).

PROVENANCE: Ex coll.: Mrs. J. Insley Blair, Tuxedo Park, New York. According to the donor's notes (MMA files), the chair ". . . belonged to the Keech or Keach family of Newport, R.I. About 1850 was taken to Burlington, Vermont. Sold by family to man in Connecticut in Sept. 1926." The chair was acquired by Mrs. Blair from Ginsburg & Levy, New York City, in 1926; exhibited at the MMA from February to November 1927 and again from 1939 until 1950; and was then given to the Museum.

CONSTRUCTION: The frame, which except for the back and the bottom has not been examined, appears similar to that at cat. no. 70 but for the straight front rail and the seat rails tenoned into the front legs. The square rear legs are continuous with the stiles; the side stretchers are pegged to the legs.

CONDITION: The walnut brown color of the legs and stretchers is visible through the partly decayed original finish. The original upholstery is retained in remarkable condition: the front and sides covered in fine Irish-stitch needlework, the once bright colors (an allover lozenge pattern in blue and green with red and yellow centers) now muted by time; the back panel worked in a surface satin, or New England laid, stitch, the colors still bright, although the bottom two inches is missing. Particularly on the back edge of the arm supports and on the bottom side edges, remnants exist of the patterned blue green woven silk tape that covered all the edges and seams, even to the piping on the wings and the raised seams on the cushion. When the back embroidery panel was opened up, the original webbing and canvas were found intact. The webbing on the bottom is in the standard lattice pattern, but with diagonal corner strips for added reinforcement. The rear legs and stiles and the seat rails have worm holes.

INSCRIPTIONS: In pencil, on back of crest rail: *Gardner Junʳ/ Newport May/1758/W.* (See p. 366 for photograph.)

72

72

DIMENSIONS: H.: overall, 46⅜ (117.8), seat, 12 (30.5); W.: seat front, 30 (76.2), seat back, 24 (61.), arms, 32⅜ (82.2), feet, 32 (81.3); D.: seat, 22¾ (57.8), feet, 25⅞ (65.7).

WOODS: Primary: walnut (front legs and all stretchers); maple (rear legs). Secondary: maple (rear stiles, crest rail, seat rails).

REFERENCES: Little, fig. 54. Andrus 1951, p. 247, right (ill.); idem 1952, p. 166 (ill.). Davidson 1967, fig. 169. Heckscher 1971a, p. 65 (ill.); idem 1971b, pp. 884 (frontispiece), 889. Bishop, p. 118; figs. 128, 128a. MMA 1976, no. 11.

Gift of Mrs. J. Insley Blair, 1950   (50.228.3)

73. Easy Chair

Massachusetts, 1760–90

THIS CHAIR TYPIFIES the later version of the classic New England easy chair. Like those of the Queen Anne type—earlier and more common—it has turned stretchers and conical arm supports. Unlike them, it has a serpentine crest rail, straight seat rails, and claw-and-ball feet. The squared knees and raked-back talons of the front legs are in the Boston manner. A Boston receipt dated 1771 was found in the upholstery of a similar chair at the Old Gaol Museum, York, Maine (Jobe and Kaye, p. 372). Practically identical to cat. no. 73 is a chair at Winterthur on whose frame is inscribed "J. Pope." Other examples, differing only in the treatment of the front stretcher, are at Dearborn (Campbell, p. 43) and at Bayou Bend (Warren, no. 90), the latter with its original Irish-stitch embroidery covering.

PROVENANCE: Ex coll.: Mrs. Giles Whiting, New York City.

CONSTRUCTION: The rear legs, chamfered above the stretchers and on the front corners below them, are continuous with the rear stiles. The stiles are tenoned into the crest rail. The wing crestings are half-lapped and dovetailed into the stiles. The arm supports are in two parts, the conical outer part nailed to the inner part. The armrests are nailed with double roseheads to their supports and to the wing stiles. Otherwise, the framing members are mortised and tenoned and, except for the lower rear rail, pegged. The front knee brackets are secured with triple roseheads; the side ones, with round-headed cut nails.

CONDITION: The legs and stretchers are a dark reddish brown in color. The soft mahogany is much scuffed. The feet once had casters. The frame is intact; modern upholsterer's strips have been added above the side and rear seat rails and in front of the rear stiles. In 1979 the frame was stripped of its modern upholstery and redone, copying in contour as well as in finishing details an intact example at the Brooklyn Museum (Jobe, fig. 25). The finish fabric illustrated here is a reproduction raspberry red worsted with pressed vermicelli pattern.

INSCRIPTIONS: In pencil, on the right wing crest rail and on the two wing stiles, three faint sets of legends, all referring to the same name: *Barton*, *Boston*, *Burton*, or *Benton*. Two have an added initial: *D* or *J*.

DIMENSIONS: H.: overall, 45 (*114.3*), seat, 12 (*30.5*); W.: seat front, 30⅛ (*76.5*), seat back, 24¾ (*62.9*), arms, 35¾ (*90.8*), feet, 31½ (*80.*); D.: seat, 24 (*61.*), feet, 27 (*68.6*).

WOODS: Primary: mahogany (front legs, front and side stretchers); maple (rear legs and stretcher). Secondary: beech (front seat rail); white pine (outer arm supports); maple (all other framing members).

Bequest of Flora E. Whiting, 1971 (1971.180.32)

73

74 See also p. 342

74. Easy Chair

Boston, 1760–90

THE FULLEST ROCOCO development of the New England easy chair is exhibited in this example, which has acanthus-leaf knee carving in addition to the serpentine cresting, square seat, and claw feet of the standard version. Easy chairs with such carved legs are rare. One (*Antiques* 115 [March 1979], inside front cover) is virtually identical to this one; of the remaining few, most have the rounded crest and front seat rails associated with the Queen Anne style (e.g., Downs 1952, no. 82). Several side chairs with similarly carved legs have Boston histories (e.g., cat. no. 13; Yehia, fig. 149), justifying for cat. no. 74 an attribution to that city. One of them (cat. no. 14) shares with this example a distinctive block-and-spindle front stretcher, suggesting that the same turner worked on both pieces.

PROVENANCE: Purchased, along with cat. no. 99, from the estate of Mrs. Henry E. Warner, Concord, Massachusetts. According to family tradition (1/16/67 letter, Margaret Warner Wagnière to MMA), the chair descended from Elizabeth Bromfield to her daughter Elizabeth Rogers; to her grandson Dr. Daniel Denison Slade of Boston, father of Henrietta (Mrs. Henry E. Warner). The chair presumably was made for the Boston merchant Henry Bromfield (1727–1820), who married Hannah Clarke in 1762. Their daughter Elizabeth (1763–1833) married Daniel Denison Rogers of Boston in 1796; their daughter Elizabeth married J.T. Slade, father of Daniel Denison Slade.

CONSTRUCTION: Above the top of the seat rails the rear legs are cut off at an angle against which rest the rear stiles, slotted into the tops of the side rails and secured from the outside with double roseheads. The seat rails are double pegged to the legs, the joints reinforced with double-nailed triangular glue blocks. Small nails secure the knee brackets. Otherwise the construction of the frame is like that at cat. no. 73.

CONDITION: The legs and stretchers, now a reddish brown in color, retain their original finish. The right foot is split. The feet have holes for casters. Nail and tack holes on the frame show that before its acquisition by the MMA the chair was reupholstered twice. It was stripped in 1971 and reupholstered in 1972 with the covering of modern red silk damask in which it is illustrated here. Except that the seat cushion is too flat, the shaping of the upholstery and the use of a woven silk tape border follow eighteenth-century precedent (see cat. no. 72).

DIMENSIONS: H.: overall, 47¾ (*121.3*), seat, 13¼ (*33.7*); W.: seat front, 32¼ (*81.9*), seat back, 23⅞ (*60.6*), arms, 35½ (*90.2*), feet, 35⅝ (*90.5*); D.: seat, 23½ (*59.7*), feet 28⅛ (*71.4*).

WOODS: Primary: mahogany. Secondary: white pine (outer arm supports, glue blocks); red maple (all other framing members).

74

REFERENCES: *MMAB* n.s. 26 (October 1967), p. 48. MMA 1975, p. 23 (ill.). Heckscher 1971, p. 7 (ill.), p. 12; idem 1971b, figs. 5 (frame), 16, 18 (drawings of construction details). MFA 1975, no. 132. For the Bromfield family, see Slade.

Friends of the American Wing Fund, 1967   (67.114.2)

75. Easy Chair

New York, 1755–90

ALTHOUGH THE C-SCROLL shape of its arms is a feature of Philadelphia work, this small easy chair can be attributed convincingly to New York. It descended in the Verplanck family of New York City and Fishkill, New York, presumably from Samuel (1739–1820). Its secondary woods are those typically found in New York-made furniture, as are the square rear legs and the method of joining the seat rails to the front legs. Moreover, its claw feet, distinguished by a squashed ball with narrow, downward-sloping talons, are of a distinctive New York type.

Similar feet are found on an easy chair with the ownership brand of Philip Van Rensselaer, of Albany (Rice, p. 21; see also cat. no. 127); on a side chair that belonged to General Philip Schuyler, also of Albany (Kirk 1972, no. 148), and on what look to be the matching corner chair (Warren, no. 87) and easy chair (Sack 5, p. 1148); on a side chair made for General Samuel Webb of New York and Connecticut (Downs 1952, no. 150); and on a pair of side chairs from the Willett family of Westchester County (cat. no. 23).

PROVENANCE: See cat. no. 24.

CONSTRUCTION: The rear legs are square. Because the massive, square seat rails are larger than the stiles of the legs to which they are tenoned, the front and rear rails are slotted into the side ones. The frame construction under the upholstery has not been examined.

CONDITION: The legs are light brown in color. Strips nailed to the side seat rails once supported a close-stool frame. In the bottom of the front seat rail are stub ends of the nails that secured the runners for the sliding unit containing the chamber pot. The conversion to such use appears to have been made in the early nineteenth century. In 1940, the chair was stripped to the frame and reglued, and new side knee brackets were made for the front legs. The chair was reupholstered with an eighteenth-century pumpkin-colored wool damask once used for curtains by the Verplanck family (a gift from family members), and in 1965 was reupholstered with an exact copy of that wool damask. The seams were covered with brass-headed nails;

75

those on the wings and back are without precedent in American easy chairs and probably do not belong.

DIMENSIONS: H.: overall, 44⅛ (*112.1*), seat, 14⅛ (*35.9*); W.: seat front, 30 (*76.2*), seat back, 25 (*63.5*), arms, 34½ (*87.6*), feet, 30⅜ (*77.2*); D.: seat, 22 (*55.9*), feet, 26⅜ (*67.*).

WOODS: Primary: walnut. Secondary: white oak (rear stiles, seat rails); white pine (arm-support cones, seat-rail strips); tulip poplar (all other framing members).

REFERENCES: Downs 1941a, p. 223 (ill.). *The Connoisseur* 109 (June 1942), p. 154. *Antiques* 119 (March 1981), p. 589.

Gift of James De Lancey Verplanck and John Bayard Rodgers Verplanck, 1939   (39.184.14)

76. Easy Chair

Philadelphia, 1745–60

ON PHILADELPHIA EASY chairs the arm supports are C-scroll-shaped; the wings have beveled front edges designed so that the upholstering could be formed into a continuous curve inside the outer edge; the seat rails are framed up with horizontal timbers like those on the city's Queen Anne chairs; and the legs are of a popular local pattern. On this Philadelphia chair, however, the back is unusually narrow in relation to its height, and the curve of the front seat rail is unusually flat at the middle. An example at Winterthur (Downs 1952, no. 78), its walnut legs with plain knees and pad feet, has identical proportions and rail configurations. A few other chairs with high backs and Queen Anne legs are known (Downs 1952, nos. 76, 77; Hornor 1935, pl. 311). All appear to be the earliest type of Philadelphia easy chair, but cat. no. 76, with claw feet, may have been made somewhat later than the others.

PROVENANCE: Ex coll.: Allan B.A. Bradley, New York City. On loan to the American Wing at the MMA from October 1924 until purchased in 1938.

CONSTRUCTION: Sketches made during the most recent reupholstering record that the crest rail is tenoned to the rear stiles; the wing crestings are half-lapped over the rear stiles; the rear stiles, their bottoms slotted into the side seat rails, are supported against the wedge-shaped tops of the rear legs; and the rear legs are rectangular with chamfered corners (features also found at cat. no. 77). The front and side seat rails are horizontally laid planks with straight inner edges; the side seat rails with their applied rear brackets are tenoned into the front rail and through the rear legs. The knee brackets are sawed out.

CONDITION: The legs have been refinished and are now a nut brown in color. The feet have holes for casters. Part of the inner edge of the front seat rail has been crudely cut away. No original stuffing or upholstery remains. After the chair came to the MMA it was covered in antique red silk damask; the fabric illustrated here was put on in 1960. Except for thick padding on the outer sides of the C-scrolled arms, the contouring of the upholstery approximates eighteenth-century practice.

DIMENSIONS: H.: overall, 46¼ (*117.5*); seat, 13¾ (*34.9*); W.: seat front, 20½ (*52.1*), seat back, 20⅞ (*53.*), arms, 33½ (*85.1*), feet, 25¾ (*65.4*); D.: seat, 22⅞ (*58.1*), feet, 28⅜ (*72.1*).

WOODS: Primary: walnut. Secondary: walnut (right stile, rear seat rail, rear brackets); maple (left stile. front and side seat rails); pine (lower rear rail); cedar (middle rear rail); tulip poplar (all other framing members).

REFERENCES: William MacPherson Hornor, "A Survey of American 'Wing Chairs,' " *The International Studio* 99 (July 1931), p. 29, fig. 5. Joseph Downs, "Three Pieces of American Furniture," *MMAB* 33 (July 1938), pp. 164–165; p. 164 (ill.).

Purchase, Joseph Pulitzer Bequest, 1938   (38.52.1)

77. Easy Chair

Philadelphia, 1750–90

THE MAJORITY of Philadelphia cabriole-leg easy chairs have similar wooden armatures supporting their upholstery. This is a classic example. Its low, broad proportions and arc-shaped front seat rail distinguish it from earlier prototypes such as cat. no. 76. The modified form appears to have been introduced by the mid-seventeen-fifties, and was available with a variety of choices in the design of the legs (see cat. no. 78). The 1772 Philadelphia list of prices describes a chair like this as "Easy Chair frame plain feet and knees without Casters" (Weil, p. 183). With legs made of walnut, as here, it cost £2-5-0; of mahogany, £2-10-0. A few other easy chairs are known with the same, inexpensive, Queen Anne-style pad feet (Hornor 1935, pl. 375; Sack 4, p. 887), and the legs of one at Winterthur have the same almost black finish (Downs 1952, fig. 75). The pad foot with raised tongue seen on the MMA example is more frequently found on Philadelphia side chairs (e.g., cat. nos. 35–37).

PROVENANCE: The chair descended in the McIlvaine family of Philadelphia until its purchase by the MMA. According to family tradition, reinforced by inscriptions (q.v.) on the rear seat rail, the needlework cover then on the chair had been worked by Anne, daughter of Caleb Emerson (died 1748) of Philadelphia. Anne married William McIlvaine (1722–1770), who emigrated from Scotland in 1745 and who later lived at Fairview, an estate near Bristol, Bucks County, Pennsylvania. Hornor (1935, p. 155) quotes what is presumably the 1770 inventory of Fairview, which lists "One Easy Chair, Eight others, and Two Stools," in the "Red Room"—a designation that referred to the room's dominant fabric color. Assuming cat. no. 77 to be the "One Easy Chair," its present red damask covering probably closely resembles the original. The chair was put on

76 See also p. 342

loan to the MMA in 1936 by Mrs. Henry van Kleeck Gilmore (Maria McIlvaine). In 1965, the Museum bought it from Francis Shippen McIlvaine, Mrs. Gilmore's brother.

CONSTRUCTION: The crest rail is tenoned to the rear stiles. The wing crestings are half-lapped over the rear stiles and nailed with triple roseheads. The rear stiles, supported against the wedge-shaped tops of the rear legs, are slotted into the side seat rails. The edges of the rectangular rear legs are chamfered. The front and side seat rails are horizontally laid planks, their inner surfaces conforming in shape to the outer ones. The front rail is lapped over and triple pegged to the side rails; the side rails are tenoned through the rear legs. Dovetail-shaped extensions of the front legs slot into the front seat rail. The vertical plank that forms the rear seat rail is double pegged. Each inner armrest board is dovetailed to the arm support, to which the outer armrest cone is nailed.

CONDITION: The legs have an opaque black finish, much worn, which may originally have been intended to simulate mahogany. The feet have brass receptacles for casters. In 1971, when the chair was stripped to the frame, its eighteenth-century floral embroidery covering (ill. *Antiques* 91 [April 1967], p. 481; *MMAB* n.s. 3 [January 1945], p. 124), ascribed to Anne Emerson, the chair's first owner, was found to have originally fitted not this chair frame but one with a narrower, higher back. Probably of English origin, it had been cut and pieced to fit. The stuffing materials were modern. Nail holes and inscriptions on the frame documented three complete reupholsterings and several re-coverings. The chair is illustrated here covered with a reproduction red silk damask.

INSCRIPTIONS: In black ink, on the inside of the back seat rail: *Emerson's Work 1740 / Repaired by E. McIlvaine 1840*. In pencil, directly below: *OK* [Repaired by] *J. Rubonis 1918 /* [Repaired by] *H.C. Rathjen 1933*. In pencil, on the front edge of the front seat rail: *Repaired by H.C. Rathjen 4/4/23 / Local #44 / Lodge 49*. In pencil, on the outside of the left wing stile: *Henry C Rathjen #99 / UIU*. Local #44 is the New York City branch of the Upholsterers, Decorators and Allied Crafts Union. Rathjen was a member in 1937.

DIMENSIONS: H.: overall, 46 (*116.8*), seat, 14⅛ (*35.9*); W.: seat front, 29 (*73.7*), seat back, 23¾ (*60.3*), arms, 35¾ (*90.8*), feet, 27¾ (*70.5*); D.: seat, 23¾ (*60.3*), feet, 27 (*68.6*).

77 See also p. 342

77

WOODS: Primary: walnut. Secondary: walnut (rear seat rail); red oak (rear stiles, right seat rail); ash (arm supports, left seat rail); maple (front seat rail); tulip poplar (arm cones); yellow pine (all other framing members).

REFERENCES: Margaret Jeffery, "Early American Embroidery," *MMAB* n.s. 3 (January 1945), pp. 120–125. James Biddle, "Collecting American art for the Metropolitan: 1961–1966," *Antiques* 91 (April 1967), pp. 480–486; p. 481 (ill.). Heckscher 1971a, pp. 64–65 (ill. frame, stripped, and construction details); idem 1971b, figs. 3, 14, 15, 17.

Rogers Fund, 1965   (65.133)

78. Easy Chair

Philadelphia, 1760–90

EXCEPT FOR ITS FRONT legs, this chair is virtually identical to cat. no. 77. With its leaf-carved knees and claw feet, it fits the description for the most expensive of easy chairs in the 1772 Philadelphia price book: "[Easy Chair frame] with Claw feet & leaves on [the knees]," costing £3-5-0 in mahogany (Weil, p. 183). Chairs with both types of legs—plain and carved—were made concurrently. As early as 1754, John Elliott, cabinetmaker, billed one Edward Shippen for "An Easy Chair frame

Carved Claw and Knee . . . 1-16-0 [and] to Making up Do . . . 1-6-0," a chair that has been identified with one now at the PMA (Hornor 1929, p. 23). On cat. no. 78, the single row of punchwork outlining the knee carving is a rare refinement (see also Hornor 1935, pl. 153; for related knee carving see *Antiques* 82 [November 1962], p. 456). A date in the mid-seventeen-sixties or after is suggested by the lively leafage, here surrounding a cabochon, on the legs of a chair that is otherwise similar to earlier forms.

PROVENANCE: According to a tradition in the donor's family (8/1/63 letter, Mrs. C.F. Dickson to MMA), the chair was acquired in about 1800 by a Benjamin Bullock, wool merchant of Philadelphia. From him it descended to his son Anthony Davis Bullock (born 1824), later a resident of Cincinnati; to his grandson James W. Bullock; to his great-granddaughter Margaret (Mrs. C.F. Dickson).

CONSTRUCTION: The rear legs are rounded in front and chamfered in back. The side seat rails, of one piece with their rear brackets, are lapped over and double pegged to the front rail. The inner surface of the front rail is rabbeted. The frame's construction is otherwise like that at cat. no. 77.

CONDITION: The legs, now a walnut brown in color, have been refinished. The feet have holes for casters. The framing elements are intact except for missing the original upholstery rails just above the side and rear seat rails. A 1936 appraisal describes the chair as "with all original filling and home spun cover, with the exception of the seat, which has been reupholstered three distinct times" (MMA files, along with a photograph sup-

78

porting that description). In 1963, the badly worn gold velvet cover was removed, and the chair was stripped to the frame and reupholstered in the antique red silk damask in which it is shown here. The upholstery approximates the contours of eighteenth-century work but for the flat inner surfaces of the wings and the omission of piping under the ornamental braid bordering the arms and wings.

DIMENSIONS: H.: overall, 46 (116.8), seat, 13¼ (33.7); W.: seat front, 29 (73.7), seat back, 23½ (59.7), arms, 37 (94.), feet, 26 (66.); D.: seat, 24¼ (61.6), feet, 28¼ (71.8).

WOODS: Primary: mahogany. Secondary: walnut (rear stiles, arm supports, seat rails); yellow pine (crest rails, wing supports, armrests); tulip poplar (armrest cones).

REFERENCES: Frances W. Robinson, "Two Centuries of Anglo-American Furniture in Ohio," *Art News* 35 (May 29, 1937), p. 12 (ill. with previous upholstery), p. 13 (attributed to William Savery). *MMAB* n.s. 23 (October 1964), p. 55 (ill.). Heckscher 1971, p. 6 (ill.), p. 12, no. 2; idem 1971b, fig. 4.

Gift of Mrs. C.F. Dickson, 1963   (63.114)

78 See also p. 342

79. Easy Chair

Charleston, South Carolina, 1760–90

THIS MASSIVE CHAIR was long attributed to New York and indeed has many characteristics of the city's cabinet-work: it is large in scale and broad of beam, its arm supports are conical, its seat rails are thick and have rounded front corners. The stiff and flat knee carving is similar to that on well-known New York chairs (e.g., cat. no. 29), as is the squashed-ball-and-claw foot (cat. no. 75). The high-shod, spade-footed rear legs also appear on New York examples (Nutting 2, no. 2055; Downs 1952, figs. 89, 90, where attributed to Philadelphia).

A more compelling case can nevertheless be made for a Charleston, South Carolina, origin for the chair. The unusual arm-support system—a single rounded piece doweled into the top of the side rail—matches that on an easy

79 See also p. 342

79

chair of similar design and with southern secondary woods now at Williamsburg (*The Williamsburg Collection of Antique Furnishings*, The Colonial Williamsburg Foundation, 1973, p. 120). Further, the rear legs of the MMA example exactly match those on an easy chair that belonged to Daniel Cannon (1726–1802), master builder of Charleston (Rosemary Niner Estes, "Daniel Cannon: A Revolutionary 'Mechanick' in Charleston," *Journal of the Museum of Early Southern Decorative Arts* 9 [May 1983], pp. 10–11, fig. 12). In addition, both chair frames make use of an auxiliary vertical arm support. Finally, another easy chair at MESDA (Helen Comstock, "Southern furniture since 1952," *Antiques* 91 [January 1967], p. 108), which has been attributed to Charleston, is related to cat. no. 79 by its knee carving.

PROVENANCE: Ex coll.: George S. Palmer, New London, Connecticut.

CONSTRUCTION: The crest rail is tenoned into the rear stiles. The wing crestings, half lapped over and nailed to the stiles, are tenoned to the wing supports, which continue through the side seat rails as large, dovetail-shaped tenons. The inner and outer surfaces of the heavy seat rails conform in shape. The rails are tenoned into the legs. The rear stiles, their tapered bottoms slotted into the side rails, are supported against the wedge-shaped tops of the square rear legs. There are large quarter-round glue blocks. The arm supports are single rounded pieces slightly tapered and doweled into the side rails. The brackets nailed to the rear legs and the front knee brackets are of similar shape. On the rear legs the ankles are rounded.

CONDITION: The legs have a brown color and a very dark old finish. Their nineteenth-century casters were removed at the MMA. The knee brackets of the right front leg are old replacements, as are the outer tips of the knee brackets of the left front leg. The left rear leg's juncture with the rails has been repaired. The frame is chewed from repeated upholsterings (see ill., frame). The right armrest has been replaced; the right rear glue block is new. No original stuffing or upholstery material remains. When the Museum acquired the chair, it had been re-covered in floral tapestry-weave material and there was no separate seat cushion. The chair was re-covered at the Museum in 1924 and again in 1962. In 1977 the chair was stripped, reupholstered, and covered in the modern yellow silk-and-cotton damask in which it is illustrated. A loose seat cushion was added. The heavy padding of the inner surface of the wings and arms, the down-filled cushion, and the woven tape sewed over the welting and onto the edges follow the precedent of easy chairs that retain their original stuffing (see cat. no. 72). The front edges of the wing framing, beveled in the Philadelphia manner, require the single-welt upholstery shown here.

DIMENSIONS: H.: overall, 48⅝ (*123.5*), seat, 14¼ (*36.2*); W.: seat front, 30½ (*77.5*), seat back, 27⅜ (*69.5*), arms, 34⅛ (*86.7*), feet, 29 (*73.7*); D.: seat, 24¾ (*62.9*), feet, 28 (*71.1*).

WOODS: Primary: mahogany. Secondary: tulip poplar (arm supports, glue blocks); red bay, or avocado (seat rails); bald cypress (all other framing elements).

REFERENCES: Nutting 2, no. 2060.

John Stewart Kennedy Fund, 1918　　　　(18.110.25)

6 Settees and Sofas

Although there is no clear demarcation between these two forms, settees are generally defined as seats with high backs and low arms for holding two or more persons, whereas the large and deep sofas that supplanted them were made for reclining. The settees referred to in the early seventeen-thirties in Philadelphia and in the late forties in New York were doubtless of the fully upholstered type which, though extremely rare, is well represented in the collection. During the third quarter of the century, upholstered settees were superseded by sofas, characteristically with a bold serpentine back—the so-called camel back—sweeping into rolled arms. The term "sofa" was first used in Philadelphia in the mid-seventeen-fifties, at which time the word "settee" began to refer only to the chairback type favored by Boston makers: not upholstered on the back or arms and having double splats that cause it to resemble two armchairs joined together. None of that type is at the Museum. Settees and sofas, sometimes made en suite with other chairs and tables, sometimes made in pairs, were almost exclusively parlor furniture. Contemporary descriptions suggest that they were usually placed not up against the wall, as might be expected, but out in the room, close by the fireplace. Both settees and sofas can lay claim to being the most costly of furniture forms after richly draped bedsteads. Prior to mid-century, leather and worsted coverings predominated, but silk damasks, often crimson in color and highlighted at the edges with brass nails, were later favored. None of the Museum's examples retains any of its original upholstery work.

80. Settee

Philadelphia, 1740–60

PROBABLY THE EARLIEST American example of the form, this upholstered settee is the only Philadelphia one known with cabriole legs and trifid-pad feet, and the only one entirely in the style of Philadelphia Queen Anne seating furniture. Stylistically, it is an amalgam of two types of cabriole-leg English settees that were in fashion in around 1715. The upholstered back and arms are adapted from fully upholstered settees (*DEF* 3, p. 87, figs. 13, 14), while the exposed wooden front seat rail and removable slip seat are like those on chair-back settees (ibid., pp. 91–92; figs. 23–26).

Structurally, the settee is a combination of two types of local chairs. The high upholstered back and the uphol-

stered C-scroll armrests are like those of Philadelphia easy chairs (e.g., cat. no. 76); the slip seat, the front legs doweled into thick horizontal seat rails, the through tenons of the side rails, and the rear stump legs are in the classic manner of the Philadelphia Queen Anne chair (e.g., cat. no. 38). The shell-carved knees and trifid feet, while typical Philadelphia motifs, are unusual enough in execution to distinguish the hand of the maker. The knees and knee brackets are flanked by raised double-beaded edges with scrolled lower ends, the lobes on the shell are separated by narrow grooves, and the surface of the three-toed feet is an unbroken curve. The only other pieces of Philadelphia seating furniture that look to be by the same hand are, as this is, objects with Logan family provenance: an easy chair (Hornor 1935, pl. 311) and two sets of side chairs (ibid., pls. 307, 310), one with shells on the knees that match those of the settee. The Logan furni-

80 See also p. 342

ture looks to be the work of an English craftsman so recently arrived in America that he had not yet entirely adjusted his style to the local taste.

PROVENANCE: Ex coll.: Louis Guerineau Myers, New York City. Myers purchased the settee in about 1924 from Lloyd M. Smith, a descendant of James Logan (1674–1751), colonial statesman and scholar. For a number of years the settee had been on exhibition at Stenton, Logan's country house, near Philadelphia, now the property of the Pennsylvania Society of Colonial Dames. Myers believed that it had been made for use in that house, and it has been widely published as such. That belief, while attractive, is probably incorrect. The inventory of Stenton, taken shortly after Logan's death in 1751, makes no mention of a settee. Moreover, Stenton was constructed between 1728 and 1734, well before the settee, which is in the fully developed Philadelphia Queen Anne style of the 1740s, could have been made. Two of Logan's five children are known to have owned settees, and this must have been made for one of them. William (1718–1776), the eldest, had in the parlor of his Second Street house at his death a "Walnut Settee" valued at £2 (Tolles, p. 401). Hannah (1719–1761), the second child, married John Smith (1722–1771) in 1748. The inventory (copy in MMA files) taken at John's death included a "Settee cover'd wᵗʰ Damask 110 [shillings]" in the parlor. It is this latter, more costly, settee that can be identified with cat. no. 80. It presumably descended to John Smith (1761–1803) of Green Hill; to John Jay Smith (born 1789) of Ivy Lodge; to Horace John Smith; to Albanus Longstreth Smith (born 1859), who used it in his rooms while a student at Haverford College (Mrs. Drayton M. Smith, 5/10/65 letter, MMA files). Albanus, his son Lloyd Muller Smith, and his grandson Drayton Muller Smith are pictured together on the settee in a photograph (copy, MMA files) taken in about 1923 at Ivy Cottage, 45 East Penn Street, Germantown, Pennsylvania.

CONSTRUCTION: The crest rail, scalloped on its upper edge, is double pegged to the side stiles, which are pieced to form rounded ears. The medial stile is pegged to the crest rail. All three stiles continue as square rear legs with chamfered edges. The rear seat rail, cut away inside to receive the middle leg, is tenoned to the outer legs. The front and side seat rails, thick horizontal boards with straight inner edges, form the balloon seat. The side rails are double pegged to the front rail and, with their rear brackets, are tenoned through the rear legs. The front corner legs continue as large dowels through the seat rails; the middle front leg is tenoned through the front rail. The knee brackets are secured with roseheads. The slip-seat frame has a dovetailed medial brace. The armrests are tenoned through the stiles.

CONDITION: The legs and seat rail have a mellow walnut brown color. The frame has been entirely reupholstered, and is illustrated here with a modern pumpkin yellow wool moreen with floral embossing, chosen because of its similarity to tiny pieces of the original wool covering found under two surviving roseheads. The middle front leg, the applied rim on the front seat rail, a small part of the side knee bracket of the right leg, and the medial brace on the slip-seat frame are replacements. The knee of the replaced middle leg looks to have been inaccurately restored. Obviously copied from the corner legs, it has a central bulge rather than following the straight line of the rail in the normal manner (e.g., cat. nos. 81, 83). There are old breaks

in the right front and middle rear legs. Early photographs of the settee (Wallace, p. 62) when it was covered with leatherette and had springs in the slip seat show it with the original seat rim, but without the middle leg. Later photographs (MMA files; Nutting I, pl. 1692) show it re-covered and without the rim. In 1958, the leg and the rim were replaced and the settee covered with antique Italian damask. In 1978, when the piece was covered with its present fabric, the springs were removed and the slip-seat frame restored.

INSCRIPTIONS: In chalk, on the back of the crest rail: a large circular mark. In pencil script (20th-century), on the top of the front seat rail: *N 3*.

DIMENSIONS: H.: overall, 45¾ (*116.2*), seat, 14⅛ (*35.9*); W.: crest, 52½ (*133.4*), seat, 56½ (*143.5*), arms, 62 (*157.5*), feet, 55¼ (*140.3*); D.: seat, 21½ (*54.6*), feet, 26¼ (*66.7*).

WOODS: Primary: walnut. Secondary: walnut, possibly English (rear seat rail); yellow pine (crest rail, arms, arm supports, slip-seat frame).

REFERENCES: Clarence W. Brazer, "Early Pennsylvania Craftsmen: Thomas Tufft 'Joyner,'" *Antiques* 13 (March 1928), pp. 200–205; fig. 9. Nutting I, pl. 1692. Myers, fig. 7; pp. 216–17. Hornor 1935, pp. 225–226. Halsey and Cornelius, fig. 53. Powel, p. 208. Davidson 1967, fig. 219. Bishop, fig. 125.

Rogers Fund, 1925 (25.115.1)

81. Settee

New York City, 1757–60
Joseph Cox (active 1756–73)

THE SETTEE ONCE BORE the trade card of Joseph Cox of Dock Street, New York, who was first heard of in America on July 19, 1756, in an advertisement in the *New-York Mercury*: "Joseph Cox, Upholsterer, from London, now living in . . . Hanover Square; Makes beds, Window Curtains, chairs, & c. and every other article in the upholstery way, in the neatest and most genteel manner" (Gottesman, p. 135).

An advertisement dated May 9, 1757, records that "Joseph Cox, upholsterer, is removed from the house he formerly lived in, to that wherein Garret Noel [a leading New York publisher and print dealer] formerly lived, in Dock-Street." Sometime during his sojourn in Dock Street, Cox ordered a printed trade card. Three years later, on May 5 and May 12, 1760, Cox announced that he had "removed his shop from The Royal Bed in Dock St. to the House opposite Mrs. Mary Derham's, Milliner, in Wall Street." In 1761, the year he was married, he became a Freeman of the City of New York (Ralston 1932, p. 208). Between 1765 and 1773 he advertised frequently; in a New York newspaper of July 13, 1767, his shop's name had been changed to "The Royal Bed and Star." Cox was an importer, among other activities. On July 29, 1765, he offered a wide selection of upholstery materials and fabrics "Just imported in the Roebuck, Capt. Smith, from London, and to be sold by Joseph Cox Upholsterer At the Royal Bed in Wall Street" (*New-York Mercury*). In later listings, 1771 to 1773, "Joseph Cox, Upholsterer, Cabinet and Chair Maker from London" was making all sorts of furniture, now including tables and case pieces (Gottesman, p. 136). Cox is last heard of in 1775, a witness to the will of one John Thurman (Ralston 1932, p. 208).

Of the three known New York upholstered cabriole-leg settees, cat. no. 81 appears to be the earliest. Its high, scallop-crested back, like that on a Philadelphia example (cat. no. 80), is in the Queen Anne tradition, whereas the others, from the Verplanck (cat. no. 82) and Beekman (Comstock, fig. 207) families, have lower backs with straight crest rails. All three have C-scroll arms and claw-and-ball feet, and the Beekman one and cat. no. 81 each have five legs, but because on every one of the three settees the legs are handled in a distinct manner, the settees look to be from three different shops. The legs of cat.

no. 81, though not identical to those on any other known New York piece, exhibit numerous local features. The uninterrupted continuation of the inner edge of the leg as the back talon of the claw is found on many New York chairs (e.g., cat. no. 27); the leaf carving on the knee compares with that on some others (e.g., Kirk 1972, figs. 140, 149); and the softly rounded talons, without articulated knuckles, are not unlike those on still others (ibid., figs. 129, 152).

Because Cox's trade card with the Dock Street address was once attached to the original webbing of cat. no. 81, the settee must have been made between 1757 and 1760—that is, during his occupancy of that site. By the claim on his card that he made "Chairs of all Sorts, in the newest Fashion," one may infer that Cox made the frames as well as the upholstery. Square rear legs are common in New York work, but not with the back extensions found on this settee. Their presence is a further implication that Cox made the frame himself, while he was still a newcomer to America and before he had fully assimilated the New York style.

81 See also p. 337

PROVENANCE: Ex coll.: Mrs. John J. Riker, New York City. The donor purchased the settee in about 1910 from an upholsterer named Giannini, in East 27 Street, New York City.

CONSTRUCTION: According to notes made when the framework was examined in 1961: The stiles, half-lapped over the crest rail at the top and pieced to form projecting ears, meet the square back legs at angled butt joints. On the rear legs, the edges are chamfered below the vertical brackets screwed to their fronts; the feet end in extended square pads. A medial back brace is pegged to the crest and upholstery rails, the latter with a pine board affixed at the bottom. The arm supports are double pegged to the side seat rails; the seat rails are tenoned into the corner legs; the central leg is tenoned into the front rail. The knee brackets are screwed to the legs.

CONDITION: The legs are a mellow walnut brown in color. Nailed to the front seat rail behind the middle leg is the stump of a poplar board, which apparently was added as a brace. A medial seat brace let into the tops of the front and rear seat rails is a modern replacement. The carved knee brackets of the left front leg and the side bracket of the right one appear to be old replacements. Upholsterer's rails have been added just above the side rails, and the top of the right rear leg has been patched where it meets the rails. The original stuffing and what may have been the original red covering remained until stripped off by the upholsterer Giannini early in this century. When the settee came to the MMA, it was again stripped to the frame, restuffed to show to advantage the scalloping of the crest rail, and covered in damask (Ralston 1932, fig. 1). In 1945, it was re-covered in leather. In 1961, the frame was restuffed and finished with the antique golden brown silk damask in which it is here illustrated.

INSCRIPTIONS: On a printed label once pasted onto the webbing and hessian of the back and then cut out and mounted separately: *Joseph Cox, Upholsterer, | from London, | At the Sign of |The Royal-Bed, | In Dock-Street, near Countjies's-Market, New York; | Makes all Sorts of Beds, both for Sea and Land; | likewise, Window Curtains, Mattresses, Easy|Chairs, Sophies, French Chairs, and Chairs of all Sorts,|in the newest Fashion.* The label (acc. no. 32.51.2) was given to the Museum with the settee. The donor (7/15/32 letter, MMA files) recalled its discovery: "In taking off the old torn tapestry which I think was red, [the upholsterer] tore that label off which he had found inside on the burlap . . . the sign was cut off or torn off by mistake, not soaked off . . . I had it framed as it was given to me." (See p. 366 for photograph.)

DIMENSIONS: H.: overall, 45¼ (*114.9*), seat, 16⅜ (*41.6*); W.: crest, 59 (*149.9*), arms, 63½ (*161.3*), seat, 57⅛ (*145.1*), feet, 58⅛ (*147.6*); D.: seat, 22 (*55.9*), feet, 27½ (*69.9*).

WOODS: Primary: mahogany. Secondary: red oak (seat rails, medial back brace, top part of rear upholstery rail); cherry (crest rail, stiles, arms); pine (bottom part of rear upholstery rail).

REFERENCES: Ralston 1932, figs. 1, 2. *The Connoisseur* 90 (November 1932), pp. 352, 353. *Antiques* 23 (April 1933), pp. 123, 124; figs. 1, 2. Davidson 1967, fig. 289.

Gift of Mrs. John J. Riker, 1932 (32.51.1)

82. Settee

New York, 1760–90

THE FLAT, SHIELDLIKE knees with shallow, scroll-carved brackets on the settee appear to be unique to the furniture with which this cabriole-leg settee is en suite—a card table (cat. no. 105) and a set of side chairs (cat. no. 24)—all probably made in the early 1760s for Samuel Verplanck's town house in Wall Street (see cat. no. 24, Provenance). The feet, large circular balls with wiry, webless talons, are, however, a distinctive New York type found on a number of other chairs and tables. In the shape of its upholstered back and arms cat. no. 82 follows a type of settee popular in England between about 1715 and 1740 (*DEF* 3, p. 98, fig. 37 and pl. VII). Another New York upholstered settee with cabriole legs (Comstock, fig. 207), now at the Department of State, Washington, D.C., descended from Dr. William Beekman (died 1770) of New York City. It is much smaller than this one and has a middle leg, features that closely follow those of its English prototypes, but it shares the Verplanck settee's straight, low back and C-scrolled arms. What is highly unexpected on cat. no. 82—all the more so on a settee that has the width of a sofa and no middle leg—is the audacious slenderness of its seat rails. Judging from the later insertion of additional seat braces, the audacity was ill advised.

PROVENANCE: See cat. no. 24.

CONSTRUCTION: The unusually thin seat rails (about one inch by three) are double pegged to the legs. Two concave seat braces are dovetailed into the bottoms of the front and rear seat rails and toenailed in place. On the elegantly shaped rear legs, the vertical side brackets are carved with scrolls like those of the front legs. The vertical front supports of the armrests are double pegged to the side seat rails. According to notes made when the framework was examined in 1965, the medial brace centered in the back is double pegged to the crest and rear seat rails.

CONDITION: The legs have a warm reddish brown color. The corner glue blocks are replacements. Three seat braces of white pine nailed to the front and rear seat rails are old additions. In 1940, when the settee was stripped to the frame, two of the carved brackets of the front legs were replaced and the left rear foot was patched. The frame was then reupholstered, and covered with eighteenth-century pumpkin-colored wool damask that had descended in the Verplanck family. In 1965, the sofa was again reupholstered and covered with a modern reproduction of the Verplanck fabric, in which it is here illustrated.

DIMENSIONS: H: overall, 40½ (*102.9*), seat, 16¼ (*41.3*); W.: crest, 70 (*177.8*), seat, 69⅞ (*177.2*), arms, 75 (*190.5*), feet, 73¼ (*186.1*); D.: seat, 23½ (*59.7*), feet, 27¾ (*70.5*).

WOODS: Primary: walnut. Secondary: white pine (arms, glue blocks); white oak (all other framing members).

82

REFERENCES: Downs 1941a, p. 221 (ill.). *The Connoisseur* 109 (June 1942), p. 154.

Gift of James De Lancey Verplanck and John Bayard Rodgers Verplanck, 1939   (39.184.1, 2)

83.   Settee

Boston, 1760–90

A PHILADELPHIA attribution, no doubt inspired in part by a supposed history of ownership there, was first advanced for the settee (Ralston 1931, p. 34); a New York origin was next suggested (Downs 1949, pl. 9). In 1952, a settee at Winterthur identical to this one in size, materials, and construction (its secondary woods characteristic of New England; its back and arm construction like that of Massachusetts easy chairs; its carved knees and claw feet with raked-back talons in the Boston manner) was

correctly identified as of Massachusetts, probably Boston, origin (Downs 1952, no. 270). The two matching settees, the only known fully upholstered Massachusetts examples having cabriole legs, are part of a small group of Boston pieces with asymmetrical C-scroll and foliate knee carving (Yehia, pp. 201–206). The carved motif was apparently adopted directly from a set of English chairs that were owned in Boston in the eighteenth century by William Phillips (MFA 1975, no. 53).

Two sets of Boston-made chairs, one set owned first by Governor Burnet and later by Governor Belcher (ibid., no. 54), the other said to have belonged to Elias Hasket Derby (Yehia, fig. 147), resemble the Phillips set except in proportion and secondary woods. The Derby family chairs and the pair of settees may have been made en suite, since the same hand is discernible in the identical carving of their legs. The asymmetrical knee motif also appears occasionally on chairs of other types (Downs 1952, no. 151) and on card tables (Biddle no. 74; *Antiques*

124 [September 1983], inside front cover) made in Boston. The consistency in the manner of construction and carving in this stylish group of pieces is convincing evidence that the furniture is all the product of the same, as yet anonymous shop.

PROVENANCE: Ex coll.: George Coe Graves, Osterville, Massachusetts. Graves purchased the settee in 1926 from Charles Woolsey Lyon, Inc., New York City. Lyon claimed that it was "from the Prevost family and once belonged to Major General Andrew Prevost of Pre-Revolutionary fame. The present family said it had been bought in 1763 in Philadelphia, near where he lived until the Revolution. It is of the Wm. Savery type of carving and is as far as we know the only such love seat" (11/1/26 bill of sale, MMA files). The censuses of 1810 and 1820 list an Andrew M. Prevost in Philadelphia County, but not those of 1790 and 1800. Lyon later claimed that he had bought the settee and its mate from the Misses Prevost, who in 1931 were residing in New York City (notes in Winterthur files of a 1960 conversation with Lyon).

CONSTRUCTION: The framework was examined in 1960, with the following findings: The crest rail—arched and serpentined at the top and arched at the bottom—is tenoned into the end stiles, with a projecting round molding conforming in shape to the top and overlapping the stiles applied along its back edge. The end stiles, pieced to form the outward curves of the ears,

continue as square rear legs tapered at the ankles and flared out at the feet. The wing supports are dovetailed and the arm supports are double pegged to the side rails. Tenoned into the crest rail and into the upholstery rail fixed above the rear seat rail is a central brace. The seat rails are tenoned into the corner legs, the joints reinforced with quadruple-nailed triangular glue blocks. The middle legs are tenoned into the seat rails, the rear one pegged, the front one double pegged. Two concave medial braces are dovetailed from below into the front and rear seat rails. The carved brackets are doubled screwed to the knees.

CONDITION: The front legs are a dark reddish brown in color; the rear legs are stained to match. The glue blocks have been renailed and the rear middle leg reset. The settee, which was covered in green damask when the MMA acquired it, was stripped to the frame in 1960, reupholstered, and covered with the antique red silk damask in which it is here illustrated. Except for thick padding on the outer sides of the arms, the contouring of the upholstery approximates eighteenth-century practice.

DIMENSIONS: H.: overall, 36⅜ (92.4), seat, 16⅜ (41.6); W.: crest, 55½ (141.), seat, 54½ (138.4), arms, 57½ (146.1), feet, 56 (142.2); D.: seat, 22⅝ (57.5), feet, 26 (66.).

WOODS: Primary: mahogany. Secondary: maple (rear legs and stiles, seat rails, rear upholstery rail, medial seat braces, arms); cedar (applied crest-rail strip, arm and wing supports, wing-

83 See also p. 335

crest rails, central brace); birch (crest rail); white pine (glue blocks).

REFERENCES: Ralston 1931, fig. 4. Halsey and Cornelius, pl. 72. Rogers, fig. 38. Downs 1949, pl. 8; idem 1952, no. 270 (ill. of the settee's mate). Margon 1954, no. 151 (ill. and measured drawings). Comstock, pl. 346. Davidson 1967, fig. 308. Bishop, fig. 218. Yehia, pp. 201–206 (related knee carving of the group discussed). MMA 1976, no. 27.

The Sylmaris Collection, Gift of George Coe Graves, 1930 (30.120.59)

84. Sofa

Philadelphia, 1760–90

THE CAMEL BACK—its crest forming a great central serpentine hump—was the most common type of sofa made in America in the second half of the eighteenth century. Several are known from Newport and New York as well as from the smaller centers, but the form had its greatest popularity in Philadelphia. On the numerous surviving examples from that city the upholstered part of the frame is distinguished by the forward slope of the rolled arms. On some of the more ambitiously conceived examples, pointed tips break the serpentine curve of the back on either side of the central hump (e.g., Downs 1952, no. 272). A few cabriole-leg sofas are known, including one made in 1783 by Thomas Tufft (Hornor 1935, pl. 231) and a

matching one signed by the upholsterer John Linton (Downs 1952, no. 273). The preferred treatment of sofas in Philadelphia, however, was the straight Marlborough leg, either molded or, as here, with cuffs. Chippendale, in his *Director* (1762 edition, pls. XXIX, XXX), illustrated Marlborough-leg sofas with serpentine backs and curved arms, but they provide no obvious inspiration for the Philadelphia version. The 1772 Philadelphia book of prices described the standard options for mahogany "Soffas Marlborough Feet":

Soffas plain feet & rails without Casters 4-10-0
Ditto with bases and brackets 5-0-0
Ditto with a fret on the Feet 7-10-0
Ditto with a fret on feet & rails and carved mouldings 10-0-0.
(Weil, p.184)

Cat. no. 84, with its plain feet, rails, bases (molded cuffs), and original casters, would have cost about £5 when new. In the valleys on either side of its stately hump is a slight flatness, as though pointed tips were missing. They were never present. The shape of its modern upholstery notwithstanding, the sofa's graceful outstretched arms have the inviting elegance of the best of these massive forms. A number of similar sofas exist. Two are at Winterthur (Downs 1952, no. 274, and acc. no. 60.1001); one is at Dearborn (Campbell, p. 14; *Antiques* 96 [December 1969], p. 845); and another is at Bayou Bend (Warren, no. 96, where incorrectly identified as Hornor, pl. 202). One at the PMA has points on its crest rail (PMA

84

1976, no. 88). The grandest of these Philadelphia sofas is that of the Chew family, thought to have been made for Governor John Penn by Thomas Affleck (Hornor 1935, pl. 258). In addition to points on its crest, the sofa has a fret on its feet and rails, and carved moldings, just as offered in the price book.

PROVENANCE: Ex coll.: Harry G. Haskell, Wilmington, Delaware. The sofa appeared in the trade several times before being purchased by the MMA from John S. Walton, Inc., New York City.

CONSTRUCTION: Judging from what can be determined through the upholstery, the frame is constructed in four separate units, in the manner of cat. no. 85. Screws in the circular ends of the crest rail secure the back unit to the arms; screws near the tops of the front corner legs secure the arms to the seat frame. The seat rails are the thickness of the legs, into which they are tenoned. There are three equally spaced concave seat braces. The legs are square. On the front ones, the molded cuffs are applied, the front and back pieces overlapping the sides. The rear legs splay back dramatically. The medial stretchers are dovetailed to the stretchers that are tenoned into the front and rear legs.

CONDITION: The legs and stretchers have a dark reddish brown color. The feet originally had casters, and large circular plugs now fill the holes that once housed them. The middle rear leg is patched at the back. The medial stretchers have been reset. The sofa frame has been entirely reupholstered. It was illustrated in 1935 and 1952 covered in a dark velvet, possibly over the original stuffing. By 1954 it had been reupholstered, and covered with a silk damask similar to the present fabric, which was put on before 1972. As shown here finished in a modern pale yellow silk damask, the upholstery reflects mid-twentieth-century taste rather than eighteenth-century upholstery practice. On the arms, the flat inner and front surfaces meet at a sharp edge with a tight little welt. Originally, the inner side would probably have been more heavily padded and rounded where it met the flat front, the seams either covered with ornamental tape or outlined with brass nails. The modern use of springs has resulted in the taut and bowed shape of the seat. The sharp edge where the fabric is stretched over the front rail would originally have been softened by an upholsterer's roll.

DIMENSIONS: H.: overall, 39¼ (99.7), seat, 13⅞ (35.2); W.: crest, 89¼ (226.7), seat, 82 (208.3), arms, 98 (248.9), feet, 82⅝ (209.9); D.: seat, 28¼ (71.8), feet, 33½ (85.1).

WOODS: Primary: mahogany. Secondary (where examined): walnut (seat rails); yellow pine (crest rail, seat braces).

REFERENCES: Hornor 1935, pp. 152, 182; pl. 202. *Antiques* 62 (September 1952), p. 193; ibid. 65 (February 1954), p. 94; ibid. 101 (March 1972), p. 414. MMA 1975, p. 22.

Purchase, Gift of Mrs. Louis Guerineau Myers, in memory of her husband, by exchange, 1972   (1972.55)

85. Sofa

Probably Philadelphia, 1760–90

THIS SOFA EXHIBITS the classic Philadelphia camel-back form. The serpentine curve is particularly graceful and the scrolled arms have a pronounced forward slant, though they lack the bold outward thrust seen at cat. no. 84. The birch and maple found in the frame are woods commonly used in New England, but the presence of yellow pine and tulip poplar and the sofa's Philadelphia ownership support an attribution to that city. On Philadelphia sofas, straight legs are normally either plain with cuffs (cat. no. 84) or tapered and molded; fluting is highly unusual. The widely spaced flutes found here are similar to those of a Philadelphia card table in the Karolik Collection (Hipkiss, no. 61). On the frame of cat. no. 85 the back is made as an individual unit—normal practice on Philadelphia sofas—but the separate arm units are less common. Also unusual is the wood finished up to the wedge-shaped tops of the rear legs, evidence that the back unit was to be completely upholstered before being slotted and screwed into place. Photographs of a sofa of identical shape and construction, with its original upholstery, document how cat. no. 85 would have looked in its first cover (ill., Heckscher 1985).

PROVENANCE: Ex coll.: Mr. and Mrs. J. Carl De La Cour, Jr., Rochester, New York. According to the donors, the sofa "was inherited from Mr. De La Cour's family in Philadelphia" (9/19/60 letter, MMA files).

CONSTRUCTION: The frame is made in four separate units: the seat frame and legs, the back, and each of the arms. On the seat frame, the concave medial brace is let, and the central front leg is tenoned, into the seat rails, which are pegged to the corner legs. The rear seat rails are tenoned to the middle rear leg. The transverse and rear stretchers are pegged to the legs. The front stretchers are tenoned into the medial stretcher and dovetailed into the side ones. The outer sides of the front legs are fluted. The wedge-shaped tops of the rear legs are rounded in back. The inner edges of all the legs are chamfered. On the back unit, the bottom rail is tenoned into the stiles; the stiles, into the crest rail; the medial brace, into the rails. The stiles rest against the tops of the rear legs, attached with large screws. Smaller screws through the rounded ends of the crest rail secure the back to the arms. On the arm units, vertical supports are nailed to the rounded armrests. Large, boltlike screws through the front legs and side seat rails secure the arm units to the seat frame.

CONDITION: The legs, much scuffed, are a fine reddish brown in color. The top of the middle rear leg is an old replacement, as probably are the middle and front stretchers. In 1973, when the frame was stripped of its later upholstery, the left rear stretcher and the corner braces let into the seat rails were replaced; upholstery-tack damage to the tops of the rear legs was repaired; and the original method of screwing together the four framing units was restored. The frame exhibits no evidence of ornamental brass nails on either arms or seat rails. The feet have holes for casters. The sofa is illustrated here without upholstery.

DIMENSIONS: H.: overall, 39¾ (*101.*), seat, 14⅜ (*36.5*); W.: crest, 87 (*221.*), arms, 88¼ (*224.2*), feet, 78 (*198.1*); D.: seat, 26⅞ (*68.3*), feet, 30½ (*77.5*).

WOODS: Primary: mahogany. Secondary: yellow pine (back framework); birch (seat rails, medial brace, back arm supports); tulip poplar (arms); maple (front arm supports).

Gift of Mr. and Mrs. J. Carl De La Cour, Jr., 1960   (60.114)

85

7 Cradle and Bedsteads

The cradle and the bedsteads are listed together as sleeping furniture, though the two forms evolved from different traditions. The type of cradle favored in the mid-eighteenth century is in shape a hooded box on short rockers. The finest examples, including the one at the Museum, are leather-covered and brass-nailed in the manner employed on trunks and coffins. A bedstead in eighteenth-century terminology referred to the wooden posts and rails that supported the mattress and hangings. Bedsteads were of two basic types: the low post and the high, or long, post. The simpler of two kinds of high post was faceted and tapered; the other was columnar—an attenuated classical column above the rails and a turned, Marlborough, or cabriole leg below. The collection, except for one folding bedstead on which are combined both low and high posts, consists entirely of the high-post kind and is heavily slanted in favor of somewhat plain examples from New England. Though they are very rare, carved, claw-footed mahogany bedsteads were made in Newport, New York, and Philadelphia, as well as Massachusetts, where the Museum's example originated. Mattresses were supported either by ropes drawn through holes in the rails—a "cord" bed—or by a canvas, or "sacking bottom," laced to pegs in the rails or to canvas strips nailed to the rails. All three types of support are to be found in the collection. The drapery curtains that enclosed the bed and covered up all but the footposts were adjusted by means of ropes through pulleys in the cornices. Miraculously, original scalloped cornices are retained on two bedsteads at the Museum. All the bedsteads are illustrated here without bedding or hangings; one has its original sacking bottom.

86. Cradle

New York City, 1762

THE EARLIEST AMERICAN leather-covered cradles were made in Boston. They have plain hoods with arched tops, and their leather coverings are secured with brass nails arranged in decorative border patterns and, often, forming the parents' initials as well as the date of the cradle's manufacture. Known Boston examples date between 1727 and 1735. A Boston-type cradle was made in 1749 for the children of Robert and Maria Sanders of Albany, New York (Blackburn 1976, no. 35); by the seventeen-sixties, a more graceful version was being made in New York City. Cat. no. 86, one of the two known New York City examples, was made for the Brinckerhoff family in 1762. The other, now at the N-YHS (ill. in Sack 1, p. 67), descended in the Livingston family, presumably made for Robert R. and Mary Livingston, who were married in 1770. The two cradles, identical in size and similar in in-ternal construction, shape, and nailing pattern (only the rockers are different), must be from the same shop. On each, the hood's sides have gracefully shaped front edges that rise to a bow-shaped cresting under the top, and the leather that sheaths the exterior is attached and framed with double rows of closely spaced brass nails that also define the cradle's outline.

American leather-covered cradles follow in the tradition of English travel chests, trunks, and coffins. Their brass-studded coverings nearly duplicate those found on trunks from the seventeenth and eighteenth centuries (*DEF* 2, p. 43). A similar ornamental effect was employed on elaborate coffins—one "covered with black velvett & finish'd with 2 rows best brass nails & 4 pairs of large strong chas'd brass handles gilt" was supplied by Chippendale in 1772 (Gilbert 1978a 1, p. 252; 2, figs. 508, 509). In Rhode Island, in the Providence cabinetmakers' 1757 table of prices (Ott 1965, p. 175), cradles are listed next to sea chests; in Massachusetts, the Hampshire price schedule of 1796 (Fales 1976, p. 286) listed them next to coffins,

86

suggesting a common craft tradition for these specialized containers.

PROVENANCE: Made for Derick (1739–1780) and Rachel Van Ranst (born 1741) Brinckerhoff of New York City, prior to the birth on March 14 of Isaac (1762–1822), the first of their eight children. Thereafter, the cradle descended in the family of the donor (*The Family of Joris Dircksen Brinckerhoff, 1638*, New York: Richard Brinckerhoff, 1887, p. 83).

CONSTRUCTION: The vertically laid headboard and the footboard are dovetailed to the side boards. Vertical battens reinforce the side boards of the hood. The hood's arched top projects slightly in rounded edges. Interior glue blocks at the front corners secure the top to the sides. The rockers, which are screwed to the bottom board from above, are joined by a rectangular stretcher whose upper edges are molded. The top and sides of the cradle are sheathed in wine red leather, with borders of brass nails. There is a separate piece of leather for each surface, except for the long sides, which have three. On them, at the horizontal medial line below the hood and at the angled vertical line near the foot are overlapping seams secured by additional rows of brass nails. The pattern of nails outlining the footboard is identical to that of the headboard. Carrying handles with pierced brass escutcheons are centered in each of the four sides.

CONDITION: The leather covering survives, though cracked, scuffed, brittle, and worn at the edges. On the right side, part of the brass escutcheon plate of the carrying handle is missing. The wood of the interior and underside was painted sometime after the leather was nailed on the outer surfaces. Originally a spring green color, the paint is much darkened. The rockers have a fine thin old finish, now with a dark mahogany red patina. Both side boards are split horizontally at the hood's narrowest point. There is a split in the arched top of the footboard.

INSCRIPTIONS: On the top, formed in brass nails: *D B R*; on the back: *1762*.

DIMENSIONS: H.: overall, 30½ (77.5); W.: hood, 19½ (49.5), base, 14 (35.6), rockers, 27½ (69.9); D.: overall, 46 (116.8), base, 32¾ (83.2).

WOODS: Primary: mahogany (rockers, stretcher). Secondary: white pine.

Gift of Cecilia E. Brinckerhoff, 1924   (24.143)

87. Bedstead

New England, 1740–90

THIS IS A GOOD EXAMPLE of the New England painted maple folding bedstead with six legs and hinged side rails. Made without certain features that could have been had at an additional cost, it is painted red, rather than another, more costly color, and, instead of having bed bolts, it is held together only by the cord that supports the mattress. But for this last feature it matches the description "[For a Bedstead] to turn against the wall, for cord,

87

screwed, painted red without [screw] caps, [£]1-8-0" in the 1792 Hartford table of prices (Lyon, p. 270). Because bedsteads of this type were meant to be furnished with floor-length curtains that met at the front of the canopy, cat. no. 87 was stripped of crewelwork hangings in 1980 and dressed properly with a reproduction blue-and-white check linen. When the bed is open, the curtains are pulled back at either side; when it is closed, the curtains cover the bed entirely, except for the footposts, which project beyond the half-canopy (see Nutting 1, no. 1467). Usually freestanding, folding bedsteads were also sometimes set within presses or bed closets (Abbott Lowell Cummings, *Bed Hangings: A Treatise on Fabrics and Styles in the Curtaining of Beds 1650–1850*, Boston, SPNEA, 1961, p. 6). John Taylor, "Upholsterer . . . from London," must have had something similar to offer when he advertised "turnup bedsteads" in New York City in 1768 (Gottesman, p. 139).

Such bedsteads demonstrate considerable variety in the handling of the legs, the headposts, and the headboard. On cat. no. 87, the square headposts, cut back above the headboard, are a distinctive departure from the common octagonal, pencil-post type. Other folding bedsteads, with high or low headposts and turned or square legs, are at Williamsburg (Greenlaw, nos. 19–21), Deerfield (Fales 1976, no. 199), and Winterthur (Sweeney, p. 29). One of the Williamsburg examples was acquired in Rhode Island, but otherwise these bedsteads are without provenance. Where in New England or how widely throughout it they were made has not yet been determined.

PROVENANCE: Ex coll.: H. Eugene Bolles, Boston.

CONSTRUCTION: The high headposts are square where they meet the headboard and rails; above, their inner surfaces are cut in, forming a smaller square shaft; below, they form octagonal legs. The low footposts are turned, as are the two additional legs. The canopy rails and angled braces are tenoned in place. The bedstead rails are square. The head rail is pegged to the headposts; the foot rail, to the left footpost. The side rails, tenoned to the corner posts and held in place by ropes laced through the rails, are sawed near the headposts in three-fingered knuckle-joint hinges. Behind the hinges, the supplemental legs are tenoned into the rail and pegged. The bed folds upward on the hinges when the bedstead closes.

CONDITION: The bedstead retains its original reddish stain finish. The headposts have been cut down five and a half inches and new mortices inserted for the canopy frame and its angled braces. There are splits in the right footpost. The bed ropes and the thin board linking the supplemental legs are modern. The bedstead is illustrated unfurnished.

INSCRIPTIONS: Incised, on the corner posts and adjacent side rails at their junctures, clockwise, from the left foot: *I* through *IIII*.

DIMENSIONS: H.: overall, 77½ (*196.9*), rails, 18 (*45.7*); W.: rails, 52¾ (*134.*), feet, 51¼ (*130.2*); D.: rails, 76 (*193.*), feet, 74½ (*189.2*).

WOODS: Primary and secondary: maple.

REFERENCES: Halsey and Tower, pl. IV, opp. p. 35 (ill. in crewelwork hangings). Ormsbee, no. 264 (line drawing). Halsey and Cornelius, fig. 47.

Gift of Mrs. Russell Sage, 1909   (10.125.335)

88. Bedstead

Southern New England, 1760–1800

OCTAGONAL BEDPOSTS, today popularly called "pencil posts," were perhaps the most common type used on eighteenth-century American bedsteads; requiring only the chamfering of the edges of a square post, they were also the simplest to make. Most examples, of maple and white pine, woods indigenous to New England, originate in that region. On cat. no. 88, painted blue green, the use of poplar for the posts and rails implies a more southerly origin, perhaps in Connecticut or New York state. A similar bedstead, at Williamsburg (Greenlaw, no. 15), is painted red, and has posts of cottonwood, a kind of poplar also found in the eastern states. Although of a modest

design, the MMA bedstead is not without optional features. In Connecticut, in the 1792 Hartford table of prices (Lyon, p. 269), additional charges are specified for bedsteads that instead of being held together solely by cords (see cat. no. 87) are secured with screws—bed bolts—and are painted a color other than the standard red, both "extras" to be found on cat. no. 88.

PROVENANCE: Ex coll.: Mrs. J. Insley Blair, Tuxedo Park, New York; Mrs. Screven Lorillard, Far Hills, New Jersey. Mrs. Blair purchased the bedstead from Collings and Collings, New York City, in 1919.

CONSTRUCTION: The four pencil posts are identical. Square where they meet the rails, they are tapered and octagonal above and straight and octagonal below. The headboard is slotted into the headposts. The head and foot rails are cut out to receive the side rails. All the rails are higher than they are wide. At their outer edges, they are molded in quarter rounds; at their inner upper edges, scratch-beaded; at their inner lower edges, beveled. The rails are tenoned into the posts and secured by bed bolts, which are screwed into nuts inserted into them from outside slots. Holes were drilled through channels on the rails to receive the bed ropes.

CONDITION: The original blue green painted finish is well preserved. The tester is missing, and both posts on the left have lost nearly an inch at the top. The rope holes in the rails have been plugged. The bed bolts are modern. The bedstead is illustrated unfurnished.

INSCRIPTIONS: Incised, on the posts and adjacent rails at their junctures, clockwise, from the right foot: *I* through *III*.

DIMENSIONS: H.: overall, 81 (*205.7*), rails, 18 (*45.7*); W.: rails, 52⅞ (*134.3*); D.: rails, 77 (*195.6*).

WOODS: tulip poplar (posts, rails); white pine (headboard).

Gift of Mrs. Screven Lorillard, 1953   (53.179.4)

88

89. Bedstead

New York, 1760–90

THIS BEDSTEAD and a mahogany one at Williamsburg (acc. no. 1960-901) have posts and headboards of identical design. Cat. no. 89 still has window cornices that match its exuberantly scalloped and decorated cornice, the latter a rare survivor that illustrates how the American bedstead of the second half of the eighteenth century looked before being draped. But for the cornice the simple painted frame would have been almost entirely covered by its hangings. The pulleys in the tester indicate that the bedstead was intended to have what Chippendale's *Director* described as "drapery curtains" (1762 edition, pl. XLVIII)—that is, curtains drawn up in draped forms next to the posts by means of lines over pulleys (ibid., pls. XLII, XLIV).

The vignettes painted on the cornices may have been inspired by printed sources: the scene on the right side, showing a hunter on horseback with a pack of hounds, is similar to one, copied almost exactly from an English hunting print, on an overmantel panel in a Franklin, Massachusetts, house (Nina Fletcher Little, *American Decorative Wall Painting, 1700–1850*, New York, E. P. Dutton & Co., 1972, figs. 31, 32). The painter of cat. no. 89's cornice was not always successful in fitting the subject matter he was borrowing into the available space, for many of the vignettes have been arbitrarily cut off by the scallops. Near the center of the cornice board at the foot, for example, only the hindquarters of a dog are included, but the slopping of the painted decoration over the scalloped edge proves that the vignette is complete as executed.

Auction advertisements in American newspapers of the mid-eighteenth century repeatedly offer sets of window curtains—always for two windows—en suite with bed hangings. Occasionally, there is specific mention of matching sets of bed and window valances or cornices: In Boston, in 1746, "A fashionable crimson Damask Furniture with Counterpain and two Sets of Window Curtains, and Vallans of the same Damask" (Dow, p. 111); in New York City, in 1769, the carver Jacob Minshall offered for sale "Bed and Window Cornicing" (Gottesman, p. 128). On cat. no. 89, the woods are those found in the middle states; the cornice decoration may be a continuation of the Hudson River valley tradition of painting in grisaille. This bedstead with its en suite window cornices is the only known existing testament of the once common practice of matching the bedroom window treatment to that of its bedstead.

PROVENANCE: Ex coll.: Mrs. J. Insley Blair, Tuxedo Park, New York.

89

CONSTRUCTION: All four turned posts are identical. On each, where the rails are tenoned into the posts, the mortices meet. The headboard is slotted into the headposts. The rectangular rails have ogee-molded outer edges and inner top edges rabbeted (the rabbet edges molded into quarter rounds) to receive turned knobs—seventeen to a side and twelve to an end—to which a sacking bottom would be laced (see cat. no. 66). The rails are secured by bed bolts, which are screwed into nuts inserted into the rails from the outside. On the tester, the boards at head and foot are tenoned into the sides; slots at either end of the foot and side boards contain wooden pulley wheels on iron axles for the cords that adjusted the swags of the curtains. Screwed to the tester boards' outer edges are the two-part cornices. The outer part, a board painted in grisaille with bucolic scenes, is scalloped along the top and rounded along the serpentine-curved bottom; the inner part is a straight-edged board whose exposed lower surface is painted the off-white background color of the outer board, to which it is screwed.

The construction of the window cornices is identical to that of the tester boards and cornices. On the bottom board of each are pulleys: on the left side of one cornice is a bank of five on a single iron rod that runs from front to back. Additional pulleys are placed at one-foot intervals across the front of the cornice, each spaced at a progressively deeper distance from the front edge and each parallel to a pulley in the left-side bank. On the second cornice, the pulley arrangement is reversed. The cornices were originally fixed to wooden wall brackets by means of pegs inserted through holes drilled at each end of the bottom board.

CONDITION: On the bedstead, the posts and rails are sanded and refinished with a dark greenish black stain. The original painted finish, similar in color, remains on the underside of the rails. The bed bolts are replacements. Filled mortices in the footposts at the same height as those for the existing headboard originally received a footboard. On each post, at thirty-nine and forty-seven inches above the floor and directly above the inner corner of the bedstead, are holes, now filled, for tiebacks. On the cornices, a number of scalloped tips have been replaced, notably at both ends on the left side and at the foot end of the right side. The painted surfaces are otherwise well preserved. The back of the cornice boards and the bottom of the tester boards have been stripped of their paint. On the window cornices, the painted surfaces are also well preserved. The entire trilobate left end is replaced on both cornices, and the underside of the horizontal bottom board has been varnished. On one, the wooden pegs are missing. The bedstead is illustrated unfurnished.

INSCRIPTIONS: Incised, on posts and rails beneath the mortice-and-tenon joints: *I* through *VIII*.

DIMENSIONS: bedstead: H.: overall, 99⅛ (*251.8*), posts, 87⅝ (*222.6*), rails, 18 (*45.7*); W.: cornice, 66 (*167.6*), rails, 57 (*144.8*), feet, 56 (*142.2*); D.: cornice, 84½ (*214.6*), rails, 77 (*195.6*), feet, 76 (*193.*); window cornice: H.: 7⅞ (*20.*); W.: top, 51¼ (*130.2*), base, 47¾ (*121.3*); D.: 4¼ (*10.8*).

WOODS: tulip poplar (posts, rails); Atlantic white cedar (bed and window cornices, tester boards); pine (headboard).

Gift of Mrs. J. Insley Blair, 1946   (46.194.6–8)

90

90. Bedstead

New England, 1760–1800

A NEW ENGLAND origin can be assumed for this bedstead from the birch and white pine of which it is made. Another bedstead, of the same woods, with similar posts and with simple serpentine cornices that were originally fabric-covered, was made sometime after 1795 for James Rundlet of Portsmouth, New Hampshire (Jobe and Kaye, no. 141). Other evidence suggests a source in central Connecticut for cat. no. 90: it has a history of ownership in Wethersfield, and its footposts are diminutive versions—even to the Marlborough feet—of the Philadelphia-inspired furniture made by Eliphalet Chapin in East Windsor, Connecticut (see cat. no. 10). Further, the types of bedsteads listed in the 1792 Hartford table of prices (Lyon, pp. 269–270) include a number of features that would seem to describe cat. no. 90: "two turn'd posts"; "moulding at the bottom of the two foot posts"; and "six pullies in the teaser."

On the bedstead, the testers, which actually have nine pulleys for drawing up the curtains, support a unique set of fabric-covered cornices that are the glory of this bedstead—the sole surviving American ones known with pierced decorative patterns. Only references to others remain, including one with "a Sett of Cutt open Cornices Rails & pullys" sold by Thomas Affleck in Philadelphia in 1770 (Wainwright, p. 44). Cat. no. 90 is one of just two bedsteads with sets of fabric-covered cornices; the other, from the Glen–Sanders House, Scotia, New York, is now at Williamsburg (*Antiques* 89 [January 1966], p. 103). On cat. no. 90, the fabric covering is antique, but appears to be a later addition. When the bedstead came to the MMA, it was equipped with valances and hangings of antique resist-blue fabric in harmony with the cornice coverings but of different designs.

PROVENANCE: Ex coll.: Mr. and Mrs. Luke V. Lockwood, Greenwich, Connecticut. The bedstead was on loan to the MMA from 1935 until its purchase in 1949. On the purchase form (5/2/49) it was described as "Made in 1751 for the John Cotton Smith house, Sharon, Connecticut." Mrs. Lockwood subsequently wrote (5/18/49, MMA files): "This bed was made for Abigail Porter who married Col. Thomas Belden in 1753 in Wethersfield Connecticut and came from the house where she lived directly to us." In 1898, the old Porter–Belden house on Main Street in Wethersfield was occupied by Miss E. E. Bidwell. Accordingly, the bedstead seems to have descended from Thomas and Abigail Belden; to Mary Belden Butler (1771–1811); to Abigail Porter Butler Bidwell (1798–1832); to Esther E. Bidwell, who was born in 1826 (Jessie Perry van Zile Belden, *Royal D. Belden and Olive Cadwell Belden*, Philadelphia, J. B. Lippincott, 1898, p. 215).

CONSTRUCTION: The four posts have turned colonettes above square pedestals. On the footposts, the colonettes begin just above the rails and have capitals formed of square blocks between multiple moldings. At the bottom are applied molded cuffs whose fronts and backs overlap the sides. On the headposts, the colonettes have neither capitals nor cuffs; their pedestals are higher and, below the rails, their inner edges are chamfered. The square rails, their outer edges molded in quarter rounds, are deeply rabbeted to receive turned knobs to which the sacking bottom was laced. The rails are tenoned into the posts and drilled to receive bed bolts; iron nuts are slotted into them from inside. The pierced and scalloped cornice boards, serpentine in front and flat in back, have beveled bottom edges to which the tester boards are screwed. Resist-blue linen is glued to the cornices and to the front edge of the tester boards. The scalloped top and the pierced openings are bound in linen tape. On the tester, the end boards are tenoned into the side boards. Three slots in each side and in the foot-end board house large wooden pulley wheels. The pulleys for the cords that control the swags of the curtains rotate on wooden dowels, set lengthwise on the side boards and at right angles on the foot-end board. At the extreme head end of each side board is a thick, five-grooved master pulley.

CONDITION: The posts and rails, a mellow honey brown in color, retain the original thin finish. The headboard is an old replacement. Two mortices, now filled, cut into each of the posts above the foot rail show that there once was a footboard. The knobs set into the rail rabbets have been crudely sawed off. The iron pins that secure the tester to the tops of the posts are modern. On the bedstead cornices, the lack of damage to the fabric covering in the course of repairs to its wooden backing, together with the paucity of tack holes at its bottom edge, where the curtains would have been nailed, suggest that it may not be the original covering. The arched top over the pierced keyhole in the right side is restored. Some of the projections on the left side may be old restorations. The resist-blue linen covering is faded and has discolored to brown. The bedstead is illustrated unfurnished.

INSCRIPTIONS: Incised, on the posts and rails beneath the mortice-and-tenon joints, counterclockwise, from the right headpost: *I* through *VIII*; at the corresponding corners of the tester boards: *I* through *IIII*.

DIMENSIONS: H.: overall, 96½ (*245.1*), posts, 87¾ (*222.9*), rails, 18 (*45.7*); W.: cornice, 56¼ (*142.9*), rails, 54¼ (*137.8*), feet, 55 (*139.7*); D.: cornice, 77¼ (*196.2*), rails, 76⅝ (*194.6*), feet, 77¼ (*196.2*).

WOODS: birch (posts, rails); white pine (cornice, tester boards).

Purchase, Joseph Pulitzer Bequest, 1949   (49.91)

91. Bedstead

Massachusetts, 1760–90

THIS IS ONE OF A SMALL group of Massachusetts bedsteads—and one of six attributable to the same shop—whose fluted columnar footposts have big claw-and-ball feet and removable knees carved with acanthus leafage and rosettes. A matching bedstead, executed by the same carver, descended in the Cunningham family of Boston (Morris sale, lot 329). Two other bedsteads, the motifs on their removable knees identical to those of cat. no. 91 but the work of a different carver, are now at Van Cortlandt Mansion in New York City and at Deerfield (Fales 1976, no. 208). The headposts of the Deerfield example, though unfluted and uncarved, have the same cabriole legs, removable knees, and columnar tops. On a bedstead from the Torrey family of Cambridge, Massachusetts, and later in the Bigelow collection (Bigelow sale, lot 126), all four carved posts are identical; on another, there are slight variations in the carving (ill. Nutting 1, no. 1497). These two bedsteads, their whereabouts unknown, complete the group of six. Other examples, while similar, look to be the work of different hands (Sack 5, pp. 1266–67, 1339). On a bedstead from the Reifsnyder collection (Nutting 1, nos. 1478, 1482), the claw feet are like those of the group, but the knee carving is in an altogether different acanthus pattern.

On cat. no. 91, the raked-back talons on the claw feet and the maple and white pine secondary woods are typical features of Massachusetts craftsmanship. Those woods, in combination with the Boston-area histories of two of the related bedsteads, suggest a Boston origin. The prototype for the group, which encompasses the richest and most splendid of all New England pre-Revolutionary bedsteads, may be one that descended in Newburyport, Massachusetts, from Nathaniel Tracy through the Perkins family (*Antiques* 54 [October 1948], p. 203). Possibly an imported example, it has footposts, with the claw feet and removable knees now associated with Massachusetts, that are surmounted in the English manner by carved balusters and cluster colonettes.

Though no evidence remains on any of these beds, the original tester frames had either fabric valances or wooden cornices painted (cat. no. 89), fabric-covered (cat. no. 90), or carved (Chippendale 1762, pl. XLIV). Cat. no. 91 now has two sets of reproduction hangings: for summer, a green-and-white checked linen; for winter, a raspberry red wool moreen. In the eighteenth century, the fabric would have been pulled up by means of cords looped through pulleys in the tester and attached to tiebacks screwed into the posts. The holes for the tiebacks remain, demonstrating that an apparatus whose function is illustrated in Chippendale's *Director* (1762 edition, pls. XLI, XLII, XLIV) originally governed the draping of the bedstead curtains.

PROVENANCE: Ex coll.: H. Eugene Bolles, Boston. The bedstead was on loan to the Kenmore Association, Fredericksburg, Virginia, between 1933 and 1978.

CONSTRUCTION: The headboard is slotted into the square,

tapering headposts. The footposts have turned and fluted colonettes above the rails; on their cabriole legs the outer edges of the claw-and-ball feet are pieced, the left half overlapping the right. Bolt holes where the square part of the posts joins the rails are covered by the projecting carved knees, which form removable caps. Each cap is held in place by means of a single screw in back that seats into an iron slot embedded in the corner of the post. On each post, at forty and forty-nine inches from the floor, are holes where tiebacks were once screwed. Iron pins projecting from the tops of the posts once secured flat tester boards. The rails, rectangular and with quarter-round molded outer edges, are tenoned into the posts and bolted. Rabbets at the inner top edge of the rails receive narrow pieces of canvas secured with roseheads through reinforcing leather strips on the sides and the foot end. Two long pieces of canvas sewn together and nailed to the head rail form the main section of the sacking bottom, which is laced to the three narrow canvas strips when the bed is assembled.

CONDITION: The bedstead has a pleasing old finish. The headposts and rails are stained a brown that was probably originally intended to match the wood of the footposts. That wood has now acquired a reddish brown patina; the headboard stain is still a dark mahogany color. The tester frame is missing. On each post, the top twelve inches was cut off and has been reattached. When the bedstead was acquired by the MMA, it had a late-nineteenth-century Federal-style painted wooden cornice (*The Antiquarian* 4 [May 1925], p. 29, ill.). The bedstead is illustrated unfurnished but with its original sacking bottom, which is laced together with modern rope.

INSCRIPTIONS: Incised, on posts and adjacent rails at their junctures, counterclockwise, from the left footpost: *I* through *VIII*; on the footposts and their knee caps: *I* (left); *II* (right).

DIMENSIONS: H.: overall, 88⅛ (*223.8*), rails, 17 (*43.2*); W.: rails, 58½ (*148.6*), feet, 61¼ (*155.6*); D.: rails, 75¾ (*192.4*), feet, 77 (*195.6*).

WOODS: Primary: mahogany (footposts, knee caps). Secondary: maple (headposts, rails); white pine (headboard).

REFERENCES: *The Antiquarian* 4 (May 1925), p. 29 (ill.). Lockwood 2, fig. 807. Lee 6, p. 296 (ill.); p. 297 (measured drawings). Marshall B. Davidson, *The American Wing: A Guide* (New York: The Metropolitan Museum of Art, 1980), fig. 88.

Gift of Mrs. Russell Sage, 1909   (10.125.336)

91

II TABLES, STANDS, AND SCREENS

8 Slab Tables

Slab tables—rectangular, four-legged tables having heavy marble tops and finished skirts on only three sides—were also known in eighteenth-century America interchangeably as marble tables, marble slab tables, marble sideboards, and sideboard tables. Cabinetmakers billed for making "frames for marble slabs." That they were made to stand against the wall and not to be moved is inherent in their design. The term "pier table" popularly used today was coined late in the eighteenth century to describe the delicate neoclassical type placed between two windows beneath a looking glass. Since neither hot dishes nor wet glasses could harm it, the marble slab top clearly made the table ideal for the serving of food and drink. Contemporary inventories usually record slab tables as in parlors, which frequently doubled as dining rooms; on the rare occasions prior to the Federal period that a separate room was actually called a "dining room," they would be found there. Documentary references, numerous after 1740, show that marble-top tables came into fashion in the colonies along with the Queen Anne style. Slab tables, particularly those with skirts cavetto-molded in the English manner, were most popular in New York; three New York tables are in the collection. The early Newport type—serpentine-skirted—is not represented at the Museum, but a later, straight-sided one is; otherwise, the tables were uncommon in New England, and none is in the collection. The complex serpentine shapes preferred among the most elaborate and costly of the rococo type are brilliantly realized in the Museum's two Philadelphia examples. The form does not seem to have been made in that city prior to the introduction of the Chippendale style.

92. Table

New York, 1740–60

THE TABLE, WHICH descended in the Verplanck family, once had a wooden top. Because all four of its sides are finished, it was probably intended to occupy the center of a room. Its pointed pad feet and rayed inlay, somewhat rural in their simplicity, lead to the speculation that it was made in the Hudson River valley for Mount Gulian, the country house that Gulian Verplanck built in about 1740 at Fishkill Landing, New York. Its front knee brackets, which match the scrolls of the splats of the Verplanck chairs (cat. no. 24) and relate to their knee brackets and those on the en suite settee (cat. no. 82) and card table (cat. no. 105), are not part of its original fabric but must have been added in an effort to bring the table up to date with the more refined chairs and tables acquired by the family in the 1760s.

PROVENANCE: See cat. no. 24.

CONSTRUCTION: The marble top has rounded front and side edges and a smoothly finished bottom surface. The frame is finished on all four sides. The solid skirts are tenoned to the legs, the joints reinforced with vertical glue blocks beveled on the inner edge. The serpentine-shaped knee brackets at the sides and rear are glued to the legs and to shaped extensions of the skirts. Dovetailed into the tops of the front and rear skirt rails are two equidistant medial braces. The eleven-rayed motif in the front skirt is of lightwood inlays alternately stained dark.

CONDITION: The frame is a reddish brown in color. The skirts have been cleaned, but the legs retain the old finish. The central rayed inlay was originally designed to have a straight bottom edge—dark at the left, light at the right—but the wood of the replaced bottom rays cannot readily be distinguished from the surrounding mahogany. The scrolled front knee brackets glued to the legs are old replacements. Behind them are visible stumps of the downward extensions of the skirts that once supported brackets like those at the sides and rear. The rear bracket on the left side and the left medial brace are replacements. The medial braces have been reset in the rails to accommodate the brass reinforcing strips now cemented beneath the marble top. The pink- and gray-veined marble top, old, but probably not original to the table, has been broken and repolished. Nail holes in the top edges of the four skirt rails are evidence that the table once had a wooden top.

INSCRIPTIONS: In chalk, on underside of marble top, predating the breaks, an illegible name. In ink (19th-century), on the top of the right medial brace: *Capt Warren*.

DIMENSIONS: H.: 29¾ (75.6); W.: top, 60⅝ (154.), skirt, 57½ (146.1), feet, 60½ (153.7); D.; top, 31⅛ (79.1), skirt, 28 (71.1), feet, 30¼ (76.8).

WOODS: Primary: mahogany. Secondary: birch (medial brace); maple (glue blocks).

Gift of James De Lancey Verplanck and John Bayard Rodgers Verplanck, 1939   (39.184.9)

92

93

93. Marble Slab Table

New York, 1750–70

THIS IS AN UNUSUALLY small version of a type of New York slab table distinguished by bold cavetto-molded skirts with mitered corners. Counterparts have descended in the Philipse (V. I. Miller, no. 36) and Mansell (*Antiques* 31 [May 1937], p. 229) families of New York. Another, from the collection of the New York painter Robert W. Weir, is now at Winterthur (Downs 1952, no. 354). A table with simple pad feet at Williamsburg may also be of New York origin (Gusler, fig. 123). On each of these tables the structural framework is hidden behind the molded mahogany skirts. A New York attribution for cat. no. 93 is supported by its Verplanck family history and its local secondary woods.

PROVENANCE: See cat. no. 24.

CONSTRUCTION: The thick marble top, with serpentine front corners, thumbnail-molded front and side edges, and an overhanging flat back edge, is rough-cut on its undersurface except for beveling at the front and sides. The skirts, cut out in a cavetto molding and a bottom bead, are mitered at the corners, backed with a triangular fillet, and glued to the front and side rails. The rails are double pegged to the leg stiles, the joints reinforced with bevel-edged vertical glue blocks. The stiles are square on the front legs, rectangular on the rear. Serpentine-shaped knee brackets are glued to the legs and rails at the front and sides. The outside corners of the knees and the middle knuckles of the feet are pieced, except on the left front knee and the left rear foot. The knees of the rear legs are flat in back.

CONDITION: The frame has a reddish brown color. The right front skirt fillet, the left rear knee bracket, and six of the eight glue blocks are replacements. The pieced middle knuckles of the front feet are restored. The badly warped top, white marble crisscrossed with gray veining, has a golden patina. Although its serpentine corners do not conform to the shape of the skirt, as would be normal practice, it appears to be original to the table.

DIMENSIONS: H.: 29 (*73.7*); W.: top, 39½ (*100.3*), skirt, 36 (*91.4*), feet, 35⅜ (*89.9*); D.: top, 24¼ (*61.6*), skirt, 21¾ (*55.2*), feet, 21 (*53.3*).

WOODS: Primary: mahogany. Secondary: white oak (rails); sweet gum (skirt fillets); white pine (glue blocks).

Gift of James De Lancey Verplanck and John Bayard Rodgers Verplanck, 1939   (39.184.10)

94. Marble Slab Table

New York, 1750–90

THE EXCEPTIONAL QUALITY of this table derives from its richly colored marble top and superbly carved knees and gadrooning. With solid straight skirts, shaped front corners, and cabriole legs, it represents a rare type of New York slab table (see also Downs 1952, no. 358). Characteristic New York features are its square and massive claw feet, the back talon continued in an unbroken line from the back edge of each leg; the crosshatched field centered at the top of its knee carving; and the sweet gum employed as one of the secondary woods. Its carved legs are identical to those of a large six-legged drop-leaf dining table from the Wick family of Morristown, New Jersey, now at Gunston Hall, Virginia (P-B sale no. 1202, 12 /2 /50, lot 672; *Antiques* 61 [February 1952], p. 126), as well as to those of a massive easy chair at Williamsburg (*Antiques* 97 [January 1970], p. 4). All three pieces must be the product of the same shop.

PROVENANCE: Said by the vendor, Mary Bergen Wesseler (11 /7 /46 letter, MMA files), to have descended to her directly through five generations of the Bergen family of Flatlands, New York. The original owner was probably Tunis Bergen (1730–1807), who married in 1760. The table would then have passed to John (1764–1824); to Cornelius (1798–1865); to John (born 1826); to Fenwick W. (1864–1939), who gave it to his daughter Mary, the vendor, on the occasion of her marriage.

CONSTRUCTION: The marble top has molded front and side edges, serpentined front corners, and a smoothly finished undersurface. The front and side skirt rails, their ends beveled to suggest canted corners, are butted against the front legs.

Reinforcing the rails, to which they are screwed, are seven-inch-long boards double pegged to the legs at one end; sawed in a serpentine at the other. The side and rear rails are double pegged to the rear legs in the normal manner, with thin vertical glue blocks reinforcing their junctures. Thick gadrooning strips are screwed and pegged to the front and side skirts. On the knees, each bracket is secured with a cut nail; the crosshatched central ground outlined by acanthus leafage with pendent bellflower on the front ones is repeated, except for the back leaf carving, on the rear ones.

CONDITION: The table frame, of fine dense wood, is a deep reddish brown in color. The right front knee bracket is a replacement. There are splits in both front claw feet. The feet have holes for casters. A medial brace connecting the front and rear rails is a replacement; dovetailed stubs remain from the original, which was removed to accommodate brass rods that now reinforce the top. The marble of the top, a single piece of yellow and rosy purple Spanish brocatelle, has been broken, and the tip of the left front corner is missing.

DIMENSIONS: H.: 28⅜ (72.1); W.: top, 43¾ (111.1), skirt, 40⅜ (102.6), feet, 42½ (108.); D.: top, 23 (58.4), skirt, 19⅜ (49.2), feet, 21¾ (55.2).

94 See also p. 343

WOODS: Primary: mahogany. Secondary: cherry (rear rail); sweet gum (rail reinforcing boards); white pine (medial brace, glue blocks).

REFERENCES: Downs 1948, p. 85 (ill.).

Purchase, Joseph Pulitzer Bequest, 1946   (46.154)

95. Marble Slab Table

Newport, 1760–90

THE MAJORITY OF NEWPORT marble slab tables, such as the one John Goddard made in 1755 for Anthony Low, have boldly serpentine skirts (Ott 1965, no. 40). A few, including this one, have straight skirts. An early straight-skirted example with turned legs and pad feet descended in the Babbitt family of Wickford, Rhode Island (ibid., no. 39); one with cabriole legs belonged to John Brown of Providence (Cooper 1971, fig. 21). The skirt of cat. no. 95

is covered with cross-grain mahogany veneers and has applied ovolo moldings, a treatment also found on a table from the Updike family of Wickford (Ott 1965, no. 41). With identical legs, except for minor differences in the design of their knee carving, the two pieces look to be by the same hand. Coincidentally, they were both once used as church altar tables.

The MMA example is unique among Rhode Island slab tables in having square-cornered skirts and a marble top partly recessed behind an applied molding; with a depth of only sixteen inches, it is also the shallowest. The table has been attributed to John Goddard because its claw feet and carved knees are similar in design to those of a tea table Goddard made for Jabez Bowen in 1763 and those of a drop-leaf table he made for James Atkinson in 1774 (Moses 1982, pp. 1130–43). On cat. no. 95, however, the knee carving—larger in scale and less assured in execution—does not compare with that of a card table in the Museum's collection (cat. no. 99), which clearly demonstrates Goddard's masterly personal touch.

95 See also p. 344

PROVENANCE: Ex coll.: Vincent D. Andrus, Greenwich, Connecticut. The table descended in the Wanton family of Newport. Joseph Wanton (1705–1780) married in 1729 and inherited the house of his father, William, in 1733. A successful merchant, he became deputy collector of customs at Newport and, from 1769 to 1775, served as governor of Rhode Island. His daughter Elizabeth married Thomas Wickham in 1762; her daughter Elizabeth married Walter Clarke Gardiner, moving with him to Hudson, New York, in 1794. As the family historian put it, "The marble-topped punch table of Governor Joseph Wanton descended to his daughter Elizabeth Wickham, and from her to her daughter, who took it to Hudson, New York, where it was used in the Episcopal church as a communion table" (Bartlett, p. 29). In Christ Church, built at Hudson in 1802–1803, "At the east end stood a wide platform, holding the altar—a simple wooden table that had come from the former mansion of the governor of Rhode Island at Newport" (De Mille, p. 10). When a new building was erected in 1854–57, the old altar was encased within a new one; yet another was installed in 1891: "When the old altar came to be taken out, the original 'Holy Table' from the first church was found within it" (ibid., p. 39). The table was moved to a side chapel, where it remained until the church was renovated in 1951. It was then placed at the head of the north aisle (photograph, MMA files). Shortly thereafter it was sold to Ginsburg & Levy, Inc., New York City, from whom the donor acquired it.

CONSTRUCTION: The marble top, fitting into a rabbet cut into the cornice molding, rests on the rails. Both top and cornice extend three-quarters of an inch beyond the rear rail. The rails are double pegged to the stiles, reinforced at each corner with a large vertical quarter-round glue block. The front and side rails are faced with vertical flitches of figured mahogany, those at the corners continuing the darker tone of the supporting legs and brackets. The quarter-round moldings glued to the skirt fronts are toenailed from below. The knees and brackets of the front legs have intaglio leaf carving; those of the rear legs are uncarved.

CONDITION: The frame has a fine patina with a dark brown mahogany color on the stiles, knee brackets, and legs, and a lighter, reddish brown color elsewhere. Both legs on the left side have old splits. On both claw feet, the tips of the front talons are restored. Though three of them have been stained, the glue blocks look to be the originals. The feet have holes for casters. The marble of the top, a single piece of gray-veined white marble with a satiny old surface, has straight sides and an unfinished undersurface.

DIMENSIONS: H.: 28 (71.1); W.: top, 48½ (123.2), skirt, 48 (121.9), feet, 50 (127.); D.: top, 16 (40.6), skirt, 15 (38.1), feet, 17 (43.2).

WOODS: Primary: mahogany, mahogany veneer. Secondary: maple (rails); white pine (glue blocks).

Bequest of Vincent D. Andrus, 1962   (62.138)

96. Marble Slab Table

Philadelphia, 1760–75

THE FRAME IS THE WORK of an accomplished craftsman, but appears to be his early and tentative essay in the Philadelphia rococo style. Though the front skirt is shaped in a sweeping double serpentine, its curves are broken by vertical joints and it is embellished with a somewhat graceless central shell; while the legs and their rounded stiles are well formed, the termination of the gadrooning at their uncarved knee brackets is visually distracting. The maker was perhaps inspired by the outline of the fully developed rococo marble top, but did not foresee all the problems it posed. These anomalous features, while awkward, are chronologically consistent with the 1761 marriage date of Benjamin Marshall, for whom the table was presumably made (see Provenance). A pair of slab tables, one at RISD, one at Bayou Bend (Fairbanks and Bates, p. 166), similar to this table in their boldly serpentine fronts and in certain details of construction, represent the form in its fully integrated rococo style.

PROVENANCE: Purchased from David David, a Philadelphia dealer who had acquired it in 1960 directly from Wyck, the Haines family house in Germantown, Pennsylvania. The table was almost certainly made for the Philadelphia merchant Benjamin Marshall (1737–1778) at about the time of his marriage, in 1761, to Sarah Lynn (1739–1797). At Marshall's death, his inventory, dated August 4, 1778 (City of Philadelphia, Register of Wills, File No. 54), included a "Marble Slab Table—£30" and a "Looking Glass Large—£10," which doubtless hung above it. Sarah Marshall's ownership is recorded in a family history nailed to the table's back skirt. The table descended from Sarah to her daughter Hannah (1765–1828), married in 1785 to Caspar Wistar Haines (1762–1801), who inherited Wyck in 1793; to their son Reuben (1786–1843); to his daughter Margaret Bowne Haines. After her marriage to Thomas Stewardson, Jr., in 1854, Margaret moved from Wyck, leaving the table behind. In a 1911 inventory of the house taken at the death of Jane R. Haines, then its occupant, the table was valued at $15; in 1947, when Jane's grandnephew Robert B. Haines and his wife took over Wyck, the table was "in the room with the large doors" (Mrs. R.B. Haines, 8/3/60 letter, MMA files).

CONSTRUCTION: The front and side edges of the marble top are molded: in front, to conform to the skirt; at the sides, in a double curve. The front skirt rail—made up of a thick timber pieced in front with a second one cut from the same log, the end joints visible in the middle of each curve—projects in exaggerated serpentines flanking a concave central panel. The rail's inner surface is roughly cut out in a central angular bay. The freestanding pierced shell is applied. The side skirts are straight. The gadrooning strips nailed to the front and side skirts are tenoned into the legs. The rails are double pegged to the legs. The shaped knee brackets are double nailed. Two medial and four diagonal corner braces are dovetailed into the tops of the rails; a single medial one, into the bottom.

96 See also pp. 344, 364

CONDITION: The frame has a mellow light reddish brown color. The top, a single piece of variegated marble in colors of black, gray, and violet, was badly broken in the 1930s and has been repaired and repolished.

INSCRIPTIONS: Typewritten, on a piece of paper nailed to rear skirt rail: *This table originally belonged to Sarah Marshall wife of Benjamin Marshall son of Christopher 1st. who died 1797 so was assigned to her great grand daughter, Margaret Haines, at the division of the household furniture at Wyck in 1843. It belongs to her children, Stewardson (card In handwriting of Jane R. Haines) copied May 1928.*

DIMENSIONS: H.: 30¼ (76.8); W.: top, 49¾ (126.4), skirt, 45¾ (116.2), feet, 48 (121.9); D.: top, 26 (66.), skirt, 24¾ (62.9), feet, 21¼ (54.).

WOODS: Primary: mahogany. Secondary: yellow pine (braces, rear rail).

REFERENCES: *MMAB* n.s. 20 (October 1961), p. 55 (ill.). Hornor 1935, pl. 208.

Purchase, The Sylmaris Collection, Gift of George Coe Graves; Gift of Mrs. Russell Sage; funds from various donors; and Rogers Fund, 1961   (61.84)

97. Marble Slab Table

Philadelphia, 1765–75

THIS REMARKABLE SLAB table is thought to have been part of the furnishings of John Cadwalader's house, the grandest in colonial Philadelphia. Though one of the richest and most finely wrought pieces of American eighteenth-century carver's work, it is not en suite with the furniture known to have been commissioned by Cadwalader between 1770 and 1772. Whereas on the card tables and chairs made for Cadwalader by Thomas Affleck and carved by James Reynolds and Bernard and Jugiez (e.g., cat. no. 59) the visual separation between the skirts and legs is maintained in the characteristic Anglo-American manner, here the two elements are integrated according to the Louis XV style into one continuous, undulating form. The carved motifs and the style of their execution are also manifestly different.

Charles Coxe, who owned a large house on Second Street not far from Cadwalader's, sold its contents at auction in May 1769. John Cadwalader's "Waste Book" records on October 10, 1769, the payment of £30 for "2 marble Slabs etc had of C. Coxe" (Wainwright, p. 122) —the only known instance of Cadwalader's acquiring furniture not specifically made for his house. If cat. no. 97 was one of the "Slabs," why it is different from the rest of John's furniture would thus be explained. In an adjacent entry in the "Waste Book" for the same day, Cadwalader records payment of £94-15 to Benjamin Randolph for furniture—the basis of the suggestion (ibid.) that Randolph made new frames for the slabs. Unfortunately, it does not follow that a table as elaborate as this one would have been created around an existing marble top, nor does the execution of the frame accord with that of any other Philadelphia work, much less any firmly documented to Randolph.

The design of cat. no. 97 looks to have been inspired by pattern-book illustrations, although here not followed as obviously as was often the case in Philadelphia. The C-scroll-carved legs are similar to those on two patterns for rectangular slab frames in Ince and Mayhew's *Universal System* of 1762 (pl. LXXIII). Related legs are found on a serpentine-front pier table in Chippendale's *Director* (1762 edition, pl. CLXX); a winged putto seated on the frame of the pier glass illustrated above it was possibly the source for the chinoiserie figure here centered on the skirt. The pierced double scrolls flanking the front knees appear to derive from plate CXCIV ("Designs of Borders for Paper Hangings &c"), a motif also borrowed by James Reynolds for the bottom of a gilt looking glass he carved for Cadwalader in 1770 (Downs 1952, no. 259).

PROVENANCE: Ex coll.: George S. Palmer, New London, Connecticut. The table descended in the Cadwalader family of Philadelphia, presumably part of the furnishings of the house on Second Street that John Cadwalader fitted up between 1769 and 1771. A 1778 inventory of the house listed "two marble plates" in the large front parlor (Wainwright, p. 66); at John's death, in 1786, there was "1 marble slab" in the front parlor and another in the back parlor (ibid., p. 72). Most of John's furnishings were inherited by his son Thomas (1779–1841), who lived

in a house at Ninth and Arch streets; they then descended to Judge John Cadwalader (1805–1879), who moved to 240 South Fourth Street in 1837. The table is illustrated in an 1889 photograph (ibid., p. 131) of one of the parlors there, when the house was occupied by Dr. Charles E. Cadwalader (1839–1907). Prior to his removal to England, in 1904, Dr. Cadwalader sold most of the family possessions at Davis & Harvey's Art Gallery. The table was described in the sale catalogue as "Handsome Antique Console Table, profusely carved, scroll legs, Egyptian marble top." It fetched $450 from the local dealer James Curran (ibid., p. 82), and was subsequently purchased by Palmer, from whom the MMA acquired it.

CONSTRUCTION: The marble top overhangs the rail in back and has molded edges that conform to the serpentine curve of the front rail and the concave shape of the sides. The frame is reinforced with short corner braces dovetailed into the tops of the rails. The front and side rails, which continue the curves of the knees, are cut from thick timbers; their inner surfaces are straight at the top and chiseled away gradually below. The front rail, carved away to form high-relief rocaille C- and S-scrolls, is built up in the middle, first at the bottom and then along the front, in order to permit the carving-out of the three-dimensional figure. The rails are double pegged to the legs, their tenons extending downward seven inches. Parts of the tenons are exposed where the bottoms of the rails were cut away, suggesting that the carving was done after the frame was assembled. The inner curves of the legs are built up with two overlapping boards. The rear legs are carved only on their outer side.

CONDITION: The table frame has a thick dark old finish. Where the carved parts have been rubbed, the luminous dark red original finish is visible. Most of the pierced carved scrollwork originally depending from the bottom of the front and side skirts has been lost; the handlelike parts on the left side and on either end of the front skirt were replaced in 1961, matching the original one that survives on the right side. The lower half of the C-scroll to the left of the central figure was also replaced. Eight additional stumps remain from lost scrollwork. The tips of the scrolls on the inner sides of the front feet are missing. The corners of the right side of the top, a single piece of black and gold Portoro marble, have been broken.

DIMENSIONS: H.: 32⅜ (82.2); W.: top, 48 (121.9), skirt, 46½ (118.1), feet, 48¼ (122.6); D.: top, 23¼ (59.1), skirt, 21⅝ (54.9), feet, 21¼ (54.).

WOODS: Primary: mahogany. Secondary: yellow pine (rear rail); walnut (corner braces).

REFERENCES: Davis & Harvey's Art Gallery, Philadelphia, sale, November 3–4, 1904, lot 168. Halsey, pp. 263; 272–273 (ill.). Herbert Cescinsky, "An English View of Philadelphia Furniture," *Antiques* 8 (November 1925), p. 272 (ill.), p. 275. "Mr. Cescinsky Talks Back," *Antiques* 9 (January 1926), pp. 11–12. Lockwood 2, fig. 764. Charles Packer, "New view on a Chippendale table," *Antiques* 62 (August 1952), p. 135 (ill.). Powel, p. 205 (ill.). Wainwright, pp. 82–83; 122–123 (table attributed to Randolph). Fairbanks and Bates, pp. 164–165 (also as Randolph).

John Stewart Kennedy Fund, 1918   (18.110.27)

97 See also pp. 344, 364

9 Card Tables

The English mania for gambling at cards, an expression of the speculative spirit rampant in the early eighteenth century, led to a similar widespread fashion in colonial America, where tables designed exclusively for gaming became a requirement in any fashionable house. Whether used for playing cards, backgammon, chess, or whatever, they were called simply card tables and were found mostly in parlors. What distinguishes a card table from other tables is its two-part hinged top and its swing rear legs that opened when the table was to be used for games. Otherwise, with its unfinished back pushed against a wall, it could double as a serving table. Dating from the 1740s and mostly in the Queen Anne style, the earliest examples made specifically for card-playing had circular tops on plain triangular or semicircular bases, but that shape was rapidly superseded by a rectangular one having straight, blocked, or serpentine skirts or turreted corners. Especially well represented in the Museum's collection are classic specimens, both early and late, from Newport and New York, but lacking is any representation of the Massachusetts type, the finest of which have elaborately embroidered playing surfaces. (Examples from that colony are somewhat less common, perhaps a reflection of the conservative New Englander's disapproval of gambling.) A Marlborough-leg version from Philadelphia is included in the collection, but there is no turret-cornered one to represent the richest phase of the Chippendale style.

98. Card Table

Newport, 1740–60

WITH THREE LEGS and a triangular frame somewhat awkwardly combined with a circular top, the form of this table is most unusual. On it, and on an example of New York attribution at Winterthur which is similar except for having a rounded frame (Downs 1952, no. 306), the top is in two pieces: one a drop leaf, the other lifting up to provide access to a storage well, presumably for housing the accoutrements of card playing. While it is possible for the entire top to be vertical (ibid., no. 305), the lack of any device to support the upper half in an upright position shows that the table was not intended to be stored in a corner in the manner of round tea tables.

The card table is unquestionably of Rhode Island origin, not just because of its Newport provenance but because of its unmistakable Newport features: the dense, purple-hued mahogany of which it is made; the maple, with characteristic signs of worm, used for the thick rails on which the rear legs swing. Two other Newport tables, similar in size and identical in basic design to English circular-top card tables fashionable in the first quarter of the eighteenth century (*DEF* 3, p. 186, figs. 8, 9), show a later development of the same unusual form (*Antiques* 106 [July 1974], p. 4; Carpenter, no. 64). On them, the rear half of the top board is hinged to fold over the front half; the front skirts are rounded to conform to the shape of the top; and the front legs have the fully developed carved knee and claw foot executed in the manner associated with John Goddard of Newport.

PROVENANCE: The table descended in the family of the donor, Mary Bancroft Coggeshall, Pleasantville, New York, presumably from Caleb Coggeshall (1709–before 1740) of Newport or from Job Coggeshall (born 1733) of Newport and Nantucket; to Caleb Coggeshall (1758–1847) of North Carolina, Newport, and New York; to George Dilwin Coggeshall (1808–1891) of New York; to Ellwood Walter Coggeshall (born 1846); to Mary Coggeshall (1880–1973).

CONSTRUCTION: The round top is divided into semicircles. The front one, attached with two closely spaced iron strap hinges to the outer rear rail, rests on the frame, secured in front by a circular brass catch, and can be lifted to give access to a storage well framed by the skirt rails. The rear half, a drop leaf attached to the front half with strap hinges at either end, completes the circular top when it is raised and the table's rear legs swing back to support it. On the triangular frame, with its obtuse front angle, the front skirts are double pegged to the front leg and dovetailed to the inner rear rail. The thick outer rear rail is divided by a pair of five-fingered knuckle-joint hinges into three parts—two swinging ones, to which the rear legs are double pegged, and a stationary middle, to which the inner rail is screwed. The swing action of the rear legs is arrested by a stop board. Knee brackets are glued to the front leg and to the fronts

98

of the rear legs. The bottom board, laid crosswise and nailed to the rabbeted bottom edges of the rails, encloses the frame.

CONDITION: The wood is a dark purplish brown in color. The knee bracket on the right leg has been replaced. The brass catch return has been restored.

DIMENSIONS: H.: 27¼ (69.2); W.: top, 35½ (90.2), skirt, 34⅜ (87.3), feet, 35 (88.9); D.: top, open, 34½ (87.6), top, closed, 17⅜ (44.1).

WOODS: Primary: mahogany. Secondary: maple (inner and outer rear rails, stop board); white pine (bottom board).

REFERENCES: For the Coggeshall family, see Charles Pierce and Russell Coggeshall, comps., *The Coggeshalls in America* (Boston: C.E. Goodspeed & Co.), 1930.

Bequest of Mary B. Coggeshall, 1972   (1973.32)

99. Card Table

Newport, 1760–85

THIS FAULTLESS TABLE has all features characteristic of Newport cabriole-leg card tables: square projecting corners; plain, unlined top boards; front legs with intaglio knee carving and open-taloned claw feet; and rear legs, with uncarved knees and pad feet, attached to hinged rails. The top and the skirt boards of the table are blocked-in, twice in front and once on the sides. On the skirts, the shallow arches at the bottom of the receding blocking are cut out to the same degree as the receding blocking is to the flanking projections, resulting in unusually harmonious proportions. Among the fewer than a dozen known tables of this type are a handful whose legs and carving show a remarkable similarity in execution. These can be associated with John Townsend. One bears his signature and the date 1762 (Cooper 1980, p. 27, fig. 24); his handwriting can be seen on another (Ott 1975, p. 946, pl. III); and a third descended in his family (Ott 1965, no. 34). Two others, one of which descended in the Slade family of Fall River, Massachusetts, are so similar as to suggest a like authorship (Sack 4, p. 1026; Ott 1968, p. 389).

The MMA table also has Slade family connections, but can be convincingly attributed to John Goddard (1723–1785) because of the similarity of its legs to those on two of his documented tables. Its rear feet, with large pads raised on high bases, match those on the pier table Goddard made in 1755 for Anthony Low (Ott 1965, no. 40), and its front legs, with carved knees and open-taloned feet, are all but identical to those on a square tea table he made for Jabez Bowen in 1763 (Downs 1952, no. 373).

PROVENANCE: Purchased, along with cat. no. 74, from the estate of Mrs. Henry E. Warner, Concord, Massachusetts, and believed to have been made for the Boston merchant Henry Bromfield (1727–1820), whose daughter Elizabeth (1763–1833) married Daniel Denison Rogers in 1796 (see Provenance, cat. no. 74). Accompanying the table, in an envelope marked "History of D.R.S.'s Table . . . ," a handwritten note: "Card Table from Daniel Denison Rogers' Mansion corner of Beacon & Mt. Vernon sts, Boston. House destroyed 1834. Mrs. Hannah (Rogers) Mason gave the table to Denison Rogers Slade in 1871 when she was moving from 63 Mt. Vernon st. to Beacon st (54). [Signed] D.R. Slade, April, 1910."

CONSTRUCTION: The two halves of the top are hinged together at the back. A tenon centered in the back edge of the stationary lower half keys into a slot in the upper half. The upper half unfolds to rest on the rear legs, which swing out to support it. The lower half is attached to the frame by three screws through the front skirt and two through the inside rear rail, and by two long glue blocks on each of the four sides. The front and side skirts, blocked-in on the outer surface and flat on the inner, are tenoned into the front legs. The inner rear rail is dovetailed to the side rails, the joints reinforced by vertical glue blocks. The thick outer rear rail is divided by a pair of seven-fingered knuckle-joint hinges into three parts—two swinging ones, to which the rear legs are double pegged, and a stationary middle one attached to the inner rear rail with four roseheads. A stop

99 See also p. 344

board nailed to the stationary part arrests the swing action. The side rails are rabbeted at the back to accommodate the rear legs. On the rear legs, the knees are uncarved and the back of the right knee is pieced. The rear knee brackets are the thickness of the legs; the front knee brackets, half as thick.

CONDITION: The original finish, now velvety, has darkened to a rust brown color; inside, the unlined playing surface retains its reddish mahogany hue. Splits in both halves of the top have been secured at the edges with splines. All but two of the screws securing the top to the frame are replaced. In 1968, the missing side knee brackets of the right front and left rear legs, the right talon of the left front foot, and five of the eight top glue blocks were replaced, and the pad feet were patched.

DIMENSIONS: H.: overall, 27¾ (*70.5*); W.: top, 33¼ (*84.5*), skirt, 31¼ (*79.4*), feet, 33⅛ (*84.1*); D.: top, open, 33¼ (*84.5*), top, closed, 16½ (*41.9*), skirt, 15¾ (*40.*), feet, 18 (*45.7*).

WOODS: Primary: mahogany. Secondary: mahogany (stop board); maple (inner and outer rear rails); chestnut (top glue blocks); white pine (corner glue blocks).

REFERENCES: *MMAB* n.s. 26 (October 1967), p. 50 (ill.). MMA 1975, p. 23. Moses 1982, figs. 21, 28, 29. For the Bromfield family, see Slade.

Friends of the American Wing Fund, 1967   (67.114.1)

100. Card Table

Newport, 1786?
John Townsend (1732–1809)

ON THIS ELEGANT and understated table, part of a small group of stop-fluted straight-legged Newport furniture, the fluting and pierced brackets are crisply cut and the crosshatching pattern incised on the lower edge of the skirts has been wrought with machinelike precision. Cat. no. 100 and two Pembroke tables, one at Winterthur (Downs 1952, no. 311) and one at the Colonial Society of Massachusetts (Moses 1981, fig. 5), objects of great refinement, are all labeled by John Townsend. A card table at the Preservation Society of Newport County, identical to the MMA example except for its simpler knee brackets and five cross braces rather than six, can be attributed to Townsend, as can at least two similar Pembroke tables (Hipkiss, no. 66; Carpenter, no. 56). Most notable among the distinctive features shared by the tables are the multiple cross braces dovetailed to the top and bottom of the lengthwise rails, the medial drawer runner fixed to

100 See also p. 345

the cross braces, and the pierced knee brackets tenoned to the legs and rails. The first two, consistently found also on Federal-style tables bearing Townsend's label, consequently serve to identify his work (Moses 1981, p. 1152).

John Townsend used three types of label. The first, from the mid-1760s, is handwritten; the second, found on a tall clock of 1789 (cat. no. 192) and a chest from 1792 (*Antiques* 59 [February 1951], p. 88), is printed; the third, on his Federal-style furniture from the 1790s, is also printed, but in a different type-font. The earliest references to Newport stop-fluted furniture—maple bedsteads—are in bills, dated 1787, from Townsend Goddard to the account of Christopher Champlin (Swan 1950, p. 449). On the paper label of Townsend's second type affixed to cat. no. 100, a date was added and has been reworked in darker ink to read 1766. Underneath, on close examination, the original figure may be interpreted as 1786, a far more plausible date.

PROVENANCE: Purchased, along with cat. nos. 139 and 192, from Clara Channing Allen, 57 Prospect Street, Northampton, Massachusetts, in whose family it descended. According to the vendor (12/8/27 letter, MMA files), "The first record of it is that it belonged to Christopher Champlin of Newport, R.I. I think probably he bought it of John Townsend as he lived in Newport at the time they were made and was married in 1763 to Miss Margaret Grant." The known references to stop-fluted furniture in the Champlin family were in Townsend Goddard's bills to Christopher (see above). The table's line of descent suggests that its first owner was probably Christopher's brother George, who bequeathed in his will: "To my wife's niece Ruth Channing, daughter of John Channing deceased, whom I took home in her infancy & have brought up and have always intended to make ample provision for and did with my wife . . . conveying to her the house and lot of land where I now live . . . also all my plate, beds, beddings, linen, and household furniture, except mahogany desk with silver furniture." The house, which was later known as the Cotton House on Cotton's Court, was moved in the 1970s to Church Street, Newport, where it is now no. 32. Ruth Channing married the Newport Congregational Church pastor Caleb Jewett Tenney, whose initials are painted on the table's underside. The furniture descended to the Tenney daughter Elizabeth, who married William Allen of Northampton, Massachusetts; to their daughter Clara Channing Allen.

CONSTRUCTION: The two top boards are hinged together at the back. The upper one opens to rest on the inner left rear leg, which swings out to support it; two tenons projecting from its back edge key into slots in the lower one. The stationary top is secured at both front and rear rails with three screws and three glue blocks. The front and side skirt rails are double pegged to the legs, each joint reinforced with a vertical glue block. All the glue blocks are rectangular and have chamfered inner edges. The outer rear rail is divided at the middle by a five-fingered knuckle-joint hinge. The right half is double pegged to the right rear leg and attached to the inner rail with four roseheads; the left half, double pegged to the left leg, forms the swing action. The inner rear rail, abutting the rear legs and glue blocks and notched to accommodate the swing leg, is joined to the front rail

by six transverse braces, three dovetailed into the rails' top edges, three into the bottom. The drawer, guided by three narrow strips attached to the upper braces, slides on a medial runner supported by two of the lower ones. On the drawer, the bottom is rabbeted to the front and side boards and overlaps the backboard; the front is cut out of the table's side rail; the opening is framed by an applied bead. On the front and side rails, the molding above the band of crosshatching is let in. The four corner legs are stop-fluted on their exposed sides and chamfered on their inner edge. The fifth, swing, leg is stop-fluted on the side visible when the top is open. The three-quarter-inch-thick pierced knee brackets are tenoned into the legs and rails, wedged in place on the rails.

CONDITION: The table, a dark reddish brown in color, has the original thin old finish. The hinged top is warped. The right rear leg has been broken. The drawer and the transverse braces have worm holes.

INSCRIPTIONS: A paper label pasted inside the drawer bottom, printed: *MADE BY / JOHN TOWNSEND / NEWPORT*; in brown ink, a double-line border, a date (1786?), and parts of the N and P of Newport. The date has been reworked in brown ink (20th-century?) to read 1766. In large painted letters (early 19th-century), on the bottom of the fixed top board and on the outside of the drawer bottom: *C J T / No 31*. (See p. 366 for photograph.)

DIMENSIONS: H.: overall, 27¼ (69.2); W.: top, 33⅞ (86.), skirt, 32¼ (81.9); D.: top, open, 33¾ (85.7), top, closed, 16⅞ (42.9), skirt, 16¼ (41.3).

WOODS: Primary: mahogany. Secondary: maple (inner and outer rear rails, medial braces); chestnut (glue blocks, drawer bottom, medial drawer runner); tulip poplar (drawer sides and back, drawer guides).

REFERENCES: Nutting I, fig. 1024. Cornelius 1928, figs. 3, 6. Halsey and Cornelius, pl. 64. Swan 1950, pp. 448–449. Moses 1981, p. 1155, figs. 6, 6a, 6b (ill. construction). For the Champlin family, see John D. Champlin, ed., "Champlin Memorial," typescript, 1903, Redwood Library and Athenaeum, Newport.

Egleston Fund, 1927   (27.161)

101. Card Table

New York, 1760–90

THE CARD TABLE, an uncarved, four-legged version of the New York serpentine-front type, has carefully chosen woods and fine, thoroughly satisfying proportions. Neither its features nor any detail of its construction can be traced to the two New York shops that produced tables of the classic types (e.g., cat. nos. 102, 103). A virtually identical example was in the Haskell collection (Haskell sale 3, lot 598).

PROVENANCE: Ex coll.: Lesley and Emma Sheafer, New York City. The donors purchased the table from Ginsburg & Levy, Inc., New York City.

101

CONSTRUCTION: The two solid figured wood halves of the top are hinged together. The upper half unfolds to rest on the left rear leg, which extends to support it. The stationary lower half is attached to the frame with screws—two through the front and rear rails, one through each side rail. The front and side skirt rails and the leg stiles are faced with vertical veneers. The thick rails, serpentine-shaped on the outside and straight on the inside, are tenoned into the front legs. The front rail is cut out at either end to accommodate the overlap of the side rails. The right side rail is double pegged to the rear leg. The left side rail is dovetailed to the inner rear rail, the joint reinforced with a glue block. The outer rear rail is divided in two by a four-part finger-joint hinge: the right side is stationary, nailed from the outside to the inner rear rail and double pegged to the right rear leg; the left, swing, side is double pegged to the left rear leg. Strips nailed to the bottom of the front and side rails form the skirt molding. Behind the brackets flanking each knee are horizontally laid rectangular glue blocks tenoned into the leg.

CONDITION: The table is a mellow light amber in color.

DIMENSIONS: H.: overall, 27⅞ (70.8); W.: top, 33⅛ (84.1); skirt, 32⅛ (81.6), feet, 34⅜ (87.3); D.: top, open, 33¼ (84.5), top, closed, 16½ (41.9), skirt, 15⅛ (38.4), feet, 19¼ (48.9).

WOODS: Primary: mahogany; mahogany veneer. Secondary: tulip poplar (front, side, and inner rear rails, glue blocks); white oak (outer rear rail).

The Lesley and Emma Sheafer Collection, Bequest of Emma A. Sheafer, 1973   (1974.356.39)

102. Card Table

New York, 1760–90

NUMEROUS EIGHTEENTH-CENTURY New York cabinetmakers and carvers produced the great variety of serpentine-sided, square-cornered card tables now known,

but most of the finest specimens fall into two readily distinguishable groups that were the products of two as yet unidentified shops (Heckscher 1973). The first group, the Van Rensselaer type, is named after cat. no. 102. The distinctive features of the type are: a deep serpentine skirt; bold, undulating gadrooning on front and side skirts; foliate knee carving on the front legs and on the outer side of each stationary rear leg; and five legs, each having a heavy, square claw-and-ball foot. The front and side skirts are typically constructed of solid mahogany, their interiors roughly contoured to follow the shape of their exteriors; the top is attached to the frame with six large screws. Except for a few examples with bunched acanthus leafage (e.g., Downs 1952, nos. 340–341), the tables of the group have C-scrolls and leafage motifs carved on their front knees. Though all are from the same shop, a number of different hands are discernible in their carving (Heckscher 1973, figs. 1–5). That of cat. no. 102 exhibits a distinctive manner, the leafage chiseled out in bold parallel cuts. The same hand executed all but identical tables now at the Art Institute of Chicago (*Antiques* 84 [September 1963], p. 226) and at the Boston MFA (Randall 1965, no. 84), as well as two others whose carving differs only in minor features, one at the MCNY (*Antiques* 69 [March 1956], p. 228, ill.) and its apparent mate (ibid. 67 [January 1955], p. 25).

PROVENANCE: Purchased at Plaza Art Galleries, New York City, from the auction of the estate of Mariana Van Rensselaer Kennedy, of New York City, by Ginsburg & Levy, Inc., which sold the table to the MMA. Because tables of this type were in fashion from the mid-1760s and because the last private owner was a direct descendant of Stephen Van Rensselaer II (1742–1769), cat. no. 102 may have been made for the Van Rensselaer Manor House at Albany, which Stephen built between 1765 and 1768. The entrance hall of the house is now installed in the American Wing at the MMA. From Stephen, the line of descent would have been to General Stephen Van Rensselaer III (1810–1864); to Cornelia Van Rensselaer Kennedy (1836–1866); to Henry Van Rensselaer Kennedy; to Mariana Van Rensselaer Kennedy.

CONSTRUCTION: The halves of the top are two solid boards hinged together at the back. The upper half unfolds to rest on the inner left rear leg, which swings out to support it. The lower half is attached to the frame with screws through the rails, two at front and back, one at each side. The inner surface is cut away: on the playing surface, to accommodate a fabric lining; at the corners, in squares to hold candlesticks; at the left of each of the four sides, in oval dishes for gaming counters. The thick, solid skirt boards, sawed out inside to conform roughly to the serpentine exteriors, are double pegged to the four corner legs. Gadrooning strips are nailed to the bottom of the front and side rails. The inner rear rail is tenoned to the rear legs. The outer rear rail is divided in half by a five-fingered knuckle-joint hinge. The stationary right part is butted to the right rear leg and nailed to the inner rear rail. The swing part is pegged to the inner left leg; behind it, in the inner rear rail, is an opening for a drawer sliding on runners nailed to the skirts (Heckscher 1973,

102 See also p. 343

figs. 6, 7). The front knees have carved C-scrolls; the outer sides of the rear knees are carved with plain acanthus leafage.

CONDITION: The dense mahogany, with its original finish, is a dark red in color. The knee brackets, except for the right front one, are replaced. The foot of the swing leg is split; its outer claw is replaced. The drawer is missing. The dark brown leather that covers the playing surface replaces the original lining, which was probably baize.

DIMENSIONS: H.: overall, 27⅞ (70.8); W.: top, 34⅛ (86.7), skirt, 32⅜ (82.2), feet, 35 (88.9); D.: top, open, 33¼ (84.5), top, closed, 16⅝ (42.2), skirt, 15½ (39.4), feet, 17¾ (45.1).

WOODS: Primary: mahogany. Secondary: white oak (outer rear rail); tulip poplar (inner rear rail, drawer slides); white pine (glue blocks).

REFERENCES: Plaza Art Galleries sale, 9/28/35, lot 427. *MMAB* n.s. 7 (Summer 1948), pp. 21, 25 (ill.). Comstock, fig. 367. Heckscher 1973, pl. II; figs. 2, 6, 7.

Purchase, Joseph Pulitzer Bequest, 1947   (47.35)

103. Card Table

New York, 1760–90

ENGLISH CARD TABLES with triple tops, inlaid backgammon boards, and wells in which to store hinged backgammon frames are not uncommon, but this is the only known one of New York origin. An examination of the parts related to the triple-top design suggests that such execution was not a standard New York practice. The swing leg is too long to be structurally sound, and the craftsman made three pairs of score marks on the swing rail before he finally established the proper placement of the tab. The table is otherwise a classic example of the second of the two distinctive groups of New York serpentine card tables (Heckscher 1973) into which most of the finest examples fall. The group, for which English prototypes are known (ibid., fig. 11), is called the Beekman

103 See also p. 343

type, after the family pair at the N-YHS (ibid., p. 981). The tables of the second group are readily distinguishable from those of the first (e.g., cat. no. 102) by the stationary top attached to the skirts with screws from above; the shallow, serpentine skirts normally veneered on pine (though here, on beech); the dainty gadrooning applied only on the front skirt; and the five legs whose ball feet have delicate, pointed claws. In addition to this one and the Beekman pair, other tables of the group are at the MCNY (*Antiques* 70 [November 1956], p. 454, ill.) and at Winterthur (Downs 1952, no. 338). All of them appear to be from the same shop, their knee carving—C-scrolls, leafage and rocaille mantels with incised peanut and pinwheel ornamentation—demonstrably all by the same hand.

PROVENANCE: Acquired for the MMA on August 21, 1937, by Ginsburg & Levy, Inc., at the house auction of the estate of Susan Weir, Garrison, New York. Robert W. Weir (1803–1889) was drawing instructor at the United States Military Academy at West Point between 1834 and 1876; when he retired from the academy faculty, he moved to Garrison. This table may be one

of the pieces of old furniture (e.g., Downs 1952, no. 354) he collected, some of it, according to family tradition, for use as studio props.

CONSTRUCTION: The top is three solid boards hinged together at the back. The uppermost unfolds to expose an inlaid light and dark-stained wooden chess and backgammon board outlined in stringing. The middle one, keying into slots in the other two by means of a tenon in its back edge, unfolds to reveal a playing surface cut out for a fabric liner and in corner squares to hold candlesticks, and, at the left of each of the four sides, in oval dishes for gaming counters. The lowest board is attached to the top of the rear rail with brass butt hinges, and can be lifted to provide access to a rectangular interior well. Because a backgammon board requires sides against which the counters can be stacked, the circular ivory plugs centered at front and back of this one held in place a two-part hinged frame that was folded up and stored in the well when not in use. The serpentine front and side skirt rails, the latter thick boards with straight inner surfaces, are mitered together where they join the front legs. The rails and the front stiles are covered with vertical flitches of figured veneers. A separate gadrooning strip is nailed to the bottom of the front rail. The rails are rabbeted at their lower edges to receive the bottom board. The thick rear rail, its top edge cut out in a rounded pen trough and two square wells for ink bot-

103

tles, is tenoned to the stiles, the joints reinforced inside with quarter-round glue blocks. The bottom of the rear rail is cut out to accommodate the inner rear leg, which is attached to the unusually long swing rail by a five-fingered knuckle-joint hinge. The swing rail extends below the other rails to the level of the knee brackets. Its top supports two boards when the lined playing surface is exposed; a tab recessed in it lifts to a greater height to support one board when the backgammon and checkerboard surface is in use. The knees of the rear legs are uncarved.

CONDITION: The table has a buildup of old, somewhat decayed finishes, and is a fine reddish brown in color. The skirt veneers and the stringing around the backgammon board have been patched and repaired. The back knee bracket of the right rear leg is a replacement, as is the lock that secures the well. The separate backgammon frame is missing. The green velvet that covers the card-playing surface is an old replacement. The original liner was probably baize.

DIMENSIONS: H.: overall, 28⅝ (72.7); W.: top, 33⅞ (86.), skirt, 32⅜ (82.2), feet, 35 (88.9); D.: top, open, 33⅝ (85.4), top, closed, 16¾ (42.), skirt, 15¾ (40.), feet, 18⅜ (46.7).

WOODS: Primary: mahogany; mahogany veneers; maple (inlaid playing surface). Secondary: beech, probably European (skirt rails); tulip poplar (bottom board); white pine (glue blocks).

REFERENCES: Joseph Downs, "New York Furniture," *MMAB* 33 (April 1938), pp. 109–110; fig. 2. Halsey and Cornelius, pl. 63. Downs 1949, pl. 26. Davidson 1967, fig. 296.

Rogers Fund, 1937 (37.122)

104. Card Table

New York, 1760–90

NEW YORK CARD TABLES with projecting rounded corners evolved from a type of table popular in England from about 1715 to 1730 (*DEF* 3, pp. 188–190). The New York tables—the so-called turret-type—have straight sides separated from the projecting circular front corners by serpentine bulges. On most examples, the skirts conform to the shape of the top, though a number with square frames are known (e.g., Downs 1952, no. 337).

Characteristic of the type is cat. no. 104, one of a small group of card tables identical in most details of design and construction and certainly all made in the same shop. Two are said to have Schuyler family histories, but though their tops, wider and deeper than that of this table, are cut from the same pattern, the two are not a pair. The front skirt of one of them (*Antiques* 81 [February 1962], p. 149) consists of vertical serpentine bulges on either side of a horizontal middle panel, and there is a hidden drawer; on the other (Sack 7, p. 1780), the front rail is faced with a single horizontal veneer and the drawer is absent. On a fourth table (P-B sale no. 1682, 5/19/56, lot

180) the small drawer centered in its front skirt is uncharacteristic in New York work. The four tables, all with uncarved rear knees, share a distinctive program of flat, somewhat ponderous carving: gadrooning on the front and side skirts and crosshatching on the front knees framed by acanthus leafage springing from the scrolled brackets. Below its knee carving, this example is further embellished with three circular drops.

PROVENANCE: Ex coll.: Louis Guerineau Myers, New York City.

CONSTRUCTION: The two halves of the top are hinged together at the back. The stationary lower half is affixed to the rails with square glue blocks. The upper half unfolds to rest on the left rear leg, which swings out to support it. The top's inner surface is cut out: on the playing surface, to accommodate a baize liner; on the circular corners, to hold candlesticks. The solid boards forming the front and side rails are dovetailed together. The front corners are built up into round turrets flanked by serpentine bulges. The turrets, through which the front legs continue, and the bulges are faced with vertical veneers. Carved gadroon strips are nailed to the bottom of the front and side rails. The inner rear rail, tenoned into the right rear leg and dovetailed to the left side rail, is nailed to the stationary half of the outer rear rail. The outer rear rail, double pegged to the stationary rear leg, is divided by a crudely sawed five-part finger-joint hinge. The swing half is double pegged to the left rear leg, which is covered by the left side rail when closed. Nailed to the front and inner rear rails is a dust board flanked by two braces which supports a small drawer accessible through the inner rear rail when the swing leg is open. The knees of both rear legs, nearly flat, have uncarved brackets.

104 See also p. 343

CONDITION: The table's soft, porous mahogany has a dark reddish brown color. There is a split in the folding top. A small part of the front gadroon strip is missing from the left side. Both front legs have split behind the knees: the left one has been reinforced with screws; the right one, with a glue block between the knee brackets. The faded green baize cover on the playing surface appears to be the original.

DIMENSIONS: H.: overall, 28⅞ (73.3); W.: top, 32⅞ (83.5), skirt, 31⅜ (79.7), feet, 33⅜ (84.8); D.: top, open, 33 (83.8), top, closed, 16½ (41.9), skirt, 15 (38.1), feet, 16½ (41.9).

WOODS: Primary: mahogany; mahogany veneers. Secondary: spruce (outer rear rail); white pine (glue blocks, drawer, drawer supports); tulip poplar (inner rear rail).

Rogers Fund, 1925   (25.115.33)

105. Card Table

New York, 1760–90

THIS TURRET-TOP TABLE descended in the Verplanck family en suite with a set of chairs (cat. no. 24) and a settee (cat. no. 82), all having similar legs—the knees with flat, shieldlike carving; the claw feet with small, distinctive rear talons. On the table, the shaping of the scrolls of the knee brackets and the design of the glue blocks differ from those of the seating furniture, suggesting that the set was the work of more than one man.

The MMA example is one of a handful of New York tables emanating from the same shop or from related

105

shops. The others of the group include a turret-top card table with solid top boards, leaf-carved knees, and a single swing leg (*Antiques* 79 [January 1961], p. 39) and two serpentine-sided rectangular tea tables with leaf-carved knees, one from the Halstead family of Rye, New York (Downs 1952, no. 374), the other illustrated in Lockwood (1901 edition, fig. 206; 1926 edition, 2, fig. 737, with gallery). All four pieces have pronounced gadrooning continued above the legs, cabriole legs with rounded and powerfully curved knees and ankles, and somewhat squat circular claw-and-ball feet with a small back talon emerging apparently independent of the leg. On cat. no. 105 the complex joinery of the folding frame—the accordion action—is meticulously realized. Accordion-action side rails, while rare on American-made card tables (see also Randall 1965, no. 79; Warren, no. 57), are not uncommon in England. Perhaps this example and the other tables of the group are the work of an English-trained craftsman recently arrived in the New World.

PROVENANCE: See cat. no. 24.

CONSTRUCTION: The top's two halves are hinged together at the back. Each is a central plank framed at front and sides by boards mitered together at the corner turrets. The lower half is screwed to the frame at the turrets and at the inner rear rail. The outer rear rail and the rear legs extend to support the unfolded upper half. The top's inner surface is cut out: on the playing surface, to accommodate a baize liner; on the circular corners, to hold candlesticks; at the left of each of the four sides, in oval dishes for gaming counters. The skirt between the turrets is the front of a drawer that opens when a wooden spring-lock nailed to the drawer bottom is released. Below the drawer and dovetailed to the vertical side rails is a horizontal board to which the gadrooning is nailed. The side rails are dovetailed to the inner rear rail. The turrets, formed of inch-thick vertical laminations at front and sides, mitered at their junctures, are wrapped in horizontal mahogany veneers. The continuous gadrooning at the front and sides is carved from boards mitered together under the turrets. The front legs have two tiers of horizontal glue blocks. The side rails are hinged to allow the table to fold; the accordion action, deployed when the rear legs and the outer rear rail are pulled out, doubles their width. Sliding wooden bolts let into the rails hold the rails rigid. The knees are carved on all four legs.

CONDITION: The table, which has a buildup of old varnishes, is a lustrous reddish brown in color. The stationary half of the top has been reattached (1979) in the original manner but with modern screws. The rear-leg knee brackets are replacements. Modern sliding brass bolts have been added to the wooden ones inside the hinged side rails. The green baize lining on the playing surface is an old replacement.

INSCRIPTIONS: Stamped, on one of a folding rail's iron hinges: *R I* [*R T?*].

DIMENSIONS: H.: overall, 28⅞ (*73.3*); W.: top, 37½ (*95.3*), skirt, 35¼ (*89.5*), feet, 36⅝ (*93.*); D.: top, open, 38 (*96.5*), top, closed, 19 (*48.3*), skirt, 18½ (*47.*), feet, 21 (*53.3*).

WOODS: Primary: mahogany; mahogany veneer. Secondary: mahogany (inner rear rail); birch (drawer front, glue blocks); tulip poplar (drawer sides, back, bottom); white pine (turret and side bulge laminations, drawer rails); Atlantic white cedar (drawer-front serpentine bulges, horizontal front board).

REFERENCES: [Downs], p. 155 (ill.). Margon 1965, p. 134 (measured drawings), p. 135 (ill.).

Gift of James De Lancey Verplanck and John Bayard Rodgers Verplanck, 1939 (39.184.12)

106. Card Table

Philadelphia, 1765–90

THE SERPENTINE SHAPE of the table's sides and front and its large front drawer, gadrooned skirts, and straight, molded Marlborough legs make it a classic example of one of Philadelphia's most popular card-table patterns. The Philadelphia cabinetmaker's price book of 1772 (Weil, p. 186) lists the prices for "Card tables with Marlborough feet" in mahogany:

Card table with a drawer without Baces or brackets	3	0 0
Ditto with baces & braqets	3	10 0
Ditto with Carved Moldings	4	0 0
Add for champing [chamfering?] the Tops	10s.	

The optional features, except for the "Baces" (cuffs), are to be seen on cat. no. 106. Though individual elements of the table's design can be found on one piece of English furniture or another, no specific prototype or engraved pattern-book source is known for this quintessentially Philadelphia form. The majority of the type have molded, and sometimes tapered, straight legs (Downs 1952, no. 346). Examples at the Boston MFA (Hipkiss, no. 62) and at the Ford Museum (Campbell, p. 10) share with this one the distinctive and identically executed twisted-rope carving centered in the leg molding; this one and the Ford Museum card table, with similar Marlborough-leg treatment, similarly figured mahogany top boards, and identical details of construction and carving, unquestionably originated in the same shop. A card table (*Antiques* 123 [April 1983], p. 725) and a Pembroke table (cat. no. 113), both with cuffs, also display the twisted-rope motif, but the carving, of a different character, cannot be attributed to any one hand.

The Philadelphia Marlborough-leg style is frequently associated with Thomas Affleck (1740–1795), the Scots cabinetmaker who emigrated to that city in 1763 (Hornor 1935, pp. 184–185). Hornor claims that Affleck made a number of card tables with Marlborough legs of various treatment (1935, pls. 255, 266), including one for his "Personal Friend" Sarah Redwood Fisher (ibid., pl. 269). For the United States Supreme Court Chamber, built in Philadelphia in 1791, Affleck made upholstered-back armchairs whose legs are also molded and have twisted-rope centers (ibid., pls. 298, 299). Though he produced much Marlborough-leg furniture, that alone does not justify an attribution of the MMA card table to him, for more than one Philadelphia maker worked in the same style.

PROVENANCE: Ex coll.: George S. Palmer, New London, Connecticut.

CONSTRUCTION: The two halves of the top are hinged together at the back. The left rear leg swings out to support the unfolded upper half. The lower half, screwed through the rails from below, is stationary; a tenon centered in its back edge keys into a slot in the upper half. The side rails are solid, their inner surfaces flat. The inner rear rail is dovetailed to the left side rail and abuts the right rear leg. On the outer rear rail, the stationary right half is nailed to the inner rail and tenoned to the leg; the left half and the rear leg tenoned to it swing out on a six-fingered knuckle-joint hinge. The horizontal rail above the front drawer is dovetailed into the tops of the front legs. On the drawer, the veneered front, its inner surface conforming to its serpentine exterior, has applied beaded edges; the drawer bottom, laid crosswise, is slotted into the front and side boards. The gadrooning, with carving arranged symmetrically around central leaf motifs on front and sides, is nailed to the skirt rails and fitted into slots in the legs. On the front legs, two sides are molded; on the rear legs, one. On all the legs, the inner edge is beveled.

CONDITION: The table is covered with a thick finish and is dark reddish brown in color. It has been extensively restored. The skillful repairs look to be the work of the Hartford firm of Robbins Brothers, which repaired a Philadelphia secretary (cat. no. 185) also from the Palmer collection. On the table, the top boards, veneered in thick matching figured mahogany, have been reconstituted. Because the grain is so similar to that on the original solid top of the Ford Museum table—both tops were apparently cut from the same log—the veneers of cat. no. 106 appear to have been sawed from its own original top boards. Except at the left front side, the pierced knee brackets are restorations. Tables of this type commonly lack rear-leg brackets, but here, since the bracket for the swing leg is in two equal parts—one nailed to the leg, the other to the side rail—as is that on another table (Hornor 1935, p. 181; pl. 290), they may be accurate copies of lost originals. The stile of the right rear leg is replaced, as are the drawer runners. The brasses are modern (early 20th-century).

DIMENSIONS: H.: overall, 28¾ (73.); W.: top, 35 (88.9), skirt, 32¾ (83.2); D.: top, open, 34 (86.4), top, closed, 17 (43.2), feet, 14½ (36.8).

WOODS: Primary: mahogany, mahogany veneer. Secondary: red oak (outer rear rail); yellow pine (inner rear rail); tulip poplar (drawer sides and back); cedar (drawer bottom).

REFERENCES: Nutting 1, fig. 1029.

John Stewart Kennedy Fund, 1918   (18.110.10)

106 See also p. 345

10 Dining Tables

In the days before separate dining rooms—in the late colonial period, generally—tables for dining, placed in the center of the room when in use and against the wall when not, had to be easy to move. Routinely described as dining tables by the seventeen-sixties and today called drop-leaf tables, this successor to the William and Mary-style gate-leg table consists of a narrow rectangular bed, or frame, to which are attached a stationary central top board with broad, hinged drop leaves and, usually, two fixed and two movable legs. Because most of the tops were rectangular, tables could be butted together. Only with the advent of the Federal period did semicircular tables become available for augmenting the basic rectangular form. Colonial dining tables could be had in almost any size, but were usually offered in six-inch increments to a frame three feet in length. The Museum's collection contains representative examples from the major cabinetmaking centers, but, save for an exceptional early Newport example and a massive, richly carved New York eight-legged table, they are without much distinction, as are the vast majority of the form.

107. Dining Table

Probably Newport, 1740–90

THE UNUSUAL DESIGN of this finely made little table does not readily fit into any known school of American cabinetwork. The table came from a member of the Schuyler family of New York, and its straight-kneed cabriole legs are indeed a feature sometimes found in New York work (e.g., Downs 1952, no. 318). The trifid pad feet, however, are of a type normally associated with Pennsylvania, and the pattern of the scalloped skirts and the scratch-beading on the leg stiles is not otherwise known. The best clues to the table's origin, therefore, are provided by the materials with which it is made. The white pine and birch suggest New England; the dense mahogany with purplish hue and areas of light-colored heartwood and the chestnut point specifically to Newport. Rhode Island merchants, John Brown of Providence in particular (Cooper 1973, pp. 328–332), not only ordered furniture in Newport but also imported it from Philadelphia, a practice that could explain the stylistic influence of that city on such a piece as this.

PROVENANCE: Purchased from the 1750 House Antiques shop, Sheffield, Massachusetts, which had acquired it from Dr. and Mrs. Frank Smith, Troy, New York. Dr. Smith bought the table from the estate of Garret Schuyler, Watervliet, New York, who had been one of his patients. In the Schuyler family of Albany, a Garret Schuyler (possibly the owner of this table), was the son of Samuel (1794–1870), son of John (1758–1852), son of Jacob, who was born in 1734.

CONSTRUCTION: The table and its supporting frame are rectangular when closed, the central top board secured with screws countersunk into the frame and, at the sides, with pairs of rectangular glue blocks. When open, the top is oval, the central board meeting the drop leaves in rule joints and attached to them with pairs of iron strap hinges. The sides of the frame are double railed. On each side, the outer rail is sawed into two parts by a finely cut seven-fingered knuckle-joint hinge. One part is stationary, double pegged to its adjacent leg and nailed with roseheads to the inner side rail; the movable part, quadruple pegged to its leg and forming the swing action, opens to support a raised leaf. The inner rail abuts the fixed leg at one end and is dovetailed to the skirt at the other, the joint reinforced with a vertical glue block.

CONDITION: The top is a reddish brown in color; the skirts and legs have an old, reddish purple patina. There is a small patch in the joint area of one drop leaf. One vertical glue block is missing.

DIMENSIONS: H.: 27¼ (69.2); W.: top, open, 39 (99.1), top, closed, 11¾ (29.8), frame, 11⅜ (28.9), feet, 11¼ (28.6); D.: top, 35½ (90.2), frame, 23⅜ (59.4), feet, 23½ (59.7).

WOODS: Primary: mahogany. Secondary: birch (outer side rails); white pine (inner side rails); chestnut (glue blocks).

REFERENCES: For the Schuyler family, see George W. Schuyler, *Colonial New York, Philip Schuyler and His Family*. 2 vols. (New York: 1885); see in particular 2, pp. 481–487.

Rogers Fund, 1934   (34.146)

108. Dining Table

Massachusetts, 1760–90

SMALL, CIRCULAR drop-leaf tables were widely made in eighteenth-century New England. An especially successful feature on this example is the rounded molding with scalloped edges that is applied to the end rails, continuing the curve of the knees. The claw feet with raked-back side talons and the crisply defined knees and skirt are details associated with rococo-spirited furniture from eastern Massachusetts, though the use of poplar for the outer rails is unusual for that region. The claw feet's rear talons are not integral to the curve of the leg, an uncommon feature also found on a table from the Hunneman family of Boston (Sack 6, p. 1452) and on some Massachusetts card tables (ibid., p. 1547; ibid. 2, p. 496). The table's legs suggest a more specific locale. The sharp-edged knees that switch abruptly to rounded legs and ankles—the so-called notched-knee treatment—are associated with the Salem area, and are displayed on numerous pieces that include Salem high chests (ibid. 6, p. 1562) and chairs with Salem histories (ibid. 4, p. 1013).

PROVENANCE: Ex coll.: Mrs. Giles Whiting, New York City.

CONSTRUCTION: When open, the table top is circular; when closed, a narrow rectangle. The top board and its flanking

leaves meet in rule joints and are secured with pairs of iron strap hinges. The central board is attached to the frame by a single screw countersunk into each of the four sides. The sides of the table frame are double railed. The outer rail is sawed in half with a six-part finger-joint hinge: one half, nailed with four roseheads to the inner rail, is double pegged to its fixed leg; the other half, double pegged to its leg, forms the swing action. The inner side rail is dovetailed to one skirt and abuts the other. The scalloping of the skirts and their molding is sawed out.

CONDITION: The table has a fine old patina. The top is reddish brown in color; the skirts and legs, reddish black. The drop-leaf hinges may be replacements. During construction, the maker cut mortices in the swing legs to receive tenons from the end rails as well as from the side, or swing, rails. Finding the mortices unnecessary, he then filled them in.

DIMENSIONS: H.: 27¼ (*69.2*); W.: top, open, 33¾ (*85.7*), top, closed, 11⅜ (*28.9*), frame, 8 (*20.3*), feet, 10¼ (*26.*); D.: top, 34 (*86.4*), frame, 24⅛ (*61.3*), feet, 25¾ (*65.4*).

WOODS: Primary: mahogany. Secondary: tulip poplar (outer side rails); white pine (inner side rails).

REFERENCES: *Antiques* 77 (January 1960), p. 90 (ill.).

Bequest of Flora E. Whiting, 1971   (1971.180.45)

108

109. Dining Table

Massachusetts, 1760–90

THIS EXAMPLE of the classic Massachusetts rectangular dining table exhibits a respectable, if uninspired, competence. In common with most drop-leaf tables of similar size from that area, it was designed with a straight-edged rectangular top so that two or more tables could be put together to form a large one.

PROVENANCE: Ex coll.: W. Gedney Beatty, Rye, New York.

CONSTRUCTION: The rectangular top consists of three rule-jointed boards of equal size. The central board is attached to the frame with glue blocks and to the drop leaves with pairs of iron strap hinges. The rectangular frame has double side rails. The outer ones, tenoned into the legs, are sawed with a six-part finger-joint hinge into two unequal pieces, the longer part nailed to the inner rail, the shorter part forming the swing action.

109

CONDITION: The table is of good, heavy wood. The top, with a slight figure in its grain, has been refinished; the table frame retains its dark old color. The glue blocks securing the top and three added at the frame's corners are modern, as are most of the hinge screws. A butterfly-shaped insert has been added underneath a split in one of the drop leaves. Three of the knee brackets are replacements. Pads have been added at the bottom of the stationary legs.

DIMENSIONS: H.: 28 (71.1); W.: top, open, 51 (129.5), top, closed, 15⅞ (40.3), frame, 14 (35.6), feet, 15⅞ (40.3); D.: top, 48 (121.9), frame, 38¼ (97.2), feet, 39⅞ (101.3).

WOODS: Primary: mahogany. Secondary: maple (outer side rails); white pine (inner side rails).

Bequest of W. Gedney Beatty, 1941   (41.160.393)

110. Dining Table

New York, 1755–90

LARGE DINING TABLES with six legs or eight, as here, were made more often in New York than anywhere else in America. Most of them have oval tops and a drawer at each end of the frame; the earliest examples have straight legs tapering to heavy, pointed pad feet. There are six-legged tables at Winterthur (Downs 1952, no. 318) and at Cherry Hill, the latter from the Viele family of Albany (Blackburn 1976, no. 84); eight-legged ones at the Abigail Adams Smith Museum, New York City; at Dearborn

(Hagler, p. 41); and at Williamsburg, a table from the Glen–Sanders family of Albany (Hendrick, no. 16). Another eight-legged table came from the Stuyvesant family, also of Albany (*Antiques* 79 [January 1961], p. 4). In his Day Book, on September 12, 1753, the New York City cabinetmaker Joshua Delaplaine records having made for Elias Desbrosses "a mahogany Dining table 5 foot 3 In. bed [frame], 8 legs, 2 draws" at a cost of £8-10-0 (J. Stewart Johnson, "New York Cabinetmaking Prior to the Revolution," Master's thesis, University of Delaware, 1964, p. 87).

A few straight-legged New York dining tables have claw-and-ball feet (*Antiques* 89 [January 1966], p. 9), including the Beekman family pair, with six legs and square tops, now at the N-YHS (acc. no. 1948.552ab). There are, in addition, at least two large dining tables with fully developed cabriole legs, leaf-carved knees, and claw feet. On a six-legged one (*Antiques* 61 [February 1952], p. 126), the knee carving matches that of a slab table (cat. no. 94) from the Bergen family of Flatlands, New York. On the other, cat. no. 110—surely in size and ornamentation the most ambitiously conceived of all New York dining tables—the carving of the gadrooning, knee leafage, and claw feet so closely matches that on sets of New York tassel-back chairs (e.g., cat. no. 28) as to suggest that the table and one of the sets were made en suite.

PROVENANCE: Ex coll.: Mr. and Mrs. Luke Vincent Lockwood, Greenwich, Connecticut.

110 See also p. 343

CONSTRUCTION: The figured central board, attached to the table frame by countersunk screws, is connected to each drop leaf by three iron strap hinges. With the leaves raised, the table top is oval. At each of the rectangular frame's four corners is a stationary leg and an adjacent swing leg. Four of the legs are cut from single pieces of wood; four are pieced on one side at knee and foot; all have astragal-beaded stile edges and carved knees and brackets. The frame has double side rails. The inner ones are double pegged to the legs. The outer ones are divided by five-fingered knuckle-joint hinges into three parts: a stationary middle one flanked by two movable ends, each pegged to an inner leg and forming the swing action. The inner rails are connected by a medial brace whose upper part—a batten with projecting dovetailed ends let into the tops of the rails—is screwed to the table top and whose lower part is a board the height of the rails, to which it is channel-dovetailed. At either end of the table frame is a drawer. The rail above it is double-tenoned into the leg stiles; the rail below it is pegged, and the gadroon strip is applied. On the drawers, the bottom boards, laid crosswise, are beveled on all four edges to slot into the drawer frame.

CONDITION: The table, now a reddish brown in color, has endured long neglect; the frame, parts of its underside weathered, bears evidence of exposure to the elements. Both drop leaves are old replacements. On their undersurface, marks from larger, more widely spaced swing rails and patches that cover the traces of four hinges show that the leaves were taken from a larger table and cut down for use here. The bottom board of one drawer and the rails on which both drawers slide are replaced. The tops of the drawer sides and backs have been partly cut away. The drawer brasses may be old replacements.

INSCRIPTIONS: In ink (late 19th-century?), on the original drawer bottom, mathematical calculations.

DIMENSIONS: H.: 29¼ (*74.3*); W.: top, open, 70 (*177.8*), top, closed, 21 (*53.3*), frame, 18⅝ (*47.3*), feet, 21¼ (*54.*); D.: top, 62 (*157.5*), frame, 51 (*129.5*), feet, 53¾ (*136.5*).

WOODS: Primary: mahogany. Secondary: mahogany (inner and outer side rails; drawer sides and backs); tulip poplar (drawer bottom); white pine (medial brace).

REFERENCES: Lockwood 2, fig. CXV. Downs and Ralston, no. 97. *MMAB* 29 (June 1934), p. 109 (ill.). Halsey and Cornelius, fig. 62. Downs 1949, pl. 20. Powel, p. 206 (ill.). Aronson, fig. 1219. Davidson 1967, fig. 292.

Purchase, Ella Elizabeth Russell Bequest, in memory of Salem Towne Russell, 1933   (33.142.1)

111. Dining Table

Philadelphia, 1740–60

THOUGH THE ARCHED and serpentine-scalloped skirts and the thumbnail-molded edges of the leg stiles on this early table are in the Philadelphia manner, the serpentined arch is unusually large, and scribe marks parallel to the curves of one skirt show that the cabinetmaker had first plotted an even larger opening. Unlike the vast ma-

jority of its fellows, which have rectangular tops (e.g., cat. no. 112), this one has a graceful oval. On the feet, the pads with tongues molded in alternate cavettos and ovolos demonstrate that feature carried to a high degree of accomplishment.

PROVENANCE: Ex coll.: W. Gedney Beatty, Rye, New York.

111

CONSTRUCTION: When the drop leaves are raised, the rule-jointed tripartite top is oval. The central part, two boards of equal width, is attached to the rectangular frame with wooden pegs, three into each end rail and one into each inner side rail, and to each of the two-board leaves, with pairs of iron strap hinges. The frame has double side rails, the outer ones sawed in half with five-fingered knuckle-joint hinges. One half is double pegged to its fixed leg and attached to the inner rail with five roseheads; the other, double pegged to its leg, forms the swing action. Each inner side rail abuts a fixed leg and is dovetailed to an end rail. On each leg, the backs of the two knee brackets are angled.

CONDITION: The table has an old finish and a mellow walnut brown color. A modern spline has been inserted between the two boards of the stationary top. The hinges on the drop leaves have been rescrewed. The stiles of the swing legs have been repaired. Three of the knee brackets are replaced. The feet have holes for casters.

INSCRIPTIONS: In chalk, on the underside of one leaf, a large calligraphic inscription: *83* or *E B* [?].

DIMENSIONS: H.: 28½ (*72.4*); W.: top, open, 59⅛ (*150.2*), top, closed, 18½ (*47.*), frame, 17¾ (*45.1*), feet, 19¼ (*48.9*); D.: top, 49 (*124.5*), frame, 38¼ (*97.2*), feet, 39¾ (*101.*).

WOODS: Primary: walnut. Secondary: yellow pine (inner side rails); white oak (outer side rails).

Bequest of W. Gedney Beatty, 1941   (41.160.367)

112

112.   Dining Table

Philadelphia, 1750–90

As HAVE MOST of its kind, this Philadelphia dining table has a rectangular top, here with the added refinement of "hollowed-out," or notched, corners. In eighteenth-century Philadelphia, this type of table was known as a "square leaf'd" dining table (Hornor 1935, p. 135), and was listed in the 1772 book of cabinetmakers' prices as "Dining table plain feet crooked." If "3 feet in the bed" (the depth of the frame), its cost in walnut was £1-17-6; if 3 feet 6 inches (the approximate size of this table), £2-5-0; "For tables with claw feet add 2.6d pʳ Claw" (Weil, p. 185). A few tables of this type are marked with the brand of cabinetmaker David Evans, who was active between 1774 and 1811 (*Antiques* 102 [October 1972], p. 505; Hummel 1955, p. 28), but otherwise no documented example is known.

PROVENANCE: Ex coll.: H. Eugene Bolles, Boston.

CONSTRUCTION: On the tripartite top, the central board meets the drop leaves in rule joints and is attached to each leaf with three iron strap hinges; it is secured to the frame by screws through two cross braces whose dovetail-shaped ends are let into the inner side rails. The rectangular frame has double side rails. The inner ones are dovetailed at both ends to the serpentine-arched skirts, the inner corners of the two fixed legs cut out to accommodate them. Each thick outer rail is divided into two parts by a six-fingered knuckle-joint hinge; one part affixed to the inner rail with six roseheads and double pegged to the stationary leg; the other, double pegged to its leg, forming the swing action. The serpentine brackets that flank each knee are triple nailed.

CONDITION: The table is a light reddish brown in color. The top has been rescrewed. Three of the knee brackets are replacements. There are breaks at the juncture of one of the swing legs and its rail and on one claw foot. The swing rails have been stained. The feet have holes for casters.

INSCRIPTIONS: In chalk, on the underside of one leaf: *Table* [?] and illegible mathematical calculations.

DIMENSIONS: H.: 28 (*71.1*); W.: top, open, 53¼ (*135.3*), top, closed, 15⅝ (*39.7*), frame, 14¼ (*36.2*), feet, 17 (*43.2*); D.: top, 48⅜ (*122.9*), frame, 40⅞ (*103.8*), feet, 43¾ (*111.1*).

WOODS: Primary: walnut. Secondary: white oak (outer side rails); yellow pine (inner side rails); maple (cross braces).

REFERENCES: Lee 5, p. 212 (ill.); p. 213 (measured drawings).

Gift of Mrs. Russell Sage, 1909   (10.125.144)

113.   Pembroke Table

Philadelphia, 1765–90

IN THE SECOND HALF of the eighteenth century, small drop-leaf tables with cross stretchers and four fixed straight legs were known as either Breakfast or Pembroke tables. Chippendale first illustrated a Breakfast Table in the 1754 edition of his *Director* (pl. XXXIII). Sheraton, in his 1803 *Cabinet Dictionary*, described the Pembroke table as a kind of breakfast table named for "the lady who first gave orders for one of them, and who probably gave the first idea of such a table to the workmen" (2, p. 284). Cat. no. 113 exemplifies the distinctively Philadelphia version of the type. With the optional features employed on it, chosen from among several listed in the Philadelphia cabinetmakers' price list of 1772 (Weil, p. 186), it would have cost £3-14-0:

Breakfast Table plain	2-15-0
Ditto with a Drawer	3-0-0
Ditto with baces & braqetes	3-5-0
Ditto with a plain Stretcher	3-10-0
Add for Scolloping the top	4s.

A handful of other Pembroke tables embellished with serpentine-sided tops are known, notably those at Winterthur (Downs 1952, nos. 313, 314), at the Wadsworth Atheneum (Comstock, fig. 359), and in the Stone collection (Rodriguez Roque, nos. 139, 140). Cat. no. 113 is unique in the group in having stump corners on its drop leaves, twisted-rope carving centered in the molded edges of its legs, and straight bases, or cuffs—all features found on a Philadelphia card table of the same style (*Antiques* 123 [April 1983], p. 725). The stump-cornered top and straight cuffs can be seen on another card table (Hipkiss, no. 61), while the molded legs with rope carving, though the work of another hand, are shared by cat. no. 106. Only two Philadelphia Pembroke tables have yet been attributed, one (Downs 1952, no. 314) branded by cabinetmaker Adam Hains (active 1788/89–1801); a plainer one said to have been made by David Evans in 1778 (Hornor 1935, pl. 257).

PROVENANCE: Ex coll.: Mr. and Mrs. Mitchel Taradash, Ardsley-on-Hudson, New York. Purchased by the MMA from Israel Sack, Inc., New York City.

CONSTRUCTION: When open, the rectangular table top has stump corners and four serpentine sides. The central board meets each narrow drop leaf at a rule joint secured with three iron strap hinges. The rectangular frame has double-railed sides. The inner ones are narrow and nailed to the outer ones; the outer ones are tenoned to the legs. Short wings—cut out of each rail in a six-fingered knuckle-joint hinge at one end, diagonal and with a finger grip at the other—swing out to support the raised leaves. Horizontal rails above and below the opening of the drawer at the front end are tenoned to the legs. Gadrooned strips are nailed to the bottom edges of the end rails and continue in slots cut into the molded surfaces of the legs. On the drawer, the front edges are scratch-beaded; the bottom, laid crosswise, is slotted into the sides and secured with glue blocks. The legs, molded and with a carved rope twist centered on their exposed surfaces, are square, with chamfered inner edges. Tenoned into the corners of the legs are saltire stretchers half-lapped and nailed at their juncture. The molded cuffs of the feet are applied.

CONDITION: The table has the original finish, now with a mellow, luminous, reddish brown patina. The left leaf, probably not often raised and thus protected from sunlight and wear, is a lighter red in color. All four pierced brackets were replaced in 1978. Glue marks and nail holes from the original brackets show that they were identical to those on a similar card table (cat. no. 106), one of which was used as the model for the copies. Except for that on the back of the left rear leg, the gadrooning around the exposed sides of the legs is restored. New glue blocks secure the top to the frame. One of the minor splits in the stationary top board is patched underneath with a butterfly-shaped insert, and there are additional splits in the stretchers where they cross and in the left rear leg where it meets the rails. Parts of the rear-leg cuffs are replaced. The fire-gilding has worn off the rococo cast drawer pull.

DIMENSIONS: H.: 28¼ (*71.8*); W.: top, open, 41½ (*105.4*), top, closed, 18⅛ (*46.*), frame, 17½ (*44.5*), feet, 18⅛ (*46.*); D.: top, 31¾ (*80.6*), frame, 28 (*71.1*), feet, 28½ (*72.4*).

WOODS: Primary: mahogany. Secondary: mahogany (inner side rails); white oak (outer side rails); tulip poplar (drawer sides, ends, runners); cedar (drawer bottom).

REFERENCES: Sack 1950, p. 249. MMA 1975, p. 22.

Purchase, Emily Crane Chadbourne Bequest, 1974   (1974.35)

113 See also p. 345

CHAPTER

11   Square Tea Tables

After mid-century, when the price of what had been a rare and costly luxury dropped, tea-drinking became widely fashionable, and special forms of tables were soon being developed to accommodate tea services. In New England, what were called square tea tables (even though they were invariably rectangular) were the prevalent type. Unlike dining and card tables, which were normally placed against the wall when not in use, these square tables, hospitably set for tea, frequently stood in the center of the parlor. The earliest Queen Anne examples have thin top boards with a broad overhang—an obvious holdover from the William and Mary style. Thereafter, in the classic form, the top was made to conform closely to the skirt, and a molded rim with concave inner side was attached to it. Plain, pad-footed tables were made in large numbers throughout New England, but carved and claw-footed examples in the Chippendale manner are exceedingly rare. The tables become progressively less common southward: unusual in New York, rare in Philadelphia. The Museum's holdings lack classic examples in the Boston Queen Anne and the later Newport style.

114. Square Tea Table

New England, 1740–60

114

ON THIS SPLENDID little table the powerful spring of the cabriole legs is continued gracefully into the deeply scalloped arches of the skirts. While the pieced and pegged knees and feet and the round-edged disks on which the pad feet are perched are individual characteristics not found on any other known example, an attribution to northern Massachusetts or southern New Hampshire may be hazarded on the basis of the skirt treatment. Here, the double ogee-arched scalloping has its closest parallel in a group of William and Mary tavern tables with stretchers and turned legs which have been associated with Essex County, Massachusetts, and Rockingham County, New Hampshire (Fales 1976, no. 295; MMA 1976, no. 8), though their arches consist of alternating cavetto and ovolo shapes instead of the small central arch flanked by serpentine curves found on this piece and also appearing on the triple-arched skirts of some New England high chests and dressing tables (e.g., cat. nos. 153, 154).

PROVENANCE: Ex coll.: H. Eugene Bolles, Boston.

CONSTRUCTION: Two pieces of wood of equal width form the top, which was originally secured to each end rail with four wooden pegs. The undersurface is rough-cut, its edges beveled to make the top appear thinner. The legs are of built-up stock. The piecing of each knee is secured with three wooden pegs; of each foot, with one. The skirt rails are double pegged. The knee brackets are glued to the skirt fronts. The absence of holes in the skirts shows that drop finials were never present.

CONDITION: The table, now a mellow honey color, was originally painted red, traces of which can be seen on the top and underneath the skirts. The old paint, the figure of the wood of the skirts partly visible through it, can be seen in a 1910 photograph (MMA files). Originally, there was an applied rim around the table top; stubs of the nails that secured it remain, and there are saw marks at each corner where its miter joint was cut in place. The top boards are now fastened to modern battens glued to the inner edge of each end rail. Only the tops of the original wooden pegs are still present. The pieced parts of two feet and of one knee bracket are replaced.

DIMENSIONS: H.: 26¼ (67.7); W.: top, 29 (73.7), skirt, 23⅜ (59.4), feet, 25⅛ (63.8); D.: top, 20½ (52.1), skirt, 15⅞ (40.3), feet, 18⅛ (46.).

WOODS: Primary: maple. No secondary woods.

REFERENCES: Lockwood 2, fig. 731.

Gift of Mrs. Russell Sage, 1909   (10.125.135)

115. Square Tea Table

Newport, 1740–60

THAT TEA TABLES of this type were very popular in Newport in the mid-eighteenth century is attested to by the large numbers of them that survive. They are all remarkably consistent in design and construction. The top is always let into the skirt frame, and the rim applied around it is almost always of the same pattern—rounded on the outside and with a broad, convex inner edge. (A table with a concave inner edge at the Brooklyn Museum is an exception.) None of the known examples are documented as to maker, locale, or date, nor do the few with family histories, this one included, provide much information. An attribution to Newport, based on stylistic affinities with case pieces from that city, is nevertheless convincing. The determining feature is the cabriole leg, which is square in section from knee to ankle and whose curve continues unbroken to the tip of the thin, pointed slipper foot.

Virtually identical leg treatment is found on a small group of Newport dressing tables, one documented to Job Townsend in 1746 (Rodriguez Roque, no. 17), and on a number of flat-topped high chests, one signed by Christopher Townsend and dated 1748 (Ott 1965, no. 57). It is therefore reasonable to suggest a date range in the mid-seventeen-forties or somewhat later for the Museum's delicate, graceful table; a logical speculation is

115

that the "Common Tea Table" valued at £7 in the Providence price list of 1756 (ibid., p. 174) may refer to one of its type. Though a few square tea tables have the characteristic Newport circular pad foot (e.g., Carpenter, no. 76), the form remained basically unchanged in Rhode Island until the seventeen-sixties, when the sides became serpentine, the knees carved, and the feet claw-and-ball. Not many of the latter are known, and none is in this collection.

116

PROVENANCE: The table descended in the family of the original owner. Stylistically, it appears to have been made in an earlier generation, but a family tradition has it that its first owner was Jacob Freese (died 1799), who married Vashti Thayer in 1773 and settled in Providence, Rhode Island. Jacob served as an officer during the revolutionary war. The table is said to have descended to Jacob II (1789–1880); to Professor Henry Simmons Frieze (1817–1889), whose name is inscribed under the top. (The spelling of the name was changed in the mid-nineteenth century.) At Henry's death, the table went to Lyman Bowers Frieze, Jr., of Staten Island, from whom it was inherited by Mr. and Mrs. Savage C. Frieze, Jr.

CONSTRUCTION: The molded rim is nailed to the solid, single-piece top. The top board's upper edge is beaded and laps over the skirts; the bottom is rabbeted to fit into the skirt well. An ovolo molding is glued to each skirt just above the bottom edge, with shaped brackets glued to the molding and to the knee. A single, roughly shaped vertical glue block reinforces each juncture of skirt board and stile.

CONDITION: The wood has a luminous mellow brown color. The side and tip of the pointed pad foot of one leg are patched. One knee bracket and four of the eight glue blocks are replacements.

INSCRIPTIONS: On undersurface of top board, in chalk: *S. Wyatt*; in pencil (19th-century): *Prof Frieze*.

DIMENSIONS: H.: overall, 25¼ *(64.1)*, top, 24⅞ *(63.2)*; W.: skirt, 30¼ *(76.8)*, feet, 31⅝ *(80.3)*; D.: skirt, 18¼ *(46.4)*, feet, 20 *(50.8)*.

WOODS: Primary: mahogany. Secondary: white pine (glue blocks).

Gift of Mr. and Mrs. Savage C. Frieze, Jr., and family, 1981 (1981.360)

116. Square Tea Table

New York, 1750–90

SQUARE TEA TABLES were made in New York in far fewer numbers than the circular, tilt-top kind. While lacking the carved knees and scalloped or gadrooned skirts typical of most of its counterparts (e.g., Downs 1952, nos. 315, 367), this one has the ample stance, blocklike claw-and-ball feet, and large, flat pine glue blocks characteristic of New York work. The somewhat square knees and the applied, convex skirt molding bear a general resemblance to the ubiquitous Newport pad-footed tea table (see cat. no. 115), reflecting the close economic and cultural ties between those two colonies.

PROVENANCE: Ex coll.: Mrs. Giles Whiting, New York City.

CONSTRUCTION: The miter joint at each corner of the top's applied rim is filled with a notched piece of wood. The two-piece top is secured to the skirts by large, rectangular glue blocks. An ovolo molding, the knee brackets glued beneath it, is nailed to each skirt just above the bottom edge. The skirts are double pegged to the legs, each juncture reinforced with a quarter-round glue block.

CONDITION: The table is reddish tan in color. The two-piece top, though atypical, appears to be the original, but the beaded edge nailed to it on all four sides below the rim is a replacement. The top may originally have been a single piece that split down the middle when the wood shrank and the tightly nailed frame would not give. If so, it may have been removed, the edges of the split trimmed and glued together, and the top reattached. Because the sides would then have been too narrow for the reduced top, the beaded edges may have been shaved off, and the new beading applied. At one time battens were screwed to the undersurface of the top, across the medial joint. Part of one knee bracket is replaced. The top glue blocks have been reset.

DIMENSIONS: H.: overall, 28⅜ (72.1), top, 27¾ (70.5); W.: skirt, 29⅞ (75.9), feet, 31⅞ (81.); D.: skirt, 18⅞ (47.9), feet, 20¼ (51.4).

WOODS: Primary: mahogany. Secondary: white pine (glue blocks).

Bequest of Flora E. Whiting, 1971   (1971.180.44)

117. Square Tea Table

Boston, 1755–90

THE SHALLOW, straight-leaf acanthus carving on this table's sharp-edged knees and the high-stepping, raked-back talons of its claw-and-ball feet are entirely in the Boston manner. Similar leg treatment is found on a sizable group of chairs that include cat. nos. 12, 13, and 74. On this last, an easy chair, and on cat. no. 117 the knee carving looks to be by the same hand. Such leg treatment, oddly, is rare on tables. Exceptions include a marble slab table at Winterthur (Downs 1952, no. 356) and this possibly unique square tea table.

PROVENANCE: Ex coll.: Lesley and Emma Sheafer, New York City. Purchased by the donors from Ginsburg & Levy, Inc., New York City. According to the dealer (receipt, 5/5/50, MMA files), "This table came down in the Taylor family of Salem, Massachusetts, and may have been made for John Wingate Taylor, a merchant of Salem in the last quarter of the 18th century."

117 See also p. 344

CONSTRUCTION: The rails are tenoned into the stiles, the junctures reinforced with vertical oblong glue blocks. A torus molding is nailed to each skirt above its lower edge. The knee brackets are nailed in place.

CONDITION: The table frame has a luminous deep reddish brown color. The top, with its applied rim, is a replacement. Of fine old wood now dark brown in color, it extends well beyond the end skirts but barely covers the side ones.

DIMENSIONS: H.: overall, 29 (73.7), top, 28¼ (71.8); W.: skirt, 28 (71.1), feet, 29½ (74.9); D.: skirt, 19⅝ (49.9), feet, 21½ (54.6).

WOODS: Primary: mahogany. Secondary: white pine (corner glue blocks).

The Lesley and Emma Sheafer Collection, Bequest of Emma A. Sheafer, 1973   (1974.356.40)

118. Square Tea Table

Portsmouth, New Hampshire, 1765–75

THE TABLE IS ONE of six similar examples all employing New England maple as a secondary wood and all attributable to a single Portsmouth cabinet shop. Five have historical associations with prominent Portsmouth families. One at the Warner House is thought to have belonged to merchant William Whipple: the "rail'd tea Table" valued at 48 shillings that appeared in his 1788 inventory along with a matching "raild [kettle] stand" worth 24 shillings (Rhoades, p. 41). Another (Lockwood 2, fig. 738), which has descended in the Wendell family with an en suite kettle stand (Biddle, no. 84), is said to have been acquired at the sale of the effects of the colony's last royal governor,

118 See also p. 345

Sir John Wentworth (1736–1820), when he fled to Nova Scotia in 1776. A third (*Antiques* 86 [July 1964], p. 58, no. 8), now at the Carnegie Institute, was owned by the merchant Stephen Chase (died 1805), and cat. no. 118 must have been made for the Cutts or Knight family (see Provenance). A tea table at the Department of State reportedly belonged to Mary Anderson Poore of Greenwood, Maine (Fairbanks and Bates, p. 172). The sixth, privately owned (Girl Scouts, no. 653), is without provenance.

Chippendale designed a rectangular tea table with arched, double-C-scroll crossed (saltire) stretchers like those on cat. no. 118 which he described as a "China Table" (*Director*, 1754 edition, pl. XXXIV; 1762 edition, pl. LI). With its shaped top, cabriole legs, and elaborate carving, it can hardly have been the direct inspiration for the New Hampshire version; rather, the American interpretation is an amalgam of features found on both English and Irish tables (Oedel, pp. 9–10): the English, with similar legs and stretchers (ill. in Anthony Coleridge, *Chippendale Furniture*, New York, Clarkson Potter, 1968, pl. 214); the Irish, with similar galleries, skirts, pierced finials, and stretchers supported by iron brackets (Hinckley, fig. 811). None of the galleries originally around the tops of all six tables seem to have survived. The solid gallery with undulating top edge, probably copied from the photograph in the Girl Scouts 1929 exhibition catalogue (that gallery itself likely a replacement), was put on cat. no. 118 prior to 1945.

PROVENANCE: According to the legend on a plaque set into one of the side rails, the table descended from the wealthy Boston Tory merchant Francis Borland (died 1775); to his grandson Joseph S. Borland (died 1875); to Louisa Marble, from whom it was purchased by A.M. Harrison (see Inscriptions). Francis Borland was the fourth husband of Phoebe Cutts of Portsmouth. Phoebe's sister Deborah was married to the Portsmouth merchant William Knight, possibly identifiable with the "W Knight" inscription on the underside of the table top (Oedel, pp. 8–9). Ginsburg & Levy, Inc., New York City,

purchased the table out of the Vassall–Longfellow House in Cambridge, Massachusetts, and first offered it for sale in 1945. It was in the collection of Ima Hogg from 1947 until shortly before 1961, when, again at Ginsburg & Levy, it was bought by the MMA.

CONSTRUCTION: The top board, projecting on all sides as an exposed torus molding, rests on the skirt rails. It is attached to the rails by nails set in through the slot around the edge that houses the gallery. The stiles and skirt rails are covered with crossbanded veneer. The beaded lower-edge molding is nailed to the bottom of the rails. On each leg, the outer surfaces are molded; the inner edge is chamfered. The pierced corner brackets are reinforced with mahogany strips. Each stretcher is a single piece dovetailed to the turned and pierced central finial, notched along the inner edge of a leg, and screwed through an iron brace driven into the leg that supports the stretcher.

CONDITION: The table is of a rich, red mahogany color. The gallery and the applied cuffs of the feet are restorations. Modern metal angle irons have been added to hold the top in place. Two of the pierced corner brackets have been mended. The brass casters are old, but may not be original to the piece.

INSCRIPTIONS: In white chalk, on the undersurface of the top: *W Knight*. Engraved on a silver plaque, probably of late nineteenth-century origin, let into one of the side rails: *This table was imported from England by Francis Borland, an English Tory, who was killed by falling from his roof while witnessing the Battle of Bunker Hill, June 17, 1775. It descended to his grandson Joseph S. Borland, who died in Somerset, Mass. May 1875. Was bequeathed to Louisa Marble, and purchased of her in August 1875 by A.M. Harrison U.S. Coast Survey.*

DIMENSIONS: H.: top, 27⅛ (68.9); W.: skirt and legs, 35 (88.9); D.: skirt and legs, 23 (58.4).

WOODS: Primary: mahogany; mahogany veneer. Secondary: maple (skirt rails).

REFERENCES: *Antiques* 48 (October 1945), p. 191 (ill.). Malcolm Vaughan, "Made in Boston or Philadelphia?," *American Collector* 15 (April 1946), pp. 5, 17. Comstock, fig. 373. Davidson 1967, fig. 309. Rhoades, pp. 41–43. Oedel.

Purchase, Mrs. Emily Crane Chadbourne Gift, 1961   (61.42)

12 Round Tea Tables

As were those of the square type, round tea tables supported on a turned pillar and three legs—a tripod base—were usually set with a tea service and placed in the center of the parlor. If the table was in the way, the top could be tilted to a vertical position and the table pushed into a corner. In addition to being called round tea tables they were known in the eighteenth century as pillar-and-claw or, simply, claw tables. Associated particularly with Philadelphia, the form was made there in great numbers, almost to the exclusion of the square type. Included in the collection are both standard models and elaborately carved bespoke pieces that run the gamut of Philadelphia types and sizes from one in the Queen Anne style being made by 1740, when "Brass tea table ketches" were offered for sale, to a carved Chippendale version with scalloped top, which was in vogue by 1755. Round tea tables were introduced by the mid-seventeen-forties into New York, where they shared the stage with square ones: the rimless tops and turned pillars typical of the region are well represented in the Museum's examples. Cabinetmakers and turners in both Philadelphia and New York virtually mass-produced legs and turned pillars for the tables. Though the form was relatively less common in New England, where most of the known types have serpentine tops, that region is represented in the collection by a marvelous octagonal-top maverick from Connecticut.

119. Round Tea Table

Philadelphia, 1740–90

ON THIS PLAIN but satisfying table, the baluster-shaped pillar with its crisp and delicate ring turnings is one of three identifiable Philadelphia types, though the bulbous part has higher, fuller shoulders than have most others of the pattern. Characteristic Philadelphia features are the molded rim of the circular top and the small, baluster-shaped pillars of the birdcage, or box. The butt ends of the legs do not exactly fit the curve of the pillar, suggesting that the legs may have been supplied by one maker, the pillar by another. An entry in the 1772 Philadelphia price book would aptly describe cat. no. 119: a walnut tea table with "plain top & feet" costing £1-15-0 (Weil, p. 187).

PROVENANCE: Ex coll.: Louis Guerineau Myers, New York City.

CONSTRUCTION: The top tilts vertically and, when horizontal, rotates freely in the manner of a modern lazy Susan. A pair of cleats laid on edge and placed at right angles to the grain are screwed to the undersurface of the top. Fixed between the cleats is a box—the so-called birdcage—which consists of two square boards connected by four small, turned pillars whose dowellike ends are wedged in place. At one end of the top board, the sides extend as dowels that fit into holes in the cleats, forming a hinge by which the top can be tilted; a brass spring catch at the other end holds the top fast in the horizontal position. The box, which rests on a molded flange at the top of the pillar, is held in place by a wooden wedge slotted through the pillar and prevented from tipping by a separate, doughnutlike collar beneath the wedge. The pillar continues as a large dowel through the box, which rotates around it.

The table top is of two equal pieces of wood joined by wooden dowels and iron pins; its molded rim is cut from the solid. The cleats, rounded on the bottom, taper toward the ends, where they are cut away in a sharp curve. The brass catch is in the shape of a pointed teardrop. On the box, score marks on the bottom board's roughly finished undersurface show how the holes for the double-wedged small pillars were plotted. The concave butt ends of the cabriole legs are dovetailed to the pillar and secured by a three-armed iron brace. The rounded pad feet are chiseled out on the bottom in bevel-edged pads.

CONDITION: The table has the original finish, now a mellow brown in color. There are numerous stains on the top, and the rim is chipped. Additional screws in the cleats are modern. The hinge part at the top of the box is an old restoration. The wedge is a replacement, as may be the collar.

INSCRIPTIONS: In white paint (20th-century), near the clasp on the box's top board: *197*.

DIMENSIONS: H.: 29 (*73.7*); diam., with grain, 34½ (*87.6*), across grain, 33½ (*85.1*); feet, span, 25½ (*64.8*).

WOODS: Primary and secondary: walnut.

REFERENCES: Margon 1949, pp. 91–94 (measured drawings).

Rogers Fund, 1925   (25.115.32)

120. Round Tea Table

Philadelphia, 1740–90

THE MOST COMMON of the three characteristic Philadelphia pillar types—the compressed ball and column—is represented here in its simplest version. The top, with a diameter of just under twenty-four inches, is but two-

119

120

thirds the size of the average tea table. The 1772 Philadelphia price book lists such a table "22 Inches with a box plain top & feet" for £1.5.0 in walnut under "folding Stands" (Weil, p. 187). As with cat. no. 119, the butt ends of the legs do not exactly fit the curve of the pillar. That, combined with the variety of woods employed in the table, suggests that the various elements were mass-produced by specialized craftsmen prior to its assembly.

PROVENANCE: Ex coll.: Louis Guerineau Myers, New York City.

CONSTRUCTION: The top, with its shallow molded rim, is cut from a solid piece of burled and striped wood. The cleats, rounded on the bottom, taper to angled ends. The brass catch is in the shape of a pointed teardrop. The box permits the table top to rotate or to tilt into a vertical position, as described at cat. no. 119. Between box and pillar is a thin leather washer. The concave butt ends of the legs are dovetailed to the pillar, the legs reinforced with a three-armed iron brace.

CONDITION: The table is a mellow brown in color. It was once covered with brown paint, which remains on the undersurface of the top and on the inside of the box. The top is much worn, especially on its molded rim. The hinge at the top of the box, made of maple and attached with three large roseheads, appears to be a replacement (18th-century). The bottoms of the feet are rotted.

DIMENSIONS: H.: 28½ (72.4); diam., with grain, 23½ (59.7), across grain, 23¼ (59.1); feet, span, 22 (55.9).

WOODS: Primary: maple (top, small pillars); beech (main pillar, legs); mahogany (top and bottom boards of box). Secondary: mahogany (cleats).

Rogers Fund, 1925   (25.115.35)

121

121. Round Tea Table

Philadelphia, 1740–90

THIS IS A CLASSIC example of the uncarved Philadelphia tea table described in the 1772 local price book as "plain Tea Table with Claw feet" and costing £3-15-0 in mahogany and £2-5-0 in walnut (Weil, p. 187). Here, the columnar shaft is thicker and squatter than the usual compressed-ball-and-column type. What further distinguishes the table—clearly the work of an exceptional craftsman—is its ball feet, which are grasped by some of the boldest and most powerful talons in all Philadelphia furniture. Similar feet are found on an otherwise totally dissimilar table in the Karolik Collection (Hipkiss, no. 58).

PROVENANCE: Ex coll.: Louis Guerineau Myers, New York City.

CONSTRUCTION: The circular top, cut out in a delicate molded rim, is made of a wide board of fine crotch figure pieced at one side with a strip, just under four inches wide, apparently cut from the same log. The cleats are rounded on the bottom and taper to cut-out ends. The brass catch is in the shape of a pointed teardrop. The box permits the table top to rotate or to tilt into a vertical position, as described at cat. no. 119. On the box, the small baluster pillars are double wedged. The concave butt ends of the legs conform precisely to the curve of the pillar, to which they are dovetailed. The joints are reinforced with a three-armed, pointed-end iron brace attached with roseheads.

CONDITION: The table is a lustrous walnut brown in color. A dark and heavy old finish remains on the undersurface of the top and legs and on parts of the box. There are two small patches in the rim. The cleats have been reattached through the top with four screws, the holes then filled. The collar and its wedge are replacements. One leg, part of its claw missing, has been reattached to the pillar; the corresponding arm of the iron brace has been replaced.

DIMENSIONS: H.: 29½ (74.9); diam., with grain, 35¾ (90.8), across grain, 35⅜ (89.9); feet, span, 27¼ (69.2).

WOODS: Primary and secondary: mahogany.

Rogers Fund, 1925   (25.115.34)

122. Round Tea Table

Philadelphia, 1740–90

AT FIRST GLANCE, the tea table appears to be identical to cat. no. 121, but its feet are higher and narrower, its pillar is thinner, and its columnar shaft is longer. Though more delicately proportioned, it lacks the other's bold stance and exceptionally well-carved feet. Different mak-

122

ers for the two tables are indicated by disparities in the shape of their cleats and the junctures of their legs and pillars and in the carving of their claw feet. Very like cat. no. 122 is a table (Sack 1, p. 200) bearing the engraved label of the Philadelphia cabinet- and chairmaker Edward James, who died in 1798.

PROVENANCE: Ex coll.: W. Gedney Beatty, Rye, New York.

CONSTRUCTION: The top, cut out in a delicate molded rim, is made of a wide board of figured wood and a narrow side piece from a different board. The cleats, rounded on the bottom, taper toward the ends. The brass catch is circular. The box permits the table top to rotate or to tilt into a vertical position, as described at cat. no. 119. The flat butt ends of the legs are dovetailed into the pillar, the joints reinforced with a three-armed iron brace.

CONDITION: The table has a deep reddish brown color under a decayed later finish. The collar is old, but from another table. The wedge is replaced.

DIMENSIONS: H.: 29¼ (74.3); diam., with grain, 35⅜ (89.9), across grain, 35 (88.9); feet, span, 24¼ (61.6).

WOODS: Primary and secondary: mahogany.

Bequest of W. Gedney Beatty, 1941   (41.160.396)

123. Round Tea Table

Philadelphia, 1760–90

THIS TABLE POSSESSES the urbanity of the best ornamentally carved Philadelphia circular tea tables. The top is a finely figured board with a delicate, crisply carved

rim; the fluting is narrow; the small-scale, naturalistic carving is discreetly placed. The table conveys an impression of controlled resilience, the result of the exceptionally high knees and, on the pillar, the unusually flattened ball. Another table (*Antiques* 63 [May 1953], p. 383; ibid. 73 [March 1958], p. 258), identical to this one in overall design and in every detail of construction—the scalloped edge of its top is even cut from the same template—can be ascribed to the same maker, though differences in the carving on the pillar and knees demonstrate that the two were not made as a pair. Carved tables described in the 1786 Philadelphia price book as having "claw feet," "Leaves on the knees," and "Scollop'd Top & Carv'd Pillar," obtainable in mahogany for £5-15-0, might well include cat. no. 123; "Fluting the pillar" cost an additional five shillings (Gillingham 1930, p. 299).

PROVENANCE: Ex coll.: Louis Guerineau Myers, New York City.

CONSTRUCTION: The high and thin rim of the single-piece top is divided into segments—eight scalloped alternating with eight plain. The cleats, rounded on the bottom and tapering toward the ends, are attached to the top with round-headed screws. The brass catch is in the shape of a pointed teardrop. The box permits the table top to rotate or to tilt into a vertical position, as described at cat. no. 119. On the pillar, the compressed ball is carved in leafage on a stippled ground; the bottom, in a ribbon-and-flower band. The legs have flat butt ends dovetailed to the pillar, the joints reinforced with a three-armed iron brace. The feet are cut out to accommodate brass casters with leather rollers.

123

123 See also p. 346

CONDITION: The table, which is remarkably well preserved, is a luminous reddish brown in color. Later finishes have been removed from the top, but there is a buildup of varnish around the carving on pillar and legs.

DIMENSIONS: H.: 27½ (*69.9*); diam., with grain, 33⅜ (*84.8*), across grain, 33 (*83.8*); feet, span, 27¼ (*69.2*).

WOODS: Primary and secondary: mahogany.

REFERENCES: Nutting I, fig. 1118. Hornor 1931, p. 39, fig. 6. Miller 2, fig. 1388 (detail). Halsey and Cornelius, pl. 68. Rogers, fig. 36. Downs 1949, no. 28. Davidson 1967, fig. 269. MMA 1976, no. 23.

Rogers Fund, 1925   (25.115.31)

124. Round Tea Table

Philadelphia, 1760–90

THE TABLE FITS into a group of Philadelphia tea tables whose pillars are in the form of a vase and a tapered column. Compared with most such examples (e.g., Hornor 1935, pls. 223, 226), this has a squatter vase and a taller and broader column; on its top, the piecrust edge is divided into eleven scalloped units rather than the usual eight or the occasional ten. The legs, fully rounded at the knees and ankles and having intertwined acanthus-frond knee carving, are distinctive. Identical legs appear on tables with compressed ball and column pillars, the top of one with a plain molded rim (Barnes and Meals, no. 118); another with an eight-unit piecrust edge (*Antiques* 21 [March 1932], p. 114). Yet another is said to have been made in 1779 by Thomas Affleck for Levi Hollingsworth (Hornor 1935, pl. 216).

PROVENANCE: Ex coll.: George Coe Graves, Osterville, Massachusetts.

CONSTRUCTION: The molded rim of the single-piece straight-grained mahogany top consists of alternating segments, eleven scalloped and eleven plain. The cleats, rounded on the bottom, taper sharply toward the ends. The box permits the table top to rotate or to tilt into a vertical position, as described at cat. no. 119. The collar of the box is secured by a tapered round peg. The concave butt ends of the legs conform to the curve of the pillar, to which they are dovetailed. A three-armed iron brace attached with roseheads reinforces the joints.

124 See also p. 346

CONDITION: The table is a tawny brown in color. Parts of the rim are patched. The hinge part of the box has been repaired. The collar looks to be modern. The brass catch, in the shape of a pointed teardrop, is an old replacement.

DIMENSIONS: H.: 28¼ (71.8); diam., with grain, 35½ (90.2), across grain, 35 (88.9); feet, span, 26 (66.).

WOODS: Primary and secondary: mahogany.

The Sylmaris Collection, Gift of George Coe Graves, 1930 (30.120.34)

125

125. Round Tea Table

New York, 1760–90

THE CUP AND FLARED SHAFT of this pillar is a pattern found on a large number of New York round tea tables and stands. The rimless top, the collarless box, and the similar cup turnings on the main pillar and on the small pillars of the box are also classic features of New York design. Less conventional are the ridges along the top edges of the legs and the elongated triangles where the balls of the feet meet the floor. Long histories of ownership in New York state accompany tables with this type of pillar: cat. no. 125, in the Verplanck family; three others, in the Van Rensselaer (Hendrick, nos. 27, 29; Blackburn 1976, no. 38).

PROVENANCE: See cat. no. 24.

CONSTRUCTION: On the underside of the top, the cleats are rounded on the bottom and at the ends. The brass catch is in the shape of a pointed teardrop. The box permits the table top to rotate or to tilt into a vertical position, as described at cat. no. 119, but here lacking the collar. The flat butt ends of the legs are dovetailed to the pillar and reinforced with a three-armed iron brace.

CONDITION: The dense heavy wood of the pillar and legs has a reddish hue, but that of the top has faded to a nut brown. The hinge part of the box, the wedge that secures the box to the pillar, and the brass catch return are replacements. The cleats and the brass catch have been rescrewed.

DIMENSIONS: H.: 27¾ (70.5); diam., with grain, 28 (71.1), across grain, 27⅝ (70.2); feet, span, 24 (61.).

WOODS: Primary and secondary: mahogany.

Gift of James De Lancey Verplanck and John Bayard Rodgers Verplanck, 1939   (39.184.11)

126. Round Tea Table

New York, 1750–90

NOT UNLIKE THAT on the somewhat larger Verplanck table (cat. no. 125), the cup-and-flared-shaft pillar is one of the standard New York turned models; the pinched claw-and-ball feet are found on most New York tripod tables and screens (e.g., cat. no. 127). Both features appear on the tea table made for Robert Sanders (1705–1765), a mayor of Albany (Blackburn 1976, no. 38), and on a firescreen at Winterthur, its original needlework marked "New York . . . 1766" (Hummel 1976, fig. 20). The unusual treatment of the rim—the fillet defining it not on the top but on the undersurface—is similar to that on a table of the same size with the brand of Philip Van Rensselaer (Blackburn 1976, no. 64). A number of full-size tea tables with this pillar design are known, including one from the Haslett family of Brooklyn (Donald A. Peirce, "New York furniture at the Brooklyn Museum," *Antiques* 115 [May 1979], p. 1000, pl. VI).

PROVENANCE: Ex coll.: The Reverend George Drew Egbert and Mrs. Egbert, Flushing, New York. On loan to the MMA from the Egbert children from 1940 until given in 1966.

CONSTRUCTION: The top tilts to a vertical position. When horizontal, the top is secured by a circular brass catch. Straight-bottomed cleats that taper to flat ends are hinged to a thick square block inserted on the top of the pillar in lieu of a box. The flat butt ends of the legs are dovetailed into the pillar.

CONDITION: The table has an old finish and a mellow reddish brown color. The brass catch return is partly restored. There are old breaks in one foot and where one leg meets the pillar. The junctures of legs and pillar are reinforced by a brace added in 1978.

126

DIMENSIONS: H.: 28 (*71.1*); diam., with grain, 24½ (*62.2*), across grain, 24⅛ (*61.3*); feet, span, 21¼ (*54.*).

WOODS: Primary and secondary: mahogany.

Given in memory of George Drew Egbert and Estelle Powers Egbert by their children, 1966   (66.108.2)

127. Round Tea Table

New York, 1770–90

ALL THE CHARACTERISTIC features of New York work can be found on this big and heavy table. The baluster-shaped shaft is the most common of three popular New York patterns; the thick circular top is rimless; the box, its small pillars also baluster-shaped, is secured to the shaft with a collarless wedge. Though these are all features that can be seen on a number of graceful tables and stands (e.g., *Antiques* 114 [December 1978], p. 1212) labeled by Thomas Burling (active 1769–1800), cabinet- and chairmaker of New York City, other evidence suggests that the table is of Albany manufacture. A knot in one of its legs implies rural work, as does the relative inelegance of its turned shaft. It bears the PVR brand signifying ownership by Philip Van Rensselaer (1749–1798), married in 1768 to Maria Sanders, whose father was a

mayor of Albany. More than twenty pieces of regional New York Chippendale-style furniture having the PVR brand are known (Blackburn 1976). All appear to have been used at Cherry Hill, the farm on the outskirts of Albany that Philip acquired around the time of his marriage and the site of a commodious house he built in 1786.

A table with the same construction and appearance, identical to this one except for its slightly smaller top, is at the Albany Institute (Rice, p. 42). It descended from Johannes Knickerbocker, who built the Knickerbocker Mansion at Schaghticoke, across the river from Albany, in 1770. Both Knickerbocker and Philip Van Rensselaer owned tall clocks with works signed "Dav^d Morras / Muchty," presumably a local man named David Morris (Rice, p. 19; Blackburn 1976, no. 39). The clocks and tables suggest that the two men routinely employed the same local craftsmen. The tripod stands and turned shafts of a small number of New York firescreens (Downs 1952, no. 241; Rodriguez Roque, no. 194), except for their size, are identical to cat. no. 127 and have similar knee carving. On another firescreen, with a more gracefully turned shaft and with the pointed pad feet of the emerging neoclassical style, the original fabric was worked in 1793 by Arriet Van Rensselaer, daughter of Maria and Philip (Blackburn 1976, no. 56).

PROVENANCE: The table descended in 1904 from Anna Eliza Van Rensselaer Hoff to Elizabeth Hoff Greene; in 1926, to Anna Greene Bates; in 1938, to the last private owner, Elizabeth Bates Carrick, Princeton, New Jersey, who put it on loan at the MMA that same year. Its prior history is uncertain. The PVR brand

127

suggests that it was part of Philip Van Rensselaer's furniture at Cherry Hill, but the 1852 inventory of the house makes no mention of it. According to family tradition (10/26/78 letter from donor, MMA files), the table had belonged to Philip's younger brother Killian (1763–1845).

CONSTRUCTION: The plain top is fashioned from a heavy board with a sweeping curve in its grain. The cleats have rounded bottom edges tapering to beveled ends. The box permits the table top to rotate or to tilt into a vertical position, as described at cat. no. 119, but here lacking the collar. The butt ends of the legs are flat where they are dovetailed to the pillar. A three-armed iron brace reinforces the joints.

CONDITION: The table is a rich red in color. Some of the old finish remains on the box and on the knee carving. When the MMA acquired it, four large, modern screws fastened the box to the top. The screws were removed in 1978, when a new brass catch was attached. It was then that the PVR brand was uncovered. An old break (18th-century?) at a knot in the ankle of one leg was repaired with an iron strap. The iron brace beneath the pillar was added later. The wedge fastening the box to the pillar is a replacement.

INSCRIPTIONS: Branded, on top board of box: PVR.

DIMENSIONS: H.: 28 (71.1); diam., with grain, 36 (91.4), across grain, 35½ (90.2); feet, span, 25½ (64.8).

WOODS: Primary and secondary: mahogany.

REFERENCES: MMAB, n.s. 26 (1967–68), p. 48 (mentioned). For the Van Rensselaer family of Cherry Hill, see Blackburn 1976; Hendrick; Benjamin Ginsburg, "The furniture of Albany's Cherry Hill," Antiques 77 (June 1960), pp. 562–566.

Gift of Elizabeth B. Carrick, 1966   (66.223)

128. Tea Table

Connecticut, 1790–1825

THIS TABLE CAN BE convincingly assigned to Connecticut, probably to the Hartford area. The use of cherry wood throughout, the naive interpretation of the pillar's design—the cup and flared shaft borrowed from New York or possibly Massachusetts—the conceit of a purely decorative, stationary box, and the unusual octagonal top all bespeak Connecticut practice and predilection for originality. The thin legs with elongated pad feet are so similar to those on a square-top table at Sturbridge (Kirk 1967, no. 170) stamped by Hartford cabinetmaker Sam-

128

128

uel Kneeland (1755–1828) as to suggest that the same man made the legs of both tables.

Though cat. no. 128 conforms to the classic pattern of the full-size tilt-top tea table popular in the second half of the eighteenth century, there is good reason to believe that it was made considerably later. The design of the pillar and the flat legs sawed from relatively narrow boards suggest features found on New England pole screens and stands from the Federal period (Montgomery, nos. 204, 373); and the painted ornament, which appears to be the table's original finish, resembles the popular "vinegar painting" of the eighteen-twenties and thirties (Fales 1972, p. 216; figs. 363, 367).

PROVENANCE: Ex coll.: Mrs. J. Insley Blair, Tuxedo Park, New York.

CONSTRUCTION: The octagonal top is formed of three boards laid diagonally to the round-bottomed, tapering cleats and to the stationary box attached to them by the dowellike hinges that allow the top to tilt vertically. The pillar continues through the box as a plain turned shaft cut to fit a square hole in the top board and secured with wooden and iron wedges. The legs are dovetailed into the pillar, their butt ends covered by a circular iron plate screwed to the pillar's bottom.

CONDITION: The surface is painted with irregular abstract patterns in vermilion on a brown ground, possibly intended to look like marble. On the top, the paint has faded to a yellow red on a brownish ground. The original colors are best preserved on the pillar on either side of the rear leg. The wooden twist latch (19th-century) that secures the top to the box replaces the original circular brass catch. One of the legs broke free of the pillar, splitting it at the bottom. The pillar was repaired with a large handmade screw (mid-19th-century?) set above the leg juncture, the area between the two front legs repainted without attempt to duplicate the original pattern. One of the attenuated slipper feet has been replaced; another has been broken.

INSCRIPTIONS: In black crayon and in pencil (20th-century), on the undersurface of the top, in several versions: 8-D and Sold.

DIMENSIONS: H.: 28 (71.1); diam., with grain, 33¼ (84.5), across grain, 32⅜ (82.2); feet, span, 24⅝ (62.6).

WOODS: Primary and secondary: cherry.

REFERENCES: Davidson 1967, fig. 183. Fales 1972, fig. 117 (as Connecticut, 1750–80).

Gift of Mrs. J. Insley Blair, 1945   (45.78.7)

13   Stands and Firescreens

Stands and firescreens were made on the same principle as round tea tables: with a single turned pillar supported on a tripod base. The size of the round tilt top determined the name of the table: those with large tops were known as tea tables; those with small ones, as stands. Stands with very small, fixed tops were for candles. In Philadelphia, cabinetmakers considered a tilt-top table with a diameter of twenty-two inches or less to be a folding stand. None of the other varieties of the type also produced occasionally in America—notably teakettle and basin stands—are in the collection. On firescreens, the turned pillar supports a pole on which a framed, fabric-covered panel can be rotated and raised or lowered. The collection includes no stand or screen from either Massachusetts or New York, but the other major urban centers are represented by pieces of the best quality.

129

129. Stand

Pennsylvania, 1740–70

AN ODD AND POSSIBLY unique combination of small tilt-top table and firescreen, the stand is made of a walnut indigenous to Pennsylvania, where it has a long history of ownership. When horizontal, the top's narrow surface seems impractical, but marks from a sewing clamp on its undersurface suggest that it once may have been used as a work table. The stand is a precursor of Federal-style wooden firescreens, which have hinged candle shelves beneath their screens: below this top is a small stationary shelf, probably intended to support a candlestick, that can be utilized when the vertical top serves as a firescreen.

Though on the stand neither the turnings of its pillar nor the shaping of its legs are recognizably American in design, the ingenuity of the total concept, combined with a tradition in the donor's family, encourages the engaging hypothesis that Benjamin Franklin himself designed the unassuming little object for his own use. Indeed, its legs match those of a four-sided music stand of Franklin's design (Nicholas B. Wainwright, *One Hundred and Fifty Years of Collecting by the Historical Society of Pennsylvania*, Philadelphia, 1974, p. 21, ill.); its legs and pillar bear comparison with those of a round tea table with the label of Philadelphia cabinetmaker William Savery (*Antiques* 94 [November 1968], p. 642).

PROVENANCE: Ex coll.: Gladys Mueller, Freeport, New York. The donor was the great-granddaughter of Sarah Franklin Bache (1744–1808), daughter of Benjamin Franklin (1706–1790), to whom, according to Bache family tradition, the table once belonged.

CONSTRUCTION: The top tilts vertically. Nailed and screwed along the length of its undersurface are a large pair of cleats, shaped at the ends and rounded on the bottom; nailed crosswise between them is a roughly shaped cleat remaining from a smaller pair. The top of the pillar continues through a thick, roughly hewn block, to which it is triple wedged. The block, square at one end and rounded at the other, is screwed to a small finished shelf of the same shape. The shelf is attached to the top by dowellike extensions at its square end let into the cleats of the top in the manner of round tea tables, and by a circular brass spring catch on its round end. The three cabriole legs are dovetailed into the base of the shaft.

CONDITION: The old finish has a dark walnut brown color. The large cleats have been rescrewed. Marks of the second cross-cleat, which presumably seated a wooden twist latch that once secured the top to the candle shelf, remain beneath the present circular spring clasp (late-19th-century). A three-armed iron brace was added under the shaft and the legs after two of the legs broke free. One of the feet has been reattached; another is replaced.

DIMENSIONS: H.: 26½ (*67.3*); diam., with grain, 30 (*76.2*), across grain, 11½ (*29.2*); feet, span, 19 (*48.3*).

WOODS: Primary and secondary: walnut.

Gift of Mrs. Alfred G. Mueller, 1956   (56.221)

130. Round Stand

Philadelphia, 1760–90

THE STAND WAS apparently made as one of a pair. According to Hornor (1931, p. 72), "Thirty odd years ago . . . the mate to the Palmer Collection gem, Fig. 5 [cat. no. 130], was ingeniously described by a loquacious individual as a 'boo-kay' table having a top made of 'fr-rills,' and sold at a public sale in Philadelphia for the now ridiculous price of 'five-eights,' an old term used in local sales amounting to *sixty-two and one half cents*."

The frill-carved rim on the top of the stand, while fairly common on English eighteenth-century tables, is not otherwise known in American furniture. The piece may nevertheless be confidently assigned to Philadelphia on the basis of its tradition of ownership in that city and the number of characteristic local features it displays: the shape of its legs and feet, the fine foliate carving on its knees, and the compressed-ball turning on its pillar. The guilloche pattern carved around the pillar's base is identical to that found on a high chest and matching dressing table (cat. nos. 166, 167), all three pieces said to have come from the same Philadelphia family. The motif also appears on a few full-size Philadelphia tea tables (Hornor 1935, pls. 222, 223). The pillar, turned in an unusual design, combines an inverted baluster with the well-known compressed ball and column shape. Similar turnings can be found on Philadelphia firescreens at Williamsburg (Acc. 1954-371) and in the Dietrich Collection (*Antiques* 125 [May 1984], p. 1119).

PROVENANCE: Ex coll.: George S. Palmer, New London, Connecticut. According to Palmer's notes (MMA files), the stand descended in the Lawrence family of Philadelphia.

CONSTRUCTION: The top is stationary, its rim richly carved in a continuous rococo ruffle defined on the inner edge by eight equal C-scroll sections. A single wide cleat is screwed to the undersurface, its bottom serpentine-shaped on either side of a raised flat center into which the pillar is doweled. The flat butt ends of the legs are joined to the pillar with dovetails.

CONDITION: The stand has a dark brown color and an old varnish finish. The cleat has been rescrewed. A modern triangular steel plate has been added to reinforce the junctures of legs and pillar.

DIMENSIONS: H.: 28¼ (71.8); diam., with grain, 21½ (54.6), across grain, 21¼ (54.); feet, span, 21 (53.3).

WOODS: Primary and secondary: mahogany.

REFERENCES: *MMAB* 13 (December 1918), p. 268, fig. 9. Hornor 1931, p. 39, fig. 5; p. 72.

John Stewart Kennedy Fund, 1918   (18.110.44)

130 See also p. 346

131. Candlestand

Norwich, Connecticut, 1770–1800

TWO STANDS, SIMILAR in size and design to cat. no. 131 but with distinct variations in carved detail, are at Winterthur (acc. nos. 59.1874.1, 2; Downs 1952, no. 284); all three, of cherry wood and made in the same manner, must be the work of the same hand. Certain features of the three stands are peculiar to furniture made in the Norwich area of Connecticut. The idiosyncratic knee carving—a symmetrical arrangement of flat, overlapping leaves, the bottom ones extended on the sides in high-relief scrolls—is found on the legs of a slab table from the Trumbull family of Norwich (Kirk 1967, no. 163); the fluted colonette with carved Corinthian capital appears on a block-front chest (ibid., no. 59) and a chest-on-chest (ibid., no. 104) also credited to Norwich.

These stands have been mistakenly attributed to Massachusetts on the basis of their carved Corinthian capitals, fluted pillars, and elongated claw feet—all features originating in work from that region—and on the basis of a nineteenth-century inscription on one of the Winterthur stands, which claims that it "was made about

the year 1778 for Samuel Hunt of Charlestown [Massachusetts] by an English soldier taken prisoner at the *Battle of Bennington* on Aug. 16, 1777 by the N.H. and Vt. Militia . . ." (Downs 1952, no. 284). The legend is improbable, and the stand's dominant characteristics are in the Norwich manner.

PROVENANCE: The stand, which descended in the same family with a New York round tea table (cat. no. 127) displaying the ownership brand of Philip Van Rensselaer, is said to have belonged originally to Killian Van Rensselaer (1763–1845), Philip's younger brother, who may have acquired it while he was a student at Yale (letters from donor, MMA files). As with the tea table, the verifiable history of the stand begins in 1904, when Anna Eliza Van Rensselaer Hoff left it to Elizabeth Hoff Greene, from whom it descended to Anna Greene Bates and, finally, to Elizabeth Bates Carrick, Princeton, New Jersey, the last private owner, who put it on loan at the MMA from 1938 until giving it in 1969.

CONSTRUCTION: The broad carved rim of the round top is cut from the solid. Screwed to the top is a circular collar scalloped in twelve lobes along its bottom edge. The turned and fluted pillar is carved with a Corinthian capital and a twist-reeded urn. The pillar, threaded at top and bottom, is screwed above into the collar and below into a platform that consists of a molded cap resting on and overlapping the circular drum. The three cabriole legs are dovetailed to the drum.

131 See also p. 346

CONDITION: The stand, dark brown in color, has a thick buildup of old varnishes now much decayed except on the flat surface of the top. The finish obscures the carving but lends to the piece an unusually pleasing aspect. The top board is split, and screw holes in its undersurface show that it has been reset several times. Two of the lobes of the collar are broken off. One leg has an old break at the ankle.

DIMENSIONS: H.: 28½ (72.4); diam., with grain, 10¼ (26.), across grain, 10 (25.4); feet, span, 17 (43.2).

WOODS: Primary and secondary: cherry.

REFERENCES: Kirk 1967, no. 154. MMA 1975, p. 24.

Gift of Elizabeth B. Carrick, 1969   (69.207)

132.   Firescreen

Philadelphia, about 1770

A SET OF FOUR identical firescreens consists of this one and others at Winterthur (Downs 1952, nos. 236, 237), at Philadelphia (PMA 1976, no. 80), and in a private collection. A fifth screen (Hornor 1935, pl. 105) is now said to be a reproduction (ibid., 1977 printing, p. xxii). The four firescreens, like most of the furniture made between 1769 and 1771 to furnish the interior of General John Cadwalader's town house on Second Street in Philadelphia (see cat. no. 59), have hairy paw feet, a feature otherwise rare in Philadelphia work. Cat. no. 132 and, apparently, one of the other screens, said to have been stored by a Cadwalader descendant in the Philadelphia Athenaeum attic in the 1940s (Carl Williams, conversation with author), have Cadwalader family histories. Consequently, it is reasonable to identify the screens with a January 14, 1771, entry in Thomas Affleck's accounts for furniture made for John Cadwalader: "To 4 Mahogany fire screens" at £2-10 each (Wainwright, p. 44). At the end of his lengthy bill, Affleck listed the separate charges of the men to whom he had subcontracted the carving: James Reynolds, carver of looking glasses, and the partners Bernard and Jugiez. The masterly carving on these screens does not relate to work attributed to Reynolds, but it does compare with documented work of Bernard and Jugiez: foliate architectural carving in the great chamber at Mount Pleasant, the MacPherson house outside Philadelphia (see PMA 1976, p. 101). It can thus be reasonably concluded that in 1770 and 1771, for John Cadwalader, Affleck made and Bernard and Jugiez carved these perfect exemplifications of the Philadelphia rococo style.

PROVENANCE: Purchased from the dealer David David of Philadelphia. According to genealogist Carl M. Williams (conversations with author, 1978, 1982), David bought the fire-

132 See also p. 346

screen from John Cadwalader Roland (died 1951) in 1949, along with an elaborate looking glass now at Winterthur (Downs 1952, no. 259). Roland had presumably inherited the screen from his mother, Anne Cadwalader Roland, great-granddaughter of General John (1742–1786).

CONSTRUCTION: The large acanthus-leaf-carved finial is doweled into the top of a pole fitted into the top of the pillar. The pillar is fashioned with a fluted shaft, a baluster turning having three units of acanthus leafage, and an urn alternately fluted and reeded. The concave butt ends of the legs are dovetailed into the bottom of the pillar, the joints reinforced by a three-armed iron plate rounded at the ends and attached with roseheads. The adjustable screen is held to the pole with brass rings and spring brackets at top and bottom. Its border, egg-and-dart carved on both front and back, is grooved to receive it.

CONDITION: The wood has the original finish, now velvety, and a dark brown color, with luminous reddish brown highlights where the carving has been rubbed. When the screen was acquired, its original fabric cover was gone. The present covers, English embroidered needlework in front and red moreen in back, were inserted in 1952. The brass clasps securing the screen to the pole are old replacements.

DIMENSIONS: H.: 62⅞ (*160.*); screen, width, 21 (*53.3*), length, 24⅞ (*63.2*); feet, span, 17¾ (*45.1*).

WOODS: Primary: mahogany. Stretcher of screen not examined.

Screen: Gifts and funds from various donors, by exchange, 1949 (49.51); Embroidered panel: Rogers Fund, 1952   (52.167)

133. Firescreen

Newport, 1760–90

NOTABLE FOR THE RICHNESS of its knee carving and for having retained its original embroidery panel, this is one of a group of four Newport firescreens all having a turned and reeded pillar that screws into a triangular platform to which are attached upright legs ending in diminutive cat's-paw feet. Between the melon-molded cap and the twist-reeded ball on this example and on a screen that has descended in the Brown family of Providence (Cooper 1971, figs. 33, 34), the mid-point of the pillar is a plain baluster turning. On the other screens—one (Ott 1965, no. 93) that belonged to Governor Wanton of Newport and one now in the Stone collection (Rodriguez Roque, no. 196)—the mid-point is a tapered and fluted shaft. The four screens are part of a larger group of Newport tripod-pedestal furniture with cat's-paw feet that also includes round tea tables and stands, basin stands, and kettle stands.

Hallmarks of the work of the Goddard and Townsend families of Newport distinguish all these stands and tables: tight, self-contained, and discreet designs, realized

133 See also p. 346

with assurance in dense mahoganies of a purplish hue. Of at least two hands discernible in this group, one may be that of John Goddard. Goddard billed James Atkinson £3 for one of the tea tables in 1774 (Carpenter, no. 79), and is said to have made for his daughter Catherine another now at the Boston MFA (Hipkiss, no. 59). The overlapping iron reinforcing straps that secure the latter's legs match those on the Brown family firescreen. Cat. no. 133, though identical to the Brown screen in design, has a different method of strapping and differently handled turning and reeding. Clearly the work of another man, it may have come from the hand of John Townsend. On this and on the two remaining firescreens, the twisted reeding of the ball is remarkably like the reeding on a kettle stand at Winterthur (Downs 1952, no. 288) attributed to Townsend on the basis of its pierced gallery, which is similar to one on a Pembroke table bearing his label (ibid., no. 311).

PROVENANCE: Ex coll.: H. Eugene Bolles, Boston.

CONSTRUCTION: The pole is fitted into the top of the turned and reeded pillar. The threaded bottom of the pillar screws into the platform, which is scratch-beaded on its top and side edges. The cabriole legs are dovetailed into the platform from below, the joints reinforced with small rectangular iron straps, each with three roseheads. The stretcher frame has a vertical medial brace to which are screwed the brass fittings that fix the adjustable screen to the pole: at the top, a broad collar with thumbscrew; at the bottom, a plain guide ring. The screen, framed by an applied half-round molding, has its original coverings: in front, cross-stitch needlework in an allover floral pattern of redbordered tan flowers with light blue green leaves and stems on a darker blue green ground; in back, silk patchwork in horizontal rows of alternating diamond and chevron-shaped pieces (ill. Carpenter, Supplement 48).

CONDITION: The heavy wood has a luminous finish, purplish brown in color. The finial, made in 1978, is a copy of an original one on an uncarved Newport firescreen of the same type (Christie's, New York, 3/10/78 sale, lot 208, ill.). The platform has a number of splits, and is patched where two of the legs broke free. The needlework is well preserved, but the silk patchwork is badly discolored and rotted.

DIMENSIONS: H.: 55⅛ (140.); screen, width, 22½ (57.2), length, 21¾ (55.2); feet, span, 17 (43.2).

WOODS: Primary: mahogany. Stretcher of screen not examined.

REFERENCES: Salomonsky, pl. 100 (measured drawings). Carpenter, no. 48; Supplement 48. Davidson 1967, fig. 468.

Gift of Mrs. Russell Sage, 1910   (10.125.422)

III CASE FURNITURE

14 Bureau Tables, Chests, and Chests-on-Chests

Chests with drawers were normally used in bedrooms to store the costly textiles and clothing whose value is attested to by the locks on each drawer. During the late colonial period the form was made in three basic types: the bureau table, the chest, and the chest-on-chest. Because the Museum's collection contains only a few of each type and because there is little chronological progression among them, each type in turn is listed by geographical origin (from north to south) and all are assembled in this one chapter. Bureau tables, now called kneehole desks or kneehole chests of drawers, are characterized by a single wide top drawer and tiers of narrow lower drawers flanking an opening that has a cupboard in back. They probably served the same purpose as dressing tables, with the small drawers holding combs and brushes and the kneehole cupboard possibly used for wig stands. The Museum's collection consists of superb examples from the major regional centers. The chest of drawers resembles the bureau table in form, but lacks its central cupboard and interior feet. Included here are fine block-fronted examples from Massachusetts and Rhode Island, unusual serpentine ones from Rhode Island and Connecticut, and a fine Philadelphia version in the rococo style, but missing is any representation of the classic Massachusetts serpentine-front chest or the typical straight-fronted New York chest with gadrooned skirt. The chest-on-chest was also referred to in eighteenth-century America as a double chest and a case upon case. It had more storage space in its lower section than had the high chest, though their functions were similar, and it was made everywhere, enjoying particular popularity in New Hampshire and in New York, where the high chest was unfashionable. Chests-on-chests from all parts of New England except Connecticut are represented at the Museum, though none demonstrates the heights of achievement attained by the makers of the Museum's New York and Philadelphia examples. A Philadelphia clothes press, rare in that city but a common form in New York, completes the chapter.

134

134. Bureau Table

Massachusetts, 1750–90

THIS BUREAU TABLE is of a block-front form widely popular in Massachusetts in the third quarter of the eighteenth century and undoubtedly made there by a number of cabinetmakers. Many have a history of descent in Boston families: a bureau table was owned by Major Thomas Melville (1751–1832) of Boston (Kennedy & Sack, no. 35). No example has been documented by its maker, but one (*Antiques* 99 [January 1971], p. 7) is branded W. WHITWELL, possibly a son of the joiner Samuel Whitwell, who died in 1727 (Kaye, p. 302). All such bureau tables have six straight bracket feet, a shallow tray drawer above a kneehole opening, and an arched, field-paneled door, but no two of them are identical. On some, the overall proportions are vertical (Nutting 1, no. 275), the blocking rounded (Hipkiss, no. 40), and the brasses Queen Anne (Greenlaw, no. 147). On others, such as cat. no. 134, the proportions are horizontal, the blocking flat, and the brasses rococo, all of which suggests that these tables date somewhat later than those of the vertical kind.

The kneehole skirt pendant and the scallops on the tray

drawer and on the bracket feet were executed in a variety of shapes. One of the most common patterns—a central semicircle flanked by ogee curves—is exhibited on many similar examples (e.g., Sack 1950, p. 151, upper right), including cat. no. 134. Also on the MMA bureau table are distinctive brasses that are shared by one very much alike except that it has drawers rather than a prospect door (*Antiques* 96 [October 1969], p. 493). The thumbnail-molded drawer edges of cat. no. 134, which also appear on a counterpart at Williamsburg (Greenlaw, no. 147), are an unusual variant on the beaded drawer openings found on most bureau tables. This one is presumed to have been purchased by the Boston merchant Thomas Dering, who married in 1756 and moved to Shelter Island in 1760. He probably acquired it sometime in the interim.

PROVENANCE: The bureau table descended in the Dering family of Shelter Island, New York, until bequeathed to the MMA. The claim (see Inscriptions) that it had belonged to Brinley Sylvester (1694–1752) is unlikely, since it is of a type that was not made much before his death. Its probable line of descent is from Thomas Dering (1720–1785), a Boston merchant who married Mary Sylvester (born 1724) in 1756; to General Sylvester Dering (1758–1820); to Nicoll H. Dering (1794–1867); to General Sylvester Dering II (born 1838), who married Ella Virginia Bristol (1842–1930), the last private owner.

CONSTRUCTION: The top has molded front and side edges; its straight back edge is without overhang. The back is two horizontal tongue and groove boards. The rails are attached to the sides with dovetails, the ends of those on the rail beneath the top drawer exposed. There are full dust boards. Above the kneehole is a shallow sliding tray. On the drawers, the inner surfaces of the fronts conform to the outer blocking; the fronts are thumbnail-molded except for the top of the large drawer and the bottom of the tray; the sides and backs are thick, with rounded tops; the bottom boards, laid crosswise, have applied runners. The skirt molding is attached to the edges of the case's bottom board and to pine strips glued beneath it. The bracket feet are reinforced with shaped glue blocks. The door and the kneehole cupboard behind it are a separate unit that can be pulled out when the tray above is removed. A single medial shelf is slotted into the unit's side boards, which are dovetailed to the top and bottom. The door has through-tenoned rails and an arched and fielded panel of figured wood. Surrounding the door are stiles and a top rail that are secured with glue blocks to the unit.

CONDITION: The dense mahogany is a deep reddish brown in color. A modern varnish, possibly that applied in 1898 (see Inscriptions), was removed in 1937. There are splits in the top and in the left side board. Scoring near the top of each side board marks the former presence of a small cavetto molding. The back bracket of the left rear leg and part of the right inner foot have been replaced.

INSCRIPTIONS: Stamped twice, on back of door's H hinges: *162.* In pencil, on bottom of removable kneehole-cupboard unit: *Finished by A. H. Evans. August 10 1898.* On a brass plate accompanying the chest: *Property of / BRINLEY SYLVESTER / of Shelter Island, N.Y. / Born Nov. 28.1694 Died Dec. 24.1752 / Presented to / The Metropolitan Museum of Art / by his G.G. Grandson, Genl. Sylvester Dering, 2nd.*

DIMENSIONS: H.: 30 *(76.2)*; W.: top, 38⅞ *(98.7)*, case, 36¼ *(92.1)*, feet, 37½ *(95.3)*; D.: top, 22⅝ *(57.5)*, case, 20¼ *(51.4)*, feet, 21½ *(54.6)*.

WOODS: Primary: mahogany. Secondary: white pine (back and bottom boards, sides flanking cupboard, dust boards); white oak (drawer sides, backs, bottoms, kneehole-cupboard unit).

REFERENCES: Miller 1, no. 906. Margon 1949, pp. 82–86 (measured drawings). Aronson, fig. 1388. For the Dering family, see Ralph G. Duvall, *The History of Shelter Island,* Shelter Island Heights, New York, 1932; Rev. Jacob E. Mallmann, *Historical Papers on Shelter Island and Its Presbyterian Church,* privately printed, 1891.

Bequest of Ella V. Dering, 1930   (30.44)

135. Bureau Table

Newport, about 1765

ON THE BASIS of similarities in design and construction to a group of labeled and dated block-and-shell four-drawer chests (see cat. no. 139), this bureau table and a number of markedly similar examples can be attributed to John Townsend (Heckscher 1982). The latter include one (*Antiques* 110 [July 1976], p. 4) now in a Chicago private collection; others are at Winterthur (Downs 1952, nos. 175, 176), at Yale (Nutting 1, no. 272), and at Bayou Bend (Warren, no. 123). Another was once exhibited at the Metropolitan Museum (MMA 1909, 2, no. 168). All of them exhibit superb quality in design, material, and workmanship. On the MMA bureau table, though the use of pine for the bottom board and chestnut for the backboard reverses Townsend's established practice, the components of the cornice molding and the construction of the feet are typical of all his labeled pieces. Except that the petals in the central Cs lack stop-fluting, the carved shells are like those on the chest dated 1765 (cat. no. 139). On the chest the subtop is screwed to the top; on the bureau table it is screwed and nailed—fastenings that predate the butterfly-shaped inserts on Townsend's later documented pieces. Because the features of the bureau table show a close resemblance to those of the 1765 chest, a comparable date for it seems reasonable.

PROVENANCE: Ex coll.: H. Eugene Bolles, Boston. In his notes (MMA files), Bolles wrote: "I bought the piece of a dealer in Exeter, N.H., named Higgins, and he bought it of a man named Pascal Allen Horton then of Stratham, N.H." According to Horton (1907 letters to Bolles, MMA files), the bureau table had belonged to his grandfather Pascal Allen, president of the Warren, Rhode Island, National Bank. In 1907 Horton sold the table to F.C. Higgins, who sold it in the same year to Bolles.

CONSTRUCTION: The solid top board, nailed and screwed to a subtop made of two boards butted together and dovetailed to the sides, is ogee-molded at the front and side edges and overhangs the back by an inch. The cornice molding is applied. Under the subtop are three separate front glue blocks and continuous side ones. The back is two horizontal boards. The rails, backed with tulip poplar, are dovetailed to the side boards. Around the drawers the rails have beaded edges; on the side boards the beading is applied. There is a dust board only under the top drawer. On the drawers, the top edges of the sides are rounded; the fronts have flat inner surfaces; the bottoms overlap the sides and back and have applied runners. On the top drawer, the projecting shells are applied and the bottom runs lengthwise; on the small drawers, the bottoms run crosswise. Behind the recessed block-and-shell kneehole door with its flat inner surface is a fixed, round-edged medial shelf. The bracket feet are glued to the bottom of the skirt molding, each foot reinforced with a vertical glue block butted to two horizontal ones. On the rear feet the back brackets are cut on the diagonal.

CONDITION: The front and sides have a fine old patina and a golden brown color. The top has been refinished and is of a reddish hue. As Bolles noted (MMA files) of the bureau table: "It is all original except a crude moulding at the top of each end on the piece when I got it; and the ends of the feet had been so poorly restored at some time that I had them done over and one back leg. I also supplied the short lower moulding with a notch under the door." It is the right rear leg that was almost entirely replaced, though one glue block is original; almost an inch on the bottom of the ogee bracket of the left rear foot and more than an inch on the bottom of each of the front feet are also the vendor's restorations. The bottom molding of each side skirt is missing. The door's upper hinge has been reset. The eighteenth-century door escutcheon is an old replacement.

INSCRIPTIONS: In pencil, on bottom of large drawer: *Bottom.* In chalk, on upper right drawer: *Mad by / — / Mahogany.* In pencil, on bottom of middle left and lower left drawers:

A; on side of lower left drawer: *Samuel Horton* [?]; *Don for J*—. Numerous other inscriptions on drawers and bottom board are illegible. In pencil, on rails below small drawers, beginning at upper left: *A* through *E*.

DIMENSIONS: H.: 34⅜ (87.3); W.: top, 36 (91.4), case, 34 (86.4), feet, 36½ (92.7); D.: top, 20½ (52.1), case, 18⅝ (47.3), feet, 20 (50.8).

WOODS: Primary: mahogany. Secondary: chestnut (large drawer bottom, glue blocks of subtop and feet); white pine (bottom board, cupboard sides); tulip poplar (all else).

REFERENCES: Lockwood 1, fig. 122. Miller 1, no. 905. Margon 1965, p. 195, bottom. Montgomery and Kane, fig. 99. Heckscher 1982, fig. 19.

Gift of Mrs. Russell Sage, 1909   (10.125.83)

135 See also p. 365

136. Bureau Table

New York, 1755–90

BUREAU TABLES of New York manufacture are rare in comparison with those from Massachusetts or Rhode Island. Though a few straight-fronted ones are known (*Antiques* 103 [February 1973], p. 231) the majority have block fronts and show influence of Massachusetts design. On them the top is set directly above the uppermost drawer and the drawers have rounded projecting blocking. Instead of the modest straight bracket feet of their Massachusetts counterparts (see cat. no. 134), New York bureau tables are almost always supported by stalwart, square, claw-and-ball feet.

Among the best of these New York examples is a distinctive group that includes cat. no. 136. All are made of fine, dense mahogany, with poplar as the sole secondary wood, and all have plain doors with *H* hinges. One, said to have been made for Philip Van Rensselaer of Cherry Hill (Comstock, no. 382; Blackburn 1976, no. 92) and now at the Albany Institute, and its mate, in a New York private collection, are similar to cat. no. 136 except that they lack the leaf carving on the sliding tray front. Curiously, the brasses of all three are identical to those used by John Townsend on his Newport chests (see cat. no. 139). Another bureau table (SPB sale no. 4156, 10/1/78, lot 370) appears different only in its knee brackets—which are replaced—and in its brasses. A fifth example, once the property of New York painter Robert W. Weir

136

and now at the Boston MFA (Hipkiss, no. 39), with different brasses, leaf carving on the front feet, and a flat rail beneath the shelf drawer, nonetheless looks to be by the maker of the rest of the group. These compact bureau tables, firmly planted on their flexed and powerful legs, are among the most assertive of New York case pieces.

PROVENANCE: Ex coll.: Harold M. and Cecile Lehman (later Cecile L. Mayer), Tarrytown, New York.

CONSTRUCTION: The overhanging front and sides of the top board have ogee-molded edges. The side boards are channel-dovetailed into the top. The back is three horizontal tongue and groove boards. Around the drawers the rails have beaded edges; the beading on the side boards is applied. There are full dust boards. On the drawers, the inner surfaces conform to the outer blocking; the thick sides and back have rounded top edges; the bottom boards, laid crosswise, are beveled to slot into the front and sides. Over the kneehole is a sliding tray drawer with acanthus leafage carved in relief on its blocked-in surface. At the back of the kneehole, a flat door of solid figured mahogany opens on a cupboard with two shelves fixed just below the height of the rails. The six legs have claw-and-ball feet and bulging knees. The knees and scalloped brackets are reinforced with conforming glue blocks screwed into the bottom board.

CONDITION: The bureau table is a dark reddish brown in color. The present finish has begun to crackle. The interiors of the drawers and cupboard are painted a muddy yellow. The lowest backboard is an old replacement; also replaced are the ogee knee brackets on the left side and that to the left of the kneehole opening. On the kneehole door the keyhole escutcheon dates from the late nineteenth century, and gold paint has been used to suggest the missing brass *H* hinges.

INSCRIPTIONS: In pencil, on small-drawer bottoms and on rails beneath, beginning at upper left: *1* through *6*. In chalk, on backboards of drawers 4 through 6: illegible markings.

DIMENSIONS: H.: 33 (*83.8*); W.: top, 34⅛ (*86.7*), case, 32 (*81.3*), feet, 35⅛ (*89.2*); D.: top, 22⅜ (*56.8*), case, 19¼ (*48.9*), feet, 21¼ (*54.*).

WOODS: Primary: mahogany. Secondary: tulip poplar.

Bequest of Cecile L. Mayer, subject to a life estate, 1962 (62.171.10)

137. Bureau Table

Pennsylvania or New Jersey, 1750–65

THE SOURCE of this bureau table is suggested by its large, splayed, ogee-bracket feet and by the poplar and cedar of which its drawers are made—characteristics of Philadelphia work that were adopted throughout eastern Pennsylvania and western New Jersey. Bureau tables from that region, while frequently mentioned in local cabinetmakers' accounts (Goyne, pp. 27–31), are not common

today. Those known have straight fronts, occasionally with fluted quarter columns. The 1772 Philadelphia price book lists: "Bureau Table with prospect dore And Squair Corners" at £6 in walnut and £7-10 in mahogany; "Ditto with Qarter Calloms" at £7 in walnut and £8-10 in mahogany (Weil, p. 189). The former describes cat. no. 137, which is square—its case width precisely matching its overall height—and has a prospect door that is tall and narrow in the mid-century manner. Most of the other known Pennsylvania bureau tables are proportionately wider and have bead-edged drawer fronts and elaborately pierced rococo or early neoclassic brasses that suggest for them a later, post-1765 date.

The visually arresting features of cat. no. 137 are its prospect door and its brasses. The door has a fielded panel with concave shoulders surmounted by a rounded top, a treatment known elsewhere only on the door of a Pennsylvania spice cabinet (David Hunt Stockwell, "The Spice Cabinets of Pennsylvania and New Jersey," *Antiques* 36 [October 1939], p. 176, fig. 7). The resulting shape, a dotted I, is repeated, where there is no keyhole, in the pierced center of the brass drawer-pull escutcheons. Similar brasses appear on a Pennsylvania bureau table at Yale (Goyne, fig. 3) and on a desk (its prospect door panel with a slight variant in the I shape), dated 1755, at the New Jersey Historical Society (*The Pulse of the People: New Jersey 1763–1789*, Trenton, New Jersey State Museum, 1976, no. 31). As has cat. no. 137, the desk has a long history in Middletown, Monmouth County, in northeastern New Jersey, far from the cultural influence of Philadelphia. Were the two pieces taken there from Philadelphia, or were they made in Middletown by Philadelphia-trained craftsmen?

PROVENANCE: The bureau table descended to the vendor, Louise Hartshorne, Middletown, New Jersey, through the Wikoff family of Monmouth County. According to a note from Miss Hartshorne (undated, MMA files), "Isaac [Wikoff, born 1739] lived in Philadelphia, father of Jacob, who was the grandfather of Miss Julia C. Wikoff . . . from whose heirs I obtained the knee hole table. William [Wikoff, born 1757] had a plantation in the West Indies. He sent the mahogany to Philadelphia where it was used for the kneehole table."

CONSTRUCTION: The front and side edges of the top are molded, the front corners are scalloped; below is an applied cavetto molding; the back has no overhang. Narrow reinforcing boards at front and back are dovetailed into the tops of the side boards. On them the top rests, secured with glue blocks. The back is two horizontal tongue and groove boards. Finishing strips are nailed to the front edges of the case and kneehole sides. In the kneehole, the side boards are dovetailed to the bottom; the stiles flanking the door have beaded edges; behind the door, at the level of the rails, are two shelves with double-beaded front edges. There are full dust boards. On the drawers, the cross-grained bottom boards are rabbeted into the sides and reinforced with applied runners; the tops of the sides are

137

rounded. The three upper drawers and the door are fitted with locks. The skirt molding is nailed to the two-piece bottom.

CONDITION: Under a partly decayed old finish the wood has a golden brown color. The finishing strips and the backboards have been renailed. On three of the drawers the molded top edge is patched. The upper shelf behind the kneehole door is missing. Except for the outer front ones the feet are old, somewhat crudely wrought replacements. The pointed tip of the outer left front foot is gone. The central brass on the top drawer is patched above the keyhole. The door escutcheon, originally made for the door of a desk and bookcase, is a replacement.

INSCRIPTIONS: In white chalk, on lower backboard: *A W[ikoff?]*. In pencil, on bottoms of small drawers and on dust boards: the numbers *1* through *6*, beginning with upper right drawer.

DIMENSIONS: H.: 31¾ (*80.6*); W.: top, 35½ (*90.2*), case, 31¾ (*80.6*), feet, 34 (*86.4*); D.: top, 20¾ (*52.7*), case, 19 (*48.3*), feet, 19¾ (*50.2*).

WOODS: Primary: walnut. Secondary: tulip poplar (backboards, small-drawer dust boards, drawer sides and backs); white pine (bottom board, large-drawer dust board, sides and shelf of kneehole); northern white cedar (drawer bottoms).

REFERENCES: *MMAB* n.s. 10 (February 1952), p. 192 (ill.). Goyne, fig. 2. *New Jersey Arts & Crafts: The Colonial Expression*, Monmouth Museum, 1972, no. 26 (ill.).

Purchase, Andrew V. and Ethel D. Stout Fund, 1951   (51.126)

138. Chest of Drawers

Massachusetts, 1750–90

DESPITE ITS CONNECTICUT history, this is a characteristic Massachusetts chest. The four-drawer block-fronted form was popular in that region, most commonly with the rounded projecting blocking and the straight bracket feet found here, but also with square projecting blocking (see cat. no. 134) or with claw-and-ball feet. On cat. no. 138 the graceful curves of the bracket feet are a distinctive variation on the standard scalloped profile (see cat. no. 134). The same configuration appears on a similar chest (*Antiques* 58 [December 1950], p. 458); a slight variation on it is found on a chest inscribed by William Frothingham of Charlestown, Massachusetts (ibid. 63 [June 1953], p. 505, where mistakenly referred to as Walter Frothingham). A chest that descended in the Otis family of Boston until acquired by the SPNEA (Jobe and Kaye, no. 14) has drawer fronts made from the same template as the Frothingham piece—similar to, but not the same as, those of cat. no. 138.

PROVENANCE: Ex coll.: Mrs. Giles Whiting, Scarborough, New York. The chest originally belonged to Jonathan Trumbull of Connecticut (see Inscriptions).

138

139. Chest of Drawers

Newport, 1765
John Townsend (1732–1809)

EIGHT KNOWN block-and-shell pieces are signed or labeled by John Townsend (Heckscher 1982). One, a small document cabinet, is undated, but it is signed in pencil in the manner Townsend employed on his earliest known works, two tables dated 1756 and 1762 (Moses 1982, pp. 1130–31). The other pieces all bear his paper labels and are dated. A slant top desk (Sack 3, pp. 790–791) and this chest of drawers were both made in 1765. Three other chests are all virtually identical to this one. One was made in 1783; its present location is unknown (Norton, p. 63, ill.); the second, dated 1791, is at Williamsburg (acc. no. G1977–225); and the third, dated 1792, is now in a private collection (ill. *Antiques* 59 [February 1951], p. 88). In addition, there are two tall clock cases, one dated 1783 (Norton, p. 63, mentioned) and the other 1789 (cat. no. 192). These pieces all demonstrate John Townsend's distinctive handling of the block-and-shell mode—a personal interpretation that changed little over a span of nearly thirty years.

The chests, all with four drawers, are remarkably alike not only in overall design and in size but also in decorative detail: the convex shells have twelve boldly shaped lobes; the concave ones, eleven; the cornices have a bead, a fillet, and a cavetto beneath the main cove molding. Similarly, there are identical details of construction: on each foot the vertical corner glue block abuts the horizontal ones instead of the bottom board, as was customary with other makers. The chests of the seventeen-nineties exhibit slight changes: in securing the top board, butterfly-shaped cleats replace screws and glue blocks; in the decoration within each shell's central C-scroll, stop-fluted petals are superseded by fluted petals over crosshatched centers; and in the brasses, shaped rococo plates give way to bail pulls with simple, circular escutcheons. Neat, compact, and harmonious in design, executed with assured and machinelike precision, chests like cat. no. 139 set the standard, never surpassed, for Newport cabinetmakers in the eighteenth century.

CONSTRUCTION: The top has molded front and side edges that overhang the case and conform to its shape. Each side board is joined to the top with a channel dovetail. On the sides, the front edges are faced with strips beaded on the inner edge. The rails have thin backings. There are no dust boards. On the drawers, the fronts are cut away in rounded curves behind the projecting blocking; the tops of the sides and backs are rounded; the bottoms are laid crosswise. Two horizontal tongue and groove boards form the back. The molded skirt, flat inside, is glued to the front of the two-piece bottom.

CONDITION: The chest has a dark reddish brown color. Except on the top, which has been refinished, the old surface is covered with a thick coat of varnish. Markings on the skirt indicate that there was once a central pendant. The bottom three inches of the right rear foot is replaced. The brasses are old, but not original.

INSCRIPTIONS: In chalk, on bottom boards, inscriptions (18th-century?) illegible but for *90* and *45*. On a sheet of paper pasted inside top drawer: *Dec. 27th–1935. Sold to Mr. Harry Arons, one block front bureau, belonged to my great grandfather, Jonathan Trumbull, Governor of Connecticut. It was left to my sister Miss Adelaide, and after her death I received same. It has always been in the Trumbull house at Lebanon.* [Signed] *Anna H. Able/Lebanon, Conn.* In ink, on another piece of paper pasted inside same drawer: *Miss — Adelaide Waller* [?]/*M.* [?] *Dutton* [?].

DIMENSIONS: H.: 30½ (77.5); W.: top, 33¾ (85.7), case, 31¾ (80.6), feet, 33¼ (84.5); D.: top, 20 (50.8), case, 17¾ (45.1), feet, 19 (48.3).

WOODS: Primary: mahogany. Secondary: white pine.

Bequest of Flora E. Whiting, 1971   (1971.180.41)

PROVENANCE: The chest, along with cat. nos. 100 and 192, was purchased from Clara Channing Allen of Northampton, Massachusetts, to whom it had descended from the original owner, George Champlin of Newport (see cat. no. 100, Provenance). A photograph of the chest in the Allen house, 57 Prospect Street, Northampton, is in the MMA files.

CONSTRUCTION: The solid top board, barely overhanging the back, has ogee-molded front and side edges. It is attached with screws and glue blocks to a subtop that consists of two broad battens dovetailed to the sides. Below the top, a separate cornice molding nailed to the front and sides covers the dovetails. The back is two horizontal tongue and groove boards nailed with roseheads. Between the drawers and dovetailed to the sides are bead-edged rails with thin backings. There are no dust boards. On the front of the top drawer the projecting shells are applied; the inner surface is flat. The other drawer fronts are blocked inside and out, a reinforcing board added behind the recessed blocking. Each drawer bottom is a single board, laid lengthwise and overlapping the sides and back, to which the runners are nailed. The tops of the drawer sides are slightly rounded. An ovolo strip is nailed to the bottom of the skirt molding between the bracket feet. Each foot has two horizontal blocks glued to the bottom board and one vertical block abutting them. The rear feet have ogee-sawed back brackets.

CONDITION: The chest has the original thin old finish, now with a mellow reddish brown patina. The left front foot has a horizontal split. The right front foot is patched in the middle of its projecting inner edge. The back bracket of the left rear foot and the bail handle of the bottom left brass are replaced.

INSCRIPTIONS: In brown ink, on a paper label centered inside top-drawer bottom: *Made by / John Townsend / Rhode Island / 1765*. In pencil, inside left side board: illegible inscriptions. In chalk, on bottom board: two large marks. (See p. 366 for photograph.)

DIMENSIONS: H.: 34½ (87.6); W.: top, 36¾ (93.3), case, 34¾ (88.3), feet, 37½ (95.3); D.: top, 20 (50.8), case, 18¾ (47.6), feet, 20¾ (52.7).

139 See also p. 365

WOODS: Primary: mahogany. Secondary: white pine (bottom, feet glue blocks); chestnut (top glue blocks); tulip poplar (all else).

REFERENCES: Cornelius 1928, pp. 72–80; p. 74 (ill.). Halsey and Cornelius, pl. 57. Rogers, fig. 47. Downs 1949, pl. 6. Powel, p. 208 (ill.). MMA 1976, fig. 13. Heckscher 1982, figs. 3, 6, 7, 11, 14.

Rogers Fund, 1927   (27.57.1)

140. Chest of Drawers

Newport, 1755–85

THIS CHEST IS ONE of a group of Newport pieces distinguished by their bold serpentine shape and solid, three-dimensional form. The only other known case piece of this type—a three-drawer chest with a virtually identical facade—is much larger and has a wooden top, four shaped corners, and four claw-and-ball feet (Fairbanks and Bates, p. 177). It has a chalk *B* inscribed in the middle drawer, as does this one, but differences in secondary woods and interior construction techniques suggest another joiner.

The MMA chest also bears comparison with the other pieces of this group: a number of marble slab tables with heavy, shaped skirts. The chest's serpentine form is duplicated on one (Carpenter, no. 71); its serpentine corner posts and raised pad rear feet are repeated on another (Ott 1965, no. 40). On the basis of the latter table, known to have been made by John Goddard in 1755, cat. no. 140 has long been attributed to that maker. The attribution is reinforced by the similarity between the chest's claw-and-ball feet—the front talons with softly articulated knuckles, the rear talon separated from the curve of the back leg with a double bulge of tendons—and those on two other documented Goddard pieces, a 1763 tea table at Winterthur (Downs 1952, no. 373) and a 1774 dining table for which Goddard's original invoice survives (Carpenter, no. 59). The design of cat. no. 140, a diminutive yet powerfully built three-drawer chest, is not characteristic of eighteenth-century American furniture. The curves of its front and sides reflected on the skirt below and its conforming marble top make it the nearest approach to a Louis XV-style commode in Colonial America—a Yankee craftsman's rendition of the "French taste."

PROVENANCE: Ex coll.: Mr. and Mrs. Charles H. Gershenson, Detroit, Michigan. The Gershensons bought the chest in about 1960 from Israel Sack, Inc., which later bought it back and sold it to the MMA. According to family tradition recorded on the label in a drawer (see Inscriptions), the chest first belonged to Robert Crooke, of Newport, who married Ann Wickham, also of Newport. From them the descent would have been to Rebecca Wickham Crooke Wood (1771–1846); to Rebecca W.C.W. Stanley (1810–1880); to Rebecca W.C.S. Falkner (1845–1895); to Rebecca W.C.F. Sutherland (1878–1926); to Christina Katharine Sutherland Fagan (born 1905); to Maurice (born 1926) and Robert (born 1928) Fagan.

CONSTRUCTION: The gray-veined white marble top, its straight back with a one-and-a-half-inch overhang, has molded front and side edges that conform to the serpentine curves of the case. The top is keyed in place by two holes in its underside that receive rounded dowels projecting from the tops of the front posts. The serpentine front corner posts continue as cabriole legs. The bead-edged rails have narrow chestnut backings. The backing of the top rail is dovetailed into the corner posts. The two middle rails are cut out around bead-edged stiles and slotted into the posts. The drawer runners overlap the rails and are slotted into the back. Drawer stops are nailed to the backs. There are no dust boards. On the drawers, the fronts' inner surfaces are slightly concave; the thick crosswise bottom boards overlap and are nailed to the sides and back. Each side of the case—three solid horizontal boards, the bottom one extending as an ovolo skirt molding—is straight on the inner surface and, on the outer, curved to repeat half of the front serpentine. The sides are tenoned into the front posts. The back, a narrow board above a wide one, is dovetailed to the side boards. The skirt rail, solid except for piecing at the center front and for applied beading, is pegged to the posts. The rear legs terminate in raised pad feet and have short stiles, which are slotted into the side boards and nailed from the back.

CONDITION: The chest has its original finish, now a lustrous deep reddish brown. There is an old break in the marble top. The drawer runners are much worn. The locks in the upper and middle drawers are missing, as are the lower right tips of their brass escutcheons.

INSCRIPTIONS: In chalk, on top-drawer backboard: *A*; middle-drawer: *B*; bottom-drawer: *C*. In pencil, on middle two rails: corresponding letters. In pencil, on top rail: *2* (a possible indication that the chest was originally one of a pair). Typewritten on a paper label (20th-century) pasted to top-drawer back: *This chest of drawers with a marble top, known in the family as the marble slab, belonged to Robert Crooke before his marriage to Anne Wickham so dates at least to 1750 or probably much earlier. This couple were the great, great, great, great grandparents of Maurice and Robert Fagan, children of Christina and Maurice Fagan.*

DIMENSIONS: H.: overall, 34¾ (88.3); W.: top, 36¾ (93.3), case, 34⅝ (88.), feet, 35 (88.9); D.: top, 21½ (54.6), case, 18¾ (47.6), feet, 19 (48.3).

WOODS: Primary: mahogany. Secondary: white pine (drawer runners, drawer stops); chestnut (all else).

REFERENCES: *Antiques* 82 (December 1962), pp. 618–619 (ill. frontispiece). Biddle, no. 47. Doris Fisher Gershenson, "Living with antiques," *Antiques* 91 (May 1967), p. 638. Sack 3, pp. 732–733. MMA 1975, p. 22.

Purchase, Emily Crane Chadbourne Bequest, Gifts of Mrs. J. Amory Haskell and Mrs. Russell Sage, by exchange, and The Sylmaris Collection, Gift of George Coe Graves, by exchange, 1972   (1972.130)

140

141. Chest of Drawers

Connecticut, 1790–1800

THE CONNECTICUT ORIGIN for the chest is suggested by the local cherry and white pine woods, the inlay patterns, and the configuration of the front. The serpentine shape of the drawer fronts terminates within the top drawer in a yokelike curve, an unusual treatment, but one employed, albeit more gracefully, on case furniture made in the Connecticut River valley by Erastus Grant of West field, Massachusetts, and George Belden of Windsor,

Connecticut (Bulkeley 1967, pp. 72–81). The barber-pole, or rope, border forming the front corners is found on another Connecticut chest (*Antiques* 105 [April 1974], p. 671) and on a secretary said to be from Hartford (ibid. 70 [October 1956], p. 307) or Norwich (ibid. 82 [July 1962], p. 21). The latter piece exhibits the same alternately light and dark stringing and rows of inlaid dark-wood diamonds found on cat. no. 141.

The largeness of this chest, nine inches higher than average and four or five inches wider than most New England examples, is emphasized by its three-drawer format. It is an unusual piece, of distinctly rural design and

141

DIMENSIONS: H.: 43 (*109.2*); W.: top, 45 (*114.3*), case, 39⅝ (*100.7*), feet, 42¼ (*107.3*); D.: top, 22¾ (*57.8*), case, 19⅞ (*50.5*), feet, 22 (*55.9*).

WOODS: Primary: cherry. Secondary: white pine.

Purchase, Mrs. Russell Sage Gift, 1970   (1970.174)

142. Chest of Drawers

Philadelphia, 1780–90

WITH CARVING CONFINED to the top edge and the quarter columns, the chest is an elegant example of the restraint that characterizes the best of Philadelphia work in the Chippendale style. Only a handful with such ornament are known: in addition to this, there are one at Winterthur (Downs 1952, no. 177) and a pair at the PMA (Hornor 1935, pl. 179). The four appear to be the work of two different shops. The first two have similar proportions and skirt moldings and may be by the same hand. In contrast to them, the pair are slightly more vertical, their skirt moldings have a different profile, their drawers have molded edges, and their feet lack applied pads.

Leaf-carved quarter columns are found on the most elaborate of Philadelphia Chippendale case pieces (cat. nos. 166–169), but the acanthus leafage alternating with rosettes on the columns of this group of chests, particularly that on cat. no. 142, lacks the sense of movement expected in rococo design. Since all four chests retain their original neoclassical-style brasses, they appear to have been made late in the century. As a consequence, their carving may be said to reflect the static quality associated with that emerging style.

PROVENANCE: Ex coll.: Mrs. J. Insley Blair, Tuxedo Park, New York; Mrs. Screven Lorillard, Far Hills, New Jersey. According to Mrs. Blair's notes (MMA files), she purchased the chest in 1930 from Willoughby Farr, of Edgewater, New Jersey. Farr had found it in Newtown, Pennsylvania.

CONSTRUCTION: The top board overhangs the back by nearly two inches and has an applied molding—a leaf-carved ovolo above a cavetto—on the front and sides. The side boards are slotted into the top. Two horizontal boards form the back. Carved quarter columns with separate capitals and bases are glued between the side boards and the front stiles. The rails, with mahogany strips facing their fronts and with drawer stops nailed to their tops, are cut out around the stiles and slotted into the sides. The full dust boards are laid lengthwise. On the drawers, the solid fronts have applied beaded edges; the bottoms, laid crosswise, are secured to the sides with closely spaced glue blocks and to the back with roseheads. The lowest drawer rides directly on the case's two-piece bottom. The front edge of the bottom is faced with a mahogany strip that forms the rail above the skirt. The skirt molding is glued to mitered framing boards, nailed under the bottom, to which the bracket feet are glued. Pads are nailed to the bottoms of the feet. Each foot has three

workmanship. The serpentine shape of the front and the claw feet, together with the naively arranged inlay—a Chippendale form with ornament in the Federal style, as were the original brasses—are an uncommon combination and suggest a date at the end of the century.

PROVENANCE: Purchased from Kenneth Hammitt Antiques, Woodbury, Connecticut.

CONSTRUCTION: The two-piece top, with molded front and side edges and a one-inch overhang in back, conforms to the chest's reverse-serpentine drawer fronts. The top is screwed to a subtop, dovetailed to the side boards, whose front, faced with cherry wood, forms the top rail. The rails between the drawers are slotted into the side boards and cut out to receive the stile boards. The stiles are inlaid with stringing, light-wood fans, and dark-wood diamonds. The upper drawers ride on rails attached to the sides and back; the lowest one rides on the bottom board. There are no dust boards. On the drawer fronts, all have scratch-beaded edges and inlaid stringing; the serpentine of the top one is applied to a straight pine backing; the others are solid, with flat inner surfaces. The keyhole on the bottom drawer is false. The top of the front skirt molding is flush with that of the bottom board, to which it is nailed. The back, two thick horizontal boards, has beveled edges. Except that they lack back brackets, the rear feet are identical to the front ones.

CONDITION: The chest, a pale reddish tan in color, has been refinished. The feet have been reglued and reinforced with screws. Each front corner talon is chewed. The shaped brackets on both rear legs are replacements, as is the skirt molding on the left side. The modern brasses are the fourth set. The original ones had a single oval escutcheon; the later ones, two smaller escutcheons, circular or oval.

142

large, shaped glue blocks. The back brackets of the rear feet are cut on the diagonal.

CONDITION: The chest, which retains its original thin finish, now somewhat decayed, has a mellow mahogany brown color. At the left, the quarter column is warped and the front bracket foot is split. At the right, the end of the skirt molding is missing, as is part of the foot pad.

DIMENSIONS: H.: 34½ (*87.6*); W.: top, 40½ (*102.9*), case, 39 (*99.1*), feet, 41½ (*105.4*); D.: top, 22⅓ (*57.2*), case, 20¼ (*51.4*), feet, 21½ (*54.6*).

WOODS: Primary: mahogany. Secondary: tulip poplar (back and dust boards, drawer sides and backs); yellow pine (bottom boards, rails behind facings, glue blocks); Atlantic white cedar (drawer bottoms).

REFERENCES: *MMAB* n.s. 11 (May 1953), p. 260 (ill.).

Gift of Mrs. Screven Lorillard, 1952   (52.195.3)

143. Chest-on-Chest on Frame

New Hampshire, about 1799

THE CHEST-ON-CHEST, with or without a separate frame, was the predominant case-furniture form made in southern New Hampshire in the late eighteenth century. Such chests from that locale are now associated with the Dunlap family of cabinetmakers.

Cat. no. 143, among the simplest of the nearly fifty examples recorded (Parsons, figs. 1–15, 20–50), is one of the few without shell-carved drawers. Its cornice, uncharacteristically small and simple, is like that on two other chests-on-chests (ibid., fig. 33; Christie's sale, 1/30/80, lot 742). The latter, except that it has four upper-case drawers rather than five, is all but identical: its original bail pulls with small oval escutcheons around each bolt suggest the type of brasses that may have been on cat. no. 143. The two chests, both with traces of the original yellow-painted surface, undoubtedly came from the same shop.

Another chest (Parsons, fig. 15) has a similar cornice, to which a classic Dunlap-type basketweave gallery top has been added. Cat. no. 143 bears no evidence of ever having had such a top; rather, all ornament is confined to the low frame. The shells and S-scrolls carved out of its front skirt are among the most characteristic motifs of New Hampshire furniture design. Here, however, their interpretation is unusual. The common Dunlap-type shell has simple flat webs between the lobes, but these shells consist of long, concave, or spoonhandle, lobes alternating with contrasting shorter convex webs—a treatment that also appears in the drawer shell of one chest (ibid., fig. 49) and in shells on the gallery tops of more elaborate examples (ibid., figs. 1, 2, 18). The standard Dunlap S-scroll has a convex surface; the scrolls on the MMA chest are concave.

Samuel Gregg (1764–1839), of New Boston, New Hampshire, has been suggested as the maker of the MMA

143

chest (ibid., p. 18). Between 1779 and 1784 he was employed by cabinetmaker John Dunlap of nearby Goffstown and Bedford, doubtless as an apprentice. His name, along with that of his father, Hugh, appears on a promissory note dated New Boston, January 17, 1799. Inscribed on one of the chest's backboards, it is presumably the draft of a proposed agreement made, for want of a piece of paper, on a board lying loose in a cabinet shop. In 1799, Gregg, probably still active as a carpenter and cabinetmaker, was serving as a justice of the peace and a selectman in New Boston.

PROVENANCE: Ex coll.: Mr. and Mrs. William H. Schubart, New York City.

CONSTRUCTION: The chest is in three parts. On the upper case: The cornice molding is nailed over the top half of a flat board that forms the frieze. The back is three horizontal tongue and groove boards. Thin rails are dovetailed to the sides. There are no dust boards. On the drawers, the solid fronts have molded edges; the thick sides and back are flat at the top; the bottom, laid lengthwise, is beveled and slotted into the front and sides. On the lower case: The midmolding is nailed on top. The uppermost rail is glued to the front of the top board. Two horizontal boards form the back. The bottom rail is nailed on top of the two-piece bottom. Otherwise, the construction is like that of the upper case. On the frame: The skirt boards, double pegged to the stiles of the disproportionately delicate legs, are surmounted by a cavetto molding. An interior arrangement consisting of large diagonal braces running from the fronts of the side rails to the middle of the back rail, the back rail itself, and strips nailed to the side rails support the chest-on-chest.

CONDITION: The chest, now a reddish tan in color, has been stripped. Traces of yellow, particularly on the underside of the frame's front skirt, remain from the chest's original paint. On the upper case, the right side of the second drawer front is repaired. The upper edge of the middle drawer front of the lower case and the bottom rear of the right side board have been patched. The brasses are modern, in the third set of holes. The original ones were placed about an inch closer to the sides of the drawers. The lock of the uppermost drawer is missing. Paper (20th-century) is pasted to the bottoms of the drawers.

INSCRIPTIONS: In ink, inside upper case back, what appears to read: *Newboston January 17th 1799 / For things Received i promissed / To pay peter Nobody the sum / of Nine Dolers and three cents / L[awful] M[oney] or With interest til paid / Witness My hand Hugh gregg / Atest Samuel gregg.* In chalk, on lower-case case bottom board: *No 2.*

DIMENSIONS: H.: overall, 79⅝ (202.3); W.: upper case, 35½ (90.2), lower case, 38 (96.5), feet, 43⅛ (109.5); D.: upper case, 17¾ (45.1), lower case, 19 (48.3), feet, 21⅞ (55.6).

WOODS: Primary: maple. Secondary: maple (rear rail and side strips of frame); white pine (all else).

REFERENCES: Parsons, p. 18; p. 29, nn. 109, 111; fig. 46. *Antiques* 98 (August 1970), p. 227, fig. 5.

Gift of Dorothy O. and Diana Schubart, in memory of William Howard Schubart, 1953   (53.198)

144. Chest-on-Chest

Massachusetts, 1750–80

THE COMBINATION of a block-fronted lower case and an upper case with fluted pilasters on either side of flat drawers is representative of a type of chest-on-chest made in Massachusetts, particularly on the North Shore. Numerous examples, the work of several shops, are known. One now at the St. Louis Museum is dated 1767 (Charles E. Buckley, "Decorative arts in the City Art Museum of Saint Louis," *Antiques* 96 [July 1969], pp. 76–81; p. 78, ill.); another, at Detroit, was signed and dated in 1774 by Nathaniel Bowen of Marblehead (Randall 1960, fig. 2; Nutting 1, no. 315, ill.); two are labeled by Benjamin Frothingham of Charlestown (Randall 1974, figs. 1, 170); a fifth, at Yale, is stamped by Nathaniel Treadwell of Beverly (Lovell, figs. 74, 75); and a sixth (ibid., fig. 76) is attributed to Abraham Watson of Salem. The type was modified in the early 1780s, when the lower-case block front was succeeded by one of serpentine or bombé shape (Randall 1965, no. 41; Vincent, fig. 125).

Though cat. no. 144 conforms in most respects to the classic type, it is the only one encountered to have stop-fluted pilasters; it is also the only one lacking a carved fan in the central top drawer. The treatment of its pediment area is unexpectedly awkward: the circular openings cramp the top of the central drawer, thereby preventing the tops of the flanking drawers from paralleling the cornice. Those problems are not present on the other examples, suggesting that cat. no. 144, which is otherwise skillfully executed in costly figured wood, may have been made before the niceties of the classic formula had been worked out.

PROVENANCE: Purchased from Collings and Collings, New York City. On loan to the Kenmore Association, Fredericksburg, Virginia, from 1931 until 1978.

CONSTRUCTION: On the upper case: The front pediment board extends behind the pilaster capitals and through the side boards. Behind it, at cornice height, a top board entirely encloses the case. The scroll pediment is enclosed on either side of the central circular openings by boxes that form a bonnet top. The rails, with thin, bead-edged facing strips, are slotted into the stile boards and their backing boards. Fluted pilasters cover the juncture of stiles and sides. Three horizontal tongue and groove boards form the back. On the drawers, the insides of the fronts are scored; the thick sides and back have beveled tops; the bottoms are laid lengthwise. On the lower case: The midmolding is nailed to the top. The back is two horizontal boards. The bead-edged rails, backed with thin boards, are dovetailed through the sides; the lowest rail rests on the two-part bottom. On the upper drawer, the interior surface of the front is flat; on the other drawers, the interior is flat at the bottom but cut away above behind the projecting blocking. The skirt molding, its interior surface conforming to the blocked

front, overlaps the bottom, to which it is secured with glue blocks. There are no dust boards.

CONDITION: The chest, now a mellow nut brown in color, retains its original, somewhat decayed finish. The central finial, the cornice molding on the left side, the thin boards enclosing the bonnet top, and the bottom three inches of the feet are all replaced. The large drawers of the upper case have new runners; one has a new backboard.

DIMENSIONS: H.: overall, 85¾ (*217.8*), pediment, 82 (*208.3*); W.: upper case, 39¾ (*101.*), lower case, 42 (*106.7*), feet, 43½ (*110.5*); D.: upper case, 18 (*45.7*), lower case, 19¾ (*50.2*), feet, 21½ (*54.6*).

WOODS: Primary: mahogany. Secondary: white pine.

REFERENCES: *MMAB* 14 (July 1919), pp. 162–163. Lee 1, p. 79 (ill.). Miller 1, no. 883.

Rogers Fund, 1919   (19.99)

144

145

145. Chest-on-Chest

Newport, 1760–90

THE CHEST-ON-CHEST typical of Rhode Island is known by the ogee-bracket feet on which it stands and by the two-part paneled tympanum and enclosed bonnet top of its broken-scroll pediment. Most examples have straight fronts and thumbnail-molded drawer edges. The more elaborate ones have three finials and, on both upper and lower cases, fluted quarter columns; those of the simple variety have a single central finial and plain front corners. Cat. no. 145, one of the latter kind, is distinguished among its modest peers (e.g., at Yale, acc. no. 1930.2162) by a pediment with carved rosettes and an unenclosed space behind its central openings.

Similar rosettes, circular and consisting of eight teardrop-shaped concave petals surrounding a prominent central knob, are found on a clock case said to have been made by John Goddard for Jabez Bowen in 1763 (Donald F. Bowen, "A Clock Case by John Goddard," *The Antiquarian* 15 [August 1930], p. 37); they also appear in virtually identical form on the cases of a number of clocks made in Providence by Edward Spaulding and Caleb Wheaton. Wheaton signed a receipt of payment for "Two Clock Cases" in 1786 on behalf of Townsend Goddard of Newport, one of John's sons (*Antiques* 24 [July 1933], p. 4). When cat. no. 145 was sold at auction in 1921, the sale catalogue attributed it to Thomas Goddard (see Provenance), another of John's sons. Thomas, who was born in 1765, could have made it, but not much before 1785. Despite evidence that about that time other members of the family were making furniture related to the chest by the carved pediment motifs, one rosette does not a Goddard make: similar ones can be found on a desk and bookcase (Ott 1965, no. 66) documented to Grindall Rawson of Providence.

PROVENANCE: Ex coll.: Mrs. Franklin Bartlett, New York City. The Bartlett auction catalogue described the chest as having been "made by Thomas Goddard of Newport, R.I., directly for the family." Bartletts are known to have been in Gloucester, Rhode Island, in the eighteenth century. The chest was bought by William Randolph Hearst. In 1941 it was purchased by the donors at the Hearst sale (*Art News* 39 [January 18, 1941], unpaged advt.).

CONSTRUCTION: On the upper case: The rosettes are screwed from behind to the pediment board; the cornice moldings are toenailed near the corners from above. In front, the tympanum boards are applied; behind, at cornice height, is a top board. Above is an enclosed bonnet that conforms to the shape of the pediment except for a rectangular cutout behind the central openings; a single horizontal board forms its back. The back of the upper case is three horizontal boards. The one-piece mid-molding is nailed to the upper case, its bottom edge rabbeted to receive the top of the lower case. On the lower case: A foot-long groove cut into the two-piece top accommodates a wooden tongue nailed to the upper-case bottom to hold it in place. The back is two horizontal boards. The skirt molding is flush with the underside of the two-piece bottom. On the rear feet, the back edge of the side brackets is shaped; the back brackets are flat boards sawed out like the front ones. On both cases, the rails, thinly faced, are dovetailed to the sides. There are no dust boards. The drawer fronts are solid; the inner surfaces of the large ones are scored. Each of the two top drawers has a wooden spring lock. The backboards of both cases are reinforced inside with vertical medial strips.

CONDITION: The chest has an old finish with a deep reddish patina. The finial is a replacement. Some of the rails and drawer fronts have minor patches. The rails have been inexpertly reglued.

INSCRIPTIONS: In pencil, on underside of lower-case top board: *Front Top*. A rough sketch of what is probably half a scroll pediment is penciled on upper-case top board. In black crayon (20th-century), on upper-case back: *178/1385*; on lower-case top: *1432-5*. On both cases, in pencil and in chalk: illegible markings.

DIMENSIONS: H.: overall, 85¼ (*216.5*); W.: upper case, 38¾ (*98.4*), lower case, 40⅛ (*101.9*), feet, 43¼ (*109.9*); D.: upper case, 19⅛ (*48.6*), lower case, 19½ (*49.5*), feet, 21¼ (*54.*).

WOODS: Primary: mahogany. Secondary: white pine (backboards, top of bonnet, feet glue blocks); tulip poplar (drawer sides and backs; medial back strips; rails between drawers); chestnut (all else).

REFERENCES: *Catalogue of the collection of Early American, English and French Furniture formed by the Late Mrs. Franklin Bartlett*, New York, American Art Association sale, January 13–15, 1921, lot 671 (ill.).

Gift of Doris Brian Hepner and Milton Hepner, subject to a life estate, 1963   (63.172)

146. Chest-on-Chest

New York, 1760–90

IN THE SECOND HALF of the eighteenth century, the chest-on-chest, along with the linen press, was a particularly fashionable piece of case furniture in New York City. This example, which descended in the Van Rensselaer family, has all the characteristic features of the fully developed type: a fretwork frieze below the cornice; canted and fluted corners in the upper case; ogee-bracket rear feet and, in front, claw-and-ball feet with leaf-carved knees and scroll-edged brackets. A similar chest-on-chest (*Antiques* 109 [January 1976], p. 61), but with a different fret pattern, uncarved lamb's-tongue terminations on the canted corners, and slightly variant knee carving, appears to be from the same shop; both chests even have the same superfluous framework for dust boards above the top drawer. A number of secretaries (Downs 1952, no. 224; Dept. of State, p. 59) and desks (Comstock, no. 327; Miller 1, no. 785) exhibit leg treatment and pierced brasses closely related to those of cat. no. 146 and may also have the same source.

On the MMA chest, the unique interlaced ogival arch fret pattern may be a replacement (see Condition) for fretwork of a distinctively New York type: an interlaced diamond pattern (see Downs 1952, no. 224; Randall 1965, no. 39); a double chain-link pattern (Dept. of State, p. 59; *Antiques* 109 [January 1976], p. 61); or a combination of both, as found on the Van Cortlandt family wardrobe (Singleton 1, opp. p. 266).

Samuel Prince, who first advertised as a cabinetmaker in the *New York Gazette* in 1772, illustrated his engraved label with a flat-top chest-on-chest with carved claw feet.

On the basis of that sketch, elaborate New York examples have often been indiscriminately associated with him. There is no justification for such an attribution for cat. no. 146, which has no specific features in common with any case pieces that bear Prince's label.

PROVENANCE: The chest-on-chest descended from father to son in the Van Rensselaer family of Claverack, Fort Crailo, and Greenbush—the Lower Manor on the east side of the Hudson River. The chest could have been made for Colonel Johannes (1708–1783); for Jeremias (1738–1764); or for Colonel John Jeremias (1762–1828). Dr. Jeremias (1793–1871) inherited Fort Crailo on his father's death in 1828, but he did not live there until 1852. He rented the house out in the interval. At that time he may have put some of the furniture into storage, which would account for the inscription (q.v.) "Dʳ VR /to be called for." The line of direct Van Rensselaer descent continues with Jeremias, Jr. (1825–1866); to Peyton Jaudon (1863–1919); to Peyton T., whose name appears on shipping labels on the chest. After his death in 1932 the chest was lent for exhibition at the Harrison Gray Otis House, Boston, until 1934, when his widow put it on loan in the American Wing, together with a set of tassel-back chairs (Downs 1952, no. 52). On Mrs. Van Rensselaer's death, in 1963, the chest descended to her brother, who then gave it to the MMA.

CONSTRUCTION: On the upper case: The crown molding and the dentils below are applied to the main cornice molding. The pierced fret and the astragal beneath it are separate pieces. The top and bottom are of two boards each; the back is of four horizontal tongue and groove boards. On the corner posts, the backs and the fluted fronts are canted at the same angle; the leaf-carved bases are cut from the solid. The rails and their thin facing strips form the fronts of the frames into which dust-board panels are slotted. Above the top drawers is an additional dustboard frame. On the sides are parallel pairs of horizontal score marks, indicating that the cabinetmaker had planned to set the drawer rails higher, but changed his mind. On the lower case: Behind the molding nailed to the top edge are the glue blocks that support the upper case. The fronts of the side boards have facing strips. The back is three horizontal boards. The structure otherwise matches that of the upper case. The skirt molding is nailed to the bottom board. The front brackets of the carved cabriole legs are wider than the side ones. The back brackets of the rear feet are cut on the diagonal. On the drawers of both cases, the solid fronts have applied beaded edges; the bottoms run lengthwise.

CONDITION: The wood has a luminous reddish brown color. The applied pierced frieze, while old, may be an early alteration: small nail holes visible at regular intervals on the surface behind it may indicate how a fretwork of different pattern was once attached. A toe is missing from the left front foot, and the bottom half of the left rear bracket foot is a replacement. The front legs, transposed and given new glue blocks at some time, were installed correctly in 1980. Some of the rails are patched above the drawer locks.

INSCRIPTIONS: On both cases the drawers are numbered from one to five, beginning at the bottom. In chalk, inside each drawer on the front, sides, and back: the drawer's number, apparently the original coding system for keeping the drawer parts in order before the piece was assembled. In brown ink, on the

146 See also p. 364

lower case top: *D^r V R one—/to be called for*. On top of the upper section, a shipping label (20th-century) printed: *From/ A. GUERRIERI/Fine Furniture and Antiques/STOCKBRIDGE, MASS.* In ink, on the label: *Mr. P. T. Van Rensselaer/c/o Metropolitan Storage Co/Massachusetts Ave/Cambridge Mass.* An identical label is nailed to the lower section top.

DIMENSIONS: H.: overall, 78¾ (*200.*); W.: upper case, 40 (*101.6*), lower case, 42¼ (*107.3*), feet, 45¼ (*114.9*); D.: upper case, 20⅛ (*51.1*), lower case, 21¼ (*54.*), feet, 23 (*58.4*).

WOODS: Primary: mahogany. Secondary: yellow pine (bottom boards of both cases, top of bottom case, framing around dust boards); white pine (bottom rail of lower case); tulip poplar (all else).

REFERENCES: Downs and Ralston, pp. xviii–xix; p. 8, no. 68. *MMAB* n.s. 24 (1965–66), p. 44. *Antiques* 91 (April 1967), p. 482 (ill.).

Gift of E. M. Newlin, 1964   (64.249.3)

147. Chest-on-Chest

Philadelphia, about 1770–75

ON THIS PIECE, a supreme manifestation of Philadelphia Chippendale case furniture, the continuous cornice beneath the pediment, the veneered drawer fronts with beaded edges, and the neoclassic design of the brasses connote a date in the seventeen-seventies or later. Of a number of related examples that can be identified as being by the same hand(s), the most striking comparison is with a secretary desk whose scroll pediment (Hornor 1935, pl. 171) is identical as to rosettes, latticework, plinth, pierced fret, and most moldings; its finial, appropriate to an article of library furniture, is a bust of John Locke. There are, in addition, two chests-on-chests with pediments that differ from that of cat. no. 147 only in the treatment of their central plinths (photographs, MMA files). The moldings between the upper and lower cases match on all three pieces. One of them, said to have belonged to Stephen Girard and now missing its finial, has the same beaded drawer fronts and neoclassic gilt brasses; the other, which descended from Vincent Loockerman (died 1785) of Dover, Delaware, has thumbnail-molded drawer fronts and a finial that consists of a carved vase of flowers. Finally, a secretary desk at Dearborn (Hornor 1935, pl. 201) and a high chest of drawers at Bayou Bend (Warren, no. 125), both said to have been made for Joseph Wharton, who died in 1775, have pierced central cartouches and flanking urn finials on pediments that otherwise match those of the preceding pieces.

147 See also p. 348

The authorship of this group of exceptional case pieces has yet to be determined. Likely possibilities, however, are Thomas Affleck the cabinetmaker and James Reynolds the carver. On cat. no. 147, the carved bird finial has a free asymmetry one might expect from a man who specialized in looking-glass frames, as Reynolds did, and the quality of its joinery would do credit to Affleck, one of Philadelphia's finest craftsmen. Further, both men are known (see Provenance) to have worked in 1772 for William Logan, who presumably commissioned the chest-on-chest.

PROVENANCE: Descended from Hannah Fox, of 339 South Broad Street, Philadelphia; to William Logan Fox, of Bleak House, Blue Bell, Pennsylvania; to Joseph M. Fox. Purchased in 1975 by the MMA from Samuel T. Freeman & Company. The chest-on-chest may have been a part of the furniture Thomas Affleck made for Sarah Logan at the time of her marriage to Thomas Fisher in 1772. The Cashbook of William Logan, at the Historical Society of Pennsylvania, records under the date April 2, 1772, that Affleck made cabinetwork for Logan's daughter Sarah at a cost of £72-15-0, of which £50 was owed to James Reynolds, carver. If cat. no. 147 is indeed part of that furniture, it presumably descended to Thomas Fisher, proprietor of Wakefield, in Germantown, Pennsylvania; to William Logan Fisher; to Elizabeth Rodman Fisher; to Mary Rodman Fisher Fox, all of Wakefield; thence to Hannah Fox, in whose town house it was seen by Emily Fox Cheston as a child in the late nineteenth century (MMA files, information prepared by Peter L.L. Strickland).

CONSTRUCTION: The chest is in three parts. The topmost unit consists of scroll pediment, cornice, and frieze. The front and back of the unit are dovetailed to the sides; the top is covered by six boards laid crosswise. On front and sides the upper halves are of pine; the lower halves are of mahogany, visible through the fretwork. The scrolls are carved from the solid. The cornice has a crown molding, a triangular core, and applied dentils; the fretwork and flanking beading are separate pieces. The pierced latticework is screwed to the solid pediment scrolls. The body of the bird finial is carved from two pieces of wood; the wings were carved separately and glued on. A rectangular tenon screwed to the back of the finial fits into a slot in the plinth. On the upper case: Quarter-round blocks are glued onto the two-piece top to locate and secure the pediment unit. The case back is formed of six horizontal tongue and groove boards. The rails are narrow boards with mahogany facings. There are full dust boards. On the lower case: The midmolding is in two parts, the upper one nailed to the top; the lower one, to the sides. Both top and bottom are made of three boards; the back, of four horizontal ones. Otherwise, the framing is like that of the upper case. Square pads with beaded edges are attached to the ogee-bracket feet. The back brackets of the rear feet are cut on the diagonal. On all the drawers, the fronts are of solid figured mahogany with applied beaded edges; the finely finished sides and back have square top edges; quarter-round mahogany blocks reinforce the junctures of sides with front; the bottoms are laid crosswise.

CONDITION: The chest, which retains its original finish remarkably undisturbed, has a luminous dark red color. The brasses have their original lemon yellow mercury gilding. The interior is virtually without wear. The skirt moldings between the side legs are patched.

DIMENSIONS: H.: overall, 97½ (247.7); W.: upper case, 41⅞ (106.4), lower case, 45⅛ (114.6), feet, 46⅞ (119.1); D.: upper case, 21⅞ (55.6.), lower case, 22⅞ (58.1), feet, 24¼ (61.6).

WOODS: Primary: mahogany. Secondary: yellow pine (back and bottom boards of upper and lower cases; glue blocks, boards backing stiles and rails); tulip poplar (drawer sides and backs, dust boards, backboard of pediment unit); Atlantic white cedar (drawer bottoms, top boards of upper and lower cases).

REFERENCES: *MMAB* n.s. 33 (Winter 1975/76), no. 17. *Philadelphia Inquirer*, Friday, March 28, 1975, p. 1. MMA 1976, no. 17. Samuel T. Freeman & Co. auction, Philadelphia, March 24–27, 1975, p. 15, lot 118.

Purchase, Friends of the American Wing and Rogers Funds; Virginia Groomes Gift, in memory of Mary W. Groomes; and Mr. and Mrs. Frederick M. Danziger, Herman Merkin, and Anonymous Gifts, 1975   (1975.91)

148. Clothes Press

Philadelphia, 1760–90

FEW PIECES OF AMERICAN furniture are as English in appearance as this clothes press: the low-slung flat broken pediment and the particular scalloped pattern of the panels of the upper doors closely resemble elements on a number of labeled case pieces made in London during the seventeen-thirties and forties by Giles Grendey (Ralph Edwards and Margaret Jourdain, *Georgian Cabinet-Makers*, London, Country Life, Ltd., 1955, pl. 51). The figured mahogany veneer in the fielded door panels, the rule joints by which the lower doors are hung, and the trays, sliding on battens attached to the doors, are all typical of English work. Nevertheless, the secondary woods, the construction and shape of the feet, and a long family history leave little doubt as to the Philadelphia origin of the piece—probably the work of a craftsman just off the boat.

The clothes press was an uncommon form in that city. One whose design is similar to this, but with flat-paneled doors, is on loan at the RIHS. Differences in detail throughout indicate that it is the work of another shop. A third example, with scroll pediment and by yet another hand, descended in the Pennington family of Philadelphia (*Antiques* 65 [March 1954], p. 172). It has trays behind doors in the upper section and a chest of drawers below. The finials on both presses—roses in a basket or vase—suggest what may once have graced cat. no. 148.

The format of the Pennington example closely resembles the description given in the 1772 Philadelphia book of prices: "Cloath press in two partes About 4 feet Square in ye frunt the dors hung with Rule Joynt & Sliding Shelves with 3 Drawers in the Loar part in side of Red Seader" (Weil, p. 191). In mahogany, it cost £15; for "a Pitch Pediment, Dentils fret & Shield," as described in the 1786 copy of the price book (Gillingham 1930, p. 302), add £6. On the MMA clothes press, the trays and the rule-jointed doors are in the lower case and the drawers in the upper case are behind doors; the description is otherwise apt.

The design of cat. no. 148 owes a debt to plates first appearing in Chippendale's *Director* in 1754. Its interior layout matches that of an elaborate flat-topped clothes press (pl. CXIII in the more common 1762 edition); its pitch pediment and projecting lower case closely resemble those of the middle section of a library bookcase (plate XCV); its cornice configuration can be seen in plate XCVI, which follows the Ionic order (pl. VIII).

The clothes press has been attributed (Carl Williams, letters, 1950, 1978, MMA files) to Thomas Affleck on the basis of the Gothic arches over a Chinese trellis in the plinth which are also found on some Marlborough-leg seating furniture (Hornor 1935, pls. 258, 285) thought to have been made by Affleck for Governor John Penn. It is by a different hand than a chest-on-chest and two secretaries having virtually identical pitch-pediments (ibid., pls. 190–193), even though one of the secretaries has doors with scalloped panels like those of cat. no. 148 and the other has a Cadwalader family history that may match it.

PROVENANCE: Purchased from Mrs. John Cadwalader, the former Margaret Nicoll of New York, when her house at 2100 Spruce Street in Philadelphia was closed. According to Carl M. Williams (letters and statements in MMA files outlining his conversations as agent in the sale with Mrs. Cadwalader and her sister-in-law Miss Sophia Cadwalader), the press, together with a hairy-paw-footed card table now at Winterthur (Downs 1952, no. 345), was a wedding present to Mrs. Cadwalader from her mother-in-law. The press was removed from 263 South Fourth Street, the law office of Judge John Cadwalader (1805–1879), his son John (1843–1925), and, finally, his grandson John, husband of Margaret Nicoll. Since the three were direct descendants of General John Cadwalader, one might speculate that the chest once belonged to him. His house in Second Street had by 1772 become one of the finest in Philadelphia, but in the extensive accounts of the furnishings made for it (Wainwright; see also cat. nos. 59, 97), there is no reference to such a piece. The press may have come from the Binneys or the McIlvaines, families of the judge's first and second wives. Alternatively—and more likely—it may have entered the Cadwalader family in the next generation, when John (1843–1925) married Mary Helen Fisher. It was through this union that the "Cadwalader" secretary, originally the property of Ann, daughter of Philadelphia mayor Charles Willing (Hornor 1935, pls. 192–193), came into the family. A more recent account has it that cat. no. 148 descended in the vendor's family and was not a Cadwalader piece at all (11/12/64 letter from Nicholas B. Wainwright to MMA).

148 See also p. 361

CONSTRUCTION: On the upper case: Cornice moldings and a central fretwork plinth are applied to the veneered pediment board that fronts the flat top. The cornice, a single molded board with a triangular core, is capped by a separate crown molding. The dentils are cut from the solid. The applied fretwork frieze has a vertical central seam. A dovetail-shaped slot behind the plinth was intended to receive a finial. Four horizontal boards form the back. On the doors, the scalloped and fielded mahogany panels have figured veneers; the mortise and tenon frames have false mitering at the corners. Inside are twelve drawers arranged in two graduated stacks. On each drawer the lengthwise-grained bottom is beveled to slot into the front and sides. Behind the scratch-beaded rails are full dust boards. On the lower case: The molding around the bottom of the upper case is attached over the veneer that covers the visible part of the two-piece top. Between the top's applied molded edges and a parallel astragal below is a sliding shelf for folding, or "pressing," linens. Three horizontal tongue and groove boards form the back. Each side is lined with a vertical board that has been sawed into four pieces. The spaces between these pieces were intended to support the projecting bottom edges of the three original sliding trays, which were pulled by heart-shaped finger grips cut in each bottom board. The trays moved in slots cut out of mahogany battens nailed to the insides of the doors; molded rule joints and three pairs of iron strap hinges on the doors held them rigidly at right angles when the trays were pulled out. The doors are like those of the upper case in construction. The top of the skirt molding is flush with that of the two-piece bottom. Pads are nailed to the bottoms of the bracket feet. The inner sides of the rear brackets are cut on the diagonal.

CONDITION: The chest, which retains the original finish, has a fine, dark, reddish patina. The finial is missing. The front half of the applied fretwork on both sides was replaced by the MMA in 1950. The top right peak of the pediment and the veneer on the top right front corner of the lower case have been patched.

Nail holes on the inner edge of the right-hand doors show that moldings once covered the central joints. The wooden moldings, visible in an old photograph in MMA files, do not look original. The bottom two of the three sliding trays are missing; early nineteenth-century wallpaper pasted on the back and sides below the existing tray suggests that the other two were discarded during that period. The brass ring pulls on the two lowest drawers and the brass knobs of the sliding shelf are modern. The lock on the lower doors is a replacement. The escutcheons on the doors are old replacements put on before the MMA acquired the piece. Those on the lower doors are eighteenth-century English rococo cast brass examples. The pattern is illustrated in an English manufacturer's catalogue of about 1780–85 (Nicholas Goodison, "The Victoria and Albert Museum's Collection of Metal-Work Pattern Books," *Furniture History* 11 [1975], fig. 28). Those on the upper doors are modern castings.

INSCRIPTIONS: In brown ink, on right side of sliding tray: *Upper one*. Stamped on one lower right door iron hinge: *IP* in a rectangle. In 1977, a small envelope (19th-century) addressed to "Miss Moss" was found partly lodged behind the wallpaper in back of the lower section.

DIMENSIONS: H.: overall, 91⅜ (232.1); W.: upper case, 40¾ (103.5), lower case, 41¾ (106.), feet, 44⅝ (113.4); D.: upper case, 14½ (36.8), lower case, 23⅛ (58.7), feet, 24¾ (62.9).

WOODS: Primary: mahogany. Secondary: yellow pine (top, back, bottom of both cases, drawer bottoms); oak (bottom of sliding tray); eastern white cedar (drawer bottoms, vertical divider between upper drawers); tulip poplar (all else).

REFERENCES: *MMAB* n.s. 10 (Summer 1951), p. 13 (ill.).

Rogers Fund, 1950   (50.114)

15 New England High Chests and Dressing Tables

Because high chests and dressing tables, today commonly called highboys and lowboys, were frequently made en suite, the two forms have been grouped together in the catalogue. These case pieces were generally used in bedrooms. The high chest—in eighteenth-century documents variously referred to as a chest of drawers, a chest of drawers on frame, or a high chest of drawers—was used to hold clothing and household linens. The dressing table, also known as a chamber table, was for storing the accoutrements of grooming, and, with a dressing glass resting on it or a looking glass hung over it, was placed against a wall between two windows so that daylight would illuminate the face and hence the mirrored reflection of the person sitting in front of it. The forms characteristic of New England emerged in Boston in the seventeen-thirties and changed little during at least a half century of popularity. The dressing table, with cabriole legs and a shell-carved drawer centered above the skirt, and the high chest, with a similarly carved drawer in the enclosed scroll pediment, are uniquely American evolutions from the characteristic William and Mary turned-leg and flat-top form. In the seventeen-thirties and forties most examples were either japanned or veneered in walnut; thereafter they were made of solid woods. The Museum's collection, though lacking any Newport pad-footed example or any East Windsor, Connecticut, interpretation of the Philadelphia type, is representative, and is notable for the number of classic examples of Boston origin, the two japanned pairs in particular.

149.   High Chest of Drawers

New England, 1730–50

THE USE OF WHITE PINE in the construction of the high chest and its matching dressing table (cat. no. 150) indicates a New England origin, and the chest's connection with the Sheafe and Gerrish families of Portsmouth, New Hampshire, suggests a specific place. The MMA set bears comparison with a set attributed to Samuel Sewall of

York, Maine (Jobe and Kaye, nos. 33, 37). Both sets have a cavetto cornice with bolection frieze in the William and Mary style, undulating front skirts, and cabriole legs without knee brackets, the rear ones forward-facing. The chest's removable bonnet top with its flamboyant inlaid stars and shell is without parallel, as in both pieces are the repetition of the top's shape in the front skirt, the lower arrangement of a single deep central drawer flanked by pairs of graduated drawers, and the arches inlaid in the drawer fronts and on the dressing table top. In spite of extensive damage and incorrect restoration to their legs, the two pieces must stand among the most venturesome creations of provincial New England cabinetmakers in the first half of the eighteenth century.

PROVENANCE: Ex coll.: Harold M. and Cecile Lehman (later Cecile L. Mayer), Tarrytown, New York. Purchased by Mr. and Mrs. Lehman at the New York auction of the Francis H. Bigelow collection in January 1924. (The high chest does not appear in the Bigelow collection album referred to at cat. no. 43, Provenance.) According to the sale catalogue, "This unusual piece was originally owned by the Sheaf family of Portsmouth, N.H." Jacob Sheafe (1715–1791), who married Hannah Seavey (1719–1773) in 1740 and moved to Portsmouth in 1742, may have been the first owner. In the nineteenth century the high chest was in Cambridgeport, now a part of Cambridge, Massachusetts, in the possession of someone named Gerrish (see Inscriptions), which, like Sheafe, is a prominent Portsmouth name. The two families were linked by marriage. Jacob Sheafe's daughter Hannah married Hugh Henderson; their daughter Hannah married Thomas Lewis; their daughter Sarah married Robert Follett Gerrish in 1848. The high chest may have descended in the same order.

CONSTRUCTION: On the bonnet top, a separate unit resting on the boards above the cornice, the veneered front is inlaid with light and dark woods forming a central shell and two pairs of compass stars joined together and framed by herringbone banding. Each of the top's circular and serpentine sections is carved from a separate, thick board, rough-hewn on its interior surface. On the upper case: The cornice is in four parts, those of the cavetto and bolection moldings veneered in light wood. The front bolection frieze is attached to a wide shallow drawer. The sides are solid wood. The back is made of two wide vertical boards with a narrow third board half-lapped between them. The drawer fronts are veneered, giving every drawer the appearance of two, each with a herringbone border and a central panel that in the top drawer is arched. The drawer sides have double-beaded top edges; the bottoms, each pegged to the drawer backboard, run lengthwise. On the lower case: The top is a single board, its grain running lengthwise. The backboard, cut out in a large ogee arch on its lower edge, is dovetailed to the solid vertical side boards. The shape of the side skirts is an exaggerated repetition of that of the front skirt. The veneered front skirt is inlaid with circular and serpentine herringbone banding. The stiles of the legs extend a short way into the case, those in front secured with glue blocks; those in back, with screws. On the central drawer the bottom runs crosswise.

CONDITION: The high chest has been refinished, and is a light brown in color except for the moldings and sides, which are a dark reddish brown. It has suffered serious indignities, but the

149

cabinetwork is basically intact. All four legs are replaced from four inches below the case. The knee stumps and their short interior stiles are probably original, although the juncture with the skirt is infelicitous. The uppermost edge of the cornice has been reworked, and the applied moldings surrounding the drawer openings appear to be later replacements. Holes and imperfections in the lightwood veneer on the drawer fronts have been filled with miniature mahogany plugs. It would seem logical that the front skirts of high chest and dressing table were, like the bonnet top, once veneered with walnut and their inlaid circles filled with compass stars, but except for minor patches the lightwood veneers all look to be original.

INSCRIPTIONS: In black paint script (19th-century), inside bonnet-top backboard and on lower-case top: *Gerrish*. Similarly, on upper-case backboards: *Gerrish./83 Green St./Cambridgeport / Mass.*

DIMENSIONS: H.: overall, 86⅜ (*219.4*); W.: upper case, 35¾ (*90.8*), lower case, 38⅞ (*98.7*), feet, 40¼ (*102.2*); D.: upper case, 17¾ (*45.1*), lower case, 19¼ (*48.9*), feet, 20¼ (*51.4*).

WOODS: Primary: walnut; veneers of walnut, burl walnut, mahogany, and lightwood. Secondary: walnut (top boards of bonnet); white pine (all else).

REFERENCES: Bigelow sale, lot 96. Nutting 2, no. 4956 (detail of bonnet top). For the Sheafe family, see *Biographical and Historical Sketches of the Sheafe and Allied Families of America*, n.p., 1923; Rev. Charles N. Sinnet, comp., *The Gerrish Genealogy*, undated ms. at New York Public Library.

Bequest of Cecile L. Mayer, subject to a life estate, 1962 (62.171.12)

150. Dressing Table

(en suite with High Chest cat. no. 149)
New England, 1730–50

PROVENANCE: Ex coll.: George Coe Graves, Osterville, Massachusetts. The piece is listed in the inventory of objects Graves offered to the MMA as: "DEN—FIRST FLOOR, item 63. Lowboy, Veneered decoration in various woods. American, probably Connecticut, mid-18th century." Where Graves got it is not known, but since the piece has had similar later alterations with its en suite high chest, the two presumably had a common provenance.

CONSTRUCTION: The top is a single pine board framed on front and sides with narrow walnut boards ovolo-molded on their outer edges. The top surface is elaborately veneered and inlaid. Within a herringbone border three large, round-arched panels are formed by crossbanding in herringbone frames. Inlaid in each corner is a quadrant of a compass star like those on the high chest's bonnet top. Otherwise, the construction is like that of cat. no. 149.

CONDITION: The top retains an old varnish finish. The front and sides, which have been refinished, are a light walnut brown in color. As is cat. no. 149, the piece is much restored. The

150

walnut legs are entirely new. The knees duplicate the original four-inch stumps on the high chest, but otherwise lack stylistic justification. The walnut framing members of the top are restorations; the herringbone border inlaid on them and the reinforcing strips below them must have been added at the same time. The moldings around the drawer openings, the beaded edge of the front skirt, and the brasses are replacements.

INSCRIPTIONS: In chalk, on the back of each drawer: the figure *3*, preceded by an arrowlike symbol.

DIMENSIONS: H.: overall, 29¾ (*75.6*); W.: top, 35¼ (*89.5*), case, 32 (*81.3*), feet, 33 (*84.5*); D.: top, 20¾ (*52.7*), case, 18 (*45.7*), feet, 18 (*45.7*).

WOODS: Primary: walnut; veneers of burl walnut, mahogany, and lightwood. Secondary: white pine.

The Sylmaris Collection, Gift of George Coe Graves, 1930 (30.120.42)

151. Dressing Table

Massachusetts, 1730–50

COMBINED IN THE COMPLEX design of this dressing table, if not totally comfortably, are a carved skirt shell with veneered drawer fronts; applied pilasters with cabriole legs. The massive shell and the pilasters appear to be the work of a hand not elsewhere known, but variations on both motifs appear on a small group of dressing tables thought to be from the Boston area. One is signed by Joseph Davis, a joiner active around that city in about

151

ers between the drawers, but no dust boards. The lower drawers, their bottom boards laid crosswise, slide on medial braces. The thick, veneered drawer fronts all have large dovetails: one on the shallow drawers, two on the deep ones. The drawer sides are double beaded at the top. The rear legs are pieced on the knees and the pad feet.

CONDITION: The dressing table has a warm nut brown patina, but it appears to have been painted at one time: the backboard is black, and traces of glossy black remain in the fluted columns, in the shell, and on the underside of the knees. On the top, though most of the original veneers remain on the edges, what was probably a pattern of walnut veneers has been replaced by a single rough-cut piece of mahogany veneer. The left front and right rear legs have been broken at the juncture of knee and stile. The pieced parts of the knee and pad of the left rear leg are replaced, as are the side knee brackets, the pendants, and the moldings flanking the central drawer. The bottoms of the two upper drawers are old restorations. The brasses are old replacements.

INSCRIPTIONS: In pencil (19th-century?), on right side of lower left drawer: *Alfred Prescott*. Stamped into back of lower left drawer brass escutcheon: *EH*.

DIMENSIONS: H.: overall, 29⅝ (*75.3*); W.: top, 34⅛ (*86.7*), case, 30⅝ (*77.8*), feet, 32¼ (*81.9*); D.: top, 21 (*53.3*), case, 18¼ (*46.4*), feet, 19 (*48.3*).

WOODS: Primary: walnut, walnut veneers; maple (legs). Secondary: walnut (front skirt core); white pine (all else).

Gift of Clarence Dillon, 1975   (1975.132.2)

1730–50 (Lovell, fig. 68); its matching high chest (Lockwood I, fig. 100) is at the Department of State. Other examples are of solid walnut with block-fronted drawers (e.g., Morse, pp. 33–34 and fig. 19; Fairbanks and Bates, p. 114).

Cat. no. 151 appears to be an early essay in the Queen Anne style. The shallow middle drawer is a feature in the waning William and Mary mode, the open arch normally found beneath the drawer here filled by the shell. In the subsequent development of the classic Queen Anne form a shell is incorporated in an enlarged central drawer (see cat. no. 157), but, probably because the juncture of pilasters above cabriole legs proved awkward, the pilasters were abandoned on dressing tables. On the upper sections of high chests (e.g., cat. nos. 157, 159), however, they long continued in use.

PROVENANCE: Ex coll.: Clarence Dillon, Far Hills, New Jersey.

CONSTRUCTION: The top is a single piece of pine veneered with mahogany (see Condition). The ovolo-molded edge on both front and sides is veneered with crossbanded walnut. The sides are single solid boards. The front stiles are encased with boards rounded and stop-fluted to give the effect of engaged columns. Bead-edged moldings are nailed around the drawer openings. The skirt board, veneered in front and with a reinforcing board glued behind the recess-carved shell, is pieced at the bottom of the shell. The flat-arched units that flank the central skirt segment are repeated on the side boards. The knee brackets are glued to the skirt boards. There are vertical divid

152.   High Chest of Drawers

Connecticut, Windsor area, about 1735

AS LATE AS 1891 this chest and its matching dressing table, whose whereabouts are now unknown, remained together (Lyon, p. 87). A high chest now at Winterthur (Downs 1952, no. 186) matches the chest in most particulars of design and construction and can confidently be assigned to the same maker. On it, the medial slides for its drawers are part of the original construction rather than the afterthought found on the lower case of cat. no. 152, which suggests that it was made somewhat later. The MMA chest, though itself undocumented, is one of a small group of case pieces bearing dates in the 1730s and with histories of ownership in the Connecticut River valley—north of Middletown, Connecticut; south of Hadley, Massachusetts; but especially around Windsor, Connecticut. It has a Windsor history (Lyon, p. 87); its Winterthur counterpart, which is dated 1736 (Hummel 1970, I, p. 897), was owned in South Windsor; and a dressing table of similar form, now at Shelburne (*Antiques* 67 [February 1955], p. 104), with cedar graining rather than imitation japanning, was found in the Phelps

152

House, Wethersfield, Connecticut (Albert Sack, conversation with author).

Three simple chests of drawers dated respectively 1735, 1737, and 1738, all found in central Massachusetts in the nineteen-thirties, appear to be closely related to the top section of cat. no. 152 in materials and construction as well as in form and type of painted decoration (Cummings, p. 192). A fourth example, undated, was found in East Windsor, Connecticut, and is now at the CHS (Kirk 1967, no. 55). Two other painted chests at the MMA (acc. nos. 38.97 and 45.78.3; ill. Kirk 1967, nos. 54, 56) have been associated with cat. no. 152, but the additional colors and different decorative motifs used on them make an attribution to the same painter unconvincing.

This is a high chest worthy to be called folk art. Its painted decoration looks to be a simplified, provincial interpretation of the japanning popular in Boston in the seventeen-thirties and forties (see cat. nos. 153–156). Its angular, exaggerated knees and straight ankles, and its large turned flat feet are an ingenuous parody of the cabriole legs of urban Massachusetts. The result is remarkable not only visually but also as a document of the speed with which the Boston Queen Anne style migrated inland and was transformed into a distinctive local style.

PROVENANCE: Ex coll.: Mrs. J. Insley Blair, Tuxedo Park, New York. The high chest, with its matching dressing table, belonged in 1891 to Edwin Simons of Hartford (Lyon, fig. 36), and was subsequently acquired by Irving Lyon. Mrs. Blair bought it from Lyon, lent it to the American Japanned Furniture exhibition at the MMA in 1933, and put it on loan in 1939.

CONSTRUCTION: On the upper case: The back is three horizontal boards, two wide and one narrow. The sides are two boards each. Their front edges have applied double beading, as do the stiles between the drawers of the top tier. The rails, double-beaded in front, are slotted into the side boards. The ogee molding nailed to the sides and front extends below the bottom board to form the base of the upper section. On the lower case: Nailed to the top of the front and sides and overlapping the two roughly planed top boards is a shallow projecting molding. The rear legs are identical to the front ones except that the back knee brackets are omitted. The backboard, side boards, and front skirt are double pegged to the stiles. The flat ogee arches flanking the deep central arch and pendants of the front skirt are repeated, with a central pendant, on the side skirts, all skirt contours outlined by an applied bead strip. The double beading around the drawer openings is also applied. The side drawers slide on medial braces. Slots cut into the corner posts and into a board nailed to the middle of the back suggest that the cabinetmaker planned to insert side runners to support the drawers, but changed his mind. On the drawers of both cases, the grain of the bottom boards runs crosswise on the small ones and lengthwise on the large ones; the bottoms overlap the sides and, except for the lower tier, have applied runner strips. The exterior of the high chest is painted black. The borders of the drawers and the individual animal and vegetable mo-

tifs sprinkled over the skirt, side boards, and drawer fronts are all in yellow, as are the ferns and other foliage painted on the legs and on the large moldings.

CONDITION: The decorative motifs, originally delicately sketched, have been heavily overpainted. In 1891 the chest was described as "crudely painted in dull yellow on black ground" (Lyon, p. 87); by 1946 it was "monochrome brown" (American Collector 16 [November 1947], frontispiece caption). The pendants, while in place in 1891 (Lyon, fig. 36), appear to be replacements. The right rear leg has been broken at the knee, and the knee bracket and most of the pad foot are replaced. The side knee bracket of the left front leg and a small part of the left rear pad foot are restored. In 1963 the ends of dovetails that projected behind the drawers were sawed off to allow the drawers to close completely.

INSCRIPTIONS: In pencil, on the backboards of the third tier of drawers: illegible markings.

DIMENSIONS: H.: overall, 62 (157.5); W.: upper case, 33¼ (84.5), lower case, 37⅜ (94.9), feet, 39⅞ (101.3); D.: upper case, 19⅝ (47.3), lower case, 22⅛ (56.2), feet, 24¼ (61.6).

WOODS: Primary: maple. Secondary: yellow pine.

REFERENCES: Lyon, p. 87; fig. 36. Downs 1933, fig. 4. Cummings, pp. 192–193, fig. 3. American Collector 16 (November 1947), frontispiece; p. 4 (ill.). Downs 1948, p. 81 (ill.). Gertrude Z. Thomas, "Lacquer: Chinese, Indian, 'right' Japan, and American," Antiques 79 (June 1961), pp. 572–575, ill. p. 575. Kirk 1967, no. 75. Margon 1971, pp. 244–245 (ill. and measured drawing).

Gift of Mrs. J. Insley Blair, 1946   (46.194.5)

153. High Chest of Drawers

Boston, about 1747

IN ALL BOSTON JAPANNED furniture only eight high chests with cabriole legs and flat tops are known, this example among them; of the three known dressing tables, its companion piece, cat. no. 154, is one of only two (with cat. no. 156) having cabriole legs. The high chest and dressing table, made en suite, are the work of the same cabinetmaker and the same japanner, but the maker's hand is not apparent in any other of the two dozen known japanned pieces. It is the delicate scale of the cornice, the slight projection of the midmolding, and, framing the drawer openings, the simple beading strip instead of the applied double-beaded molding characteristic of the William and Mary style that make the cabinetwork of this high chest distinctive. These features, in combination with the Queen Anne-type brasses (albeit engraved in the

William and Mary manner), suggest a date of manufacture later than that of most Boston japanned furniture, a hypothesis confirmed by the "July 1747" painted on the dressing table.

On the drawers of the upper case of this high chest and of a flat-top one at Winterthur (Downs 1952, no. 187) the basket centered in the second tier and the carriage centered in the fourth tier are notably alike. On a bonnet-top high chest at the New Haven Colony Historical Society (Rhoades and Jobe, pp. 1084–85) the pilasters and winged cherubs that flank painted shells in the recessed arches of the upper and lower central drawers and the splotching of the black paint that forms the tortoiseshell background of the side panels all match those of cat. no. 153. Although extensive paint losses on both the Winterthur and the New Haven pieces compound the difficulty in identifying the painting styles of the different hands, the similarity in a number of the decorative motifs on them and on the MMA high chest reflects the close collaboration within eighteenth-century Boston's community of japanners.

PROVENANCE: Ex coll.: H. Eugene Bolles, Boston. According to Bolles's notes (MMA files), the high chest and its matching dressing table were "bought by Koopman [a Boston dealer] at the auction of Peter Parley Estate in Jamaica Plain [the western part of Roxbury]. I was not able to attend the auction, and bought them several days afterwards from Koopman."

CONSTRUCTION: On the upper case: The cornice moldings are in three parts; in front, a large maple cove is attached to the pine front board of a wide, shallow drawer. The top and backboards are each of two pieces, those of the latter horizontal and with tongue and groove joints. Between the drawers are partial dust boards fronted with inch-deep rails, double-beaded at the front edges, which are slotted into the side boards, their ends exposed. The front edges of the side boards are faced in maple, and maple beading strips are applied at the sides of the drawer openings. The lowest drawer slides directly on the bottom board. Under the bottom board thick runner strips are attached at front and sides; the high bottom molding is attached to them and to the side boards. On the lower case: The shallow projecting molding is nailed to the front and side rails, on which the upper case rests. Within this framework are two rough-hewn top boards laid crosswise. The two-piece backboard and the side boards reinforced at the joints with glue blocks are triple pegged to the stiles. Each side skirt is cut out in a flat arch identical to those on the front skirt. The front skirt is double pegged to the corner posts. The double-beaded rails and stiles between the drawers are dovetailed into the corner posts and skirt. The drawer openings adjacent to the skirt and the corner posts have applied beading. The sides of the knees and pad feet are pieced. The knees of the rear legs do not extend beyond the backboard. On the drawers: The fronts are all solid, except on the cove drawer. The top edges of the sides are double beaded. The bottom boards, their grain running crosswise, extend over the sides and have applied runner strips.

The high chest is entirely painted in a tortoiseshell pattern created with bold black streaks on a vermilion ground. Raised ornament—gilded gesso—appears on the drawer fronts, front skirt, and front corner posts. The other ornament is painted in shades of gold and green directly onto the tortoiseshell ground. The cornice is painted: on the cyma recta molding, with a row of leaves; on the cove molding, with large floral motifs on panels of alternating gold color and tortoiseshell. The drawer fronts are treated individually, each with three or four separate motifs within a simple painted border—the larger the drawer, the larger and more complex the motifs. On the lower central drawer, a painted shell in a recessed round arch is flanked by pilasters and surrounded by winged cherubs. Painted on each side of the upper case are a large and a small floral arrangement framed by a plain border. On either side of the lower case are wavelike guilloche panels and a central, double-bordered floral arrangement.

CONDITION: The high chest's decoration is remarkably well preserved, but has darkened to a somber, reddish brown hue. The painted background is generally intact except for areas above the brasses on the bottom drawer of the upper case and on the right-hand drawer of the lower case. Some of the gesso ornament has been restored. The japanning was stabilized and cleaned in 1983–84. According to Bolles (12/23/1909 letter, MMA files), "There were one or two small pieces [of the applied lacquer decoration] not larger than one's finger nail off the piece when it arrived at Davenport's. . . . Of course, the old applied lacquer, especially where it is raised up, is very dry and shaky. When I got this piece a few spots near the base were missing, and they were very well restored by a man who lives near Boston."

The turned pendants on the skirt are 1978 reproductions based upon those on a japanned high chest at Boston (Randall 1965, no. 52). The upper edge of the cavetto molding nailed to the top of the lower case is restored. The runners of the large drawers and the lower backboard of the upper case are replaced. A 1913 photograph (Lockwood 1, fig. 79) shows the chest lacking three of its brasses and with two that do not match. These have been replaced. The brass knob on the lower central drawer is a replacement; marks on the wood have been left by a ring pull with circular escutcheon.

INSCRIPTIONS: In chalk, inside upper-case bottom board: *B*; on drawer backboards of both cases, except for the cove drawer, beginning at top: *1* through *4*.

DIMENSIONS: H.: overall, 70¼ (*178.4*); W.: upper case, 36 (*91.4*), lower case, 38 (*96.5*), feet, 39⅝ (*100.7*); D.: upper case, 19⅞ (*50.5*), lower case, 20⅞ (*53.*), feet, 21 (*53.3*).

WOODS: Primary: maple; white pine (side boards). Secondary: white pine.

REFERENCES: Lockwood 1, fig. 79. Nutting 1, no. 343. MMA 1930, no. 14. Salomonsky, pl. 92 (measured drawing). Fales 1974, fig. 42.

Gift of Mrs. Russell Sage, 1909 (10.125.58)

154. Dressing Table

(en suite with High Chest cat. no. 153)
Boston, 1747

PROVENANCE: See cat. no. 153.

CONSTRUCTION: The top is three boards of equal width, with thumbnail molding on all four edges (partly shaved off on the back) and with notched front corners. The top is attached with glue blocks to the back and side boards, these double pegged to the corner posts, the joints reinforced with glue blocks. The knees and pad feet are pieced on the sides of the front legs and on the backs of the rear legs. The front skirt, blocked-in below the arch of the center drawer, is pegged to the front posts. There are no dust boards or dividers between the lower drawers. The top edges of the drawer sides are flat. The top is painted in an allover tortoiseshell pattern on which, formed in gesso, are two closely juxtaposed pagodalike pavilions with a bridge at the lower left and two figures in a boat at the lower right. The scene is framed in a border formed by diapered gold panels in the middle of the front and back and at the

corners. Otherwise the table is made and painted in the same manner as cat. no. 153.

CONDITION: The painted decoration, while generally well preserved, is much worn on the surface of the top, where most of the gilding is gone from the raised gesso figures. There, the only gold-painted border panels clearly visible are those at the back, in the middle and at the right. The japanning was stabilized and cleaned in 1983–84. All that remained of the original skirt pendants was a maple stump on the right side, and in 1978 new drops were made (see cat. no. 153, Condition). The knee brackets, except for that on the side of the right front leg, are replaced, as is the pieced part of the left rear pad foot. The brasses on the lower drawers are copies of the originals on the matching high chest, but the single pull on the top drawer is an old one removed from the same piece (ill. Lockwood 1, fig. 80). Single holes, now filled, at either side of the top drawer indicate that it once had two pulls. There are marks on the paint in the blocked-in central drawer from a circular escutcheon and its drop.

INSCRIPTIONS: In black paint, on the bottom edge of the left side board: *July 1747.*

154

DIMENSIONS: H.: overall, 30⅝ (77.8); W.: top, 33⅞ (86.), case, 30⅛ (76.5), feet, 31⅝ (80.3); D.: top, 21⅛ (53.7), case, 17⅞ (45.4), feet, 19¼ (48.9).

WOODS: Primary: maple; white pine (side boards). Secondary: white pine.

REFERENCES: Lockwood 1, fig. 80. Fales 1974, fig. 43.

Gift of Mrs. Russell Sage, 1909   (10.125.68)

155. High Chest of Drawers

Boston, 1730–50

THE HIGH CHEST, one of six known Boston japanned examples with bonnet tops and cabriole legs (see Greenlaw, no. 80), is en suite with a dressing table (cat. no. 156) and a looking glass (cat. no. 210). On high chest and dressing table the cabinetwork is identical; the painted decoration on all three pieces is by the same hand. A high chest at Bayou Bend (Warren, no. 68), remarkably similar to cat. no. 155 in design, construction, and japanning, must be by the same craftsmen. The most visible features in the japanning of both high chests—the sketchy, jagged quality of the painted ornament on the cornice moldings, and the large irregular masses of gesso in the central designs on the side panels—are not apparent in any other Boston japanned work. Thomas Johnston (1708–1767) has been suggested as the decorator (Brazer, fig. 4; Davidson 1967, p. 148) because of the similarity between the cherubs in the high chests' pediments and those on the trade card he engraved for himself in 1732 (S. Hitchings, "Thomas Johnston," *Boston Prints and Printmakers 1670–1775*, Boston, 1973, p. 87, fig. 37). This of itself is insufficient evidence for a firm attribution, for though Johnston is the best known of all Boston japanners, no documented example of his painted furniture has yet been found.

The design of the MMA high chest and dressing table is in the early Queen Anne style. The legs have unusual lobate knee brackets and rounded pad feet raised on straight-sided bases, features also found on two flat-top japanned high chests (Fales 1974, fig. 35; *Antiques* 112 [July 1977], p. 97). The bonnet top of cat. no. 155 has a cramped look: the upper shell drawer (actually a door) is very tall; the circular openings above it, very small. The John Pimm high chest at Winterthur (Downs 1952, no. 188) has a similarly tall upper drawer within an immensely high pediment. The remaining three high chests have pediments with more pleasing proportions, their shell drawers horizontal in emphasis and typical of the fully developed Massachusetts high chest of mid-century (cat. no. 159). The pagodalike finials of cat. no. 155, probably based on those found on English japanned secretaries such as the one owned by General James Bow-

doin (1726–1790) of Boston (Fales 1974, figs. 46, 47), are the only original ones known to survive on American japanned furniture. On the high chest, the hinged door that opens onto a cupboard is unique. The chest and the rest of the en suite japanned pieces seem to fit the description in the 1730 inventory of Henry Guineau of Boston (Lyon, p. 90): "A Japan'd chest drawers Cabinet in one. A Looking Glass and table varnished in red, £50."

PROVENANCE: According to a tradition in the family, a William and Mary-style Boston japanned high chest, a japanned dressing glass imported from England (MMA acc. nos. 40.37.3, 5), this high chest and its matching dressing table (cat. no. 156) and looking glass (cat. no. 210) originally belonged to Benjamin Pickman (1708–1773), merchant of Salem (Downs 1940, pp. 147–148). Pickman married Love Rawlins in 1731, and in 1750 moved into the great house at 165 Essex Street, Salem (Fiske Kimball, *Domestic Architecture of the American Colonies and of the Early Republic*, New York, 1922, p. 91, fig. 63), where the pieces are said to have been used. They probably descended through Pickman's son Benjamin (1740–1819); to his grandson Thomas (1773–1817); to Thomas's daughter Mary, who married George Bailey Loring of Salem in 1851. Irving Whitall Lyon knew the pieces when they "belonged to the late Dr. George B. Loring" (Lyon, p. 89). The set subsequently descended to Lawrence Dwight (died 1918); to his fiancée, Harriet Amory, later Mrs. Warwick Potter, who sold it to the MMA in 1940.

CONSTRUCTION: On the upper case: Each side is of one wide and one narrow board with a thick maple strip applied to the front edge. There are four horizontal backboards. The upper one, which backs the space above the drawers and extends through the side boards, is cut out behind the pediment's open top in an inverted round arch. The board fronting the pediment is pierced below the broken scroll by a pair of small, circular, applied-bead-edged openings; its ends extend through the side boards. The two-piece cornice molding is continued a short way into the pediment opening. In the opening, the sides are straight at the top and sharply angled outward below. The shell-carved drawer centered in the top tier is actually a door—a thick board with a blocked-out arch on the inner surface behind the shell. The door, hinged at the right side, opens onto a removable cupboard unit containing three arch-topped cubbyholes over a single drawer. The drawers of the chest slide on thick dust boards slotted into the sides and faced with maple strips, except for the bottom drawer, which rides on slides above the case's bottom boards. The upper case stands on continuous glue blocks attached beneath the front and sides of the bottom boards and on the bottom molding nailed to them.

On the lower case: The top is of three cross-grained boards fitted around the corner posts and rabbeted into the top edges of the side boards and the front rail, with a boldly projecting two-piece molding nailed to the edges. The sides and backboards are triple pegged to the corner posts. The flat arch on each of the side skirts repeats those between the pendants on the single-pegged front skirt. The knee brackets are glued to the skirt boards. The stiles and rails between the drawers are slotted together. Under each top drawer is a dust board laid lengthwise and fixed with glue blocks between the runners. On the drawers of both cases, the cross-grained bottom boards extend over the sides and have applied runners.

The chest is painted in vermilion streaked with black to simulate tortoiseshell. Raised gesso ornament, painted and gilded, is applied to the drawer fronts, front corner posts, skirt rail, and side boards. The other ornament—in shades of green and gold—is painted directly onto the tortoiseshell background. In the cornice, the moldings are divided into panels of alternating gold and tortoiseshell decorated with floral motifs. Two large and three small sad-faced cherubs fill the pediment area. Festooned Ionic pilasters and pairs of cherubs with crossed wings ornament the carved shell drawers. The cupboard unit and the inside of the door are japanned in gold on a vermilion ground. Each drawer front has a series of separate painted decorative motifs and a painted border. On each of the upper case sides, within a wide border, is a large vignette: a willow tree shading a cluster of buildings. On the lower case, a large floral arrangement between rinceau borders adorns each side.

CONDITION: The painted surfaces were restored in 1983–84. Much of the original decoration was found to be intact under discolored varnishes and later, heavy-handed overpainting. The pediment area (finials, cornice, tympanum, shell door, and interior cupboard), the lower shell drawer and front skirt, and the entire left side are particularly well preserved. The stiles and rails flanking the drawers are repainted, as is much of the right side, and there are extensive background paint losses on the legs and the uncarved drawer fronts. The molded edges of the drawers were originally gilded. In 1984, because traces of gold were found on the drawer handles, the brasses were lacquered to match. The woodwork is in good condition. The skirt pendants, made in 1978, are copied from those on a dressing table at Deerfield (Fales 1976, fig. 428). The beaded strip outlining the front and side skirts, the molded top edge of the lower shell drawer, and the knee brackets on the rear legs are replacements. All the drawers are lined with tan paper (19th-century).

INSCRIPTIONS: On the upper left drawer of the lower case: a pencil sketch of a squat bonnet-top high chest, partly obliterated. In chalk, on back of bottom shell drawer: *W E*. In pencil, beginning at the upper left, the backs of the uncarved drawers and their corresponding dust boards are numbered *1* through *10*. Stamped on backs of escutcheon plates of brass drawer pulls, beginning at upper left: *1* through *14*; on the keyhole escutcheon plates: *3, 5, 7, 8, 9*. Pasted on the paper that lines the bottom drawer of the upper case is one page of a personal letter (early 20th-century) that refers to Lawrence Dwight (see Provenance).

DIMENSIONS: H.: overall, 86½ *(219.7)*, pediment, 84½ *(214.6)*; W.: upper case, 37¾ *(95.9)*, lower case, 38¼ *(97.2)*, feet, 40 *(101.6)*; D.: upper case, 19¾ *(50.2)*, lower case, 20⅞ *(53.)*, feet, 21½ *(54.6)*.

WOODS: Primary: maple (moldings, uncarved drawer fronts, strips facing upper-case rails and front edges of side boards); birch (legs); white pine (side boards, pediment and skirt boards, rails and stiles between drawers of lower case, stiles between drawers of upper case). Secondary: white pine.

REFERENCES: Lyon, p. 89; fig. 38. Downs 1933, p. 43 (ill.); idem 1940, fig. 2. Halsey and Cornelius, fig. 51. *Antiques* 50 (October 1946), p. 251, fig. 20. Powel, p. 203. Comstock, fig. 184. Davidson 1967, fig. 194. Fales 1972, fig. 97; idem 1974, fig. 40.

Purchase, Joseph Pulitzer Bequest, 1940   (40.37.1)

156. Dressing Table

(en suite with High Chest cat. no. 155)
Boston, 1730–50

PROVENANCE: See cat. no. 155.

CONSTRUCTION: The sides and backboard are double pegged to the corner posts. The front skirt, its flat arches repeated on the side boards, is pegged. The rails and stiles flanking the drawers are slotted into each other and into the corner posts and skirt. There are no dust boards or dividers between the drawers. The top edges of the drawer sides are flat; the drawer bottoms, their grain running crosswise, extend over the sides and have attached runners.

CONDITION: The japanned finish, which had suffered widespread flaking and subsequent crude overpainting, was stabilized in 1983–84. On the front, only on the rail, stiles, right corner post, skirt center, and shell-drawer winged cherubs is the original japanning well preserved. On the left side, the wavelike guilloche patterns on the stiles are intact, as is the gold lambrequin motif on the right rear leg. The dressing table has sustained extensive structural damage. The top board, installed in 1940, was apparently copied from that on cat. no. 154 to replace an earlier restoration (Lyon, fig. 39). The pendent skirt brackets, copied from the originals remaining on cat. no. 155, were also restored in 1940. The skirt's beaded edge and turned pendants were added in 1978, the former on the basis of nail holes found in the bottom edge of the skirt, the latter duplicating ones on a gilded-shell dressing table at Deerfield (Fales 1976, fig. 428). The front left and rear left knee brackets are replaced.

DIMENSIONS: H.: overall, 29¾ *(75.6)*; W.: top, 33¾ *(85.7)*, case, 30 *(76.2)*, feet, 31 *(78.7)*; D.: top, 21⅛ *(53.7)*, case, 17⅞ *(45.4)*, feet, 18⅝ *(47.3)*.

WOODS: Primary: maple (uncarved drawer fronts); birch (legs); white pine (carved drawer front, case sides, skirt, stiles and rails between drawers). Secondary: white pine.

REFERENCES: Lyon, fig. 39 (ill. with its English shaving stand). Downs 1940. Powel, p. 202 (ill.). Davidson 1967, fig. 193. Fales 1972, fig. 98; idem 1974, fig. 41.

Purchase, Joseph Pulitzer Bequest, 1940   (40.37.2)

157. High Chest of Drawers

Boston, 1730–50

AMONG THE MASSACHUSETTS high chests with bonnet tops and fluted pilaster strips this is one of a handful with figured walnut veneers inlaid with stars and stringing and with carved and gilded shells in the central drawer fronts. (The compass star and unusual checkerboard stringing inlay are also found on a child's desk, cat. no. 172; a dressing table, cat. no. 158, has similar, if simplified, stringing and shell ornamentation.) The hand

that made the high-chest shells appears to be the one that also carved the central drawer of an otherwise plain dressing table (*Antiques* 91 [April 1967], p. 411).

Three other high chests of this type (Comstock, fig. 183; Flayderman sale, lot 437; Randall 1965, no. 54) and two dressing tables (Fales 1976, figs. 427, 428) all have a more naturalistic type of shell not unlike those found on some japanned high chests (cat. no. 155), but otherwise admit to much variety in detail (Randall 1965, no. 54) and were doubtless the product of a number of shops. All either have Boston family histories or were found in that locale. One, at the Boston MFA, is signed and dated 1739 by Ebenezer Hartshorne (ibid.). Hartshorne was a joiner in Charlestown between about 1729 and 1743, but also had business interests in nearby Boston (Richard H. Randall, Jr., and Martha McElman, "Ebenezer Hartshorne, cabinetmaker," *Antiques* 87 [January 1965], pp. 78–79).

The account books of Boston cabinetmakers in the seventeen-thirties document many of the precise decorative details found on cat. no. 157, and thus suggest when the piece was made: in 1733, gilding of two carved shells; in 1738, "a Case of drawers soled ends and stringed" and a desk inlaid with a star (Jobe, pp. 16–20). On cat. no. 157, the exquisite detailing of its veneers, inlays, and carving, as well as its fine old finish, make it noteworthy among its peers.

156

157 See also pp. 352, 363

155 See also pp. 352, 363

PROVENANCE: Ex coll.: H. Eugene Bolles, Boston. According to Bolles's notes (MMA files), "It was bought by me of a private family in Boston. The woman told me her husband had been a furniture mover, and when moving some well-to-do family many years ago, they gave it to her husband because it was in such poor condition."

CONSTRUCTION: On the upper case: Each two-piece, solid wood side is inlaid with narrow crossbanded veneering at front and back and has a six-point star inlaid within a large arched central panel formed by triple stringing. There are three wide horizontal backboards: the uppermost, cut out in a square behind the pediment opening, extends through the side boards to the crossbanded veneer. The bonnet top is enclosed. The pediment board has matched veneers inlaid with four-point compass stars. On either side of the drawers are four-fluted pilasters flanked with crossbanding and stringing. The facing of the rails is half an inch thick. The only dust board is under the upper tier of drawers. On the lower case: The midmolding is nailed to the top edges of the front and sides. The top consists of two thin lengthwise-grained boards enclosed at the front by the upper rail and at the sides with pine strips pierced by the back stiles. Each front leg and its stile is of one piece of wood. The stiles of the rear legs are pieced halfway up the case. The rear knees do not extend beyond the backboard. The knee brackets are glued to the skirts. The backboard is triple pegged to the stiles. The side boards are quadruple pegged in back and pegged in front, their crossband veneering defined at front and back with the triple stringing that also outlines the shape of their flat-arched skirts. Inlaid on each side is a central, six-point compass star. In front, the rails and the stiles between the drawers are solid wood. Stringing outlines the veneered skirt and the crossbanded front stiles. The veneered drawer fronts are framed in quadruple stringing (checkerboard sections of light and dark wood between lightwood borders) and in applied walnut strips with thumbnail-molded edges. Each wide drawer is veneered to look like two. The shells on the upper and lower central drawers are cut out on the stippled and dark-stained ground of a recessed arch. On the shells, plain pointed sections alternate with long, hollowed-out lobes topped with bellflowers. The top edges of the drawer sides are rounded. The drawer bottoms, their grain running crosswise, extend over the drawer sides and have applied runner strips. The bottom drawers slide on medial braces.

CONDITION: The chest has a lustrous and mellow light brown patina. According to Bolles's notes (MMA files), the high chest "was very much shaken and some of the veneer gone, but no substantial part was gone, and it was restored after I bought it." Bolles had the two missing side finials, the turned skirt drops, and the top of the right pilaster replaced. (Presumably, the tops of the original side finials were gilded like that of the central one.) All the large drawers have new runners, and some of the slides have been reversed. All drawer interiors have been varnished. The bottom of the upper left drawer is replaced. The brasses on the two small upper drawers are antique replacements. The wooden knob on the lower shell drawer, while old, is not visible in the MMA's earliest photograph.

INSCRIPTIONS: In chalk, on lower-case backboard, in large letters: *Back*; on backboards of upper-case drawers, beginning at top left: *1* through *6*; on back of upper shell drawer: *M*. On bottom of upper shell drawer and on upper-case bottom board:

illegible inscriptions. In pencil (19th-century?), on upper-case middle backboard: *Photo/May 11th, 76*.

DIMENSIONS: H.: overall, 90 (*238.6*), pediment, 86 (*218.4*); W.: upper case, 39⅛ (*99.4*), lower case, 42½ (*108.*), feet, 44 (*111.8*); D.: upper case, 19⅝ (*49.9*), lower case, 21½ (*54.6*), feet, 22¼ (*56.5*).

WOODS: Primary: walnut; walnut veneer. Secondary: white pine.

REFERENCES: Lockwood 1, fig. 94. MMA 1930, no. 16. Jobe, fig. 16.

Gift of Mrs. Russell Sage, 1909   (10.125.62)

158. Dressing Table

Boston, 1730–50

THE DRESSING TABLE and cat. no. 157 are based on the same model and were doubtless built in the same immediate locale. The drawers of both pieces are of identical construction and their brasses of identical pattern, which may indicate the work of one joiner. In most other details, however, the two are not alike. The handling of the ornamental veneers, inlays, and carved shells appears to be the work of different men. In contrast to that of the high chest, the dressing table's plain stringing is all but invisible, and the elements of its shell are large in scale and crude in execution. (Similar shells appear on a mahogany high chest [Christie's, 10/13/84 sale, lot 300 G].) Because of these differences and because the two pieces have no common history prior to their entering the Bolles collection, they cannot be considered as having been made en suite.

PROVENANCE: Ex coll.: H. Eugene Bolles, Boston. Bolles's notes (MMA files) record that the piece "almost matched the above [cat. no. 157], but [is] not its mate. It was bought some years after the other from a dealer in Boston who said he got it in the South."

CONSTRUCTION: The top is two boards ovolo-molded on all four edges. The boards of the front skirt are unusually thick. On each double-pegged side board the skirt is cut out in a flat arch flanked by ogee curves. The backboard is double pegged to the stiles. All four legs and stiles are continued to the top in one piece. The rear knees extend beyond the backboard. The knee brackets are glued over the skirt veneers. The rails and stiles between the drawers are of solid wood. On the drawers, the cross-grained bottom extends over the sides; the top edges of the sides are rounded; the lower drawers ride on medial braces. The veneered side boards are bordered at top and sides with triple stringing and diagonal crossbanding; the contour of each skirt is similarly bordered. Triple stringing follows the front skirt outline and bisects the diagonal crossbanding of the stiles. The veneered fronts of the drawers are framed by stringing and applied walnut strips with thumbnail-molded edges.

CONDITION: The dressing table, which has been refinished, is light brown in color. Most of the gilding of the carved shell is worn down to the gesso or the wood. Except for some of the ovolo edge molding, the veneered surface of the top was replaced for Bolles. The top is attached to the frame with modern screws. The front legs have been strengthened with corner braces. The side bracket of the left rear leg is replaced. A small part of the right front pad foot is patched, and the pads of the left front and right rear feet have splits. A medial brace has been added under the top drawer. Although Bolles thought them original, the skirt pendants, crudely fashioned from solid walnut, look to be replacements. The plinth of the one on the right has been repaired. The drawer interiors have been varnished.

INSCRIPTIONS: On backboard: *72.598* (in chalk, 20th-century); part of a shipping label from The Art Institute of Chicago.

DIMENSIONS: H.: overall, 29¾ (*75.6*); W.: top, 33¾ (*85.7*), case, 30 (*76.2*), feet, 31 (*78.7*); D.: top, 20⅝ (*52.4*), case, 17⅞ (*45.4*), feet, 19½ (*49.5*).

WOODS: Primary: walnut; walnut veneer. Secondary: white pine.

Gift of Mrs. Russell Sage, 1909　　(10.125.72)

158　See also p. 353

159.　High Chest of Drawers

Massachusetts, 1760–70

CIRCULAR PEDIMENT openings, tripartite flat-arched front skirts, fanlike carvings of central drawer fronts, and attenuated cabriole legs are characteristic of large numbers of high chests made throughout Massachusetts and Connecticut during the middle years of the century. One by Ebenezer Hartshorne is dated 1739 (Randall 1965, no. 54); one by a John Brooks is dated 1769 (*Antiques* 56 [November 1949], p. 311). Dressing tables of the same general design were also popular (see cat. no. 160).

On this example, the corkscrew finials and fluted pilasters of the upper case are in the Boston manner, as are those of cat. no. 157, which is made of walnut and probably dates from the seventeen-thirties. Cat. no. 159, however, is made of mahogany highlighted with elaborate large brasses; its pilasters have capitals and bases; the edges of its drawer openings are beaded; and it has been assembled with cut nails. With these rococo-inspired refinements, the high chest can be assigned a date in the seventeen-sixties.

PROVENANCE: Ex coll.: H. Eugene Bolles, Boston. Bolles acquired the high chest at auction in Boston.

CONSTRUCTION: On the upper case: There are three wide horizontal backboards; the uppermost, which incorporates the bonnet top, has a large square section cut out behind the pediment's central opening. The top consists of the boards framing the opening and the thin boards enclosing the bonnet top. The pediment board continues behind the blocks of the pilaster frieze. Extending into the pediment area is the large central top drawer cut out in a fanlike shell within an arch. Five-fluted pilasters, each with a separate capital and base, are nailed to thin strips flanking the drawers. The rails, faced with beaded strips, are let into the side boards. Beneath the top tier of drawers is a dust board. Blocks nailed to the drawer backs serve as drawer stops. On the lower case: Instead of top boards, side rails and an extension of the top rail support the upper case. The backboard is dovetailed to the side boards. The side skirts are cut out in flat arches. The sides and back are rabbeted to receive the stiles of the legs; the rear ones extending a third of the way up the case, the front ones, a quarter of the way. On the front, the stiles are faced with mahogany. The flat-arched skirt board is cut in, conforming to the arch of the central drawer. Large triangular glue blocks, their bottom edges following the serpentine curve of the knee brackets, reinforce the juncture of stiles and case elements. The rails, like those of the upper case, are faced with beaded strips. There are no dust boards or dividers between the bottom drawers. On the drawers: The fronts vary in thickness; the thin fronts of the small bottom drawers are backed with pine; the sides, double-beaded at the top edges, are thin; the outer surface of the bottom boards and backboards are rough-cut.

CONDITION: The fine old finish is a deep and lustrous red. The right-side finial and the turned pendent acorn at the right on the skirt are replacements made for Bolles. The front of the upper shell drawer, while original, is browner in color than the others and has a different grain. There is minor splitting and discoloration on the right front side of the upper case. Many of the drawer slides are replacements. Part of the pad of the right rear foot is patched.

INSCRIPTIONS: In chalk, on lower-case backboard: an indecipherable mark or monogram. In pencil (19th-century?), inside lower left drawer: *ESDAY 18/1   EA[S?]TERDAY 16.*

DIMENSIONS: H.: overall, 88¾ (*225.4*), pediment, 84¾ (*215.3*); W.: upper case, 38¼ (*97.2*), lower case, 40½ (*102.9*), feet, 41 (*104.1*); D.: upper case, 19⅜ (*49.2*), lower case, 21⅝ (*54.9*), feet, 22½ (*57.2*).

WOODS: Primary: mahogany. Secondary: white pine.

REFERENCES: Lockwood 1, fig. 95. Lee 1, p. 77 (measured drawings); p. 78 (ill.). MMA 1930, no. 13. Salomonsky, pl. 93 (measured drawing).

Gift of Mrs. Russell Sage, 1909   (10.125.63)

160. Dressing Table

New England, 1740–90

AN ORIGIN IN Connecticut is suggested by the cherry wood of which the dressing table is made and by the wide overhang and the finished edges on all four sides of its top. Other features of its design are from perhaps the most popular of Massachusetts patterns: the skirts shaped in flat arches and the finely rayed shell cut into the bottom of the central drawer above a blocked-in skirt. The treatment of the shell is not unlike that on a high chest signed by Massachusetts cabinetmaker Benjamin Frothingham and on its matching dressing table, both at Winterthur (Randall 1974, fig. 155). See also cat. no. 159.

PROVENANCE: Ex coll.: Mr. and Mrs. Edward S. Harkness, New London, Connecticut.

159 See also pp. 353, 363

160 See also p. 353

CONSTRUCTION: The top, made of one broad and one narrow board and with notched corners, is screwed to the frame. The back and side boards are pegged to the stiles, five pegs at each joint. The front skirt is doubled pegged, once through the stile, once through the knee. The drawer bottoms are slotted into the front and side boards and nailed to the back with roseheads. On the top and central drawers the grain on the bottom runs lengthwise; on the other drawers it runs crosswise.

CONDITION: The piece, reddish in color, has been refinished. The top has been reattached a number of times. The skirt below the shell is patched. Both pendent finials and the knee blocks flanking the left front leg are replacements. The brasses, smaller than the originals, are modern replacements. At one time an escutcheon was centered in the top drawer.

DIMENSIONS: H.: overall, 30½ (*77.5*); W.: top, 34⅝ (*88.*), case, 27 (*68.6*), feet, 28½ (*72.4*); D.: top, 22¼ (*56.5*), case, 17¼ (*43.8*), feet, 19⅜ (*49.2*).

WOODS: Primary: cherry; maple (front skirt). Secondary: white pine.

Bequest of Mary Stillman Harkness, 1950   (50.145.359)

161. High Chest of Drawers

Newport, 1760–80

THOUGH A CLASSIC example of the Newport bonnet-top type, this high chest has a number of atypical features. It is the only one known with knee carving on all four legs; with open-cut talons grasping the balls of all four feet; and with an additional small cavetto-and-ovolo-molded strip nailed above the midmolding. More than by any of these features, however, the high chest is distinguished by the discreet allover pattern formed by the so-called plum-pudding graining of its pediment panels and drawer fronts, the latter embellished by brasses whose open centers are framed in curvilinear contours. The acanthus-leaf knee carving emerges directly from the stiles in a manner found elsewhere only on the Abraham Redwood pier table (Carpenter, no. 73) and on a triple-top card table (*Antiques* 114 [October 1978], p. 620). The skirt shell is contained within a round arch, a characteristic of early Newport furniture in the Queen Anne style, but the unbordered reeding of the shell's center is a unique detail.

To assign the high chest to a specific maker is not now possible, but a high chest signed by Benjamin Baker of Newport (Cooper 1980, fig. 25) appears to be a close relative. Both bonnet tops are constructed in the same manner, and both chests have highly individual pierced brasses that look to be the work of one man. Cat. no. 161 is much smaller than comparable Boston examples (e.g., cat. nos. 157, 159). It is tall and lean, in contrast to the more massive, three-dimensional high chests with quarter columns that have been attributed to John Townsend (Heckscher 1982, fig. 21), and it is executed in a crisp, hard-edged style. In the characteristic Newport manner, the lower case stands high in relation to the upper case, which has only four tiers of drawers. Its august bonnet notwithstanding, the effect of the chest is dainty and delicate, even prim.

PROVENANCE: Ex coll.: Rear Admiral and Mrs. E. P. Moore, Washington, D.C. The Moores purchased the chest from Israel Sack, Inc., New York City.

CONSTRUCTION: On the upper case: The bonnet top is enclosed except for circular openings in front and a narrow crosswise slot on top. The slot is flanked by cornice moldings that continue almost to the solid horizontal backboard. The bonnet is strengthened by those moldings and by medial braces at each side beneath the top boards. On the pediment board, which is dovetailed to the side boards, the molded edges of the circular openings and the panels that conform to the shape of the bonnet are applied. The plinth supporting the turned finial is quadruple-fluted on three sides. Below the bonnet, the solid top board of the case is dovetailed to the sides, as are the rails, which are faced with half-inch strips. The back is two wide horizontal boards. The two-part midmolding is nailed to the front and sides of the upper case; its overlap holds the case in place. On the lower case: There is no top board. On the side boards, to which the backboard is dovetailed, the skirts are cut in ogee arches. The front stiles have facing strips. The front skirt shell is carved from the solid. The stiles flanking the small central drawer are dovetailed to the rail above it. The legs, secured with glue blocks, continue halfway up the case as interior stiles. The relief carving on the knees of the front legs is repeated on the sides of the back legs. On all the drawers, the framing members are thin; the sides have rounded top edges; the bottoms, the grain running lengthwise on the large ones and crosswise on the small, extend over the side boards; the runners are applied. There are no dust boards.

CONDITION: The high chest is refinished but has a rich reddish brown color. The original finial is missing about two inches of its top; the knob appears to be the stump of a twisted flame that has been crudely rasped into its present shape. There are minor repairs or patches to the drawer fronts, front stiles, and skirt shell. The legs are secured with modern screws.

INSCRIPTIONS: In chalk, on back of top right drawer: a mark consisting of what appears to be an *R* [*K*?] within a *D*; on the middle large drawer: illegible marks.

DIMENSIONS: H.: overall, 84⅛ (*213.6*), pediment, 81½ (*207.*); W.: upper case, 36½ (*92.7*), lower case, 37⅞ (*96.2*), feet, 40 (*101.6*); D.: upper case, 18⅛ (*46.*), lower case, 19 (*48.3*), feet, 21⅜ (*54.3*).

WOODS: Primary: mahogany. Secondary: white pine (top boards of bonnet); chestnut (all else).

REFERENCES: Ott 1965, no. 62; idem 1965a, no. 13.

Gift of Mrs. E. P. Moore, in memory of Rear Admiral E. P. Moore, USN, 1980   (1980.139)

161 See also pp. 344, 363, 365

CHAPTER

16 Pennsylvania High Chests and Dressing Tables

High chests and dressing tables were nearly as popular in Pennsylvania and in Philadelphia's orbit as in New England. Despite an occasional trace of New England influence, an unmistakable Philadelphia type rapidly emerged. The earliest cabriole-leg high chests, doubtless introduced during the seventeen-thirties at the same time as the Queen Anne chair, are typically of solid walnut and have either a flat top or a bonnet top with a large drawer centered in the pediment, a front skirt sawed out in a complexly scalloped arch, and Spanish or trifid feet. Manufacture of the Queen Anne high chest continued through the colonial period with only a few modifications, such as claw feet, but a form evolved in the Chippendale style that was to be one of the most magnificent of American furniture types. The earliest Chippendale examples (one dated 1753) are of mahogany, and have a shell drawer in a broken-scroll pediment, large drawers flanked by fluted quarter columns, an oversize bottom drawer with smaller drawers on either side, leaf-carved knees, and claw feet. In the succeeding phase the pediment shell drawer is replaced by applied carving; in the final phase, in a perfectly harmonious design, the scroll pediment is separated from the drawers by a continuous cornice. The Museum's collection contains only one Queen Anne example—an unusual child-size high chest with a Boston-style bonnet top—but the more fully developed style is brilliantly represented by two pairs of high chests and dressing tables and the most elaborate of Lancaster dressing tables, a Pennsylvania-German interpretation of the form.

162. Child's High Chest of Drawers

Pennsylvania, 1735–60

SOMEWHAT LESS THAN half the standard size and doubt-less made for a child, this diminutive high chest must be one of the earliest of Pennsylvania bonnet-top examples. Both upper and lower parts have full dust boards, and secondary woods of walnut, cedar, and yellow pine—construction features common to Pennsylvania. Stylistic-ally, however, the high chest combines characteristics from both New England and the Middle Colonies. The enclosed bonnet top follows the classic Massachusetts pattern: a large, shell-carved central drawer below two circular pediment openings that flank the plinth of a cen-tral finial. In shape, the shell has direct parallels with those on certain full-size japanned case pieces (e.g., cat.

162

nos. 155, 156); in execution, it is not unlike the fan motif carved into the top drawer of many Massachusetts case pieces (e.g., cat. no. 159). The squat cabriole legs with tri-fid feet, though normally without so angular a knee, are commonly found on high chests and dressing tables from the Pennsylvania area. The brasses are identical to those on a Spanish-footed spice chest from Chester County, Pennsylvania (Schiffer, fig. 153). The scalloped skirt, with its unusual central fish-tail pendant between pairs of di-minutive semicircles, appears on a few fine Philadelphia dressing tables (e.g., Girl Scouts, no. 566; Sack 1, p. 195), including one that has been attributed to Philadelphia cabinetmaker William Savery on the basis of a history of descent in his family (Samuel W. Woodhouse, Jr., "Philadelphia Cabinet Makers," *PMA Bulletin* 20 [Janu-ary 1925], pp. 62–63).

Another such stylistic hybrid, all but identical to cat. no. 162 in size and in the Massachusetts-type design of its bonnet top, shell drawer, and upper section, has distinct variations in the lower part: a tripartite skirt design with turned pendants in the New England manner, and Span-ish feet rather than trifid, an alternative in Pennsylvania (PMA 1976, no. 21). Thomas Stapleford (died 1739), a cabinetmaker trained in Boston and later employed in Philadelphia, has been suggested as a likely candidate for its maker (ibid., where referred to as Stapleton). Al-though a causal relationship between the two high chests is suggested by their scale and stylistic similarities, the dif-ferences in their primary and secondary woods and in most of their construction details rule out a definite attri-bution either to the same maker or to the same shop.

PROVENANCE: Ex coll.: Harold M. and Cecile Lehman (later Cecile L. Mayer), Tarrytown, New York. According to notes in the possession of the life tenant, the high chest was purchased from Jacob Margolis, a New York City dealer.

CONSTRUCTION: On the upper case: The bonnet top is fully enclosed except for the area behind the central finial, where the thin roofing boards are cut in from the front in a shallow arch. The back is in three parts: a single horizontal board behind the pediment, a narrow horizontal board dovetailed to the blocks that support the top board behind the side cornice moldings, and a single vertical board behind the drawer area. Strips are nailed to the front edges of the side boards. The four shallow upper drawers lock by means of springs that can be released through holes in the dust boards. On the lower case: The boards of front, back, and sides are double pegged to the stiles. The thin top board, its grain running lengthwise, is framed by the two-piece midmolding. On the drawers, the top edges of the sides and back are rounded; the bottom edges are rabbeted to receive the bottom boards, which on the wide drawers are lengthwise-grained. There are full dust boards throughout.

CONDITION: The high chest has been refinished and has a nut brown color. The finials look to be old replacements. The top of the shell drawer, the upper half of the midmolding, and four drawer bottoms have been restored. The knee brackets are gone. The scalloping on the side skirts may have been added after the chest was made.

DIMENSIONS: H.: pediment, 41½ (*105.4*); W.: upper case, 18⅛ (*46.*), lower case, 19⅝ (*49.9*), feet, 21 (*53.3*); D.: upper case, 11 (*27.9*), lower case, 11⅞ (*30.2*), feet, 12⅞ (*32.7*).

WOODS: Primary: cherry. Secondary: sweet gum (upper-case drawer sides and backs); yellow pine (upper-case top and bottom boards, lower-case back and large drawer bottom); white pine (upper-case backboards, all dust boards); white cedar (upper-case drawer bottoms, lower-case top); walnut (lower-case drawer sides and backs, small-drawer bottoms).

Bequest of Cecile L. Mayer, subject to a life estate, 1962 (62.171.9)

163. Dressing Table

Philadelphia, 1755–90

THIS IS ONE OF A GROUP of Philadelphia high chests and dressing tables that show such marked similarities in design and construction as to suggest a common workshop. On all the pieces of the group the carving is similar: on the central drawer, a recessed shell with an undulating lobate border and a few bold stop flutes within sketchily carved ribs; superimposed on the shell, flanked by sprigs of leafage, a central rosette in high relief, its center plain to receive the drawer pull; the background of the shell filled in with punchwork like that above the leaf carving on the knee brackets. All the pieces have skirts sawed out in scallops, with only minor variations in the treatment at center front, and rococo brasses with pierced, latticelike patterns.

A high chest (now lacking its upper section) at the Department of State, with figured mahogany drawer fronts nearly identical to those of cat. no. 163, appears to have been made en suite with it (*Antiques* 91 [April 1967], p. 409). A rocaille shell applied at the middle of the high chest's front skirt suggests what once may have been on the MMA example (see Condition). Similar shells are found on the skirts of other high chests in the group (Miller 1, no. 660; *Antiques* 103 [May 1973], p. 893). On these high chests and on another, from the Cowell family, now at the PMA (acc. no. 27.91.1) can be seen the same scalloped openings, applied carving, and pierced central cartouches within scrolled tops. (For other pieces in the group see Lockwood 1904, pl. XCV; Landman, p. 933; Miller 1, no. 712; Sack 3, p. 633.)

PROVENANCE: Ex coll.: George Coe Graves, Osterville, Massachusetts. According to the New York dealer Morris Schwartz (1932 notes, MMA files), the dressing table was in "The Smith Collection sold in Connecticut years ago." It was on loan between 1954 and 1959 to the Museum of Fine Arts, Richmond, Virginia; between 1963 and 1980, to the American Museum in Britain.

163 See also p. 350

CONSTRUCTION: The two-piece top overhangs the back by half an inch. The front stiles, inset with fluted quarter columns, are backed with pine strips. The sides and the two horizontal backboards are triple pegged to the rear stiles. The skirts are scalloped, the curves on the side boards repeated at either end of the front skirt. The central semicircular lobe on the front skirt is pieced. The tenon of one of the stiles flanking the shell drawer extends through the skirt. There are no dust boards. The lower drawers are separated by narrow uprights. On the drawers, the sides are slightly rounded at the top edges; on the bottoms, the grain runs crosswise. All the knee brackets are smoothly sawed out at the sides and on the angled backs. On the rear legs, the side brackets are of a simple, uncarved serpentine shape. There are no back brackets.

CONDITION: The dressing table, of dense, even-grained wood, was refinished many years ago and is now a sun-faded light brown in color. The top boards are screwed to new rails that have been added inside at sides and back. On the shell drawer, the tips of the lower applied fronds are missing. Tiny nail holes in the front skirt board may indicate where applied carving was once attached. The drawers have new runner strips.

DIMENSIONS: H.: overall, 30⅝ (77.8); W.: top, 35⅞ (91.1), case, 32½ (82.6), feet, 34½ (87.6); D.: top, 20⅝ (52.4), case, 18¼ (46.4), feet, 20 (50.8).

WOODS: Primary: mahogany. Secondary: yellow pine (backboards, drawer slides); tulip poplar (drawer sides and backs); white cedar (drawer bottoms).

REFERENCES: Margon 1954, no. 49; idem 1965, p. 140 (ill.).

The Sylmaris Collection, Gift of George Coe Graves, 1930 (30.120.61)

164 See also p. 350

164. Dressing Table

Pennsylvania or Delaware, 1760–90

THE DRESSING TABLE once belonged to James Read of Delaware. A high chest similar in design (see SPB sale no. 3804, 11/8/75, lot 1258) has a history of descent in the Eckard family from the Signer George Read (1733–1798), brother to James. The two pieces have in common a number of features not normally found on Philadelphia dressing tables and high chests: an upper drawer deeper than the lower ones flanking the shell drawer, fluted quarter columns that start at the same height as the lower drawer openings rather than close to the knees, and side skirts scalloped in flattened ogee arches—a New England feature found in Philadelphia only on pad- or Spanish-footed high chests and dressing tables. These anomalies suggest that the pieces may have been bought by the Reads from a Delaware cabinetmaker who worked in the Philadelphia manner. A number of related pieces (Downs 1952, no. 196; N-YHS, acc. no. 1959.84; *Antiques* 105 [January 1974], p. 96) are all apparently from the same shop.

PROVENANCE: Ex coll.: Lesley and Emma Sheafer, New York City. Said to have descended from the original owner, James Read (1743–1822) of New Castle, Delaware; to his daughter, Susan Read Eckard (died 1861); and thereafter in the Eckard family until purchased by Ginsburg & Levy, Inc., New York City, from whom the donors bought it in 1949.

CONSTRUCTION: The inner surfaces of the top and side boards are rough-cut. A separate cavetto molding is attached below the top. On the back is a narrow board above a wide one secured to each stile with three pairs of pegs. In front, the rails are pegged to the stiles; the skirt is double pegged. There are dust boards under all but the shell drawer. The one under the upper drawer is laid lengthwise, those under the small side drawers are laid crosswise and supported at front and back by triangular glue blocks. The dividers between the lower drawers are nailed to the backboard with large roseheads. The rear knees are carved like the front ones, but only on the sides. The front board of the shell drawer is unusually thin. The drawer dovetails are sloppily cut.

CONDITION: The modern varnish finish on the dark, reddish brown wood has begun to craze. The warped top has been reattached to the frame with new glue blocks and cross braces. The frame appears to have been apart. The knee brackets back of the right rear leg and at the side of the left front leg are replaced. The drawers have been reassembled and their interiors varnished. On the central drawer, the tips of some of the acanthus leafage and the long triple-budded stems at either side have been restored, the latter approximating those on the George Read high chest. On the front skirt, the tip of the right-hand scroll is replaced.

DIMENSIONS: H.: overall, 28¾ (73.); W.: top, 33⅝ (85.4), case, 31 (78.7), feet, 32⅜ (82.2); D.: top, 19¾ (50.2), case, 18⅜ (46.7), feet, 19⅞ (50.5).

WOODS: Primary: mahogany. Secondary: yellow pine (backboards, dividers between lower drawers); tulip poplar (drawer sides and backs, dust boards); Atlantic white cedar (drawer bottoms).

REFERENCES: Charles Simms, "A Fine 18th Century Philadelphia Lowboy," *American Collector* 17 (March 1948), pp. 5, 22 (ill. p. 5).

The Lesley and Emma Sheafer Collection, Bequest of Emma A. Sheafer, 1973   (1974.356.41)

165. High Chest of Drawers

Philadelphia, 1755–90

IN A NUMBER of important features this high chest is closely related to such famous ones as the Van Pelt (Downs 1952, no. 195) and the Karolik (Hipkiss, no. 33), and to certain chests-on-chests (Downs 1952, no. 184; *Antiques* 69 [January 1956], inside front cover). The features include the boldly scrolled pediment with squashed circular openings, the cartouche with projecting molded plinth, the extensive applied rocaille carving of the tympanum, the richly figured mahogany veneers of the thumbnail-molded drawer fronts, the motifs of the knee carving and the treatment of the knee brackets, the shape of the scalloping of the side boards, and the frilly shell carved into the bottom drawer. The Van Pelt high chest, its legs and side skirts and its knee carving identical to those of cat. no. 165, must be from the same shop. Although different in a number of construction details, a high chest at the Minneapolis Institute (acc. no. 31.21), with notable similarities to the MMA high chest in its pediment treatment and carving and in its simple front skirt, must also be from the same shop. What appears to be cat. no. 165's matching dressing table has been advertised (*Antiques* 55 [February 1949], p. 106; ibid. 100 [October 1971], p. 464; ibid. 105 [January 1974], p. 1). Another dressing table (Sack 3, p. 736) has similar knees and side skirts, but looks to have been carved by a different hand. In the pediment of the MMA high chest the leaf carving with its distinctive beading in the center looks to be a free interpretation of plate 2 in P. Baretti's *New Book of Ornaments . . . for . . . Carvers* (London, 1762, ill. in *Furniture History* 11 [1975], pl. 151). The 1766 edition of the book was advertised in the *Boston Newsletter*, July 1, 1767, but its existence in Philadelphia is not documented.

Joseph Moulder, the original owner, was listed in 1764 as a joiner (see Provenance), which might imply that he was involved with the manufacture of cat. no. 165 and the related case pieces, but evidence of his serious participation in the furniture trade is lacking. His name appeared

in the Tax Rolls of 1769, that time without occupation; two years later, in his will, he was called "Sail-maker." His inventory (copy, MMA files) contains no joiner's tools.

PROVENANCE: Ex coll.: George S. Palmer, New London, Connecticut. Joseph Moulder, the original owner of the high chest, was born at Marcus Hook in about 1722. He married Sarah Carlisle (sister of silversmith Abraham) in about 1756. In the Proprietary Tax Rolls of 1764 (Pennsylvania Archives, Series II [1879], p. 177), he is listed as a joiner. He later served as a captain in the Continental Army. On Christmas Eve, 1776, in command of the battery, he was one of the soldiers who crossed the Delaware River to engage in the Battle of Trenton. In his will of 1771 (File no. 254, Register of Wills, Philadelphia), he left everything to his wife and children. After his death in 1779 the December 22 inventory of his estate included "1 Chest of Drawers . . . 15-0-0" (presumably, this piece), as well as "1 Mahogany dressing Table . . . 2-0-0." The latter, though proportionately less expensive, may refer to a matching dressing table. Sarah died in 1791, and the high chest went to her daughter Elizabeth, who had married Gerard Vogels in 1783. The evidence for this and for the subsequent history of the chest is a statement (MMA files) by Gerard R. Vogels to Ferdinand Keller, a cabinetmaker, restorer, and sometime antique dealer in Philadelphia. Dated October 4, 1905, it reads:

This is to certify that the Case of Mahoginy Drawers and Two high back chairs purchased by you of me this day were originally the property of my Great Grandfather Jos Moulder who served as Captain of Artilley during our Revolution   Captain Moulder crossed the Delaware to Trenton N.J with Genl Geo Washington   The above named articles were inherited by me and May be fully relied upon as above represented—

Gerard R. Vogels
To F Keller.

There are notes on the back of Vogel's letter: "The mahogany veneered high boy that I bought of Macy for $1400⁰⁰ finely carved top and legs—Geo S Palmer Feb 1906," and, in a different hand, "Highboy was sent to Mr. Hicks, New Bedford Mass." Evidently, Palmer did not buy the piece directly from Keller.

CONSTRUCTION: On the upper case: The bonnet top is enclosed on each side of the central space; behind it, the three-piece horizontal backboard is cut out to conform to the general shape of the front. At cornice height is an enclosing top board. The side cornices are molded boards over triangular pine cores. The tympanum carving is applied. Below the pediment, six horizontal boards form the back. The fluted quarter columns inserted between the front stiles and the side boards have separate capital blocks. The dust boards are laid lengthwise. The stiles between the upper drawers have exposed tenons. On the lower case: The top is seven boards laid crosswise and glued together within the framing boards. Below it is a central medial brace. The side boards, triple pegged to the stiles, are reinforced with triangular glue blocks. The top rail is pegged; the front skirt is double pegged. The runners for the shell drawer and the vertical dividers of the lower three drawers are slotted into the horizontal two-piece backboard. There are no dust boards. The thick knee brackets are carved at the sides, sawed flat at the back, and secured with roseheads. All drawer fronts are of mahogany

165 See also pp. 347, 349, 350

faced with figured veneers except that of the shell drawer, which is carved from the solid. The drawer sides are rabbeted to receive both the crosswise bottom boards and the runners.

CONDITION: A rich reddish brown color is visible under the present thick, somewhat crazed varnish. The bottom of the cartouche is split and patched. The pediment rosettes and the flame finials are replacements, as are the tips of some of the leafage in the tympanum and on the shell drawer and the tip of the left scroll of the front skirt. The high chest was at one time dismantled. The cornice moldings are now screwed from the front, the holes plugged. The thin wooden covers enclosing the bonnet are modern. A strip of wood has been let into the back edge of the right side of the upper case. Most of the glue blocks behind the stiles and quarter columns are replaced, as are the strips framing the back and side edges of the lower case's top board. The interiors of all the drawers have been varnished. All the drawers have new runners except for those of the upper two tiers. Medial braces have been inserted in the bottoms of the larger drawers.

INSCRIPTIONS: In pencil, on backs of narrow drawers: location marks *L* or *R*. In brown ink (19th-century), on lower-case central top board, in large capital letters sans serif: *LUISE*. Glued to each section's backboard, a Palmer Bros. Co. shipping label and a paper label inscribed *G S Palmer*.

DIMENSIONS: H.: overall, 97¾ (*248.3*), pediment, 88¼ (*224.2*); W.: upper case, 41¼ (*104.8*), lower case, 42¼ (*107.3*), feet, 44½ (*113.*); D.: upper case, 23 (*58.4*), lower case, 23⅞ (*60.6*), feet, 25½ (*64.8*).

WOODS: Primary: mahogany; mahogany veneer. Secondary: yellow pine (upper-case top, bottom, back; lower-case back; bonnet-top sides); tulip poplar (drawer sides and backs, upper-case dust boards); northern white cedar (lower-case top, partitions flanking shell drawer, drawer bottoms); oak (lower-case glue blocks).

REFERENCES: MMA 1909, 2, no. 162; ill. facing p. 64. Halsey, pp. 256–257; fig. 3 (attributed to Savery). Lockwood 1, fig. 104. MMA 1930, no. 18. Margon 1965, p. 110. Kennedy & Sack, no. 43. For Joseph Moulder, see J. W. Jordan, *Colonial Families of Philadelphia*, New York and Chicago, 1911, 1, pp. 642–643.

John Stewart Kennedy Fund, 1918   (18.110.60)

166. High Chest of Drawers

Philadelphia, 1760–90

THE MOST COSTLY high chests listed in the 1772 Philadelphia price book are a "Chest on a frame Claw feet & leaves on the knees & Shell Drawer in ye frame (£20)" and "Ditto Drawers Scroul pedement hed Carved work Not to Exceed £3-10 (£21)." Tables "to Suit" cost £6 (Weil, p. 181). These perfectly describe cat. nos. 166 and 167, except that for them, perhaps the most elaborate and richly carved of all Philadelphia case furniture, the cost of the carving doubtless exceeded £3-10. Finely proportioned and splendidly executed, the two pieces are worthy mon-

uments of the Philadelphia school. Conversely, nowhere is the inherent awkwardness of the combination of plain drawer fronts and carved tympanum more apparent.

The MMA matched pair are related to several other examples. A smaller version of the high chest (its program of carving apparently identical, except that its quarter columns are fluted) was in 1974 in a private collection in Wilmington, Delaware. The ornament on a dressing table at Minneapolis (Nutting 1, no. 429) is also similar, even to the unusual guilloche-carved top edge, though the work is demonstrably not by the same hand. The guilloche with a meander pattern below it also appears on the base of a high chest now at Yale (ibid., no. 434), and the punchwork on the knees is the same as that on a high chest at Minneapolis (acc. no. 31.21). The shell in the lower central drawer is carved with frill-like lobes in a pattern employed by a number of Philadelphia carvers (see also cat. nos. 164, 165), and the motif of pairs of C-scrolls on the outer edges of the front skirt is repeated on a number of finely carved Philadelphia high chests (e.g., Downs 1952, no. 197). Evidently a number of men made case furniture in this mode.

PROVENANCE: Ex coll.: George S. Palmer, New London, Connecticut. According to Palmer, this piece (as well as its companion, cat. no. 167, and a tripod stand, cat. no. 130) descended in the Lawrence family of Philadelphia. Hornor's reference (1935, p. 109) to the "Law–Palmer" highboy apparently should read "Lawrence–Palmer." At the time of Palmer's death, his friend and fellow collector Henry W. Erving recalled of his collection and of these pieces in particular:

... I was pretty well acquainted with every piece except the new high-boy and low-boy which he purchased after following it through *three* generations. And let me say that when he went out to St. Louis on one occasion to look at it, he admired the center finial so much that the dear old lady took it off and insisted that he should keep it. She wanted to give it to him, but he was fine enough to utterly refuse it and tell her never to let the piece be dismantled. But evidently she did at some time, because it was gone when I first saw the piece.
(Isham 1934, p. 64)

CONSTRUCTION: On the upper case: The bonnet top is enclosed by boards on each side of the open space; the horizontal backboard is cut out in a serpentine curve below the central opening. At cornice height is an enclosing top board. The side cornice moldings have triangular pine cores. The carving in the tympanum area of the pediment is applied except for the C-scrolls, the leafage, and the circular punchwork framing center openings. The drawers are flanked by narrow stiles with separate carved quarter columns. Full dust boards run lengthwise. The back is three horizontal tongue and groove boards. On the lower case: Three thin, cross-grained boards form the top. The ogee-molded and guilloche-carved upper piece of the midmolding is nailed to poplar strips nailed onto the top boards. Applied separately below are a cavetto molding and meanders. The side boards and the two-piece backboard are quadruple pegged to the stiles. The skirts are carved from the solid. The double C-scrolls below the small drawers are re-

166 See also pp. 347, 349, 351

peated on the side skirts. The background of the knee carving has circular punchwork. The rear legs are carved only on the sides. The knee brackets are sawed out on the sides and flat in back. Below the upper drawer is a cross-grained dust board. The dividers between the bottom drawers have exposed double tenons. On all the drawers of the high chest the fronts are solid, the sides have rounded top edges and closely spaced dovetails, and the grain of the bottom boards runs crosswise.

CONDITION: The high chest, which was stripped in 1937, has a reddish brown color. The central cartouche, the side finials, and the rosettes were missing when the chest was acquired by the MMA. In 1949, replacement parts based upon the originals on the Cowell family high chest (see cat. no. 163) were carved. The front of the top drawer of the lower case is badly warped. Minor repairs have been made to the left side edge of that drawer and the third one from the top. Small pieces of the carving applied to the tympanum and to the shell drawer are replaced or missing. On the shell drawer the original brass knob (see cat. no. 167) has been replaced. The drawers have been varnished on the sides and interiors.

INSCRIPTIONS: Incised, on upper right drawer bottom: *Right.* In chalk, on drawer bottoms: *1* through *11*; on bottom of second drawer from the top: *6/3/2.* Pasted on upper-case back, a Palmer Bros. Co. shipping label.

DIMENSIONS: H.: overall, 99 (*251.5*), pediment, 89¾ (*228.*); W.: upper case, 41½ (*105.4*), lower case, 43½ (*110.5*), feet, 45½ (*115.6*); D.: upper case, 21¾ (*55.2*), lower case, 22½ (*57.2*), feet, 25 (*63.5*).

WOODS: Primary: mahogany. Secondary: yellow pine (top beneath bonnet, upper-case bottom, lower-case backboards); tulip poplar (drawer sides and backs); Atlantic white cedar (upper-case backboards, lower-case top, dust boards, drawer bottoms, dividers between small drawers of bottom tier).

REFERENCES: Halsey, pp. 258–262; fig. 4 (attributed to William Savery). Nutting 1, no. 361. Lee 1, p. 83. MMA 1930, no. 17. Isham 1934, p. 64. Hornor 1935, p. 109.

John Stewart Kennedy Fund, 1918   (18.110.6)

167. Dressing Table

(en suite with High Chest cat. no. 166)
Philadelphia, 1760–90

THE DRESSING TABLE is a smaller version of the lower half of its companion high chest. The construction features are so similar on both pieces as to indicate the same woodworker. But for minor variances in the quarter columns and at the middle of the front skirt the carved motifs are identical, if of different execution. The rocaille mantels growing out of the C-scrolls on the high chest's front skirt, for example, have a fluidity lacking in the

167

stiff, static ones on the dressing table. As if to make up for his deficient skill, the carver of the latter elaborated the background of the central skirt cartouche with punchwork.

PROVENANCE: See cat. no. 166.

CONSTRUCTION: The two-piece top, which overhangs one and a half inches in the back, has front and side edges carved in a guilloche pattern. The side boards and the two-piece backboard are triple pegged to the stiles. Below the upper drawer is a cross-grained dust board. The construction is otherwise like that of cat. no. 166.

CONDITION: The surface finish is identical to that of cat. no. 166. Both boards of the top have been reattached with new glue blocks. The rear board may be a replacement. There are minor patches to the edges of the drawer fronts and to the meander. The tips of most of the applied acanthus-leaf fronds on the shell drawer are missing. The sides and interiors of the drawers have been varnished, and new runner strips added.

DIMENSIONS: H.: overall, 31¾ (80.6); W.: top, 33¾ (85.7), case, 32 (81.3), feet, 34 (86.4); D.: top, 21¾ (55.2), case, 19¼ (48.9), feet, 21 (53.3).

WOODS: Primary: mahogany. Secondary: yellow pine (backboards, dividers between drawers); tulip poplar (drawer sides and backs); Atlantic white cedar (drawer bottoms, dust board).

REFERENCES: Halsey, pp. 260–261; fig. 5 (attributed to William Savery). Lee 1, p. 76 (ill.). Rogers, fig. 44. Downs 1949, no. 5. Nutting 1, no. 423.

John Stewart Kennedy Fund, 1918   (18.110.7)

168. High Chest of Drawers

Philadelphia, 1762–90

THIS HIGH CHEST has long been acknowledged as one of the supreme examples of American furniture in the Chippendale style. The design of the top, with a continuous horizontal cornice separating the scroll pediment from the drawers, resolves the often awkward relationship between these parts (see cat. no. 166). The elegant proportions, the carefully chosen figured wood of the drawer fronts, and the delicate, discreetly placed and highly naturalistic carving—in the pediment scrolls the asymmetrical leafage seems to grow out of the architectural elements—merit panegyrics.

The chest was first attributed to the newly discovered cabinetmaker William Savery (Halsey, p. 262). Following the purchase of its matching dressing table (cat. no. 169) it was reappraised (Downs 1932, p. 260). Downs, though he spoke of the carved central bust as "La Pompadour, so called because of its French character," was the first to

notice the influence of English pattern books on the chest's design. He attributed the piece to Benjamin Randolph on the basis of the carving. That attribution was discredited a short while later by Hornor (1935, pp. 93–95), though he too called the chest the "Pompadour" or the "Madame Pompadour"—names that are still in use. The most recent evaluation (Smith 1971, p. 901) convincingly associates the carving of the bust with that of two other Philadelphia finial busts (ibid., figs. 4–6); less convincing is Smith's reaffirmation of the Randolph attribution based on supposed similarities in the carving of the high chest and the so-called sample easy chair at the PMA (ibid., p. 901).

The design concept of cat. no. 168 is characteristic of a number of the finest custom-made pieces of Philadelphia rococo furniture. On what is a uniquely American high-chest form the maker has unabashedly bestowed whole designs taken directly from fashionable English pattern books, the most obvious of which is the swan- and serpent-carved drawer copied line for line from a design for a chimneypiece tablet in Thomas Johnson's *New Book of Ornaments*, published in London in 1762 (Helena Hayward, "Newly-Discovered Designs by Thomas Johnson," *Furniture History* 11 [1975], pp. 40–42, pl. 100). Other borrowings come from a number of plates in the third edition of Chippendale's *Director*, also published in 1762: the general scheme of a portrait bust within a pediment from whose scroll ends leafage springs is from plate CVIII (a desk and bookcase); the precise mixture and configuration of cornice moldings and dentils is taken from plate CVII (another desk and bookcase). The draped-urn finial in the same plate inspired the flanking finials on the Pompadour, and the midmoldings—a cavetto and ovolo—look to be from either of two clothes presses (pls. CXXIX and CXXX).

The major design motifs of the high chest and dressing table are to be found on only two other known pairs. The straight cornice, fretwork frieze, leaf-carved quarter columns, and pictorial carving on the lower drawer find their closest parallels in the Howe family pair (PMA 1976, nos. 104a, b; Comstock, no. 312); a dressing table at the Boston MFA (Hipkiss, no. 55) and what appears to be the base of its matching high chest, now at the Department of State (Nutting 1, fig. 435), are of the same design, but neither pair is attributable to the maker of the Pompadour. The Chippendale cornice employed on cat. no. 168 appears with slight variations on the flat pediments of a few secretaries (Horner 1935, pl. 94) and chests-on-chests (*Antiques* 67 [February 1955], p. 99), which, like the Pompadour, have pierced leafage and diapered plinths supporting bust finials. The pediment of the Pompadour is an integral part of the upper case. Because the upper-case top board is the height of the side cornices and

168 See also pp. 348, 349, 351

the tympanum is pierced, part of the top board had to be cut away. The separate pediment unit characteristic of fully developed Philadelphia case furniture (see cat. no. 147) may have evolved after craftsmen simplified this somewhat cumbersome method of construction.

PROVENANCE: Ex coll.: George S. Palmer, New London, Connecticut. The early history of the high chest is not known. Rough manuscript notes (20th-century) on the Daniel Barnes family of New Haven and Litchfield, Connecticut, under the heading "Incomplete Genealogy of Pompadour highboy and lowb," are in MMA files, but who prepared the notes or the documentation linking cat. nos. 168 and 169 to the Barnes family is not given. The high chest appears to have entered the antique furniture market about the time of the nation's Centennial. The Charles G. Angeroth, Jr., whose name is inscribed with the date 1878 on the back of the high chest can be identified with one listed as a furniture dealer at 1829 South Street in the Philadelphia directories of 1869 and 1870. The other inscribed name, Frank E. Lay, cannot be matched in the directories, but a number of cabinetmakers and woodworkers named Lay were active in Philadelphia in the second half of the nineteenth century. Palmer probably acquired the high chest between 1909 (it was not lent with his other great pieces to the MMA Hudson–Fulton Celebration in that year) and 1913, when Lockwood first published it and identified it as belonging to Palmer.

CONSTRUCTION: On the upper case: The top and bottom have three boards each; the back, five horizontal ones. Glue blocks with canted corners reinforce the junction of side boards, quarter columns, and front stiles. The rails abut the stiles and continue behind them to the side boards. Two-piece dust boards are laid lengthwise and slotted into the side boards. The drawers ride directly on the dust boards. Mahogany drawer stops are nailed to the tops of the front rails. The pediment board begins above the top tier of drawers, extends upward behind the cornice and the scroll pediment, and is carved with pierced leafage in the tympanum area. On the pediment board the fretwork, the cornice moldings, and the diaper-carved plinth supporting the central finial bust are applied. The cornice is a single molded board with a triangular core and, at each side, a separate crown molding. The cornice and pediment dentils are cut from the solid. The bust and rounded pedestal are carved from a block of wood unfinished in back and attached to the plinth with a single large, rectangular tenon. The swag-draped urns of the side finials, unfinished in back and with turned tops and bottoms, are carved from the solid.

On the lower case: The three-piece top, its grain running lengthwise, is framed with narrow strips onto which the midmolding is nailed. The fretwork below is applied. The side boards are triple pegged to the stiles; the two-piece backboard is quadruple pegged. The quarter columns are let into the front stiles. The front skirt is carved from the solid; the side skirts are sawed in scallops that ascend to a central pointed arch. There are no dust boards. On the central bottom drawer the front is solid figured wood embellished with applied carving. The dividers between the drawers are slotted into the backboards. The knees of the front legs and the sides of the rear ones are identically carved. The knee brackets are flat in back. On all the uncarved drawers of the high chest, the fronts are mahogany with mahogany veneer and an applied beaded edge. The drawer bottoms, cross-grained, are slotted into the sides.

CONDITION: The high chest has had extensive surface and ornamental restoration but retains its integrity. Unlike many of the other important pieces acquired from the Palmer collection, this one had not been restored when the MMA bought it. (It is illustrated in its unrestored state in the 1913 edition of Lockwood [fig. 107] and in Nutting 1 [no. 364].) The upper and lower case frames show no inner restoration, though all the drawers have been painted bright yellow inside. Exterior restoration was done at different times under the MMA's supervision. In 1927, nineteenth-century wooden knobs were replaced with English rococo gilt cast bronze pulls. The ones on the drawer below the midmolding, originally placed in line with those of the upper case, are now directly above those of the lower tier. Rococo keyhole escutcheons were added to the large drawers, but were subsequently replaced. The original fretwork survives only across the front of the cornice and in the middle at the lower-case top. The remainder was added in 1932 at the same time that new tops, based on plate XCII in the third edition of Chippendale's Director (1762), were turned for the urn finials. Between 1953 and 1955, the missing carving was replaced: the topmost leafage fronds of the broken-scroll pediment terminals; the heads of the swans in the large bottom drawer (the original head of the one probably turned back toward the other, as in cat. no. 169); and the front corners of the cornice. The high chest was then entirely refinished, emerging a glossy light reddish brown.

INSCRIPTIONS: In chalk, inside upper-case backboards and on both sides of lower-case bottom right drawer: John H—. In pencil (19th-century), on lower-case backboards, under a layer of varnish: 1776 / Centential / Frank E. Lay; below, apparently in the same hand: 7777 / 6666 [someone's attempt to perfect an eighteenth-century style of numbering?] and 1878 / Chas G Angeroth Jr. Pasted over varnish on back: what remains of a Palmer Bros. Co. shipping label.

DIMENSIONS: H.: overall, 91¾ (233.), pediment molding, 85½ (217.2); W.: upper case, 41⅛ (104.5), lower case, 42⅝ (108.3), feet, 44⅝ (113.4); D.: upper case, 21⅝ (54.9), lower case, 22½ (57.2), feet, 24⅝ (62.6).

WOODS: Primary: mahogany; mahogany veneer. Secondary: yellow pine (upper-case top and bottom, backboards); tulip poplar (drawer sides and backs); northern white cedar (lower-case top boards, dust boards, dividers between bottom drawers, drawer bottoms).

REFERENCES: Lockwood (1913 edition), fig. 107 (ill. unrestored). Halsey, pp. 264–265; fig.7 and drawings of carving on drawer and skirt. Nutting 1, no. 364. MMA 1930, no. 19. Downs 1932, pp. 259–262; fig. 4. Hornor 1935, pp. 93–95. Halsey and Cornelius, fig. 67. Downs 1949, no. 4. Powel, p. 204 (ill.). Margon 1965, pp. 38–39 (ill. and measured drawings). Davidson 1967, fig. 276; idem 1970, p. 228, fig. 6 (bust ill.), p. 229 (history given is that of cat. nos. 166, 167). Smith 1971, pp. 901–902; fig. 4.

John Stewart Kennedy Fund, 1918   (18.110.4)

169. Dressing Table

(en suite with High Chest cat. no. 168)
Philadelphia, 1762–90

WHILE UNQUESTIONABLY fashioned to match cat. no. 168, the dressing table has numerous differences in construction details from those of the high chest, suggesting that different men were occupied in the manufacture of the two pieces. The carving, though superficially identical, also appears to be the work of two different hands: a greater depth and sense of liveliness is exhibited in that of the dressing table.

PROVENANCE: Purchased in 1932 from a Roy K. Smith, Amityville, Long Island, New York.

CONSTRUCTION: The top, a single piece of solid, finely figured crotch mahogany, is attached to the frame with square glue blocks. Beneath its molded front and side edges is a small cavetto molding above an applied fret. The two backboards are triple pegged to the back stiles. The side boards are sawed out in flattened ogee arches, their junctures with the stiles reinforced with quarter-round glue blocks. The drawer bottoms extend beyond the backboard as drawer stops. The construction otherwise approximates that of cat. no. 168.

CONDITION: The old varnish was carefully removed from the dressing table in 1933, revealing a fine reddish brown patina. There are splits in the figured top board. Missing carving was replaced at the MMA in 1979: the central part of the carved skirt beneath the pierced opening, based upon that of cat. no. 168, and the heads of the serpent and the two swans on the central drawer, based upon Johnson's engraved design (see cat. no. 168). The fretwork, missing on either side beneath the top, was re-created at the same time. The beaded edge on the left side of the carved drawer is replaced. In 1933 old brasses were installed in the original holes, replacing mid-nineteenth-century wooden knobs. The feet have holes for casters.

INSCRIPTIONS: In white chalk, on large lower-drawer bottom: a large *B*; on lower right drawer bottom: a smaller *B*. Cut into right side board of lower left drawer: the simply sketched outline of a central-chimney house.

DIMENSIONS: H.: 31¼ (*79.4*); W.: top, 35⅜ (*89.9*), case, 33¾ (*85.7*), feet, 35⅞ (*91.1*); D.: top, 21⅜ (*54.3*), case, 19⅜ (*49.2*), feet, 21⅜ (*54.3*).

WOODS: Primary: mahogany; mahogany veneer. Secondary: yellow pine (backboards, drawer runners, glue blocks); tulip poplar (drawer sides and backs); northern white cedar (drawer bottoms, dividers between bottom drawers).

REFERENCES: Downs 1932, pp. 259–262 (attributed to Benjamin Randolph). Powel, p. 205 (ill.). Davidson 1967, fig. 275.

Morris K. Jesup Fund, 1932   (32.93)

169

170. Dressing Table

Pennsylvania, Lancaster area, 1780–1810

IN GENERAL DESIGN, this dressing table is in the characteristic Philadelphia manner, but in construction and interpretation deviates from it dramatically. Tulip poplar is the sole secondary wood rather than one used in combination with yellow pine and cedar, and the drawers slide on their bottom boards instead of on runners. On the exterior, the differences are even greater: the undulating front skirt hangs ponderously, and the entire skirt board is covered in stylized, snakelike leaves and flowers carved in relief against a stippled ground. The same dogged excess carries over .into the meander vine pattern on the quarter columns and the applied carving that flanks the central drawer's shell.

Not surprisingly, therefore, the piece at one time was considered to be Philadelphia workmanship of inferior quality (Halsey, p. 262); later, even its authenticity was questioned (1930 letter, MMA files). Pediments carved in the same relief manner are found on a number of tall clocks thought to be from Lancaster County because their dials are signed by Lancaster makers (Snyder 1974, figs. 5–7). Further, a high chest with the same style of carving in its pediment, though by a different hand, is signed by a member of the Lind family of Lancaster (idem 1975, p. 972; fig. 9). The dressing table can consequently be attributed to Lancaster Borough, the largest inland town in eighteenth-century America, where some 160 carpenters, joiners, and cabinetmakers are known to have been active between 1760 and 1810 and furniture highly carved in the same manner as cat. no. 170 to have

been made after the Revolution and as late as 1810 (idem 1974, p. 1063). For many years, case furniture with allover relief carving in the pediments or on the skirt boards was attributed to Jacob Bachman of Lancaster (Dreppard), an attribution later disproved (Snyder 1974).

Of the approximately twenty pieces now known in the group, three look to have been carved by the same hand. The first is a high chest, promised to the Heritage Center of Lancaster County, whose lower section closely resembles in design and construction that of the second, cat. no. 170, this the most elaborate of all Lancaster County dressing tables. The third is a dressing table with a skirt board of similar shape, but uncarved (*Antiques* 68 [August 1955], p. 89). Leafage on its shell drawer is highlighted by areas of scratch-carved parallel shading identical to that found on the first two.

PROVENANCE: Ex coll.: George S. Palmer, New London, Connecticut. The table was on loan from the MMA to the Dey Mansion, Preakness, New Jersey, from 1938 to 1969.

CONSTRUCTION: The two-piece top, with incised egg-and-dart-carved quarter-round molding on its front and side edges and a two-inch overhang in back, is secured to the frame with large square glue blocks. The sides and backboard are triple pegged to the stiles. In front, the rails are pegged; the skirt, its allover carving cut from the solid, is double pegged. The side skirts are sawed out in serpentine curves and a small central arch. The knee carving on the front legs is repeated on the sides of the rear legs. The backs of the rear legs are partly carved. The six knee brackets, flat in back, are nailed with double roseheads. The quarter columns with their capitals and bases are single pieces let into the front stiles. There are no dust boards or dividers between the drawers. The pegged stiles flanking the shell drawer have exposed tenons. The drawers have finely cut dovetails and ride on cross-grained bottom boards that extend over the sides and back.

CONDITION: The dressing table, which has been stripped and refinished, is a dark red in color. The top has been reset with a modern medial brace added beneath it. The fronts of the three lower drawers have been built up at the bottom edge. Some of the drawer slides are replacements. The brasses are old, but at least the third set. Plugged holes on the top drawer show that the earlier brasses were set much farther in from the ends.

INSCRIPTIONS: In pencil (20th-century), on back of top drawer: *Mat over D.M. Alter*; inside lower right-hand drawer, on a paper label (20th-century): *292* crossed out and changed to *190*. Pasted on backboard: a Palmer Bros. Co. shipping label.

DIMENSIONS: H.: overall, 29⅝ (75.3); W.: top, 34½ (87.6), case, 33 (83.8), feet, 35½ (90.2); D.: top, 21⅝ (54.9), case, 19⅛ (48.6), feet, 21¼ (54.).

WOODS: Primary: mahogany. Secondary: tulip poplar.

REFERENCES: Halsey, pp. 262–263; fig. 6. Nutting 1, no. 437 (attributed to Philadelphia). Snyder 1974, p. 1057, figs. 3, 12b (dovetail).

John Stewart Kennedy Fund, 1918   (18.110.2)

170 See also pp. 349, 351

17   Desks

Desks of the late colonial period, almost always made with a slant top—then known as a fall—are of two types: those made in one piece and usually about forty-five inches in height, and those with a separate upper-case unit. Both types appear to have been known as scrutoirs or scriptors (anglicized versions of the French *escritoire*, "writing desk") in New England until the seventeen-forties. Thereafter, and elsewhere in America, those of the first kind were commonly called desks or, sometimes, writing desks. Those of the second, two-piece kind, called desks and bookcases, are described separately. Desks consist of a hinged slant top that opens to form a writing surface (usually thirty-three inches from the floor) and to reveal interior small drawers and cubbyholes for holding pens, pencils, and paper; a central, prospect door is often present; below the slant top is a series of large drawers. Used for keeping household accounts and correspondence that could be concealed and secured behind the slant top, the desks were placed more often in parlors than in bedchambers. Only New England examples are present at the Museum: they are arranged in this chapter according to the treatment of their facades, beginning with the straight front and followed by the serpentine and blocked types particularly favored in that region. Smaller desks were made for children, as demonstrated here by three of varying dimensions, but full-size examples of the popular straight-front types from New York, Philadelphia, and the South are not represented in the Museum's collection, nor is the adult desk-on-frame form sometimes made in New England and the middle colonies.

171

171. Child's Desk

New England, 1725–60

THIS DESK IS of the smallest size in which children's desks were made in eighteenth-century New England. The dimensions are the same as those of one that descended in the Jordan and Gay families of Biddeford, Maine (SPB sale no. 4590Y, 5/1/81, lot 941), which has certain earlier features—bun feet and, instead of a top drawer, a well accessible from the inside. The brasses of both desks are identical, and, since they measure the same as brasses used on full-scale pieces, they appear disproportionate; on the top drawer of cat. no. 171 they even extend beyond the bottom edge. The escutcheons stamped with decorative patterns and the wire handles attached with iron cotter pins are in the William and Mary style and suggest an early date, but the crisp quarter round of the skirt moldings and the elegant curves of the bracket feet have a rococo, post-seventeen-fifties character. The feet and moldings were possibly installed to replace the bun feet of a desk made twenty or thirty years earlier: the walnut of which they are made is at variance with the other primary wood, and scribe marks on the bottom boards do not line up with the present feet.

PROVENANCE: Ex coll.: H. Eugene Bolles, Boston.

CONSTRUCTION: The slant top opens on iron hinges to rest on one-piece lopers, revealing an interior divided into three equal sections, each having two cubbyholes above a drawer opening. The rails between the exterior drawers are dovetailed into the side boards. There are no dust boards. The drawers have thick sides and bottoms. On the latter, the grain runs lengthwise. The back of the desk is two vertical pine boards half-lapped together and slotted into the top and sides of the case. The feet are nailed to the bottom board and to the skirt molding nailed to its sides. On each rear leg the back bracket, its inner edge cut diagonally, is rabbeted into the side bracket.

CONDITION: The desk has a pleasing light brown patina; traces of red, especially on the pine cubbyholes, suggest that it was once entirely stained that color. The top and side boards and the drawer fronts have worm holes. The bracket feet look to be of eighteenth-century date, but behind each of them are scribe marks and evidence of previous, larger glue blocks and, possibly, different feet. The three small interior drawers are missing. All but one of the scalloped tops of the cubbyholes are replaced. The bottom part of the brass keyhole escutcheon on the top drawer is broken off, and the lock is missing. The iron cotter pins of the handles have been replaced.

INSCRIPTIONS: In pencil (20th-century), inside middle drawer: — — Brick house. In red pencil (20th-century), on exterior of bottom drawer: Bottom.

DIMENSIONS: H.: overall, 21⅞ (55.6), writing surface, 15⅜ (39.1); W.: case, 18 (45.7), feet, 18¾ (47.6); D.: case, 10¼ (26.), feet, 10¾ (27.3).

WOODS: Primary: maple; walnut (skirt molding, bracket feet). Secondary: yellow pine (rear-foot brackets); white pine (all else).

REFERENCES: Richmond Huntley, "Small Furniture Made Early," American Collector 3 (June 1935), pp. 1, 9; p. 11 (ill.). Toller, p. 63; pl. 18.

Gift of Mrs. Russell Sage, 1909   (10.125.93)

172. Child's Desk on Frame

Desk, Massachusetts, 1730–50
Frame, Philadelphia, 1740–60

THIS MAPLE DESK, with its inlaid compass star, stringing of alternating light and dark wood, and exclusive use of white pine for secondary woods, is characteristic of Massachusetts. The frame, made entirely of walnut and standing on trifid feet, is typically Pennsylvania. Because both parts are of eighteenth-century manufacture and fit together perfectly, this dichotomy can have but one explanation: a child's desk made in Massachusetts sometime between 1730 and 1750 was taken a few years later to Pennsylvania, where a high frame was added in order to elevate the writing surface for an older child.

When the desk is lifted out of its frame, the holes of the nails that secured the original molded skirt and bracket feet are visible on its bottom edge. The desk's original appearance is suggested by a related example with a compass inlay but no stringing (*Antiques* 106 [July 1974], inside back cover) that stands on straight bracket feet and has a plain, molded skirt. Another three-drawer Massachusetts child's desk on a frame of Pennsylvania origin was offered for sale in the nineteen-twenties (ibid. 4 [July 1923], p. 49). The desk part is similar in size and design to this one's except that its stamped brasses are of an earlier type; the legs of the frame are identical to these, but the skirt is scalloped and the molded juncture with the desk is much less bold. Similar to the MMA example are two New England child-size desks (Downs 1952, no. 216; Randall 1965, no. 56) that were originally made to stand on frames having boldly scalloped skirts and tapered turned legs.

The inlaid ornament on cat. no. 172 relates to that on a small group of case pieces from the Boston area, most of them of the highest quality. The star, or compass, inlay on the slant top has eight points, each forming an elongated four-sided diamond made up of four pieces of alternating dark and light wood. Similar stars with four or six points are inlaid on a Massachusetts high chest (cat. no. 157); stars with seven or thirteen points are found on a Connecticut desk (cat. no. 178). The stringing inlay used by Boston makers was usually of three parallel strips—light, dark, light (see cat. no. 158)—but the stringing on cat. no. 172 is more complex. Of the four parallel bands, the outer ones are continuous strips of light wood; the inner ones, checkerboard sections of light and dark wood. Identical inlay is known on only a few other American-made pieces, including a card table (Warren, no. 57) and a high chest (cat. no. 157), both from around Boston.

PROVENANCE: Ex coll.: Miss Jane E. Lockwood; Mrs. Luke Vincent Lockwood, Riverside, Connecticut. Purchased by the MMA at the 1942 auction of Mrs. Lockwood's collection.

CONSTRUCTION: Behind the hinged slant top with its inlaid border and central compass pattern is an interior divided into four large cubbyholes, each with a scalloped crest and a small drawer below. The case back is two vertical boards half-lapped together. The solid rails, the uppermost faced with a walnut strip, are slotted through the side boards. There are no dust boards. Stringing borders identical to the one on the slant top are inlaid on the drawer fronts. The cross-grained drawer bottoms are slotted into the front and nailed over the sides and back; their runners are applied. On the separate frame, the molded top edge is in two parts: the upper one fixed to the top of the rails; the lower one, to the sides. The rails are pegged to the legs.

CONDITION: The wood is a mellow walnut brown in color. On the slant top, the upper half of the left edge has been patched. Parts of the compass-star inlay were replaced in 1977. The walnut veneer facings on the front edge of each side board are modern replacements. The frame replaces the original bracket feet and applied skirt molding (see above); the side

172

brackets of its front legs are modern replacements. The lock receptacle centered in the desk's top board has been patched.

INSCRIPTIONS: In brown ink, inside bottom drawer: illegible markings.

DIMENSIONS: H.: overall, 35⅛ (*89.2*), writing surface, 27½ (*69.9*), desk, 21⅞ (*55.6*), frame, 14½ (*36.8*); W.: desk, 21½ (*54.6*), frame, 22⅜ (*56.8*), feet, 24 (*61.*); D.: desk, 11⅝ (*29.5*), frame, 12¼ (*31.1*), feet, 13⅝ (*34.6*).

WOODS: Primary: walnut (frame, desk slant top, lopers, drawer fronts, front rails between drawers); walnut veneer (facing of top rail); maple (top and side boards, top rail, fronts of interior drawers, light-wood stringing). Secondary: white pine.

REFERENCES: Lockwood 1, fig. 245. P-B sale no. 404, November 7, 1942, lot 194. Downs 1944, p. 80 (as Pennsylvania). *Antiques* 47 (January 1945), p. 50 (as Pennsylvania). Toller, p. 90; pl. 48 (as Philadelphia).

Purchase, Joseph Pulitzer Bequest, 1942   (42.139)

173 See also p. 354

173. Desk on Frame

Connecticut, 1787?

RATHER THAN HAVING attached feet, a goodly number of full-size Connecticut desks and secretaries rest on separate low frames that are vestigial survivals of the high stands found on many William and Mary- and Queen Anne-style desks (Kirk 1967, nos. 114–116, 122). The frame of cat. no. 173 has distinctive serpentine-scalloped skirts and small, springy cabriole legs on pad feet that provide a graceful freshness to an otherwise solid and businesslike form.

Some clearly related desks are from the same locale, if not from the same shop. The frame of a mahogany example (Barnes and Meals, no. 75) matches cat. no. 173 except for the carved shell in the middle of its skirt; similar to the mahogany one is a desk at the Brooklyn Museum with a history of ownership in Hartford (*Antiques* 63 [March 1953], p. 167; Kirk 1967, no. 115). The feet of a secretary desk reputedly purchased in Hartford and now at the Ford Museum (Kirk 1967, no. 125) are like those of cat. no. 173; the desk interiors are also alike but for the secretary's prospect door.

Serpentine-scalloped skirts also appear on a high chest and matching dressing table (ibid., nos. 81, 179) said to have belonged to Ezekiel Porter of Wethersfield, just south of Hartford. On the basis of these shared features

an attribution to the Hartford area may be hazarded for the MMA desk. The unusual shell and reeded oval sunburst on the drawers of its removable central unit typify the imaginative use to which Connecticut makers put a small number of decorative motifs.

PROVENANCE: Ex coll.: Walter Hosmer, Hartford; H. Eugene Bolles, Boston.

CONSTRUCTION: Behind the hinged slant top are two groups of four cubbyholes. Above each cubbyhole is a shallow pencil drawer whose bottom is dovetailed into the scallop-edged front; below each group is a double tier of blocked-in drawers. In the middle is a removable central unit having a cubbyhole with a drawer above and below (the latter with an elegantly wrought eleven-rayed shell) and, on either side, a fixed split spindle stained to resemble ebony. Behind the spindles are vertical document slots accessible from the rear when the unit is removed. The desk has three horizontal tongue and groove backboards and a single bottom board. The rails are dovetailed into the sides. There are no dust boards. The drawers' thick framing members have huge dovetails; on the drawer bottoms the grain runs lengthwise. On the separate frame, the rails are double pegged to the leg stiles. Pine battens, nailed with roseheads to the side rails, support two boards on which the desk rests. The boards are kept in place by the applied top molding.

CONDITION: The wood is a reddish brown in color. A strip two inches wide has been replaced at the bottom of the slant top. Patches on the writing surface indicate the location of two previous sets of hinges. The front of the second drawer has been refaced on the extreme left. The side strips on which the drawers slide have been replaced. Behind the modern brasses are dark shadows left by previous, rococo-style ones. The removable interior unit may be from another eighteenth-century desk to accommodate which the beaded flanking boards were made thinner. A thumbhole in the unit's top was for the purpose of releasing a spring lock that is not present on the desk. The reeded oval rosette behind the knob of the top drawer and the ribbed plinth for the knob of the bottom drawer may be later embellishments. The document slots are new.

INSCRIPTIONS: In white chalk, on right side of removable prospect door unit: *October / 6* [?] *1787*; on bottoms of pencil drawers: *1* through *8*; on bottoms of upper cubbyhole drawers: *1* through *4*. A paper label (20th-century) pasted inside upper right cubbyhole drawer printed: *Included in the collection of Antique Furniture transferred to Mr. H. E. Bolles, and Mr. Geo. S. Palmer.* In brown ink, on label: *A Cherry Secretary, Bandy feet* [signed] *Walter Hosmer.* In pencil (20th-century), on bottom of drawer no. 8: *What cheer / 1636 / Roger Williams / 1919*, together with an anchor in a circle.

DIMENSIONS: H.: overall, 45 (*114.3*), writing surface, 33⅝ (*85.4*); W.: case, 35½ (*90.2*), frame, 37⅝ (*95.7*), feet, 39⅝ (*100.7*); D.: case, 18 (*45.7*), frame, 19¼ (*48.9*), feet, 20¼ (*51.4*).

WOODS: Primary: cherry. Secondary: cherry (bottom board); white pine (all else).

Gift of Mrs. Russell Sage, 1909   (10.125.76)

174. Desk

Massachusetts, 1760–90

THE CAREFULLY CHOSEN figured mahoganies and the classic proportions of this desk suggest an urban maker. That he was of eastern Massachusetts origin is indicated by the bird's-talon claws and sharp-cornered knees of the feet, the large brasses and carrying handles, and the use of mahogany and white pine, all features typical of that region. The shaping of the front, with its projecting center and receding sides, can be found only on a few other straight-sided desks and secretaries (e.g., cat. no. 175; Sack 4, p. 952; *Antiques* 108 [September 1975], p. 339; ibid. 110 [September 1976], p. 511). The urbane reverse-serpentine beginning after a blocklike definition at the drawer edges is a technique more usually found in conjunction with bombé-shaped case furniture, where the regular serpentine (e.g., cat. no. 179) was never used. The legs of cat. no. 174 and those of a bombé-serpentine chest (Lockwood 1, fig. 129) look to be by the same hand. The interior of the desk is the simplest of New England types. Because some secretary desks with fronts of this shape have Boston histories (Warren, no. 134; Vincent, fig. 135), all of them are generally attributed to that city.

PROVENANCE: Ex coll.: H. Eugene Bolles, Boston.

CONSTRUCTION: The hinged slant top, a solid piece of richly figured wood with batten ends, opens to rest on pine lopers having thick mahogany fronts. Inside, flanking the flat prospect door, split spindles in the form of colonettes with acorn finials are fastened to removable document slots; on either side are four cubbyholes over two tiers of plain drawers. Behind the door is a wide cubbyhole with a scallop-fronted pencil drawer above and a plain drawer below. The front boards of the desk's four large drawers are serpentine-shaped inside and out. The grain runs crosswise on the drawer bottoms. There are no dust boards. The bead-edged rails between the drawers are blind-slotted into the sides and reinforced behind with pine strips. There are four horizontal backboards. The legs extend through the bottom board. The rear feet have only three talons. The front skirt molding, its inner surface straight, overlaps the bottom board.

CONDITION: The desk has a fine reddish brown color. There are deep gouges in the surface of the top board. A patch has been inserted in the top board and a thin strip added to the bottom edge of the slant top. On the drawers, the large ones have new runners; the bottom of the lowest drawer has been patched. The hinges on the prospect door are modern replacements. The bottom two drawers are missing their locks.

INSCRIPTIONS: In pencil, on bottom of drawer behind prospect door: a lengthy but illegible inscription; on back and bottom boards of large drawers: *1* through *4*, beginning at the top. The small drawers are similarly numbered.

174 See also p. 354

DIMENSIONS: H.: overall, 44 (*111.8*), writing surface, 33 (*83.8*); W.: case, 41½ (*105.4*), feet, 44½ (*113.*); D.: case, 22¾ (*57.8*), feet, 24¼ (*61.6*).

WOODS: Primary: mahogany. Secondary: white pine.

REFERENCES: Lee 2, p. 179 (measured drawings); p. 180 (ill.).

Gift of Mrs. Russell Sage, 1909   (10.125.92)

175. Desk

Massachusetts, 1760–90

IN OVERALL DESIGN this example is closely related to cat. no. 174 and probably also originated in Boston. Both desks have plain interiors, bold and angular claw-and-ball feet, and the rare reverse-serpentine front. Here, however, instead of beginning at a point somewhat in from the drawer edges, the serpentine starts its curve directly, if imperceptibly, at them. A visible rail above the skirt molding increases the impression of weight conveyed by the desk, and it is its drawer fronts rather than its slant top that have the most richly figured mahogany. The interior, for the most part, is in the simplest New England manner. The serpentine-curved frame of the

175 See also p. 354

paneled prospect door appears in the more elaborate interiors of a few other desks (P-B sale no. 1534, 10/9/54, lot 173; Sack 3, p. 737), on a bureau table (*Antiques* 111 [January 1977], p. 4), and on English prototypes, where it is used around mirrors (*DEF* 1, p. 135, fig. 34). Most often found on the large upper doors of secretaries (cat. nos. 179, 180, 183), it is a favorite Massachusetts motif.

PROVENANCE: Ex coll.: H. Eugene Bolles, Boston.

CONSTRUCTION: Centered behind the hinged slant top, the prospect door and flanking plain pilasters form a single removable unit secured by a wooden spring catch set into the desk's top board. The shaped panel on the door is rectangular in back. Inside the door is a cubbyhole over a single blocked-in drawer. When the unit is removed, its back panel slides upward to reveal two vertical document slots flanking three shallow drawers. The desk has no dust boards. On the large drawers, the solid fronts are contoured inside and out; the grain on the bottoms runs crosswise. The beaded rails between the drawers are backed with pine strips. The rear feet have only three talons.

CONDITION: The desk is a deep reddish brown in color. There have been minor repairs: a narrow mahogany strip nailed to the upper front edge of the top large drawer; a new bottom board on the third drawer; and new runners on all the large drawers. Parts are missing from three of the four thin scalloped dividers between the cubbyholes. The wooden spring securing the prospect-door unit is a replacement. Modern battens have been nailed to the outer surface of the removable unit's sliding back. The brasses are old, but from two different sets. The prospect door lacks its keyhole escutcheon. Most of the drawer locks are replacements.

INSCRIPTIONS: In chalk, on underside of bottom drawer: *Doratu*[?] or *Donatio*[?]. In brown ink, on top drawer in back of removable interior unit: *300*. In pencil, on large drawer bottoms: *4* through *7*, each with an *X* mark below. In pencil (19th-century), on small top drawer second from left: *$63—Due*.

DIMENSIONS: H.: overall, 44¾ (*113.7*), writing surface, 33 (*83.8*); W.: case, 42½ (*108.*), feet, 47¼ (*120.*); D.: case, 21⅞ (*55.6*), feet, 24¾ (*62.9*).

WOODS: Primary: mahogany. Secondary: white pine.

REFERENCES: Lockwood 1, fig. 286.

Gift of Mrs. Russell Sage, 1909   (10.125.80)

176. Desk

Massachusetts, 1760–90

THE DESK IS SOME eight inches lower and narrower than the norm, but much larger than child-size (see cat. nos. 171, 172). Judging by Lydian Haraden's proprietary inscriptions, the young lady seems to have found it just right. A number of full-size desks of similar interior and exterior design and distinctive shell-carved skirt pendant look to be from the same shop (e.g., Anderson Galleries sale no. 4214, 12/12–14/35, lot 445; Haskell sale 1, lot 717). One of them (*Antiques* 86 [November 1964], p. 529), like this one but with additional small drawers and a different skirt molding, is inscribed: "This Botet of Benjⁿ Reead July 26–1771 / Price £10-0-0 L M." The name may refer to an owner, since no Benjamin Read has been identified as a Massachusetts cabinetmaker. On cat. no. 176, the square top corners of the blocking and the delicate claw feet flanked by large bolection brackets are in the Salem manner, suggesting the origin of this stylish little object.

PROVENANCE: Ex coll.: George S. Palmer, New London, Connecticut. The desk is said to have been bought in Hartford by the dealer Morris Schwartz (information from Bernard Levy, July 1983).

CONSTRUCTION: The desk top is dovetailed to the sides. The hinged slant top opens to rest on pine lopers having thick mahogany fronts. Inside, on either side of the recessed-block-and-shell prospect door is a sliding document slot faced with an applied colonette crowned by a gilded acorn finial and having scallop-topped side boards; a double cubbyhole over a flat drawer; and a pair of recessed-blocked drawers surmounted by a drawer with a twelve-lobed shell. When the prospect door is opened, an additional set of block-and-shell drawers is revealed. On the desk, the bead-edged rails, reinforced behind with narrow boards, are slotted into the side boards. Mahogany strips are nailed to the side boards' front edges. There are no dust boards. The inner surfaces of the drawer fronts are sawed out at canted angles behind the blocking. On the drawers, the sides are beaded on their top inner surfaces; on the bottoms, the grain runs crosswise. Behind the desk's recessed central blocking the thick single-piece skirt molding extends as a giant dovetail into the bottom board. The cabriole legs and shaped brackets are attached to a frame—the sides, pine boards; the front, pine and mahogany glue blocks—on the bottom board's underside. The rear legs have thick curved back brackets. The applied skirt pendant, a dished-out thirteen-lobed shell, is reinforced with a rounded glue block.

CONDITION: The desk is a dark reddish brown in color. The flat top, slant top, and sides have been refinished; the wood otherwise has the original finish and, particularly around the brasses, a lustrous patina. The slant top is patched around the hinges. On the legs, the side glue blocks are replaced. The side skirt moldings have been reattached.

INSCRIPTIONS: In brown ink, on backs of left-hand interior drawers, beginning at the top: *1* through *4*. On drawer no. 4, in brown ink: *EHC*; in pencil: *ACS*. Numerous writings, both ancient and modern, on all the small drawers. Except for various numbers in chalk, all are illegible. In pencil, in an early 19th-century hand, on the sides of the two document slots: *M A C Ds Drawer/to keep new/pencil in.—L A Haraden's/Draw to keep her/pens in./Lydian Haraden's/Draw to keep her/pens in.*

DIMENSIONS: H.: overall, 36⅛ (*91.8*), writing surface, 26¾ (*67.9*); W.: case, 30 (*76.2*), feet, 32⅜ (*82.2*); D.: case, 17¼ (*43.8*), feet, 18½ (*47.*).

WOODS: Primary: mahogany. Secondary: white pine.

REFERENCES: Miller 1, no. 893. Nutting 1, no. 635.

John Stewart Kennedy Fund, 1918   (18.110.56)

176 See also p. 355

177. Desk

Boston, 1760–90

OF A COMMON Massachusetts form and without exceptional carving, the desk nonetheless exhibits wonderful quality. The even-grained, dense mahogany is finely wrought, as is the thickly framed pine interior. The desk's overall massive scale is continued in the squatness of its feet and its interior columns. Several of its design and construction features—the rounded top corners of the drawer blocking, the large size of the claw feet, the stepped interior with stiffly carved fanlike shells, the molded skirt dovetailed into the bottom board—suggest a Boston provenance (Lovell, pp. 112–115). In contrast, the exposed dovetails where the rails join the side boards are more typical of Newport work (ibid., pp. 85–86); the blocked slant top, of Salem (ibid., p. 120). The brasses are of a pattern frequently found on fine Massachusetts case pieces. A seemingly identical desk is dated 1786 (Barry A. Greenlaw, "American furniture in Houston collections," *Antiques* 116 [September 1979], p. 553, pl. XIII); another, with slightly different brasses, has been advertised (*Antiques* 83 [February 1963], p. 137). Both look to be by the maker of cat. no. 177.

177 See also p. 355

Though other examples have similar interiors, their slant tops are without blocking and the handling of their colonettes and the shaping of their feet bespeak different makers. One of the desks, at Yale (Lovell, fig. 80), descended in the Winthrop family of Boston; another is at the Boston MFA (Hipkiss, no. 24) together with a bombé secretary (ibid., no. 21) that descended from Gibbs Atkins of Boston. A simpler version of the stepped interior was used by Benjamin Frothingham of Charlestown, Massachusetts, on a desk with serpentine front and ogee-bracket feet (Randall 1974, fig. 165; see also cat. no. 180). Although the block front is a characteristically New England feature, an English prototype displays a facade remarkably similar to that of cat. no. 177 (Percy Macquoid, *A History of English Furniture: The Age of Mahogany*, London, 1906, figs. 39, 40). The similarity is so marked that an American attribution was once assigned to the English example (Miller 1, p. 480).

PROVENANCE: Ex coll.: Mrs. Giles Whiting, Scarborough, New York.

CONSTRUCTION: The top board is half-lapped and mitered to the side boards. The two wide, horizontal backboards are reinforced inside with a vertical medial brace. The hinged slant top, a single blocked piece slotted into flanking battens, opens to rest on mahogany lopers having applied fronts. Inside, the bottom tier of plain drawers is stepped; above it, inward-blocked drawers capped by carved shells alternate with outward-blocked drawers under paired cubbyholes. On these interior drawers the cross-grained bottom boards extend beyond the backboards to act as stops. The half columns on the document slots are applied. On the sides of the slots, the tops are rounded; on the sides of the drawers, they are chamfered.

On the desk, the bead-edged rails are dovetailed into the side boards and backed with narrow boards. There are no dust boards. On the large drawers, the fronts are cut away inside at canted angles behind the projecting blocking; the cross-grained bottom boards are slotted into the front and sides. The underside of the bottom of the desk is framed on front and sides by boards, mitered together, to which the knee brackets are attached. The molded front skirt is cut out in a large dovetail that extends into the bottom board; similarly, each foot continues through it as a square tenon.

CONDITION: The desk has a lustrous dark brown patina. Behind the slant top the wood has the unfilled grain and reddish hue of the original thin finish. The writing surface is patched where a hinge has been removed. Two small parts of the molded and scalloped central skirt ornament are missing. The left front leg has a split, and the left-side runners on the middle two large drawers are new. The bottom of one of the large drawers is lined with sheets from a Massachusetts newspaper (see Inscriptions); the others are lined with plain, nineteenth-century paper.

INSCRIPTIONS: In white chalk, on underside of lowest large drawer, a partly obliterated inscription appears to read: *R. Forrester.* Incised, on upper backboard: a series of compass marks. Lining the bottom of second drawer from the bottom are pages from the Boston newspaper *Columbian Centinel* of January 17, 1821.

DIMENSIONS: H.: overall, 44½ (*113.*), writing surface, 33 (*83.8*); W.: case, 42 (*106.7*), feet, 46 (*116.8*); D.: case, 22¾ (*57.8*), feet, 25 (*63.5*).

WOODS: Primary: mahogany. Secondary: white pine.

REFERENCES: Helen Comstock, "Furniture in the collection of Mrs. Giles Whiting," *Antiques* 69 (March 1956), p. 230, fig. 4.

Bequest of Flora E. Whiting, 1971   (1971.180.40)

178. Desk

Colchester, Connecticut, 1769
Benjamin Burnham (about 1737–about 1773)

WELL KNOWN SINCE its first publication (Lyon 1891), this is probably the most ambitiously conceived of all Connecticut desks and certainly the most fully documented. Yet it remains an enigmatic masterpiece. The inscription unequivocally declares it to have been made in 1769 by Benjamin Burnham, who had apprenticed in "Felledlfey," generally interpreted as Philadelphia, but in neither design nor construction does a single feature of the desk, with the possible exception of the overall shape of the claw foot, demonstrate any of that city's influence. Rather, the combination of bracket feet in back with claw-and-ball feet in front suggests New York; the stop-fluting on the pilasters and the pattern of the brasses, Newport; and the use of cherry and the treatment of the decorative motifs, Connecticut. For all that, the main inspiration is unquestionably Boston: the compass inlays (see cat. no. 157); the amphitheaterlike interior (see cat. no. 183); the fronts of the large drawers, round-blocked outside and angular in, and the dovetail juncture of skirt molding and bottom board (see cat. no. 177).

Benjamin Burnham was not an uncommon name in eighteenth-century New England, but the maker of cat. no. 178 has been reasonably identified (Bulkeley 1967, pp. 28–33) as one who worked in Colchester, Connecticut. Remarkably little is known about him. According to the 1903 *History of Tolland and Windham County* (ibid., quoted p. 30), "The Grandfather [Benjamin Burnham] of Griswold Burnham was a cabinetmaker of Colchester, Conn., and some of his handiwork is still in the possession of his descendants." (No such pieces have been located.) The 1784 Colchester Vital Records documents Burnham's marriage to a "Catherin Trumble" in 1770 or 1771 (ibid.), and family tradition has it that Burnham left the county before the birth of his son in 1773. He may have been one of two Benjamin Burnhams born in or near Ipswich, Massachusetts, in 1737 and 1739 (ibid., p. 31). The normal apprenticeship of seven years began in that

178 See also pp. 355, 364

era at age fourteen, which would place the maker of cat. no. 178 in Philadelphia between 1751 and 1758 or 1753 and 1760. When he moved to Colchester is not known.

The MMA desk is the only documented example of his work. A New England Queen Anne flat-top high chest with "Benjamin Burnham" chalked on the back (*Antiques* 105 [February 1974], p. 277) bears no stylistic resemblance to cat. no. 178 and looks to be the work of

another, earlier hand. George Palmer, the desk's last private owner, claimed that its maker worked in Hebron, an adjoining town to which the Burnham family moved from Colchester in about 1800 (Myers and Mayhew, pp. 112–113).

A number of case pieces share distinctive stylistic similarities with cat. no. 178, and must originate, if not in the same shop, in the same locale. A slightly simplified version of the desk, originally the property of Eliphalet Bulkeley (born 1746) of Colchester, bears what may be the signature of Samuel Loomis (1748–1813), a later Colchester cabinetmaker (ibid., no. 32). A child's desk on frame (Lockwood 1, fig. 248) has an interior that repeats almost exactly that of the MMA desk. The highly individual leg treatment of cat. no. 178 is also found on a group of three-drawer chests with block-and-shell fronts. One (Kirk 1967, no. 62) has identical gouged knee carving; another (Downs 1952, no. 172) was found in Colchester; a third, from the Bulkeley family, is said to have been purchased by the clockmaker Thomas Harland after 1773 (Myers and Mayhew, no. 34). In addition, a bonnet-top chest-on-chest at the Ford Museum (Kirk 1967, no. 100) and another, with a Colchester history, at Deerfield (Fales 1976, fig. 439), have related feet. A group of Connecticut desks and secretaries (Sack 5, pp. 1314–15; *Antiques* 98 [August 1970], p. 216) have similarly arranged interiors, though less elaborately realized. A desk on frame at one time in the MMA collection (Nutting 1, no. 632) has incised knee carving and three inlaid six-point compass stars in its slant top, both features also found on cat. no. 178. Which of these related pieces were made by Burnham and which by other Colchester-area makers has yet to be determined.

PROVENANCE: Ex coll.: George S. Palmer, New London, Connecticut. In 1891, this desk "was lately bought from an estate in Hartford, Conn., and is now a part of the [Walter] Hosmer Collection of that city" (Lyon, p. 121; fig. 50). Palmer bought it from Hosmer.

CONSTRUCTION: The top board of the desk is dovetailed into the side boards. Three compass stars—the outer ones with seven points; the middle one, thirteen—are inlaid toward the upper edge of the hinged slant top. On the opened desk, the side battens of the writing surface are notched twice to accommodate the bulging drawer unit. Flanking the central section and above the three tiers of interior drawers are eight cubbyholes, each having a shell-carved pencil drawer with a pierced and scalloped lower edge and a bottom reinforced in order to receive the knob. The drawers, their fronts serpentine in section, are in an amphitheaterlike arrangement, projecting at the sides and receding in a series of curves toward the middle; the bottom tier is stepped. In the central section, the four blocked-in drawers (the shallow bottom one false) are flanked by narrow slots, each divided into three fluted drawers. The grain of the drawer bottoms runs crosswise. On the desk, two boards form the left side, one the right. The stop-fluted pilasters flanking the drawers are cut from single boards glued to the side boards' front

edges and extending through the inside top board. The edges of the applied loper fronts have projecting thumbnail moldings. The beaded rails let into the pilaster boards and slotted into the side boards are without backing strips. There are no dust boards. The front of the top drawer is flat on the inner surface, cut away only to receive the shafts of the brasses. The other drawer fronts are sawed out inside, their corners canted behind the projecting blocking. The grain runs crosswise on the drawer bottoms. The complexly molded skirt is a single thick board that extends into the bottom board as a giant dovetail behind the central concave blocking. The front feet are pieced at the back and at one side. The back brackets of the rear feet are plain boards, diagonally cut. The boards forming glue blocks behind the feet are nailed to the bottom board.

CONDITION: The wood is light reddish brown in color. The incised carving on the legs is highlighted by a buildup of the dark old finishes that have been cleaned from the rest of the desk. The top board is patched where the lock is received, and there are patches on the slant top: a one-inch strip at the bottom and two wedge-shaped inserts, apparently to repair shrinkage cracks, where the main board is mitered to the side battens. Some pieces of the inlay of the compass stars have been replaced. At the level of each of the rails on the right side of the case is a square patch. The tip of the middle scroll on the left front leg is missing. The legs have been reglued to the bottom board a number of times, and the backboards have been renailed.

INSCRIPTIONS: In brown ink, centered on underside of bottom board, in an eighteenth-century hand: *This Desk was maid in the | year of 1769 Buy Benjn Burnam, | that sarvfed his time in Felledlfey.* Incised inside backboard of many of the small drawers is a circle. Chalked inside backboard of each of the large drawers is a circle pierced by the apex of a triangle. Part of a printed Palmer Bros. Co. shipping label is pasted on the top backboard. (See p. 366 for photograph.)

DIMENSIONS: H.: overall, 49¾ (126.4), writing surface, 35 (88.9); W.: case, 40¾ (103.5), feet, 44½ (113.); D.: case, 22¼ (56.5), feet, 24½ (62.2).

WOODS: Primary: cherry. Secondary: cherry (drawer runners and case glue blocks); white pine (drawer sides, backs, bottoms, feet glue blocks); tulip poplar (backboards, bottom board, dark- and light-wood inlays).

REFERENCES: Lyon, p. 121; fig. 50. Dyer, fig. 7 (caption erroneously put with fig. 3). Lockwood 1, fig. 264. Downs 1949, no. 7. Bjerkoe, pp. 54–55; pl. XVIII, no. 1. Bulkeley 1958, pp. 85–89; idem 1959, pp. 62–63; idem 1967, pp. 28–33. Davidson 1967, fig. 324. Kirk 1967, no. 121. Myers and Mayhew, pp. 4–7, 32, 34, 111–113.

John Stewart Kennedy Fund, 1918   (18.110.58)

CHAPTER

18 Desks and Bookcases

A separate bookcase unit having hinged doors opening onto shelves, cubbyholes, and slots in any combination, added to the desk unit previously described, created an ancillary form. Until the end of the late colonial period the doors were usually paneled with wood or looking glass, suggesting that the shelves were intended not so much to display as to store the books or the packets of papers they held. Among the largest and most impressive pieces of American furniture, desks and bookcases were a symbol of their owners' mercantile and intellectual achievements. The collection is especially rich in New England examples—fine block-fronted ones from Boston, Salem, and Newport in particular. The terms "secretary" or "secretary bookcase" by which the desks are commonly known today were introduced in England only in the seventeen-eighties to describe desks in which the writing surface is provided not by the slant top, as here, but by the unfolded front of the upper drawer.

179. Desk and Bookcase

Massachusetts, Salem area, 1794

NEITHER PARTICULARLY elaborate nor unusual in design, this desk and bookcase nevertheless has excellent proportions and, derived from the carefully chosen tiger-stripe maple of which it is made, a lively decorative charm rarely equaled in New England case furniture. It is one of a number of similar serpentine-front New England secretaries that have been convincingly associated with a single cabinet shop (Young). Who the cabinetmaker was

179 See also p. 356

and where he worked are still matters for conjecture, although available evidence suggests an origin in Massachusetts for some of the pieces, including this one, and in New Hampshire for others. A bonnet-top desk and bookcase formerly in the Cluett collection (ibid., fig. 4) is identical to cat. no. 179 in most details of design and construction. Both secretaries are of a typical Massachusetts pattern, and certain of their features—the silhouetted convex scallop shell centered below the skirt and, on the Cluett example, the tiny circular disks at the juncture of the scroll cornice and the rounded openings below—are characteristic of Salem. Further, both pieces have Massachusetts histories: the Cluett one is said to have descended from Henry Waters of Salem, and the MMA one, which is dated 1794, reputedly belonged in the early nineteenth century to Jonathan Warner of Hardwick.

Three other secretaries, while demonstrably associated with the same shop, appear to have been made in Gilmanton, New Hampshire, a few years later than the first two. (A logical hypothesis is that the cabinetmaker moved from Salem to Gilmanton, which is north of Concord, after 1794.) All three desks have histories of ownership in New Hampshire. Two of them are inscribed with the date 1799 and the place Gilmanton; the inscriptions appear to be in the same hand as the date on the MMA desk. One of the two, that at the Currier Gallery (ibid., fig. 2) is very like the Salem examples, even to the decorative exploitation of the wood's tiger-stripe grain; the only stylistic difference is in its pendent shell, which is fanlike rather than the typical Salem scallop. The second desk is inscribed "T [?] Cogswell / 1799 /——— manton." (Efforts to link this Cogswell with one of the Massachusetts cabinetmakers of that name have not been successful.) On it, the same fanlike skirt motif is employed, but the desk is made of plain cherry and has a different interior arrangement and ogee-bracket feet (ibid., fig. 5). The same foot treatment is found on the third New Hampshire desk, an even simpler example in plain maple (ibid., fig. 1). Of these five secretaries, all but the one signed by Cogswell have between their central inner colonettes two drawers whose removal permits access to a secret drawer (ibid., fig. 4A)—an arrangement so distinctive as to suggest the same unknown maker's hand.

PROVENANCE: Ex coll.: Mrs. J. Insley Blair, Tuxedo Park, New York; Mrs. Screven Lorillard, Far Hills, New Jersey. Mrs. Blair purchased the desk from the New York dealer Charles R. Morson in October 1927. According to her records, "In the early nineteenth century the secretary stood in the homestead of Jonathan Warner at Hardwick, Mass., and it always remained in possession of the Warner family." Presumably this was the Jonathan Warner born in Hardwick in 1763 and married to Sally Paige in 1789.

CONSTRUCTION: On the bookcase unit: The molded cornice is fashioned from a single board, with a separate molded strip nailed just above the door opening. On the doors, the rail tenons project through the stiles. The door frames have serpentine inner edges, but the panels that back them are square. Inside, across the top, are seven cubbyholes. Below them, stacks of three cubbyholes flank the central area, which contains a full-length shelf over a medial divider to which a half-length shelf is attached. Thin scalloped dividers separate the top row of cubbyholes; thick boards with double-beaded fronts separate the other compartments. The joints of the bookcase backboards are concealed by the fixed shelves. On the desk unit: Behind the hinged slant top, the small drawers are plain, except for the central top one, which is carved with a fluted shell. The molded baseboard on which the drawers are stacked and the dividers and rails between them are maple-stained pine. Behind the two small square middle drawers at the bottom and attached to the vertical strip that separates them is a hidden drawer accessible when the drawers are removed and the strip is pulled out. The document slots that flank the middle drawers are fronted with turned colonettes. Each desk side is two vertical boards; the back is two horizontal ones. The beaded rails are dovetailed to the sides. The lopers are solid. There are no dust boards. On the drawers, the fronts are shaped inside and out; the bottom boards are laid crosswise. The desk's bottom board is flush with the top of the one-piece front skirt, through which the legs continue as square tenons. Diagonally cut back brackets are tenoned into the rear legs. On both bookcase and desk units, carefully chosen striped maple is used on the exterior front surfaces, plain maple on all the others. The finish surfaces, including the interiors, have been washed with a reddish brown stain.

CONDITION: The original red finish has faded to a golden hue. The scalloped crestings of all the cubbyholes in the upper unit and of that second from the left in the lower unit are replacements, as are the brass keyhole escutcheons on the doors. An 1876 tax bill from the City of Hallowell, Maine, made out to an A.J. Lynn, and a promissory note dated April 13, 1888, from one Warren H. Calley to Lynn were found in the central compartment of the desk when it arrived at the MMA.

INSCRIPTIONS: In chalk, on bookcase-unit back: *1794 / I* [?] *Back*; on desk-unit back: *October 17th D 1794*; on top right front corner of each divider in bookcase upper tier and on dividers and drawers of desk interior: sequences of Roman numerals.

DIMENSIONS: H.: overall, 84 (*213.4*), writing surface, 33 (*83.8*); W.: upper case, 40⅛ (*101.9*), lower case, 42¼ (*107.3*), feet, 45¾ (*116.2*); D.: upper case, 12⅛ (*30.8*), lower case, 23¼ (*59.1*), feet, 25¼ (*64.1*).

WOODS: Primary: maple. Secondary: white pine.

REFERENCES: Young, pp. 478–485; fig. 3 (with bookcase open), fig. 3A (chalk inscription). For Jonathan Warner, see Lucius R. Paige, *History of Hardwick, Massachusetts*, Boston, 1883, pp. 523–524.

Gift of Mrs. Screven Lorillard, 1953   (53.179.1)

180. Desk and Bookcase

Massachusetts, Newburyport area, 1760–90

MANY FEATURES typical of Boston work are seen in this secretary. The bookcase unit, with its flat, scallop-paneled doors and flanking pilasters surmounted by a continuous denticulated cornice and a separate broken-scroll pediment, follows the model of the George Bright secretary at the Boston MFA (Randall 1965, no. 64), as does the stepped arrangement of the interior drawers; the slightly squashed shape of the circular pediment openings

180 See also p. 356

is paralleled in those of the John Cogswell chest-on-chest of 1782 in the same collection (Vincent, fig. 125). The MMA secretary nevertheless lacks the crisp, vigorous lines and naturalistic carving found on the best Boston examples. The irregular thirteen-rayed rosette beneath the central finial and the softness of execution of the flamelike finials and pendent skirt fan indicate either a lesser carver or an interpretation of Boston design executed beyond the city's borders.

On the desk unit, the serpentine drawer fronts and ogee-bracket feet are similar to those found on three desks labeled by Benjamin Frothingham (1734–1809) of Charlestown, Massachusetts (Randall 1974, figs. 163–167). A visual relationship between cat. no. 180 and a secretary for which Abner Toppan of Newburyport, Massachusetts, is said to have billed the Bannister family in 1795 (Swan 1945, fig. 6; Jobe and Kaye, fig. I-32) is even more compelling. In addition to a notable similarity in the drawer fronts and bracket feet of both pieces, their twisted finial flames and the pinwheel rosettes in their scroll pediments and beneath their central finials look to be by the same hand. Toppan billed the Bannister family in 1795 for another case piece stylistically related to cat. no. 180—a serpentine chest-on-chest (Swan 1945, fig. 7). The handling of certain elements common to all three pieces demonstrates a consistent personal style, which justifies a tentative attribution of the MMA secretary to Abner Toppan's shop. A block-front desk (*Antiques* 86 [July 1964], p. 10), said to date from 1773 and to have a Newburyport history, has baluster-shaped colonettes on its document slots identical to those on the MMA desk and bookcase. That link, while shedding no further light on the identity of the secretary's maker, at least supports its suggested Newburyport provenance.

PROVENANCE: Ex coll.: H. Eugene Bolles, Boston. According to Bolles's notes (MMA files), "It was bought by me of a dealer in Boston." The secretary was on loan from the MMA to the Kenmore Association, Fredericksburg, Virginia, from 1931 to 1978.

CONSTRUCTION: On the bookcase unit: The finials are in two parts, the upper carved, the lower turned. The bonnet is enclosed at the back. At each end of the scroll pediment the rosette and a small part of the molding are cut from the same separate block. The unit's top and bottom boards are dovetailed to the sides in the normal manner; visible inside the bookcase are finished top and bottom boards slotted into the sides just above and below the doors. The door frames are pegged together. Their outer edges are scratch-beaded; their inner edges, backed by rectangular panels of figured wood, are scalloped; and fluted pilasters are nailed to their outer stiles. The left door is pieced on its inner edge. The bookcase interior is neatly finished. Three stationary shelves with bead-edged mahogany fronts are fitted from behind into slots in the sides. The three horizontal tongue and groove backboards are mahogany-stained on their inner surface. On the desk unit: The hinged slant top opens to rest on solid lopers. In the interior, the plain bottom tier of drawers is stepped; above are recessed-blocked drawers—plain ones capped by carved shells alternating with serpentine ones under triple cubbyholes. The document slots are faced with half columns. The front edges of the desk sides are faced with mahogany strips. The three vertical backboards are half-lapped together. There are no dust boards. The inner surfaces of the large drawer fronts conform to the outer serpentine shape, except for that of the top drawer, which is flat. The top edges of the drawer sides are flat. On the drawer bottoms the grain runs lengthwise. The skirt molding extends below the bottom board. The bracket feet, their glue blocks rectangular, are screwed to the skirt molding. The back brackets of the rear legs are sawed out in half arches.

CONDITION: The mahogany has a rich brown patina and a thin old shellac finish. At the time the piece was acquired the vendor's notes (MMA files) record it as "... unrestored. All three top ornaments are original." The plinth supporting the middle finial has been repaired; the shell on the skirt, reattached; the runners of the large drawers, renewed. The lower shelf in the bookcase unit has been removed and the slots in the side boards filled in. The interior cubbyholes originally had scalloped crests. The brass drawer pulls are old replacements, those on the bottom drawer from a different set from the others. The keyhole escutcheons are modern. The brass pull on the right upper interior drawer is missing. A keyhole has been cut into the shell of the upper middle drawer.

INSCRIPTIONS: In chalk, outside bookcase back: *C Brabry* [?] and *Bd* [?]; on desk-unit bottom board, what is probably a repetition of the above, now illegible; on desk-unit middle backboard: *Br*. In brown ink, on rail between the two central interior drawers: 25 *foot*.

DIMENSIONS: H.: overall, 89¾ (228.), writing surface, 32 (81.3); W.: upper case, 39¾ (101.), lower case, 42½ (108.), feet, 45 (114.3); D.: upper case, 10¾ (27.3), lower case, 22 (55.9), feet, 23½ (59.7).

WOODS: Primary: mahogany. Secondary: white pine.

REFERENCES: Lockwood 1, fig. 288. Salomonsky, pl. 86 (measured drawing).

Gift of Mrs. Russell Sage, 1909   (10.125.79)

181.   Desk and Bookcase

Salem, Massachusetts, about 1779
Workshop of Nathaniel Gould (1734–1782)

THIS IS ONE of the supreme manifestations of the characteristic Massachusetts block-front desk with scroll-pediment bookcase and round-arched doors (Lovell, figs. 86–89). A number of its features consistently appear on case pieces with Salem histories: the sharp square corners of the projecting blocking; the tiny carved pinwheels at the termination of the broken-pediment moldings; the scallop shell centered in the skirt; and the extended, bulging brackets of the feet. It is one of three secretaries, identical in size and in almost every feature of design and construction, unquestionably from the same shop. The other two are at Amherst College (Lewis A. Shephard, *American Art at Amherst*, Middletown, Connecticut, Wesleyan University Press, 1978, p. 245) and in a private Houston collection (*Antiques* 93 [January 1968], p. 74). The Amherst piece has applied shells that are incorrect replacements and straight bracket feet, but its doors and slant top and those of cat. no. 181 were sawed from the same magnificent figured mahogany log. On the Houston piece, which descended in the Stearns family of Salem, parts of the interior have been reworked and the finials replaced (Sack 1, p. 25). A fourth secretary, at the Art Institute of Chicago (Rogers, figs. 45, 46), though of the same general design and possessed of an identical applied pediment shell, differs in numerous details, and looks to be by a different hand.

A number of block-front desks, several with Salem histories, exhibit such unequivocal similarities of design and construction as to indicate a common origin with the three secretaries. One (Lovell, fig. 84) is signed by Henry Rust (born 1737), a cabinetmaker in Salem as well as in Boston and Beverly; another (Lockwood 1, fig. LVII) is now at the Ford Museum. (For others, see *Antiques* 55 [June 1949], p. 399; ibid. 91 [February 1967] and 112 [October 1977], inside front covers.) The same distinctive claw feet and skirt shell also appear on a number of bombé desks, including one made for Elias Hasket Derby of Salem (Sack 3, p. 595), and on bombé chests, including one from the Charles Waters family of Salem (Downs 1952, no. 166).

On the MMA secretary is the enigmatic inscription, "Nath Gould not his work." Its meaning can only be surmised. Nathaniel Gould was the richest cabinetmaker in Salem and the only one in Massachusetts known to have owned a copy of Chippendale's *Director*. At his death, in 1781, he was styled "Gent," suggesting that he himself no longer did manual labor (*Antiques* 97 [January 1970], p. 52). Might his social pretensions have inspired one of the journeymen in his shop to record for posterity that this splendid desk, although sold by Gould, was in fact made by a disaffected workman? (And did Henry Rust, whose signed desk so closely resembles cat. no. 181, work in Gould's shop?) Near the inscription is what appears to be the date 1779. Between 1777 and 1779 Gould was supplying furniture to the Derby family. A desk and bookcase of this quality would have been altogether appropriate for the house of that distinguished and prosperous family. While there is insufficient evidence to prove such a provenance for this piece (the Derby–Gould accounts at the Essex Institute list no secretary), the existence until

recently (see Condition) on its pediment of carved figures attributed to the workshop of John and Simeon Skillin, Boston, about 1790 (Swan 1931, p. 343), is provocative, since the Skillins worked extensively for Elias Hasket Derby.

PROVENANCE: Ex coll.: H. Eugene Bolles, Boston. According to Bolles's notes (MMA files): "It was bought by me of a Boston dealer, who said it came from a family near Exeter, N.H., and formerly belonged to Oliver Putnam of Newburyport. His book plate found in it was offered to me." Two of Putnam's engraved bookplates (now in the MMA Department of Prints and Photographs) were acquired with the desk. According to inscriptions of 1888 on the secretary, it was acquired at auction by Thorndike Putnam (1787–1858) and descended to Henry Putnam (1817–1878) and Oliver Putnam (1844–1897). Thorndike was a son of Oliver Putnam (1753–1798) of Newburyport, Massachusetts.

CONSTRUCTION: On the bookcase unit: The bonnet is enclosed except in the center. Bolection frieze units and a central shell motif are glued to the pediment front. Below, fluted pilasters with separate bases and capitals are affixed to the stiles of the doors. The round-arched doors have conforming panels that are fielded in front and flat in back. Inside, behind their arched tops, are concave shells, each having twenty ribs; below are three graduated, bead-edged shelves above a row of five drawers. Scalloped dividers form eleven cubbyholes on the top shelf and five slots on each of the lower shelves. A candle slide is centered below each door. On the desk unit: The blocking of the hinged slant top is cut from the solid. Inside, the two lower tiers of drawers have shaped fronts; the bottom tier is slightly stepped; and the document slots are faced with turned colonettes. On the prospect door, the arched and fielded panel is cut from the solid and the hinges have shaped inner straps. The door opens onto three recessed-blocked drawers, the upper two identical to those flanking the cubbyholes. Below the writing surface, beaded rails backed with narrow pine strips are dovetailed into the sides of the case. There are no dust boards. On the drawers, the fronts are solid; behind the projecting blocking, their inner surfaces are roughly cut away in shallow, angular sections; the top edges of their sides and backs are double beaded. The desk's bottom board is built up at front and sides with mitered pine strips to which the feet and the scalloped brackets are glued. The scallop shell on the shaped skirt pendant is applied. On the sides of both units are brass carrying handles.

CONDITION: The secretary has a marvelous, lustrous, reddish brown patina. Bolles described the desk's state when he got it: "The finish was black with age and dirt, but otherwise it was in very good condition. The cabinet work only required overhauling, some re-glueing, etc., and other minor repairs. To save the old color which was rich under the scale of dirt, I had the old finish rubbed down by hand nearly to the surface of the wood instead of having it scraped" (MMA files). On the bookcase unit, the uppermost four inches of the back and top boards of the bonnet has been replaced. The carved pediment shell has a horizontal split. In 1975, a two-inch section at the top of the central finial's plinth was restored, following the pattern of the Houston secretary. The typical Massachusetts-type corkscrew finials were added at the same time, the side ones replacing draped figures of Peace and Plenty probably carved about 1790

by the Skillins of Salem. (In an earlier MMA restoration, a caduceus replaced what was likely an olive branch in the left hand of Peace.) The central finial, however, may originally have consisted of a large ball above a cup-shaped urn like that on the Amherst secretary. On the left door is a candle burn, and a narrow wooden strip has been added on the door's inner edge. Inside, the two central vertical dividers in the bottom shelf are missing and the tops of the two right-hand drawers below have been patched. The molded fronts of the candle slides have been repaired and their runners and the adjacent backboard replaced. On the desk unit, there are splits in the crotch mahogany board of the right side and in the right rear leg. Inside the slant top, the left shell drawer is new; the front of that on the right has been patched; the brass pull on the drawer below has been reset; and a filler strip has been added to the left side of the prospect door. The runners of the four large outer drawers are replaced. The brasses of the large drawers were replaced in 1940 with the present antique ones, which are similar to those found on related Salem pieces.

INSCRIPTIONS: Incised, in neat script on top board of desk unit: *Nath Gould not his work*; in crude script: *Joseph Gould and 1779* [?]. In chalk, on right-hand drawer, second inside tier, an inscription that may read: *Mrs T G pound R*. In pencil, on top drawer inside prospect door: *Oliver Putnam / Hampstead N.H. / Oct. 17—1888 / This desk was bought by my Grandfather / at an Auction in Derry* [New Hampshire] *before / I can remember*. In pencil, on right-hand drawer, third inside tier: *Oliver Putnam / Hampstead / N H / Jany 29 1888*. (See p. 366 for photograph.)

DIMENSIONS: H.: overall, 105 (266.7), pediment, 100¾ (255.9), writing surface, 32½ (82.6); W.: upper case, 40¼ (102.2), lower case, 42 (106.7), feet, 45 (114.3); D.: upper case, 11½ (29.2), lower case, 22 (55.9), feet, 24 (61.).

WOODS: Primary: mahogany. Secondary: white pine.

REFERENCES: Kimball, pp. 194–196 (figures formerly on pediment attributed to McIntire). Lockwood 1, fig. 267. Swan 1931, fig. 11 (former pediment figures attributed to John and Simeon Skillin). Fiske Kimball, "The Estimate of McIntire," *Antiques* 21 (January 1932), pp. 23–25. Paul H. Burroughs, "Two Centuries of Massachusetts Furniture," *American Collector* 6 (September 1937), pp. 4, 5, 10–13; ill., p. 10 (desk attributed to William King of Salem). Downs 1949, no. 2. Powel, p. 207 (ill.). Aronson, fig. 1050. Lovell, fig. 87; p. 125. MMA 1976, no. 12. For the Putnam family, see Eben Putnam, *A History of the Putnam Family in Scotland and America*, Salem, Massachusetts, 1892.

Gift of Mrs. Russell Sage, 1909 (10.125.81)

182. Desk and Bookcase

New England, 1760–90

A RURAL NEW ENGLAND origin for cat. no. 182 is suggested by its squat proportions and by its legs, which are exaggeratedly curved and too tiny. A Connecticut feature is its cherry primary wood, but in overall design this example conforms to a well-known type of Massachu-

setts secretary having round-arched paneled bookcase doors and block-fronted drawers. Moreover, its tradition of ownership with Timothy Dexter of Newburyport would point to a place of origin on the North Shore of Massachusetts.

The joinery is good, but a number of construction details suggest that the builder was working by trial and error in an effort to create a block-front desk and bookcase based on a fleeting acquaintance with an urban masterpiece such as cat. no. 181. The bottom of the desk unit, rather than consisting of one or more identical pieces of wood, is made up of a thick, rough-sawed pine plank and a cherry board. Inside the slant top, the maker apparently intended originally to step out the lower tiers of drawers, but then changed course. As a result, the pine board under the drawer-and-cubbyhole unit intrudes into the cherry of the writing surface, and the slots in the side boards that receive the rails between the drawers extend too far forward and have been filled in. The gilded ball finials, probably acquired from a turner or a gilder, are similar to those on a Connecticut chest-on-chest (Downs 1952, no. 179), though that type of ornament is normally found only on English or New York tall clock cases (*DEF* 2, pl. IV, fig. 41, facing p. 114).

PROVENANCE: Ex coll.: H. Eugene Bolles, Boston. According to a tradition in the family of the previous owner, the desk and bookcase originally belonged to "Lord" Timothy Dexter of Newburyport, Massachusetts. Dexter (1747–1806) moved to Newburyport in 1769 and there set up as a leather dresser. He married a woman of means the following year, which would have enabled him to purchase this secretary of somewhat pretentious design. In 1791, when he suddenly became rich through currency speculation, he dubbed himself "Lord" Timothy Dexter and adopted the grand and eccentric manner of living for which he is remembered. Mrs. Hattie Putnam Campbell, of Hudson, New Hampshire, gave the following account (letters to Bolles, April 1904, MMA files): The desk was purchased in Newburyport from Timothy Dexter by her great-grandmother Edna Hopkinson Saunders, who, upon her marriage to Thomas Andrews, took the desk to Hudson, New Hampshire. On Andrews's death, in 1847, Mrs. Andrews gave the desk to John M. Saunders of Nashua, New Hampshire, from whom it passed to his sister Edna H.S. Putnam of Hudson (Mrs. Campbell's mother). After Mrs. Putnam's death the desk was sold for $51 in Nashua (3/19/1898) by auctioneer H.F. Dane to Lee L. Powers, a Boston dealer. The broadside announcing the auction of the desk as "once the property of 'Lord' Timothy Dexter" is in the MMA collection. Powers sold the desk to Bolles in 1904.

CONSTRUCTION: On the bookcase unit: The bonnet is enclosed at the back. A single horizontal backboard extends to the bottom of the cornice, below which are three vertical backboards. The bottom board is slotted into the front and side boards about an inch above their juncture with the desk. The outer edges of the double-pegged door frames are molded. The fielded door panels are flat in back. Inside, behind the doors' arched tops, are concave, twelve-ribbed shells above a row of

181 See also pp. 356, 358

ten cubbyholes whose dividers, like those of cat. no. 181, are scalloped. Except for a row of drawer openings at the bottom, the balance of the interior is subdivided into square side spaces flanking a broad center that contains an adjustable shelf. The interior partitions are of pine stained to match the cherry wood of the shells. On the desk unit: The left side is two boards; the right side, three. The bottom is two boards: a front one of cherry that continues as the front skirt molding; a rear, wider one of pine. The back is two vertical boards whose beveled edges are slotted into the top and sides. Behind the hinged slant top is a plain interior having three stacks of blocked-in drawers alternating with two sets of paired cubbyholes over a plain drawer. On the drawers, the sides, their top edges beaded, are lap-joined to the front and backboards. Below the writing surface, the rails are attached with exposed dovetails. On the large drawers, the fronts are contoured inside and out; the projecting blocking is applied; the sides have rounded top edges; the grain of the bottom boards runs lengthwise. The feet, their side brackets secured with roseheads, continue as square stiles into the bottom boards.

CONDITION: The secretary has a glowing red patina. According to Bolles's notes (MMA files), "The secretary was restored after I bought it. The cabinet work was good, and . . . only minor repairs and restoration were required." The ball finials retain the original gilding. The pointed top spire of the central fin-

ial and the tops of the scroll pediment cornice flanking it are restorations; the tops of the boards behind are missing. (A photograph, MMA files, of the piece when auctioned in 1898 shows a board nailed across the top of the truncated pediment just above the ball of the central finial.) There are patches in the bottom of the pediment board and at the top of the projecting blocking of the second large drawer. On the back of the right door panel is a rough-hewn rectangular cutout. The molded front of the right loper is new, as are the scalloped tops of the cubbyholes and two of the knee brackets. The runners of the large drawers, the drawer slides, and half the backboards of the desk unit are replaced. The legs have been reset.

INSCRIPTIONS: Crudely incised, on backboard behind bonnet top, large letters (19th-century): *M* and *S* (a reference to John M. Saunders?). In chalk, on bookcase backboard: *Photo* (for 1898 auction?).

DIMENSIONS: H.: overall, 86⅝ (220.), writing surface, 31¾ (80.6); W.: upper case, 40 (101.6), lower case, 42 (106.7), feet, 44½ (113.); D.: upper case, 12¼ (31.1), lower case, 22⅛ (56.2), feet, 23¾ (60.3).

WOODS: Primary: cherry. Secondary: cherry (bottom of bookcase unit, front board of desk bottom); white pine (all else).

REFERENCES: Lockwood 1, fig. 265. Dyer, fig. 6. Miller 1, no. 903.

Gift of Mrs. Russell Sage, 1909　　　　　　　　(10.125.82)

183. Desk and Bookcase

Boston, 1765–90

IN EIGHTEENTH-CENTURY Boston the secretary desk held pride of place. Perhaps a symbol of the fusion of commerce and culture, it was the most costly and important piece of household furniture. Cat. no. 183 is the only known instance where the bombé and block-front shapes are used together. An unusually monumental and ornate example, it combines features of the earlier and later styles of the form. The desk part bears comparison with that of some half-dozen other Boston bombé secretaries with straight-sided drawers, amphitheaterlike interiors, and bracket feet, a style of desk made during the seventeen-fifties and sixties. One documented example, at the Department of State, was signed by Benjamin Frothingham in 1753 (Vincent, fig. 97). Another, the work of James McMillian, who died in 1769 (ibid., fig. 101, incorrectly, with claws), has ogee-bracket feet with leaf carving that looks to have been executed by the same artisan who worked on the feet of cat. no. 183. While no other leaf-carved bracket feet are known, similar carving appears on the claw feet of the George Bright secretary at the Boston MFA (Randall 1965, fig. 64D), a secretary that also shares with cat. no. 183 an unusual feature: three secret drawers in a well below a removable prospect-door unit.

182　See also pp. 357, 363

Whereas the design of the bottom part of cat. no. 183 looks backward stylistically, that of the upper part is typical of a later type of Boston secretary. The doors, instead of having the round-arched tops and fielded wooden panels common in the seventeen-fifties (e.g., Vincent, fig. 97), form scalloped frames, originally with mirror-glass panels, flanked by fluted pilasters with carved Corinthian capitals. A scroll pediment was common on early Boston secretaries, but on later ones a flat, broken pediment (e.g., Warren, no. 134) was occasionally employed. That on cat. no. 183, the sides of the tympanum filled with solid wood triangles, is duplicated on a desk and bookcase dated 1771 and thought to have descended from the same William Greenleaf (Vincent, pp. 186, 190; figs. 132, 133) who was the known owner of cat. no. 183. Another, at the Maryland Historical Society (Gregory R. Weidman, *Furniture in Maryland, 1740–1940*, Baltimore, Maryland Historical Society, 1984, no. 24), is missing a pediment that was probably similar to that of cat. no. 183, for the two secretaries are otherwise remarkably alike. The chest-on-chest that Charles Apthorp imported to Boston before 1758 (Vincent, fig. 102) exhibits a flat pediment with carved cornice moldings and a bombé drawer section with carved corners. These features also appear on the MMA secretary, demonstrating that its Boston maker adhered unusually closely to imported English fashion.

PROVENANCE: Ex coll.: George S. Palmer, New London, Connecticut. A tradition in the Pope family, printed on the back of 1880 photographs (see Condition), has it that the secretary was purchased in London between 1750 and 1760 for £100 by William Greenleaf (1724/25–1803), High Sheriff of Suffolk County, Massachusetts. A London origin is belied by the desk's unmistakable Boston features, but Greenleaf's ownership is documented in extensive family correspondence dating as far back as 1856 (MMA files). He is said to have lent it to the Vassall (later Longfellow) House in Cambridge in 1776, when the house was Washington's headquarters. Thereafter, the secretary descended from Greenleaf to his daughter Elizabeth Greenleaf Pope (1749–1841); to her son Thomas Pope (1789–1872); to his son William Greenleaf Eliot Pope. In 1881, it was purchased and shipped to St. Louis, Missouri, by R. J. Lackland, whose widow bequeathed it in 1892 to the Reverend Edward R. Pope of Rochester, Minnesota. In 1893, it was exhibited as "Washington's desk" on the second floor of the Massachusetts Building at the World's Columbian Exposition in Chicago. That same year it was purchased by Palmer for $500 and shipped to Edwin Simons & Company in Hartford, Connecticut. The claim that the desk has no proven family history (Vincent, p. 186, n. 29) seems thus without foundation.

CONSTRUCTION: On the bookcase unit: The broken pediment, its moldings screwed to the solid tympanum boards, is flat in back. A complete entablature is formed by the carved architrave and cornice moldings, the latter built up with three separate boards around a rectangular core. Fluted pilasters with separate capitals and bases are nailed to the doors. The doors have egg-and-dart-carved scalloped inner edges. In the interior,

a central section containing two adjustable shelves is surrounded on three sides by identical cubbyholes—nine across the top and four tiers of pairs on each side—with a row of four plain drawers on the bottom. The shelves and cubbyhole dividers have beaded mahogany fronts. Six horizontal boards form the back of the case. The entire unit stands on narrow strips glued under the bottom board at front and sides. On the desk unit: Each side is in two parts: a single solid plank, its inner surface roughly chiseled (cf. Vincent, fig. 120) to conform to the outer bombé shape, and behind it a thick strip with a straight inner edge to which the three horizontal backboards are nailed. The hinged slant top has thick figured veneers on both surfaces. On the outer surface, at each end, are crossbanded veneers. The mahogany lopers have thick applied fronts. Centered in the amphi-

183 See also pp. 360, 364

theaterlike interior is a solid block-and-shell prospect door flanked by fixed pilasters; behind the door is a cubbyhole with a scalloped pencil drawer above and a blocked-in drawer below. When the pencil drawer is removed, its supporting shelf slides forward to expose a fingerhole to a wooden spring that releases the entire unit. A rectangular well leading to three small drawers is then revealed, and the document slots behind the pilasters become accessible from the rear. The desk's beaded rails, backed with narrow boards, are dovetailed into the sides. There are no dust boards. On the drawers, the fronts are blocked inside and out; the thin side boards have double-beaded tops; the bottom boards are laid crosswise. A shelf behind the top drawer houses the three small drawers that are accessible only through the well below the prospect-door unit. The bracket feet, all similarly carved, are affixed to the skirt molding and to boards that frame the underside of the two-piece bottom.

CONDITION: The secretary, now a dark wine red in color, was restored and refinished for Palmer by Simons & Company of Hartford (see Provenance). It has been entirely reassembled. The interior of the bookcase unit has been stained and varnished. All the drawers have been sanded inside and out. The crown molding of the cornice on the left side and the beaded edge on the right door are replacements. There are breaks at the ankles on all four feet; the left front foot has a patch near the ankle; and the back brackets of the rear feet are replaced. On the doors, the capitals over the pilasters are unlike the Corinthian capitals normally employed on Boston secretaries (e.g., Vincent, fig. 132) and look to be early nineteenth-century replacements carved in the neoclassic fashion. The fielded wood panels were added in about 1900 on the recommendation of the Providence collector Charles V. Pendleton, who wrote Palmer (9/17/1898 letter, MMA files): "I should put mahogany panels in your bookcase doors without hesitation. . . . Your book-case is a very interesting piece and I spent much time examining it, & am willing to stake my reputation as an antique crank that the doors originally had moulded panels." Pendleton's conviction notwithstanding, cat. no. 183 was almost certainly originally made with looking-glass door panels in the manner of a number of equally elaborate Boston secretaries (Randall 1965, no. 64; Vincent, fig. 132). Stereoscopic photographs from 1880 (MMA files) show the piece with looking-glass panels in place. The Reverend E. R. Pope wrote to Palmer immediately after having sold the desk to him. In his letters (1893–94, MMA files), he said: "As far as I know these mirrors were in the secretary when it was made" and "I am quite confident that the glasses were always in the doors. No one has any other recollection or tradition about it." The secretary, when first acquired by the MMA, was displayed with a bust of Shakespeare in the pediment. The two objects were unrelated.

INSCRIPTIONS: In chalk, on bookcase-unit bottom board: *Boston* and *H. Rechards*, the latter superimposed on the former; on desk-unit bottom board: *H. Rechards*; on backboards of some of the small drawers: random numbers. Pasted on backboards of both units, printed Palmer Bros. Co. shipping labels.

DIMENSIONS: H.: overall, 93½ (237.5), writing surface, 30⅜ (77.2); W.: upper case, 40 (101.6), lower case, 45⅝ (115.9), feet, 44¾ (113.7); D.: upper case, 12⅛ (30.8), lower case, 24⅝ (62.6), feet, 24¼ (61.6).

WOODS: Primary: mahogany; mahogany veneer. Secondary: white pine.

REFERENCES: MMA 1909, 2, no. 166. Lockwood 1, fig. 280. Miller 1, nos. 898, 899. Halsey and Cornelius, fig. 61. Downs 1949, no. 1. Nutting 1, fig. 687 (ill. open and with bust of Shakespeare). Aronson, fig. 1051.

John Stewart Kennedy Fund, 1918   (18.110.3)

184. Desk and Bookcase

Newport, 1760–90

THIS IS ONE OF TEN known Newport desks and bookcases with block-and-shell treatment in both upper and lower sections. Though none are signed or dated, three are generally believed to have been made for the brothers Joseph, John, and Nicholas Brown (a fourth, for Moses Brown, was apparently long ago destroyed by fire). Two others have histories of ownership in the Potter family of Kingston, Rhode Island. On the MMA secretary the Z H cut into the right-hand loper may refer to Zephaniah Heath, married in Newport in 1764, or to Zephaniah Hathaway, who was listed in the 1774 state census—the only persons with those initials then recorded in Newport.

On the basis of details of design and construction the secretaries can be said to have been produced by at least two separate shops and can be divided into two groups, the first group consisting of four desks that include the Brown family pieces—Joseph's, at RIHS (Ott 1965, no. 67); John's, at Yale (Cooper 1973, pp. 338–339, pl. II); and Nicholas's, still with the Brown family (Isham 1927, fig. 6). The distinguishing characteristics of the four are: open pediments, pediment moldings terminating in rosettes, urn-and-corkscrew finials, large C-scrolls centered in the shells, and unusually tall tripartite bookcase units having movable shelves in an interior divided vertically by two fixed partitions. Joseph Brown's secretary is unique in the group not only in having a fourth drawer, with shell carving, but also thumbnail-molded drawer edges and shells confined within circles, both features found in early Rhode Island case furniture. The fourth secretary of the group (Hipkiss, no. 19), though not as tall as the Brown family examples, looks for the most part to be by the same hand. John Goddard has been suggested as the maker on the basis of a letter he wrote to Nicholas Brown in 1766 regarding a "desk and Bookcase" (Cooper 1973, p. 334).

The second group, comprising six secretaries, is the product of a different hand or hands. The group characteristics are: broken-scroll pediments with completely enclosed bonnet tops, cornice moldings that turn at a right angle into the pediment opening, final urns with fluted petals, and tripartite upper sections having fixed shelves.

184 See also pp. 359, 363, 365

The exterior shells are not unlike those on two bureau tables, one labeled by Edmund Townsend (Hipkiss, no. 38), the other once owned by Daniel Goddard (Sack 2, pp. 506–507). The MMA secretary is the first of three in the second group that are identical except for minor differences in the treatment of their bookcase interiors (see Construction). That of the second, at Bayou Bend (Warren, no. 135), differs only in having arched cubbyholes at the top and drawers at the bottom, in the Massachusetts manner; that of the third, at Winterthur (Downs 1952, no. 232), is of cedar, and the scallops of its vertical dividers have a different profile and are movable. The three remaining secretaries of the group have interiors similar to that of the Winterthur desk, but their bonnets and feet are different: one, in the Pendleton Collection (Lockwood 1, fig. 274), has an open pediment reminiscent of the Brown family pieces, somewhat flat blocking in the bonnet, and an additional skirt molding between the feet; the other two are Potter family secretaries, one at the Boston MFA (Randall 1965, no. 62), one at RISD (Carpenter, no. 43). On the Potter pieces, the flat panels in the bonnet area are entirely without blocking, the finial urns have concave sides, the skirts have the additional molding, and the desks look to be the work of one shop. Whether that was the shop of John Goddard, as claimed for the RISD desk by Goddard's son in 1813 (ibid.), remains to be proved. What is certain is that not one of the ten secretary desks displays any of the consistent personal characteristics of the work of John Townsend, the best documented of all Newport cabinetmakers.

PROVENANCE: Ex coll.: Richard A. Canfield, New York City. Canfield was an early collector (Stillinger, pp. 114–117). The secretary was purchased by the MMA from Luke Vincent Lockwood as executor of the Canfield estate.

CONSTRUCTION: On the bookcase unit: The urns of the three-part finials are fluted, the central one cut away at its juncture with the facing board, the fluting on the side ones not completed in back. The top third of the entirely enclosed bonnet is cut away at a forty-five-degree angle at the back, undoubtedly to accommodate the cornice of the room for which the secretary was intended. The two shaped and blocked panels within the pediment area are applied, as are the sides and the framing moldings of the circular openings above them. The central door of the unit is hinged to the door on the left. The recessed block-and-shell on the central door is cut from a single board with a plain flat back; on the flanking doors, the projecting blocks and shells, two separate pieces, are applied. When closed and locked, the three doors are secured inside to two thick mahogany vertical partitions that subdivide the interior space. The doors open to reveal between the partitions a symmetrical, fixed arrangement of cubbyholes—four tiers in the middle and five tiers on the sides—whose thin mahogany vertical dividers are scalloped. The back of the unit is made up of three vertical boards. On the desk unit: The recessed middle shell of the hinged slant top is cut from the solid; the flanking projecting shells and blockings are separate applied pieces. Behind the

slant top, blocked-out drawers beneath triple cubbyholes topped by pencil drawers alternate with the blocked-in shell-carved prospect door and drawers at either end. Behind the prospect door, which is backed with a thin mahogany board, are three graduated, recessed-blocked drawers. In the writing surface, a well with a sliding cover opens into the uppermost of the large drawers. There are no dust boards. Between the drawers, beaded rails reinforced behind with chestnut strips are dovetailed to the desk's sides; the sides have applied beading at the drawer openings. On the drawers, the solid fronts are blocked inside and out, the interior central part built up with an applied board; the top drawer's upper corners are cut out to receive the lopers; the bottom drawer slides on thick strips nailed to the two boards of the desk bottom. The back of the unit consists of three horizontal boards. Each bracket foot is reinforced with two horizontal glue blocks abutting a central, vertical one.

CONDITION: The exterior of the secretary, a slightly faded brown in color, now has a highly polished modern finish; the interior retains the original reddish color and finish. The rounded side edges of the slant top have been replaced. The top of the left front corner of the cornice, the left edge of the large middle drawer, the lower back edge of the right side, and the tip of the blocking on the left front foot are patched. The vertical backboards of the bookcase unit have been reset; the top board of the desk back is replaced. The large drawers have new runners. The brasses on the large drawers are old but not original.

INSCRIPTIONS: Incised, on outer edge of right-hand loper: Z H; on top edge: A M. In ink, on a paper tab on upper right bookcase cubbyhole: P, possibly the shelf mark of the first owner. In pencil, on desk's top board: Moved by / Thos Kernant [?] June 6—1906; in white chalk: an illegible inscription. In pencil, on desk's uppermost backboard: Upper Part; marks and labels referring to the MMA Hudson–Fulton Celebration in 1909.

DIMENSIONS: H.: overall, 99⅛ (251.8), writing surface, 31½ (80.); W.: upper case, 39⅜ (100.), lower case, 41⅝ (105.7), feet, 44⅛ (112.1); D.: upper case, 12¼ (31.1), lower case, 23¾ (60.3), feet, 25¾ (65.4).

WOODS: Primary: mahogany. Secondary: mahogany (sides and back of small drawers); chestnut (backboards, rail reinforcements, bottom boards of desk unit); white pine (bottoms of large drawers); yellow pine (bottom board of bookcase unit); tulip poplar (top board of desk unit, sides of large drawers); cedar (bottoms of small drawers).

REFERENCES: MMA 1909, 2, no. 170. Lockwood 1, p. 246 (attributed to John Goddard); fig. 275. Malcolm A. Norton, "Three Block-Front Secretaries," Antiques 11 (March 1927), pp. 192–194; fig. 1. The Antiquarian 8 (April 1927), p. 33 (ill.). Lee 2, p. 183 (measured drawings); p. 184 (ill.). Ormsbee, p. 49; pl. XVIII (attributed to John Goddard). Salomonsky, pl. 87 (measured drawings). Miller 1, no. 896. Halsey and Cornelius, pl. 59. Downs 1949, no. 3. Davidson 1967, fig. 319.

Rogers Fund, 1915   (15.21.2)

185. Desk and Bookcase

Philadelphia, 1765–90

ON THIS SECRETARY DESK, the continuous cornice with fretwork frieze surmounted by a central bust finial in a broken-scroll pediment, the square-paneled bookcase doors, and the highly figured mahogany used throughout the piece, even in the severely plain desk interior, are characteristics of the Chippendale form as interpreted in Philadelphia.

The secretary nevertheless has certain unusual features: fretwork carving on the bookcase door frames, found elsewhere only on the Cadwalader family secretary (Hornor 1935, pl. 193), and the addition of a separate plinth unit below the bookcase unit, the latter an anomaly shared with a secretary having the same fret design (*Antiques* 6 [October 1924], p. 179). Chippendale's *Director* illustrates prototypes for the handling of the separate plinth (pl. LXXX, 1754 edition; pl. CIX, 1762 edition), while Ince and Mayhew's *Universal System* of 1762 provides the exact source for the fretwork design (pl. XL). The most unusual feature, and one apparently unique to the MMA secretary, is the presence of doors in front of sliding trays on the desk unit, as illustrated in plate CVII of the *Director* (1762 edition).

At least one of the hands that worked on cat. no. 185 (the one particularly identifiable in the fashioning of the pediment top) can be detected in a number of other Philadelphia case pieces, pointing to a common origin. The cornice moldings and patterns of applied fretwork on a high chest at the Smithsonian (Comstock, no. 313) and on a chest-on-chest at Philadelphia (PMA 1976, no. 76) are the same as those on the MMA secretary. Identical moldings and fretwork and, in addition, similar swirl-carved terminals are found on three other case pieces: a secretary in Washington (Smith 1970, p. 771, fig. 7) and two whose pediments are illustrated in Hornor (1935, pls. 120, 126). Though the pediment of the MMA secretary does not now stand as tall as they and lacks the rococo leafage that appears on the solid board in their tympanum area, it displays so many elements similar to theirs that its unrestored top (see Condition) may originally have been identical. The technique used in modeling the pediment bust has caused it to be associated with six other finely wrought portrait busts found on Philadelphia furniture (Smith 1971, p. 903), including that on the Department of State desk and bookcase already related to the MMA example.

PROVENANCE: Ex coll.: George S. Palmer, New London, Connecticut. The desk was sold to the MMA by Palmer, who had bought it in March 1898 from William Meggat, a dealer in Wethersfield, Connecticut. The transaction has been related by

185 See also pp. 357, 363

Henry Erving, another Connecticut collector (Isham 1934, pp. 63–64), who described the desk: ". . . that superb cabinet-top scrutoire of absolutely Chippendale features, with beautiful feet and a carved bust for a center finial. Meggat was very anxious to have me buy it . . . I could have bought the whole thing, and easily, for $75 and Meggat would have been greatly pleased to have me do so, but I knew that I could never afford to have it repaired as it properly should be. I think Palmer told me subsequently that he had Patrick Stevens of Robbins do the work and it cost about $600 [see Inscriptions]. What he paid for the piece originally, I never knew, or if he did tell me, I have utterly forgotten—but it was a very wonderful piece." Meggat, in writing Palmer about the secretary (3/21/1898 letter, MMA files), claimed that "it was found in New Jersey, back from Camden near Philadelphia was 100 year in that one Family."

CONSTRUCTION: The secretary is in four parts. The framing members of the first part—the unit formed by the scroll pediment, cornice, and fretwork—are dovetailed together. The cornice is made up of three mahogany moldings around a pine core. The applied fretwork has a vertical seam at center front. The female portrait bust, carved from the solid, is doweled into the upper of two separate plinths (see Condition). The inner edges of the side boards are beveled to overlap the sides of the bookcase section below. On the bookcase unit (the second part), the fretwork on the door frames is carved from the solid. In the bookcase interior, the side boards, their front edges molded with a small quarter round, have ten slots cut into them for movable shelves. The bookcase has four horizontal backboards. The dovetailed boards of the plinth unit (the third part) have fretwork carved from the solid; the plinth is screwed to both the bookcase section above and the desk unit below. On the desk unit (the fourth part), the right side consists of two boards. The hinged slant top is veneered on both sides; the veneers forming its battenlike ends are laid in the same direction. Beaded edges are applied on all sides. In the unadorned interior, the mahogany fronts of the small drawers are veneered with figured mahogany; the central prospect-door unit can be pulled out to provide access to three cedar boxes stacked directly behind. There are dust boards beneath the large drawer. The doors below are veneered on both sides with figured mahogany. Steel hinges and rule joints hold the opened doors at right angles to support three trays that slide out on slots cut into the doors' inner surfaces. The ogee-bracket feet are built up with large, horizontal pine glue blocks.

CONDITION: The secretary, a reddish brown color under a thick varnish, has been extensively restored. In 1898, Robbins Brothers charged Palmer for 994 hours of labor, including "making trays & trimming" (see Inscriptions). The trays are behind the lower doors; the trimming probably included the applied carving on the lower doors and the fretwork on the upper doors. The charge for making the brass handles for the large drawer was listed separately. The extent of the repairing and scraping done was not specified, but the appearance of this desk and bookcase looks to have been transformed in a number of ways. The scroll pediment has been reduced in height, and the finial bust is mounted on two modern plinth blocks rather than on a single block above an upward continuation of the tympanum board. The doors of the bookcase unit have been reworked. The fielded panels are new, replacing either plain flat wooden panels (e.g., Hummel 1976, fig. 86) or, more likely, glazing bars and glass (e.g., Smith 1970, fig. 7), as suggested by

pegs visible in the framing members. The fretwork on the framing members, carved from the solid rather than applied, in the usual manner, may have been added. The interior shelves are new. The doors of the desk section may be original, if reveneered, since the hinges are old and there is no evidence that drawers were once present and replaced later by trays. The serpentine molding and leaf carving applied to the doors, not characteristic of eighteenth-century work, must be new. An applied molding appears to have been inserted at one time in a horizontal slot cut into the side boards at the level of the writing surface and now filled in. The molding below the large drawer is new, as are the scalloped boards above the cubbyholes in the interior writing area. The prospect door has been veneered, and the removable unit behind it—a cubbyhole with scalloped pencil drawer above and recessed-blocked drawer below—looks to be modern. The single large drawer, its interior fitted with partitions, has been entirely rebuilt. The bottom inch-and-a-half of the feet has been replaced.

INSCRIPTIONS: In pencil, inside the back of desk unit: an illegible inscription. Pasted, on bottom of large drawer, a printed paper receipt from Robbins Brothers, Makers and Dealers in Modern and Antique Furniture, 209 Main Street, Hartford, Connecticut, made out (December 29, 1898) to Mr. George S. Palmer:

To 994 hours labour rep[air]ing scraping & making trays & trimming Ant Mahogany Secretary & bookcase	40cs	397.60
Stock. making brass handles engraving & lacquiring same 2 locks 3 keys 1 pr butts &c		15.40
finishing same		19.00
2 Crates & packing		3.00
		435.00
By discount in 994 hours @5cts	49.70	385.30

A red pencil inscription (20th-century?) on bottom of small lower left interior desk drawer: *Thos D B.*

DIMENSIONS: H.: overall, 96⅝ (*245.4*), writing surface, 29½ (*74.9*); W.: upper case, 35⅝ (*90.5*), lower case, 37½ (*95.3*), feet, 40½ (*102.9*); D.: upper case, 12⅛ (*30.8*), lower case, 23⅜ (*59.4*), feet, 24¾ (*62.9*).

WOODS: Primary: mahogany. Secondary: yellow pine (top and bottom boards of upper and lower cases); red cedar (interior-drawer sides and backs); white oak (backboards of pediment and plinth); tulip poplar (prospect-door unit); northern white cedar (backboards of upper and lower cases).

REFERENCES: Halsey, pp. 266–267; fig. 8. Lockwood 1, fig. 283. Isham 1934, pp. 62–64 (quotes Henry Erving). Nutting 1, no. 686. Davidson 1970, pp. 229–230; fig. 7. Smith 1971, p. 903 (finial bust discussed and ill.). Richard H. Saunders, "Collecting American decorative arts in New England, Part II: 1876–1910," *Antiques* 110 (October 1976), pl. III; pp. 756, 759.

Rogers Fund, 1918   (18.110.1)

186. Desk and Bookcase

New York, eastern Long Island, 1786

THOUGH THIS DESK AND BOOKCASE is neatly made and has crisp and fine moldings, its overall proportions and detailing proclaim it to be the product of an ambitious rural craftsman. The broad, massive lower section with but three large drawers stands on delicate feet that seem too small, and the bookcase unit, as if truncated to fit a low-ceilinged house, is disproportionately squat. The star inlays and the stepped interior drawers suggest a Massachusetts influence, but the large cavetto-molded cornice, canted corners, claw feet, and, on the rear feet, pointed pads raised on high disks are variants of details sometimes found on furniture from New York City or Long Island. A flat-top maple high chest (*Antiques* 113 [February 1978], p. 335) has identical brasses, rear feet, and canted and fluted corner posts, as well as a similar cornice. Apparently by the maker of cat. no. 186, the chest was purchased from a house sale in New York state (Elizabeth R. Daniel, 9/4/78 letter, MMA files). The origin suggested for cat. no. 186 by its history in eastern Long Island—which is halfway between New York and Boston—would explain the desk's stylistic mix.

PROVENANCE: In an "Oral History of the Desk—Written Out for the First Time" by Harriet A. Bedell in September 1933 (a framed, typed copy was formerly affixed behind the bookcase doors), the desk is recorded as having been made for Goldsmith Davis of Selden, Long Island, and the walnut tree from which it was made cut down in 1783 and sawed into planks at Patchogue. Three years later the planks were purportedly shipped to New York City to be made into the desk. The date is confirmed by the inlaid inscription (q.v.), but the place of manufacture is not borne out by the desk's design. The presumed line of descent from Goldsmith Davis is to his daughter Sophira Davis (Mrs. Charles Floyd); to her cousin Bryant Goldsmith Norton; to his daughter Mary Esther Norton (Mrs. Stephen Bedell); to her daughters Harriet A. and Jeannette N. Bedell.

CONSTRUCTION: On the bookcase unit: The cornice is built up of two molded boards with dentil blocks glued on below. Six vertical tongue and groove boards form the back. The canted corner posts, fluted and terminating in lamb's-tongues, are glued to the front edges of the side boards. On the doors, the juncture is covered by a molding applied to the door on the right; the flat panels are round-arched inside and out. The interior space extends both above and below the doors, subdivided by three fixed shelves. The narrow top shelf, just below the cornice level, has a plain central divider. Scalloped dividers separate the second shelf into four equal sections; the third, into three; the bottom, into two. On the desk unit: The top is framed with a three-part molding whose concave bottom section conceals a shallow drawer the width of the desk and accessible only from the rear. The sides of the drawer are slotted into the front board and half-lapped to the back. Below the drawer are four vertical tongue and groove backboards. The hinged slant top

186 See also p. 357

opens to reveal a central prospect door flanked by pairs of cubbyholes capped by scalloped pencil drawers. Below each cubbyhole is a double tier of plain drawers. At the bottom is a stepped row of three large drawers. The wide prospect door has an applied wooden knob centered in an eight-point inlaid lightwood star. Behind the door, a wider version of one of the cubbyhole units is flanked by fluted-front sliding document slots. The slots' side boards have scalloped top edges. Each desk-unit side is two pieces of wood slotted to receive the rails and the board behind the writing surface, the latter secured on each side by two large recessed and plugged roseheads. The molded fronts of the lopers are applied. There are no dust boards. Square wooden pegs attach the solid skirt molding to the bottom board. The scalloped brackets are double tenoned to the legs and nailed to the bottom board.

CONDITION: The desk and bookcase retains its original thin finish, now a mellow nut brown in color. On the bookcase unit, the interior has beeen painted red (19th century); the front of the lower shelf was cut away to accommodate the framed history formerly screwed inside the doors. The feet have holes for casters. Part of the pad of the left rear foot has been replaced. The iron catches for the left-hand door and the locks for the prospect door and the bottom drawer are missing.

INSCRIPTIONS: Inlaid, in slant-top desk lid: *GD* and *1786*. In chalk, across inside back of each drawer: an arc-shaped mark; on bottom of pencil drawer second from left: an illegible inscription. Pasted in pencil drawer second from right, an unidentified newspaper clipping marked "Jan 6 '06," on the subject of a gravestone at West Patchogue, Long Island.

DIMENSIONS: H.: overall, 79¾ (*202.6*), writing surface, 30 (*76.2*); W.: upper case, 39⅞ (*101.3*), lower case, 42 (*106.7*), feet, 44 (*111.8*); D.: upper case, 12¾ (*32.4*), lower case, 23½ (*59.7*), feet, 25¼ (*64.1*).

WOODS: Primary: walnut. Secondary: walnut (front and sides of concealed drawer); maple (corner posts of bookcase unit); chestnut (sides of interior drawers); white pine (backboard of bottom drawer); yellow pine (all else).

REFERENCES: Downs 1944, p. 79 (ill.). *Antiques* 47 (January 1945), p. 50.

Gift of Jeannette N. Bedell, 1943   (43.150)

19 Clocks

The standard clock-type in eighteenth-century America was the tall clock, popularly referred to since the late nineteenth century as the grandfather clock. The case is the cabinetmaker's solution to the problem of housing the extraordinarily accurate long pendulum that was developed in England in the sixteen-sixties. The case's three-part design—bonnet, shaft, and pedestal, of clearly classical inspiration—is thoroughly practical. The bonnet encloses the clock movement and dial, protecting them from dust and dirt; the shaft has the width to accommodate the swing of the pendulum; and the shaft and pedestal together achieve the height necessary for the drop of the weights over an eight-day period. Still largely unidentifiable cabinetmakers created the cases, but had nothing to do with the actual mechanism; that was produced by clockmakers, who customarily signed their works. The first American tall-clock cases were made in about 1700, but few can be dated before the seventeen-twenties. The earliest at the Museum—one showing a strong William and Mary influence—houses a clock by Benjamin Bagnall, the best of the first-generation Boston makers. The collection, though richest in the block-fronted-shaft-door type from New England, contains most of the major regional kinds; examples of japanned Boston and early flat-top Philadelphia Queen Anne cases are the only serious omissions. The manufacture of smaller timepieces began toward the end of the late colonial period. At the Museum is one of the earliest wall clocks of a type invented by the Willards of Grafton and Roxbury, Massachusetts; also present is a signed example of the two-part shelf clock associated with David Williams of Newburyport. Lacking is any representation of the bracket clock, a type of shelf clock popular in England and occasionally made in colonial America.

187. Tall Clock

Boston, 1725–40
Movement by Benjamin Bagnall (1689–1773)

BENJAMIN BAGNALL was Boston's first important clockmaker. Born in England in 1689, he settled in Boston in 1713 (Nutting 3, p. 487), where, in 1717–18, he made a town clock for the New Brick Meeting-House; seventeen years later he was voted the sum of £10 to maintain it for one year. Benjamin junior and Samuel (see cat. no. 188) followed their father as clockmakers. Bagnall, who was also active in trade, became a prominent citizen of Boston. In 1737, the *New England Weekly Journal* reported the marriage of Benjamin junior, "eldest son of Mr. Benjamin Bagnall, of this Town, Merchant," and added that "the vast Concourse of People of all Perswations who came to see the Solemnity" had included the governor and members of the council. Years later, at Bagnall's death, the *Boston News-Letter* of 15 July 1773 described him as "watchmaker of this Town, aged 84 yrs., one of the people called Quakers. . . . honest and upright in his Dealings . . . and a good citizen; he acquired the Regard and Esteem of all who had the Pleasure of his Acquaintance" (Partridge, pp. 29–30).

Most of the cases housing Benjamin Bagnall's clocks have sarcophagus tops and are made of pine, either veneered with figured walnut or japanned. One of the latter, now stripped of its painted ornament, bears the engraved 1732 label of Thomas Johnston, japanner (Harvard Tercentenary, no. 257, pl. 46). The MMA clock, which is veneered, has a number of unusual features: arched moldings above the bonnet side lights, all moldings cut across the grain from thick slices of walnut, and pierced fretwork in the spandrels above the bonnet door—a feature found on another of Benjamin's clock cases (Fairbanks and Bates, p. 116). The ogee-molded sarcophagus top, a conjectural restoration, may be incorrect: the molded part is wider and the flat top narrower than those of known examples (ibid.). A sarcophagus top that consists of a large ovolo molding above a raised plinth (Palmer 1928, fig. 9) is more common on Boston clock cases. The latter type appears on a London clock case that otherwise closely parallels the MMA example, even to the fretwork in the spandrels above the bonnet door (Cescinsky and Webster, fig. 179).

The known clocks by Benjamin Bagnall have dials in the English manner: either the square type of about 1700 or the arched type of 1730–35 (ibid., figs. 56, 57). Cat. no. 187 is one of the latter group. Known Bagnall dials are all stylistically datable before 1740 (one is recorded [Lyon, p. 253] as having a case dated 1722), implying that by that time he had turned away from clockmaking to

187

pursue his mercantile interests. The Reverend Elisha Williams (1694–1755), who is said to have owned cat. no. 187 (see Provenance), was born in Massachusetts, graduated from Harvard College in 1711, and moved to central Connecticut by 1714. If this was indeed his clock, he probably acquired it between 1725 and 1739, when he was rector of Yale College.

PROVENANCE: Ex coll.: Walter Hosmer, Hartford; H. Eugene Bolles, Boston. As reported by Lyon (p. 253), "This clock has a well-authenticated history of having belonged to the Reverend Elisha Williams, President of Yale College from 1725 to 1739." According to Bolles's notes (MMA files), he purchased the clock from Hosmer in 1894.

CONSTRUCTION: On the bonnet: The flat cornice consists of a two-part core overlaid with two separate ogee moldings formed of thick, crossbanded veneers. The pierced-fret spandrels flanking the arch of the door are glued onto a fabric backing. The front colonettes are part of the door frame. At the rear are turned quarter columns. The horizontally veneered side boards are joined across the top at cornice height by two dovetailed battens. The tall side lights are arched. On the shaft: The door, a pine board with battens at top and bottom, is faced with four flitches of figured veneer that are framed by herringboned and crossbanded borders. The sides are faced with plain horizontal veneers. On the pedestal, the moldings are similar to those of the bonnet; the veneering, to that of the shaft door. The feet are cut out in scallops in front and in arches at the sides. On the clock: The brass dial has separate cast spandrels—masks in the corners and dolphins in the lunette. The chapter and seconds rings are silvered, as is the name and strike/silent boss in the lunette. The movement is an eight-day rack and snail striking clock with anchor-recoil escapement. The movement has five turned pillars and, except for the rough casting marks on the front plate, is finely finished.

CONDITION: The case, now dark brown in color, has a thick varnish finish, partly crazed. The finials and molded sarcophagus top above the flat cornice are replaced. According to Bolles's notes (MMA files), "Mr. Hosmer told me the pagoda design at the top of the clock was restoration. As I recall it, he said he and Dr. Lyon thought it should be done in that way." The pierced fretwork above the bonnet door has been patched; its yellow silk damask backing is a 1965 replacement. Walnut strips have been nailed to the inner edges of the shaft door, and the veneer is patched at the hinges. The feet, the bottom inch restored, have been re-veneered. The keyhole escutcheon on the door was copied from that on the case of a Samuel Bagnall clock (Sack 3, p. 641).

INSCRIPTIONS: Engraved in center of dial lunette: *Benjamⁿ / Bagnall / Boston*. A paper label (20th-century) pasted inside back of case printed: *Included in the collection of Antique Furniture transferred to Mr. H. E. Bolles, and Mr. Geo. S. Palmer. It is the original piece illustrated in "Colonial Furn[iture of] New England," by Dr. Lyons.* In pencil, on label: *Tall Clock made by Benjamin Bagnall.*

DIMENSIONS: H.: cornice, 87 (*221.*); W.: cornice, 20⅝ (*52.4*), shaft, 12½ (*31.8*), pedestal, 16⅜ (*41.6*), feet, 18½ (*47.*); D.: cornice, 11⅜ (*28.9*), shaft, 7 (*17.8*), pedestal, 9⅛ (*23.2*), feet, 10¼ (*26.*); Dial, less lunette: 12 × 12 (*30.5 × 30.5*).

WOODS: Primary: walnut, walnut veneer. Secondary: white pine.

REFERENCES: Lyon, p. 253; fig. 111. Moore 1911, p. 149; fig. 89. Nutting 1924, fig. 90. Nutting 2, no. 3243. Palmer 1928, fig. 8. Partridge, pp. 26–31 (Benjamin Bagnall biography); p. 27 (ill.).

Gift of Mrs. Russell Sage, 1909   (10.125.388)

188. Tall Clock

Boston, 1740–60
Movement by Samuel Bagnall (active 1740–60)

THIS CLOCK BEARS the applied, engraved nameplate of Samuel Bagnall of Boston on a dial that is a particularly fine example of a type made in England beginning about 1730 (Cescinsky and Webster, fig. 57). Practically nothing is known about Samuel, son of Benjamin Bagnall (see cat. no. 187), save that he was born in 1715, sometime after his brother Benjamin, Jr. He could not have been a clockmaker in his own right much before 1740.

Clocks by Samuel Bagnall are rare. One is in a case comparable to that of cat. no. 187 (Sack 3, p. 641), and references exist to others: in Lyon (p. 254), those belonging to Mrs. W. R. Dupee and to Ebenezer Gay; in Partridge (p. 30), those in the G. Winthrop Brown and the Arthur R. Robertson collections. The clock case of cat. no. 188, with its disproportionately small bonnet and cramped arched cornice, is a modest housing for such a well-executed dial. On the shaft, the flat-top door with applied ovolo-molded edge and the mitered frame of the opening around it are characteristic of clock cases from Pennsylvania and New Jersey. Because the tops of the side boards on which the seat board rests have been restored, there is no way of telling if the clock and the case have always been together or were assembled sometime after their individual manufacture.

PROVENANCE: Ex coll.: George S. Palmer, New London, Connecticut.

CONSTRUCTION: On the bonnet: The top is a flat board spanning the side boards behind the arched front. The front colonettes are attached to the hinged door; the quarter columns at the rear are nailed to extensions of the side boards. Above the colonettes, the horizontal front and side boards are mitered together. On the shaft: The thick front boards, mitered around the door opening, lap over the side boards and are nailed to them; inside are long, rectangular glue blocks, one to each side. The side boards, with interior cutouts to accommodate the swing of the pendulum, continue to the base. On the pedestal, the thick vertical front and side boards are pieced. On the clock:

188

The brass dial has separate cast spandrels, silvered nameplate, and silvered chapter, seconds, and strike /silent rings. The dial is cut out to receive the compass star in the lunette and to reveal the calendar wheel above the numeral VI. The movement is a finely finished eight-day rack and snail striking clock with anchor-recoil escapement.

CONDITION: The case has been stripped and refinished and now has a walnut brown color. The basic case is original (the interior is in untouched condition), but certain parts have been reworked or replaced. The applied molding that frames the shaft door is new, as is the keyhole escutcheon; the unusually small cove moldings above and below the shaft and on the pedestal base look reworked. There may originally have been a molded foot. The bun feet on the clock when it was acquired by the MMA were old replacements and have been removed.

INSCRIPTIONS: Engraved on nameplate on dial: *Sam¹ Bagnall / Boston*. Pasted on backboard: a fragment of a Palmer Bros. Co. shipping label.

DIMENSIONS: H.: overall, 84⅜ (*214.3*); W.: cornice, 17¼ (*43.8*), shaft, 11⅝ (*29.5*), pedestal, 14⅛ (*35.9*), base, 15 (*38.1*); D.: cornice, 10¼ (*26.*), shaft, 7⅝ (*19.4*), pedestal, 8⅞ (*22.5*), base, 9½ (*24.1*); Dial, less lunette: 12 × 12 (*30.5 × 30.5*).

WOODS: Primary: walnut. Secondary: white pine.

REFERENCES: Nutting 1924, no. 79. Palmer 1928, fig. 11. Nutting 2, fig. 3242. Partridge, p. 31 (ill.). Distin and Bishop, fig. 44.

John Stewart Kennedy Fund, 1918   (18.110.63)

189. Dwarf Tall Clock

Newport, 1755–65
Movement by Thomas Claggett
(about 1730–1797)

THOMAS CLAGGETT, son of William (see cat. no. 190), was active as a clockmaker in Newport between about 1752 and 1776. After the Revolution he removed to Providence and started a school "to teach the use of the Back Sword" (Providence *Gazette*, 21 June 1779). He died in 1797, having been found "in a nude state in Dyre's swamp" (quoted in Champlin 1976, p. 68). There are only ten known clock movements signed by Thomas (ibid., p. 65), all having arched dials but otherwise showing much variety. Among them only the dials of cat. no. 189 and of one now at Winterthur (Lockwood 2, fig. CXXVIII) are alike, both featuring the type of cast cherub spandrels common on late-seventeenth-century English clocks. The cases of the two clocks are also of similar design: both smaller than the standard size but larger than most miniature versions; both constructed, in the manner of a full-size tall clock, with a separate bonnet having a hinged glazed door (the typical miniature tall clock has a one-piece case with door in back). Differences in the secondary woods, moldings, and most construction details nevertheless suggest that the two cases were the work of different hands. (A third dwarf clock, its whereabouts unknown, has been mentioned [Champlin 1976, p. 62].)

The MMA clock's broken-scroll pediment with turned bosses and filled-in center, the scalloped top edge of the door, and the tripartite pedestal are also found on one full-size Thomas Claggett clock case (ibid., p. 73; cover ill.). This was apparently the archetypal housing for Claggett's earlier clocks. The treatment of pediment and door is characteristic of that found on tall clocks from the English Midlands (Nutting 2, no. 3291; Cescinsky and Webster, figs. 217–220).

Four of Claggett's works are in cases that represent Newport clock-case design in its full maturity, each having an arched top, a similarly arched door, a plain pedestal, and ogee-bracket feet. The doors of two are plain; those of two others are block-fronted and with carved shells. Of the plain-door cases, one now at Sturbridge carries the manuscript label of cabinetmaker Benjamin Baker (1737–1822). The case is accompanied by a statement, written by Thomas Claggett, that guarantees the movement it contains "to be a good clock" (Champlin 1976, figs. 1, 2). The warrant, dated 1772, proves that these Newport cases were the housings for his later clocks.

PROVENANCE: Ex coll.: George S. Palmer, New London, Connecticut.

CONSTRUCTION: On the bonnet: The top is entirely enclosed with thin boards that conform to the shape of the broken-scroll pediment. The unit's horizontal backboard is rabbeted to receive the arch-topped backboard of the shaft. Above the fluted colonettes are thick front and side boards, joined with exposed dovetails, to which the cornice moldings are attached. The turned bosses are nailed from behind with roseheads. On the shaft: The front boards of shaft and pedestal are half-lapped over the side boards. The pedestal, framed out from the shaft, is in three parts of graduated height. On the clock: The cast brass dial has a separate silvered chapter ring, name boss, and a calendar ring visible through the aperture above the numeral VI. The six cast cupid spandrels are screwed on from behind. The movement, with anchor-recoil escapement and a winding drum of only thirteen grooves, runs for about seven days.

CONDITION: The dark reddish brown-colored case, now with a thick varnish finish, has been extensively restored. The bottom boards and the base moldings of the bonnet have been rebuilt. On top of the shaft, where the bonnet is received, the front edge of the cavetto molding has been restored. Inside, at front and sides of the pedestal, a later, boxlike framework of pine boards has been attached. The case's original backboard extends to the level of the quarter-round midmolding. There, its bottom edge has been beveled to join an added board five and a half inches high. The front and side boards of the upper part of the pedestal also terminate in beveled edges where they meet the lower boards. Below, though the wood is old, everything may have been replaced. Comparison with two closely related

Thomas Claggett clock cases—the one at Winterthur, similar in size to this one; the other, full-size (Champlin 1976, cover ill.)— suggests that originally the case stood on a continuous straight molded base and the upper part of the pedestal may have continued to where two bottom moldings were fixed close together (cf. cat. no. 190). The entire interior has been stained. The finials are original, but in previously published illustrations are shown installed with the rounded central section inverted. The backboard has a deep trough to receive the end (now cut off) of the crutch that guided the clock's pendulum. The shaft door has new hardware. The spandrels have been reattached to the dial.

INSCRIPTIONS: Engraved on boss in arched top of dial: *Thomas / Claggett / Newport*. Scratched on backs of cupid spandrels: *II, III, V, VI, X, *.*

189

DIMENSIONS: H.: overall, 61 (*154.9*); W.: cornice, 13⅞ (*35.2*), shaft, 9 (*22.9*), pedestal, 11⅝ (*29.5*), feet, 14½ (*36.2*); D.: cornice, 7¾ (*19.7*), shaft, 5½ (*14.*), pedestal, 6⅞ (*17.5*), feet, 8 (*20.3*); Dial, less lunette, 7 × 7 (*17.8 × 17.8*).

WOODS: Primary: mahogany. Secondary: white pine (bonnet top and back, seat board); spruce (backboard).

REFERENCES: Nutting 1924, fig. 75. Cornelius 1926, pl. XXXI, facing p. 124. Burl N. Osburn and Bernice B. Osburn, *Measured Drawings of Early American Furniture*, Milwaukee, Wisconsin, The Bruce Publishing Co., 1926, pp. 63–65 (ill. and measured drawings). Nutting 2, no. 3244. Salomonsky, pl. 101 (measured drawings). Palmer 1928, pl. 17. Schiffer, pp. 138–139; ill. p. 144. Champlin 1976, pp. 57–68 (biography of maker; p. 62, ref. to clock).

John Stewart Kennedy Fund, 1918   (18.110.30)

190. Tall Clock

Newport, 1745–50
Movement by William Claggett (1696–1749)

WILLIAM CLAGGETT, who was born in Wales, came to Boston in about 1708. He advertised as a clockmaker in 1715, and the next year removed to Newport, where he achieved prominence as a merchant, author, engraver, printer, musical-instrumentmaker, and clockmaker. With more than fifty examples of his clockmaking known, the evolution of his work and of the cases that house it is easily traceable (see Lockwood 2, pp. 282–286).

Claggett's earliest dials are square, with cast urn and eagle spandrels; his rectangular engraved nameplate is set above the numeral VI and the date aperture; and the movements, as a rule, are housed in cases having sarcophagus tops and stepped bottoms (e.g., Randall 1965, no. 200). The second type of Claggett dial constitutes the great majority of his known oeuvre and is identical to the first except for the addition of an arched top that contains, between dolphin spandrels, a strike/silent lever (Carpenter, no. 29), a dial marking the high tide at Newport and with a subsidiary moon phase (Nutting 2, no. 3249), or a name boss (Lockwood 2, fig. CXXXVII). The dials of the second group are housed in various types of cases, most of which have sarcophagus tops. On Claggett's third type of dial the arch is filled with a large painted moon phase with the nameplate, now narrow and conforming to the shape of the arch, above it. Cat. no. 190 is typical of the third group except that on it, as on a clock said to have belonged to Claggett himself (Champlin 1974, p. 161), there are subsidiary dials in the upper corners: on the left, for the time of the high tide at Newport; on the right, the strike/silent lever. On two other examples, both in japanned cases with sarcophagus

190 See also p. 362

tops, subsidiary dials occupy all four corners (Nutting 2, no. 3245; Champlin 1974, p. 183).

On the MMA clock the dial, from Claggett's mature period, is housed in what is stylistically the most advanced of the cases for his works. The block-and-shell door is identical to that found on a case with a sarcophagus top that houses a Claggett clock of the second type (Failey, no. 74). The broken-scroll pediment over an arched cornice (ignoring subsequent changes to the pediment and the addition of fluted quarter columns, see Condition) is known on no other Claggett clock case. However, two clocks by James Wady, Claggett's son-in-law and former apprentice, who carried on the clock business after Claggett's death, in 1749, are housed in cases that closely resemble that of cat. no. 190 (Downs 1952, no. 202; Ott 1965, no. 76). All three have broken-scroll pediments over arched cornices, and blocked doors whose shell treatment is similar to that found on the documented work of Job Townsend in the late seventeen-forties—a desk (*Antiques* 80 [December 1961], p. 502), a secretary at RISD (Carpenter, no. 44), and a dressing table datable to 1746 (Rodriguez Roque, no. 17). Entries by both Townsend (one for "2 pairs Clock Case Hinges" [Champlin 1974, p. 169]) and Claggett that appear in a 1733–34 Day Book at the NHS reinforce the possibility that Claggett, and later Wady, employed Job Townsend to make the cases for their clocks.

PROVENANCE: Ex coll.: George Coe Graves, Osterville, Massachusetts. The donor purchased the clock from Charles Woolsey Lyon, Inc., in 1929. The bill was annotated: "It was made for Governor Wetmore, a colonial governor of Rhode Island—descended to the late William Boerum Wetmore of Newport, was purchased from this estate by Wm. Hiram Burlingham of Bristol, R.I. from whom Clapp & Graham of New York City purchased it for us." None of Rhode Island's colonial governors was named Wetmore.

CONSTRUCTION: On the bonnet: Over the arched dial is a broken-scroll pediment above an arched pediment. On the pediment, behind the middle of the fabric-backed fret, a thick, cut-out front board is dovetailed to horizontal side pieces nailed to the thin side boards, these extending to the upper cornice and pierced with rectangular lights. There is a flat top board where the broken-scroll pediment cornice begins. Except behind the finial and its triple-fluted plinth the pediment is enclosed by the backboard and the bonnet top. Colonettes with brass capitals, bases, and stop-fluting are attached to the door frame. On the shaft: The arched door, with recessed block-and-shell front and flat back, is a single piece of wood. The front and side boards are overlaid with the pedestal boards, the front half-lapped over the sides. On the clock: The cast brass dial has separate silvered chapter ring, seconds ring, subdials in each of the upper spandrels, and engraved arched nameplate. The spandrels are rough-cast. The movement, an eight-day rack and snail striking clock with anchor-recoil escapement, a moon phase, and a tide dial, has five turned pillars, all pinned, and an unusually large front plate, apparently cast for use in a musical movement but here turned on its side.

CONDITION: The case has been refinished and now has a light reddish brown color. At some time prior to its acquisition by the MMA changes were made to it, resulting in an altered appearance of the shaft and, possibly, of the broken-scroll pediment and base molding. The shaft's original square corners have been embellished with fluted quarter columns having brass capitals and stop-fluting. In contrast to those of standard design (e.g., cat. no. 192), these are uncommonly close to the door, extend too far down the waist, and, rather than being a separate unit, are carved from the vertical side and front boards, exposing in the latter tenons, now patched over, from the horizontal rail above the door. The broken-scroll pediment and its enclosing bonnet have been reworked in old wood. If they were originally like those on the two other known cases of this type, both with movements by Claggett's son-in-law James Wady, the pediment would have been squatter and its front board covered with a pierced fret similar to that on the arched pediment below (see Downs 1952, no. 202, or Ott 1965, no. 76). Marks on the top of the bonnet indicate that there were originally three finials. The present one was made in 1937. The colonettes on the bonnet door may originally have been plain. The boards behind the replaced lowest base molding are cut out in a flat arch, suggesting the shape of the original molding. The backboard has been cut down and refitted, and a second board added below it. Narrow strips have been added to the top of the bold cove molding that supports the bonnet and to the backs of the thumbnail moldings on the shaft door. The door hinges have been replaced. Glue blocks have been added behind the quarter columns.

INSCRIPTIONS: Engraved on arched nameplate fixed to lunette of dial: *William Claggett Newport*. In pencil (18th-century?), on seat board: *N F/I 32*. In chalk, on case backboard, modern inscriptions: *14 Day N 03 / Feb ru 12 fl [oor?]*; incised below: *Moses [?] P—tkin*.

DIMENSIONS: H.: overall, 104½ (*265.4*); W.: cornice, 20½ (*52.1*), shaft, 13⅞ (*35.2*), pedestal, 18 (*45.7*), base, 20⅜ (*51.8*); D.: cornice, 10¾ (*27.3*), shaft, 7¼ (*18.4*), pedestal, 9½ (*24.1*), base, 10½ (*26.7*); Dial, less lunette, 12 × 12 (*30.5 × 30.5*).

WOODS: Primary: mahogany. Secondary: tulip poplar (boards of bonnet top and back, shaft backboard); red maple (bonnet runners, seat board).

REFERENCES: Ralston 1931, p. 36. For William Claggett, see Champlin 1974, pp. 159–190.

The Sylmaris Collection, Gift of George Coe Graves, 1930 (30.120.17)

191. Tall Clock

Newport, 1750–60
Movement by Gawen Brown (1719–1801),
Boston

GAWEN BROWN ARRIVED in Boston from London in 1749. Between 1752 and 1773 some seventeen of his newspaper advertisements point to an active business in the selling of clocks and watches, some by his own hand, many imported (Dow, pp. 134–137). For much of the

191

time between 1776 and 1781 Brown was active in the Massachusetts military, where he attained the rank of lieutenant colonel. How diligently he pursued the trade of clockmaker after the Revolution is not known.

For the dials of his clocks Brown employed three different types of lunettes: those with a painted rocking ship; those with a strike /silent lever (both types with shaped applied nameplate above the numeral VI); and those with a nameplate boss. His earliest dials may be of the rocking-ship type found on cat. no. 191, since their spandrels consistently feature the urn and eagle common on English dials of the early eighteenth century (the spandrels on his other types are of a later, rococo pattern). The dial of cat. no. 191 was originally a square one, to which the arched top was added, probably by Brown himself. A clock illustrated in Hansen (p. 2) has an identical dial, except that the rocking ship faces in the opposite direction. Another, this one at Winterthur (Fales 1974, fig. 36), differs only in having an inscription on the chapter ring and a seconds dial rather than a moon phase. Housed in a magnificent japanned case, the clock may date from between 1749 and 1752, when Brown was keeping his shop at Thomas Johnston's, the japanner in Brattle Street, Boston.

Brown's clocks are usually in Boston cases, but cat. no. 191's case is a Newport one, a simpler version of cat. no. 192. To determine when case and movement were conjoined is not possible, but the "Proud" inscription (q.v.) may indicate a connection with the Proud cabinetmaking family working in Newport throughout the eighteenth century. The bonnet, with its well-proportioned cornice, is bold and handsome, but the shaft and base become progressively plainer, perhaps the result of later restoration. On the door, the somewhat flat, open-centered shell narrower than the blocking below it looks to be an early (about 1755–60) example of the Newport type. Another Gawen Brown rocking-ship clock, now in a private collection, has a Newport case that lacks the block-and-shell door but has cove moldings above and below the shaft identical to those of cat. no. 191— a possible indication that the moldings of the MMA clock, though not in original condition, conform to the original design.

PROVENANCE: Ex coll.: Louis Guerineau Myers, New York City.

CONSTRUCTION: On the bonnet: The cornice molding is blocked-out above the molded central key block. Under the thin boards of the arched top is a central medial brace. The turned colonettes flanking the door are fully fluted; at the rear are fluted split spindles. Each side consists of four vertical pieces of wood framing a rectangular light. The bonnet back is rabbeted to receive the square-topped backboard of the shaft. On the shaft: The front boards extend over the sides. The block-and-shell door, flat in back, is a solid piece of wood. On the clock:

The rectangular brass dial has applied cast urn and eagle spandrels. The separate chapter ring and nameplate are silvered, as are the engraved moon face visible in the circular opening beneath the numeral XII; the lunar cycle ring, visible in the rectangular window beneath I; and the calendar date ring, within the rectangular window above VI. The arched lunette, a separate piece of brass, is painted with a seascape, a background for the rocking ship. The movement is an eight-day rack and snail striking clock with anchor-recoil escapement.

CONDITION: The case has been refinished, the glowing red of the dense mahogany now barely visible through glossy brown varnish. The bonnet is intact, but small circular holes in the top of the cornice suggest that there were at one time three brass finials. The arched part of the dial is partly repainted. The lower part of the clock case has been extensively restored. The bottom moldings and the bracket feet are replacements; the large cove moldings above and below the shaft are reworked or replaced. The opening for the shaft door has been narrowed by strips added at either side; similarly, square fillets have been added to the sides of the front board of the pedestal. The shaft is patched around the door hinges. The hinges are the third set.

INSCRIPTIONS: Engraved on dial nameplate: *G Brown/ BOSTON*. In white chalk, inside backboard, large script letters: *J. Marvin [Norwin or Narvin?]/Apponaug [?]*. Crudely incised (18th century?), on guide strip nailed to right side board behind bonnet top: *B [?] R T Proud*. Record of clock repairs scratched on back of brass lunette of dial: *Nov [?] 15 1841* (in one hand); *John J. Tanner/June th29 1857/January 11 / Sydney Maine* (in another hand).

DIMENSIONS: H.: overall, 91⅜ (*232.1*); W.: cornice, 21⅛ (*53.7*), shaft, 13⅞ (*35.3*), pedestal, 17¾ (*45.1*), feet, 19¾ (*50.2*); D.: cornice, 10½ (*26.7*), shaft, 7 (*17.8*), pedestal, 8⅞ (*22.5*), feet, 9⅞ (*25.1*); Dial, less lunette, 12 × 12 (*30.5 × 30.5*).

WOODS: Primary: mahogany. Secondary: chestnut (backboards of bonnet and shaft, medial brace in bonnet top); white pine (bonnet top).

REFERENCES: For Gawen Brown, see Hansen.

Rogers Fund, 1925 (25.115.42)

192. Tall Clock

Newport, 1789
Case by John Townsend (1732–1809)
Movement by William Tomlinson,
London (active 1733)

PERHAPS THE PERFECT Rhode Island tall clock, this beautifully proportioned and executed case with its wonderful old finish is signed and dated by the cabinetmaker. It is one of only two recorded clock cases that carry the label of John Townsend; the location of the other, dated 1783, is unknown (Norton, p. 63). The 1789 date on the label of the MMA clock was misread as 1769 until

recently (Ott 1968, pp. 388–389). The workmanship is entirely consistent with that of Townsend's other documented case furniture (Heckscher 1982). The coved cornice moldings duplicate those of the labeled chests (see cat. no. 139); the shell has an even number of lobes; the lobes are boldly undulating; the C-shaped center has fluting above a crosshatched field, in the manner of the later block-front chests; the remains of the original chestnut brackets of the rear feet are ogee-shaped and rabbeted into the side brackets; and the framing elements are worked with machinelike precision.

The arched-top case with block-and-shell door is of a type widely popular in Newport and Providence. None of the other known examples exhibit characteristics of John Townsend's workmanship. Unlike cat. no. 192, most have pedestals with canted front corners and square, raised front panels (Greenlaw, no. 83; Ott 1965, nos. 78, 79). On the MMA clock the case postdates the movement, which is by William Tomlinson, of London, who was made a master in the English clockmakers' guild in 1733. The brass dial with ringed winding holes is in a style peculiar to early eighteenth-century English work; by the time this case was made, in 1789, the fashion had shifted to painted iron dials. There is, however, no reason to question the case's originality to the movement, since it shows no sign of having been modified to accommodate the dial. The movement may have been in Newport in 1789 in an old-fashioned case, and Townsend commissioned to make a more up-to-date one for it. Other London-made movements and dials, notably those by William Creak (Sack 3, p. 706) and Marmaduke Storrs (Ott 1965, no. 79), also housed in fine Newport block-and-shell cases, demonstrate that such practice was not unusual. A number of English clock cases made in the seventeen-seventies and containing London movements of a generation earlier (Cescinsky and Webster, fig. 228) are typified by a hollow-cornered raised panel on the front of the pedestal and by stop-fluted colonettes and quarter columns (the stop-fluting, like that of cat. no. 190, achieved with brass rods). These could well be the inspiration for their Newport counterparts.

PROVENANCE: Purchased, along with cat. nos. 100 and 139, from Clara Channing Allen, 57 Prospect Street, Northampton, Massachusetts, to whom it had descended from the original owner, George Champlin, of Newport (see cat. no. 100, Provenance). The clock was taken to Northampton prior to 1865, when John Hamun (?) recorded that he had cleaned the movement (see Inscriptions). A photograph of the clock in the Allen house is in the MMA files.

CONSTRUCTION: On the bonnet: The cornice molding is blocked-out above the fluted central key block and is attached, as are the side boards (these having exposed dovetails), to the unusually thick arched front board. Under the thin boards of

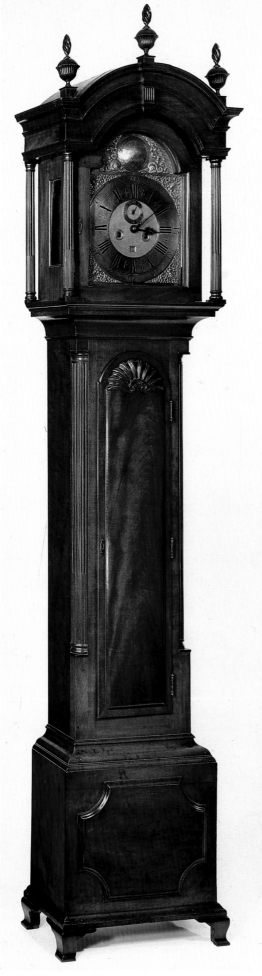

the arched top is a central medial brace. Each finial is turned in three parts, with the stop-fluted urn part sawed flat in back. The frame of the door is pegged together and flanked in front by turned, stop-fluted colonettes; at the rear are thin, stop-fluted split spindles. Large rectangular side lights in the side boards give view onto the clock movement. The bonnet backboard is rabbeted to receive the arch-topped backboard of the shaft. On the shaft: The moldings at top and bottom have triangular cores. A single, finely finished diagonal block joining the front and side boards is screwed in place behind each stop-fluted quarter column. The capitals, bases, and plinth blocks are separate pieces. On the door, the projecting blocking and the carved shell are separate pieces fixed to a frame formed by the mitered mortise and tenon rails and stiles and reinforced by a dovetailed central horizontal brace. On the pedestal, the front is framed by stiles double tenoned into rails that are the width of the case. The raised, horizontally laid, hollow-cornered panel has an applied molded edge. The side boards are dovetailed to receive the bottom board. The back brackets of the rear legs are ogee-shaped. On the clock: The brass dial has separate cast spandrels and silvered chapter ring, seconds ring, and name boss. The movement is an eight-day rack and snail striking clock with anchor-recoil escapement. Its plates are secured with five turned posts—the four outer ones pinned, the fifth, inner one plate-latched. The ends of the seat board are gently tapered so as not to be visible through the side lights.

CONDITION The case has the original finish with a rich translucent brown patina. The twisted tops of the finials replace Federal-period brass urn finials added at one time to the existing originals and visible in an old photograph (see Provenance). The right rear foot and the chestnut brackets behind both rear feet are original above the bottom inch; the other feet are replacements made in 1973. The bottom board has been replaced.

INSCRIPTIONS: A paper label pasted in upper center of backboard printed: MADE BY / JOHN TOWNSEND; below, handwritten in brown ink: *Newport Rhode Island 1789*. Engraved on dial name boss: *William / Tomlinson / London*. In chalk, on backboard behind movement, a characteristic Townsend mark: A with superimposed *M* [?]. In pencil and in ink, on seat board, a record of maintenance of movement: *Jan 29* [?] *1825 / cleaned Dec^m 27–1831 By J.S. / October 20th 1839 / J.S. — [King or Krig or Ring?] Aug 17th 1847 / cleaned—1887 G H C / John Hamun [Hanum?] Northampton Mass / cleaned / Sept 11th 1865 / cleaned—/Sept 4 1878.* (See p. 366 for photograph.)

DIMENSIONS: H.: overall, 98¼ (*249.6*), pediment, 91⅝ (*232.7*); W.: cornice, 22 (*55.9*), shaft, 13¾ (*34.9*), pedestal, 17⅞ (*45.4*), feet, 19⅞ (*50.5*); D.: cornice, 11⅛ (*28.3*), shaft, 7 (*17.8*), pedestal, 9 (*22.9*), feet, 10¼ (*26.*); Dial, less lunette, 12 × 12 (*30.5 × 30.5*).

WOODS: Primary: mahogany. Secondary: chestnut (backboards, glue blocks, molding cores, rear-leg back brackets); tulip poplar (bonnet top); maple (seat board).

REFERENCES: Cornelius 1928, fig. 2. Lee 6, p. 294 (ill.); p. 295 (measured drawings). Halsey and Cornelius, fig. 58. Downs 1947, fig. 7. Palmer 1928, no. 18. Nutting 2, no. 3265. Davidson 1967, fig. 315. Ott 1968, p. 389. Heckscher 1982, pp. 1146, 1148, 1150; fig. 4.

Rogers Fund, 1927   (27.57.2)

193. Tall Clock

Roxbury, Massachusetts, 1772
Movement by Benjamin Willard (1743–1803)
and Simon Willard (1754–1849)

WITH FREE AND SPIRITED engraving on its dial, a flat
board naively suggesting a scroll pediment, and a block-
and-shell door rare in Massachusetts work, this is a particularly appealing New England tall clock. It is also remarkably well documented. The engraving on the dial
records that it was made in 1772 for James Mears in
Roxbury, Massachusetts, by Benjamin Willard—his
hundred-and-thirty-first clock. Copperplate engraving
on the movement also identifies it as having been made in
Roxbury for Mears. The movement, however, is also
marked "number 9," which can be read as the ninth made
by Benjamin's brother Simon; below, in an annotation
signed and dated 1833, Simon scratched the information
that he had made the clock in his seventeenth year, that is,
in about 1770. (The Aaron Willard who cleaned it in 1845
[see Inscriptions] was Simon's nephew.) The collaboration of Benjamin and Simon Willard on this clock is plausible, for Simon later credited his teaching to Benjamin,
who was ten years his senior (Willard, p. 2). Simon further remarked that the man (said to have been an English-
man named Morris) to whom he was apprenticed at the
age of twelve knew little or nothing about the art of
clockmaking. If he was the same man as the John Morris
whose name appears with Simon's on the pendulum bob,
they were still working together in 1770/71. Afterward,
Simon and Benjamin probably worked in tandem from
about 1771 to 1775, the year Simon attained his majority
and presumably set up on his own.

A clock with a similarly inscribed bob was auctioned in
the early nineteen-twenties (Daniel J. Steele, "The Clocks
of Simon Willard," *Antiques* 1 [February 1922], p. 69).
The dial and case of what is probably the same clock
(Charles Messer Stow, "Simon Willard, Maker of
Clocks," *The Antiquarian* 6 [April 1926], pp. 36–41; ill.
p. 36) are a less elaborate version of those of cat. no. 193.
The engraved dial is signed by Simon. A number of other
clocks with dials and cases closely related to cat. no. 193
are known. All are signed by Benjamin, either at Roxbury
or at Grafton, and many are numbered (Palmer 1967,
figs. 8, 9; *The Antiquarian* 15 [October 1930], p. 12). Except for the embellishment of its case with a distinctive
block-and-shell door and flanking quarter columns,
found elsewhere only on a case housing a Connecticut
clock (Nutting 1924, no. 84), cat. no. 193 is a characteristic example of the clocks made by Benjamin and Simon
Willard individually or together during the years of their
collaboration. The housings of the Willards' numbered

193 See also p. 362

clocks have a character and foot treatment known from English prototypes (e.g., Cescinsky and Webster, fig. 231). In overall design and specific detail, however, they are so similar as to suggest a single source. An advertisement in the *Boston Gazette*, September 12, 1774, suggests that that source may have been Benjamin's own shop (quoted in Dow, pp. 145–146): "Inquire of Benja. Willard, Clock & Watch Maker in Roxbury Street near Boston, Where all sorts of Clocks are made in the newest Form. . . . Also Clock Cases are made in the same Place, in various Forms and in the best Manner, and cheaper than can be purchas'd in London."

PROVENANCE: Ex coll.: Dr. and Mrs. Brooks H. Marsh, New York City. The donors acquired the clock from Israel Sack, Inc., New York City. The clock was made in 1772 for James Mears, one of four generations of tanners in Roxbury. His house was at the corner of Eustis and Old Town streets (Francis Drake, *The Town of Roxbury*, Roxbury, Massachusetts, privately printed, 1878, pp. 142, 370).

CONSTRUCTION: On the bonnet: The top is enclosed with thin boards that conform in shape to the shallow arch of the cornice. The arched cornice molding and the five-fluted plinths beneath each of the brass finials are nailed to the thin pediment board scratch-beaded around its broken scroll. Above the colonettes the front board of the pediment overlaps thick side pieces, screwed to the bonnet's side boards, to which the backboard is dovetailed. The side boards, pierced with arched lights, are tenoned through the bottom boards. The colonettes flanking the hinged door have brass capitals and bases and, except in back, are fluted (on the right side, eight flutes, six with brass stop-fluting; on the left, six flutes with brass stop-fluting and one unfinished one). At the back are attenuated engaged quarter colonettes. On the shaft: The recessed blocking and rayed shell on the door are carved from the solid. The hinges continue inside the door as shaped straps. The door is flanked by narrow boards that overlap the shaft sides above and below the fluted quarter columns. Glued behind each quarter column is a single long block to which triangular glue blocks are added above and below the door opening. During construction, pieces were added to the side boards so that they could receive the clock's seat board. The cove molding above the door is reinforced with a horizontal pine board. The backboard has a shallow arched top. On the pedestal, the horizontal front board is half-lapped over the vertical side boards. The base moldings, except for the applied quarter-round foot pads, are cut from a single board. On the clock: The brass dial is engraved with chapter and seconds rings and with rococo foliate designs in the spandrels and around the date aperture above the numeral VI. The hemispheres below the moon phase in the arched lunette are plain. The movement is an eight-day rack and snail striking clock with anchor-recoil escapement.

CONDITION: The case has a fine honey color beneath which the original deep red of the mahogany is still apparent. Shallow square indentations at the front corners of the top mark where plinth blocks once stood beneath the side finials. The base molding on the right side has been broken, and part of the rear bracket foot replaced. The quarter-round foot pads have been reattached. When the clock was acquired by the MMA, in 1976,

the dial was polished brass, but traces of the original silvering remained. The dial was resilvered in 1978.

INSCRIPTIONS: Engraved, on clock dial, in lunette: *Warrentd For Mr James Mears 1772*; within seconds circle: *No 131*; in central circle: *Benjan Willard / Roxbury / Fecit*. Engraved, in copperplate hand, on front plate of movement: *for Mr Jams Meears / Roxbury / No 9*. Scratched on front plate of movement: *Made by Simon Willard / in his 17th year / Cleaned by him in August 10th / 1833 / in his 81th year; Cleand by Aaron Willard / Feb 22 / 45; J. F. Fisher / 1881 / 923 Washon St; E H F cld by C W H / Nov 15 1869 / Ditto Mar 24 74 B*. Raised letters cast into lead of pendulum bob: • *IOHN* • *MORRIS 1771 / 1770 CLOCK PENDULEM* • *1770 / I.S* • *WILLARD : IOHN* • *MORRIS*. Ink inscriptions, where legible, on seat board: *M. Weld Jr. / Aug 15 1868 / 2d House beyond the house / RR Station—*.

DIMENSIONS: H.: overall, 95¼ *(241.9)*; W.: cornice, 21⅞ *(55.6)*, shaft, 15 *(38.1)*, pedestal, 19 *(48.3)*, feet, 21 *(53.3)*; D.: cornice, 9¾ *(24.8)*, shaft, 7 *(17.8)*, pedestal, 9 *(22.9)*, feet, 10⅜ *(26.4)*; Dial, less lunette, 13¼ × 13¼ *(33.7 × 33.7)*.

WOODS: Primary: mahogany. Secondary: cherry (bonnet runners, seat-board supports); white pine (all else).

REFERENCES: *Antiques* 57 (January 1950), p. 3 (ill.). Sack 1950, pp. 124–125.

Gift of Dr. and Mrs. Brooks H. Marsh, 1976   (1976.341)

194. Tall Clock

Norwich, Connecticut, about 1775
Movement by Thomas Harland (1735–1807)

IN 1773, THOMAS HARLAND emigrated from London and established a clock shop in Norwich, Connecticut. His advertisement on December 9 of that year in *The Norwich Packet* announced that he made watches and clocks, also "Clock faces engraved and finished for the trade" (Hoopes, p. 83). Judging from an advertisement of the following year in which he thanks his clients for their patronage, his business was an immediate success. In 1779, he married, and he built a house in Norwich that was to remain his home for the rest of his life. After the Revolution, in 1787, he again advertised watches and clocks. He also sought an apprentice, and tradition has it that by 1790 he was employing several of them. Harland's shop was destroyed by fire in 1795, but he rebuilt it and continued in business until his death in 1807.

Several clocks by Harland are known. With few exceptions, their dials are of a distinctive type: a single flat piece of brass engraved with chapter ring and rococo foliate spandrel designs and then silvered, with a separate seconds dial and a calendar aperture in the center. The movement is attached to the dial with screws or rivets visible from the front. The dial of cat. no. 194 is a character-

194 See also pp. 362, 363

istic example except for the separate recessed brass plate within the chapter ring. On the movement, the pin-type count wheel is also typical, though the crudely cast plates are unexpected for an artisan generally thought to be the most skillful of the early Connecticut clockmakers.

Cat. no. 194 is probably one of Harland's first American products. The earliest identified one, at the Wadsworth Atheneum (Hoopes, fig. 44), is said to have been made in 1774 for Samuel Leffingwell, the man Harland first boarded with in Norwich (Moore 1911, p. 101). On another clock, at the Department of State, the dial is signed and dated "Tho⁵. Harland / Norwich / 1776" (Charles F. Montgomery, "Furniture," *The American Art Journal* 7 [May 1975], p. 57). Cat. no. 194's case must also be from the mid-seventeen-seventies to judge by the 1775 New London newspaper pasted in its bonnet (see Inscriptions). Another Harland clock, this one at the Ford Museum (Palmer 1967, fig. 20), was made for Joshua Hall. The cases housing Harland's clocks are all of a distinctive type: an arched top with scalloped crest, cornice moldings consisting of an ovolo above a cavetto, and, at the top of the pedestal, a scalloped board. The design is one favored by other Connecticut clockmakers (Hoopes, fig. 49; Palmer 1967, fig. 21). Remarkable parallels between the typical Harland case and dial and those of Benjamin Willard in Massachusetts (see cat. no. 193) suggest an as yet undocumented working relationship between these two celebrated New England clockmakers.

PROVENANCE: Ex coll.: George S. Palmer, New London, Connecticut.

CONSTRUCTION: On the bonnet: The cornice moldings are glued to thick side boards each joined to the backboard with a single large dovetail. The top, enclosed with thin boards, conforms to the arch of the cornice. The scalloped boards above the pediment, reinforced behind with angular glue blocks, are slotted into the rectangular, six-fluted plinths supporting the finials. The colonettes flanking the door are incompletely fluted (thirteen flutes on the right one, twelve on the left) and have brass capitals and bases. At the rear are narrow flanking boards with turned quarter colonettes. The side boards have arched lights. On the shaft: The front boards overlap the thin side boards of both shaft and pedestal. Beneath the cove at the juncture of the two parts is a scalloped molding. The base moldings and bracket feet are all of a piece, except for the applied pads on the feet. The backboard is arched at the top. On the clock: The cast brass dial is engraved with chapter ring and, in the spandrels, with rococo foliage. The area of the dial within the chapter ring is cut away. Attached behind the opening is a separate piece of brass on which the seconds ring and rococo foliage are engraved; a separate calendar wheel is visible in the semicircular aperture. The movement is an eight-day striking clock with anchor escapement and pin-type count wheel. The pendulum stem and the pulleys are of wood. The front plate is imperfectly cast: a large circular brass patch was probably inserted to correct for casting faults. The two baluster-shaped upper pillars are brass; the two lower ones, steel.

CONDITION: The case has a fine old finish and a deep reddish brown patina. A few case parts have been replaced: the bottom inch of the central finial, the extreme right front section of the scalloped pedestal board, the glass of the bonnet door, the hardware of the shaft door, and the bottom board. The dial has been resilvered except for the separate piece within the chapter ring, which is polished brass; most of the hour hand is replaced, based on an old photograph of the original; the pendulum crutch has been repaired.

INSCRIPTIONS: Engraved, in arch over lunette of dial: THOMAS HARLAND NORWICH. On rounded top of bonnet hood, pasted to inner surface, presumably as dustproofing, the torn left half of the front page of *The Connecticut Gazette; and the Universal Intelligencer* for Friday, April 13, 1775. The newspaper was published in New London.

DIMENSIONS: H.: overall, 93¾ (238.1); W.: cornice, 21⅛ (53.7), shaft, 14¾ (37.5), pedestal, 18 (45.7), feet, 21 (53.3); D.: cornice, 10 (25.4), shaft, 7⅜ (18.7), pedestal, 9¼ (23.5), feet, 10½ (26.7); Dial, less lunette, 12¼ × 12¼ (31.1 × 31.1).

WOODS: Primary: mahogany. Secondary: white pine.

REFERENCES: Nutting 1924, fig. 67. Palmer 1928, fig. 59. Nutting 2, no. 3340. For Thomas Harland biography, see Moore 1911, pp. 101–103; Hoopes, pp. 83–88.

John Stewart Kennedy Fund, 1918   (18.110.29)

195. Tall Clock

New Hampshire, 1775–92
Case attributed to Major John Dunlap
(1746–1792)

THE HOUSING OF THIS CLOCK is one of the rural wonders of American cabinetwork. Contrasted with the eighteenth-century norm, the proportions of its fat shaft, squat pedestal, and high claw-and-ball feet are bizarre, and its pediment rosettes, tapered cornice moldings, and twist-turned colonettes standing free of the cornice above give it a decidedly whimsical air. Despite the idiosyncrasies of its design, the case is crafted with consummate skill. The dovetailing of the top and bottom boards to the sides and the lap joints securing the quarter columns of the shaft are more accomplished details of construction than are usually found even in urban work.

A clock case at Amherst College (Parsons, fig. 76), markedly similar and certainly by the same hand, differs from cat. no. 195 mainly in having a shaft even broader and a pedestal even shorter, narrow barber-pole stringing around the door, and intertwined vines inlaid on its shaft door. The Amherst clock descended until the nineteen-thirties in the Bedford, New Hampshire, family of cabinetmaker Major John Dunlap, presumably the "House Clock 14£" listed in the inventory of his estate (ibid., p. 36). Its case has consequently been attributed to him

(ibid., fig. 76), and, if the attribution is correct, then cat. no. 195 is also by his hand.

From the late seventeen-sixties until his death in 1792, Major John practiced cabinetmaking (see also cat. nos. 19 and 143), first at Goffstown and then, after 1777, at Bedford. No clocks are recorded in his surviving account book, covering the years 1768–87, but in his ciphering book he gives "Dementions for Making a Clock Cace"—dimensions followed neither in the Amherst clock case nor in this one. Distinctive decorative motifs on the housings of the clocks are shared with a sizable number of case pieces found in towns where Major John or his younger brother Samuel worked. The "flowered" ogee-carved moldings are repeated in the cornice of a room, now at Winterthur, from the Zachariah Chandler house, Bedford, which was executed by Major John in 1777 (Parsons, fig. 102). The similarly carved base molding and the claw feet are like those on a desk found at Goffstown and now at the Currier Gallery (ibid., fig. 64); and the rosettes in the pediment resemble those on a chest-on-chest from Bedford now at the New Hampshire Historical Society (ibid., fig. 3; fig. G, p. 14). Only one other Dunlap-type tall clock case is known; it was found at Amherst, New Hampshire (information, MMA files, supplied by Charles Parsons, 8/3/82). The molding at the top of its shaft and the compass star in its pedestal are similar to those of cat. no. 195, but otherwise it is just a typical New England Federal-style case. On cat. no. 195, the painted dial appears to be a replacement (see Condition), probably for an engraved brass dial by Jonathan Mulliken (1746–1782) of Newburyport, Massachusetts, similar to that on Major John's own clock at Amherst College.

PROVENANCE: The tall clock was sold at a modest house auction in Wakefield, Massachusetts, in 1964. Between that time and 1981, when it appeared at auction in New York, it was owned by the dealers Philip Budrose, Marblehead, Massachusetts; John Walton, Jewett City, Connecticut; and Alexander Acevedo, New York City. According to a modern label on the case (see Inscriptions), the clock was once owned by Robert Wallace, son of "Ocean-born Mary." Mary Wilson (1720–1814), born on a ship en route to America from Ireland, grew up in Londonderry, New Hampshire, where in 1742 she married James Wallace. Their son Robert (1749–1815) served as state legislator from the town of Henniker, to which he moved in 1776. The furnishings of the great house he built nearby presumably included cat. no. 195.

CONSTRUCTION: On the bonnet: The front board forms a broken-scroll pediment above the dial's arched door. The carved cornice moldings taper toward the attached rosettes, behind which is centered a smaller rosette that projects from a round stem. The stem separates below the rosette into two branches, each with a dangling rosette wired to it. The flat top board is dovetailed to the side boards. The double-pegged dial door, its overlapping beaded edge applied, is flush with the

195 See also p. 363

front board; on either side are spiral-turned colonettes that instead of supporting the cornice terminate an inch in front of it. At the rear are fluted quarter columns. On the shaft: The door's molded edge is like that of the dial door. The fluted quarter columns on either side cover the joint where the front boards partly overlap the side boards, obviating the need for glue blocks. The side boards continue to the bottom of the pedestal, where a bottom board was once dovetailed to them. The principal backboard continues down to a horizontal one beginning just below the molding at the top of the pedestal. On the pedestal, the claw-and-ball feet continue as stiles to that molding. Front, side, and back boards are pegged to the stiles. Two inlay patterns are employed: a zigzag bordered by five-part stringing that frames both doors and forms a panel in the pedestal and, in the shaft door, three compass stars. On the dial door are hinges that continue inside as shaped straps; on the shaft door are simple butt hinges. On the clock: The dial plate is iron, painted, and without a false plate behind. The lunette is a separate piece attached with riveted straps. The movement is an eight-day rack and snail striking clock with anchor-recoil escapement.

CONDITION: The case has a mellow light brown color. The backs of the rosettes retain traces of a dark finish. The glass of the dial door is cracked. On each front foot the uppermost front-bracket scallop is broken off. The bottom board is missing. The molded edge on the bottom of the door is replaced. The lock in the shaft door is an old replacement; of the two keyholes, the original, inner one has a diamond-shaped sheet brass escutcheon. The clock movement here illustrated in the case has a painted dial on which the calendar ring above the number VI is repainted. The seat board and the tops of the side boards on which it rests are modern. The dial is probably of American manufacture, since it is crudely done in comparison with the English dials routinely imported at the end of the eighteenth century, but it is nevertheless not original to the case. In 1964 the clock case was accompanied by a one-piece engraved brass dial similar to the one on the Amherst College clock (Parsons, fig. 76), signed by Jonathan Mulliken of Newburyport, Massachusetts (8/3/82 information, MMA files, from Charles S. Parsons; see also Parsons, *New Hampshire Clocks & Clockmakers*, Exeter, New Hampshire, Adams Brown Co., 1976, p. 24, where dial is the "other one" referred to). The following year the clock case was advertised (*Antiques* 87 [March 1965], p. 240) with the painted dial now in it. In 1981, when the case was auctioned (SPB sale no. 4590Y, lot 1007), it housed a brass dial with separate chapter ring and cast spandrels and bearing a nameplate, which appears spurious, engraved "John Mulliken / NewburyPort." That dial and the painted one were both subsequently acquired by the MMA together with the case. The original Mulliken clock has not been found.

INSCRIPTIONS: In pencil, on shaft door, recording maintenance: *S March 30 17*; *July 29 1841 / S W G—*; *S [I?] P Chase / Feb 1 1862*. Typewritten, on a paper label (20th-century) on shaft door: *This clock once belonged to Robert Wallace, son of 'Ocean-born Mary' Wallace.*

DIMENSIONS: H.: overall, 85 (*215.9.*); W.: cornice, 23¼ (*59.1*), shaft, 15 (*38.1*), pedestal, 17¾ (*45.1*), feet, 19¾ (*50.2*); D.: cornice, 11⅛ (*28.3*), shaft, 8 (*20.3*), pedestal, 9⅜ (*23.8*), feet, 10½ (*26.7*); Dial, less lunette, 12 × 12 (*30.5 × 30.5*).

WOODS: Primary: cherry. Secondary: white pine.

REFERENCES: *Antiques* 87 (March 1965), p. 240 (ill.). SPB sale no. 4590Y, April 29–May 1, 1981, lot 1007 (ill.). Samuel Pennington, "Tick Tock: The Tale of a (Two Faced) Clock," *Maine Antique Digest*, August 1981, pp. 24A–25A. Parsons, p. 15, fig. 1 (ill. inlay detail). For the Wallace family, see Leander W. Cogswell, *History of the Town of Henniker* [New Hampshire], Concord, 1880, pp. 756–758.

Gift of Alexander Acevedo, 1981   (1981.160.1)

196. Dwarf Tall Clock

Plymouth, Massachusetts, 1780–90
Movement by Caleb Leach (active 1776–90)

CALEB LEACH IS SAID to have been active in Plymouth between 1776 and 1790 (Palmer 1928, p. 231), but nothing is known about his life. Examples of his work include a shelf clock with silvered dial (*Antiques* 59 [May 1951], p. 333) and a tall clock in a private collection. The housing for cat. no. 196, somewhat larger than that of most miniature tall clocks but about half the height of a standard one, has a separate bonnet rather than the single unit with door in back typical of most miniatures. Since the clock appears always to have been in this case, and the case has urn and spire finials and oval door escutcheons that show the influence of the Federal style, the movement must date from near the end of Leach's career.

PROVENANCE: Ex coll.: George Coe Graves, Osterville, Massachusetts.

CONSTRUCTION: On the bonnet: Thin top boards are nailed to the hollow-arched board rising behind the cornice and to a board of similar shape at the back that is rabbeted to receive the arched top of the shaft backboard. The three brass finials stand on square wooden plinths. Turned colonettes at the front and quarter columns at the rear support the cornice moldings. There are no side lights. The stepped plinths above the cornice are veneered. The bonnet is secured to the backboard with an iron hook and eye. On the shaft: The boards framing the door opening are butted together and overlap the sides. A continuous glue block reinforces the joint on each side of the door opening. The sides of the shaft continue to the bottom of the pedestal. The front is also continued, but with a pine board. Attached to this interior framework at each corner are thick posts to which are nailed the pedestal's mitered front and side boards, their top edges molded in quarter rounds. The base moldings and ogee-bracket feet are cut from single pieces of wood. In back is a single bracket foot running the width of the pedestal. On the clock: The silvered brass dial, engraved with a seconds ring beneath the numeral XII and a calendar ring above VI, is screwed to the movement. The movement is an eight-day rack and snail striking clock with anchor-recoil escapement. It has a nine-inch pendulum formed from a strip of hammered brass. The posts are baluster-shaped; the bell is mounted vertically.

CONDITION: The case has a pleasing aspect. The wood, walnut brown in color, has an old, somewhat decayed finish. There are patches above the iron hook-eye on the left side of the bonnet and on the molding below. A new piece has been added to the front of the shaft adjacent to the lock. The spire of one finial, the seat board, the glass of the bonnet door, and the shaft-door escutcheon are replaced. The side boards have been built up to receive the seat board. The backs of the rear feet have been chamfered so as to fit the clock into a corner. The bottom board and three of the foot glue blocks are missing.

INSCRIPTIONS: Engraved in lunette of dial: *Caleb Leach / PLYMOUTH.*

DIMENSIONS: H.: overall, 47 (*119.4*); W.: cornice, 11⅜ (*28.9*), shaft, 7⅜ (*18.7*), pedestal, 10⅜ (*26.4*), feet, 10⅞ (*27.6*); D.: cornice, 5⅝ (*14.3*), shaft, 3¾ (*9.4*), pedestal, 5¼ (*13.3*), feet, 6 (*15.2*); Dial, less lunette: 6 × 6 (*15.2 × 15.2*).

WOODS: Primary: mahogany. Secondary: oak (bonnet backboard); maple (shaft backboard); white pine (all else).

REFERENCES: Arthur Collani, "How to Build a Reproduction of a Famous Old-Time American Grandmother's Clock," *The Home Craftsman*, March–April 1951, pp. 35–37; 48 (includes complete working drawings). Distin and Bishop, fig. 154 .

The Sylmaris Collection, Gift of George Coe Graves, 1930 (30.120.49)

196

197. Tall Clock

New York, 1730–50
Movement by Henry Hill

EIGHTEENTH-CENTURY CLOCKS and clock cases of New York manufacture are remarkably rare. On this example the elaborately engraved dial is the only one known to be signed by Henry Hill, an otherwise elusive individual. Hill must have worked in New York City, since clockmakers then inscribed their dials with the name of the city or town, not with that of the colony. Alterations to the cornice and base notwithstanding, the case is typical of American clocks made in the mid-Atlantic states during the second quarter of the eighteenth century. The style apparently originated in the Philadelphia area, and many examples from that city are known. One clock of the type, at Winterthur (Fairbanks and Bates, p. 62), with a movement by Isaac Pearson of Burlington, New Jersey, is dated 1723. Others, including a second one at Winterthur and one at the Bowne House in Flushing (see Failey, no. 14), are by Anthony Ward, who moved from Philadelphia to New York City in 1724. These clocks have dials similar to that of cat. no. 197: in the spandrels, putti supporting a crown; on the chapter ring, an outer circle enclosing Arabic numerals and wide enough to accommodate the maker's name engraved between 25 and 35 and, centered at the spandrels, engraved motifs which on cat. no. 197 are rosettes. These are features characteristic of English clock-dial design of about 1705–10 (Cescinsky and Webster, figs. 51, 52), though on cat. no. 197 the solid shaft door with its arched top and thumbnail-molded edges and the somewhat fussy baluster turnings of the colonettes proclaim the Queen Anne style, and justify a mid-century date.

PROVENANCE: Ex coll.: Mrs. J. Insley Blair, Tuxedo Park, New York.

CONSTRUCTION: On the bonnet: The front and side boards, to which the cornice moldings are nailed, are mitered together. The turned colonettes flanking the dial are one with the double-pegged door. At the rear, nailed to the side boards, are turned quarter columns and molded strips. The side boards, double tenoned and pegged to the bottom rails, have rectangular lights. On the shaft: The front boards framing the door and pegged to the sides are mortised and tenoned at miter joints. There are no glue blocks. The moldings above and below the door are in two pieces. The hinges continue inside the door as shaped straps. The pedestal has an interior framework. At the top, its horizontal members are mortised and tenoned to vertical corner posts; to it are pegged the pedestal's front and side boards, with the front board also nailed to the sides. The backboard is nailed on with roseheads. The seat board is a four-inch-thick block. On the clock: The brass dial has separate cast and lacquered spandrels and a separate silvered chapter ring around a floral-engraved center that contains a calendar aperture above the nu-

197

meral VI. The movement is a thirty-hour rack and snail striking clock with anchor-recoil escapement.

CONDITION: The case has a fine mellow brown patina. The top and bottom have been altered: the boards forming the flat top and the part of the backboard behind the bonnet are replaced, and thin strips have been added to the top edge of the cornice molding. There may originally have been a stepped sarcophagus top (e.g., Edwin A. Battison and Patricia E. Kane, *The American Clock 1725–1865: The Mabel Brady Garvan and Other Collections at Yale University*, Greenwich, Connecticut, 1973, no. 26). The mahogany claw-and-ball feet and the ovolo molding have replaced what was probably a straight molded base. The bottom board is missing. The interior shaped strap of the lower shaft-door hinge has been patched.

INSCRIPTIONS: Engraved on chapter ring: HEN^Y HILL NEW YORK. Scratched on back of brass dial: *5880*. Stamped on butt of each hinge of shaft door: *217*.

DIMENSIONS: H.: overall, 82½ (209.6); W.: cornice, 19⅜ (49.2), shaft, 14 (35.6), pedestal, 17⅛ (43.5); D.: cornice, 9⅞ (25.1), shaft, 8 (20.3), pedestal, 9¾ (24.8); Dial, 12 × 12 (30.5 × 30.5).

WOODS: Primary: walnut. Secondary: tulip poplar (backboard); red oak (seat board); white oak (pedestal interior frame).

REFERENCES: *MMAB* n.s. 7 (Summer 1948), p. 20. Downs 1948, p. 82 (ill.). Joan S. Wilson, "Mid-18th Century New York Clock 'by' Henry Hill," *American Collector* 17 (December 1948), pp. 5, 21.

Gift of Mrs. J. Insley Blair, 1947   (47.103.3)

198. Tall Clock

Philadelphia, 1750–60
Movement by John Wood, Sr.
(active 1734–60)

JOHN WOOD, WHO DIED IN 1760, and his son John junior (1736–1793) were both clockmakers in eighteenth-century Philadelphia. In 1734 the silversmith Joseph Richardson billed John senior "To Ingraving 6 name pieces. . . .5 Clock Faces . . . " (Hornor 1935, p. 55). John senior is also known to have ordered a clock case from the cabinetmaker Henry Clifton in 1750 (ibid., p. 127). At Wood's death a decade later his stock included fourteen eight-day clocks valued at £140. John junior inherited his father's thriving business, including the shop at Front and Chestnut streets that had originally belonged to Peter Stretch, Philadelphia's first important clockmaker.

Though the simple signature "John Wood" or "Jno Wood" that appears on the dials of their clocks does not distinguish between father and son, both dial and case of cat. no. 198 look to predate 1760, and thus are probably the work of the father. The dial, subsequently brought up

to date by the addition of an arched moon phase, is a type that was popular in England in about 1710–15. The case looks to date from the seventeen-fifties, the decade during which Chippendale features began to appear in Philadelphia on Queen Anne forms. The scroll-arched pediment with leaf carving and flame finials, the freestanding colonettes on the bonnet, and the quarter columns on the shaft are features associated with the Chippendale style; Queen Anne in character are the enclosed bonnet with its unpierced central shell (cf. cat. no. 162), the absence of fluting on colonettes and quarter columns, the round-arched door, and the use of walnut—especially the figured piece chosen for the shaft door.

A similar case now at the Department of State houses a clock by Emanuel Rouse, who was active in Philadelphia from 1747 to 1768. The mahogany used for its case and the presence of a scallop-arched door on it suggest that it was made in the seventeen-sixties, somewhat later than cat. no. 198. The two clocks share a distinctive closed bonnet and carved-shell treatment, but because on the MMA clock the hood of the bonnet projects farther than normal and the shaft and base are unusually wide, the clock is endowed with unusual presence and stature.

PROVENANCE: Ex coll.: W. Gedney Beatty, Rye, New York. The clock descended in the family of Joseph Barber until Beatty acquired it. Barber (about 1763–1830) was born in Princeton, New Jersey. In 1788, the year of his marriage to Jane McCob, he bought a farm near Montgomery Village, Orange County, New York. (The farm was one of the sites where mastodon bones were exhumed in 1793 by the painter Charles Willson Peale.) According to a manuscript bill of sale (photostat, MMA files), Barber purchased the clock for £25 on March 30, 1789, from John McAudey of Beekman Township, Dutchess County, New York. The case's Montgomery, New York, shipping label (see Inscriptions) substantiates its ownership in New York state.

CONSTRUCTION: On the bonnet: The fully enclosed top conforms to the shape of the arched cornice. The cornice, made of three separate moldings, breaks at the middle. The shell and leaf carving at the front is applied. The projecting arched hood is supported at the front by freestanding turned colonettes and at the rear by split spindles. Immense dovetails, exposed on the front, join the hood's horizontal side and front boards. The bonnet's side boards, double-tenoned through the bottom rail, are pierced with arched lights. On the shaft: On either side of the door—a plank of figured walnut with molded edges—are plain quarter columns secured with large glue blocks. The cove moldings have applied astragals. Between the quarter columns on the pedestal is a projecting rectangular panel cut from two pieces of the same figured board. The back brackets of the rear feet are reinforced with laminated horizontal glue blocks. At the lower end of the backboard is a narrow horizontal extension. On the clock: The lunette arch and the hemispheres under the moon face, the hemispheres faced with pieces cut from cast spandrels, are separate pieces of brass brazed onto the square dial plate below. The plate is in two parts, the open space behind the chapter ring spanned by radiating copper strips. The

198 See also pp. 362, 363

finely chased and lacquered cast spandrels and the silvered chapter and seconds rings are applied. The movement is an eight-day rack and snail striking clock with anchor-recoil escapement.

CONDITION: The case has a lustrous mellow brown patina. In the pediment carving, the tips of some of the leaves and parts of the strapwork leading from behind the shell to the middle finial are missing. The bottom board and most of the hardware on the shaft door have been replaced. The back edges of the rear legs have been chamfered to fit the clock into a corner, and molded pads have been added beneath all the ogee-bracket feet. The tops of the side boards on which the seat board rests were cut off, presumably when the clock was first fitted into the case. The seconds hand on the dial is replaced.

INSCRIPTIONS: Engraved on bottom edge of dial's chapter ring: *JN.º WOOD PHILADELPHIA*. Incised, on bonnet backboard: compass-drawn circles (used to plot the shape of the arched top); sketched in chalk: part of a scroll pediment. Scratched into case backboard, near top: *Joshe Barber*. Pasted to backboard, a late nineteenth-century shipping label printed: *Wells Fargo & Co / EXPRESS. / FROM / Montgomery N.Y.*

DIMENSIONS: H.: overall, 107½ (*273.1*); W.: cornice, 23½ (*59.7*), shaft, 15⅜ (*39.1*), pedestal, 20⅛ (*51.1*); D.: cornice, 11⅜ (*28.9*), shaft, 7¾ (*19.7*), pedestal, 10¼ (*26.*); Dial, less lunette, 13 × 13 (*33. × 33.*).

WOODS: Primary: walnut. Secondary: tulip poplar (bonnet backboard); white pine (all else).

REFERENCES: Palmer 1928, fig. 36. Nutting 2, fig. 3285. *NYGBS Record* 62 (1931), p. 126 (history of clock given). Marshall B. Davidson, "On Time in America," *MMAB* n.s. 3 (December 1944), pp. 105–109 (bonnet and dial ill.).

Bequest of W. Gedney Beatty, 1941   (41.160.369)

199. Tall Clock

Philadelphia, 1765–90
Movement by William Huston (about 1730–1791)

WILLIAM HUSTON was born in America, probably in Philadelphia, and advertised as clockmaker between 1754 and 1777 (Palmer 1928, p. 218). Referred to as "watchmaker" in 1767 and as "c'lk ma'r" in 1774 (PMA 1976, p. 94), he presumably carried on his trade until his death in 1791. He built a house in Philadelphia on Front Street, south of Chestnut, but lost it in a sheriff's sale (George H. Eckhardt, *Pennsylvania Clocks and Clockmakers*, New York, Bonanza Books, 1955, p. 180). Huston's father and the clockmaker John Wood, Sr. (see cat. no. 198), were close friends, which has led to the suggestion that Huston learned the trade from Wood (PMA 1976, p. 94).

This clock case, representative of the classic Philadelphia Chippendale type, conforms to a description in that city's 1772 book of prices: "[Clock Case] with Scrol pedement hed . . . Collom . . . £10" (Weil, p. 192). A number of Philadelphia clock cases appear to have a common authorship with it. An identical case houses an unsigned clock (*PMB* 19 [May 1924], p. 154, pl. V, left). On the applied pediment of a case housing a clock by Burrows Dowdney (Conger, p. 95; figs. 19, 20), the carving is by a different hand, but the case itself, attributed without foundation to Thomas Affleck (ibid.), has the same boldly vertical scrolled pediment, ogee moldings rather than the usual cove above and below the shaft, and pedestal panel with extended circular corners—all elements that distinguish the work of the unidentified maker of cat. no. 199. A number of cases with the same features but without pediment carving contain clocks by William Huston (e.g., P-B sale no. 2026, 3/24/61, lot 127), though pediment carving on the case of another Huston clock, otherwise notably different, is identical (*Antiques* 112 [July 1977], inside back cover). Two clocks by Huston are in labeled cases: the first, by Nathaniel Dowdney (Ruth B. Davidson, "Living with antiques," *Antiques* 67 [March 1955], p. 236, ill.), bears no comparison with cat. no. 199; the other, by Edward James (PMA 1976, no. 74), exhibits certain parallels in the construction of its bonnet, but not enough to warrant an attribution.

On the MMA clock, the inner edge of the chapter ring is scalloped and the minute-division band is arched, in the Dutch manner, between the Arabic numbers. These features are atypical in Huston's oeuvre, for his dials are usually English in treatment (ibid., see ill.). Apparently he had his name engraved on the separate seconds ring of an imported Dutch dial that he used with his clock movement.

PROVENANCE: Ex coll.: Verna Belli, Pipersville, Pennsylvania. Miss Belli acquired the clock from Asa Worthington, whose mother was said to be a direct descendant of Samuel Powel. No Asa Worthington appears in the Powel or Hare family genealogies. Powel was the last colonial mayor of Philadelphia. The upstairs back parlor from his house on South Third Street is now in the American Wing at the MMA. He died without issue in 1793, leaving the bulk of his estate to his wife, Elizabeth Willing Powel. A tall clock, possibly this one, is included in the 1830 inventory taken at her death. Mrs. Powel's nephew, who changed the order of his name to John Hare Powel at her request, was her principal heir. He removed most of the property to Powelton, a country house outside Philadelphia, from which it was later dispersed among the family.

CONSTRUCTION: On the bonnet: The front board forms a broken-scroll pediment to which the cornice moldings and carved C-scrolls and leafage are applied. The flat top is a rough-cut mahogany board. Dovetails join the side and front boards of the pediment; the side boards are joined in back by a batten dovetailed to them just below the top. On all four corners of the bonnet are freestanding colonettes: those in front with twelve

199 See also pp. 362, 363

flutes; those in back with seven (left) and nine (right). The bonnet door can be locked by means of an iron sliding bolt attached to the shaft and accessible through the shaft door. The bonnet side boards, triple tenoned through the bottom boards, are pierced with arched lights. On the shaft: The solid figured mahogany door is flanked by fluted quarter columns, each reinforced with two long glue blocks. The moldings above and below the shaft are in two parts. Rails tenoned into the stiles frame the front of the pedestal to receive a raised panel of figured wood having extended circular corners and molded edges. The glue blocks on the ogee-bracket feet are carved to follow the shape of the scalloped brackets. The back brackets of the rear legs are of mahogany cut on the diagonal. On the clock: The cast spandrels on the brass dial are applied. The ring that encloses the painted rocking ship in the lunette is silvered, as are the chapter ring and subsidiary seconds dial. Above the numeral VI is a date aperture. The movement is an eight-day rack and snail striking clock with anchor-recoil escapement. The rocking ship is attached to the verge anchor. The movement has five pillars.

CONDITION: The case retains much of the original red color of the mahogany, but the figure of the wood is partly lost under a later finish. At one time the scroll pediment was sawed off on a level with the bottom of the circular openings. The original pieces were later reattached, except for the carved bracket below the central finial and the top of the leaf directly under it, which are restorations. The large pierced brass keyhole escutcheon on the shaft door is old, but of a type found on the doors of desks and bookcases (e.g., PMA 1976, no. 84); it probably replaces a smaller, original one. The bottom board, the lower right part of the backboard, the shaft-door hinges, and the right-foot glue blocks are replacements. The underside of the case has been painted brown. A hole that may once have secured a maker's name plaque above the calendar aperture in the dial plate has been plugged. The rocking ship is newly painted. Behind it, the brass plate engraved with the setting sun may have been added.

INSCRIPTIONS: Engraved on the clock dial, in subsidiary dial beneath the numeral XII: *Willm Huston / Philadelphia*; in lunette: *Tempus et Aestus / neminem expectant* ["Time and Tide wait for no one"]. On back of wooden liner framing dial: an illegible chalk inscription, partly lost when the arch was cut out of the board. Chiseled into bonnet bottom: *I M*. In chalk, on outside of backboard: a script monogram that may combine the letters *T* and *H* [?] and words which may be partly read as *G— Ragn* [?] *– – / Jacobus N— / R—*. In brown ink (18th-century?), inside backboard: *S* [?] *Hamilton*; in chalk: *Milton / of Maneyunk —* [a town on the Schuylkill river northwest of Philadelphia] */ Jan 26 / 1864*. Painted in white and almost filling pedestal back: *1872*. In pencil, on shaft door: *Em Eddy rep / Sept 4–7 / cleaned Dec 7 72*.

DIMENSIONS: H.: overall, 105 (266.7); W.: cornice, 22 (55.9), shaft, 13½ (34.3), pedestal, 18¼ (46.4), feet, 19¾ (50.2); D.: cornice, 11¾ (29.8), shaft, 7⅝ (19.4), pedestal, 9¾ (24.8), feet, 10½ (26.7); Dial, less lunette, 12 × 12 (30.5 × 30.5).

WOODS: Primary: mahogany. Secondary: mahogany (seat board); tulip poplar (backboard); white pine (glue blocks).

REFERENCES: Downs 1948, p. 83 (ill.). George B. Tatum, *Philadelphia Georgian: The City House of Samuel Powel*, Middletown, Connecticut, Wesleyan University Press, 1976, p. 111, fig. 59.

Morris K. Jesup Fund, 1948   (48.99)

200. Wall Clock

Grafton, Massachusetts, 1772–82
Movement by Aaron Willard (1757–1844)

THIS IS ONE OF NEARLY two dozen known examples of what is the earliest form of the New England wall clock. Cat. no. 200, two clocks at Winterthur (Montgomery, no. 155 and acc. no. 57.920), one at Deerfield (Fales 1976, fig. 522), and one at Sturbridge (acc. no. 57.1.68) are signed on the dial by Aaron Willard; all the rest are signed by Simon Willard (see cat. no. 193). A variant was made by Timothy Sibley, of Sutton, Massachusetts (Rodriguez Roque, no. 39).

Simon Willard was active as a clockmaker by the early seventeen-seventies; Aaron, his younger brother, by the mid-seventeen-seventies. About Aaron's early life little is known. In 1775, he served in the Grafton militia. He appeared on the Roxbury Tax Lists in 1783, and as a resident of Roxbury, on the outskirts of Boston, in the 1790 census. In 1792 he bought an estate on the Neck in Boston, where by 1798 he had relocated his shop. He carried on the business until the eighteen-twenties (Willard, pp. 85–93). Simon and Aaron both worked in Grafton and in Roxbury. Two of Simon's wall clocks (ibid., pl. 16; *Antiques* 76 [November 1959], p. 438) and one of Aaron's (*Antiques* 75 [March 1959], p. 284) are inscribed "Grafton," but none is marked "Roxbury." Apparently, all these clocks were made in Grafton between about 1772 and 1782, after which the two Willards settled in Roxbury.

The Willard wall clocks are much alike. Except for one, all have a circular brass dial, like that of a large watch, centered somewhat awkwardly in the narrowest part of a bell-shaped glass in the door of a delicate cabinet. (The exception, at Sturbridge, has a bell-shaped brass dial with moon phase in the upper part; cat. no. 200 is the only one with a date aperture.) The scroll-footed upper case appears to stand on a plain rectangular pedestal, but that is illusory: the pedestal, which covers the pendulum and the weight, actually hangs from the backboard. Each clock of the group shows some variation in the shaping of the pierced crest (though that of the MMA clock is similar to another [Schorsch, color plate 6]) and scroll feet, as well as in the finishing of the edge of the frame around the glass. The design of these clocks was

200

the basis not for later wall clocks such as the famous "Banjo" patented by Simon in 1802 but for the Massachusetts shelf clock. A small number of clocks in the unmistakable scroll-footed type of upper cabinet actually stand on footed pedestals (e.g., Distin and Bishop, figs. 196, 216). On them, the circular dials have been raised to fit into the rounded part of the bell-shaped glass. From there to the characteristic Federal shelf clock in which Aaron Willard specialized (ibid., no. 200) was but a short step.

PROVENANCE: Ex coll.: George Coe Graves, Osterville, Massachusetts.

CONSTRUCTION: The case is in two parts. On the upper case: The movement, and above it the bell, are screwed to a thick backboard. The backboard is sawed out in a keyhole-shaped opening to receive the movement and pendulum, the latter covered by a separate board visible below the dial. The bonnet enclosing the clock is a single unit hinged to the backboard at the right side and latched to it at the left. The bell-shaped glass is framed by boards whose borders are pierced. The side boards are slotted into the top board and dovetailed to the bottom board. The board forming the scrolled feet is applied. On the lower case: The case is formed of an open-back box, the front

board overlapping the sides. The molded boards of top and bottom, the bottom thick and cut out on the inside surface to give play to the pendulum, are nailed in place. The case is suspended from iron rods that are implanted at the top, where the sides extend outward, and that fit into slots cut out of the upper-case backboard. On the clock: The brass dial is engraved and silvered. Below the numeral XII is a seconds dial; above VI, a calendar aperture. Small screws outside III and IX attach the dial to the cast brass rim edged in rope-twisting. The movement, a thirty-hour timepiece with dead-beat escapement, strikes once on the hour; it has circular plates and three pillars.

CONDITION: The upper case retains its old, decayed finish. Parts of the pierced strapwork of the crest have been restored; other parts of the strapwork at the top and on the sides are missing (Montgomery, no. 156, displays what may be the original configuration). The brass finial on the right is a replacement, as is the glass of the door. There are minor patches on the door's pierced border. The upper part of the case is otherwise well preserved. On the lower case, the molded bottom has been reattached and the finish cleaned, presumably after the clock-weight fell and displaced it. The lower case is now screwed to the upper-case backboard. Both parts of the clock were probably originally mounted on a separate pine backboard, now missing. On the clock, the seconds hand is replaced. The lead weight is modern.

INSCRIPTIONS: Engraved on dial between the numerals IIII and VIII: *Aaron Willard.*

DIMENSIONS: H.: overall, 23½ (59.7); W.: upper case, 6½ (16.5), midmoldings, 8⅞ (22.5), lower case, 7¼ (18.4); D.: upper case, 2¼ (5.7), midmolding, 3 (7.6), lower case, 2¾ (7.); Dial, diam., 4½ (11.4).

WOODS: Primary and secondary: mahogany.

REFERENCES: Barr 1951, p. 371, fig. 3 (ill. movement); idem 1959, p. 283 (ill.); idem, "An 'Unique' Willard Timepiece," *Bulletin of the National Association of Watch and Clock Collectors* 9 (December 1959), p. 17 (ill. case); p. 18 (ill. movement). Distin and Bishop, fig. 508.

The Sylmaris Collection, Gift of George Coe Graves, 1930 (30.120.52)

201. Shelf Clock

Newburyport, Massachusetts, 1792–1800
Movement by David Wood (1766–about 1850)

DAVID WOOD, WHO WAS born in Newburyport, Massachusetts, advertised in 1792 that he had "Set up a shop in Market Square, near Rev. Andrews' Meeting House" (Palmer 1928, p. 313). Three years later, at age twenty-nine, he married. In 1824 he again advertised, this time "New and second hand clocks for sale at the shop to which he has recently moved . . ." (ibid.). Little else is known of his life. Wood made tall clocks, but he is best known for the numerous shelf clocks that perpetuate his name. The majority of them have painted dials and are housed in veneered and inlaid Federal-style cases (e.g., Distin and Bishop, no. 206). Cat. no. 201 stands apart in having a silvered dial and a case decorated with three-dimensional architectural motifs—pilasters and a keystone arch—rather than with inlaid ornament. Stylistically, the clock appears to be one of Wood's earliest.

This distinctive type of case is known in a number of other examples: with movements by David Wood (Sack 1950, p. 131, right; Essex Institute, acc. no. 121.136); by Daniel Balch, Jr., of Newburyport (Schorsch, p. 117, no. 19-3); and by William Fitz, who was born in Newburyport and moved to Portsmouth, New Hampshire, in 1791 (Distin and Bishop, figs. 193, 194). Some, like cat. no. 201, have sarcophagus tops, others have broken-scroll pediments; some have silvered dials, others, painted. In all other respects, however, the cases housing these clocks are remarkably alike.

201

PROVENANCE: Ex coll.: George Coe Graves, Osterville, Massachusetts. Graves purchased the clock from Charles Woolsey Lyon, Inc., New York City, in 1926 (bill, MMA files) and gave it to the MMA in 1930. The clock was on loan to the Baltimore Museum of Art from 1952 to 1977.

CONSTRUCTION: The case is in two parts. On the upper case: The hollow sarcophagus top formed from a mitered, molded board is capped by a thin bead-edged board and a stepped block. Behind the cornice molding is a top board dovetailed to side boards veneered in mahogany and having arched windows. The tenons of the door frame are exposed. Thick posts and rails with veneered fronts and applied pilasters frame the door opening. The molded base rests on the beaded top edge of the lower case. On the lower case: The door's fluted pilasters and keystone arch are applied. The door is veneered; the boards framing its opening are solid. The veneered side boards are dovetailed to the bottom board. The fluted pilasters encasing the front corners and framing the rear edges continue behind the applied base molding. The backboard is secured with cut nails. On the clock: The brass dial is engraved and silvered. The movement is a timepiece that strikes once on the hour.

CONDITION: The case, which has been stripped, is a light reddish brown in color. The glass has been replaced. The lower door is warped. The brass finial is modern (1978), copied from one illustrated in the Sack Collection (4, p. 948) and replacing a large brass finial, added in 1930, of the type normally found on Massachusetts tall clock cases of the Federal period. The clock has been illustrated, with that finial, standing on a carved bracket that does not belong to it (Distin and Bishop, fig. 192).

INSCRIPTIONS: Engraved in lunette of dial: *David Wood / Newbury Port*. In pencil, on backboard behind bell: *Cleaned June 12th 1862 / By H. Withorell*; on inside of shaft door: *Cleaned By Wm Jacobs 5-31 /67*.

DIMENSIONS: H.: overall, 31½ (*80.*); W.: upper case, 8¾ (*22.2*), lower case, 10½ (*26.7*), base, 12¼ (*31.1*); D.: upper case, 4⅝ (*11.8*), lower case, 5¼ (*13.3*), base, 6¼ (*15.9*); Dial, less lunette, 5 × 5 (*12.7 × 12.7*).

WOODS: Primary: mahogany; mahogany veneer. Secondary: white pine.

REFERENCES: Distin and Bishop, fig. 192.

The Sylmaris Collection, Gift of George Coe Graves, 1930 (30.120.53)

20 Miscellaneous Case Forms

Included here are pieces that do not fit comfortably into any of the catalogue's other case-furniture chapters. The storage box with its Queen Anne-style molding and inlay is a holdover from a form that went out of fashion when drawers in case furniture became the norm. The dressing glass, knife boxes, and bentside spinets are characteristically English forms made only rarely in the colonies because either they were cheaper to import or there was no market for them. The writing table, a composite of a number of Chippendale designs, is without precedent in American furniture. The corner cupboards from the Eastern Shore of Virginia are exceptional in that they are freestanding. Elsewhere, such pieces were normally built into the paneling of a room and thus not furniture in the true sense.

202

202. Box

New England, 1735–60

SMALL BOXES DATING from the mid-eighteenth century are uncommon. The inlay patterns on this example suggest a Boston-area origin: the compass stars are a simplified version of the kind that was introduced in that city in the seventeen-thirties (see cat. no. 157), and the stringing, made of alternating light- and dark-wood parallelograms, is a crude version of a type sometimes found there (see cat. no. 207). A nineteenth-century history of ownership in Rhode Island is implied by the presence of Newport newspapers pasted inside the box (see Inscriptions).

PROVENANCE: Ex coll.: John E. Walton, Dobbs Ferry, New York.

CONSTRUCTION: The front and side edges of the two-piece top are thumbnail-molded, with an applied cove molding nailed on from below. The top moves on iron loops set into its back edge that engage cotter pins in the backboard. The boards of front and back are half-lapped over the side boards and nailed. The two-piece bottom, to which the cavetto base molding is nailed, overlaps and is nailed to the sides. The box is raised on two trestlelike supports, each roughly sawed out at the bottom in a shallow arch to form two rectangular feet. Pieces of lightwood, alternately dark-stained, form the decorative inlays.

CONDITION: The wood has a mellow brown color. The top, which is waterstained, has a shim crudely inserted between its two parts. The applied cavetto moldings at either end, three of the points of the top's inlaid compass star, and the cotter pins that attach the iron loops to the backboard are replacements.

INSCRIPTIONS: Inside top: illegible ink markings and numbers. Lining the sides and bottom of the interior are fragments of Newport, Rhode Island, newspapers, one dated 1821, another 1824. Glued over the joint on the inside of the two-piece top: a strip of paper from the *New York Weekly Times* of Saturday, March 22, 1862.

DIMENSIONS: H.: 7⅝ (*19.4*); W.: top, 15¾ (*40.*), case, 15 (*38.1*), skirt, 16⅛ (*41.*); D.: top, 8⅝ (*21.9*), case, 8¼ (*21.*), skirt, 9 (*22.9*).

WOODS: Primary: walnut; maple inlays. Secondary: walnut.

Gift of John E. Walton, in memory of his grandfather Homer L. Hoyt, 1972   (1972.237)

203. Knife Cases (Set of Three)

New York City, 1765–95

THIS TYPE OF KNIFE BOX, with boldly shaped front and sloping lid, was popular in England beginning in the late seventeenth century, and cases like these, veneered with mahogany and embellished with silver mounts, were popular there beginning in the late seventeen-sixties (*DEF* 2, p. 275, fig. 3). Advertisements of John Clark, "Shagreen and Mahogany Case-Maker" (Gottesman, pp. 111–112), in New York City newspapers between 1767 and 1774 prove that such pieces, although exceedingly rare, were also made in America. The New York attribution of cat. no. 203 is substantiated by the tulippoplar secondary wood and the silver mounts bearing the mark FUETER, for one of the family of New York City silversmiths.

Daniel Christian Fueter (1720–1785), a native of Switzerland, worked in New York from 1754 to 1769. Daniel's son Lewis was in partnership with him in the years preceding 1769, and carried on the craft thereafter; Daniel, Jr., was listed in the 1786–1806 New York Directories, though no pieces marked by him are known. The works of Daniel, Sr., and Lewis are distinguished by their initialed marks. The mounts on these boxes have been attributed to Lewis (*Antiques* 65 [February 1954], p. 99; Andrus 1955, p. 228) and to Daniel, Jr. (Darling, p. 81), either of which is plausible, since the case mounts are in the elaborate rococo manner of the seventeen-seventies and eighties.

Although generally fashioned in pairs, knife cases were also sold in threes. In 1769, John Cadwalader purchased from London "Two Mahogany Cases for knives lined & laced with Silver and ornamented with Silver Furniture" weighing 17 oz. 11dwt. for £13.4 and "one Dº," the furniture weighing 9 oz. 16dwt., for £6.17.6 (Wainwright, p. 81). The third case was larger, having heavier mounts and costing more than each of the others. In this set, by contrast, the odd case is smaller.

PROVENANCE: The cases were purchased in 1954 by Ginsburg & Levy, Inc. (from which the MMA acquired them that same year), directly out of the 2 East 79 Street, New York City, house of the late Augustus Van Horne Stuyvesant, Jr. (1870–1953). The cases are thought to have come down in the Stuyvesant line. Presumably they were made for Nicholas William Stuyvesant (1722–1780), a bachelor, or for his brother

203

Petrus (1727–1805), who married Margaret Livingston in 1764. They could also have been made for the latter's son Nicholas William (1769–1833), who married Catherine L. Reade in 1795. The direct line of descent was then to Gerard (1805–1859), who married Susan Rivington Van Horne in 1836; to Augustus Van Horne Stuyvesant (1838–1918), who married Harriet LeRoy Steward in 1864; to the last owner.

CONSTRUCTION: The three cases are en suite. Two are matching; the third is smaller and exhibits modest differences in the shape of its front and top and in the arrangement of its interior slots. Each case is a rectangular box, made of pine and veneered with mahogany (plain on the back and bottom and figured elsewhere), with serpentine front and canted top front edge. All junctures of top and sides are outlined with applied quarter rounds painted black. On the large cases, the angle of the top is so steep that its molded edge is overlapped by the silver lock escutcheon. The top, hinged in back, opens to expose a slanted surface partitioned to hold knives and other flatware. The larger cases have thirty-one openings; the smaller one, thirty-six. The dividers parallel to the back extend to the bottom; those at right angles are shallow. The lining is a mellow rusty rose velvet, with the openings and the corner seams outlined in silver braid. On each case are silver mounts consisting of two hinges, a lifting handle with escutcheon, a two-part lock with escutcheon, three claw-and-ball feet, and

two carrying handles. The hinges and lifting handle are identical on the three cases; the other mountings are scaled down for the small one. The left-side carrying handle of the small case and that of one of the large ones have been transposed. Because the holes cut into their sides to receive the stems of the handle supports are not interchangeable, the mix-up must have occurred when the cases were being made. The case illustrated is one of the large ones.

CONDITION: The wood has a fine old patina and a rich reddish color. Pieces of the narrow applied beading on the lower edge of the top are replaced on all the cases. A similar applied beading originally framed the bottom of each, but survives only in parts under the silver foot mounts of all three cases and on the back of the small one. There are small patches in the mahogany veneer at the right front on both the large cases, and the right rear divider strip is missing from inside one of them. The interiors, including the velvet and the silver braid, are otherwise well preserved.

INSCRIPTIONS: On the bottom of each of the silver rear-leg mounts: *FUETER* in a rectangle.

DIMENSIONS: large cases: H.: 14⅝ (*37.2*); W.: 8¾ (*22.2*); D.: 8⅞ (*22.5*); small case: H.: 13¼ (*33.7*); W.: 8 (*20.3*); D.: 7¾ (*19.7*).

WOODS: Primary: mahogany; mahogany veneer. Secondary: white pine (cores of sides, tops, bottoms); tulip poplar (interior dividers).

REFERENCES: *Antiques* 65 (February 1954), p. 99. Andrus 1955, p. 228. Aronson, fig. 833. Darling, p. 81 (ill. Feuter mark).

Morris K. Jesup Fund, 1954   (54.24.1–3)

204. Dressing Glass

Boston, 1760–90

A LOOKING GLASS mounted on a box stand that resembled a miniature chest of drawers was a popular form in England throughout the eighteenth century (*DEF* 2, pp. 352–357). Examples made in America before the Federal period are rare; even rarer are those with bombé-shaped stands. On cat. no. 204, the bold scalloping of the frame's crest and the dancing, flamelike appearance of the carved and gilded leafage in the central pierced opening proclaim the rococo taste of the seventeen-seventies, but the stand is executed with the straight-sided drawers that were present on the Boston bombé case pieces introduced two decades earlier. The shape of the bombé, the handling of the bracket feet and the central skirt pendant, and the treatment of the drawers are not unlike those of a secretary, now at the Department of State, made in 1753 by Benjamin Frothingham (1734–1809) and D. Sprage of Boston (Vincent, fig. 97). Three other bombé dressing glasses, each with a single drawer, have twist-turned posts with corkscrew finials supporting small mirror frames, two of them gilded. On one, at Winterthur (ibid., fig. 122), the drawer is straight-sided; on the other two (ibid., fig. 123, and Nutting 2, no. 3210), the drawer sides conform to the bombé, in the later Boston manner. The looking glass on cat. no. 204, much larger than any of the others, creates an overall effect not only assertive but, for such a small object, monumental.

PROVENANCE: Ex coll.: Harold M. and Cecile Lehman (later Cecile M. Mayer), Tarrytown, New York.

CONSTRUCTION: The scalloped horizontal crest board, glued to the top of the frame and reinforced with blocks, is vertically veneered. Its gilded central leaf carving is cut from the solid except for the projecting top frond. Around the mirror glass, the miter-jointed frame has a shallow applied molding with a carved and gilded inner border. On each rounded upper corner the molding is cut on the diagonal from a separate piece of wood. A vertical backboard protects the silvered glass. Between backward-slanted uprights slotted into the solid top board of the bombé chest the frame pivots on two thumbscrews that can be tightened to hold the glass at the desired angle. On the chest, the solid bombé side boards, straight on the inside, are dovetailed to the top board. The beading around the drawer openings is cut from the solid. On the drawers, the tops of the thin sides are rounded; the bottoms, laid crosswise, fit into rabbets on the front and sides. The chest's vertical backboards are nailed to the top and sides and to blocks, glued to the bottom board, that serve as drawer stops. The skirt molding is nailed to the edges of the bottom board. Each molded foot has three shaped glue blocks.

CONDITION: The wood of the dressing-glass stand has a buildup of varnishes and a rich dark brown patina. The gilt border and leaf carving on the frame have been varnished. The chest, its top board split, is badly warped. Some of the scrolled tips on the crest have been re-veneered. Two of the glue blocks on the feet are replaced. The glass's silvering is intact. The brass

204

finials and thumbscrews are modern. Each side drawer has a central hole and two holes with cotter-pin marks in addition to the present brasses, which are old replacements. The central-drawer lock is missing.

INSCRIPTIONS: In chalk, on outside of backboard: a number of numerical computations. Incised, on central-drawer back: compass marks.

DIMENSIONS: H.: overall, 33 *(83.8)*, frame, 25½ *(64.8)*, chest, 7½ *(19.1)*; W.: frame, 17⅜ *(44.1)*, chest, 22 *(55.9)*, feet, 22¼ *(56.5)*; D.: chest, 9¾ *(24.8)*, feet, 10 *(25.4)*; Glass, 17 × 15½ *(43.2 × 39.4)*.

WOODS: Primary: walnut (chest); walnut veneer (mirror frame). Secondary: walnut (foot glue blocks); white pine (all other framing members).

REFERENCES: Bondome, "The Home Market: The Box Toilet Mirror," *Antiques* 3 (March 1923), pp. 133–134. Nutting 2, no. 3206.

Bequest of Cecile L. Mayer, 1962   (62.171.14)

205. Writing Table

Philadelphia, 1760–85

WRITING TABLES are almost unheard of in eighteenth-century American furniture. This example, with its complexly shaped front and massive straight legs, has no known counterpart. The secondary woods, however, indicate a Middle-Colonies origin, and the Philadelphia family history, the Marlborough legs, and the ornateness of the design are compelling evidence of its source. The table combines features from a number of plates in the third edition of Chippendale's *Director* (1762). The design of the case front—a single wide blocked-in central drawer above an arched kneehole flanked by two tiers of serpentine-fronted drawers—is copied almost line for line from the writing table of plate LXXII; the gadrooning even matches the full-size detail shown at the left side of the illustration. Only the legs and the treatment of the kneehole spandrels are different. The table's

205

straight, stocky legs were inspired by the square legs, also carved out with astragal-ended panels, of plate LXXIV, another writing table, while the diapering appears to have been adapted from the spandrels on the cabinet of plate CXXI.

Physical evidence on cat. no. 205 indicates that at the rear of the flat top there once was an upper part, of which a hearsay description is recorded: "Between the time that it was sold by Mr. Moskowitz and Mr. Lyon the top had been converted from a sloping writing top with a series of pigeon-holes rising to a flat-topped writing table as it now stands" (Joseph Downs, undated notes, MMA files). The description of a "sloping writing top" is probably erroneous, but the mention of "a series of pigeon-holes rising" immediately recalls the illustration of the upper section of plate LXXII, with Chippendale's caption: "A Writing-Table, with Drawers in the under Part. In the Middle of the upper Part are small Drawers, and Pigeon-Holes, and a Place for Books." If the maker of cat. no. 205 was as faithful to the *Director*'s published designs for the upper part as he was for the lower, he would have modeled the missing section after that of either plate LXXII or plate LXXV, the only writing tables with superstructures. No matter which of the two he chose, there can be no doubt that this superb example of American cabinetwork was originally made as a "writing table" after Chippendale's designs.

PROVENANCE: Ex coll.: George Coe Graves, Osterville, Massachusetts. According to Hornor (1935, p. 178), the table descended in the Wistar and Wister families. In the early 1900s it was acquired by James A. Murphy, a Philadelphia collector, supposedly "from a Chinaman to whom it had been given by one of the Wister family of Philadelphia. At that time it was in a dilapidated condition having been relegated to the barn" (Joseph Downs, undated notes, MMA files). Mrs. Murphy wrote after her husband's death that he had sold the table to the Philadelphia dealer David Moskowitz (undated letter to Downs, MMA files). It was subsequently owned by Thomas Curran and Charles Woolsey Lyon, two other dealers, before being acquired by Graves.

CONSTRUCTION: The top, made up of one wide and one narrow board, has rounded front corners; its molded front and side edges conform to the shape of the frame below. The square legs, with chamfered inner edges, continue to the top; to them the side boards are tenoned and the backboard double pegged. The bottom rails, twelve inches in depth, are tenoned into the front legs and the side boards and are dovetailed to the kneehole sides, thus supporting the drawers and the kneehole arch. The kneehole side boards, their front edges faced with mahogany strips, form the stiles between the drawers. Joining them at the back is a horizontal board that encloses the kneehole space. Around the bottom edges of the kneehole opening and the front and sides of the case is continuous gadrooning, which on the shaped fronts of the bottom rails is carved from the solid and is elsewhere applied. Behind the rails, under each drawer, are full dust boards. The concave, diaper-cut arched board over the kneehole opening is fashioned from two vertical pieces of wood glued to a horizontal mahogany backing. The drawer fronts, sawed from thick boards and straight in back, are faced with vertical veneers and framed with applied beaded edges. The drawer bottoms, laid crosswise, are secured with glue blocks in front and with roseheads in back.

CONDITION: The wood of the writing table is now a reddish blond color. The table has been subjected to stripping and alterations as well as to restorations. The top, originally secured with glue blocks, is now screwed in place. There are multiple plugged or filled screw and nail holes through it, particularly at the front corners. The five-inch-wide rear board of the top is a replacement. Five pairs of square nail holes in the backboard and rear stiles mark where wooden battens once secured a superstructure above the top board. There is no evidence of knee brackets at the junctures of legs and skirts. The cuffs of the feet, missing in a photograph (MMA files) of the table when it was in the donor's possession, are replacements, as are parts of the gadrooning on the right front leg and two inches at the front on the right side of the kneehole. Bisected dovetails and replaced beading at the top of each of the three upper drawers attest that at an earlier time, probably when the superstructure was removed, a strip three-eighths of an inch thick was sawed off to allow for the insertion of a fixed rail between the drawers and the top. As a consequence, the brasses on those drawer fronts appear to be located too far up. There are patches to the veneer of the middle drawer. On the right-hand drawer, filler strips have been added between the pieces of veneer. The brasses are replaced.

INSCRIPTIONS: In chalk, inside center-drawer backboard: *B X.* The drawer sides are numbered in chalk for assembly.

DIMENSIONS: H.: 29¾ (*75.6*); W.: top, 49¾ (*126.4*), frame, 46¾ (*118.8*), feet, 47¾ (*121.3*); D.: top, 25 (*63.5*), frame, 23 (*58.4*), feet, 23¾ (*60.3*).

WOODS: Primary: mahogany. Secondary: yellow pine (backboard, vertical dividers between drawers); sweet gum (drawer sides and backs); Atlantic white cedar (drawer bottoms); tulip poplar (dust boards).

REFERENCES: Hornor 1935, pp. 123, 178, 180–181, 186; pl. 116. Downs 1949, pl. 23. Comstock, fig. 403. Davidson 1967, fig. 283.

The Sylmaris Collection, Gift of George Coe Graves, 1932 (32.125.1)

206. Bentside Spinet

Philadelphia, 1739
Johannes Gottlob Clemm (1690–1762)

THE BENTSIDE, OR TRANSVERSE, spinet was introduced into England from Italy in the third quarter of the seventeenth century. The earliest dated English example is by Thomas Hitchcock in 1660. By 1700 the spinet had superseded the rectangular virginal as the common domestic

206 See also p. 366

keyboard instrument. With only minor changes, it was made continuously into the seventeen-eighties as a smaller and cheaper alternative to the harpsichord, with which it shared a similar mechanism that plucked the strings to produce the sound.

Cat. no. 206 is the only instrument now known by Johannes Clemm. Clemm (or Klemm, as he is also known) was born in 1690 in Germany, near Dresden, and studied theology before turning to organ-building. In 1733 he emigrated to America, settling near Philadelphia. A receipt for £3, dated August 6, 1735, on account from Peter Boynton of that city, is signed by John Klemm, organmaker (Hornor 1935, pl. 70). Clemm built the organ for Trinity Church in New York in the years 1739–41, and in 1746, in association with organ-builder and portrait-painter Gustavus Hesselius, installed an organ in the Moravian Church at Bethlehem, Pennsylvania. In Nazareth, in 1758, he began a collaboration with David Tannenberg (who was to become the leading organ-builder of eighteenth-century Pennsylvania) that was to continue until Clemm's death on May 5, 1762.

This spinet is the earliest known one made in America. Thus, despite the ignominy of once having been turned into an exhibition case, it has an important place among the incunabula of American furniture. Its bent side, of solid wood rather than veneered, suggests the influence of continental spinet design rather than English practice (for which see cat. no. 207). In place of a trestle-type support is a stand with turned legs joined by rails at the top and by box stretchers below. Of eighteenth-century date, it is apparently original to the spinet, although the marks on the bottom that would prove the mutuality of the two are not distinct enough to be conclusive.

PROVENANCE: Ex coll.: Mrs. J. Amory Haskell, Red Bank, New Jersey. Purchased by the MMA at the Haskell sale in 1944.

CONSTRUCTION: The spinet and its stand are separate units. On the spinet: The top is hinged in back. The bottom is three pine boards laid parallel to the keyboard, under which the first two are united by large butterfly-shaped inserts. Strips of paper, covered with inscriptions and calculations and probably torn from an eighteenth-century account book, are pasted over the joint between the bottom and bentside boards and around an interior one behind the nameboard to seal the sound box. The sharp curve of the bentside board was created by the compressing of a series of vertical saw cuts, or kerfs, on its inner surface. The removable nameboard, with inset rectangular light-wood nameplate, is slotted into the boards flanking the keyboard. On the stand: Let into the top rails on either side of the front leg are two exposed-end medial braces that extend diagonally to the rear rail. The rails and stretchers are pegged to the three legs.

CONDITION: Both spinet and stand have been stripped and refinished. The former is a walnut brown in color; the latter, a pale tan. The case is much altered. Most of the interior mechanism was removed when the spinet was made into a display case. When the MMA purchased the instrument at auction, the catalogue noted that "the top is glazed and lined in olive velours to form a vitrine." The top, its glass now replaced with a wooden panel, is modern. Patches in the backboard, or spine, mark the place of the two hinges of the original top. The fallboard, which was hinged to the top and could be lowered to cover the keyboard, is missing. Screw holes in the center of the board below the keyboard show where the fallboard clasp was received. At one time, presumably when the present top was added, a keyhole and lock were inserted over the nameplate. The velours has been removed from the interior. There are traces of vermilion paint on the edge of the soundhole centered in the soundboard, but the decorative rose that covered it is gone. The strings, bridge, jacks, jack rail and left bracket, and hitch pins are missing. The original four-and-a-half-octave keyboard (the compass F–C) has been replaced by a nineteenth-century one. The stand has been apart and repegged.

INSCRIPTIONS: In brown ink, on nameboard, in Gothic script: *Johannes Clemm fecit Philadelphia 1739.*

DIMENSIONS: H.: overall, 33½ (*85.1*), case, 8 (*20.3*), stand, 25½ (*64.8*); W.: case, 73¼ (*186.7*), stand, 61½ (*156.2*); D.: case, 27 (*68.6*), stand, 18¼ (*46.4*).

WOODS: Primary: walnut; maple (legs); yellow pine (rails, stretchers of stand). Secondary: walnut (pin block, upper and lower jack guides); Atlantic white cedar (soundboard).

REFERENCES: Hornor 1935, p. 66. Haskell sale 5, lot 669. Downs 1945, p. 66. *American Collector* 15 (April 1946), p. 13 (ill.). *Antiques* 93 (April 1968), p. 489, fig. 12a. Boalch, p. 25. For Clemm biographies, see Orpha Ochse, *The History of the Organ in the United States*, Bloomington, Indiana, 1975, pp. 15–18; John Ogasapian, *Organ Building in New York City: 1700–1900*, Braintree, Massachusetts, 1977, pp. 3–5.

Rogers Fund, 1944 (44.149)

207. Bentside Spinet

Boston, 1769
John Harris (active 1730–69)

SPINETS WERE SO RARELY made in colonial America that it was newsworthy when one was. On September 18, 1769, the *Boston-Gazette, and Country Journal* reported:

> It is with Pleasure we inform the Publick, That a few Days since / was ship'd for Newport, a very curious Spinet, being the first / ever made in America; the performance of the

ingenious Mr. John / Harris, of Boston (Son to the late Mr. Joseph Harris, of London, / Harpsichord and Spinet Maker, deceas'd) and in every Respect / does Honour to that Artist, who now carries on said Business at his / House a Few Doors Northward of Dr. Clark's, North-End, Boston.

(also quoted in Dow, in slightly different form, p. 301)

There is every reason to believe that the instrument referred to is cat. no. 207, for it and the one mentioned in the announcement were both made in Boston by John Harris and were both in Newport in the eighteenth century. In addition, cat. no. 207 has been identified with the news report quoted, at least since 1895 (Earle, pp. 225–226). With the exception of one bought in 1772 by the Boston merchant Isaac Smith, no Boston-made spinet by John Harris is recorded. Indeed, the only other known eighteenth-century Massachusetts stringed keyboard instrument is a spinet by Samuel Blyth of Salem (Fales 1965, no. 49).

John Harris was one of a prominent family of London musical-instrument makers. A number of spinets and harpsichords dated in the seventeen-fifties and made by Joseph Harris, John's father, survive (Boalch, p. 60). John himself is recorded as having made three spinets in London (ibid.), and he may be the man listed in Mortimer's *Universal Directory* (London, 1763) as "Maker of the Armonica" (Boalch, pp. 59–60). He moved to Boston in 1768. According to an advertisement in the *Boston Chronicle* on May 16 of that year:

> From London, John Harris, who is just arrived in Capt. Calef, begs / leave to inform the public, that he *makes* and *sells* all sorts of *Harpsichords* and *Spinnets*. Likewise mends,

207 See also p. 366

repairs, new strings, / and tunes the said instruments, in the best and neatest manner. . . . He / lives at Mr. John Moore's, next door to Dr. Clarke's in the North end.

Similar advertisements, on July 4 and November 14, report Harris as living at "Mr. Gavin Brown's Watchmaker [see cat. no. 191] North-side of *King Street*."

The following year John made cat. no. 207. The instrument is in the classic English bentside-spinet form. It differs little from those made in mid-eighteenth-century London by members of the Harris family. Moreover, in many particulars—the pattern of the ornamental brass hardware, for example—it is notably like one signed by Baker Harris, dated 1770, now in London (Raymond Russell, *Catalogue of Musical Instruments, Victoria and Albert Museum, Vol. I, Keyboard Instruments*, London, 1968, fig. 23), and another signed by William Harris, dated 1766, now at the St. Louis Museum (acc. no. 286:55). The latter retains its original stand, which is similar to that of cat. no. 207. The nameplate John Harris used here—oblong with shaped and pointed ends and Gothic lettering—is similar to English ones, if somewhat cruder. What sets the MMA spinet apart is the bold barber-pole banding that surrounds the mahogany side panels; the use of a number of American woods in the interior; and the unequivocal inscription on the nameboard. Otherwise, the instrument might be of English manufacture.

Carpenter (no. 50) has suggested that the stand, which stylistically could have originated either in Boston or in Newport, may have been made in Newport after the spinet's arrival. That attractive theory is unlikely. The stand is so similar to known English ones, particularly that at St. Louis, that it must have been made under the direct supervision of the instrumentmaker. Disassembled, it would have been easily transportable. There was apparently a limited market for American-made spinets, and no uniquely American version of the form evolved.

PROVENANCE: Ex coll.: Mr. and Mrs. Jess Pavey, Detroit, Michigan; Mr. and Mrs. Walter B. Robb, Buffalo, New York. Mr. and Mrs. Pavey bought the spinet in about 1941 from the dealer David Stockwell; Mr. and Mrs. Robb sold it in 1975 to Israel Sack, Inc., New York City, from which the MMA acquired it. According to family tradition (letter, Elizabeth Breese McIlvaine to David Stockwell, 2/16/50, copy, MMA files), the spinet is said to have been first owned by the merchant Francis Malbone (1728–1785) and his wife, Margaret, whose great brick house still stands on Thames Street in Newport, and the instrument to have been given to their daughter Mary (1771–1815) on her marriage to William Crooke (1760–1832) in 1796. Credence is lent to that belief by William Crooke's engraved card, which is attached to the spinet key (see Inscriptions). At Mary Crooke's death, there being no issue, the spinet was supposedly transferred to her sister Elizabeth Malbone (1755–1832), who was married to Major John Breese (1738–1799) of Newport. From them, the line of descent was to Thomas Breese (1793–1846) and to his last surviving child,

Francis Malbone Breese (1837–1912). A photograph (19th-century, copy, MMA files) shows the spinet in the parlor of the eighteenth-century John Gidley house at Thames and Gidley streets, which was purchased by an Edward Breese in 1825 (Antoinette F. Downing and Vincent J. Scully, Jr., *The Architectural Heritage of Newport Rhode Island 1640–1915*, rev. ed., New York, Clarkson N. Potter, 1967, pp. 71–72). In 1877, the same spinet was reported to be the property of Miss Catharine Crook, 11 Spring Street, Newport (Dow, p. 301), and indeed the inventory of Katherine M. Crooke's estate (February 25, 1881, Newport Rhode Island Probate Records 33, p. 617) does list a spinet valued at $20. Again, in 1895, cat. no. 207 was noted as being in the Edward Breese house (Earle, p. 226). In 1906, when the house was demolished, Francis Malbone Breese removed the parlor paneling and the spinet to a house at 31 Old Beach Road in Newport. A photograph (MMA files) shows the spinet in the alcove especially designed for it; the paneling has since been installed at Winterthur. On Francis Breese's death, in 1912, the spinet descended to his niece Elizabeth Malbone Breese McIlvaine, of Downingtown, Pennsylvania, who sold it to David Stockwell.

CONSTRUCTION: The spinet and the stand are separate units. On the spinet: The top, its molded edge nailed from below, consists of four boards laid parallel to the keyboard and butted together. It is attached to the backboard, or spine, with three hinges that continue inside as shaped straps; three similar hinges attach the round-edged fallboard to it. The keyboard can be locked by means of a brass clasp centered in the bottom edge of the fallboard's plain outer surface. The nameboard, with the nameplate centered in crossbanded veneers, slots into place behind the keyboard. The veneer pattern on the nameboard, on the board above it, and on the bentside boards and the sides consists of mahogany panels framed with barber-pole banding and crossbanded borders. The soundboard is of eight pieces of wood. It is laid parallel to the keyboard, as are the bottom boards. On the stand: The trapezial trestle-type stand has two pairs of baluster-turned supports that terminate in cabriole legs and pad feet; the knees and pads of those at the right pieced out on one side; of those at the left, on two sides. Both pairs of legs are joined together at the top by a thick cleat and above the knees by a thick rail with one molded top edge, the rails attached with iron bed bolts to a long medial rail. The stand is thus easily disassembled for shipping. Small projecting knobs, two on top of each cleat, correspond to indentations in the bottom of the spinet, fixing the correct juxtaposition of the two parts. The range of the instrument is F–F, five octaves (the lowest F-sharp is absent).

CONDITION: The spinet has a fine mellow reddish brown patina. As a result of shrinkage there are wide spaces between the boards that form the top. The battens screwed to its underside are later additions. The mechanism is complete. The black keys, some of the white-key ivories, and the jack-rail rest appear to be old replacements. The arcades on the key fronts were originally gilded. The lower guide was added when the box guide was found to be inadequate.

INSCRIPTIONS: In brown ink, on nameboard, in Gothic script: *John Harris. Boston New England fecit*. In chalk, on belly rail: *back loose over*. Engraved, on a paper card (19th-century) attached with an old strip of green velvet to the spinet lock's iron key, recto: *William Crooke*; in brown ink, verso: *Key to / Spinnet* (ill. Carpenter, p. 208).

DIMENSIONS: H.: overall, 32¾ (*83.2*), case, 9⅛ (*23.2*), stand, 23½ (*59.7*); W.: case, 79⅜ (*201.6*), stand, 48 (*121.9*); D.: case, 30½ (*77.5*), stand, 23 (*58.4*).

WOODS: Primary: mahogany; maple [?] (light-wood inlays); mahogany veneer (side boards, nameboard, jack rail). Secondary: white oak (core of bent side and sides flanking keyboard); white pine (boards of bottom and spine, cores of nameboard, jack rail, and keys); Atlantic white cedar (soundboard); cherry (jack socket); apple or other fruit wood (jacks); birch (location knobs in top of stand).

REFERENCES: Earle, pp. 225–226. Dow, p. 301. *Antiques* 62 (November 1952), p. 348. Carpenter, no. 50; Supplement 50. Gaines, p. 489. Boalch, pp. 59–60. MFA 1975, no. 135. Sack 5, pp. 1212–13. *Antiques* 109 (March 1976), inside front cover.

Purchase, Anonymous Gift, Friends of the American Wing Fund, Sansbury-Mills, Dodge, and Pfeiffer Funds, and funds from various donors, 1976   (1976.229)

208. Corner Cupboard

Virginia, 1780–1800

ON THIS EXAMPLE, the doors—the upper one glazed, the lower one paneled—and the fluted pilaster boards facing the canted sides of the front are typical of dozens of corner cupboards made between about 1740 and 1820 on the Eastern Shore of Virginia (Melchor, Lohr, and Melchor, figs. 66–100). Many of them, including this one, were originally painted green with white highlights. Cat. no. 208 is unusual only in having three rather than four tiers of panes. The cupboard has been associated with a few others, which, while more elaborate or refined, have similar moldings (ibid., figs. 66–68). All share two peculiar features: on the pilasters the first flute is cut into the front corner, and all the flute endings are concave. Of the cupboards of the group, three made with roseheads appear to be of mid-century date. Cat. no. 208, constructed with cut nails, was probably made toward the end of the century.

PROVENANCE: Ex coll.: Mrs. Robert W. de Forest, New York City. Purchased by the donor from the Brooklyn dealer Charles Morson in 1922, at which time the cupboard was thought to be Pennsylvania German.

CONSTRUCTION: The triangular cupboard is made in one piece. The facing boards of the three chamfered corners and the fronts and backs of the three-board sides continue to the floor. Fluted pilaster strips are nailed to the canted front boards; across them extend the moldings of cornice, middle, and base. The top and bottom are single pieces of wood. Behind the paneled lower door are two thin, plain-fronted shelves.

CONDITION: The cupboard has been stripped, and the waxed pine has turned a reddish brown color. Traces of the original

green and white paint remain, showing that the elements highlighted in white were the shallow cavettos in the cornice and projecting midmolding, and the beveled edges of the bottom door panels and their surrounding moldings (Melchor, Lohr, and Melchor, pl. 7, illustrates a similar, intact paint pattern). The shelves behind the upper door have been replaced; the original top one was two inches higher than the upper glazing bar. A replacement for the rotted bottoms of the rear boards has been installed. The present door hinges are the third set. Originally there were large *H*-shaped wrought-iron hinges nailed in place and painted the green of the cupboard. The lower door was originally fitted with a lock and a small brass escutcheon plate, now replaced, and with a wooden twist latch, now gone, nailed to the stile near the top of the door. The turned knob is a later addition. The upper door appears to have been originally secured by a wooden twist latch, now missing, just below the present brass knob.

208

INSCRIPTIONS: Pasted to bottom board, part of a printed shipping label (19th-century): *Princess Anne, Md. (N.Y.P + N.)*; ink-stamped: *89-81-03*.

DIMENSIONS: H.: 81½ (*207*.); W.: cornice, 41 (*104.1*), case, 40 (*101.6*); D.: 20 (*50.8*).

WOODS: Primary and secondary: yellow pine.

REFERENCES: Melchor, Lohr, and Melchor, fig. 69; figs. 69a, 69b (molding profiles).

Gift of Mrs. Robert W. de Forest, 1933   (34.100.11)

209. Corner Cupboard

Virginia, 1750–90

THE GLAZED UPPER DOOR with arched panes on top and the fluted pilasters at the sides clearly place cat. no. 209 with its numerous fellows made on the Eastern Shore of Virginia, but this corner cupboard has a stateliness and presence found in no other. It is taller and narrower than the norm (cf. cat. no. 208), having five tiers of panes in the door rather than four or three, and is made of walnut rather than of painted pine. (For another example in walnut, see Melchor, Lohr, and Melchor, fig. 71.) The pilasters on a painted corner cupboard with a history across Chesapeake Bay in Gloucester County, Virginia (MESDA research file S-2625), have fluting and multiple applied moldings similar to those of cat. no. 209 (Melchor, Lohr, and Melchor, fig. 73). The two cupboards are apparently by the same hand.

PROVENANCE: Ex coll.: Louis Guerineau Myers, New York City.

CONSTRUCTION: The freestanding cupboard was constructed in a similar manner to cat. no. 208 except that the side boards are single pieces of wood cut out in an arch at the bottom. The cornice molding is in four parts; the midmolding is a single piece except for the applied projecting ovolo. The top and bottom boards and the three scallop-fronted shelves behind the glazed door are single pieces of wood attached with roseheads to the sides and back. The frames of the doors and the door openings are pegged. Behind the lower door is a single shelf with simple blocked-in front.

CONDITION: The cupboard has a dark golden brown color and a fine patina. The piece has been sawed in half behind the projecting applied ovolo of the midmolding. The original bottom shelf of the upper cupboard now forms the bottom of the upper case; old boards have been added to create the top of the lower section. The interior of the upper cupboard has been painted brown. The tips of the central scallops of the middle shelf have broken off. Part of the edge of the fielded-door panel on the right is patched. The bottom of the backboard, which forms the rear foot, is rotted. The front feet are slightly reduced in height. The door pulls, locks, and eighteenth-century escutcheons are replacements. The original lock on the upper door remains in situ just below the handle, but the keyhole has been plugged and the plain small escutcheon plate is missing.

INSCRIPTIONS: Stamped, on backs of door hinges: *16*.

DIMENSIONS: H.: 87¼ (*221.6*); W.: cornice, 39½ (*100.3*), case, 36 (*91.4*); D.: 16 (*40.6*).

WOODS: Primary: walnut. Secondary: yellow pine.

REFERENCES: Nutting 1, fig. 524. Lee 3, p. 299 (measured drawings); p. 300 (ill.). Margon 1949, pp. 13–15 (measured drawings; molding profiles). Davidson 1967, fig. 205. Melchor, Lohr, and Melchor, figs. 74, 74a-c (molding and shelf profiles).

Rogers Fund, 1925   (25.115.30)

209

IV FRAMES

21 Looking Glasses

Looking glasses, or simply glasses—today called mirrors—were fixtures in most eighteenth-century American homes. Their logical place in both bedchambers and parlors was between two windows. Very few American-made looking-glass frames have been identified; the great majority of the wooden frames and all the mirror glass were imported from England or, to a lesser extent, from the continent. The origin of a frame is readily determined by its secondary woods: for American examples, eastern white pine; for English ones, mainly Scotch pine and spruce. With few exceptions, the looking glasses in the collection are of English manufacture and are not included in this book. Those present are New England in origin and Queen Anne in style: a simple, sconcelike pair, a wonderfully intact japanned example, and a looking glass on a box stand (the dressing glass mentioned at Chapter 20). Not in the collection is any Philadelphia carved rococo frame.

210

210. Looking Glass

Boston, 1730–50

THE LOOKING GLASS and its en suite high chest and
dressing table (cat. nos. 155, 156), all with a history of descent in the Pickman and Loring families of Salem and all
constructed of New England woods, were decorated by
the same hand. The japanner's individual style is most apparent in those areas where the looking-glass frame and
the high chest are similar. The moldings, for example, are
divided into rectangles on both pieces: floral motifs on
tortoiseshell alternating with jagged cloudlike designs on
gold. Though the Boston japanner Robert Davis has been
suggested (Brazer, pp. 208–210) as the maker of other
American looking glasses, cat. no. 210 is the only one
now known of unquestionable Boston manufacture. This
most magnificent domestic example is large in size and
contains bevel-edged mirror glasses. So well preserved
that it retains its smooth and shining lacquerlike appearance, it must demonstrate the original finish of all its
counterparts.

PROVENANCE: See cat. no. 155.

CONSTRUCTION: The scalloped crest consists of a thin horizontal board secured with a glue block to the curved top of the
frame, and two thin, vertical side boards half-lapped to it from
behind. The upper part of the beveled, two-piece glass overlaps
the lower. The framing members and their applied front moldings conform to the shape of the glass. On the framing members, retangular in section, the sides are half-lapped over the
tops and bottoms and nailed from behind. The front molding
overlaps the crest boards slightly and the glass by half an inch.
Made in six parts, it has vertical joints between the top and side
pieces and horizontal joints where the shaped upper sides meet
the straight lower sides. The vertical backboard, its shape following that of the frame, is roughly planed both inside and out.
The exterior parts of the frame are painted in a tortoiseshell
pattern—black streaks on a vermilion ground. On the crest, the
ribs of the shell, the strapwork above it, and the chinoiserie figure and buildings are built up with gesso and gilded. On the
molding, raised bronze-colored gilt floral motifs superimposed
on the tortoiseshell ground alternate with motifs painted in
black on panels of lemon-colored gilt.

CONDITION: The japanning is wonderfully intact. The face
and hands of the chinoiserie figure and the painted border
outlining the scroll top, apparently once silvered, are now tar-
nished. Two old splits in the horizontal crest board were repaired with rows of small glue blocks, with additional glue
blocks securing the crest boards and the mirror glass to the
frame. The glasses have never been out of the frame. The silvering is well preserved. The backboard has been renailed.

INSCRIPTIONS: In chalk, on backboard: a line repeating the
curved outline of the frame. In brown ink, on Boston MFA paper labels (20th-century), on backboard: 52.17 / Dwight; on upper framing member: T.L.1059 / Mrs. Amory (in reference to
Mrs. William Amory's consignment for restoration, 1920–23).

DIMENSIONS: frame: H.: 57½ (*146.1*); W.: 19⅛ (*48.6*); D.: 1¼ (*3.2*); glass, upper part, 13¾ × 16 (*34.9 × 40.6*), lower part, 34 × 16 (*86.4 × 40.6*).

WOODS: Primary: white pine. The molded border has not been examined.

REFERENCES: Downs 1940, p. 146 (mentioned).

Purchase, Joseph Pulitzer Bequest, 1940　　　　(40.37.4)

211. Looking Glasses (Pair)

New England, 1740–90

OF DIMINUTIVE SIZE and exaggerated verticality, each of the mirrors is suited only to reflecting the light of a single candle. Except that they have never been fitted with the brass candle holders that would have been screwed to the scalloped bottom of the frame, they are characteristic of sconces, or wall lights, which were routinely made in pairs in the eighteenth century (Nutting 2, nos. 2787–89, 2833, 2861–62, 2864). The pair must originally have hung on a wall behind candlesticks placed on a mantel or a piece of furniture. American examples are very rare, but the white pine of which these two are made indicate a New England origin. A larger but otherwise similar example is complete with its candle holder (Sack 6, p. 1625).

PROVENANCE: Ex coll.: Louis Guerineau Myers, New York City. A photograph (MMA files) shows the pair of looking glasses hanging above a mantel in Myers's house.

CONSTRUCTION: On each frame: The rectangular sides, extending at top and bottom to the beginning of the scalloping, are half-lapped over and nailed to the thick horizontal boards above and below. Each thick board, cut away in a bevel-edged triangular block behind its sawed-out scalloping, is faced with vertical veneers. The mirror opening is framed with applied moldings whose shaped upper corners, applied to separate, diagonally veneered pieces, are butted against the top and side strips. The rectangular mirror glass is secured with glue blocks. The vertical backboard is nailed on.

CONDITION: Each frame is covered with a thick buildup of old finishes, now much darkened and decayed; the narrow inner molding retains its original black paint. The sides are stained black. Some of the tips of the scalloping are patched, and there are splits in the veneers. The mirror-glass silvering is remarkably well preserved. The backboard has been renailed. The hanging mechanism, probably a wire looped through two closely spaced holes centered above the glass, is missing.

DIMENSIONS: frame: H.: 19 (*48.3*); W.: 5¼ (*13.3*); D.: ⅞ (*2.*); glass: 11¾ × 4 (*29.8 × 10.2*).

WOODS: Primary: walnut; walnut veneer. Secondary: white pine (frame, backboard).

Rogers Fund, 1925　　　　(25.115.40, 41)

211

22 Picture Frames

The frames that protected and enhanced the portraits hanging in late colonial houses were among their most elaborate and costly furnishings. Frames for pictures, like those for looking glasses, were more often imported into colonial America than made there. Only three among all the frames in which the Museum's eighteenth-century American portraits are displayed can, on the basis of the native eastern white pine used in them, be adjudged to be of local manufacture. Still with the pastels by Copley original to them, these examples of the carver's art must be considered among the fullest expressions of the rococo spirit in American furniture.

212. Picture Frames (Pair)

Boston, 1767–69

THE FRAMES ENCLOSE matching pastel portraits of Ebenezer Storer (1699–1761) and his wife, Mary Edwards Storer (1700–1771), painted by John Singleton Copley between about 1767 and 1769 (Prown). Ebenezer's was a posthumous portrait. Copley frequently supplied frames for his sitters' portraits (Ward, pp. 16–20; Cooper 1980, p. 139), most of them elaborately carved and gilded rococo examples, some imported, others locally made. The American white pine used for the superbly carved Storer frames indicates local manufacture. Many details of their design match those of the frames, also of white pine and apparently by the same carver, on Copley's large, forty-by-fifty-inch oils of Mr. and Mrs. Isaac Smith, painted in 1769 and now at Yale (Ward, fig. 1). Mrs. Smith, née Elizabeth Storer, was Mary and Ebenezer's eldest daughter.

During his celebrated 1771 New York trip, about two years after having completed the Smith portraits, Copley called upon his half brother Henry Pelham to supply him with frames. On October 11, regarding small frames such as those of cat. no. 212, he wrote, "Let me know what you paid Welch for carving and Whiting for gilding" (quoted in Ward, p. 18). He was undoubtedly referring to John Welch (1711–1789), who was a well-known Boston carver (Yehia, pp. 213, 215), and to Stephen Whiting (1728–1789), a framemaker, japanner, and gilder of the same city (Brazer, p. 213). Both men were leading craftsmen and could well have made the Storer frames.

212

PROVENANCE: The framed portraits descended from the subjects to Elizabeth Storer Smith (1726–1786); to William Smith (1755–1816); to Thomas Smith; to William Vincent Smith (1840–1920), who changed his name to William Smith Carter in 1881; to Theodore Parkman Carter, from whom the MMA acquired them.

CONSTRUCTION: On each frame: Each of the four sides is in two parts. The first part is a thick board carved out in a deep cove with leaf streamers and rosettes, and, bordering the picture, in a gadrooned inner edge. The second part, a thin rim embellished at the corners and in the middle of each side with carved acanthus leafage, is nailed to the outer front edge of the thick board, the leafage covering large spaces cut away at corresponding points in the latter. The carving is finished with gilded gesso; the sides are painted yellow.

CONDITION: On each frame: The gilding, for the most part the original, is a yellow gold in color. Screw holes remain in the top from two rings from which the frame was originally suspended. On one: The top left rosette and the tip of the lower left corner are gone; the bottom cove is split. On the other: The two top rosettes and the tips at the middle of the right side and the lower right corner are gone.

INSCRIPTIONS: In brown ink, on a paper label (19th-century) pasted on one backboard: *Ebenezer Storer. | Of Sudbury Street. | Boston. | Born 1699—Died 1761*; on the other: *Mrs Ebenezer Storer. | Her Maiden Name | was Mary Edwards. | Born 1700. Died 1771.*

DIMENSIONS: frame: H.: 30½ (*77.5*); W.: 24½ (*62.2*); D.: 2½ (*6.4*); opening, 23 × 16¾ (*58.4 × 42.5*).

WOODS: Primary and secondary: white pine.

REFERENCES: Hermann Warner Williams, Jr., "Two Early Pastels by Copley," *MMAB* 36 (June 1941), pp. 136–140. Prown 1, pp. 62–67, 230; pls. 234, 235. Ward, pp. 16–19. For the Storer family, see Malcolm Storer, *Annals of the Storer Family*, Boston, 1927.

Purchase, Thomas J. Watson Gift, 1940   (40.161.1, 2)

213

213. Picture Frame

Boston, about 1765

IN THIS FRAME is a pastel portrait of Mrs. Edward Green, of Boston, painted by John Singleton Copley in 1765. Mrs. Green, née Mary Storer, was one of the daughters of Ebenezer and Mary Storer, whose portraits Copley painted between about 1767 and 1769 (cat. no. 212). The gilded frames of all three portraits, rococo in style and carved from white pine, are of American manufacture. The general similarities of the three notwithstanding, this frame is the work of a less accomplished carver.

PROVENANCE: Ex coll.: Mrs. David Murray, New Brunswick, New Jersey. The MMA purchased the frame with the portrait from Mrs. Murray.

CONSTRUCTION: See cat. no. 212. Between the acanthus-scrolled corners, the thin rim is in the form of a bead. In place of a gadroon, the inner border is leaf-carved.

CONDITION: Though the frame has been badly broken, all the original parts survive. The mitered joints at each corner have been rebuilt behind the carved leafage. A steel armature has been added to reinforce the frame. The gessoed surface has been regilded.

INSCRIPTIONS: Signed, at lower left of portrait: *John S. Copley / fect 1765*. Fragments of newspaper pasted to back of stretcher. In brown ink, on a paper label (19th-century) pasted to backboard: *A Pastel of Mary Storer of Boston. / Painted by Copley 1766. belonging / to Mrs. David Murray / New Brunswick / New Jersey.* On a separate label: *Murray.* On a printed paper label (19th-century): *Return to T. A. Wilmurt & Son, 34 East 13th Street, NEW YORK.*

DIMENSIONS: frame: H.: 29½ (74.9); W.: 24½ (69.2); D.: 2¾ (7.); opening, 22¼ × 16⅜ (56.5 × 41.6).

WOODS: Primary and secondary: white pine.

REFERENCES: *MMAB* 3 (February 1908), pp. 37–38. Prown 1, p. 216.

Purchase, Curtis Fund, 1908   (08.1)

PHOTOGRAPHIC DETAILS

11 Massachusetts

83 Boston

83 Boston

12 Boston

13 Boston

14 Boston

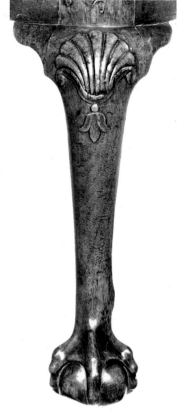

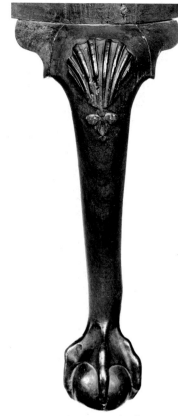

6 New England

7 New England

8 New England

9 Newport

21 New York

22 New York

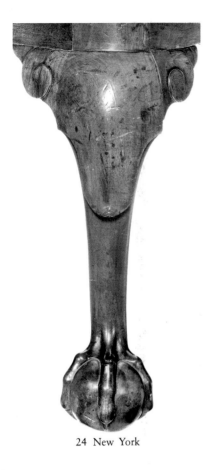

24 New York

81 New York

81 New York

34 New York

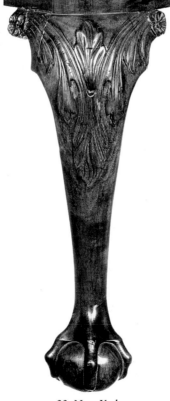

23 New York

28 New York

36 Philadelphia

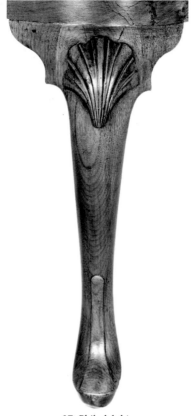

37 Philadelphia

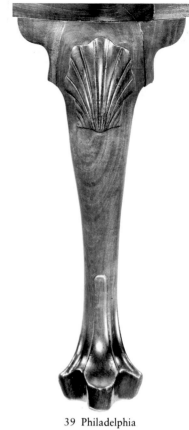

39 Philadelphia

40 Philadelphia

41 Philadelphia

42 Philadelphia

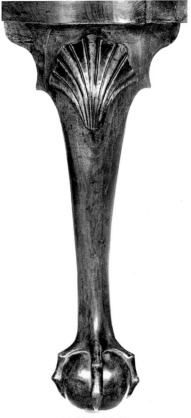

44 Philadelphia

45 Philadelphia

46 Philadelphia

47 Philadelphia

48 Philadelphia

56 Philadelphia

49 Philadelphia

50 Philadelphia

53 Philadelphia

51 Philadelphia

61 Philadelphia

60 Philadelphia

54 Philadelphia

55 Philadelphia

57 Philadelphia

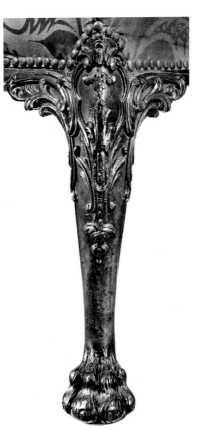

52 Philadelphia

58 Philadelphia

59 Philadelphia

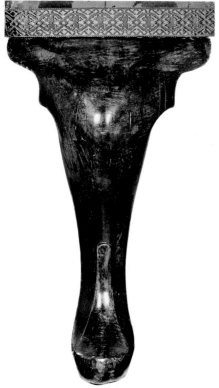

77 Philadelphia

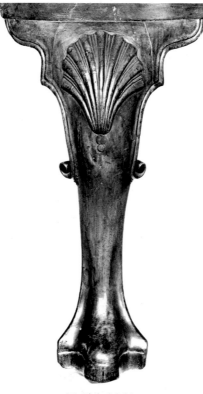

80 Philadelphia

76 Philadelphia

78 Philadelphia

79 Charleston

74 Boston

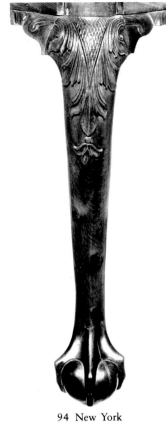

110 New York

94 New York

104 New York

102 New York

103 New York

95 Newport

99 Newport

161 Newport

117 Boston

96 Philadelphia

97 Philadelphia

118 Portsmouth

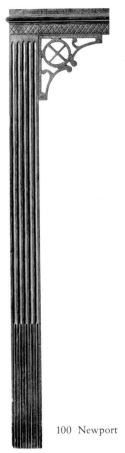

100 Newport

106 Philadelphia

113 Philadelphia

124 Philadelphia

123 Philadelphia

130 Philadelphia

132 Philadelphia

133 Newport

131 Norwich

165 Philadelphia

166 Philadelphia

147 Philadelphia

168 Philadelphia

166 Philadelphia

168 Philadelphia

165 Philadelphia

170 Lancaster

163 Philadelphia

164 Pennsylvania

165 Philadelphia

166 Philadelphia

168 Philadelphia

170 Lancaster

153 Boston

155 Boston

157 Boston

158 Boston

159 Massachusetts

160 New England

173 Connecticut

174 Massachusetts

175 Massachusetts

176 Massachusetts

177 Boston

178 Colchester

179 Massachusetts

180 Newburyport

181 Salem

182 New England

185 Philadelphia

186 Long Island

181 Salem

184 Newport

183 Boston

148 Philadelphia

190 Newport

192 Newport

193 Roxbury

194 Norwich

198 Philadelphia

199 Philadelphia

155 Boston   184 Newport   182 New England   198 Philadelphia

157 Boston   192 Newport   194 Norwich   185 Philadelphia

159 Massachusetts   161 Newport   195 New Hampshire   199 Philadelphia

183 Boston

183 Boston

146 New York

178 Colchester

96 Philadelphia

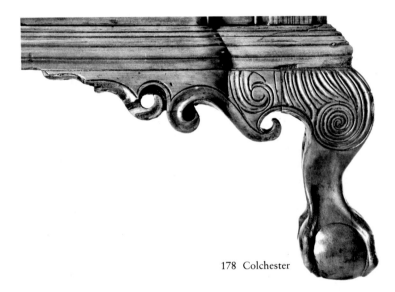

97 Philadelphia

139 Newport

135 Newport

184 Newport

161 Newport

81 New York

192 Newport

100 Newport

181 Salem

139 Newport

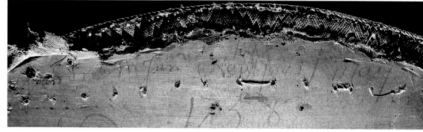

72 Newport

178 Colchester

206 Philadelphia

207 Boston

SHORT TITLES AND ABBREVIATIONS

Albany Institute
Albany Institute of History and Art, Albany, New York

Andrus 1951
Vincent D. Andrus. "Some Recent Gifts of Early New England Furniture" *The Metropolitan Museum of Art Bulletin* n.s. 9 (May 1951), pp. 241–248.

Andrus 1952
Vincent D. Andrus. "American Furniture from the Blair Collection." *The Magazine Antiques* 61 (February 1952), pp. 164–167.

Andrus 1955
Vincent D. Andrus. "Recent Accessions for the American Wing." *The Metropolitan Museum of Art Bulletin* n.s. 13 (March 1955), pp. 225–230.

Aronson
Joseph Aronson. *The Encyclopedia of Furniture.* New York: Crown Publishers, 1965.

Barnes and Meals
Jairus B. Barnes and Moselle Taylor Meals. *American Furniture in the Western Reserve.* Cleveland: The Western Reserve Historical Society, 1972.

Barr 1951
Lockwood Barr. "Willard's Experimental Banjo Models." *Bulletin of the National Association of Watch and Clock Collectors* 9 (June 1951), pp. 370–377.

Barr 1959
Lockwood Barr. "The forerunner of the Willard banjo." *The Magazine Antiques* 75 (March 1959), pp. 282–285.

Bartlett
John Russell Bartlett. *History of the Wanton Family of Providence, Rhode Island.* Providence: Sidney S. Rider, 1978.

Bayou Bend
The Bayou Bend Collection, Houston, Texas

Beckerdite
Luke Beckerdite. "Philadelphia carving shops: Part I: James Reynolds." *The Magazine Antiques* 125 (May 1984), pp. 1120–33.

Biddle
James Biddle. *American Art from American Collections.* New York: The Metropolitan Museum of Art, 1963.

Bigelow sale
Colonial Furniture: The Superb Collection of Mr. Francis Hill Bigelow. New York: American Art Association, January 17, 1924.

Bishop
Robert Bishop. *Centuries and Styles of the American Chair: 1640–1970.* New York: E. P. Dutton & Co., 1972.

Bjerkoe
Ethel Hall Bjerkoe. *The Cabinetmakers of America.* Garden City, New York: Doubleday & Co., 1957.

Blackburn 1976
Roderic H. Blackburn. *Cherry Hill: The History and Collections of a Van Rensselaer Family.* Albany: Historic Cherry Hill, 1976.

Blackburn 1981
Roderic H. Blackburn. "Branded and stamped New York furniture." *The Magazine Antiques* 119 (May 1981), pp. 1130–45.

Boalch
Donald H. Boalch. *Makers of the Harpsichord and Clavichord, 1440–1840.* Oxford: Clarendon Press, 1974.

Brazer
Esther Stevens Brazer. "The Early Boston Japanners." *The Magazine Antiques* 43 (May 1943), pp. 208–211.

Bulkeley 1958
Houghton Bulkeley. "Benjamin Burnham of Colchester, Cabinetmaker." *The Connecticut Historical Society Bulletin* 23 (July 1958), pp. 85–89.

Bulkeley 1959
Houghton Bulkeley. "Benjamin Burnham of Colchester, Cabinetmaker." *The Magazine Antiques* 76 (July 1959), pp. 62–63.

Bulkeley 1967
Houghton Bulkeley. *Contributions to Connecticut Cabinet Making.* Bloomfield: The Connecticut Historical Society, 1967.

Butler
Joseph T. Butler. *Sleepy Hollow Restorations: A Cross-Section of the Collections.* Tarrytown, New York: Sleepy Hollow Press, 1983.

Campbell
Christopher M. Campbell. *American Chippendale Furniture 1755–1790.* Dearborn, Michigan: The Edison Institute, 1975.

Carnegie Institute
Museum of Art, Carnegie Institute, Pittsburgh, Pennsylvania

Carpenter
Ralph E. Carpenter, Jr. *The Arts and Crafts of Newport, Rhode Island: 1640–1820.* Newport: Preservation Society of Newport County, 1954.

Cescinsky and Hunter
Herbert Cescinsky and George Leland Hunter. *English and American Furniture.* Garden City, New York: Garden City Publishing Co., 1929.

Cescinsky and Webster
Herbert Cescinsky and Malcolm R. Webster. *English Domestic Clocks.* New York: Bonanza Books, 1968.

Champlin 1974
Richard L. Champlin. "High Time: William Claggett and His Clockmaking Family." *Newport History* 47 (Summer 1974), pp. 159–190.

Champlin 1976
Richard L. Champlin. "Thomas Claggett: Silversmith, Swordsman, Clock-maker." *Newport History* 49 (Summer 1976), pp. 57–68.

Cherry Hill
Historic Cherry Hill, Albany, New York

Chippendale
Thomas Chippendale. *The Gentleman & Cabinet-Maker's Director.* 3rd ed. London, 1762. Reprint. New York: Dover Publications, 1966.

CHS
Connecticut Historical Society, Hartford

CINOA
The Grand Gallery at The Metropolitan Museum of Art. The International Confederation of Dealers in Works of Art, Sixth International Exhibition. New York, October 19, 1974–January 5, 1975.

Comstock
Helen Comstock. *American Furniture: Seventeenth, Eighteenth, and Nineteenth Century Styles.* New York: The Viking Press, 1962.

Conger
"Chippendale Furniture in the Department of State Collection." *The American Art Journal* 8 (May 1976), pp. 84–98.

Cooper 1971
Wendy A. Cooper. "The Furniture and Furnishings of John Brown, Merchant of Providence, 1736–1803." Master's thesis, University of Delaware, 1971.

Cooper 1973
Wendy A. Cooper. "The purchase of furniture and furnishings by John Brown, Providence Merchant: Part I: 1760–1788." *The Magazine Antiques* 103 (February 1973), pp. 328–337.

Cooper 1977
Wendy A. Cooper. "American Chippendale Chairback Settees: Some Sources and Related Examples." *The American Art Journal* 9 (November 1977), pp. 34–45.

Cooper 1980
Wendy A. Cooper. *In Praise of America: American Decorative Arts, 1650–1830.* New York: Alfred A. Knopf, 1980.

Cornelius 1926
Charles Over Cornelius. *Early American Furniture.* New York: The Century Co., 1926.

Cornelius 1928
Charles Over Cornelius. "John Townsend: An Eighteenth-Century Cabinet-Maker." *Metropolitan Museum of Art Studies* 1 (1928), pp. 72–80.

Cummings
J. L. Cummings. "Painted chests from the Connecticut valley." *The Magazine Antiques* 34 (October 1938), pp. 192–193.

Currier Gallery
The Currier Gallery of Art, Manchester, New Hampshire

DAPC
Decorative Arts Photograph Collection, The Henry Francis du Pont Winterthur Museum, Winterthur, Delaware

Darling
Herbert Darling. *New York State Silversmiths.* Eggertsville, New York: The Darling Foundation, 1964.

Davidson 1967
Marshall B. Davidson. *The American Heritage History of Colonial Antiques.* New York: American Heritage Publishing Co., 1967.

Davidson 1970
Marshall B. Davidson. "Those American Things." *Metropolitan Museum Journal* 3 (1970), pp. 219–233.

Dearborn
Greenfield Village and Henry Ford Museum, Dearborn, Michigan

Deerfield
Historic Deerfield, Inc., Deerfield, Massachusetts

DEF
Percy Macquoid and Ralph Edwards. *The Dictionary of English Furniture From the Middle Ages to the Late Georgian Period.* 3 vols. London and New York: Country Life; Charles Scribner's Sons, 1924; vol. 3, 1927.

De Mille
Rev. George E. De Mille. *Christ Church in the City of Hudson, 1802–1952.* Hudson, New York: privately printed, 1952.

Department of State
Jane W. Pool, ed. *Guidebook to Diplomatic Reception Rooms.* Washington, D.C.: Department of State, 1973.

Distin and Bishop
William Distin and Robert Bishop. *The American Clock.* New York: E. P. Dutton & Co., 1976.

Dow
George Francis Dow. *The Arts & Crafts in New England, 1704–1775.* Topsfield, Massachusetts: Wayside Press, 1927. Reprint. New York: Da Capo Press, 1967.

Downs 1932
Joseph Downs. "A Philadelphia Lowboy." *Bulletin of the Metropolitan Museum of Art* 27 (December 1932), pp. 259–262.

Downs 1933
Joseph Downs. "American Japanned Furniture." *Bulletin of the Metropolitan Museum of Art* 28 (March 1933), pp. 42–48.

Downs 1940
Joseph Downs. "American Japanned Furniture." *Bulletin of the Metropolitan Museum of Art* 35 (July 1940), pp. 145–148.

Downs 1941
Joseph Downs. "The Verplanck Drawing Room." *American Collector* 10 (November 1941), pp. 8–9.

Downs 1941a
Joseph Downs. "The Verplanck Room." *Bulletin of the Metropolitan Museum of Art* 36 (November 1941), pp. 218–224.

Downs 1944
Joseph Downs. "Recent Additions to the American Wing." *The Metropolitan Museum of Art Bulletin* n.s. 3 (November 1944), pp. 78–83.

Downs 1945
Joseph Downs. "Recent Additions to the American Wing." *The Metropolitan Museum of Art Bulletin* n.s. 4 (October 1945), pp. 66–72.

Downs 1947
Joseph Downs. "The furniture of Goddard and Townsend." *The Magazine Antiques* 52 (December 1947), pp. 427–431.

Downs 1948
Joseph Downs. "Recent Additions to the American Wing." *The Metropolitan Museum of Art Bulletin* n.s. 7 (November 1948), pp. 79–85.

Downs 1949
Joseph Downs. *American Chippendale Furniture: A Picture Book*. Rev. ed. New York: The Metropolitan Museum of Art, 1949.

Downs 1952
Joseph Downs. *American Furniture, Queen Anne and Chippendale Periods in the Henry Francis du Pont Winterthur Museum*. New York: Macmillan Co., 1952.

[Downs]
[Joseph Downs.] "New York furniture from the Verplanck Family." *The Connoisseur* 109 (June 1942), pp. 145–147, 160.

Downs and Ralston
Joseph Downs and Ruth Ralston. *A Loan Exhibition of New York State Furniture with Contemporary Accessories*. New York: The Metropolitan Museum of Art, 1934.

Drepperd
Carl W. Drepperd. "Furniture Masterpieces by Jacob Bachman." *American Collector* 14 (October 1945), pp. 6–9, 16, 20.

Dyer
Walter A. Dyer. "John Goddard and His Block-Fronts." *The Magazine Antiques* 1 (May 1922), pp. 203–208.

Earle
Alice Morse Earle. *Colonial Dames and Good Wives*. 1895. Reprint. New York: Macmillan Co., 1924.

Eberlein and Hubbard
Harold Donaldson Eberlein and Courtlandt Van Dyke Hubbard. *Portrait of a Colonial City: Philadelphia 1760–1838*. Philadelphia: Lippincott, 1939.

Elder
William Voss Elder III. *Maryland Queen Anne and Chippendale Furniture of the Eighteenth Century*. Baltimore: The Baltimore Museum of Art, 1968.

Essex Institute
Salem, Massachusetts

Failey
Dean F. Failey et al. *Long Island Is My Nation: The Decorative Arts & Craftsmen, 1640–1830*. Setauket, New York: Society for the Preservation of Long Island Antiquities, 1976.

Fairbanks and Bates
Jonathan L. Fairbanks and Elizabeth Bidwell Bates. *American Furniture: 1620 to the Present*. New York: Richard Marek Publishers, 1981.

Fales 1965
Dean A. Fales, Jr. *Essex County Furniture: Documented Treasures from Local Collections, 1660–1860*. Salem, Massachusetts: Essex Institute, 1965.

Fales 1972
Dean A. Fales, Jr. *American Painted Furniture, 1660–1880*. New York: E. P. Dutton, 1972.

Fales 1974
Dean A. Fales, Jr. "Boston Japanned Furniture." In *Boston Furniture of the Eighteenth Century*. Edited by Walter Muir Whitehill, Brock Jobe, and Jonathan Fairbanks. Boston: Colonial Society of Massachusetts, 1974, pp. 49–70.

Fales 1976
Dean A. Fales, Jr. *The Furniture of Historic Deerfield*. New York: E. P. Dutton, 1976.

Flayderman sale
Colonial Furniture, Silver, and Decorations: The Collection of the late Philip Flayderman. New York: American Art Association, January 2–4, 1930.

Furniture History
The Journal of the Furniture History Society, Leeds, England

Gaines
Edith Gaines. "The Robb collection of American furniture: Part II." *The Magazine Antiques* 93 (April 1968), pp. 484–489.

Gilbert 1978
Christopher Gilbert. *Furniture at Temple Newsam House and Lotherton Hall*. 2 vols. Bradford and London: Lund Humphries, 1978.

Gilbert 1978a
Christopher Gilbert. *The Life and Works of Thomas Chippendale*. 2 vols. New York: Macmillan Co., 1978.

Gillingham 1930
Harold E. Gillingham. "Benjamin Lehman, A Germantown Cabinetmaker." *The Pennsylvania Magazine of History and Biography* 54 (1930), pp. 288–306.

Gillingham 1936
Harold E. Gillingham. "James Gillingham, Philadelphia Cabinetmaker." *The Magazine Antiques* 29 (May 1936), pp. 200–201.

Girl Scouts
Loan Exhibition of Eighteenth and Nineteenth Century Furniture & Glass . . . for the Benefit of the National Council of Girl Scouts, Inc. New York, American Art Galleries, September 25–October 9, 1929.

Gottesman
Rita Susswein Gottesman, comp. *The Arts and Crafts in New York, 1726–1776: Advertisements and News Items from New York City Newspapers*. New York: The New-York Historical Society, 1938.

Goyne
Nancy A. Goyne. "The Bureau Table in America." *Winterthur Portfolio* 3 (1967), pp. 24–36.

Greenlaw
Barry A. Greenlaw. *New England Furniture at Williamsburg.* Williamsburg, Virginia: The Colonial Williamsburg Foundation, 1974.

Gusler
Wallace B. Gusler. *Furniture of Williamsburg and Eastern Virginia, 1710–1790.* Richmond: Virginia Museum, 1979.

Hagler
Katharine Bryant Hagler. *American Queen Anne Furniture: 1720–1755.* Dearborn, Michigan: The Edison Institute, 1976.

Halsey
R. T. H. Halsey. "William Savery, the Colonial Cabinet-Maker, and His Furniture." *Bulletin of the Metropolitan Museum of Art* 13 (December 1918), pp. 254–267.

Halsey and Cornelius
R. T. H. Halsey and Charles O. Cornelius. *A Handbook of the American Wing.* 7th ed. rev. New York: The Metropolitan Museum of Art, 1942.

Halsey and Tower
R. T. H. Halsey and Elizabeth Tower. *The Homes of Our Ancestors As Shown in the American Wing of The Metropolitan Museum of Art.* Garden City, New York: Doubleday, Page and Co., 1925.

Hansen
David Hansen. "Gawen Brown, Soldier and Clockmaker." *Old-Time New England* 30 (July 1939), pp. 1–9.

Harvard Tercentenary
Catalogue of Furniture, Silver, Pewter, Glass, Ceramics, Paintings, Prints, Together with Allied Arts and Crafts of the Period 1636–1836. Cambridge: Harvard University Press, 1936.

Haskell sale
The Americana Collection of the Late Mrs. J. Amory Haskell. Part 1, April 26–29; Part 2, May 17–20; Part 3, October 11–14; Part 4, November 8–11; Part 5, December 6–9, 1944; Part 6, February 13–16, 1945. New York: Parke-Bernet Galleries.

Heckscher 1971
Morrison H. Heckscher. *In Quest of Comfort: The Easy Chair in America.* New York: The Metropolitan Museum of Art, 1971.

Heckscher 1971a
Morrison H. Heckscher. "In Quest of Comfort: The Easy Chair in America." *The Metropolitan Museum of Art Bulletin* n.s. 30 (October/November 1971), pp. 64–65.

Heckscher 1971b
Morrison H. Heckscher. "Form and frame: new thoughts on the American easy chair." *The Magazine Antiques* 100 (December 1971), pp. 886–893.

Heckscher 1973
Morrison H. Heckscher. "The New York serpentine card table." *The Magazine Antiques* 103 (May 1973), pp. 974–983.

Heckscher 1982
Morrison H. Heckscher. "John Townsend's block-and-shell furniture." *The Magazine Antiques* 121 (May 1982), pp. 1144–52.

Heckscher 1985
Morrison H. Heckscher. "Eighteenth-century American Upholstery Techniques: Easy Chairs, Sofas, and Settees." In *Proceedings from the Conference on Historical Upholstery and Drapery.* Boston: Museum of Fine Arts. Forthcoming.

Hendrick
Robert E. P. Hendrick. *The Glen-Sanders Collection from Scotia, New York.* Williamsburg, Virginia: Colonial Williamsburg, 1966.

Hepplewhite
George Hepplewhite. *The Cabinet-Maker & Upholsterer's Guide.* 3rd ed. London: I. & J. Taylor, 1794. Reprint. New York: Dover Publications, 1969.

Hinckley
F. Lewis Hinckley. *A Dictionary of Antique Furniture.* New York: Bonanza Books, 1953.

Hipkiss
Edwin J. Hipkiss. *Eighteenth-Century American Arts: The M. and M. Karolik Collection.* Cambridge: Harvard University Press for the Museum of Fine Arts, Boston, 1941.

Hoopes
Penrose R. Hoopes. *Connecticut Clockmakers of the Eighteenth Century.* New York: Dodd, Mead & Company, 1930.

Hornor 1929
W. M. Hornor, Jr. "The Diverse Activities of John Elliott." *The International Studio* 93 (August 1929), pp. 21–25, 76–78.

Hornor 1931
W. M. Hornor, Jr. "A Study of American Piecrust Tables." *The International Studio* 99 (June 1931), pp. 38–40, 71–72.

Hornor 1935
William MacPherson Hornor, Jr. *Blue Book: Philadelphia Furniture.* Privately printed, 1935. Reprint. Washington, D.C.: Highland House Publishers, 1977.

Hornor 1935a
William MacPherson Hornor, Jr. *A Loan Exhibition of Authenticated Furniture of the Great Philadelphia Cabinet-Makers.* Philadelphia: The Pennsylvania Museum of Art, 1935.

Household Furniture
Household Furniture in the Present Taste . . . by a Society of Upholsterers, Cabinet-makers, etc. 2nd ed. London, 1762. Reprint. East Ardsley, England: E. P. Publishing, Ltd., 1978.

Hummel 1955
Charles F. Hummel. "The Influence of Design Books upon the Philadelphia Cabinetmakers, 1760–1820." Master's thesis, University of Delaware, 1955.

Hummel 1968
Charles F. Hummel. *With Hammer in Hand: The Dominy Craftsmen of East Hampton, New York.* Charlottesville: The University Press of Virginia, 1968.

Hummel 1970
Charles F. Hummel. "Queen Anne and Chippendale furniture in the Henry Francis du Pont Winterthur Museum." *The Magazine Antiques* 97 (June 1970), pp. 896–903, Part I; ibid. 98 (December 1970), pp. 900–907, Part II; ibid. 99 (January 1971), pp. 98–107, Part III.

Hummel 1976
Charles F. Hummel. *A Winterthur Guide to American Chippendale Furniture*. New York: Crown Publishers, 1976.

Ince and Mayhew
William Ince and John Mayhew. *The Universal System of Household Furniture*. London, 1762.

Isham 1927
Norman M. Isham. "John Goddard and His Work." *Bulletin of the Rhode Island School of Design* 15 (April 1927), pp. 14–24.

Isham 1934
Norman M. Isham. "In Memoriam: George Shepard Palmer." *The Walpole Society Note Book 1934*. Boston: The Walpole Society, 1934, pp. 61–69.

Jobe
Brock Jobe. "The Boston Furniture Industry 1720–1740." In *Boston Furniture of the Eighteenth Century*. Edited by Walter Muir Whitehill, Brock Jobe, and Jonathan Fairbanks. Boston: Colonial Society of Massachusetts, 1974, pp. 3–48.

Jobe and Kaye
Brock Jobe and Myrna Kaye. *New England Furniture: The Colonial Era: Selections from the Society for the Preservation of New England Antiquities*. Boston: Houghton Mifflin Company, 1984.

Johnston, P.
Phillip Johnston. "Eighteenth- and nineteenth-century American furniture in the Wadsworth Atheneum." *The Magazine Antiques* 115 (May 1979), pp. 1016–27.

Johnston, W.
William R. Johnston. "Anatomy of the Chair: American regional variations in eighteenth-century styles." *The Metropolitan Museum of Art Bulletin* n.s. 21 (November 1962), pp. 118–129.

Kane
Patricia E. Kane. *300 Years of American Seating Furniture: Chairs and Beds from the Mabel Brady Garvan and Other Collections at Yale University*. Boston: New York Graphic Society, 1976.

Kaye
Myrna Kaye. "Eighteenth-Century Boston Furniture Craftsmen." In *Boston Furniture of the Eighteenth Century*. Edited by Walter Muir Whitehill, Brock Jobe, and Jonathan Fairbanks. Boston: Colonial Society of Massachusetts, 1974, pp. 267–302.

Kennedy & Sack
Age of the Revolution and Early Republic in Fine and Decorative Arts: 1750–1824. New York: Kennedy Galleries, Inc., and Israel Sack, Inc., 1977.

Kihn
Phyllis Kihn. "Connecticut Cabinetmakers." Part I. *The Connecticut Historical Society Bulletin* 32 (October 1967), pp. 97–144.

Kimball
Fiske Kimball. "Some Carved Figures by Samuel McIntire." *Bulletin of The Metropolitan Museum of Art* 18 (August 1923), pp. 194–196.

Kindig
Joseph K. Kindig III. *The Philadelphia Chair: 1685–1785*. Harrisburg, Pennsylvania: The Historical Society of York County, 1978.

Kirk 1967
John T. Kirk. *Connecticut Furniture, Seventeenth and Eighteenth Centuries*. Hartford: The Wadsworth Atheneum, 1967.

Kirk 1972
John T. Kirk. *American Chairs: Queen Anne and Chippendale*. New York: Alfred A. Knopf, 1972.

Kirk 1982
John T. Kirk. *American Furniture and the British Tradition to 1830*. New York: Alfred A. Knopf, 1982.

Landman
Hedy B. Landman. "The Pendleton House at the Museum of Art, Rhode Island School of Design." *The Magazine Antiques* 107 (May 1975), pp. 923–938.

Lee
Anne Lee. Part I: "Colonial Furniture." *Good Furniture and Decoration* 34 (February 1930), pp. 73–84. Part II: "The Desk." Ibid. (April 1930), pp. 177–188. Part III: "The Cupboard: The Sideboard." Ibid. (June 1930), pp. 297–306. Part IV: "The Chair." Ibid. 35 (August 1930), pp. 63–74. Part V: "The Table." Ibid. (October 1930), pp. 209–220. Part VI: "The Mirror: The Bed: The Clock." Ibid. (December 1930), pp. 289–298.

Levy
Bernard Levy and S. Dean Levy. *"Opulence and Splendor": The New York Chair 1690–1830*. New York: Bernard & S. Dean Levy, Inc., 1984.

Little
Frances Little. *Early American Textiles*. New York: The Century Co., 1931.

Lockwood
Luke Vincent Lockwood. *Colonial Furniture in America*. New York: Charles Scribner's Sons, 1901. Rev. ed. 2 vols. 1926.

Lockwood 1904
Luke Vincent Lockwood. *The Pendleton Collection*. The Rhode Island School of Design, 1904.

Lockwood 1907
Luke Vincent Lockwood. *A Collection of English Furniture of the XVII & XVIII Centuries*. New York: Tiffany Studios, 1907.

Lorimer sale
Important American & English Furniture Collected by the Late George Horace Lorimer. Part 1, March 29–April 1; Part 2, October 24–28, 1944. New York: Parke-Bernet Galleries.

Loughlin
David Loughlin. *The Case of Major Fanshawe's Chairs*. New York: University Books, 1978.

Lovell
Margaretta Markel Lovell. "Boston Blockfront Furniture." In *Boston Furniture of the Eighteenth Century*. Edited by Walter Muir Whitehill, Brock Jobe, and Jonathan Fairbanks. Boston: Colonial Society of Massachusetts, 1974, pp. 77–137.

Lyon
Irving Whitall Lyon. *The Colonial Furniture of New England*. Boston and New York: Houghton Mifflin & Co., 1891. Reprint. New York: E. P. Dutton, 1977.

Manwaring
Robert Manwaring. *The Cabinet and Chair-maker's Real Friend and Companion*. London, 1765.

Margon 1949
Lester Margon. *Construction of American Furniture Treasures*. New York: Home Craftsman Publishing Corporation, 1949.

Margon 1954
Lester Margon. *World Furniture Treasures*. New York: Reinhold Publishing Corp., 1954.

Margon 1965
Lester Margon. *Masterpieces of American Furniture 1620–1840*. New York: Architectural Book Publishing Co., 1965.

Margon 1971
Lester Margon. *More American Furniture Treasures*. New York: Architectural Book Publishing Co., 1971.

MCNY
Museum of the City of New York

Melchor, Lohr, and Melchor
James R. Melchor, N. Gordon Lohr, Marilyn S. Melchor. *Eastern Shore, Virginia, Raised Panel Furniture*. Norfolk, Virginia: The Chrysler Museum, 1982.

MESDA
Museum of Early Southern Decorative Arts, Winston-Salem, North Carolina

MFA
Museum of Fine Arts, Boston, Massachusetts

MFA 1975
Jonathan Fairbanks et al. *Paul Revere's Boston: 1735–1818*. Boston: Museum of Fine Arts, 1975.

MHS
Massachusetts Historical Society, Boston, Massachusetts

Miller
Edgar G. Miller, Jr. *American Antique Furniture: A Book for Amateurs*. 2 vols. Baltimore: Lord Baltimore Press, 1937.

Miller, V. I.
V. Isabelle Miller. *Furniture by New York Cabinetmakers: 1650 to 1860*. New York: Museum of the City of New York, 1957.

Minneapolis
The Minneapolis Institute of Arts, Minneapolis, Minnesota

MMA
The Metropolitan Museum of Art, New York, New York

MMA 1909
The Hudson–Fulton Celebration: Catalogue of an Exhibition Held in The Metropolitan Museum of Art. 2 vols. New York, 1909.

MMA 1930
The American High Chest. New York: The Museum Press, 1930.

MMA 1975
The Metropolitan Museum of Art: Notable Acquisitions 1965–1975. New York: The Metropolitan Museum of Art, 1975.

MMA 1976
A Bicentennial Treasury: Masterpieces from the Metropolitan. New York: The Metropolitan Museum of Art, 1976. Reprinted from *The Metropolitan Museum of Art Bulletin* n.s. 33 (Winter 1975/76).

MMAB
Metropolitan Museum of Art Bulletin

Montgomery
Charles F. Montgomery. *American Furniture: The Federal Period, in the Henry Francis du Pont Winterthur Museum*. New York: The Viking Press, 1966.

Montgomery and Kane
Charles F. Montgomery and Patricia E. Kane, eds. *American Art: 1750–1800: Towards Independence*. Boston: New York Graphic Society, 1976.

Moore 1903
N. Hudson Moore. *The Old Furniture Book*. Frederick A. Stokes, 1903. Reprint. New York: Tudor Publishing Co., 1935.

Moore 1911
N. Hudson Moore. *The Old Clock Book*. New York: Frederick A. Stokes, 1911.

Morris sale
The Contents of The Lindens. New York: Christie, Manson & Woods International, Inc., 1983.

Morse
Frances Clary Morse. *Furniture of the Olden Time*. New York: Macmillan Co., 1902.

Moses 1981
Liza Moses and Michael Moses. "Authenticating John Townsend's later tables." *The Magazine Antiques* 119 (May 1981), pp. 1152–63.

Moses 1982
Liza Moses and Michael Moses. "Authenticating John Townsend's and John Goddard's Queen Anne and Chippendale tables." *The Magazine Antiques* 121 (May 1982), pp. 1130–43.

Myers
Louis Guerineau Myers. "Queen Anne Chairs of Colonial Days." *The Magazine Antiques* 22 (December 1932), pp. 213–217.

Myers sale 1921
The Louis Guerineau Myers Collection. New York: American Art Galleries, February 24–26, 1921.

Myers sale 1932
The Private Collection of the Late Louis Guerineau Myers. New York: American Art Association, April 7–9, 1932.

Myers and Mayhew
Minor Myers, Jr., and Edgar deN. Mayhew. *New London County Furniture, 1640–1840.* New London, Connecticut: The Lyman Allyn Museum, 1974.

Naeve
Milo M. Naeve. "Daniel Trotter and his ladder-back chairs." *The Magazine Antiques* 76 (November 1959), pp. 442–445.

New Hampshire Historical Society
Concord, New Hampshire

Newport History
Bulletin of the Newport Historical Society, Newport, Rhode Island

New York State History Collection
Albany, New York

NHS
Newport Historical Society, Newport, Rhode Island

Norton
Malcolm A. Norton. "More Light on the Block-Front." *The Magazine Antiques* 3 (February 1923), pp. 63–66.

Nutting
Wallace Nutting. *Furniture Treasury.* 3 vols. Framingham, Massachusetts: Old America Co., 1928–1933. Reprint. New York: Macmillan Co., 1954.

Nutting 1924
Wallace Nutting. *The Clock Book.* Framingham, Massachusetts: Old America Co., 1924.

NYGBS
New York Genealogical and Biographical Society, New York, New York

N-YHS
The New-York Historical Society, New York, New York

Oedel
William Oedel. "The Francis Borland Tea Table." Research paper, written at Yale University, 1974.

Old-Time New England
Bulletin of the Society for the Preservation of New England Antiquities, Boston

Ormsbee
Thomas Hamilton Ormsbee. *Early American Furniture Makers.* New York: Tudor Publishing Co., 1930.

Ott 1965
Joseph K. Ott. *The John Brown House Loan Exhibition of Rhode Island Furniture.* Providence: The Rhode Island Historical Society, 1965.

Ott 1965a
Joseph K. Ott. "The John Brown House Loan Exhibition of Rhode Island Furniture." *The Magazine Antiques* 87 (May 1965), pp. 564–571.

Ott 1968
Joseph K. Ott. "John Townsend, a chair, and two tables." *The Magazine Antiques* 94 (September 1968), pp. 388–390.

Ott 1969
Joseph K. Ott. "Recent Discoveries Among Rhode Island Cabinetmakers and Their Work." *Rhode Island History* 28 (Winter 1969), pp. 3–25.

Ott 1969a
Joseph K. Ott. "More Notes on Rhode Island Cabinetmakers and Their Work." *Rhode Island History* 28 (May 1969), pp. 49–52.

Ott 1969b
Joseph K. Ott. "Still More Notes on Rhode Island Cabinetmakers and Allied Craftsmen." *Rhode Island History* 28 (November 1969), pp. 111–121.

Ott 1975
Joseph K. Ott. "Some Rhode Island furniture." *The Magazine Antiques* 107 (May 1975), pp. 940–951.

Palmer 1928
Brooks Palmer. *The Book of American Clocks.* New York: Macmillan Co., 1928.

Palmer 1967
Brooks Palmer. *A Treasury of American Clocks.* New York: Macmillan Co., 1967.

Palmer sale
The George S. Palmer Collection. New York: Anderson Galleries, October 18–20, 1928.

Parsons
Charles S. Parsons. *The Dunlaps and Their Furniture.* Manchester, New Hampshire: The Currier Gallery of Art, 1970.

Partridge
Albert E. Partridge. "Benjamin Bagnall of Boston, Clockmaker." *Old-Time New England* 26 (July 1935), pp. 26–31.

P-B
Parke-Bernet, Inc., New York, New York

Philipse Manor
Philipse Manor Hall State Historic Site, Yonkers, New York

PMA
Philadelphia Museum of Art, Philadelphia, Pennsylvania

PMA 1976
Philadelphia: Three Centuries of American Art. Philadelphia: Philadelphia Museum of Art, 1976.

PMB
Bulletin of the Philadelphia Museum of Art

Powel
Lydia Bond Powel. "The American Wing." *The Metropolitan Museum of Art Bulletin* n.s. 12 (March 1954), pp. 194–216.

Price
Lois Olcott Price. "Furniture Craftsmen and the Queen Anne Style in Eighteenth Century New York." Master's thesis, University of Delaware, 1977.

Prime 1929
Alfred Coxe Prime, comp. *The Arts & Crafts in Philadelphia, Maryland, and South Carolina, 1721–1785.* Series One. Topsfield, Massachusetts: The Walpole Society, 1929.

Prime 1932
Alfred Coxe Prime, comp. *The Arts & Crafts in Philadelphia, Maryland, and South Carolina, 1786–1800.* Series Two. Topsfield, Massachusetts: The Walpole Society, 1932.

Prown
Jules David Prown. *John Singleton Copley.* 2 vols. Cambridge: Harvard University Press, 1966.

Ralston **1931**
Ruth Ralston. "The Exhibition in the American Wing of an Anonymous Gift." *Bulletin of The Metropolitan Museum of Art* 26 (February 1931), pp. 30–38.

Ralston 1932
Ruth Ralston. "A Settee from the Workshop of Joseph Cox." *Bulletin of The Metropolitan Museum of Art* 27 (September 1932), pp. 206–208.

Randall 1960
Richard H. Randall, Jr. "An Eighteenth Century Partnership." *The Art Quarterly* 23 (Summer 1960), pp. 152–161.

Randall 1963
Richard H. Randall, Jr. "Boston Chairs." *Old-Time New England* 54 (Summer 1963), pp. 12–20.

Randall 1965
Richard H. Randall, Jr. *American Furniture in the Museum of Fine Arts Boston.* Boston: Museum of Fine Arts, 1965.

Randall 1966
Richard H. Randall, Jr., "The finest American masonic Senior Warden's Chair." *The Connoisseur* 162 (April 1966), pp. 286–287.

Randall 1974
Richard H. Randall, Jr. "Benjamin Frothingham." In *Boston Furniture of the Eighteenth Century.* Edited by Walter Muir Whitehill, Brock Jobe, and Jonathan Fairbanks. Boston: Colonial Society of Massachusetts, 1974, pp. 223–249.

Reifsnyder sale
Colonial Furniture: The Superb Collection of the Late Howard Reifsnyder. New York: American Art Association, April 24–27, 1929.

Reynolds
Helen Wilkinson Reynolds. *Dutchess County Doorways and Other Examples of Period-Work in Wood: 1730–1830.* New York: William Farquahar Payson, 1931.

Rhoades
Elizabeth Adams Rhoades. "Household Furnishings: Portsmouth, New Hampshire, 1750–75." Master's thesis, University of Delaware, 1972.

Rhoades and Jobe
Elizabeth Rhoades and Brock Jobe. "Recent discoveries in Boston japanned furniture." *The Magazine Antiques* 105 (May 1974), pp. 1082–91.

Rice
Norman S. Rice. *New York Furniture Before 1840 in the Collection of the Albany Institute of History and Art.* Albany: Albany Institute of History and Art, 1962.

RIHS
Rhode Island Historical Society, Providence, Rhode Island

RISD
Museum of Art, Rhode Island School of Design, Providence, Rhode Island

Rodriguez Roque
Oswaldo Rodriguez Roque. *American Furniture at Chipstone.* Madison: The University of Wisconsin Press, 1984.

Rogers
Meyric R. Rogers. *American Interior Design.* New York: Bonanza Books, 1947.

Sack
American Antiques from Israel Sack Collection. 7 vols. Washington, D.C.: Highland House Publishers, 1981–1983.

Sack 1950
Albert Sack. *Fine Points of Furniture, Early American.* New York: Crown Publishers, 1950.

Sack sale
One Hundred Important American Antiques: Colonial and Early Federal Furniture, Silver, and Porcelains Acquired from Notable Collections by Israel Sack. New York: Anderson Galleries, January 9, 1932.

Salomonsky
Verna Cook Salomonsky. *Masterpieces of Furniture Design.* Grand Rapids, Michigan: Periodical Publishing Co., 1931.

Schiffer
Herbert F. Schiffer and Peter B. Schiffer. *Miniature Antique Furniture.* Wynnewood, Pennsylvania: Livingston Publishing Co., 1972.

Schorsch
Anita Schorsch. *The Warner Collector's Guide to American Clocks.* New York: The Main Street Press, 1981.

Schuyler Mansion
Schuyler Mansion State Historic Site, Albany, New York

Schwartz 1968
Marvin D. Schwartz. *American Interiors, 1675–1885: A Guide to the American Period Rooms in the Brooklyn Museum.* New York: The Brooklyn Museum, 1968.

Schwartz 1976
Marvin D. Schwartz. *American Furniture of the Colonial Period.* New York: The Metropolitan Museum of Art, 1976.

Shaffer
Douglas H. Shaffer. *Clocks.* Washington, D.C.: Smithsonian Institution, 1980.

Shelburne
Shelburne Museum, Inc., Shelburne, Vermont

Shephard
Lewis A. Shephard. *American Art at Amherst.* Middletown, Conn.: Wesleyan University Press, 1978.

Sheraton
Thomas Sheraton. *The Cabinet Dictionary.* London: W. Smith, 1803. Reprint. Edited by Wilford P. Cole and Charles F. Montgomery. 2 vols. New York: Praeger Publishers, 1970.

Singleton
Esther Singleton. *The Furniture of Our Forefathers.* 2 vols. New York: Doubleday, Page and Co., 1900–1901.

Slade
Daniel Denison Slade. "The Bromfield Family." *New England Historical and Genealogical Register* 26 (1872), pp. 39–43.

Smith 1970
Robert C. Smith. "Masterpieces of early American furniture at the United States Department of State." *The Magazine Antiques* 98 (November 1970), pp. 766–772.

Smith 1971
Robert C. Smith. "Finial busts on eighteenth-century Philadelphia furniture." *The Magazine Antiques* 100 (December 1971), pp. 900–905.

Smithsonian
National Museum of American History, Smithsonian Institution, Washington, D.C.

Snyder 1974
John J. Snyder, Jr. "The Bachman attributions: a reconsideration." *The Magazine Antiques* 105 (May 1974), pp. 1057–65.

Snyder 1975
John J. Snyder, Jr. "Carved Chippendale case furniture from Lancaster, Pennsylvania." *The Magazine Antiques* 107 (May 1975), pp. 964–975.

Solis-Cohen
Lita Solis-Cohen. "Expensive Seat." *Maine Antique Digest,* December 1982, pp. 14A–15A.

SPB
Sotheby Parke Bernet, Inc., New York, New York

SPNEA
Society for the Preservation of New England Antiquities, Boston, Massachusetts

Stillinger
Elizabeth Stillinger. *The Antiquers.* New York: Alfred A. Knopf, 1980.

Stokes
I.N. Phelps Stokes, comp. *The Iconography of Manhattan Island: 1498–1909.* 6 vols. New York: Robert H. Dodd, 1915–28.

Stone
Stanley Stone. "Rhode Island furniture at Chipstone." Part I. *The Magazine Antiques* 91 (February 1967), pp. 207–213; Part II. Ibid. (April 1967), pp. 508–513.

Sturbridge
Old Sturbridge Village, Sturbridge, Massachusetts

Swan 1931
Mabel M. Swan. "A Revised Estimate of McIntire." *The Magazine Antiques* 20 (December 1931), pp. 338–343.

Swan 1945
Mabel M. Swan. "Newburyport Furnituremakers." *The Magazine Antiques* 47 (April 1945), pp. 222–225.

Swan 1950
Mabel Munson Swan. "John Goddard's Sons." *The Magazine Antiques* 57 (June 1950), pp. 448–449.

Sweeney
John A. H. Sweeney. *The Treasure House of Early American Rooms.* New York: The Viking Press, 1963.

Toller
Jane Toller. *Antique Miniature Furniture in Great Britain and America.* Newton, Massachusetts: Charles T. Bradford, 1966.

Tolles
Frederick B. Tolles. "Town House and Country House, Inventories from the Estate of William Logan, 1776." *The Pennsylvania Magazine of History and Biography* 82 (October 1958), pp. 397–410.

Van Cortlandt Manor
Croton-on-Hudson, New York

Vincent
Gilbert T. Vincent. "The Bombé Furniture of Boston." In *Boston Furniture of the Eighteenth Century.* Edited by Walter Muir Whitehill, Brock Jobe, and Jonathan Fairbanks. Boston: Colonial Society of Massachusetts, 1974, pp. 137–196.

Wadsworth Atheneum
Hartford, Connecticut

Wainwright
Nicholas B. Wainwright. *Colonial Grandeur in Philadelphia: The House and Furniture of General John Cadwalader.* Philadelphia: The Historical Society of Pennsylvania, 1964.

Wallace
Philip B. Wallace. *Colonial Houses.* New York: Architectural Book Publishing Co., 1931.

Ward
Barbara M. Ward and Gerald W. R. Ward. "The Makers of Copley's Picture Frames: A Clue." *Old-Time New England* 67 (Summer–Fall 1976), pp. 16–19.

Warren
David B. Warren. *Bayou Bend: American Furniture, Paintings, and Silver from the Bayou Bend Collection.* Houston: The Museum of Fine Arts, 1975.

Weil
Martin Eli Weil. "A Cabinetmaker's Price Book." *Winterthur Portfolio* 13 (1979), pp. 175–192.

Willard
John Ware Willard. *Simon Willard and His Clock.* Boston: privately printed, 1911. Reprint. New York: Dover Publications, 1968.

Williams
Carl M. Williams. "Thomas Tufft and His Furniture for Richard Edwards." *The Magazine Antiques* 54 (October 1948), pp. 246–247.

Williamsburg
Colonial Williamsburg, Williamsburg, Virginia

Winchester
Alice Winchester. "The Dunlap Dilemma." *The Magazine Antiques* 46 (December 1944), pp. 336–339.

Winterthur
The Henry Francis du Pont Winterthur Museum, Winterthur, Delaware

Woodhouse 1927
S. W. Woodhouse, Jr. "Benjamin Randolph of Philadelphia." *The Magazine Antiques* 11 (May 1927), pp. 366–371.

Woodhouse 1930
S. W. Woodhouse, Jr. "More About Benjamin Randolph." *The Magazine Antiques* 17 (January 1930), pp. 21–25.

Yale
Yale University Art Gallery, Mabel Brady Garvan collection, New Haven, Connecticut

Yehia
Mary Ellen Hayward Yehia. "Ornamental Carving on Boston Furniture of the Chippendale Style." In *Boston Furniture of the Eighteenth Century.* Edited by Walter Muir Whitehill, Brock Jobe, and Jonathan Fairbanks. Boston: Colonial Society of Massachusetts, 1974, pp. 197–222.

Young
M. Ada Young. "Five secretaries and the Cogswells." *The Magazine Antiques* 88 (October 1965), pp. 478–485.

Zimmerman 1979
Philip D. Zimmerman. "A Methodological Study in the Identification of Some Important Philadelphia Chippendale Furniture." *Winterthur Portfolio* 13 (1979), pp. 193–208.

Zimmerman 1980
Philip D. Zimmerman. "The Artifact as Historical Source Material: A Comparative Study of Philadelphia Chippendale Chairs." Master's thesis, University of Delaware, 1980.

Zimmerman 1981
Philip D. Zimmerman. "Workmanship as Evidence: A Model for Object Study." *Winterthur Portfolio* 16 (Winter 1981), pp. 283–307.

GENERAL INDEX

The names printed in heavy type are those of eighteenth-century American craftsmen.

Affleck, Thomas, 24, 25, 94, 99, 107, 118, 143, 150, 162, 175–176, 195, 204, 228, 229, 308
Angeroth, Charles G., Jr., 260
Apthorp, Charles (Boston), 21, 63, 281
Apthorp family (New York City), 31, 62, 63
Armitt, Joseph, 87–89
Ash, Colonel, 87
Ash, Gilbert, 68
Atkins, Gibbs, 270
Atkinson, James, 159, 206

Babbitt family (Wickford, R.I.), 159
Bachman, Jacob, 262
Bagnall, Benjamin, Jr., 290, 291
Bagnall, Benjamin, Sr., 290–291
Bagnall, Samuel, 290, 291
Baker, Benjamin, 247, 293
Balch, Daniel, Jr., 311
Bannister family (Newburyport, Mass.), 276
Baretti, P., 253
Barnard, Anna, 47
Barnard, Joseph, 46
Barnes, Philena, 71
Beekman, Margaret, see Livingston, Margaret Beekman
Beekman, Dr. William, 139
Beekman family (New York City), 23, 63, 138, 171–172, 180
Belcher, Governor (Jonathan), 140
Bergen family (Flatlands, N.Y.), 180
Bernard and Jugiez, 107, 162, 204
Bigelow, Francis Hill, 28, 151
Blair, Natalie K. (Mrs. J. Insley Blair), 30, 39–41
Blyth, Samuel, 319
Bogart family (Roslyn, N.Y.), 67
Bolles, H. Eugene, 28, 29, 31, 74, 244
Bowdoin, Gen. James, 240
Bowen, Jabez, 159, 166, 224
Bowen, Nathaniel, 223
Bowman, Jonathan, 56
Boynton, Peter, 318
Bright, George, 56, 122, 275, 280
Brinckerhoff family (New York City), 146
Bromfield, Henry, 63
Brooks, John, 245
Brown, Gawen, 295–296, 297, 320
Brown, G. Winthrop, 291
Brown, John, 44, 159, 178, 282

Brown, Joseph, 282
Brown, Moses, 42, 282
Brown, Nicholas, 282
Brown family (Providence, R.I.), 205, 206, 284
Bulkeley, Eliphalet, 272
Bulkeley, Houghton, 39
Burling, Thomas, 197
Burnap, Daniel, 46
Burnet, Governor, 140
Burnham, Benjamin, 270–272
Burnham, Catherin Trumble, 270
Burnham, Griswold, 270

Cadwalader, Elizabeth Lloyd, 107
Cadwalader, Gen. John, 99, 104, 107, 161–162, 204, 313
Cadwalader, Lambert, 107
Cadwalader family (Philadelphia), 104, 107, 229, 285
Cannon, Daniel, 134
Carpenter family (Philadelphia), 108
Champlin, Christopher, 168
Chandler, Zachariah, 302
Chapin, Aaron, 46, 47
Chapin, Eliphalet, 46, 47, 114–115, 150
Chapin family (East Windsor, Conn.), 22
Chase, S (I?) P, 303
Chase, Stephen, 189
Chestney, James, 61
Cheston, Emily Fox, 228
Chew, Benjamin, 118
Chew family (Philadelphia), 118, 143
Chippendale, Thomas, 19, 21, 24, 25, 72, 97, 99–100, 101, 103, 105, 109, 117–118, 142, 149, 151, 162, 182, 189, 220, 229, 258, 277, 285, 316–317
Claggett, Thomas, 292, 293
Claggett, William, 292, 294–295
Clark, John, 313
Clarke, Anna Barnard, 47
Clarke, Joseph, 47
Clarke, Thomas B., 27, 71, 84, 104
Clarkson, Matthew, 72
Clemm, Johannes Gottlob, 317–319
Clifton, Henry, 306
Cogill, Charles B., 92, 93
Cogswell, John, 25, 276
Cogswell, T.(?), 274
Cooper, Isaac, 97

Copley, John Singleton, 27, 63, 331, 332
Coryell, Emanuel, I, 96
Coryell, Emanuel, II, 96
Courtenay, Hercules, 24
Coutant, David, 61
Cowell family (Philadelphia), 251
Cox, Joseph, 22, 137–139
Cox family (Piping Rock, N.Y.), 72
Coxe, Charles, 162
Creak, William, 297
Crommelin, Judith, see Verplanck, Judith Crommelin
Cunningham family (Boston), 151
Custard, Amelia Foulke, 82
Cutts family (Portsmouth, N.H.), 189

Davids, Eliza, 100
Davis, Cummings, 26
Davis, Joseph, 233
Davis, Robert, 328
de Forest, Mrs. Robert W., 29
de Forest, Robert W., 27, 28
Delaplaine, Joshua, 180
Derby, Elias Hasket, 140, 277
Derby, Mrs. Elmer G., 39
Derham, Mary, 137
Dering, Gen. Sylvester, 211
Dering, Gen. Sylvester, II, 211
Dering, Thomas, 210
Desbrosses, Elias, 180
De Wolf family (Bristol, R.I.), 52
Dexter, Timothy, 279
Dickinson, John, 97
Dowdney, Burrows, 308
Dunlap, Maj. John, 58, 222, 302
Dunlap, Samuel, 58, 302
Dunlap family (New Hampshire), 221–222

Eckard family (New Castle, Del.), 252
Eddy family (Warren, R.I.), 113
Edwards family (Philadelphia), 104–105
Ellery, William, 36
Elliott, John, 131
Evans, David, 182

Fisher, J.F., 300
Fisher, Sarah Redwood, 175
Fitz, William, 311
Fleeson, Plunket, 23, 107

377

INDEX OF DONORS AND FORMER OWNERS